HARRAP'S
FIVE LANGUAGE DICTIONARY

English-French-German-Italian-Spanish

HARRAP

FIVE-LANGUAGE DICTIONARY

Compilers: Monika Eberhard, Ursula Guidi, Beatrix Haag,
Nicola Petersen, Marcus Rathbone, Hildegard Schulte-Umberg,
Montserrat Vancells
Designer: Inga Koch

First published in Great Britain 1991
by HARRAP BOOKS Ltd
Chelsea House, 26 Market Square, Bromley, Kent BR1 1NA

© 1991 Compact Verlag München

ISBN 0 245-60346-8

ISBN 0-13-387986-0 (United States)

Printed in Germany

FOREWORD

The steady growth of international communication – particularly within today's unified Europe – means that knowledge of foreign languages is becoming an increasingly important requirement in all areas of life. This new dictionary meets the demand for a practical, up-to-date reference source by providing the user with access to a general vocabulary of 20,000 headwords and 80,000 translations in five major European languages: English, French, German, Italian and Spanish.

The multilingual integration of all the headwords within a single alphabetical sequence makes it quick and easy to look up a particular word and its translations in any of the five languages.

Convenient and comprehensive, this international dictionary will prove an invaluable reference for all day-to-day communication needs.

ABBREVIATIONS

D= GERMAN
E= ENGLISH
F= FRENCH
I= ITALIAN
ES= SPANISH
f= feminine
m= masculine
n= neuter

	D	E	F	I	Es
a (Es)	nach	after/to	après/selon	a/in/verso/dopo	—
a¹ (I)	an	at/on/by	à/près de	—	junto a
a² (I)	nach	after/to	après/selon	—	a/hacia/después
à (F)	an	at/on/by	—	a/in/su	junto a
ab (D)	—	from	à partir de/dès	da	a partir de/de
abajo¹ (Es)	herunter	down	en bas	giù	—
abajo² (Es)	nieder	inferior	bas(se)	in basso	—
abajo³ (Es)	unten	downstairs	dessous	sotto/giù	—
abandonner¹ (F)	aufgeben	give up	—	rinunciare	renunciar
abandonner² (F)	verlassen	leave	—	lasciare	dejar
abarrotado (Es)	überfüllt	crowded	bondé(e)	pieno(a) zeppo(a)	—
a bassa voce (I)	leise	quietly	à voix basse	—	sin ruido
abbassare (I)	senken	lower	baisser	—	bajar
abbastanza¹ (I)	genug	enough	assez	—	bastante
abbastanza² (I)	ziemlich	quite	assez	—	bastante
abbestellen (D)	—	cancel	décommander	annullare	anular el pedido de
abbezahlen (D)	—	pay off	payer à tempérament	pagare a rate	pagar a plazos
abbiegen (D)	—	turn off	tourner	svoltare	torcer
abbigliamento (I)	Kleidung f	clothing	habits m pl	—	vestuario m
abblasen (D)	—	call off	annuler	disdire	anular
abbozzo (I)	Entwurf m	outline	esquisse f	—	proyecto m
abbracciare (I)	umarmen	embrace	embrasser	—	abrazar
abbreviation (E)	Abkürzung f	—	abréviation f	abbreviazione f	abreviatura f
abbreviazione (I)	Abkürzung f	abbreviation	abréviation f	—	abreviatura f
abbrustolire (I)	rösten	roast	griller	—	tostar
Abend (D)	—	evening	soir m	sera f	noche f
Abendessen (D)	—	supper	dîner m	cena f	cena f
abends (D)	—	in the evening	le soir	di sera	por la tarde
Abenteuer (D)	—	adventure	aventure f	avventura f	aventura f
aber (D)	—	but	mais	ma	pero
abergläubisch (D)	—	superstitious	superstitieux (-euse)	superstizioso(a)	supersticioso(a)
abertura (Es)	Eröffnung f	opening	ouverture f	apertura f	—
abfahren (D)	—	depart	partir (de)	partire	salir
Abfahrt (D)	—	departure	départ m	partenza f	salida f
Abfall (D)	—	rubbish	déchets m pl	immondizia f	basura f
Abfalleimer (D)	—	bin	poubelle f	pattumiera f	cubo de la basura m
Abflug (D)	—	take-off	décollage m	decollo m	despegue m
abhängen (D)	—	depend	dépendre	dipendere	depender
abholen (D)	—	pick up	aller chercher	andare a prendere	recoger
abierto¹ (Es)	geöffnet	open	ouvert(e)	aperto(a)	—
abierto² (Es)	offen	open	ouvert(e)	aperto(a)	—
abile¹ (I)	clever	clever	futé(e)	—	listo(a)
abile² (I)	geschickt	skilful	habile	—	mañoso(a)
ability (E)	Fähigkeit f	—	capacité f	capacità f	capacidad f
abitante¹ (I)	Bewohner m	inhabitant	habitant m	—	habitante m
abitante² (I)	Einwohner m	inhabitant	habitant m	—	habitante m

	D	E	F	I	Es
abitare (I)	wohnen	live	habiter	—	vivir
abituale (I)	gewöhnlich	usual	habituel(le)	—	habitual
abituare (I)	gewöhnen, sich	get used to	habituer, se	—	acostumbrarse
abitudine (I)	Gewohnheit *f*	habit	habitude *f*	—	costumbre *f*
Abitur (D)	—	German school leaving examinations	baccalauréat *m*	maturità *f*	bachillerato *m*
Abkürzung (D)	—	abbreviation	abréviation *f*	abbreviazione *f*	abreviatura *f*
abladen (D)	—	unload	décharger	scaricare	descargar
able (E)	imstande	—	capable	capace	en condiciones
ablehnen (D)	—	reject	refuser	rifiutare	rehusar
ablenken (D)	—	distract	distraire	distrarre	desviar
Abmachung (D)	—	agreement	accord *m*	accordo *m*	acuerdo *m*
abnehmen[1] (D)	—	lose weight	maigrir	dimagrire	adelgazar
abnehmen[2] (D)	—	take away	décrocher	staccare	descolgar
abnutzen (D)	—	wear out	user	consumare	desgastar
abogado (Es)	Rechtsanwalt *m*	lawyer	avocat *m*	avvocato *m*	—
abominable (E)	abscheulich	—	affreux(-euse)	disgustoso(a)	horrible
about[1] (E)	etwa	—	environ	pressappoco	unos
about[2] (E)	ungefähr	—	environ	pressappoco	aproximadamente
above[1] (E)	darüber	—	au dessus	sopra	por encima
above[2] (E)	oben	—	en haut	sopra	arriba
abraten (D)	—	warn	déconseiller	sconsigliare	desaconsejar
abrazar (Es)	umarmen	embrace	embrasser	abbracciare	—
abrebotellas (Es)	Flaschenöffner *m*	bottle opener	ouvre-bouteilles *m*	apribottiglie *m*	—
Abreise (D)	—	departure	départ *m*	partenza *f*	salida *f*
abreisen (D)	—	leave	partir	partire	salir
abréviation (F)	Abkürzung *f*	abbreviation	—	abbreviazione *f*	abreviatura *f*
abreviatura (Es)	Abkürzung *f*	abbreviation	abréviation *f*	abbreviazione *f*	—
abricot (F)	Aprikose *f*	apricot	—	albicocca *f*	albaricoque *m*
abrigo (Es)	Mantel *m*	coat	manteau *m*	cappotto *m*	—
abril (Es)	April *m*	April	avril *m*	aprile *m*	—
abrir (Es)	öffnen	open	ouvrir	aprire	—
abroad (E)	Ausland *n*	—	étranger *m*	estero *m*	extranjero *m*
abrupt (D)	—	abrupt	subit(e)	improvviso(a)	súbito(a)
abrupt (E)	abrupt	—	subit(e)	improvviso(a)	súbito(a)
abrüsten (D)	—	disarm	désarmer	disarmare	desarmar
Absage (D)	—	refusal	refus *m*	risposta negativa *f*	negativa *f*
abschalten (D)	—	switch off	éteindre	spegnere	desconectar
abscheulich (D)	—	abominable	affreux(-euse)	disgustoso(a)	horrible
Abschied (D)	—	parting	adieux *m pl*	addio *m*	despedida *f*
abschleppen (D)	—	take in tow	remorquer	rimorchiare	remolcar
Abschleppwagen (D)	—	breakdown service	dépanneuse *f*	carro soccorso *m*	coche-grúa *m*
absence (E)	Abwesenheit *f*	—	absence *f*	assenza *f*	ausencia *f*
absence (F)	Abwesenheit *f*	absence	—	assenza *f*	ausencia *f*
Absender (D)	—	sender	expéditeur *m*	mittente *m*	remitente *m*
absent (E)	abwesend	—	absent(e)	assente	ausente
absent (F)	abwesend	absent	—	assente	ausente
Absicht (D)	—	intention	intension *f*	intenzione *f*	intención *f*

	D	E	F	I	Es
absichtlich (D)	—	intentionally	exprès	apposta	adrede
absolument (F)	unbedingt	absolutely	—	assolutamente	absolutamente
absolutamente (Es)	unbedingt	absolutely	absolument	assolutamente	—
absolutely (E)	unbedingt	—	absolument	assolutamente	absolutamente
abspülen (D)	—	wash up	faire la vaisselle	sciacquare	lavar
abstammen (D)	—	be descended	descendre	discendere	descender
Abstand (D)	—	distance	distance f	distanza f	distancia f
absteigen (D)	—	dismount	descendre	scendere	descender
abstellen (D)	—	turn off	arrêter	spegnere	desconectar
Absturz (D)	—	crash	chute f	caduta f	caída f
abstürzen (D)	—	crash	faire une chute	precipitare	caer a tierra
absurdo[1] (Es)	Unsinn m	nonsense	bêtises f pl	nonsenso m	—
absurdo[2] (Es)	unsinnig	nonsensical	insensé(e)	insensato(a)	—
Abteil (D)	—	compartment	compartiment m	scompartimento m	compartimiento m
Abteilung (D)	—	department	département m	reparto m	departamento m
abuela (Es)	Großmutter f	grandmother	grand-mère f	nonna f	—
abuelo (Es)	Großvater m	grandfather	grand-père m	nonno m	—
abuelos (Es)	Großeltern pl	grandparents	grands-parents m pl	nonni m pl	—
a buon mercato (I)	billig	cheap	bon marché(e)	—	barato(a)
aburrido (Es)	langweilig	boring	ennuyeux(-euse)	noioso(a)	—
aburrirse (Es)	langweilen, sich	get bored	ennuyer, se	annoiarsi	—
abus (F)	Mißbrauch m	abuse	—	abuso m	abuso m
abusar (Es)	mißbrauchen	abuse	abuser de	abusare	—
abusare (I)	mißbrauchen	abuse	abuser de	—	abusar
abuse[1] (E)	mißbrauchen	—	abuser de	abusare	abusar
abuse[2] (E)	Mißbrauch m	—	abus m	abuso m	abuso m
abuser de (F)	mißbrauchen	abuse	—	abusare	abusar
abuso (Es)	Mißbrauch m	abuse	abus m	abuso m	—
abuso (I)	Mißbrauch m	abuse	abus m	—	abuso m
abwärts (D)	—	downwards	en bas	in giù	hacia abajo
abwaschen (D)	—	wash off	laver	lavar via	lavar
abwechseln (D)	—	take turns	alterner	alternarsi	alternar
abwesend (D)	—	absent	absent(e)	assente	ausente
Abwesenheit (D)	—	absence	absence f	assenza f	ausencia f
abziehen (D)	—	subtract	soustraire	sottrarre	restar
acabar[1] (Es)	erledigen	take care of	régler	sbrigare	—
acabar[2] (Es)	enden	end	finir	finire	—
acampar (Es)	zelten	camp	camper	campeggiare	—
à carreaux (F)	kariert	checked	—	a quadretti	a cuadros
a casa (Es)	nach Hause	home	à la maison	a casa	—
a casa[1] (I)	daheim	at home	à la maison	—	en casa
a casa[2] (I)	nach Hause	home	à la maison	—	a casa
a causa de (Es)	wegen	because of	à cause de	a causa di	—
a causa di (I)	wegen	because of	à cause de	—	a causa de
à cause de (F)	wegen	because of	—	a causa di	a causa de
accadere[1] (I)	geschehen	happen	arriver	—	ocurrir
accadere[2] (I)	vorkommen	occur	exister	—	suceder

accanto a

	D	E	F	I	Es
accanto a (I)	neben	beside/next to	près de	—	al lado de
accelerare (I)	beschleunigen	accelerate	accélérer	—	acelerar
accelerate (E)	beschleunigen	—	accélérer	accelerare	acelerar
accélérer (F)	beschleunigen	accelerate	—	accelerare	acelerar
accendere[1] (I)	anmachen	put on	allumer	—	encender
accendere[2] (I)	anzünden	light	allumer	—	encender
accendere[3] (I)	anstellen	turn on	mettre en marche	—	poner
accendere[4] (I)	einschalten	switch on	allumer	—	conectar
accendersi (I)	zünden	ignite	allumer, se	—	encender
accendino (I)	Feuerzeug n	lighter	briquet m	—	mechero m
accent (E)	Akzent m	—	accent m	accento m	acento m
accent (F)	Akzent m	accent	—	accento m	acento m
accento (I)	Akzent m	accent	accent m	—	acento m
accept (E)	annehmen	—	accepter	accettare	aceptar
acceptance (E)	Annahme f	—	réception f	accettazione f	aceptación f
accepter (F)	annehmen	accept	—	accettare	aceptar
accès[1] (F)	Zutritt m	admission	—	accesso m	acceso m
accès[2] (F)	Zugang m	access	—	entrata f	entrada f
acceso (Es)	Zutritt m	admission	accès m	accesso m	—
access (E)	Zugang m	—	accès m	entrata f	entrada f
accesso (I)	Zutritt m	admission	accès m	—	acceso m
accettare[1] (I)	annehmen	accept	accepter	—	aceptar
accettare[2] (I)	übernehmen	take over	reprendre	—	tomar posesión de
accetazione (I)	Annahme f	acceptance	réception f	—	aceptación f
accettazione bagagli (I)	Gepäckannahme f	luggage desk	enregistrement des bagages m	—	recepción de equipajes f
acchiappare[1] (I)	erwischen	catch	attraper	—	atrapar
acchiappare[2] (I)	fangen	catch	attraper	—	coger
acciaio (I)	Stahl m	steel	acier m	—	acero m
accident (E)	Unfall m	—	accident m	incidente m	accidente m
accident (F)	Unfall m	accident	—	incidente m	accidente m
accident de voiture (F)	Autounfall m	car accident	—	incidente stradale m	accidente de automóvil m
accidente (Es)	Unfall m	accident	accident m	incidente m	—
accidente de automóvil (Es)	Autounfall m	car accident	accident de voiture m	incidente stradale m	—
acción (Es)	Tat f	deed	action f	azione f	—
acclimater, se (F)	einleben, sich	settle into	—	ambientarsi	familiarizarse
accoglienza (I)	Aufnahme f	reception	accueil m	—	acogida f
accogliere (I)	aufnehmen	receive	accueillir	—	recibir
accommodation (E)	Unterkunft f	—	logement m	alloggio m	hospedaje m
accompagnare[1] (I)	begleiten	accompany	accompagner	—	acompañar
accompagnare[2] (I)	mitgehen	go along with	accompagner	—	acompañar
accompagner[1] (F)	begleiten	accompany	—	accompagnare	acompañar
accompagner[2] (F)	mitgehen	go along with	—	accompagnare	acompañar
accompany (E)	begleiten	—	accompagner	accompagnare	acompañar
acconsentire (I)	zustimmen	agree	être d'accord	—	consentir
acconto (I)	Anzahlung f	deposit	acompte m	—	primer pago m
accord[1] (F)	Abmachung f	agreement	—	accordo m	acuerdo m

	D	E	F	I	Es
accord² (F)	Verständigung *f*	agreement	—	accordo *m*	acuerdo *m*
accordarsi (I)	einigen, sich	agree	mettre d'accord, se	—	ponerse de acuerdo
accorder (F)	gewähren	grant	—	concedere	conceder
accordo¹ (I)	Abmachung *f*	agreement	accord *m*	—	acuerdo *m*
accordo² (I)	Verständigung *f*	agreement	accord *m*	—	acuerdo *m*
accorgersi di (I)	merken	notice	remarquer	—	notar
account (E)	Konto *n*	—	compte *m*	conto *m*	cuenta *f*
accrocher (F)	aufhängen	hang up	—	appendere	colgar
accueil (F)	Aufnahme *f*	reception	—	accoglienza *f*	acogida *f*
accueillir (F)	aufnehmen	receive	—	accogliere	recibir
accuracy (E)	Genauigkeit *f*	—	exactitude *f*	precisione *f*	exactitud *f*
accurato (I)	sorgfältig	careful	soigneux(-euse)	—	cuidadoso(a)
aceite (Es)	Öl *n*	oil	huile *f*	olio *m*	—
aceituna (Es)	Olive *f*	olive	olive *f*	oliva *f*	—
acelerar (Es)	beschleunigen	accelerate	accélérer	accelerare	—
acento (Es)	Akzent *m*	accent	accent *m*	accento *m*	—
aceptación (Es)	Annahme *f*	acceptance	réception *f*	accettazione *f*	—
aceptar¹ (Es)	annehmen	accept	accepter	accettare	—
aceptar² (Es)	übernehmen	take over	reprendre	accettare	—
acera (Es)	Gehweg *m*	pavement	trottoir *m*	marciapiede *m*	—
acercarse (Es)	nähern, sich	approach	approcher, se	avvicinarsi	—
acero (Es)	Stahl *m*	steel	acier *m*	acciaio *m*	—
acertar (Es)	gelingen	succeed	réussir	riuscire	—
aceto (I)	Essig *m*	vinegar	vinaigre *m*	—	vinagre *m*
achat¹ (F)	Einkauf *m*	shopping	—	spesa *f*	compra *f*
achat² (F)	Kauf *m*	purchase	—	acquisto *m*	compra *f*
acheter (F)	kaufen	buy	—	comprare	comprar
acheteur (F)	Käufer *m*	buyer	—	acquirente *m*	comprador *m*
acht (D)	—	eight	huit	otto	ocho
achtgeben (D)	—	take care	faire attention	badare	atender
Achtung! (D)	—	attention!	attention!	attenzione!	¡atención!
achtzehn (D)	—	eighteen	dix-huit	diciotto	dieciocho
achtzig (D)	—	eighty	quatre-vingts	ottanta	ochenta
acid (E)	Säure *f*	—	acide *m*	acido *m*	ácido *m*
acide (F)	Säure *f*	acid	—	acido *m*	ácido *m*
ácido (Es)	Säure *f*	acid	acide *m*	acido *m*	—
acido¹ (I)	sauer	sour	aigre	—	agrio(a)
acido² (I)	Säure *f*	acid	acide *m*	—	ácido *m*
acier (F)	Stahl *m*	steel	—	acciaio *m*	acero *m*
Acker (D)	—	field	champ *m*	campo *m*	campo *m*
aclimatarse (Es)	anpassen, sich	adapt	adapter, se	adattarsi	—
acogida (Es)	Aufnahme *f*	reception	accueil *m*	accoglienza *f*	—
acompañar¹ (Es)	begleiten	accompany	accompagner	accompagnare	—
acompañar² (Es)	mitgehen	go along with	accompagner	accompagnare	—
acompte (F)	Anzahlung *f*	deposit	—	acconto *m*	primer pago *m*
à condition que (F)	vorausgesetzt	provided	—	presumendo	supuesto
aconsejar (Es)	raten	advise	conseiller	consigliare	—
acostumbrarse (Es)	gewöhnen, sich	get used to	habituer, se	abituare	—

	D	E	F	I	Es
acqua (I)	Wasser *n*	water	eau *f*	—	agua *f*
acquaintance (E)	Bekannter *m*	—	ami *m*	conoscente *m*	conocido *m*
acqua minerale (I)	Mineralwasser *n*	mineral water	eau minérale *f*	—	agua mineral *f*
acqua potabile (I)	Trinkwasser *n*	drinking water	eau potable *f*	—	agua potable *f*
acquavite (I)	Schnaps *m*	spirits	eau-de-vie *f*	—	aguardiente *m*
acque (I)	Gewässer *n*	waters	eaux *f pl*	—	aguas *f pl*
acquérir (F)	erwerben	acquire	—	acquistare	adquirir
acquire[1] (E)	besorgen	—	procurer	procurare	conseguir
acquire[2] (E)	erwerben	—	acquérir	acquistare	adquirir
acquirente (I)	Käufer *m*	buyer	acheteur *m*	—	comprador *m*
acquistabile (I)	erhältlich	available	en vente	—	que puede adquirirse
acquistare (I)	erwerben	acquire	acquérir	—	adquirir
acquisto (I)	Kauf *m*	purchase	achat *m*	—	compra *f*
across[1] (E)	hinüber	—	de l'autre côté	di là	hacia el otro lado
across[2] (E)	quer	—	en travers	di trasverso	al través
act[1] (E)	darstellen	—	représenter	rappresentare	representar
act[2] (E)	handeln	—	agir	agire	obrar
act[3] (E)	verfahren	—	procéder	procedere	proceder
acteur (F)	Schauspieler *m*	actor	—	attore *m*	actor *m*
actif[1] (F)	aktiv	active	—	attivo(a)	activo(a)
actif[2] (F)	tätig	active	—	attivo(a)	activo(a)
action (F)	Tat *f*	deed	—	azione *f*	acción *f*
actitud (Es)	Einstellung *f*	attitude	attitude *f*	atteggiamento *m*	—
active[1] (E)	aktiv	—	actif(-ive)	attivo(a)	activo(a)
active[2] (E)	tätig	—	actif(-ive)	attivo(a)	activo(a)
actividad (Es)	Tätigkeit *f*	activity	activité *f*	attività *f*	—
activité (F)	Tätigkeit *f*	activity	—	attività *f*	actividad *f*
activity (E)	Tätigkeit *f*	—	activité *f*	attività *f*	actividad *f*
activo[1] (Es)	aktiv	active	actif(-ive)	attivo(a)	—
activo[2] (Es)	fleißig	diligent	travailleur(-euse)	diligente	—
activo[3] (Es)	lebendig	alive	vivant(e)	vivo(a)	—
activo[4] (Es)	tätig	active	actif(-ive)	attivo(a)	—
actor (E)	Schauspieler *m*	—	acteur *m*	attore *m*	actor *m*
actor (Es)	Schauspieler *m*	actor	acteur *m*	attore *m*	—
actually (E)	eigentlich	—	en fait	in fondo	en realidad
actualmente (Es)	nun	now	maintenant	adesso	—
a cuadros (Es)	kariert	checked	à carreaux	a quadretti	—
acuerdo[1] (Es)	Abmachung *f*	agreement	accord *m*	accordo *m*	—
acuerdo[2] (Es)	Verständigung *f*	agreement	information *f*	accordo *m*	—
adapt (E)	anpassen, sich	—	adapter, se	adattarsi	aclimatarse
adapter, se (F)	anpassen, sich	adapt	—	adattarsi	aclimatarse
adattarsi (I)	anpassen, sich	adapt	adapter, se	—	aclimatarse
adatto[1] (I)	geeignet	suitable	approprié(e)	—	indicado(a)
adatto[2] (I)	passend	suitable	assorti(e)	—	apropiado(a)
adatto[3] (I)	zweckmäßig	suitable	approprié(e)	—	adecuado(a)
add[1] (E)	anbauen	—	ajouter	ampliare	ampliar
add[2] (E)	hinzufügen	—	ajouter	aggiungere	añadir

	D	E	F	I	Es
addestramento (I)	Ausbildung f	education	formation f	—	formación f
addestrare (I)	ausbilden	educate	former	—	instruir
addieren (D)	—	add up	additionner	sommare	sumar
addio (I)	Abschied m	parting	adieux m pl	—	despedida f
additionner (F)	addieren	add up	—	sommare	sumar
addormentarsi (I)	einschlafen	fall asleep	endormir, se	—	adormecerse
addossare (I)	aufbürden	burden	charger	—	cargar
address[1] (E)	adressieren	—	adresser	indirizzare	poner las señas en
address[2] (E)	Anschrift f / Adresse f	—	adresse f	indirizzo m	dirección f
add up (E)	addieren	—	additionner	sommare	sumar
adecuado (Es)	zweckmäßig	suitable	approprié(e)	adatto(a)	—
adelantar (Es)	überholen	overtake	doubler	sorpassare	—
¡adelante! (Es)	los!	off!	allons-y!	avanti!	—
adelante[1] (Es)	vorwärts	forward(s)	en avant	avanti	—
adelante[2] (Es)	weiter	further	plus éloigné(e)	più ampio(a)	—
adelgazar (Es)	abnehmen	lose weight	maigrir	dimagrire	—
además (Es)	außerdem	besides	en outre	inoltre	—
adentro (Es)	herein	in	vers l'intérieur	dentro	—
Ader (D)	—	vein	veine f	vena f	vena f
adesso[1] (I)	jetzt	now	maintenant	—	ahora
adesso[2] (I)	nun	now	maintenant	—	actualmente
ad est (I)	östlich	eastern	d'est	—	al este
a destra (I)	rechts	right	à droite	—	a la derecha
adhesivo (Es)	Klebstoff m	glue	colle f	colla f	—
adicional (Es)	zusätzlich	in addition	supplémentaire	supplementare	—
adieux (F)	Abschied m	parting	—	addio m	despedida f
¡adiós![1] (Es)	wiedersehen!	good-bye!	au revoir!	arrivederci!	—
¡adiós![2] (Es)	wiederhören!	good-bye!	au revoir!	a risentirci!	—
adivinanza (Es)	Rätsel n	riddle	devinette f	enigma m	—
adivinar (Es)	raten	guess	deviner	indovinare	—
adjust (E)	einstellen	—	régler	regolare	ajustar
Adler (D)	—	eagle	aigle m	aquila f	águila f
admettre (F)	zulassen	permit	—	permettere	permitir
administración (Es)	Verwaltung f	administration	administration f	amministrazione f	—
administration (E)	Verwaltung f	—	administration f	amministrazione f	administración f
administration (F)	Verwaltung f	administration	—	amministrazione f	administración f
admirar (Es)	bewundern	admire	admirer	ammirare	—
admire (E)	bewundern	—	admirer	ammirare	admirar
admirer (F)	bewundern	admire	—	ammirare	admirar
admission (E)	Zutritt m	—	accès m	accesso m	acceso m
a dónde (Es)	wohin	where to	où	dove	—
adoquinado (Es)	Pflaster n	pavement	pavé m	lastricato m	—
adorar (Es)	anbeten	worship	adorer	adorare	—
adorare (I)	anbeten	worship	adorer	—	adorar
adorer (F)	anbeten	worship	—	adorare	adorar
adormecerse (Es)	einschlafen	fall asleep	endormir, se	addormentarsi	—
ad ovest (I)	westlich	western	de l'ouest	—	occidental

	D	E	F	I	Es
adquirir (Es)	erwerben	acquire	acquérir	acquistare	—
adrede (Es)	absichtlich	intentionally	exprès	apposta	—
Adresse (D)	—	address	adresse f	indirizzo m	dirección f
adresse (F)	Anschrift f / Adresse f	address	—	indirizzo m	dirección f
adresser (F)	adressieren	address	—	indirizzare	poner las señas en
adressieren (D)	—	address	adresser	indirizzare	poner las señas en
à droite (F)	rechts	right	—	a destra	a la derecha
aduana (Es)	Zoll m	customs	douane f	dogana f	—
adult (E)	Erwachsener m	—	adulte m	adulto m	adulto m
adulte[1] (F)	erwachsen	grown up	—	adulto(a)	adulto(a)
adulte[2] (F)	Erwachsener m	adult	—	adulto m	adulto m
adulto[1] (Es)	erwachsen	grown up	adulte	adulto(a)	—
adulto[2] (Es)	Erwachsener m	adult	adulte m	adulto m	—
adulto[1] (I)	erwachsen	grown up	adulte	—	adulto(a)
adulto[2] (I)	Erwachsener m	adult	adulte m	—	adulto m
advance booking (E)	Vorverkauf m	—	location f	vendita anticipata f	venta anticipada f
advantage (E)	Vorteil m	—	avantage m	vantaggio m	ventaja f
adventure (E)	Abenteuer n	—	aventure f	avventura f	aventura f
adversaire (F)	Gegner m	opponent	—	avversario m	adversario m
adversario (Es)	Gegner m	opponent	adversaire m	avversario m	—
advertir (Es)	warnen	warn	prévenir de	ammonire	—
advertise (E)	werben	—	faire de la publicité	fare propaganda	hacer propaganda
advertisement[1] (E)	Annonce f	—	annonce f	annuncio m	anuncio m
advertisement[2] (E)	Inserat n	—	annonce f	inserzione f	anuncio m
advertisement[3] (E)	Reklame f	—	publicité f	réclame f	anuncio m
advertising (E)	Werbung f	—	publicité f	pubblicità f	publicidad f
advice (E)	Rat m	—	conseil m	consiglio m	consejo m
advise (E)	raten	—	conseiller	consigliare	aconsejar
aereo (I)	Flugzeug n	aeroplane	avion m	—	avión m
aérer (F)	lüften	air	—	arieggiare	ventilar
aeroplane (E)	Flugzeug n	—	avion m	aereo m	avión m
aéroport (F)	Flughafen m	airport	—	aeroporto m	aeropuerto m
aeroporto (I)	Flughafen m	airport	aéroport m	—	aeropuerto m
aeropuerto (Es)	Flughafen m	airport	aéroport m	aeroporto m	—
a este lado (Es)	herüber	over	par ici	da questa parte	—
afectuoso (Es)	herzlich	cordial	cordial(e)	cordiale	—
afeitar (Es)	rasieren	shave	raser	fare la barba	—
affair (E)	Angelegenheit f	—	affaire f	affare m	asunto m
affaire (F)	Angelegenheit f	affair	—	affare m	asunto m
affamato (I)	hungrig	hungry	affamé(e)	—	hambriento(a)
affamé (F)	hungrig	hungry	—	affamato(a)	hambriento(a)
affare (I)	Angelegenheit f	affair	affaire f	—	asunto m
affascinante[1] (I)	charmant	charming	charmant(e)	—	encantador(a)
affascinante[2] (I)	entzückend	delightful	ravissant(e)	—	encantador(a)
affascinato (I)	entzückt	delighted	ravi(e)	—	encantado(a)
affaticare (I)	anstrengen	make an effort	faire des efforts	—	cansar
Affe (D)	—	ape	singe m	scimmia f	mono m

	D	E	F	I	Es
affermare (I)	behaupten	assert	affirmer	—	afirmar
affermer (F)	verpachten	lease out	—	affittare	arrendar
afferrare¹ (I)	ergreifen	seize	saisir	—	coger
afferrare² (I)	greifen	seize	saisir	—	coger
affettato (I)	Aufschnitt *m*	cold meat	charcuterie *f*	—	loncha *f*
affiche (F)	Plakat *n*	poster	—	affisso *m*	cartel *m*
affidabile (I)	zuverlässig	reliable	sûr(e)	—	de confianza
affilare (I)	schärfen	sharpen	aiguiser	—	afilar
affirmer (F)	behaupten	assert	—	affermare	afirmar
affisso (I)	Plakat *n*	poster	affiche *f*	—	cartel *m*
affittare¹ (I)	mieten	rent	louer	—	alquilar
affittare² (I)	verpachten	lease out	affermer	—	arrendar
affittare³ (I)	vermieten	rent	louer	—	alquilar
affitto (I)	Miete *f*	rent	loyer *m*	—	alquiler *m*
affondare¹ (I)	sinken	sink	couler	—	hundirse
affondare² (I)	versinken	sink	enfoncer, se	—	hundirse
affrancare (I)	frankieren	stamp	affranchir	—	franquear
affrancatura (I)	Porto *n*	postage	port *m*	—	franqueo *m*
affranchir (F)	frankieren	stamp	—	affrancare	franquear
affrettarsi (I)	beeilen, sich	hurry up	dépêcher, se	—	darse prisa
affreux (F)	abscheulich	abominable	—	disgustoso(a)	horrible
afilar (Es)	schärfen	sharpen	aiguiser	affilare	—
afirmación (Es)	Aussage *f*	statement	déclaration *f*	dichiarazione *f*	—
afirmar (Es)	bejahen	agree with	répondre par l'affirmative à	approvare	—
aflojar (Es)	nachlassen	slacken	apaiser, se	allentare	—
à fond (F)	gründlich	thorough	—	a fondo	a fondo
a fondo (Es)	gründlich	thorough	à fond	a fondo	—
a fondo (I)	gründlich	thorough	à fond	—	a fondo
afortunado (Es)	erfolgreich	successful	avec succès	pieno(a) di successi	—
afoso (I)	schwül	sultry	lourd(e)	—	sofocante
Africa (E)	Afrika	—	Afrique *f*	Africa *f*	Africa *f*
Africa (Es)	Afrika	Africa	Afrique *f*	Africa *f*	—
Africa (I)	Afrika	Africa	Afrique *f*	—	Africa *f*
Afrika (D)	—	Africa	Afrique *f*	Africa *f*	Africa *f*
Afrique (F)	Afrika	Africa	—	Africa *f*	Africa *f*
after¹ (E)	nachdem	—	après que	dopo	después que
after² (E)	nach	—	après/selon	a/in/verso/dopo	a/hacia/después
afternoon (E)	Nachmittag *m*	—	après-midi *m*	pomeriggio *m*	tarde *f*
afterwards¹ (E)	danach	—	après	poi/dopo	después
afterwards² (E)	darauf	—	dessus/ensuite	dopo/su	encima
afterwards³ (E)	nachher	—	ensuite	dopo	después
afuera¹ (Es)	außen	outside	au dehors	fuori	—
afuera² (Es)	draußen	outside	dehors	fuori	—
again¹ (E)	nochmals	—	encore une fois	di nuovo	otra vez
again² (E)	wieder	—	de nouveau	di nuovo	de nuevo
against (E)	gegen	—	contre	contro	contra
against it (E)	dagegen	—	contre cela	contro	contra

	D	E	F	I	Es
à gauche (F)	links	left	—	a sinistra	a la izquierda
age (E)	Alter n	—	âge m	età f	edad f
âge (F)	Alter n	age	—	età f	edad f
agence de voyages (F)	Reisebüro n	travel agency	—	agenzia turistica f	agencia de viajes f
agent de police (F)	Polizist m	policeman	—	poliziotto m	policía m
agenzia turistica (I)	Reisebüro n	travel agency	agence de voyages f	—	agencia de viajes f
aggiungere (I)	hinzufügen	add	ajouter	—	añadir
agglomerato (I)	Siedlung f	settlement	cité f	—	colonia f
aggressione (I)	Überfall m	raid	attaque f	—	asalto m
agir (F)	handeln	act	—	agire	obrar
agire (I)	handeln	act	agir	—	obrar
agitar¹ (Es)	schütteln	shake	secouer	agitare	—
agitar² (Es)	aufregen	excite	énerver	agitare	—
agitare¹ (I)	aufregen	excite	énerver	—	agitar
agitare² (I)	schütteln	shake	secouer	—	agitar
agité (F)	aufgeregt	excited	—	eccitato(a)	excitado(a)
aglio (I)	Knoblauch m	garlic	ail m	—	ajo m
agneau (F)	Lamm n	lamb	—	agnello m	cordero m
agnello (I)	Lamm n	lamb	agneau m	—	cordero m
ago (I)	Nadel f	needle	aiguille f	—	aguja f
agosto (Es)	August m	August	août m	agosto m	—
agosto (I)	August m	August	août m	—	agosto m
agotado (Es)	erschöpft	exhausted	épuisé(e)	esausto(a)	—
agradable¹ (Es)	angenehm	pleasant	agréable	gradevole	—
agradable² (Es)	mild	mild	doux(douce)	mite	—
agradable³ (Es)	nett	nice	joli(e)	carino(a)	—
agradecer (Es)	danken	thank	remercier	ringraziare	—
agradecer algo (Es)	bedanken	say thank you	remercier	ringraziare	—
agradecido (Es)	dankbar	grateful	reconnaissant(e)	grato(a)	—
agradecimiento (Es)	Dank m	thanks	remerciement m	ringraziamento m	—
agrandar (Es)	vergrößern	enlarge	agrandir	ingrandire	—
agrandir (F)	vergrößern	enlarge	—	ingrandire	agrandar
agréable¹ (F)	angenehm	pleasant	—	gradevole	agradable
agréable² (F)	gemütlich	comfortable	—	comodo(a)	cómodo(a)
agree¹ (E)	ausmachen	—	convenir	stabilire	convenir
agree² (E)	einigen, sich	—	mettre d'accord, se	accordarsi	ponerse de acuerdo
agree³ (E)	übereinstimmen	—	être d'accord	concordare	estar de acuerdo
agree⁴ (E)	zustimmen	—	être d'accord	acconsentire	consentir
agreed (E)	einverstanden	—	d'accord	d'accordo	de acuerdo
agreement¹ (E)	Abmachung f	—	accord m	accordo m	acuerdo m
agreement² (E)	Verständigung f	—	accord m	accordo m	acuerdo m
agree upon (E)	vereinbaren	—	convenir de	fissare	convenir
agree with (E)	bejahen	—	répondre par l'affirmative à	approvare	afirmar
agricoltore (I)	Landwirt m	farmer	agriculteur m	—	agricultor m
agriculteur (F)	Landwirt m	farmer	—	agricoltore m	agricultor m
agricultor (Es)	Landwirt m	farmer	agriculteur m	agricoltore m	—

	D	E	F	I	Es
agrio (Es)	sauer	sour	aigre	acido(a)	—
agua (Es)	Wasser *n*	water	eau *f*	acqua *f*	—
agua mineral (Es)	Mineralwasser *n*	mineral water	eau minérale *f*	acqua minerale *f*	—
aguantar (Es)	aushalten	bear	supporter	sopportare	—
agua potable (Es)	Trinkwasser *n*	drinking water	eau potable *f*	acqua potabile *f*	—
aguardiente (Es)	Schnaps *m*	spirits	eau-de-vie *f*	acquavite *f*	—
aguas (Es)	Gewässer *n*	waters	eaux *f pl*	acque *f pl*	—
águila (Es)	Adler *m*	eagle	aigle *m*	aquila *f*	—
aguja (Es)	Nadel *f*	needle	aiguille *f*	ago *m*	—
agujero (Es)	Loch *n*	hole	trou *m*	buco *m*	—
ahead (E)	voraus	—	en avant	avanti	delante
ähneln (D)	—	resemble	ressembler	assomigliare	parecer
ahnen (D)	—	suspect	douter, se	supporre	suponer
ähnlich (D)	—	similar	semblable	simile	parecido(a)
Ahnung (D)	—	presentiment	pressentiment *m*	presentimento *m*	presentimiento *m*
ahogarse (Es)	ertrinken	drown	noyer, se	annegare	—
ahora (Es)	jetzt	now	maintenant	adesso	—
ahora mismo (Es)	soeben	just now	à l'instant même	poco fa	—
ahorrar (Es)	sparen	save	économiser	risparmiare	—
aide (F)	Hilfe *f*	help	—	aiuto *m*	ayuda *f*
aider (F)	helfen	help	—	aiutare	ayudar
aider qn (F)	behilflich sein	help s.b.	—	aiutare	ayudar a alguien
aigle (F)	Adler *m*	eagle	—	aquila *f*	águila *f*
aigre (F)	sauer	sour	—	acido(a)	agrio(a)
aiguille (F)	Nadel *f*	needle	—	ago *m*	aguja *f*
aiguiser (F)	schärfen	sharpen	—	affilare	afilar
ail (F)	Knoblauch *m*	garlic	—	aglio *m*	ajo *m*
aile (F)	Flügel *m*	wing	—	ala *f*	ala *f*
ailleurs (F)	woanders	elsewhere	—	altrove	en otra parte
aimable¹ (F)	freundlich	friendly	—	gentile	amistoso(a)
aimable² (F)	liebenswürdig	kind	—	gentile	gentil
aimer¹ (F)	lieben	love	—	amare	amar
aimer² (F)	mögen	like	—	piacere	querer
aîné (F)	ältere(r,s)	elder	—	maggiore	mayor
ainsi (F)	so	like this	—	cosí	así
air¹ (E)	lüften	—	aérer	arieggiare	ventilar
air² (E)	Luft *f*	—	air *m*	aria *f*	aire *m*
air (F)	Luft *f*	air	—	aria *f*	aire *m*
aire (Es)	Luft *f*	air	air *m*	aria *f*	—
air mail (E)	Luftpost *f*	—	poste aérienne *f*	posta aerea *f*	correo aéreo *m*
airport (E)	Flughafen *m*	—	aéroport *m*	aeroporto *m*	aeropuerto *m*
aiutare¹ (I)	behilflich sein	help s.b.	aider qn	—	ayudar a alguien
aiutare² (I)	helfen	help	aider	—	ayudar
aiuto (I)	Hilfe *f*	help	aide *f*	—	ayuda *f*
ajo (Es)	Knoblauch *m*	garlic	ail *m*	aglio *m*	—
ajouter¹ (F)	anbauen	add	—	ampliare	ampliar
ajouter² (F)	hinzufügen	add	—	aggiungere	añadir
ajustar (Es)	einstellen	adjust	régler	regolare	—

	D	E	F	I	Es
Aktenmappe (D)	—	file	porte-documents *m*	cartella *f*	cartera *f*
aktiv (D)	—	active	actif(-ive)	attivo(a)	activo(a)
Akzent (D)	—	accent	accent *m*	accento *m*	acento *m*
ala (Es)	Flügel *m*	wing	aile *f*	ala *f*	—
ala (I)	Flügel *m*	wing	aile *f*	—	ala *f*
a la derecha (Es)	rechts	right	à droite	a destra	—
a la izquierda (Es)	links	left	à gauche	a sinistra	—
à la maison[1] (F)	daheim	at home	—	a casa	en casa
à la maison[2] (F)	nach Hause	home	—	a casa	a casa
alambre (Es)	Draht *m*	wire	fil de fer *m*	filo metallico *m*	—
alargar[1] (Es)	strecken	stretch	allonger	stendere	—
alargar[2] (Es)	verlängern	extend	prolonger	allungare	—
alarm clock (E)	Wecker *m*	—	réveil *m*	sveglia *f*	despertador *m*
a la sombra (Es)	schattig	shady	ombragé(e)	ombroso(a)	—
a la vez (Es)	gleichzeitig	simultaneous	en même temps	contemporaneo(a)	—
albaricoque (Es)	Aprikose *f*	apricot	abricot *m*	albicocca *f*	—
albergo (I)	Hotel *n*	hotel	hôtel *m*	—	hotel *m*
albern (D)	—	foolish	sot(te)	sciocco(a)	tonto(a)
albero (I)	Baum *m*	tree	arbre *m*	—	árbol *m*
albicocca (I)	Aprikose *f*	apricot	abricot *m*	—	albaricoque *m*
alcalde (Es)	Bürgermeister *m*	mayor	maire *m*	sindaco *m*	—
alcanzar[1] (Es)	erreichen	reach	atteindre	raggiungere	—
alcanzar[2] (Es)	reichen	pass	passer	passare	—
alcanzar[3] (Es)	treffen	hit	toucher	colpire	—
alcohol (E)	Alkohol *m*	—	alcool *m*	alcol *m*	alcohol *m*
alcohol (Es)	Alkohol *m*	alcohol	alcool *m*	alcol *m*	—
alcol (I)	Alkohol *m*	alcohol	alcool *m*	—	alcohol *m*
alcool (F)	Alkohol *m*	alcohol	—	alcol *m*	alcohol *m*
alcuni[1] (I)	einige	some	quelques	—	algunos(as)
alcuni[2] (I)	etliche	several	quelques	—	algunos(as)
al di là (I)	jenseits	beyond	de l'autre côté	—	al otro lado
al di sotto di (I)	unter	under	sous	—	debajo de
alegrarse (Es)	freuen, sich	be glad	être heureux(-euse)	rallegrarsi	—
alegre (Es)	munter	lively	éveillé(e)	vivace	—
alegría (Es)	Freude *f*	joy	joie *f*	gioia *f*	—
alemán[1] (Es)	deutsch	German	allemand(e)	tedesco(a)	—
alemán[2] (Es)	Deutscher *m*	German	Allemand *m*	tedesco	—
Alemania (Es)	Deutschland	Germany	Allemagne *f*	Germania *f*	—
alergia (Es)	Allergie *f*	allergy	allergie *f*	allergia *f*	—
al este (Es)	östlich	eastern	d'est	ad est	—
à l'extérieur (F)	auswärts	out(wards)	—	fuori	fuera
alfabeto (Es)	Alphabet *n*	alphabet	alphabet *m*	alfabeto *m*	—
alfabeto (I)	Alphabet *n*	alphabet	alphabet *m*	—	alfabeto *m*
alfombra (Es)	Teppich *m*	carpet	tapis *m*	tappeto *m*	—
algo[1] (Es)	etwas	something	quelque chose	qualcosa	—
algo[2] (Es)	irgend etwas	something	n'importe quoi	qualsiasi cosa	—
algodón[1] (Es)	Baumwolle *f*	cotton	coton *m*	cotone *m*	—

	D	E	F	I	Es
algodón² (Es)	Watte f	cotton wool	ouate f	ovatta f	—
alguien (Es)	jemand	somebody	quelqu'un	qualcuno	—
alguno (Es)	irgend jemand	somebody	n'importe qui	qualcuno	—
algunos¹ (Es)	etliche	several	quelques	alcuni(e)	—
algunos² (Es)	einige	some	quelques	alcuni(e)	—
aliment (F)	Speise f	food	—	cibo m	comida f
alimentación¹ (Es)	Ernährung f	nourishment	nourriture f	alimentazione f	—
alimentación² (Es)	Verpflegung f	catering	nourriture f	vitto m	—
alimentar (Es)	ernähren	feed	nourrir	nutrire	—
alimentari¹ (I)	Eßwaren pl	foodstuffs	produits alimentaires m pl	—	comestibles m pl
alimentari² (I)	Lebensmittel pl	food	alimentation f	—	alimentos m pl
alimentation (F)	Lebensmittel pl	food	—	alimentari m pl	alimentos m pl
alimentazione¹ (I)	Ernährung f	nourishment	nourriture f	—	alimentación f
alimentazione² (I)	Essen n	food	repas m	—	comida f
alimentazione³ (I)	Nahrung f	food	nourriture f	—	nutrición f
alimento (Es)	Kost f	food	nourriture f	cibo m	—
alimentos (Es)	Lebensmittel pl	food	alimentation f	alimentari m pl	—
à l'instant même (F)	soeben	just now	—	poco fa	ahora mismo
à l'intérieur (F)	drinnen, innen	inside	—	dentro	dentro
à l'intérieur de (F)	innerhalb	within	—	entro	dentro de
a little (E)	bißchen	—	un peu	un po	un poquito
alive (E)	lebendig	—	vivant(e)	vivo(a)	vivo(a)
aliviarse (Es)	erholen, sich	recover	reposer, se	rimettersi	—
Alkohol (D)	—	alcohol	alcool m	alcol m	alcohol m
all (E)	alle	—	tous(toutes)	tutti(e)	todos(as)
al lado de (Es)	neben	beside	près de	accanto a	—
alle (D)	—	all	tous(toutes)	tutti(e)	todos(as)
allée (F)	Auffahrt f	drive	—	salita d'ingresso f	entrada f
allegro (I)	lustig	funny	marrant(e)	—	divertido(a)
allein (D)	—	alone	seul(e)	solo(a)	solo(a)
Allemagne (F)	Deutschland	Germany	—	Germania f	Alemania f
allemand (F)	deutsch	German	—	tedesco(a)	alemán(-ana)
Allemand (F)	Deutscher m	German	—	tedesco m	alemán m
allentare (I)	nachlassen	slacken	apaiser, se	—	aflojar
aller (F)	gehen	go	—	andare	andar
aller bien (F)	passen	suit	—	stare bene	venir bien
aller chercher¹ (F)	abholen	pick up	—	andare a prendere	recoger
aller chercher² (F)	holen	fetch	—	andare a prendere	traer
allergia (I)	Allergie f	allergy	allergie f	—	alergia f
Allergie (D)	—	allergy	allergie f	allergia f	alergia f
allergie (F)	Allergie f	allergy	—	allergia f	alergia f
allergy (E)	Allergie f	—	allergie f	allergia f	alergia f
aller plus loin (F)	weitergehen	go on	—	proseguire	proseguir
aller, s'en (F)	weggehen	go away	—	andare via	marcharse
alles (D)	—	everything	tout	tutto	todo
allevare (I)	züchten	breed	élever	—	criar
allgemein (D)	—	general	général(e)	generale	general

	D	E	F	I	Es
allí¹ (Es)	dort	there	là/y	là	—
allí² (Es)	da	there	là/ici	qui/là	—
allmählich (D)	—	gradual	graduel(le)	graduale	gradual
allô! (F)	hallo!	hello!	—	pronto!	¡diga!
alloggio (I)	Unterkunft f	accommodation	logement m	—	hospedaje m
all one colour (E)	einfarbig	—	uni(e)	monocolore	de un solo color
allonger (F)	strecken	stretch	—	stendere	alargar
allons-y! (F)	los!	off!	—	avanti!	¡adelante!
allontanare (I)	entfernen	remove	éloigner	—	quitar
allora (I)	damals	at that time	à cette époque	—	entonces
allow¹ (E)	erlauben	—	permettre	permettere	permitir
allow² (E)	gestatten	—	permettre	permettere	permitir
Alltag (D)	—	everyday life	vie quotidienne f	vita quotidiana f	vida cotidiana f
all the same (E)	egal	—	égal(e)	uguale	igual
allumer¹ (F)	anzünden	light	—	accendere	encender
allumer² (F)	anmachen	put on	—	accendere	encender
allumer³ (F)	einschalten	switch on	—	accendere	conectar
allumer, se (F)	zünden	ignite	—	accendersi	encender
allumette (F)	Streichholz n	match	—	fiammifero m	cerilla f
allungare (I)	verlängern	extend	prolonger	—	alargar
almacén (Es)	Lager n	store	magasin m	magazzino m	—
al massimo (I)	höchstens	at the most	tout au plus	—	a lo sumo
almendra (Es)	Mandel f	almond	amande f	mandorla f	—
almeno¹ (I)	mindestens	at least	au moins	—	por lo menos
almeno² (I)	wenigstens	at least	au moins	—	por lo menos
almohada (Es)	Kopfkissen n	pillow	oreiller m	guanciale m	—
almond (E)	Mandel f	—	amande f	mandorla f	almendra f
Almosen (D)	—	alms	aumône f	elemosina f	limosna f
alms (E)	Almosen n	—	aumône f	elemosina f	limosna f
a lo largo de (Es)	entlang	along	le long de	lungo	—
alone (E)	allein	—	seul(e)	solo(a)	solo(a)
along (E)	entlang	—	le long de	lungo	a lo largo de
a long time ago (E)	längst	—	depuis bien longtemps	da molto	hace mucho
alors (F)	damals	at that time	—	allora	entonces
a lo sumo (Es)	höchstens	at the most	tout au plus	al massimo	—
a lot of (E)	viel	—	beaucoup de	molto(a)	mucho(a)
al otro lado¹ (Es)	drüben	over there	de l'autre côté	dall'altra parte	—
al otro lado² (Es)	jenseits	beyond	de l'autre côté	al di là	—
Alphabet (D)	—	alphabet	alphabet m	alfabeto m	alfabeto m
alphabet (E)	Alphabet n	—	alphabet m	alfabeto m	alfabeto m
alphabet (F)	Alphabet n	alphabet	—	alfabeto m	alfabeto m
alpinista (Es)	Bergsteiger m	mountaineer	alpiniste m	alpinista m	—
alpinista (I)	Bergsteiger m	mountaineer	alpiniste m	—	alpinista m
alpiniste (F)	Bergsteiger m	mountaineer	—	alpinista m	alpinista m
alquilar¹ (Es)	mieten	rent	louer	affittare	—
alquilar² (Es)	vermieten	rent	louer	affittare	—
alquiler (Es)	Miete f	rent	loyer m	affitto m	—

	D	E	F	I	Es
already (E)	bereits/schon	—	déjà	già	ya
alrededor (Es)	herum	around	autour	intorno	—
alrededor de (Es)	um	at/around	autour de/à	intorno a/a	—
alrededores (Es)	Umgebung f	surroundings	environs m pl	dintorni m pl	—
als (D)	—	when	quand	quando	cuando
also (D)	—	therefore	donc	dunque/quindi	así
also (E)	auch	—	aussi	anche/pure	también
al sur (Es)	südlich	southern	au sud	a sud	—
alt (D)	—	old	vieux, vieil, vieille	vecchio(a)	viejo(a)
alt! (I)	halt!	stop!	stop!	—	¡alto!
alta marea (I)	Flut f	high tide	marée haute f	—	marea alta f
alta montagna (I)	Hochgebirge n	high mountain-chain	haute montage f	—	montañas elevadas f pl
alta stagione (I)	Hochsaison f	high season	pleine saison f	—	temporada alta f
altavoz (Es)	Lautsprecher m	loudspeaker	haut-parleur m	altoparlante m	—
Alter (D)	—	age	âge m	età f	edad f
alteration (E)	Umbuchung f	—	transfert m	riporto m	cambio m
ältere (D)	—	elder	aîné(e)	maggiore	mayor
alternar (Es)	abwechseln	take turns	alterner	alternarsi	—
alternarsi (I)	abwechseln	take turns	alterner	—	alternar
alterner (F)	abwechseln	take turns	—	alternarsi	alternar
altertümlich (D)	—	dated	antique	antico(a)	antiguo(a)
altezza (I)	Höhe f	height	hauteur f	—	altura f
although (E)	obwohl/obgleich	—	bien que	benché	aunque
altmodisch (D)	—	old-fashioned	démodé(e)	fuori moda	pasado(a) de moda
alto (Es)	hoch	up/high	haut(e)	alto(a)	—
¡alto! (Es)	halt!	stop!	stop!	alt!	—
alto (I)	hoch	up/high	haut(e)	—	alto(a)
altogether (E)	insgesamt	—	dans l'ensemble	complessivamente	en suma
altoparlante (I)	Lautsprecher m	loudspeaker	haut-parleur m	—	altavoz m
al través (Es)	quer	across	en travers	di trasverso	—
altrettanto (I)	ebenfalls	as well	aussi	—	también
altrimenti (I)	sonst	otherwise	autrement	—	por lo demás
altro (I)	andere(r,s)	other	autre	—	otra(o)
altrove (I)	woanders	elsewhere	ailleurs	—	en otra parte
altura (Es)	Höhe f	height	hauteur f	altezza f	—
alumno (Es)	Schüler m	pupil	élève m	scolaro m	—
always[1] (E)	immer	—	toujours	sempre	siempre
always[2] (E)	stets	—	toujours	sempre	siempre
alzare[1] (I)	erheben	raise	lever	—	elevar
alzare[2] (I)	heben	lift	soulever	—	levantar
alzarsi (I)	aufstehen	get up	lever, se	—	levantarse
amable (Es)	lieb	sweet	gentil(le)	caro(a)	—
ama de casa (Es)	Hausfrau f	housewife	femme de maison f	casalinga f	—
amande (F)	Mandel f	almond	—	mandorla f	almendra f
amanecer (Es)	dämmern	dawn	poindre	spuntare	—
amapola (Es)	Mohn m	poppy	coquelicot m	papavero m	—
amar (Es)	lieben	love	aimer	amare	—

	D	E	F	I	Es
amare (I)	lieben	love	aimer	—	amar
amargo[1] (Es)	bitter	bitter	amer(-ère)	amaro(a)	—
amargo[2] (Es)	herb	bitter	âcre	amaro(a)	—
amarillo (Es)	gelb	yellow	jaune	giallo(a)	—
amaro[1] (I)	bitter	bitter	amer(-ère)	—	amargo(a)
amaro[2] (I)	herb	bitter	âpre	—	amargo(a)
ambasciata (I)	Botschaft f	embassy	ambassade f	—	embajada f
ambassade (F)	Botschaft f	embassy	—	ambasciata f	embajada f
ambientarsi (I)	einleben, sich	settle into	acclimater, se	—	familiarizarse
ambiente (I)	Umwelt f	environment	environnement m	—	medioambiente m
ambos (Es)	beide	both	tous/toutes les deux	entrambi	—
ambulance (E)	Krankenwagen m	—	ambulance f	ambulanza f	ambulancia f
ambulance (F)	Krankenwagen m	ambulance	—	ambulanza f	ambulancia f
ambulancia (Es)	Krankenwagen m	ambulance	ambulance f	ambulanza f	—
ambulanza (I)	Krankenwagen m	ambulance	ambulance f	—	ambulancia f
amélioration (F)	Besserung f	improvement	—	miglioramento m	restablecimiento m
améliorer (F)	verbessern	improve	—	migliorare	mejorar
a memoria (Es)	Andenken n	souvenir	souvenir m	ricordo m	—
a memoria (I)	auswendig	by heart	par cœur	—	de memoria
aménager (F)	einrichten	fit out	—	arredare	equipar
amenazar[1] (Es)	drohen	threaten s.b.	menacer	minacciare	—
amenazar[2] (Es)	androhen	threaten	menacer	minacciare	—
amenazar[3] (Es)	bedrohen	threaten	menacer	minacciare	—
a menudo (Es)	oft	often	souvent	spesso	—
amer (F)	bitter	bitter	—	amaro(a)	amargo(a)
America (E)	Amerika n	—	Amérique f	America f	América f
América (Es)	Amerika n	America	Amérique f	America f	—
America (I)	Amerika n	America	Amérique f	—	América f
America del Nord (I)	Nordamerika n	North America	Amérique du Nord f	—	América del Norte f
América del Norte (Es)	Nordamerika n	North America	Amérique du Nord f	America del Nord f	—
américain (F)	amerikanisch	American	—	americano(a)	americano(a)
American (E)	amerikanisch	—	américain(e)	americano(a)	americano(a)
americano (I)	amerikanisch	American	américain(e)	—	americano(a)
americano (Es)	amerikanisch	American	américain(e)	americano	—
Amerika (D)	—	America	Amérique f	America f	América f
amerikanisch (D)	—	American	américain(e)	americano(a)	americano(a)
Amérique (F)	Amerika n	America	—	America f	América f
Amérique du Nord (F)	Nordamerika n	North America	—	America del Nord f	América del Norte f
ameublement (F)	Einrichtung f	furnishing	—	arredamento m	mobiliario m
a mezzogiorno (I)	mittags	at midday	à midi	—	mediodía
ami[1] (F)	Freund m	friend	—	amico m	amigo m
ami[2] (F)	Bekannter m	acquaintance	—	conoscente m	conocido m
amicizia (I)	Freundschaft f	friendship	amitié f	—	amistad f
amico[1] (I)	befreundet	friendly	ami(e)	—	amigo(a)
amico[2] (I)	Freund m	friend	ami m	—	amigo m
ami de (F)	befreundet	friendly	—	amico(a)	amigo(a) de
à midi (F)	mittags	at midday	—	a mezzogiorno	mediodía

	D	E	F	I	Es
amigo (Es)	Freund *m*	friend	ami *m*	amico *m*	—
amigo de (Es)	befreundet	friendly	ami(e) de	amico(a)	—
amistad (Es)	Freundschaft *f*	friendship	amitié *f*	amicizia *f*	—
amistoso (Es)	freundlich	friendly	aimable	gentile	—
amitié (F)	Freundschaft *f*	friendship	—	amicizia *f*	amistad *f*
ammalarsi (I)	erkranken	get ill	tomber malade	—	enfermar
amministrazione (I)	Verwaltung *f*	administration	administration *f*	—	administración *f*
ammirare (I)	bewundern	admire	admirer	—	admirar
ammobiliare (I)	möblieren	furnish	meubler	—	amueblar
ammobiliato (I)	möbliert	furnished	meublé(e)	—	amueblado(a)
ammonire[1] (I)	mahnen	warn	exhorter	—	notificar
ammonire[2] (I)	warnen	warn	prévenir de	—	advertir
amor (Es)	Liebe *f*	love	amour *m*	amore *m*	—
amore (I)	Liebe *f*	love	amour *m*	—	amor *m*
amount (E)	Betrag *m*	—	montant *m*	somma *f*	importe *m*
amour (F)	Liebe *f*	love	—	amore *m*	amor *m*
amoureux (F)	verliebt	in love	—	innamorato(a)	enamorado(a)
Ampel (D)	—	traffic lights	feux *m pl*	semaforo *m*	semáforo *m*
ampliar (Es)	anbauen	add	ajouter	ampliare	—
ampliare (I)	anbauen	add	ajouter	—	ampliar
amplio[1] (Es)	breit	broad	large	largo(a)	—
amplio[2] (I)	weit	far	éloigné(e)	—	ancho(a)
ampoule (F)	Glühbirne *f*	light bulb	—	lampadina *f*	lámpara *f*
Amt (D)	—	office	bureau *m*	ufficio *m*	oficio *m*
amtlich (D)	—	official	officiel(le)	ufficiale	oficial
amueblado (Es)	möbliert	furnished	meublé(e)	ammobiliato(a)	—
amueblar (Es)	möblieren	furnish	meubler	ammobiliare	—
amuser, se (F)	amüsieren, sich	enjoy o.s.	—	divertirsi	divertirse
amüsieren, sich (D)	—	enjoy o.s.	amuser, se	divertirsi	divertirse
an (D)	—	at/on/by	à/près de	a/in/su	junto a
añadir (Es)	hinzufügen	add	ajouter	aggiungere	—
Ananas (D)	—	pineapple	ananas *m*	ananas *m*	piña *f*
ananas (F)	Ananas *f*	pineapple	—	ananas *m*	piña *f*
ananas (I)	Ananas *f*	pineapple	ananas *m*	—	piña *f*
anatra (I)	Ente *f*	duck	canard *m*	—	pato *m*
anbauen[1] (D)	—	add	ajouter	ampliare	ampliar
anbauen[2] (D)	—	cultivate	cultiver	coltivare	cultivar
anbeten (D)	—	worship	adorer	adorare	adorar
anbieten (D)	—	offer	offrir	offrire	ofrecer
anbringen (D)	—	fasten	fixer	fissare	colocar
anche (I)	auch	also/too	aussi	—	también
ancho (Es)	weit	far	éloigné(e)	largo(a)	—
ancora (I)	noch	still	encore	—	aún/todavía
and (E)	und	—	et	e	y
andar[1] (Es)	gehen	go	aller	andare	—
andar[2] (Es)	geben	give	donner	dare	—
andare[1] (I)	fahren	drive	conduire	—	conducir
andare[2] (I)	gehen	go	aller	—	andar

	D	E	F	I	Es
andare a prendere[1] (I)	abholen	pick up	aller chercher	—	recoger
andare a prendere[2] (I)	holen	fetch	aller chercher	—	traer
andare a trovare (I)	besuchen	visit	rendre visite à	—	visitar
andare avanti (I)	vorangehen	go ahead	marcher devant	—	pasar adelante
andare a vela (I)	segeln	sail	faire de la voile	—	navegar a vela
andare in fretta (I)	eilen	hurry	dépêcher, se	—	darse prisa
andare insieme (I)	mitgehen	go along with	accompagner	—	acompañar
andare via (I)	weggehen	go away	s'en aller	—	marcharse
Andenken (D)	—	souvenir	souvenir *m*	ricordo *m*	recuerdo *m*
andere (D)	—	other	autre	altro(a)	otra(o)
andererseits (D)	—	on the other hand	d'autre part	d'altra parte	por otra parte
ändern (D)	—	change	changer	cambiare	cambiar
anders (D)	—	different	différent(e)	differente	diferente
anderthalb (D)	—	one and a half	un(e) et demi(e)	uno(a) e mezzo	uno(a) y medio(a)
androhen (D)	—	threaten	menacer	minacciare	amenazar
âne (F)	Esel *m*	donkey	—	asino *m*	burro *m*
anello (I)	Ring *m*	ring	bague *f*	—	sortija *f*
Anfang (D)	—	beginning	commencement *m*	inizio *m*	inicio *m*
anfangen (D)	—	start	commencer	cominciare	empezar
Anfänger (D)	—	beginner	débutant(e)	principiante *m*	principiante *m*
anfitrión (Es)	Gastgeber *m*	host	hôte *m*	ospite *m*	—
anfordern (D)	—	request	demander	esigere	pedir
Angabe (D)	—	information	information *f*	indicazione *f*	información *f*
ange (F)	Engel *m*	angel	—	angelo *m*	ángel *m*
angeblich (D)	—	pretended	prétendu(e)	presunto(a)	supuesto(a)
angeboren (D)	—	inborn	inné(e)	innato(a)	innato(a)
Angebot (D)	—	offer	offre *f*	offerta *f*	oferta *f*
angel (E)	Engel *m*	—	ange *m*	angelo *m*	ángel *m*
ángel (Es)	Engel *m*	angel	ange *m*	angelo *m*	—
Angelegenheit (D)	—	affair	affaire *f*	affare *m*	asunto *m*
angeln (D)	—	fish	pêcher	pescare	pescar con caña
angelo (I)	Engel *m*	angel	ange *m*	—	ángel *m*
angenehm (D)	—	pleasant	agréable	gradevole	agradable
anger (E)	Wut *f*	—	colère *f*	rabbia *f*	rabia *f*
Angestellter (D)	—	employee	employé *m*	impiegato *m*	empleado *m*
anglais (F)	englisch	English	—	inglese	inglés(-esa)
Anglais (F)	Engländer *m*	Englishman	—	inglese *m*	inglés *m*
Angleterre (F)	England *n*	England	—	Inghilterra *f*	Inglaterra *f*
angolo (I)	Ecke *f*	corner	coin *m*	—	esquina *f*
angreifen (D)	—	attack	attaquer	attaccare	atacar
angry (E)	ärgerlich	—	fâché(e)	arrabbiato(a)	enfadado(a)
Angst (D)	—	fear	peur *f*	paura *f*	miedo *m*
ängstlich (D)	—	fearful	peureux(-euse)	pauroso(a)	miedoso(a)
anhaben (D)	—	have on	porter	indossare	llevar
anhalten (D)	—	stop	arrêter	fermare	parar
Anhalter (D)	—	hitch-hiker	auto-stoppeur *m*	autostoppista *m*	autoestopista *m*
animado (Es)	belebt	lively	animé(e)	animato(a)	—

	D	E	F	I	Es
animal (E)	Tier n	—	animal m	animale m	animal m
animal (Es)	Tier n	animal	animal m	animale m	—
animal (F)	Tier n	animal	—	animale m	animal m
animale (I)	Tier n	animal	animal m	—	animal m
animato (I)	belebt	lively	animé(e)	—	animado(a)
animé (F)	belebt	lively	—	animato(a)	animado(a)
ánimo (Es)	Gemüt n	disposition	disposition f	animo m	—
animo (I)	Gemüt n	disposition	disposition f	—	ánimo m
ankle (E)	Knöchel m	—	cheville f	caviglia f	tobillo m
ankommen (D)	—	arrive	arriver	arrivare	llegar
Ankunft (D)	—	arrival	arrivée f	arrivo m	llegada f
Anlage (D)	—	plant	construction f	impianto m	establecimiento m
Anlaß (D)	—	occasion	occasion f	occasione f	ocasión f
anmachen (D)	—	put on	allumer	accendere	encender
anmelden (D)	—	announce	annoncer	annunciare	anunciar
annaffiare (I)	gießen	water	arroser	—	regar
Annahme[1] (D)	—	acceptance	réception f	accettazione f	aceptación f
Annahme[2] (D)	—	assumption	supposition f	supposizione f	suposición f
année (F)	Jahr n	year	—	anno m	año m
annegare (I)	ertrinken	drown	noyer, se	—	ahogarse
annehmen[1] (D)	—	accept	accepter	accettare	aceptar
annehmen[2] (D)	—	suppose	supposer	supporre	suponer
anniversaire (F)	Geburtstag m	birthday	—	compleanno m	cumpleaños m
anno (I)	Jahr n	year	année f	—	año m
annoiarsi (I)	langweilen, sich	get bored	ennuyer, se	—	aburrirse
Annonce (D)	—	advertisement	annonce f	annuncio m	anuncio m
annonce[1] (F)	Anzeige f	announcement	—	annuncio m	anuncio m
annonce[2] (F)	Annonce f	advertisement	—	annuncio m	anuncio m
annonce[3] (F)	Inserat n	advertisement	—	inserzione f	anuncio m
annonce[4] (F)	Meldung f	report	—	annuncio m	aviso m
annoncer[1] (F)	ansagen	announce	—	annunciare	anunciar
annoncer[2] (F)	anmelden	announce	—	annunciare	anunciar
annoncer[3] (F)	melden	report	—	annunciare	declarar
annotare (I)	notieren	note down	noter	—	anotar
announce[1] (E)	ansagen	—	annoncer	annunciare	anunciar
announce[2] (E)	anmelden	—	annoncer	annunciare	anunciar
announcement (E)	Anzeige f	—	annonce f	annuncio m	anuncio m
annoy[1] (E)	ärgern	—	fâcher	arrabbiare	enfadar
annoy[2] (E)	belästigen	—	importuner	importunare	molestar
annuaire du téléphone (F)	Telefonbuch n	phone book	—	elenco telefonico m	guía telefónica f
annual (E)	jährlich	—	annuel(le)	annuale	anual
annuale (I)	jährlich	annual	annuel(le)	—	anual
annuel (F)	jährlich	annual	—	annuale	anual
annuire (I)	nicken	nod	faire un signe de la tête	—	inclinar la cabeza
annul (E)	annullieren	—	annuler	annullare	anular
annuler (F)	annullieren	annul	—	annullare	anular
annullare[1] (I)	annullieren	annul	annuler	—	anular

	D	E	F	I	Es
annullare² (I)	abbestellen	cancel	décommander	—	anular el pedido de
annullieren (D)	—	annul	annuler	annullare	anular
annunciare¹ (I)	ansagen	announce	annoncer	—	anunciar
annunciare² (I)	anmelden	announce	annoncer	—	anunciar
annunciare³ (I)	melden	report	annoncer	—	declarar
annuncio¹ (I)	Anzeige f	announcement	annonce f	—	anuncio m
annuncio² (I)	Annonce f	advertisement	annonce f	—	anuncio m
annuncio³ (I)	Meldung f	report	annonce f	—	aviso m
año (Es)	Jahr n	year	année f	anno m	—
Año Nuevo (Es)	Neujahr n	New Year	nouvel an m	Capodanno m	—
a nord (I)	nördlich	northerly	du nord	—	del norte
anotar (Es)	notieren	note down	noter	annotare	—
anpassen, sich (D)	—	adapt	adapter, se	adattarsi	aclimatarse
anprobieren (D)	—	try on	essayer	provare	probar
anrechnen (D)	—	charge	compter	mettere in conto	poner en cuenta
Anruf (D)	—	call	coup de téléphone m	chiamata f	llamada f
anrufen (D)	—	ring up	téléphoner	telefonare	llamar por teléfono
ansagen (D)	—	announce	annoncer	annunciare	anunciar
anschauen (D)	—	look at	regarder	guardare	mirar
anscheinend (D)	—	seemingly	apparemment	apparentemente	aparentemente
Anschluß (D)	—	connection	correspondance f	coincidenza f	conexión f
Anschrift (D)	—	address	adresse f	indirizzo m	dirección f
ansehen (D)	—	look at	regarder	guardare	mirar
Ansicht (D)	—	opinion	avis m	opinione f	opinión f
Ansichtskarte (D)	—	postcard	carte postale f	cartolina f	tarjeta postal f
anständig (D)	—	decent	convenable	decente	decente
anstatt (D)	—	instead of	au lieu de	invece di	en vez de
anstellen (D)	—	turn on	mettre en marche	accendere	poner
anstoßen (D)	—	bump	heurter	urtare	empujar
anstrengen (D)	—	make an effort	faire des efforts	affaticare	cansar
anstrengend (D)	—	tiring	fatigant(e)	faticoso(a)	fatigoso(a)
Anstrengung (D)	—	strain	effort m	fatica f	esfuerzo m
answer¹ (E)	antworten	—	répondre	rispondere	responder
answer² (E)	Antwort f	—	réponse f	risposta f	respuesta f
answer³ (E)	beantworten	—	répondre à	rispondere a	responder a
anteayer (Es)	vorgestern	day before yesterday	avant-hier	l'altro ieri	—
anterior (Es)	vorhergehend	preceding	précédent	precedente	—
antes¹ (Es)	eher	sooner	plus tôt	prima	—
antes² (Es)	früher	earlier	autrefois	prima	—
antes³ (Es)	vorher	before	avant	prima	—
antes⁴ (Es)	zuvor	before	auparavant	prima	—
antes que¹ (Es)	bevor	before	avant que	prima che	—
antes que² (Es)	ehe	before	avant que	prima che	—
antico (I)	altertümlich	dated	antique	—	antiguo(a)
antigüedades (Es)	Antiquitäten pl	antiques	antiquités f pl	oggetti antichi m	—
antiguo (Es)	altertümlich	dated	antique	antico(a)	—
antipasto (I)	Vorspeise f	appetizer	hors-d'œuvre m	—	primer plato m

	D	E	F	I	Es
antique (F)	altertümlich	dated	—	antico(a)	antiguo(a)
antiques (E)	Antiquitäten pl	—	antiquités f pl	oggetti antichi m	antigüedades f pl
Antiquitäten (D)	—	antiques	antiquités f pl	oggetti antichi m	antigüedades f pl
antiquités (F)	Antiquitäten pl	antiques	—	oggetti antichi m	antigüedades f pl
Antrag (D)	—	application	demande f	domanda f	solicitud f
Antwort (D)	—	answer	réponse f	risposta f	respuesta f
antworten (D)	→	answer	répondre	rispondere	responder
anual (Es)	jährlich	annual	annuel(le)	annuale	—
anular¹ (Es)	abblasen	call off	souffler	disdire	—
anular² (Es)	annullieren	annul	annuler	annullare	—
anular³ (Es)	tilgen	erase	effacer	estinguere	—
anular el pedido de (Es)	abbestellen	cancel	décommander	annullare	—
anunciar¹ (Es)	anmelden	announce	annoncer	annunciare	—
anunciar² (Es)	ansagen	announce	annoncer	annunciare	—
anuncio¹ (Es)	Annonce f	advertisement	annonce f	annuncio m	—
anuncio² (Es)	Anzeige f	announcement	annonce f	annuncio m	—
anuncio³ (Es)	Inserat n	advertisement	annonce f	inserzione f	—
anuncio⁴ (Es)	Reklame f	advertisement	publicité f	réclame f	—
anwenden (D)	—	apply	employer	impiegare	usar
Anwesen (D)	—	premises	domaine m	podere m	posesión f
anwesend (D)	—	present	présent(e)	presente	presente
any (E)	beliebig	—	n'importe quel	qualsiasi	a voluntad
Anzahl (D)	—	number	nombre m	numero m	número m
Anzahlung (D)	—	deposit	acompte m	acconto m	primer pago m
Anzeige¹ (D)	—	announcement	annonce f	annuncio m	anuncio m
Anzeige² (D)	—	denunciation	dénonciation f	denuncia f	denuncia f
anziehen (D)	—	put on	mettre	indossare	ponerse
Anzug (D)	—	suit	costume m	vestito m	traje m
anzünden (D)	—	light	allumer	accendere	encender
août (F)	August m	August	—	agosto m	agosto m
apagar¹ (Es)	ausmachen	switch off	éteindre	spegnere	—
apagar² (Es)	auslöschen	extinguish	éteindre	estinguere	—
apagar³ (Es)	löschen	extinguish	éteindre	spegnere	—
apaiser, se (F)	nachlassen	slacken	—	allentare	aflojar
aparato (Es)	Apparat m	apparatus	appareil m	apparecchio m	—
aparcar (Es)	parken	park	garer	parcheggiare	—
aparecer (Es)	erscheinen	appear	apparaître	apparire	—
aparente (Es)	anscheinend	seemingly	apparemment	apparentemente	—
apart (E)	auseinander	—	séparé(e)	separato(a)	lejos/ distante
à part (F)	extra	extra	—	a parte	separado(a)
a parte (I)	extra	extra	à part	—	separado(a)
a partir de (Es)	ab	off	à partir de/dès	da	—
à partir de (F)	ab	off	—	da	a partir de/de
ape (E)	Affe m	—	singe m	scimmia f	mono m
à peine (F)	kaum	hardly	—	appena	apenas
apellido (Es)	Nachname m	surname	nom de famille m	cognome m	—
apenas (Es)	kaum	hardly	à peine	appena	—

	D	E	F	I	Es
aperto¹ (I)	geöffnet	open	ouvert(e)	—	abierto(a)
aperto² (I)	offen	open	ouvert(e)	—	abierto(a)
apertura (I)	Eröffnung f	opening	ouverture f	—	abertura f
a pesar de (Es)	trotz	despite	malgré	nonostante	—
apestar (Es)	stinken	stink	puer	puzzare	—
apetito (Es)	Appetit m	appetite	appétit m	appetito m	—
Apfel (D)	—	apple	pomme f	mela f	manzana f
Apfelsine (D)	—	orange	orange f	arancia f	naranja f
aplastar (Es)	zerdrücken	squash	écraser	sgualcire	—
aplaudir (Es)	klatschen	applaud	applaudir	battere le mani	—
aplauso (Es)	Beifall m	applause	applaudissements m pl	applauso m	—
aplazar (Es)	verschieben	postpone	remettre	rimandare	—
apologize (E)	entschuldigen, sich	—	excuser, se	scusarsi	disculparse
apology (E)	Entschuldigung f	—	excuse f	scusa f	disculpa f
apostar (Es)	wetten	bet	parier	scommettere	—
Apotheke (D)	—	chemist's	pharmacie f	farmacia f	farmacia f
apoyar (Es)	unterstützen	support	soutenir	assistere	—
apoyo (Es)	Unterstützung f	support	soutien m	sostegno m	—
apparaître (F)	erscheinen	appear	—	apparire	aparecer
Apparat (D)	—	apparatus	appareil m	apparecchio m	aparato m
apparatus (E)	Apparat m	—	appareil m	apparecchio m	aparato m
apparecchio¹ (I)	Apparat m	apparatus	appareil m	—	aparato m
apparecchio² (I)	Gerät n	appliance	appareil m	—	utensilio m
appareil¹ (F)	Apparat m	apparatus	—	apparecchio m	aparato m
appareil² (F)	Gerät n	appliance	—	apparecchio m	utensilio m
appareil photo (F)	Fotoapparat m	camera	—	macchina fotografica f	máquina fotográfica f
apparemment (F)	anscheinend	seemingly	—	apparentemente	aparentemente
apparence (F)	Aussehen n	appearance	—	aspetto m	aspecto m
apparentemente (I)	anscheinend	seemingly	apparemment	—	aparentemente
apparire (I)	erscheinen	appear	apparaître	—	aparecer
appartamento (I)	Wohnung f	flat	appartement m	—	piso m
appartement (F)	Wohnung f	flat	—	appartamento m	piso m
appartenere (I)	gehören	belong	appartenir	—	pertenecer
appartenir (F)	gehören	belong	—	appartenere	pertenecer
appassire (I)	welken	wither	faner, se	—	marchitarse
appear (E)	erscheinen	—	apparaître	apparire	aparecer
appearance (E)	Aussehen n	—	apparence f	aspetto m	aspecto m
appeler¹ (F)	nennen	call	—	chiamare	nombrar
appeler² (F)	rufen	shout	—	chiamare	llamar
appeler, se (F)	heißen	be called	—	chiamarsi	llamarse
appena¹ (I)	kaum	hardly	à peine	—	apenas
appena² (I)	sobald	as soon as	dès que	—	tan pronto como
appendere (I)	aufhängen	hang up	accrocher	—	colgar
Appetit (D)	—	appetite	appétit m	appetito m	apetito m
appétit (F)	Appetit m	appetite	—	appetito m	apetito m
appetite (E)	Appetit m	—	appétit m	appetito m	apetito m
appetito (I)	Appetit m	appetite	appétit m	—	apetito m

	D	E	F	I	Es
appetizer (E)	Vorspeise *f*	—	hors-d'œuvre *m*	antipasto *m*	primer plato *m*
applaud (E)	klatschen	—	applaudir	battere le mani	aplaudir
applaudir (F)	klatschen	applaud	—	battere le mani	aplaudir
applaudissements (F)	Beifall *m*	applause	—	applauso *m*	aplauso *m*
applause (E)	Beifall *m*	—	applaudissements *m pl*	applauso *m*	aplauso *m*
applauso (I)	Beifall *m*	applause	applaudissements *m pl*	—	aplauso *m*
apple (E)	Apfel *m*	—	pomme *f*	mela *f*	manzana *f*
appliance (E)	Gerät *n*	—	appareil *m*	apparecchio *m*	utensilio *m*
application[1] (E)	Antrag *m*	—	demande *f*	domanda *f*	solicitud *f*
application[2] (E)	Bewerbung *f*	—	candidature *f*	domanda d'impiego *f*	aspiración *f*
apply[1] (E)	anwenden	—	employer	impiegare	usar
apply[2] (E)	bewerben, sich	—	poser sa candidature	concorrere	presentarse
apporter (F)	mitbringen	bring (along)	—	portare con sé	traer
apposta (I)	absichtlich	intentionally	exprès	—	adrede
apprendista (I)	Lehrling *m*	apprentice	apprenti *m*	—	aprendiz *m*
apprendre[1] (F)	erfahren	learn	—	venire a sapere	enterarse
apprendre[2] (F)	lernen	learn	—	imparare	aprender
apprenti (F)	Lehrling *m*	apprentice	—	apprendista *m*	aprendiz *m*
apprentice (E)	Lehrling *m*	—	apprenti *m*	apprendista *m*	aprendiz *m*
approach[1] (E)	entgegenkommen	—	venir à la rencontre	venire incontro	venir al encuentro
approach[2] (E)	nähern, sich	—	approcher, se	avvicinarsi	acercarse
approcher, se (F)	nähern, sich	approach	—	avvicinarsi	acercarse
approprié[1] (F)	geeignet	suitable	—	adatto(a)	indicado(a)
approprié[2] (F)	zweckmäßig	suitable	—	adatto(a)	adecuado(a)
approuver (F)	billigen	approve of	—	approvare	aprobar
approvare[1] (I)	bejahen	agree with	répondre par l'affirmative à	—	afirmar
approvare[2] (I)	billigen	approve of	approuver	—	aprobar
approvare[3] (I)	genehmigen	approve	autoriser	—	permitir
approve (E)	genehmigen	—	autoriser	approvare	permitir
approve of (E)	billigen	—	approuver	approvare	aprobar
approvvigionare (I)	versorgen	provide	fournir	—	proveer
appuntamento (I)	Verabredung *f*	date	rendez-vous *m*	—	cita *f*
appuntito (I)	spitz	pointed	pointu(e)	—	puntiagudo(a)
âpre (F)	herb	bitter	—	amaro(a)	amargo(a)
aprender (Es)	lernen	learn	apprendre	imparare	—
aprendiz (Es)	Lehrling *m*	apprentice	apprenti *m*	apprendista *m*	—
après[1] (F)	danach	afterwards	—	poi/dopo	después
après[2] (F)	nach	after/to	—	a/in/verso/dopo	a/hacia/después
après-demain (F)	übermorgen	day after tomorrow	—	dopodomani	pasado mañana
après-midi (F)	Nachmittag *m*	afternoon	—	pomeriggio *m*	tarde *f*
après que (F)	nachdem	after	—	dopo	después que
apretar (Es)	drücken	press	presser	premere	—
apribottiglie (I)	Flaschenöffner *m*	bottle opener	ouvre-bouteilles *m*	—	abrebotellas *m*
apricot (E)	Aprikose *f*	—	abricot *m*	albicocca *f*	albaricoque *m*

	D	E	F	I	Es
Aprikose (D)	—	apricot	abricot *m*	albicocca *f*	albaricoque *m*
April (D)	—	April	avril *m*	aprile *m*	abril *m*
April (E)	April *m*	—	avril *m*	aprile *m*	abril *m*
aprile (I)	April *m*	April	avril *m*	—	abril *m*
aprire (I)	öffnen	open	ouvrir	—	abrir
aprobar (Es)	billigen	approve of	approuver	approvare	—
apropiado (Es)	passend	suitable	assorti(e)	adatto(a)	—
aproximadamente (Es)	ungefähr	about	environ	pressappoco	—
apuesta (Es)	Wette *f*	bet	pari *m*	scommessa *f*	—
a quadretti (I)	kariert	checked	à carreaux	—	a cuadros
a quarter (E)	Viertel *n*	—	quart *m*	quarto *m*	cuarto *m*
aquel (Es)	jene(r,s)	that	ce, cette	quello(a)	—
aquí[1] (Es)	her	here	ici	qua/qui/da	—
aquí[2] (Es)	hier	here	ici	qui	—
aquila (I)	Adler *m*	eagle	aigle *m*	—	águila *f*
araignée (F)	Spinne *f*	spider	—	ragno *m*	araña *f*
araña (Es)	Spinne *f*	spider	araignée *f*	ragno *m*	—
arancia[1] (I)	Apfelsine *f*	orange	orange *f*	—	naranja *f*
arancia[2] (I)	Orange *f*	orange	orange *f*	—	naranja *f*
Arbeit (D)	—	work	travail *m*	lavoro *m*	trabajo *m*
arbeiten (D)	—	work	travailler	lavorare	trabajar
Arbeiter (D)	—	worker	ouvrier *m*	operaio *m*	trabajador *m*
arbeitslos (D)	—	unemployed	en chômage	disoccupato(a)	desempleado(a)
Arbeitslosigkeit (D)	—	unemployment	chômage *m*	disoccupazione *f*	desempleo *m*
arbitre (F)	Schiedsrichter *m*	referee	—	arbitro *m*	árbitro *m*
arbitrio (Es)	Zoll *m*	duty	droits de douane *m pl*	dazio *m*	—
árbitro (Es)	Schiedsrichter *m*	referee	arbitre *m*	arbitro *m*	—
arbitro (I)	Schiedsrichter *m*	referee	arbitre *m*	—	árbitro *m*
árbol (Es)	Baum *m*	tree	arbre *m*	albero *m*	—
arbre (F)	Baum *m*	tree	—	albero *m*	árbol *m*
arbusto (Es)	Strauch *m*	bush	buisson *m*	cespuglio *m*	—
arder (Es)	brennen	burn	brûler	bruciare	—
area (E)	Fläche *f*	—	surface *f*	area *f*	área *f*
area (I)	Fläche *f*	area	surface *f*	—	área *f*
arena (Es)	Sand *m*	sand	sable *m*	sabbia *f*	—
argent[1] (F)	Geld *n*	money	—	denaro *m*	dinero *m*
argent[2] (F)	Silber *n*	silver	—	argento *m*	plata *f*
argent de poche (F)	Taschengeld *n*	pocket money	—	denaro per le piccole spese *m*	dinero de bolsillo *m*
argento (I)	Silber *n*	silver	argent *m*	—	plata *f*
ärgerlich (D)	—	angry	fâché(e)	arrabbiato(a)	enfadado(a)
ärgern (D)	—	annoy	fâcher	arrabbiare	enfadar
argomento (I)	Argument *n*	argument	argument *m*	—	argumento *m*
Argument (D)	—	argument	argument *m*	argomento *m*	argumento *m*
argument[1] (E)	Argument *n*	—	argument *m*	argomento *m*	argumento *m*
argument[2] (E)	Streit *m*	—	dispute *f*	lite *f*	disputa *f*
argument (F)	Argument *n*	argument	—	argomento *m*	argumento *m*

	D	E	F	I	Es
argumento (Es)	Argument *n*	argument	argument *m*	argomento *m*	—
aria (I)	Luft *f*	air	air *m*	—	aire *m*
árido (Es)	dürr	skinny	maigre	secco(a)	—
arieggiare (I)	lüften	air	aérer	—	ventilar
arise (E)	entstehen	—	naître	nascere	surgir
a risentirci! (I)	wiederhören!	good-bye!	au revoir!	—	¡adiós!
arm (D)	—	poor	pauvre	povero(a)	pobre
Arm (D)	—	arm	bras *m*	braccio *m*	brazo *m*
arm (E)	Arm *m*	—	bras *m*	braccio *m*	brazo *m*
arma (Es)	Waffe *f*	weapon	arme *f*	arma *f*	—
arma (I)	Waffe *f*	weapon	arme *f*	—	arma *m*
armadio¹ (I)	Kleiderschrank *m*	wardrobe	garde-robe *f*	—	armario ropero *m*
armadio² (I)	Schrank *m*	cupboard	armoire *f*	—	armario *m*
armario (Es)	Schrank *m*	cupboard	armoire *f*	armadio *m*	—
armario ropero (Es)	Kleiderschrank *m*	wardrobe	garde-robe *f*	armadio *m*	—
Armband (D)	—	bracelet	bracelet *m*	bracciale *m*	pulsera *f*
armchair (E)	Sessel *m*	—	fauteuil *m*	poltrona *f*	sillón *m*
arme (F)	Waffe *f*	weapon	—	arma *f*	arma *m*
Ärmel (D)	—	sleeve	manche *f*	manica *f*	manga *f*
Ärmelkanal (D)	—	Channel	Manche *f*	Manica *f*	Canal de la Mancha *m*
armoire (F)	Schrank *m*	cupboard	—	armadio *m*	armario *m*
aroma (Es)	Duft *m*	scent	odeur *f*	profumo *m*	—
aromatico (I)	würzig	spicy	épicé(e)	—	aromático(a)
aromático (Es)	würzig	spicy	épicé(e)	aromatico(a)	—
around (E)	herum	—	autour	intorno	alrededor
arrabbiare (I)	ärgern	annoy	fâcher	—	enfadar
arrabbiato¹ (I)	ärgerlich	angry	fâché(e)	—	enfadado(a)
arrabbiato² (I)	wütend	furious	furieux(-euse)	—	furioso(a)
arrampicarsi (I)	klettern	climb	grimper	—	escalar
arrange (E)	arrangieren	—	arranger	arrangiare	organizar
arranger (F)	arrangieren	arrange	—	arrangiare	organizar
arrange to meet (E)	verabreden	—	prendre rendez-vous	darsi appuntamento	concertar una cita
arrangiare (I)	arrangieren	arrange	arranger	—	organizar
arrangieren (D)	—	arrange	arranger	arrangiare	organizar
arredamento (I)	Einrichtung *f*	furnishing	ameublement *m*	—	mobiliario *m*
arredare (I)	einrichten	fit out	aménager	—	equipar
arreglar (Es)	aufräumen	clear away	ranger	mettere in ordine	—
arrendar (Es)	verpachten	lease out	affermer	affittare	—
arrepentirse (Es)	bereuen	regret	regretter	pentirsi	—
arrest (E)	verhaften	—	arrêter	arrestare	detener
arrestare (I)	verhaften	arrest	arrêter	—	detener
arrêt (F)	Haltestelle *f*	stop	—	fermata *f*	parada *f*
arrêter¹ (F)	aufhören	stop	—	cessare	terminar
arrêter² (F)	anhalten	stop	—	fermare	parar
arrêter³ (F)	ausschalten	switch off	—	spegnere	desconectar
arrêter⁴ (F)	abstellen	turn off	—	spegnere	desconectar
arrêter⁵ (F)	verhaften	arrest	—	arrestare	detener

	D	E	F	I	Es
arriba (Es)	oben	above	en haut	sopra	—
arrière-grands-parents (F)	Urgroßeltern *pl*	great-grandparents	—	bisnonni *m pl*	bisabuelos *m pl*
arriesgar (Es)	riskieren	risk	risquer	rischiare	—
arrival (E)	Ankunft *f*	—	arrivée *f*	arrivo *m*	llegada *f*
arrivare[1] (I)	ankommen	arrive	arriver	—	llegar
arrivare[2] (I)	eintreffen	arrive	arriver	—	llegar
arrivare a (I)	gelangen	attain	arriver à	—	conseguir
arrive[1] (E)	ankommen	—	arriver	arrivare	llegar
arrive[2] (E)	eintreffen	—	arriver	arrivare	llegar
arrivederci! (I)	wiedersehen!	good-bye!	au revoir!	—	¡adiós!
arrivée (F)	Ankunft *f*	arrival	—	arrivo *m*	llegada *f*
arriver[1] (F)	ankommen	arrive	—	arrivare	llegar
arriver[2] (F)	eintreffen	arrive	—	arrivare	llegar
arriver[3] (F)	geschehen	happen	—	accadere	ocurrir
arriver[4] (F)	passieren	happen	—	succedere	pasar
arriver à (F)	gelangen	attain	—	arrivare a	conseguir
arrivo (I)	Ankunft *f*	arrival	arrivée *f*	—	llegada *f*
arroser (F)	gießen	water	—	annaffiare	regar
arrostire (I)	braten	roast	rôtir	—	asar
arrostito (I)	gebraten	fried	rôti(e)	—	asado(a)
arrosto (I)	Braten *m*	roast	rôti *m*	—	asado *m*
arrow (E)	Pfeil *m*	—	flèche *f*	freccia *f*	flecha *f*
arroz (Es)	Reis *m*	rice	riz *m*	riso *m*	—
arrugginire (I)	rosten	rust	rouiller	—	oxidarse
arrugginito (I)	rostig	rusty	rouillé(e)	—	oxidado(a)
arruinar (Es)	verderben	ruin	détruire	rovinare	—
Art[1] (D)	—	way	manière *f*	modo *m*	manera *f*
Art[2] (D)	—	species	espèce *f*	specie *f*	especie *f*
art (E)	Kunst *f*	—	art *m*	arte *f*	arte *m*
art (F)	Kunst *f*	art	—	arte *f*	arte *m*
arte (Es)	Kunst *f*	art	art *m*	arte *f*	—
arte (I)	Kunst *f*	art	art *m*	—	arte *m*
artesanía (Es)	Handwerk *n*	craft	métier *m*	artigianato *m*	—
artesano (Es)	Handwerker *m*	craftsman	artisan *m*	artigiano *m*	—
article (E)	Artikel *m*	—	article *m*	articolo *m*	artículo *m*
article (F)	Artikel *m*	article	—	articolo *m*	artículo *m*
articolo (I)	Artikel *m*	article	article *m*	—	artículo *m*
artículo (Es)	Artikel *m*	article	article *m*	articolo *m*	—
artificial (E)	künstlich	—	artificiel(le)	artificiale	artificial
artificial (Es)	künstlich	artificial	artificiel(le)	artificiale	—
artificiale (I)	künstlich	artificial	artificiel(le)	—	artificial
artificiel (F)	künstlich	artificial	—	artificiale	artificial
artigianato (I)	Handwerk *n*	craft	métier *m*	—	artesanía *f*
artigiano (I)	Handwerker *m*	craftsman	artisan *m*	—	artesano *m*
Artikel (D)	—	article	article *m*	articolo *m*	artículo *m*
artisan (F)	Handwerker *m*	craftsman	—	artigiano *m*	artesano *m*
artist (E)	Künstler *m*	—	artiste *m*	artista *m*	artista *m*

	D	E	F	I	Es
artista (Es)	Künstler *m*	artist	artiste *m*	artista *m*	—
artista (I)	Künstler *m*	artist	artiste *m/f*	—	artista *m/f*
artiste (F)	Künstler *m*	artist	—	artista *m*	artista *m/f*
Arznei (D)	—	medicine	médicament *m*	medicina *f*	medicina *f*
Arzt (D)	—	doctor	médecin *m*	medico *m*	médico *m*
a saber (Es)	nämlich	namely	à savoir	cioè	—
asado[1] (Es)	Braten *m*	roast	rôti *m*	arrosto *m*	—
asado[2] (Es)	gebraten	fried	rôti(e)	arrostito(a)	—
asaltar (Es)	überfallen	raid	attaquer	assalire	—
asalto (Es)	Überfall *m*	raid	attaque *f*	aggressione *f*	—
asar (Es)	braten	roast	rôtir	arrostire	—
as a result of (E)	infolge	—	par suite de	in seguito a	por
à savoir (F)	nämlich	namely	—	cioè	a saber
ascend (E)	aufsteigen	—	monter	salire	subir
ascenseur (F)	Fahrstuhl *m*/Lift *m*	elevator	—	ascensore *m*	ascensor *m*
ascensor (Es)	Fahrstuhl *m*/Lift *m*	elevator	ascenseur *m*	ascensore *m*	—
ascensore (I)	Fahrstuhl *m*/Lift *m*	elevator	ascenseur *m*	—	ascensor *m*
Asche (D)	—	ash	cendre *f*	cenere *f*	ceniza *f*
Aschenbecher (D)	—	ashtray	cendrier *m*	portacenere *m*	cenicero *m*
asciugamano (I)	Handtuch *n*	towel	serviette *f*	—	toalla *f*
asciugare (I)	trocknen	dry	sécher	—	secar
asciutto (I)	trocken	dry	sec(sèche)	—	seco(a)
ascoltare (I)	zuhören	listen	écouter	—	escuchar
ascoltatore (I)	Hörer *m*	listener	auditeur *m*	—	oyente *m*
asegurar (Es)	versichern	assure	assurer	assicurare	—
aseo (Es)	Pflege *f*	care	soins *m pl*	cura *f*	—
asesinato (Es)	Mord *m*	murder	meurtre *m*	assassinio *m*	—
as far as (E)	soweit	—	autant que	fin dove	hasta tanto
ash (E)	Asche *f*	—	cendre *f*	cenere *f*	ceniza *f*
ashtray (E)	Aschenbecher *m*	—	cendrier *m*	portacenere *m*	cenicero *m*
así[1] (Es)	also	therefore	donc	dunque/quindi	—
así[2] (Es)	so	like this	ainsi	così	—
asidero (Es)	Griff *m*	handle	poignée *f*	maniglia *f*	—
asiento[1] (Es)	Sitzplatz *m*	seat	place assise *f*	posto a sedere *m*	—
asiento[2] (Es)	Sitz *m*	seat	siège *m*	sede *f*	—
asilo (infantile) (I)	Kindergarten *m*	nursery school	jardin d'enfants *m*	—	jardin de infancia *m*
a sinistra (I)	links	left	à gauche	—	a la izquierda
asino (I)	Esel *m*	donkey	âne *m*	—	burro *m*
asistir a (Es)	beistehen	stand by s.b.	assister	assistere	—
as is well known (E)	bekanntlich	—	comme on sait	com'è noto	como es sabido
ask[1] (E)	auffordern	—	inviter	invitare	invitar
ask[2] (E)	fragen	—	demander	domandare	preguntar
as long (E)	solange	—	tant que	finché	en tanto que
asociación (Es)	Verein *m*	club	association *f*	associazione *f*	—
asombrar (Es)	wundern	wonder	étonner, se	stupire	—
asombrarse (Es)	staunen	be astonished	étonner, se	stupirsi	—
aspecto[1] (Es)	Aussehen *n*	appearance	apparence *f*	aspetto *m*	—

	D	E	F	I	Es
aspecto² (Es)	Miene *f*	expression	mine *f*	aspetto *m*	—
asperger (F)	spritzen	squirt	—	spruzzare	salpicar
aspettare¹ (I)	erwarten	expect	attendre	—	esperar
aspettare² (I)	warten	wait	attendre	—	esperar
aspetto¹ (I)	Aussehen *n*	appearance	apparence *f*	—	aspecto *m*
aspetto² (I)	Miene *f*	expression	mine *f*	—	expresión *f*
aspiración (Es)	Bewerbung *f*	application	candidature *f*	domanda d'impiego *f*	—
aspirador (Es)	Staubsauger *m*	vacuum-cleaner	aspirateur *m*	aspirapolvere *m*	—
aspirapolvere (I)	Staubsauger *m*	vacuum-cleaner	aspirateur *m*	—	aspirador *m*
aspirateur (F)	Staubsauger *m*	vacuum-cleaner	—	aspirapolvere *m*	aspirador *m*
assaggiare (I)	versuchen	try	essayer	—	probar
assalire (I)	überfallen	raid	attaquer	—	asaltar
assassinio (I)	Mord *m*	murder	meurtre *m*	—	asesinato *m*
assegno (I)	Scheck *m*	cheque	chèque *m*	—	cheque *m*
assegno turistico (I)	Reisescheck *m*	traveller's cheque	chèque de voyage *m*	—	cheque de viaje *m*
assente (I)	abwesend	absent	absent(e)	—	ausente
assenza (I)	Abwesenheit *f*	absence	absence *f*	—	ausencia *f*
asseoir, se (F)	hinsetzen	sit down	—	sedersi	sentarse
assert (E)	behaupten	—	affirmer	affermare	afirmar
assetato (I)	durstig	thirsty	assoiffé(e)	—	sediento(a)
assez¹ (F)	genug	enough	—	abbastanza	bastante
assez² (F)	ziemlich	quite	—	abbastanza	bastante
assicurare (I)	versichern	assure	assurer	—	asegurar
assicurazione (I)	Versicherung *f*	insurance	assurance *f*	—	seguro *m*
assiette (F)	Teller *m*	plate	—	piatto *m*	plato *m*
assigner (F)	vorladen	summon	—	citare in giudizio	citar
assister (F)	beistehen	stand by s.b.	—	assistere	asistir a
assistere¹ (I)	beistehen	stand by s.b.	assister	—	asistir a
assistere² (I)	unterstützen	support	soutenir	—	apoyar
association (F)	Verein *m*	club	—	associazione *f*	asociación *f*
associazione (I)	Verein *m*	club	association *f*	—	asociación *f*
assoiffé (F)	durstig	thirsty	—	assetato(a)	sediento(a)
assolutamente (I)	unbedingt	absolutely	absolument	—	absolutamente
assomigliare (I)	ähneln	resemble	ressembler	—	parecer
as soon as (E)	sobald	—	dès que	appena	tan pronto como
assorti (F)	passend	suitable	—	adatto(a)	apropiado(a)
assortire (I)	sortieren	sort	trier	—	clasificar
assume (E)	voraussetzen	—	supposer	presupporre	suponer
assumere (I)	einstellen	employ	recruter	—	emplear
assumption (E)	Annahme *f*	—	supposition *f*	supposizione *f*	suposición *f*
assurance (F)	Versicherung *f*	insurance	—	assicurazione *f*	seguro *m*
assurdo (I)	sinnlos	senseless	insensé(e)	—	inútil
assure (E)	versichern	—	assurer	assicurare	asegurar
assurer (F)	versichern	assure	—	assicurare	asegurar
Ast (D)	—	branch	branche *f*	ramo *m*	rama *f*
asta (I)	Stange *f*	pole	barre *f*	—	barra *f*
astiquer (F)	polieren	polish	—	lucidare	pulir

	D	E	F	I	Es
astucieux (F)	schlau	clever	—	astuto(a)	astuto(a)
astuto (I)	schlau	clever	astucieux(-euse)	—	astuto(a)
astuto (Es)	schlau	clever	astucieux(-euse)	astuto(a)	—
a sud (I)	südlich	southern	du sud	—	al sur
asunto (Es)	Angelegenheit f	affair	affaire f	affare m	—
asustar (Es)	erschrecken	frighten	effrayer	spaventare	—
as well as (E)	sowohl	—	aussi bien	tanto…quanto	tanto…
at¹ (E)	um	—	autour de/à	intorno a/a	alrededor de/a las
at² (E)	bei	—	chez/près de	da/presso	cerca de/junto a
at³ (E)	an	—	à/près de	a/in/su	junto a
atacar (Es)	angreifen	attack	attaquer	attaccare	—
at all¹ (E)	irgend	—	d'une façon ou d'une autre	in qualche modo	cualquiera
at all² (E)	überhaupt	—	en général	in genere	en general
atar (Es)	binden	bind	attacher	legare	—
ataúd (Es)	Sarg m	coffin	cercueil m	bara f	—
atelier (F)	Werkstatt f	workshop	—	officina f	taller m
atelier de réparation d'autos (F)	Autowerkstatt f	repair shop	—	autofficina f	taller de reparaciones m
Atem (D)	—	breath	respiration f	fiato m	respiro m
à temps (F)	rechtzeitig	in time	—	in tempo	a tiempo
¡atención! (Es)	Achtung!	attention!	attention!	attenzione!	—
atender¹ (Es)	sorgen	worry about	occuper de, se	prendersi cura di	—
atender² (Es)	achtgeben	take care	faire attention	badare	—
atento (Es)	aufmerksam	attentive	attentif(-ive)	attento(a)	—
aterrizaje (Es)	Landung f	landing	atterrissage m	atterraggio m	—
aterrizar (Es)	landen	land	atterrir	atterrare	—
atestiguar (Es)	bescheinigen	certify	attester	attestare	—
at first (E)	zuerst	—	d'abord	dapprima	primero
a third (E)	Drittel n	—	tiers m	terzo m	tercio m
at home (E)	daheim	—	à la maison	a casa	en casa
a tiempo (Es)	rechtzeitig	in time	à temps	in tempo	—
at last (E)	endlich	—	enfin	finalmente	finalmente
at least¹ (E)	mindestens	—	au moins	almeno	por lo menos
at least² (E)	wenigstens	—	au moins	almeno	por lo menos
at least³ (E)	zumindest	—	au moins	per lo meno	por lo menos
atmen (D)	—	breathe	respirer	respirare	respirar
at midday (E)	mittags	—	à midi	a mezzogiorno	a mediodía
at nighttime (E)	nachts	—	la nuit	di notte	por la noche
atormentar (Es)	quälen	torture	torturer	tormentare	—
atraer (Es)	locken	attract	attirer	attirare	—
atrapar (Es)	erwischen	catch	attraper	acchiappare	—
atrás (Es)	zurück	back	de retour	indietro	—
à travers (F)	hindurch	through	—	attraverso	a través de
atravesar (Es)	überqueren	cross	traverser	attraversare	—
a través de (Es)	hindurch	through	à travers	attraverso	—
atreverse (Es)	wagen	dare	oser	osare	—
atrevido (Es)	frech	cheeky	insolent(e)	sfacciato(a)	—
atributo (Es)	Eigenschaft f	quality	qualité f	qualità f	—

	D	E	F	I	Es
atropellar (Es)	überfahren	run over	écraser	investire	—
attaccare (I)	angreifen	attack	attaquer	—	atacar
attacher (F)	binden	bind	—	legare	atar
attack (E)	angreifen	—	attaquer	attaccare	atacar
attain (E)	gelangen	—	arriver à	arrivare a	conseguir
attaque (F)	Überfall *m*	raid	—	aggressione *f*	asalto *m*
attaquer[1] (F)	angreifen	attack	—	attaccare	atacar
attaquer[2] (F)	überfallen	raid	—	assalire	asaltar
atteggiamento (I)	Einstellung *f*	attitude	attitude *f*	—	actitud *f*
atteindre (F)	erreichen	reach	—	raggiungere	alcanzar
attendant (E)	Wärter *m*	—	gardien *m*	custode *m*	guarda *m*
attendre[1] (F)	erwarten	expect	—	aspettare	esperar
attendre[2] (F)	warten	wait	—	aspettare	esperar
attentif (F)	aufmerksam	attentive	—	attento(a)	atento(a)
attention! (E)	Achtung!	—	attention!	attenzione!	¡atención!
attention! (F)	Achtung!	attention!	—	attenzione!	¡atención!
attentive (E)	aufmerksam	—	attentif(-ive)	attento(a)	atento(a)
attento (I)	aufmerksam	attentive	attentif(-ive)	—	atento(a)
attenzione! (I)	Achtung!	attention!	attention!	—	¡atención!
atterraggio (I)	Landung *f*	landing	atterrissage *m*	—	aterrizaje *m*
atterrare (I)	landen	land	atterrir	—	aterrizar
atterrir (F)	landen	land	—	atterrare	aterrizar
atterrissage (F)	Landung *f*	landing	—	atterraggio *m*	aterrizaje *m*
Attest (D)	—	certificate	certificat *m*	certificato *m*	certificado *m*
attestare (I)	bescheinigen	certify	attester	—	atestiguar
attestation (F)	Bescheinigung *f*	certificate	—	certificato *m*	certificado *m*
attester (F)	bescheinigen	certify	—	attestare	atestiguar
at that time (E)	damals	—	à cette époque	allora	entonces
at the front (E)	vorn(e)	—	devant	davanti	delante
at the most (E)	höchstens	—	tout au plus	al massimo	a lo sumo
attimo (I)	Augenblick *m*	moment	instant *m*	—	momento *m*
attirare (I)	locken	attract	attirer	—	atraer
attirer (F)	locken	attract	—	attirare	atraer
attitude (E)	Einstellung *f*	—	attitude *f*	atteggiamento *m*	actitud *f*
attitude (F)	Einstellung *f*	attitude	—	atteggiamento *m*	actitud *f*
attività (I)	Tätigkeit *f*	activity	activité *f*	—	actividad *f*
attivo[1] (I)	aktiv	active	actif(-ive)	—	activo(a)
attivo[2] (I)	tätig	active	actif(-ive)	—	activo(a)
attore (I)	Schauspieler *m*	actor	acteur *m*	—	actor *m*
attract (E)	locken	—	attirer	attirare	atraer
attraper[1] (F)	erwischen	catch	—.	acchiappare	atrapar
attraper[2] (F)	fangen	catch	—	acchiappare	coger
attraversare (I)	überqueren	cross	traverser	—	atravesar
attraverso (I)	hindurch	through	à travers	—	a través de
atún (Es)	Thunfisch *m*	tuna	thon *m*	tonno *m*	—
auberge[1] (F)	Gasthaus *n*	inn	—	osteria *f*	posada *f*
auberge[2] (F)	Wirtshaus *n*	inn	—	osteria *f*	restaurante *m*
au cas où (F)	falls	in case	—	qualora	en caso de que

	D	E	F	I	Es
auch (D)	—	also/too	aussi	anche/pure	también
aucun (F)	keine(r,s)	none	—	nessuno(a)	ninguno(a)
au dehors (F)	außen	outside	—	fuori	afuera
au-dehors (F)	hervor	forth	—	fuori	delante
audience (E)	Publikum n	—	spectateurs m pl	pubblico m	público m
auditeur (F)	Hörer m	listener	—	ascoltatore m	oyente m
auf (D)	—	on/on top/onto	sur	su/sopra	sobre/en/hacia
aufbewahren (D)	—	keep	garder	conservare	guardar
aufbürden (D)	—	burden	charger	addossare	cargar
Aufenthalt (D)	—	stay	séjour m	soggiorno m	estancia f
Auffahrt[1] (D)	—	drive	allée f	salita d'ingresso f	entrada f
Auffahrt[2] (D)	—	slip road	bretelle d'accès f	entrata f	vía de acceso f
auffallen (D)	—	be noticeable	faire remarquer, se	dare nell'occhio	llamar la atención por algo
auffordern (D)	—	ask	inviter	invitare	exigir
Aufführung (D)	—	performance	représentation f	recita f	representación f
Aufgabe (D)	—	task	tâche f	incarico m	tarea f
Aufgang (D)	—	staircase	montée f	scala f	subida f
aufgeben (D)	—	give up	abandonner	rinunciare	renunciar
aufgeregt (D)	—	excited	agité(e)	eccitato(a)	excitado(a)
aufhängen (D)	—	hang up	accrocher	appendere	colgar
aufhören (D)	—	stop	arrêter	cessare	terminar
aufladen (D)	—	load	charger	caricare	cargar
auflösen (D)	—	dissolve	dénouer	sciogliere	deshacer
aufmerksam (D)	—	attentive	attentif(-ive)	attento(a)	atento(a)
Aufnahme[1] (D)	—	reception	accueil m	accoglienza f	acogida f
Aufnahme[2] (D)	—	photograph	photographie f	fotografia f	fotografía f
aufnehmen[1] (D)	—	receive	accueillir	accogliere	recibir
aufnehmen[2] (D)	—	photograph	photographier	fotografare	fotografiar
aufpassen (D)	—	pay attention	faire attention	fare attenzione	prestar atención
aufräumen (D)	—	clear away	ranger	mettere in ordine	arreglar
aufrecht (D)	—	upright	droit(e)	diritto(a)	derecho(a)
aufregen (D)	—	excite	énerver	agitare	agitar
aufregend (D)	—	exciting	énervant(e)	eccitante	emocionante
aufrichtig (D)	—	honest	sincère	onesto(a)	sincero(a)
Aufschnitt (D)	—	cold meat	charcuterie f	affettato m	fiambre m
Aufseher (D)	—	guard	gardien m	custode m	vigilante m
Aufstand (D)	—	rebellion	soulèvement m	insurrezione f	revuelta f
aufstehen (D)	—	get up	lever, se	alzarsi	levantarse
aufsteigen (D)	—	ascend	monter	salire	subir
aufwachen (D)	—	wake up	réveiller, se	svegliarsi	despertarse
aufwachsen (D)	—	grow up	grandir	crescere	criarse
aufwärts (D)	—	upwards	vers le haut	in su	hacia arriba
aufwecken (D)	—	wake up	réveiller	svegliare	despertar
Aufzug (D)	—	elevator	ascenseur m	ascensore m	ascensor m
Auge (D)	—	eye	œil m (yeux pl)	occhio m	ojo m
Augenarzt (D)	—	eye specialist	oculiste m	oculista m	oculista m
Augenblick (D)	—	moment	instant m	attimo m	momento m

	D	E	F	I	Es
augenblicklich (D)	—	instantaneous	instantané(e)	instantaneo(a)	instantáneo(a)
augmenter¹ (F)	erhöhen	raise	—	innalzare	elevar
augmenter² (F)	vermehren	increase	—	aumentare	aumentar
augmenter³ (F)	zunehmen	increase	—	aumentare	aumentar
auguri (I)	Glückwunsch *m*	congratulations	félicitations *f pl*	—	felicitaciones *f pl*
August (D)	—	August	août *m*	agosto *m*	agosto *m*
August (E)	August *m*	—	août *m*	agosto *m*	agosto *m*
aujourd'hui (F)	heute	today	—	oggi	hoy
au lieu de¹ (F)	anstatt	instead of	—	invece di	en vez de
au lieu de² (F)	statt	instead	—	invece di	en vez de
aumentar¹ (Es)	vermehren	increase	augmenter	aumentare	—
aumentar² (Es)	zunehmen	increase	augmenter	aumentare	—
aumentare¹ (I)	vermehren	increase	augmenter	—	aumentar
aumentare² (I)	zunehmen	increase	augmenter	—	aumentar
au milieu (F)	mitten	in the middle	—	in mezzo	en medio
au milieu de (F)	inmitten	in the middle of	—	in mezzo a	en medio de
au moins¹ (F)	mindestens	at least	—	almeno	por lo menos
au moins² (F)	wenigstens	at least	—	almeno	por lo menos
au moins³ (F)	zumindest	at least	—	per lo meno	por lo menos
aumône (F)	Almosen *n*	alms	—	elemosina *f*	limosna *f*
aún (Es)	noch	still	encore	ancora	—
aunque (Es)	obwohl/ obgleich	although	bien que	benché	—
aunt (E)	Tante *f*	—	tante *f*	zia *f*	tía *f*
auparavant (F)	zuvor	before	—	prima	antes
au revoir!¹ (F)	wiederhören!	good-bye!	—	a risentirci!	¡adiós!
au revoir!² (F)	wiedersehen!	good-bye!	—	arrivederci!	¡adiós!
auricular (Es)	Hörer *m*	receiver	récepteur *m*	ricevitore *m*	—
aus (D)	—	off/from/ out of	de/par/hors de	da/di	de/por
ausbilden (D)	—	educate	former	addestrare	instruir
Ausbildung (D)	—	education	formation *f*	addestramento *m*	formación *f*
Ausdruck (D)	—	expression	expression *f*	espressione *f*	término *m*
ausdrücklich (D)	—	explicit	exprès(-esse)	espresso(a)	explícito(a)
auseinander (D)	—	apart	séparer	separato(a)	lejos/distante
ausencia (Es)	Abwesenheit *f*	absence	absence *f*	assenza *f*	—
ausente (Es)	abwesend	absent	absent(e)	assente	—
Ausflug (D)	—	outing	excursion *f*	gita *f*	excursión *f*
Ausfuhr (D)	—	export	exportation *f*	esportazione *f*	exportación *f*
ausführen (D)	—	export	exporter	esportare	exportar
ausführlich (D)	—	detailed	détaillé(e)	dettagliato(a)	detallado(a)
ausfüllen (D)	—	fill in	remplir	riempire	llenar
Ausgang (D)	—	exit	sortie *f*	uscita *f*	salida *f*
ausgebucht (D)	—	fully booked	complet(-ète)	esaurito(a)	completo(a)
ausgehen (D)	—	go out	sortir	uscire	salir
ausgenommen (D)	—	except	exepté	eccetto	excepto
ausgeschlossen (D)	—	impossible	hors de question	escluso(a)	imposible
ausgezeichnet (D)	—	excellent	excellent(e)	eccellente	excelente
aushalten (D)	—	bear	supporter	sopportare	aguantar

	D	E	F	I	Es
auskennen, sich (D)	—	know one's way about	connaître, s'y	conoscere	conocer a fondo
Auskunft (D)	—	information	renseignement *m*	informazione *f*	información *f*
auslachen (D)	—	laugh at	rire de qn	deridere	reírse de
ausladen (D)	—	unload	décharger	scaricare	descargar
Ausland (D)	—	abroad	étranger *m*	estero *m*	extranjero *m*
Ausländer (D)	—	foreigner	étranger *m*	straniero *m*	extranjero *m*
ausländisch (D)	—	foreign	étranger(-ère)	straniero(a)	extranjero(a)
ausleihen (D)	—	lend	prêter	dare in prestito	prestar
auslöschen (D)	—	extinguish	éteindre	estinguere	apagar
ausmachen[1] (D)	—	agree	convenir	stabilire	convenir
ausmachen[2] (D)	—	switch off	éteindre	spegnere	apagar
Ausnahme (D)	—	exception	exception *f*	eccezione *f*	excepción *f*
auspacken (D)	—	unpack	défaire	disfare	deshacer
Ausreise (D)	—	departure	départ *m*	partenza *f*	salida *f*
ausrichten (D)	—	pass on a message	transmettre	riferire	comunicar
ausrufen (D)	—	exclaim	crier	esclamare	exclamar
ausruhen (D)	—	rest	reposer, se	riposare	descansar
Aussage (D)	—	statement	déclaration *f*	dichiarazione *f*	afirmación *f*
ausschalten (D)	—	switch off	arrêter	spegnere	desconectar
aussehen (D)	—	look	avoir l'air	avere l'aspetto	parecer
Aussehen (D)	—	appearance	apparence *f*	aspetto *m*	aspecto *m*
außen (D)	—	outside	au dehors	fuori	afuera
außer (D)	—	except	hors de	eccetto	salvo
außerdem (D)	—	besides	en outre	inoltre	además
außergewöhnlich (D)	—	exceptional	exceptionnel(le)	straordinario(a)	excepcional
außerhalb (D)	—	out of	hors de	fuori di	fuera de
äußerlich (D)	—	external	externe	esterno(a)	superficial
außerordentlich (D)	—	extraordinary	extraordinaire	straordinario(a)	extraordinario(a)
aussi[1] (F)	auch	also/too	—	anche/pure	también
aussi[2] (F)	ebenfalls	likewise	—	altrettanto	también
aussi bien (F)	sowohl	as well as	—	tanto...quanto	tanto...
Aussicht (D)	—	view	vue *f*	vista *f*	vista *f*
Aussprache[1] (D)	—	discussion	discussion *f*	discussione *f*	discusión *f*
Aussprache[2] (D)	—	pronunciation	prononciation *f*	pronuncia *f*	pronunciación *f*
aussprechen (D)	—	pronounce	prononcer	pronunciare	pronunciar
aussteigen (D)	—	get off	descendre	scendere	bajar
ausstellen (D)	—	exhibit	exposer	esporre	exponer
Ausstellung (D)	—	exhibition	exposition *f*	esposizione *f*	exposición *f*
aussuchen (D)	—	select	choisir	scegliere	escoger
Austausch (D)	—	exchange	échange *m*	scambio *m*	cambio *m*
austauschen (D)	—	exchange	échanger	scambiare	cambiar
austeilen (D)	—	distribute	distribuer	distribuire	distribuir
Auster (D)	—	oyster	huître *f*	ostrica *f*	ostra *f*
Austria (E)	Österreich *n*	—	Autriche *f*	Austria *f*	Austria *f*
Austria (Es)	Österreich *n*	Austria	Autriche *f*	Austria *f*	—
Austria (I)	Österreich *n*	Austria	Autriche *f*	—	Austria *f*
austríaco[1] (Es)	österreichisch	Austrian	autrichien(ne)	austriaco(a)	—

	D	E	F	I	Es
austríaco² (Es)	Österreicher m	Austrian	Autrichien m	austriaco m	—
austriaco¹ (I)	österreichisch	Austrian	autrichien(ne)	—	austríaco(a)
austriaco² (I)	Österreicher m	Austrian	Autrichien m	—	austríaco m
Austrian¹ (E)	österreichisch	—	autrichien(ne)	austriaco(a)	austríaco(a)
Austrian² (E)	Österreicher m	—	Autrichien m	austriaco m	austríaco m
ausüben (D)	—	practise	exercer	esercitare	ejercer
Ausverkauf (D)	—	sale	soldes m pl	saldi m pl	liquidación f
ausverkauft (D)	—	sold out	épuisé(e)	esaurito(a)	vendido(a)
Auswahl (D)	—	choice	choix m	scelta f	elección f
auswählen (D)	—	choose	choisir	scegliere	eligir
auswandern (D)	—	emigrate	émigrer	emigrare	emigrar
auswärts (D)	—	out(wards)	à l'extérieur	fuori	fuera
Ausweis (D)	—	passport	pièce d'identité f	documento d'identità m	documento de identidad m
auswendig (D)	—	by heart	par cœur	a memoria	de memoria
ausziehen¹ (D)	—	take off	enlever	levare	quitarse
ausziehen² (D)	—	move out	déménager	sloggiare	mudarse
autant que (F)	soweit	as far as	—	fin dove	hasta tanto
auteur (F)	Autor m	author	—	autore m	autor(a) m(f)
author (E)	Autor m	—	auteur m	autore m	autor(a) m(f)
authorities (E)	Behörde f	—	autorités f pl	autorità f pl	autoridades f pl
authority (E)	Vollmacht f	—	procuration f	delega f	poder m
authorization (E)	Genehmigung f	—	autorisation f	permesso m	permiso m
autista¹ (I)	Chauffeur m	chauffeur	chauffeur m	—	chófer m
autista² (I)	Fahrer m	driver	conducteur m	—	conductor m
Auto (D)	—	car	voiture f	automobile f / macchina f	coche m
Autobahn (D)	—	motorway	autoroute f	autostrada f	autopista f
autobús¹ (Es)	Bus m	bus	bus m	autobus m	—
autobús² (Es)	Omnibus m	omnibus	autobus m	autobus m	—
autobus (F)	Omnibus m	omnibus	—	autobus m	autobús m
autobus¹ (I)	Bus m	bus	bus m	—	autobús m
autobus² (I)	Omnibus m	omnibus	autobus m	—	autobús m
autoestopista (Es)	Anhalter m	hitch-hiker	auto-stoppeur m	autostoppista m	—
autofficina (I)	Autowerkstatt f	repair shop	atelier de réparation d'autos m	—	taller de reparaciones m
Automat (D)	—	vending machine	distributeur automatique m	distributore automatico m	distribuidor automático m
automatical (E)	automatisch	—	automatique	automatico(a)	automático(a)
automatico (I)	automatisch	automatic	automatique	—	automático(a)
automático (Es)	automatisch	automatic	automatique	automatico(a)	—
automatique (F)	automatisch	automatic	—	automatico(a)	automático(a)
automatisch (D)	—	automatic	automatique	automatico(a)	automático(a)
automne (F)	Herbst m	autumn	—	autunno m	otoño m
automobile (I)	Auto n	car	voiture f	—	coche m
autopista (Es)	Autobahn f	motorway	autoroute f	autostrada f	—
Autor (D)	—	author	auteur m	autore m	autor(a) m(f)
autor (Es)	Autor m	author	auteur m	autore m	—
autore (I)	Autor m	author	auteur m	—	autor(a) m(f)

	D	E	F	I	Es
autoridades (Es)	Behörde f	authorities	autorités f pl	autorità f pl	—
autorisation (F)	Genehmigung f	authorization	—	permesso m	permiso m
autoriser (F)	genehmigen	approve	—	approvare	permitir
autorità (I)	Behörde f	authorities	autorités f pl	—	autoridades f pl
autorités (F)	Behörde f	authorities	—	autorità f pl	autoridades f pl
autoroute (F)	Autobahn f	motorway	—	autostrada f	autopista f
autoservicio (Es)	Selbstbedienung f	self service	libre-service m	self-service m	—
auto-stoppeur (F)	Anhalter m	hitch-hiker	—	autostoppista m	autoestopista m
autostoppista (I)	Anhalter m	hitch-hiker	auto-stoppeur m	—	autoestopista m
autostrada (I)	Autobahn f	motorway	autoroute f	—	autopista f
Autounfall (D)	—	car accident	accident de voiture m	incidente stradale m	accidente de automóvil m
autour (F)	herum	around	—	intorno	alrededor
autour de (F)	um	at/around	—	intorno a/a	alrededor de/a las
Autowerkstatt (D)	—	repair shop	atelier de réparation d'autos m	autofficina f	taller de reparaciones m
autre (F)	andere(r,s)	other	—	altro(a)	otra(o)
autrefois (F)	früher	earlier	—	prima	antes
autrement (F)	sonst	otherwise	—	altrimenti	por lo demás
Autriche (F)	Österreich n	Austria	—	Austria f	Austria f
autrichien (F)	österreichisch	Austrian	—	austriaco(a)	austríaco(a)
Autrichien (F)	Österreicher m	Austrian	—	austriaco	austríaco m
autumn (E)	Herbst m	—	automne m	autunno m	otoño m
autunno (I)	Herbst m	autumn	automne m	—	otoño m
available[1] (E)	erhältlich	—	en vente	acquistabile	que puede adquirirse
available[2] (E)	vorhanden	—	présent(e)	disponibile	presente
avaler (F)	schlucken	swallow	—	inghiottire	tragar
avancer (F)	vorgehen	proceed	—	procedere	proceder
avant (F)	vorher	before	—	prima	antes
avantage (F)	Vorteil m	advantage	—	vantaggio m	ventaja f
avant-dernier (F)	vorletzte(r,s)	one before last	—	penultimo(a)	penúltimo(a)
avant-hier (F)	vorgestern	day before yesterday	—	l'altro ieri	anteayer
avanti[1] (I)	voraus	ahead	en avant	—	delante
avanti[2] (I)	vorwärts	forward(s)	en avant	—	adelante
avanti! (I)	los!	off!	allons-y!	—	¡adelante!
avant que[1] (F)	bevor	before	—	prima che	antes que
avant que[2] (F)	ehe	before	—	prima che	antes que
avanzare (I)	übrigbleiben	be left	rester	—	quedar
avare (F)	geizig	mean	—	avaro(a)	avaro(a)
avaro (I)	geizig	mean	avare	—	avaro(a)
avaro (Es)	geizig	mean	avare	avaro(a)	—
avec (F)	mit	with	—	con	con
avec cela (F)	damit	with it	—	con questo	con ello
a veces (Es)	manchmal	sometimes	quelquefois	talvolta	—
avec plaisir (F)	gern	willingly	—	volentieri	con gusto
avec succès (F)	erfolgreich	successful	—	pieno(a) di successi	afortunado(a)
avenir (F)	Zukunft f	future	—	futuro m	futuro m

	D	E	F	I	Es
aventura (Es)	Abenteuer *n*	adventure	aventure *f*	avventura *f*	—
aventure (F)	Abenteuer *n*	adventure	—	avventura *f*	aventura *f*
average (E)	durchschnittlich	—	moyen(ne)	medio(a)	medio(a)
aver bisogno di[1] (I)	benötigen/ brauchen	need	avoir besoin de	—	necesitar
aver bisogno di[2] (I)	bedürfen	need	nécessiter	—	necesitar
avere (I)	haben	have	avoir	—	tener
avere freddo (I)	frieren	be cold	avoir froid	—	tener frío
avere intenzione di (I)	vorhaben	intend	avoir l'intention de	—	tener la intención de
avere l'aspetto (I)	aussehen	look	avoir l'air	—	parecer
avere (I) **(l')intenzione di** (I)	beabsichtigen	intend	avoir l'intention de	—	proyectar
avere luogo (I)	stattfinden	take place	avoir lieu	—	tener lugar
avería (Es)	Panne *f*	breakdown	panne *f*	panna *f*	—
aves (Es)	Geflügel *n*	poultry	volaille *f*	pollame *m*	—
aveugle (F)	blind	blind	—	cieco(a)	ciego(a)
avión (Es)	Flugzeug *n*	aeroplane	avion *m*	aereo *m*	—
avion (F)	Flugzeug *n*	aeroplane	—	aereo *m*	avión *m*
avis (F)	Ansicht *f*	opinion	—	opinione *f*	opinión *f*
avisar (Es)	benachrichtigen	inform	informer	informare	—
aviso (Es)	Meldung *f*	report	annonce *f*	annuncio *m*	—
avispa (Es)	Wespe *f*	wasp	guêpe *f*	vespa *f*	—
avocat (F)	Rechtsanwalt *m*	lawyer	—	avvocato *m*	abogado *m*
avoid (E)	meiden/vermeiden	—	éviter	evitare	evitar
avoir (F)	haben	have	—	avere	tener
avoir besoin de (F)	benötigen/ brauchen	need	—	aver bisogno di	necesitar
avoir confiance (F)	vertrauen	trust	—	fidarsi	confiar
avoir froid (F)	frieren	be cold	—	avere freddo	tener frío
avoir honte (F)	schämen	be ashamed	—	vergognarsi	tener vergüenza
avoir l'air (F)	aussehen	look	—	avere l'aspetto	parecer
avoir le droit (F)	dürfen	be allowed	—	potere	poder
avoir lieu (F)	stattfinden	take place	—	avere luogo	tener lugar
avoir l'intention de[1] (F)	beabsichtigen	intend	—	avere (l')intenzione di	proyectar
avoir l'intention de[2] (F)	vorhaben	intend	—	avere intenzione di	tener la intención de
avoir un rhume (F)	erkältet sein	have a cold	—	essere raffreddato(a)	estar acatarrado(a)
avoisinant (F)	benachbart	neighbouring	—	vicino	vecino
à voix basse (F)	leise	quietly	—	a bassa voce	sin ruido
a voluntad (Es)	beliebig	any	n'importe quel	qualsiasi	—
avouer (F)	gestehen	confess	—	confessare	confesar
avril (F)	April *m*	April	—	aprile *m*	abril *m*
avveduto (I)	besonnen	sensible	réfléchi(e)	—	sensato(a)
avvenimento (I)	Ereignis *n*	event	événement *m*	—	suceso *m*
avventura (I)	Abenteuer *n*	adventure	aventure *f*	—	aventura *f*
avversario (I)	Gegner *m*	opponent	adversaire *m*	—	adversario *m*
avvicinarsi (I)	nähern, sich	approach	approcher, se	—	acercarse
avvocato (I)	Rechtsanwalt *m*	lawyer	avocat *m*	—	abogado *m*

	D	E	F	I	Es
avvolgere¹ (I)	einwickeln	wrap up	envelopper	—	envolver
avvolgere² (I)	wickeln	wind	enrouler	—	envolver
awake (E)	wach	—	réveillé(e)	sveglio(a)	despierto(a)
away¹ (E)	fort	—	parti	via	lejos
away² (E)	weg	—	pas là	via	fuera
ayer (Es)	gestern	yesterday	hier	ieri	—
ayuda (Es)	Hilfe f	help	aide f	aiuto m	—
ayudar (Es)	helfen	help	aider	aiutare	—
ayudar a alguien (Es)	behilflich sein	help s.b.	aider qn	aiutare	—
ayunar (Es)	fasten	fast	jeûner	digiunare	—
ayuntamiento (Es)	Rathaus n	town hall	mairie f	municipio m	—
azafata (Es)	Stewardeß m	stewardess	hôtesse de l'air f	hostess f	—
azione (I)	Tat f	deed	action f	—	acción f
azúcar (Es)	Zucker m	sugar	sucre m	zucchero m	—
azul (Es)	blau	blue	bleu(e)	blu	—
Baby (D)	—	baby	bébé m	bebè m	bebé m
baby (E)	Baby n	—	bébé m	bebè m	bebé m
bac (F)	Fähre f	ferry	—	traghetto m	transbordador m
baccalauréat (F)	Abitur n	German school leaving examinations	—	maturità f	bachillerato m
bachelor (E)	Junggeselle m	—	célibataire m	scapolo m	soltero m
bachillerato (Es)	Abitur n	German school leaving examinations	baccalauréat m	maturità f	—
baciare (I)	küssen	kiss	embrasser	—	besar
bacio (I)	Kuß m	kiss	baiser m	—	beso m
back¹ (E)	Rücken m	—	dos m	schiena f	espalda m
back² (E)	zurück	—	de retour	indietro	atrás
backen (D)	—	bake	faire cuire	cuocere (al forno)	cocer (al horno)
Bäckerei (D)	—	bakery	boulangerie f	panetteria f	panadería f
backwards (E)	rückwärts	—	en arrière	in dietro	marcha atrás
bacon (E)	Speck m	—	lard m	lardo m	tocino m
Bad (D)	—	bath	bain m	bagno m	baño m
bad¹ (E)	schlecht	—	mauvais(e)	cattivo(a)	malo(a)
bad² (E)	übel	—	mauvais(e)	cattivo(a)	malo(a)
badare (I)	achtgeben	take care	faire attention	—	atender
Badeanzug (D)	—	swimsuit	maillot de bain m	costume da bagno m	traje de baño m
Badehose (D)	—	swimming trunks	maillot slip de bain m	costume da bagno m	bañador m
Bademeister (D)	—	baths attendant	maître baigneur m	bagnino m	bañero m
baden (D)	—	bathe	baigner, se	fare il bagno	bañarse
Badewanne (D)	—	bath tub	baignoire f	vasca da bagno f	bañera f
Badezimmer (D)	—	bathroom	salle de bains f	stanza da bagno f	cuarto de baño m
bad luck (E)	Pech n	—	malchance f	sfortuna f	mala suerte f
baffi (I)	Schnurrbart m	moustache	moustache f	—	bigote m
bag (E)	Tüte f	—	sac m	sacchetto m	bolsa f
bagage à main (F)	Handgepäck n	hand-luggage	—	bagaglio a mano m	equipaje de mano m
bagages (F)	Gepäck n	luggage	—	bagaglio m	equipaje m

	D	E	F	I	Es
bagaglio (I)	Gepäck n	luggage	bagages m pl	—	equipaje m
bagaglio a mano (I)	Handgepäck n	hand-luggage	bagage à main m	—	equipaje de mano m
bagnato (I)	naß	wet	mouillé(e)	—	húmedo(a)
bagnino (I)	Bademeister m	baths attendant	maître baigneur m	—	bañero m
bagno (I)	Bad n	bath	bain m	—	baño m
bague (F)	Ring m	ring	—	anello m	sortija f
Bahnhof (D)	—	station	gare f	stazione f	estación f
Bahre (D)	—	stretcher	brancard m	barella f	camilla f
baigner, se (F)	baden	bathe	—	fare il bagno	bañarse
baignoire (F)	Badewanne f	bath tub	—	vasca da bagno f	bañera f
bailar (Es)	tanzen	dance	danser	ballare	—
baille (Es)	Tanz m	dance	danse f	ballo m	—
bain (F)	Bad n	bath	—	bagno m	baño m
baiser (F)	Kuß m	kiss	—	bacio m	beso m
baisser[1] (F)	herabsetzen	lower	—	diminuire	rebajar
baisser[2] (F)	senken	lower	—	abbassare	bajar
bajar[1] (Es)	aussteigen	get off	descendre	scendere	—
bajar[2] (Es)	hinuntergehen	descend	descendre	scendere	—
bajar[3] (Es)	senken	lower	baisser	abbassare	—
bajo (Es)	niedrig	low	bas(se)	basso(a)	—
bake (E)	backen	—	faire cuire	cuocere (al forno)	cocer (al horno)
bakery (E)	Bäckerei f	—	boulangerie f	panetteria f	panadería f
balai (F)	Besen m	broom	—	scopa f	escoba f
balance (F)	Waage f	scales	—	bilancia f	balanza f
balancer, se (F)	schaukeln	swing	—	dondolare	columpiarse
balanza (Es)	Waage f	scales	balance f	bilancia f	—
balayer[1] (F)	fegen	sweep	—	scopare	barrer
balayer[2] (F)	kehren	sweep	—	scopare	barrer
balbettare (I)	stottern	stutter	bégayer	—	tartamudear
balcón (Es)	Balkon m	balcony	balcon m	balcone m	—
balcon (F)	Balkon m	balcony	—	balcone m	balcón m
balcone (I)	Balkon m	balcony	balcon m	—	balcón m
balcony (E)	Balkon m	—	balcon m	balcone m	balcón m
bald (D)	—	soon	bientôt	presto	pronto
bald (E)	kahl	—	chauve	calvo(a)	calvo(a)
Balkon (D)	—	balcony	balcon m	balcone m	balcón m
Ball (D)	—	ball	balle f	palla f	pelota f
ball (E)	Ball m	—	balle f	palla f	pelota f
ballare (I)	tanzen	dance	danser	—	bailar
balle (F)	Ball m	ball	—	palla f	pelota f
ballo (I)	Tanz m	dance	danse f	—	baile f
bambino (I)	Kind n	child	enfant m	—	niño m
bambola (I)	Puppe f	doll	poupée f	—	muñeca f
bañador (Es)	Badehose f	swimming trunks	maillot slip de bain m	costume da bagno m	—
banana (E)	Banane f	—	banane f	banana f	plátano m
banana (I)	Banane f	banana	banane f	—	plátano m

	D	E	F	I	Es
Banane (D)	—	banana	banane *f*	banana *f*	plátano *m*
banane (F)	Banane *f*	banana	—	banana *f*	plátano *m*
bañarse (Es)	baden	bathe	baigner, se	fare il bagno	—
banca (I)	Bank *f*	bank	banque *f*	—	banco *m*
banco (Es)	Bank *f*	bank	banque *f*	banca *f*	—
banco di vendita (I)	Ladentisch *m*	counter	comptoir *m*	—	mostrador *m*
banconota (I)	Schein *m*	note	billet *m*	—	billete *m*
Band (D)	—	ribbon	bandeau *m*	nastro *m*	cinta *f*
band[1] (E)	Kapelle *f*	—	orchestre *m*	banda *f*	banda *f*
band[2] (E)	Schar *f*	—	bande *f*	schiera *f*	grupo *m*
banda (Es)	Kapelle *f*	band	orchestre *m*	banda *f*	—
banda (I)	Kapelle *f*	band	orchestre *m*	—	banda *f*
bandage (E)	Binde *m*	—	bandage *m*	fascia *f*	faja *f*
bandage (F)	Binde *m*	bandage	—	fascia *f*	faja *f*
bande (F)	Schar *f*	band	—	schiera *f*	grupo *m*
bandeau (F)	Band *n*	ribbon	—	nastro *m*	cinta *f*
bandeja (Es)	Tablett *n*	tray	plateau *m*	vassoio *m*	—
bande magnétique (F)	Tonband *n*	tape	—	nastro magnetico *m*	cinta magnetofónica *f*
bandera[1] (Es)	Fahne *f*	flag	drapeau *m*	bandiera *f*	—
bandera[2] (Es)	Flagge *f*	flag	pavillon *m*	bandiera *f*	—
bandiera[1] (I)	Flagge *f*	flag	pavillon *m*	—	bandera *f*
bandiera[2] (I)	Fahne *f*	flag	drapeau *m*	—	bandera *f*
bañera (Es)	Badewanne *f*	bath tub	baignoire *f*	vasca da bagno *f*	—
bañero (Es)	Bademeister *m*	baths attendant	maître baigneur *m*	bagnino *m*	—
Bank (D)	—	bank	banque *f*	banca *f*	banco *m*
bank (E)	Bank *f*	—	banque *f*	banca *f*	banco *m*
baño (Es)	Bad *n*	bath	bain *m*	bagno *m*	—
banque (F)	Bank *f*	bank	—	banca *f*	banco *m*
baptême (F)	Taufe *f*	baptism	—	battesimo *m*	bautizo *m*
baptism (E)	Taufe *f*	—	baptême *m*	battesimo *m*	bautizo *m*
Bär (D)	—	bear	ours *m*	orso *m*	oso *m*
bara (I)	Sarg *m*	coffin	cercueil *m*	—	ataúd *m*
barato (Es)	billig	cheap	bon marché(e)	a buon mercato	—
barba (Es)	Bart *m*	beard	barbe *f*	barba *f*	—
barba (I)	Bart *m*	beard	barbe *f*	—	barba *f*
barbe (F)	Bart *m*	beard	—	barba *f*	barba *f*
barbilla (Es)	Kinn *n*	chin	menton *m*	mento *m*	—
barca (I)	Boot	boat	bateau *m*	—	bote *m*
barcaza (Es)	Kahn *m*	barge	barque *f*	chiatta *f*	—
barco (Es)	Schiff *n*	ship	navire *m*	nave *f*	—
barcollare[1] (I)	taumeln	reel	tituber	—	vacilar
barcollare[2] (I)	wanken	stagger	chanceler	—	vacilar
barella (I)	Bahre *f*	stretcher	brancard *m*	—	camilla *f*
barge (E)	Kahn *m*	—	barque *f*	chiatta *f*	barcaza *f*
Bargeld (D)	—	cash	espèces *f pl*	contanti *m pl*	dinero al contado *m*
barque (F)	Kahn *m*	barge	—	chiatta *f*	barcaza *f*

	D	E	F	I	Es
barre (F)	Stange *f*	pole	—	asta *f*	vara *f*
barrel (E)	Tonne *f*	—	tonneau *m*	botte *f*	barril *m*
barrer[1] (Es)	fegen	sweep	balayer	scopare	—
barrer[2] (Es)	kehren	sweep	balayer	scopare	—
barrera (Es)	Schranke *f*	barrier	barrière *f*	sbarra *f*	—
barrier (E)	Schranke *f*	—	barrière *f*	sbarra *f*	barrera *f*
barrière (F)	Schranke *f*	barrier	—	sbarra *f*	barrera *f*
barril (Es)	Tonne *f*	barrel	tonneau *m*	botte *f*	—
barro (Es)	Schlamm *m*	mud	boue *f*	fango *m*	—
Bart (D)	—	beard	barbe *f*	barba *f*	barba *f*
barzelletta (I)	Witz *m*	joke	plaisanterie *f*	—	chiste *m*
bas[1] (F)	Strumpf *m*	stocking	—	calza *f*	media *f*
bas[2] (F)	niedrig	low	—	basso(a)	bajo(a)
bas[3] (F)	nieder	inferior	—	in basso	abajo
base (E)	Grundfläche *f*	—	base *f*	base *f*	base *f*
base[1] (Es)	Basis *f*	basis	base *f*	base *f*	—
base[2] (Es)	Grundfläche *f*	base	base *f*	base *f*	—
base[1] (F)	Basis *f*	basis	—	base *f*	base *f*
base[2] (F)	Grundfläche *f*	base	—	base *f*	base *f*
base[1] (I)	Basis *f*	basis	base *f*	—	base *f*
base[2] (I)	Grundfläche *f*	base	base *f*	—	base *f*
basilare (I)	grundsätzlich	fundamental	par principe	—	por principio
Basis (D)	—	basis	base *f*	base *f*	base *f*
basis (E)	Basis *f*	—	base *f*	base *f*	base *f*
basket (E)	Korb *m*	—	panier *m*	cesto *m*	cesta *f*
bassa marea (I)	Ebbe *f*	low tide	marée basse *f*	—	marea baja *f*
bassa stagione (I)	Vorsaison *f*	low season	basse saison *f*	—	pretemporada *f*
basse saison (F)	Vorsaison *f*	low season	—	bassa stagione *f*	pretemporada *f*
basso (I)	niedrig	low	bas(se)	—	bajo(a)
bastante[1] (Es)	genug	enough	assez	abbastanza	—
bastante[2] (Es)	ziemlich	quite	assez	abbastanza	—
bastar (Es)	genügen	suffice	suffire	bastare	—
bastare (I)	genügen	suffice	suffire	—	bastar
bastón (Es)	Stock *m*	stick	bâton *m*	bastone *m*	—
bastone (I)	Stock *m*	stick	bâton *m*	—	bastón *m*
basura (Es)	Abfall *m*	rubbish	déchets *m pl*	immondizia *f*	—
bateau (F)	Boot	boat	—	barca *f*	bote *m*
batería (Es)	Batterie *f*	battery	batterie *f*	batteria *f*	—
bath (E)	Bad *n*	—	bain *m*	bagno *m*	baño *m*
bathe (E)	baden	—	baigner, se	fare il bagno	bañarse
bathroom (E)	Badezimmer *n*	—	salle de bains *f*	stanza da bagno *f*	cuarto de baño *m*
baths attendant (E)	Bademeister *m*	—	maître baigneur *m*	bagnino *m*	bañero *m*
bath tub (E)	Badewanne *f*	—	baignoire *f*	vasca da bagno *f*	bañera *f*
bâtiment (F)	Gebäude *n*	building	—	edificio *m*	edificio *m*
bâton (F)	Stock *m*	stick	—	bastone *m*	bastón *m*
battere[1] (I)	pochen	knock	frapper	—	golpear
battere[2] (I)	schlagen	hit	battre	—	golpear

	D	E	F	I	Es
battere a macchina (I)	tippen	type	taper (à la machine)	—	escribir a máquina
battere le mani (I)	klatschen	applaud	applaudir	—	aplaudir
batteria (I)	Batterie f	battery	batterie f	—	batería f
Batterie (D)	—	battery	batterie f	batteria f	batería f
batterie (F)	Batterie f	battery	—	batteria f	batería f
battery (E)	Batterie f	—	batterie f	batteria f	batería f
battesimo (I)	Taufe f	baptism	baptême m	—	bautizo m
battre (F)	schlagen	hit	—	battere	golpear
battre, se (F)	kämpfen	fight	—	combattere	luchar
Bau (D)	—	construction	construction f	costruzione f	construcción f
Bauch (D)	—	stomach	ventre m	pancia f	vientre m
bauen (D)	—	build	construire	costruire	construir
Bauer (D)	—	farmer	paysan m	contadino m	campesino m
Bauernhof (D)	—	farmhouse	ferme f	fattoria f	granja f
Baum (D)	—	tree	arbre m	albero m	árbol m
Baumwolle (D)	—	cotton	coton m	cotone m	algodón m
bautizo (Es)	Taufe f	baptism	baptême m	battesimo m	—
bavarder (F)	schwatzen	chatter	—	chiacchierare	charlar
be (E)	sein	—	être	essere/stare	ser/estar
beabsichtigen (D)	—	intend	avoir l'intention de	avere (l')intenzione di	proyectar
beach (E)	Strand m	—	plage f	spiaggia f	playa f
beachten (D)	—	take notice of	considérer	osservare	prestar atención a
be allowed (E)	dürfen	—	avoir le droit	potere	poder
Beamter (D)	—	civil servant	fonctionnaire m	impiegato statale m	funcionario m
bean (E)	Bohne f	—	haricot m	fagiolo m	judía f
beantworten (D)	—	answer	répondre à	rispondere a	responder a
bear[1] (E)	aushalten	—	supporter	sopportare	aguantar
bear[2] (E)	Bär m	—	ours m	orso m	oso m
bear[3] (E)	ertragen	—	supporter	sopportare	soportar
beard (E)	Bart m	—	barbe f	barba f	barba f
be ashamed (E)	schämen	—	avoir honte	vergognarsi	tener vergüenza
be astonished (E)	staunen	—	étonner, se	stupirsi	asombrarse
beau (F)	schön	beautiful	—	bello(a)	hermoso(a)
beaucoup de[1] (F)	viele	many/a lot of	—	molti(e)	muchos(as)
beaucoup de[2] (F)	viel	a lot of	—	molto(a)	mucho(a)
beau-frère (F)	Schwager m	brother-in-law	—	cognato m	cuñado m
beauftragen (D)	—	instruct	charger de	incaricare	encargar
beauté (F)	Schönheit f	beauty	—	bellezza f	belleza f
beautiful (E)	schön	—	beau, bel, belle	bello(a)	hermoso(a)
beauty (E)	Schönheit f	—	beauté f	bellezza f	belleza f
beaux-parents (F)	Schwiegereltern pl	parents-in-law	—	suoceri m pl	suegros m pl
bebé (Es)	Baby n	baby	bébé m	bebè m	—
bébé (F)	Baby n	baby	—	bebè m	bebé m
bebè (I)	Baby n	baby	bébé m	—	bebé m
beber (Es)	trinken	drink	boire	bere	—
bebida (Es)	Getränk n	drink	boisson f	bevanda f	—

	D	E	F	I	Es
be called (E)	heißen	—	appeler, se	chiamarsi	llamarse
because (E)	weil	—	parce que	perché	porque
because of (E)	wegen	—	à cause de	a causa di	a causa de
be cold (E)	frieren	—	avoir froid	avere freddo	tener frío
become (E)	werden	—	devenir	diventare	llegar
bed (E)	Bett *n*	—	lit *m*	letto *m*	cama *f*
bedanken (D)	—	say thank you	remercier	ringraziare	agradecer algo
bedauern (D)	—	regret	regretter	deplorare	lamentar
Bedauern (D)	—	regret	regret *m*	dispiacere *m*	compasión *f*
bedecken (D)	—	cover	couvrir	coprire	cubrir
bedeckt (D)	—	covered	couvert(e)	coperto(a)	cubierto(a)
be defeated (E)	unterliegen	—	être vaincu(e) par qn	soccombere	sucumbir
be descended (E)	abstammen	—	descendre	discendere	descender
bedeuten (D)	—	mean	signifier	significare	significar
bedeutend (D)	—	significant	important(e)	importante	importante
Bedeutung (D)	—	meaning	signification *f*	significato *m*	significado *m*
bedienen (D)	—	serve	servir	servire	servir
Bedienung (D)	—	service	service *m*	servizio *m*	servicio *m*
Bedingung (D)	—	condition	condition *f*	condizione *f*	condición *f*
bedrohen (D)	—	threaten	menacer	minacciare	amenazar
bedroom (E)	Schlafzimmer *n*	—	chambre à coucher *f*	camera da letto *f*	dormitorio *m*
bedürfen (D)	—	need	nécessiter	aver bisogno di	necesitar
Bedürfnis (D)	—	need	besoin *m*	bisogno *m*	necesidad *f*
beef (E)	Rindfleisch *n*	—	viande de bœuf *f*	carne di manzo *f*	carne de vaca *f*
beeilen, sich (D)	—	hurry up	dépêcher, se	affrettarsi	darse prisa
beeinflussen (D)	—	influence	influencer	influenzare	influir
beenden (D)	—	stop	terminer	terminare	terminar
beer (E)	Bier *n*	—	bière *f*	birra *f*	cerveza *f*
beerben (D)	—	inherit from	hériter	ereditare	heredar
Beerdigung (D)	—	funeral	enterrement *m*	funerale *m*	entierro *m*
beetle (E)	Käfer *m*	—	coléoptère *m*	coleottero *m*	escarabajo *m*
Befehl (D)	—	order	ordre *m*	ordine *m*	mando *m*
befestigen (D)	—	fasten	fixer	fissare	sujetar
befinden, sich (D)	—	feel	trouver, se	trovarsi	encontrarse
before[1] (E)	bevor	—	avant que	prima che	antes que
before[2] (E)	ehe	—	avant que	prima che	antes que
before[3] (E)	vor	—	devant/avant	davanti a	delante de
before[4] (E)	vorher	—	avant	prima	antes
before[5] (E)	zuvor	—	auparavant	prima	antes
before noon (E)	Vormittag *m*	—	matinée *f*	mattina *f*	mañana *f*
befreundet (D)	—	friendly	ami(e)	amico(a)	amigo(a)
befriedigen (D)	—	satisfy	satisfaire	soddisfare	satisfacer
befürchten (D)	—	fear	craindre	temere	temer
begabt (D)	—	gifted	doué(e)	dotato(a)	dotado(a)
bégayer (F)	stottern	stutter	—	balbettare	tartamudear
begegnen (D)	—	meet	rencontrer	incontrare	encontrar

	D	E	F	I	Es
begeistern (D)	—	inspire	enthousiasmer	entusiasmare	entusiasmar
begeistert (D)	—	enthusiastic	enthousiaste	entusiasta	entusiasta
begin (E)	beginnen	—	commencer	cominciare	empezar
Beginn (D)	—	beginning	commencement m	inizio m	principio m
beginnen (D)	—	begin	commencer	cominciare	empezar
beginner (E)	Anfänger m	—	débutant	principiante m	principante m
beginning[1] (E)	Anfang m	—	commencement m	inizio m	inicio m
beginning[2] (E)	Beginn m	—	commencement m	inizio m	principio m
be glad (E)	freuen, sich	—	être heureux (-euse)	rallegrarsi	alegrarse
begleiten (D)	—	accompany	accompagner	accompagnare	acompañar
begreifen (D)	—	comprehend	comprendre	comprendere	comprender
begrenzen (D)	—	limit	limiter	limitare	limitar
begrüßen (D)	—	greet	saluer	salutare	saludar
behalten (D)	—	keep	garder	tenere	retener
Behälter (D)	—	container	récipient m	recipiente m	recipiente m
behandeln (D)	—	treat	traiter	trattare	tratar
Behandlung (D)	—	treatment	traitement m	trattamento m	tratamiento m
behaupten (D)	—	assert	affirmer	affermare	afirmar
behave (E)	benehmen, sich	—	comporter, se	comportarsi	comportarse
behaviour (E)	Benehmen n	—	conduite f	comportamento m	comportamiento m
behilflich sein (D)	—	help s.b.	aider qn	aiutare	ayudar a alguien
behind (E)	hinten	—	derrière	dietro	detrás
behind it (E)	dahinter	—	derrière	dietro	detrás
Behörde (D)	—	authorities	autorités f pl	autorità f pl	autoridad f
bei (D)	—	at/near	chez/près de	da/presso	cerca de/ junto a
beide (D)	—	both	tous/toutes les deux	entrambi(e)	ambos(as)
Beifahrer (D)	—	passenger	passager m	passeggero m	pasajero m
Beifall (D)	—	applause	applaudissements m pl	applauso m	aplauso m
Beilage (D)	—	supplement	supplément m	supplemento m	suplemento m
Beileid (D)	—	condolence	condoléances f pl	condoglianza f	pésame m
Bein (D)	—	leg	jambe f	gamba f	pierna f
beinahe (D)	—	nearly	presque	circa/quasi	casi
being (E)	Wesen n	—	être m	essere m	ser m
Beispiel (D)	—	example	exemple m	esempio m	ejemplo m
beißen (D)	—	bite	mordre	mordere	morder
beistehen (D)	—	stand by s.b.	assister	assistere	asistir a
Beitrag (D)	—	contribution	contribution f	contributo m	cuota f
bejahen (D)	—	agree with	répondre par l'affirmative à	approvare	afirmar
bekannt (D)	—	well known	connu(e)	conosciuto(a)	conocido(a)
Bekannter (D)	—	aquaintance	ami m	conoscente m	conocido m
bekanntlich (D)	—	as is well known	comme on sait	com'è noto	notoriamente
Bekenntnis (D)	—	confession	confession f	confessione f	confesión f
beklagen (D)	—	deplore	plaindre de, se	lamentare	quejarse
bekommen (D)	—	get	recevoir	ricevere	recibir
belästigen (D)	—	annoy	importuner	importunare	molestar

	D	E	F	I	Es
be late (E)	verspäten	—	être en retard	ritardare	llevar retraso
belebt (D)	—	lively	animé(e)	animato(a)	animado(a)
be left (E)	übrigbleiben	—	rester	avanzare	quedar
beleidigen (D)	—	insult	offenser	offendere	ofender
Beleidigung (D)	—	insult	offense f	offesa f	ofensa f
beleuchten (D)	—	illuminate	éclairer	illuminare	iluminar
Beleuchtung (D)	—	lighting	éclairage m	illuminazione f	iluminación f
belga (Es)	Belgier m	Belgian	Belge m	belga m	—
belga (I)	Belgier m	Belgian	Belge m	—	belga m
Belge (F)	Belgier m	Belgian	—	belga m	belga m
Belgian (E)	Belgier m	—	Belge m	belga m	belga m
Bélgica (Es)	Belgien n	Belgium	Belgique f	Belgio f	—
Belgien (D)	—	Belgium	Belgique f	Belgio f	Bélgica f
Belgier (D)	—	Belgian	Belge m	belga m	belga m
Belgio (I)	Belgien n	Belgium	Belgique f	—	Bélgica f
Belgique (F)	Belgien n	Belgium	—	Belgio f	Bélgica f
Belgium (E)	Belgien n	—	Belgique f	Belgio f	Bélgica f
Belieben (D)	—	will	plaisir m	piacere m	placer m
beliebig (D)	—	any	n'importe quel	qualsiasi	a voluntad
beliebt (D)	—	popular	populaire	popolare	estimado(a)
believe (E)	glauben	—	croire	credere	creer
bell[1] (E)	Glocke f	—	cloche f	campana f	campana f
bell[2] (E)	Klingel f	—	sonnette f	campanello m	timbre m
belle-mère (F)	Schwiegermutter f	mother-in-law	—	suocera f	suegra f
belle-sœur (F)	Schwägerin f	sister-in-law	—	cognata f	cuñada f
belleza (Es)	Schönheit f	beauty	beauté f	bellezza f	—
bellezza (I)	Schönheit f	beauty	beauté f	—	belleza f
bello (I)	schön	beautiful	beau, bel, belle	—	hermoso(a)
belohnen (D)	—	reward	récompenser	premiare	recompensar
Belohnung (D)	—	reward	récompense f	ricompensa f	recompensa f
belong (E)	gehören	—	appartenir	appartenere	pertenecer
belt[1] (E)	Gurt m	—	ceinture f	cinghia f	cinturón m
belt[2] (E)	Gürtel m	—	ceinture f	cintura f	cinturón m
bemerken (D)	—	notice	remarquer	notare	darse cuenta
be mistaken (E)	irren	—	tromper, se	sbagliare	equivocarse
bemitleiden (D)	—	pity	plaindre	compatire	compadecerse de
bemühen, sich (D)	—	make an effort	efforcer, se	sforzarsi	esforzarse
Bemühung (D)	—	effort	effort m	sforzo m	esfuerzo m
benachbart (D)	—	neighbouring	avoisinant(e)	vicino(a)	vecino(a)
benachrichtigen (D)	—	inform	informer	informare	avisar
benachteiligen (D)	—	disadvantage	désavantager	svantaggiare	perjudicar
benché (I)	obwohl/obgleich	although	bien que	—	aunque
bend[1] (E)	biegen	—	plier	piegare	doblar
bend[2] (E)	Kurve f	—	virage m	curva f	curva f
bene (I)	wohl	well	bien	—	bien
Benehmen (D)	—	behaviour	conduite f	comportamento m	comportamiento m
benehmen, sich (D)	—	behave	comporter, se	comportarsi	comportarse

	D	E	F	I	Es
beneiden (D)	—	envy	envier	invidiare	envidiar
benessere (I)	Wohl n	welfare	bien m	—	bienestar m
beni (I)	Güter f	goods	marchandises f pl	—	bienes f pl
be noticeable (E)	auffallen	—	faire remarquer, se	dare nell'occhio	llamar la atención
benötigen (D)	—	need	avoir besoin de	aver bisogno di	necesitar
benutzen (D)	—	use	utiliser	usare	usar
benvenuto (I)	willkommen	welcome	bienvenu(e)	—	bienvenido(a)
Benzin (D)	—	petrol	essence f	benzina f	gasolina f
benzina (I)	Benzin n	petrol	essence f	—	gasolina f
beobachten (D)	—	observe	observer	osservare	observar
be of use (E)	taugen	—	convenir pour	essere portato(a)	valer
be on strike (E)	streiken	—	faire grève	scioperare	hacer huelga
bequeath (E)	vererben	—	léguer	lasciare in eredità	transmitir hereditariamente
bequem (D)	—	comfortable	confortable	comodo(a)	cómodo(a)
Bequemlichkeit (D)	—	convenience	confort m	comodità f	comodidad f
bere (I)	trinken	drink	boire	—	beber
berechnen (D)	—	charge	calculer	calcolare	calcular
bereit (D)	—	ready	prêt(e)	pronto(a)	dispuesto(a)
bereits (D)	—	already	déjà	già	ya
bereuen (D)	—	regret	regretter	pentirsi	arrepentirse
Berg (D)	—	mountain	mont m	monte m	montaña f
bergab (D)	—	downhill	en descendant	in discesa	cuesta abajo
bergauf (D)	—	uphill	en montant	in salita	cuesta arriba
Bergsteiger (D)	—	mountaineer	alpiniste m	alpinista m	alpinista m
Bericht (D)	—	report	rapport m	relazione f	relación f
berichten (D)	—	report	faire un rapport	riferire	informar
berretto (I)	Mütze f	cap	casquette f	—	gorra f
Beruf (D)	—	profession	profession f	professione f	profesión f
beruhigen (D)	—	calm	calmer, se	calmare	calmar
berühmt (D)	—	famous	célèbre	famoso(a)	famoso(a)
berühren (D)	—	touch	toucher	toccare	tocar
besar (Es)	küssen	kiss	embrasser	baciare	—
beschädigen (D)	—	damage	endommager	danneggiare	deteriorar
Beschädigung (D)	—	damage	endommagement m	danno m	deterioro m
beschaffen (D)	—	get	procurer	procurare	proporcionar
beschäftigen (D)	—	occupy/employ	occuper	occupare	ocupar
beschäftigt (D)	—	busy	occupé(e)	occupato(a)	ocupado(a)
bescheiden (D)	—	modest	modeste	modesto(a)	modesto(a)
bescheinigen (D)	—	certify	attester	attestare	atestiguar
Bescheinigung (D)	—	certificate	attestation f	certificato m	certificado m
beschleunigen (D)	—	accelerate	accélérer	accelerare	acelerar
beschließen (D)	—	decide	décider	decidere	decidir
beschreiben (D)	—	describe	décrire	descrivere	describir
beschützen (D)	—	protect	protéger	proteggere	proteger
Beschwerde (D)	—	complaint	plainte f	reclamo m	reclamación f
beschweren, sich (D)	—	complain	plaindre, se	lamentarsi	quejarse

	D	E	F	I	Es
Besen (D)	—	broom	balai *m*	scopa *f*	escoba *f*
besetzt (D)	—	engaged	occupé(e)	occupato(a)	ocupado(a)
besichtigen (D)	—	have a look at	visiter	visitare	visitar
beside (E)	neben	—	près de	accanto a	al lado de
besides (E)	außerdem	—	en outre	inoltre	además
be silent (E)	schweigen	—	taire, se	tacere	callar
Besitz (D)	—	possession	propriété *f*	proprietà *f*	posesión *f*
besitzen (D)	—	possess	posséder	possedere	poseer
Besitzer (D)	—	owner	propriétaire *m*	proprietario *m*	proprietario *m*
beso (Es)	Kuß *m*	kiss	baiser *m*	bacio *m*	—
besoin (F)	Bedürfnis *n*	need	—	bisogno *m*	necesidad *f*
besondere (D)	—	special	spécial(e)	straordinario(a)	extraordinario(a)
besonders (D)	—	especially	surtout	particolarmente	sobre todo
besonnen (D)	—	sensible	réfléchi(e)	avveduto(a)	sensato(a)
besorgen (D)	—	acquire	procurer	procurare	conseguir
besprechen (D)	—	discuss	discuter	discutere	discutir
besser (D)	—	better	meilleur(e)	meglio	mejor
Besserung (D)	—	improvement	amélioration *f*	miglioramento *m*	restablecimiento *m*
best (E)	beste(r,s)	—	meilleur(e)	migliore	óptimo(a)
bestätigen (D)	—	confirm	confirmer	confermare	confirmar
beste (D)	—	best	meilleur(e)	migliore	óptimo(a)
bestellen (D)	—	order	commander	ordinare	pedir
bestimmt (D)	—	definitely	certainement	certamente	ciertamente
Besuch (D)	—	visit	visite *f*	visita *f*	visita *f*
besuchen (D)	—	visit	rendre visite à	andare a trovare	visitar
Besucher (D)	—	visitor	visiteur *m*	visitatore *m*	visitante *m*
bet[1] (E)	wetten	—	parier	scommettere	apostar
bet[2] (E)	Wette *f*	—	pari *m*	scommessa *f*	apuesta *f*
bête[1] (F)	dumm	stupid	—	stupido(a)	tonto(a)
bête[2] (F)	doof	daft	—	scemo(a)	estúpido(a)
beten (D)	—	pray	prier	pregare	rezar
bêtises (F)	Unsinn *m*	nonsense	—	nonsenso *m*	absurdo *m*
beträchtlich (D)	—	considerable	considérable	considerevole	notable
Betrag (D)	—	amount	montant *m*	somma *f*	importe *m*
betray (E)	verraten	—	trahir	tradire	traicionar
betreffen (D)	—	concern	concerner	riguardare	concernir
betreten (D)	—	enter	entrer dans	entrare	entrar
betrinken, sich (D)	—	get drunk	enivrer, se	ubriacarsi	emborracharse
Betrug (D)	—	fraud	tromperie *f*	inganno *m*	engaño *m*
betrügen (D)	—	cheat	tromper	ingannare	engañar
betrunken (D)	—	drunk	soûl(e)	ubriaco(a)	borracho(a)
Bett (D)	—	bed	lit *m*	letto *m*	cama *f*
better (E)	besser	—	meilleur(e)	meglio	mejor
betún (Es)	Schuhcreme *f*	shoe polish	cirage *m*	lucido per scarpe *m*	—
between (E)	zwischen	—	entre	tra/fra	entre
beunruhigen (D)	—	disturb	inquiéter	preoccupare	inquietar
beurre (F)	Butter *f*	butter	—	burro *m*	mantequilla *f*

51

bientôt

	D	E	F	I	Es
beurteilen (D)	—	judge	juger	giudicare	juzgar
bevanda (I)	Getränk n	drink	boisson f	—	bebida f
Bevölkerung (D)	—	population	population f	popolazione f	población f
bevor (D)	—	before	avant que	prima che (di)	antes que
bevorzugen (D)	—	prefer	préférer	perferire	preferir
bewachen (D)	—	guard	garder	sorvegliare	vigilar
bewegen (D)	—	move	bouger	muovere	mover
Bewegung (D)	—	movement	mouvement m	movimento m	movimiento m
bewegungslos (D)	—	motionless	immobile	immobile	inmóvil
Beweis (D)	—	proof	preuve f	prova f	prueba f
beweisen (D)	—	prove	prouver	provare	probar
bewerben, sich (D)	—	apply	poser sa candidature	concorrere	presentarse
Bewerbung (D)	—	application	candidature f	domanda d'impiego f	solicitud f
Bewohner (D)	—	inhabitant	habitant m	abitante m	habitante m
bewölkt (D)	—	cloudy	couvert(e)	nuvoloso(a)	nublado(a)
be worth (E)	gelten	—	valoir	valere	valer
be worth while (E)	lohnen	—	en valoir la peine	valere la pena	valer la pena
bewundern (D)	—	admire	admirer	ammirare	admirar
bewußt (D)	—	deliberate	délibéré(e)	intenzionale	intencionado
beyond (E)	jenseits	—	de l'autre côté	al di là	al otro lado
bezahlen (D)	—	pay	payer	pagare	pagar
Bezahlung (D)	—	payment	paiement m	pagamento m	pago m
beziehen (D)	—	cover	recouvrir	ricoprire	tapizar
Beziehung[1] (D)	—	relation	rapport m	relazione f	relación f
Beziehung[2] (D)	—	relationship	relation f	rapporto m	relaciones f pl
biancheria (I)	Wäsche f	washing	linge m	—	ropa f
biancheria intima (I)	Unterwäsche f	underwear	sous-vêtements m pl	—	ropa interior f
bianco (I)	weiß	white	blanc(he)	—	blanco(a)
bibbia (I)	Bibel f	Bible	Bible f	—	Biblia f
Bibel (D)	—	Bible	Bible f	bibbia f	Biblia f
Bible (E)	Bibel f	—	Bible f	bibbia f	Biblia f
Bible (F)	Bibel f	Bible	—	bibbia f	Biblia f
Biblia (Es)	Bibel f	Bible	Bible f	bibbia f	—
bicchiere (I)	Glas n	glass	verre m	—	vaso m
bicicleta (Es)	Fahrrad n	bicycle	bicyclette f	bicicletta f	—
bicicletta (I)	Fahrrad n	bicycle	bicyclette f	—	bicicleta f
bicycle (E)	Fahrrad n	—	bicyclette f	bicicletta f	bicicleta f
bicyclette (F)	Fahrrad n	bicycle	—	bicicletta f	bicicleta f
biegen (D)	—	bend	plier	piegare	doblar
bien (Es)	wohl	well	bien	bene/forse	—
bien[1] (F)	wohl	well	—	bene/forse	bien
bien[2] (F)	Wohl n	welfare	—	benessere m	bienestar m
bienes (Es)	Güter f	goods	marchandises f pl	beni m pl	—
bienestar (Es)	Wohl n	welfare	bien m	benessere m	—
bien que (F)	obwohl/obgleich	although	—	benché	aunque
bientôt (F)	bald	soon	—	presto	pronto

	D	E	F	I	Es
bienvenido (Es)	willkommen	welcome	bienvenu(e)	benvenuto(a)	—
bienvenu (F)	willkommen	welcome	—	benvenuto(a)	bienvenido(a)
Bier (D)	—	beer	bière *f*	birra *f*	cerveza *f*
bière (F)	Bier *n*	beer	—	birra *f*	cerveza *f*
bieten (D)	—	offer	offrir	offrire	ofrecer
big (E)	groß	—	grand(e)	grande	grande
bigliettaio (I)	Schaffner *m*	conductor	contrôleur *m*	—	revisor *m*
biglietto (I)	Fahrkarte *f*	ticket	billet *m*	—	billete *m*
biglietto non vincente (I)	Niete *f*	blank	mauvais numéro *m*	—	número sin premio *m*
bigote (Es)	Schnurrbart *m*	moustache	moustache *f*	baffi *m pl*	—
bijoutier (F)	Juwelier *m*	jeweller	—	gioielliere *m*	joyero *m*
bijoux (F)	Schmuck *m*	jewellery	—	gioielli *m pl*	joyas *f pl*
bilancia (I)	Waage *f*	scales	balance *f*	—	balanza *f*
Bild (D)	—	picture	image *f*	immagine *f*	cuadro *m*
bilden (D)	—	form	former	formare	formar
Bildhauer (D)	—	sculptor	sculpteur *m*	scultore *m*	escultor *m*
Bildung[1] (D)	—	formation	formation *f*	formazione *f*	formación *f*
Bildung[2] (D)	—	education	éducation *f*	istruzione *f*	educación *f*
bilingual (E)	zweisprachig	—	bilingue	bilingue	bilingüe
bilingue (F)	zweisprachig	bilingual	—	bilingue	bilingüe
bilingue (I)	zweisprachig	bilingual	bilingue	—	bilingüe
bilingüe (Es)	zweisprachig	bilingual	bilingue	bilingue	—
bilis (Es)	Galle *f*	gall	fiel *m*	cistifellea *f*	—
bill (E)	Rechnung *f*	—	facture *f*	fattura *f*	factura *f*
billet[1] (F)	Fahrkarte *f*	ticket	—	biglietto *m*	billete *m*
billet[2] (F)	Schein *m*	note	—	banconota *f*	billete *m*
billete[1] (Es)	Fahrkarte *f*	ticket	billet *m*	biglietto *m*	—
billete[2] (Es)	Fahrschein *m*	ticket	ticket *m*	biglietto *m*	—
billete[3] (Es)	Schein *m*	note	billet *m*	banconota *f*	—
billig (D)	—	cheap	bon marché(e)	a buon mercato	barato(a)
billigen (D)	—	approve of	approuver	approvare	aprobar
billion (E)	Milliarde *f*	—	milliard *m*	miliardo *m*	mil millones *m*
bin (E)	Abfalleimer *m*	—	poubelle *f*	pattumiera *f*	cubo de la basura *m*
binario (I)	Gleis *n*	track	voie *f*	—	vía *f*
bind (E)	binden	—	attacher	legare	atar
Binde (D)	—	bandage	bandage *m*	fascia *f*	faja *f*
binden (D)	—	bind	attacher	legare	atar
binoculars (E)	Fernglas *n*	—	jumelles *f pl*	cannocchiale *m*	gemelos *m pl*
biondo (I)	blond	blond	blond(e)	—	rubio(a)
bird (E)	Vogel *m*	—	oiseau *m*	uccello *m*	pájaro *m*
Birne (D)	—	pear	poire *f*	pera *f*	pera *f*
biro (E)	Kugelschreiber *m*	—	stylo à bille *m*	biro *f*	bolígrafo *m*
biro (I)	Kugelschreiber *m*	biro	stylo à bille *m*	—	bolígrafo *m*
birra (I)	Bier *n*	beer	bière *f*	—	cerveza *f*
birth (E)	Geburt *f*	—	naissance *f*	nascita *f*	nacimiento *m*
birthday (E)	Geburtstag *m*	—	anniversaire *m*	compleanno *m*	cumpleaños *m*

	D	E	F	I	Es
bis (D)	—	until	jusqu'à	fino a	hasta
bisabuelos (Es)	Urgroßeltern *pl*	great-grandparents	arrière-grands-parents *m pl*	bisnonni *m pl*	—
bisbigliare (I)	flüstern	whisper	chuchoter	—	cuchichear
biscotte (F)	Zwieback *m*	rusk	—	fette biscottate *f pl*	bizcocho *m*
biscotti (I)	Gebäck *n*	pastry	pâtisserie *f*	—	pastas *f pl*
biscotto (I)	Keks *m*	biscuit	biscuit *m*	—	galleta *f*
biscuit (E)	Keks *m*	—	biscuit *m*	biscotto *m*	galleta *f*
biscuit (F)	Keks *m*	biscuit	—	biscotto *m*	galleta *f*
bisher (D)	—	so far	jusqu'à présent	finora	hasta ahora
bisnonni (I)	Urgroßeltern *pl*	great-grandparents	arrière-grands-parents *m pl*	—	bisabuelos *m pl*
bisogno (I)	Bedürfnis *n*	need	besoin *m*	—	necesidad *f*
bißchen (D)	—	a little	un peu	un po'	un poquito
bistro (F)	Kneipe *f*	pub	—	osteria *f*	tasca *f*
bite (E)	beißen	—	mordre	mordere	morder
bitte (D)	—	please	s'il vous plaît	prego	por favor
Bitte (D)	—	request	demande *f*	domanda *f*	ruego *m*
bitten (D)	—	request	demander	pregare	rogar
bitter (D)	—	bitter	amer(-ère)	amaro(a)	amargo(a)
bitter[1] (E)	bitter	—	amer(-ère)	amaro(a)	amargo(a)
bitter[2] (E)	herb	—	âpre	amaro(a)	amargo(a)
bizarre (F)	seltsam	strange	—	strano(a)	extraño(a)
bizcocho (Es)	Zwieback *m*	rusk	biscotte *f*	fette biscottate *f pl*	—
black (E)	schwarz	—	noir(e)	nero(a)	negro(a)
blackberry (E)	Brombeere *f*	—	mûre *f*	mora *f*	zarzamora *f*
blackmail (E)	Erpressung *f*	—	chantage *m*	ricatto *m*	chantaje *m*
bladder (E)	Blase *f*	—	vessie *f*	vescica *f*	vejiga *f*
blade (E)	Klinge *f*	—	lame *f*	lama *f*	cuchilla *f*
blame (E)	vorwerfen	—	reprocher	rimproverare	echar en cara
blanc (F)	weiß	white	—	bianco(a)	blanco(a)
blanchisserie (F)	Wäscherei *f*	laundry	—	lavanderia *f*	lavandería *f*
blanco (Es)	weiß	white	blanc(he)	bianco(a)	—
blank (E)	Niete *f*	—	mauvais numéro *m*	biglietto non vincente *m*	número sin premio *m*
blanket (E)	Decke *f*	—	couverture *f*	coperta *f*	techo *m*
Blase[1] (D)	—	bladder	vessie *f*	vescica *f*	vejiga *f*
Blase[2] (D)	—	bubble	bulle *f*	bolla *f*	burbuja *f*
blasen (D)	—	blow	souffler	soffiare	soplar
blaß (D)	—	pale	pâle	pallido(a)	pálido(a)
Blatt (D)	—	leaf	feuille *f*	foglia *f*	hoja *f*
blau (D)	—	blue	bleu(e)	blu	azul
blé (F)	Weizen *m*	wheat	—	frumento *m*	trigo *m*
Blech (D)	—	sheet metal	tôle *f*	latta *f*	chapa *f*
bleed (E)	bluten	—	saigner	sanguinare	sangrar
bleiben (D)	—	stay	rester	rimanere	quedarse
Bleistift (D)	—	pencil	crayon *m*	matita *f*	lápiz *m*
blesser[1] (F)	verletzen	injure	—	ferire	herir

	D	E	F	I	Es
blesser[2] (F)	verwunden	wound	—	ferire	herir
blessure[1] (F)	Verletzung *f*	injury	—	ferita *f*	herida *f*
blessure[2] (F)	Wunde *f*	wound	—	ferita *f*	herida *f*
bleu (F)	blau	blue	—	blu	azul
Blick (D)	—	look	regard *m*	sguardo *m*	vista *f*
blicken (D)	—	look	regarder	guardare	mirar
blind (D)	—	blind	aveugle	cieco(a)	ciego(a)
blind (E)	blind	—	aveugle	cieco(a)	ciego(a)
blinken (D)	—	flash	clignoter	lampeggiare	emitir reflejos
Blitz (D)	—	lightning	éclair *m*	lampo *m*	rayo *m*
blond (D)	—	blond	blond(e)	biondo(a)	rubio(a)
blond (E)	blond	—	blond(e)	biondo(a)	rubio(a)
blond (F)	blond	blond	—	biondo(a)	rubio(a)
blood (E)	Blut *n*	—	sang *m*	sangue *m*	sangre *f*
bloom (E)	blühen	—	fleurir	fiorire	florecer
bloß (D)	—	only	seulement	soltanto	sólo
blouse (E)	Bluse *f*	—	chemisier *m*	camicetta *f*	blusa *f*
blow[1] (E)	blasen	—	souffler	soffiare	soplar
blow[2] (E)	Stoß *m*	—	coup *m*	spinta *f*	empujón *m*
blow[3] (E)	Schlag *m*	—	coup *m*	colpo *m*	golpe *m*
blu (I)	blau	blue	bleu(e)	—	azul
blue (E)	blau	—	bleu(e)	blu	azul
blühen (D)	—	bloom	fleurir	fiorire	florecer
Blume (D)	—	flower	fleur *f*	fiore *m*	flor *f*
Blumenkohl (D)	—	cauliflower	chou-fleur *m*	cavolfiore *m*	coliflor *f*
blusa (Es)	Bluse *f*	blouse	chemisier *m*	camicetta *f*	—
Bluse (D)	—	blouse	chemisier *m*	camicetta *f*	blusa *f*
Blut (D)	—	blood	sang *m*	sangue *m*	sangre *f*
bluten (D)	—	bleed	saigner	sanguinare	sangrar
boarding house (E)	Pension *f*	—	pension *f*	pensione *f*	pensión *f*
boarding school (E)	Internat *n*	—	internat *m*	collegio *m*	internado *m*
boat (E)	Boot *n*	—	bateau *m*	barca *f*	bote *m*
boca (Es)	Mund *m*	mouth	bouche *f*	bocca *f*	—
bocca (I)	Mund *m*	mouth	bouche *f*	—	boca *f*
bocciolo (I)	Knospe *f*	bud	bourgeon *f*	—	yema *f*
boceto (Es)	Skizze *f*	sketch	esquisse *f*	schizzo *m*	—
bocina (Es)	Hupe *f*	horn	claxon *m*	clacson *m*	—
boda[1] (Es)	Hochzeit *f*	wedding	mariage *m*	nozze *f pl*	—
boda[2] (Es)	Heirat *f*	marriage	mariage *m*	matrimonio *m*	—
Boden (D)	—	floor	terre *f*	terra *f*	suelo *m*
body[1] (E)	Körper *m*	—	corps *m*	corpo *m*	cuerpo *m*
body[2] (E)	Karosserie *f*	—	carrosserie *f*	carrozzeria *f*	carrocería *f*
bœuf[1] (F)	Ochse *m*	ox	—	bue *m*	buey *m*
bœuf[2] (F)	Rind *n*	cow	—	manzo *m*	buey *m*
Bohne (D)	—	bean	haricot *m*	fagiolo *m*	judía *f*
boire (F)	trinken	drink	—	bere	beber
bois (F)	Holz *n*	wood	—	legno *m*	madera *f*

	D	E	F	I	Es
boisson (F)	Getränk *n*	drink	—	bevanda *f*	bebida *f*
boîte[1] (F)	Dose *f*	tin	—	scatola *f*	lata *f*
boîte[2] (F)	Schachtel *f*	box	—	scatola *f*	caja *f*
boîte aux lettres (F)	Briefkasten *m*	letterbox	—	cassetta postale *f*	buzón *m*
boîte de nuit (F)	Nachtlokal *n*	(night) club	—	night *m*	local nocturno *m*
bolígrafo (Es)	Kugelschreiber *m*	biro	stylo à bille *m*	biro *f*	
bolla (I)	Blase *f*	bubble	bulle *f*	—	burbuja *f*
bollettino metereologico (I)	Wetterbericht *m*	weather report	bulletin météorologique *m*	—	informe metereológico *m*
bolsa (Es)	Tüte *f*	bag	sac *m*	sacchetto *m*	—
bolsa de compra (Es)	Einkaufstasche *f*	shopping bag	sac à provision *m*	borsa della spesa *f*	—
bolso[1] (Es)	Handtasche *f*	handbag	sac à main *m*	borsetta *f*	—
bolso[2] (Es)	Tasche *f*	handbag	sac *m*	borsa *f*	—
bolt (E)	Riegel *m*	—	verrou *m*	catenaccio *m*	cerrojo *m*
bomba (Es)	Pumpe *f*	pump	pompe *f*	pompa *f*	—
bon[1] (F)	Gutschein *m*	voucher	—	buono *m*	vale *m*
bon[2] (F)	gut	good/well	—	buono(a)/bene	bueno(a)/bien
Bonbon (D)	—	sweet	bonbon *m*	caramella *f*	caramelo *m*
bonbon (F)	Bonbon *n*	sweet	—	caramella *f*	caramelo *m*
bondé (F)	überfüllt	crowded	—	pieno(a) zeppo(a)	abarrotado(a)
bone (E)	Knochen *m*	—	os *m*	osso *m*	hueso *m*
bonito (Es)	hübsch	pretty	joli(e)	carino(a)	—
bon marché[1] (F)	billig	cheap	—	a buon mercato	barato(a)
bon marché[2] (F)	preiswert	inexpensive	—	conveniente	económico(a)
book[1] (E)	buchen	—	retenir	prenotare	reservar
book[2] (E)	Buch *n*	—	livre *m*	libro *m*	libro *m*
book[3] (E)	vormerken	—	prendre note de	prendere nota di	tomar nota
book[4] (E)	vorbestellen	—	réserver	prenotare	hacer reservar
book-keeping (E)	Buchhaltung *f*	—	comptabilité *f*	contabilità *f*	contabilidad *f*
bookshop (E)	Buchhandlung *f*	—	librairie *f*	libreria *f*	librería *f*
Boot (D)	—	boat	bateau *m*	barca *f*	bote *m*
boot[1] (E)	Kofferraum *m*	—	coffre *m*	portabagagli *m*	maletero *m*
boot[2] (E)	Stiefel *m*	—	botte *f*	stivale *m*	bota *f*
bord[1] (F)	Rand *m*	brim	—	margine *m*	borde *m*
bord[2] (F)	Ufer *n*	shore/bank	—	riva *f*	orilla *f*
borde (Es)	Rand *m*	brim	bord *m*	margine *m*	—
borgen (D)	—	lend	prêter	prestare	prestar
boring (E)	langweilig	—	ennuyeux(-euse)	noioso(a)	aburrido(a)
born (E)	geboren	—	né(e)	nato(a)	nacido(a)
borracho (Es)	betrunken	drunk	soûl(e)	ubriaco(a)	—
borsa (I)	Tasche *f*	handbag	sac *m*	—	bolso *m*
borsa della spesa (I)	Einkaufstasche *f*	shopping bag	sac à provision *m*	—	bolsa de compra *f*
borsetta (I)	Handtasche *f*	handbag	sac à main *m*	—	bolso *m*
bosco (I)	Wald *m*	forest	forêt *f*	—	bosque *m*
böse (D)	—	wicked	méchant(e)	cattivo(a)	malo(a)
bosque[1] (Es)	Forst *m*	forest	forêt *f*	foresta *f*	—
bosque[2] (Es)	Wald *m*	forest	forêt *f*	bosco *m*	—

	D	E	F	I	Es
boss (E)	Chef *m*	—	patron *m*	capo *m*	jefe *m*
bota (Es)	Stiefel *m*	boot	botte *f*	stivale *m*	—
bote (Es)	Boot *n*	boat	bateau *m*	barca *f*	—
botella (Es)	Flasche *f*	bottle	bouteille *f*	bottiglia *f*	—
bote neumático (Es)	Schlauchboot *n*	(rubber) dinghy	canot pneumatique *m*	canotto pneumatico *m*	—
both (E)	beide	—	tous/ toutes les deux	entrambi(e)	ambos(as)
botón (Es)	Knopf *m*	button	bouton *m*	bottone *m*	—
Botschaft[1] (D)	—	message	message *m*	messaggio *m*	mensaje *m*
Botschaft[2] (D)	—	embassy	ambassade *f*	ambasciata *f*	embajada *f*
botte (F)	Stiefel *m*	boot	—	stivale *m*	bota *f*
botte (I)	Tonne *f*	barrel	tonneau *m*	—	barril *m*
bottiglia (I)	Flasche *f*	bottle	bouteille *f*	—	botella *f*
bottle (E)	Flasche *f*	—	bouteille *f*	bottiglia *f*	botella *f*
bottle opener (E)	Flaschenöffner *m*	—	ouvre-bouteilles *m*	apribottiglie *m*	abrebotellas *m*
bottone (I)	Knopf *m*	button	bouton *m*	—	botón *m*
bouche (F)	Mund *m*	mouth	—	bocca *f*	boca *f*
boucher (F)	Metzger *m*	butcher	—	macellaio *m*	carnicero *m*
boucherie (F)	Metzgerei *f*	butcher's	—	macelleria *f*	carnicería *f*
boucle (F)	Locke *f*	curl	—	riccio *m*	rizo *m*
bouclier (F)	Schild *n*	shield	—	scudo *m*	escudo *m*
boue (F)	Schlamm *m*	mud	—	fango *m*	barro *m*
bouée de sauvetage (F)	Rettungsring *m*	lifebelt	—	salvagente *m*	salvavidas *m*
bouffer (F)	fressen	eat	—	mangiare	devorar
bouger (F)	bewegen	move	—	muovere	mover
bougie (F)	Kerze *f*	candle	—	candela *f*	vela *f*
bouillon (F)	Brühe *f*	broth	—	brodo *m*	caldo *m*
boulangerie (F)	Bäckerei *f*	bakery	—	panetteria *f*	panadería *f*
bouquet (F)	Strauß *m*	bunch	—	mazzo *m*	ramo *m*
bourgeois (E)	spießig	—	bourgeois(e)	da piccolo(a) borghese	pequeño(a) burgués(-esa)
bourgeois (F)	spießig	bourgeois	—	da piccolo(a) borghese	pequeño(a) burgués(-esa)
bourgeon (F)	Knospe *f*	bud	—	bocciolo *m*	yema *f*
bouteille (F)	Flasche *f*	bottle	—	bottiglia *f*	botella *f*
bouton (F)	Knopf *m*	button	—	bottone *m*	botón *m*
bowl (E)	Schüssel *m*	—	jatte *f*	scodella *f*	fuente *f*
box[1] (E)	Kiste *f*	—	caisse *f*	cassetta *f*	caja *f*
box[2] (E)	Loge *f*	—	loge *f*	palco *m*	palco *m*
box[3] (E)	Schachtel *f*	—	boîte *f*	scatola *f*	caja *f*
boy (E)	Junge *m*	—	garçon *m*	ragazzo *m*	chico *m*
bracciale (I)	Armband *n*	bracelet	bracelet *m*	—	pulsera *f*
braccio (I)	Arm *m*	arm	bras *m*	—	brazo *m*
bracelet (E)	Armband *n*	—	bracelet *m*	bracciale *m*	pulsera *f*
bracelet (F)	Armband *n*	bracelet	—	bracciale *m*	pulsera *f*
brain (E)	Hirn *n*	—	cerveau *m*	cervello *m*	cerebro *m*
brake[1] (E)	bremsen	—	freiner	frenare	frenar
brake[2] (E)	Bremse *f*	—	frein *m*	freno *m*	freno *m*

	D	E	F	I	Es
brancard (F)	Bahre f	stretcher	—	barella f	camilla f
branch¹ (E)	Ast m	—	branche f	ramo m	rama f
branch² (E)	Filiale f	—	succursale f	filiale f	sucursal f
branch³ (E)	Zweig m	—	branche f	ramo m	rama f
branche¹ (F)	Ast m	branch	—	ramo m	rama f
branche² (F)	Zweig m	branch	—	ramo m	rama f
Brand (D)	—	fire	incendie m	incendio m	incendio m
brand (E)	Marke f	—	marque f	marca f	marca f
bras (F)	Arm m	arm	—	braccio m	brazo m
braten (D)	—	roast	rôtir	arrostire	asar
Braten (D)	—	roast	rôti m	arrosto m	asado m
brauchen (D)	—	need	avoir besoin de	aver bisogno di	necesitar
braun (D)	—	brown	marron	marrone	marrón
Braut (D)	—	bride	mariée f	sposa f	novia f
brav (D)	—	good	gentil(le)	bravo(a)	bueno(a)
brave (E)	tapfer	—	courageux(-euse)	coraggioso(a)	valiente
bravo (I)	brav	good	gentil(le)	—	bueno(a)
brazo (Es)	Arm m	arm	bras m	braccio m	—
bread (E)	Brot n	—	pain m	pane m	pan m
break¹ (E)	brechen	—	casser	rompere	romper
break² (E)	Pause f	—	pause f	pausa f	pausa f
breakdown (E)	Panne f	—	panne f	panne f	avería f
breakdown van (E)	Abschlepp-wagen m	—	dépanneuse f	carro attrezzi m	camión grúa m
breakfast (E)	Frühstück n	—	petit-déjeuner m	colazione f	desayuno m
break in (E)	einbrechen	—	cambrioler	fare irruzione	irumpir
breast (E)	Brust f	—	poitrine f	petto m	pecho m
breath (E)	Atem m	—	respiration f	fiato m	respiro m
breathe (E)	atmen	—	respirer	respirare	respirar
brechen (D)	—	break	casser	rompere	romper
breed (E)	züchten	—	élever	allevare	criar
breit (D)	—	broad	large	largo(a)	amplio(a)
Breite (D)	—	width	largeur f	larghezza f	extensión f
Bremse (D)	—	brake	frein m	freno m	freno m
bremsen (D)	—	brake	freiner	frenare	frenar
brennen (D)	—	burn	brûler	bruciare	arder
bretelle d'accès (F)	Auffahrt f	slip road	—	entrata f	vía de acceso f
brick (E)	Ziegel m	—	brique f	mattone m	ladrillo m
bride (E)	Braut f	—	mariée f	sposa f	novia f
bridge (E)	Brücke f	—	pont m	ponte m	puente m
Brief (D)	—	letter	lettre f	lettera f	carta f
Briefkasten (D)	—	letterbox	boîte aux lettres f	cassetta delle lettere f	buzón m
Briefmarke (D)	—	stamp	timbre m	francobollo m	sello m
bright (E)	hell	—	clair(e)	chiaro(a)	claro(a)
brillar (Es)	glänzen	shine	briller	splendere	—
Brille (D)	—	glasses	lunettes f pl	occhiali m pl	gafas f pl
briller (F)	glänzen	shine	—	splendere	brillar
brim (E)	Rand m	—	bord m	margine m	borde m

	D	E	F	I	Es
bring (along) (E)	mitbringen	—	apporter	portare con sé	traer
bring back (E)	zurückbringen	—	rapporter	riportare	devolver
bringen (D)	—	fetch	porter	portare	llevar
brique (F)	Ziegel *m*	brick	—	mattone *m*	ladrillo *m*
briquet (F)	Feuerzeug *n*	lighter	—	accendino *m*	mechero *m*
broad (E)	breit	—	large	largo(a)	amplio(a)
broadcast (E)	senden	—	transmettre	trasmettere	transmitir
broadcasting (E)	Rundfunk *m*	—	radio *f*	radio *f*	radiodifusión *f*
brocca (I)	Krug *m*	jug	cruche *f*	—	jarro(a) *m(f)*
brochure (E)	Prospekt *n*	—	prospectus *m*	dépliant *m*	prospecto *m*
brodo (I)	Brühe *f*	broth	bouillon *m*	—	caldo *m*
broken (E)	kaputt	—	cassé(e)	rotto(a)	roto(a)
broken piece (E)	Scherbe *f*	—	tesson *m*	coccio *m*	pedazo *m*
broma¹ (Es)	Spaß *m*	fun	plaisir *m*	scherzo *m*	—
broma² (Es)	Scherz *m*	joke	plaisanterie *f*	scherzo *m*	—
Brombeere (D)	—	blackberry	mûre *f*	mora *f*	zarzamora *f*
bromear (Es)	spaßen	joke	plaisanter	scherzare	—
broom (E)	Besen *m*	—	balai *m*	scopa *f*	escoba *f*
brosse (F)	Bürste *f*	brush	—	spazzola *f*	cepillo *m*
brosse à dents (F)	Zahnbürste *f*	toothbrush	—	spazzolino da denti *m*	cepillo de dientes *m*
Brot (D)	—	bread	pain *m*	pane *m*	pan *m*
Brötchen (D)	—	roll	petit pain *m*	panino *m*	panecillo *m*
broth (E)	Brühe *f*	—	bouillon *m*	brodo *m*	caldo *m*
brother (E)	Bruder *m*	—	frère *m*	fratello *m*	hermano *m*
brother-in-law (E)	Schwager *m*	—	beau-frère *m*	cognato *m*	cuñado *m*
brothers and sisters (E)	Geschwister *pl*	—	frère(s) et sœur(s) *pl*	fratelli *m pl*	hermanos *m pl*
brouillard (F)	Nebel *m*	fog	—	nebbia *f*	niebla *f*
brown (E)	braun	—	marron	marrone	marrón
bruciare¹ (I)	brennen	burn	brûler	—	arder
bruciare² (I)	verbrennen	burn	brûler	—	quemar
Brücke (D)	—	bridge	pont *m*	ponte *m*	puente *m*
Bruder (D)	—	brother	frère *m*	fratello *m*	hermano *m*
Brühe (D)	—	broth	bouillon *m*	brodo *m*	caldo *m*
bruire (F)	rauschen	rush	—	mormorare	susurrar
bruit¹ (F)	Geräusch *n*	sound	—	rumore *m*	ruido *m*
bruit² (F)	Krach *m*	noise	—	chiasso *m*	ruido *m*
bruit³ (F)	Lärm *m*	noise	—	rumore *m*	ruido *m*
bruja (Es)	Hexe *f*	witch	sorcière *f*	strega *f*	—
brûler¹ (F)	brennen	burn	—	bruciare	arder
brûler² (F)	verbrennen	burn	—	bruciare	quemar
Brunnen (D)	—	fountain	fontaine *f*	fontana *f*	fuente *f*
brush¹ (E)	Bürste *f*	—	brosse *f*	spazzola *f*	cepillo *m*
brush² (E)	Pinsel *m*	—	pinceau *m*	pennello *m*	pincel *m*
Brust (D)	—	breast	poitrine *f*	petto *m*	pecho *m*
brutto (I)	häßlich	ugly	laid(e)	—	feo(a)
bubble (E)	Blase *f*	—	bulle *f*	bolla *f*	burbuja *f*

	D	E	F	I	Es
buccia (I)	Schale *f*	peel	peau *f*	—	piel *f*
bucear (Es)	tauchen	dive	plonger	immergere	—
Buch (D)	—	book	livre *m*	libro *m*	libro *m*
buchen (D)	—	book	retenir	prenotare	reservar
Buchhaltung (D)	—	book-keeping	comptabilité *f*	contabilità *f*	contabilidad *f*
Buchhandlung (D)	—	bookshop	librairie *f*	libreria *f*	librería *f*
Buchstabe (D)	—	letter	lettre *f*	lettera *f*	letra *f*
buchstabieren (D)	—	spell	épeler	sillabare	deletrear
bucket (E)	Eimer *m*	—	seau *m*	secchio *m*	cubo *m*
buco (I)	Loch *n*	hole	trou *m*	—	agujero *m*
buco della chiave (I)	Schlüsselloch *n*	keyhole	trou de la serrure *m*	—	ojo de la cerradura *m*
bud (E)	Knospe *f*	—	bourgeon *m*	bocciolo *m*	yema *f*
budino (I)	Pudding *m*	pudding	flan *m*	—	flan *m*
bue (I)	Ochse *m*	ox	bœuf *m*	—	buey *m*
bueno¹ (Es)	brav	good	gentil(le)	bravo(a)	—
bueno² (Es)	gut	good/well	bon(ne)/bien	buono(a)/bene	—
buey¹ (Es)	Ochse *m*	ox	bœuf *m*	bue *m*	—
buey² (Es)	Rind *n*	cow	bœuf *m*	manzo *m*	—
Bügeleisen (D)	—	iron	fer à repasser *m*	ferro da stiro *m*	plancha *f*
bügeln (D)	—	iron	repasser	stirare	planchar
Bühne (D)	—	stage	scène *f*	palcoscenico *m*	escenario *m*
build (E)	bauen	—	construire	costruire	construir
building (E)	Gebäude *n*	—	bâtiment *m*	edificio *m*	edificio *m*
buio¹ (I)	finster	dark	sombre	—	oscuro(a)
buio² (I)	Finsternis *f*	darkness	obscurité *f*	—	oscuridad *f*
buisson (F)	Strauch *m*	bush	—	cespuglio *m*	arbusto *m*
bull (E)	Stier *m*	—	taureau *m*	toro *m*	toro *m*
bulle (F)	Blase *f*	bubble	—	bolla *f*	burbuja *f*
bulletin (F)	Zeugnis *n*	report	—	pagella *f*	informe *m*
bulletin météorologique (F)	Wetterbericht *m*	weather report	—	bollettino metereologico *m*	informe meteorológico *m*
bummeln (D)	—	stroll	flâner	girellare	callejear
bump (E)	anstoßen	—	heurter	urtare	empujar
bunch (E)	Strauß *m*	—	bouquet *m*	mazzo *m*	ramo *m*
Bundeskanzler (D)	—	Federal Chancellor	chancelier fédéral *m*	cancelliere federale *m*	canciller federal *m*
Bundesstraße (D)	—	Federal Highway/ main road	route nationale *f*	strada statale *f*	carretera nacional *f*
bunt (D)	—	coloured	coloré(e)	variopinto(a)	de colores
buono¹ (I)	gut	good	bon(ne)	—	bueno(a)
buono² (I)	Gutschein *m*	voucher	bon *m*	—	vale *m*
burbuja (Es)	Blase *f*	bubble	bulle *f*	bolla *f*	—
burden (E)	aufbürden	—	charger	addossare	cargar
bureau¹ (F)	Amt *n*	office	—	ufficio *m*	oficio *m*
bureau² (F)	Büro *n*	office	—	ufficio *m*	oficina *f*
bureau de change (E)	Wechselstube *f*	—	bureau de change *m*	ufficio di cambio *m*	casa de cambio *f*
bureau de change (F)	Wechselstube *f*	bureau de change	—	ufficio di cambio *m*	casa de cambio *f*
bureau de poste (F)	Postamt *n*	post office	—	ufficio postale *m*	oficina de correos *f*

	D	E	F	I	Es
bureau des objets trouvés (F)	Fundbüro n	lost property office	—	ufficio oggetti smarriti m	oficina de objetos perdidos f
Burg (D)	—	fortress	château fort m	rocca f	fortaleza f
bürgerlich (D)	—	civil	civil(e)	civile	civil
Bürgermeister (D)	—	mayor	maire m	sindaco m	alcalde m
burn[1] (E)	brennen	—	brûler	bruciare	arder
burn[2] (E)	verbrennen	—	brûler	bruciare	quemar
Büro (D)	—	office	bureau m	ufficio m	oficina f
burro (Es)	Esel m	donkey	âne m	asino m	—
burro (I)	Butter f	butter	beurre m	—	mantequilla f
Bursche (D)	—	fellow	garçon m	ragazzo m	chico m
burst (E)	platzen	—	éclater	scoppiare	reventar
Bürste (D)	—	brush	brosse f	spazzola f	cepillo m
Bus (D)	—	bus	bus m	autobus m	autobús m
bus (E)	Bus m	—	bus m	autobus m	autobús m
bus (F)	Bus m	bus	—	autobus m	autobús m
buscar (Es)	suchen	look for	chercher	cercare	—
bush (E)	Strauch m	—	buisson m	cespuglio m	arbusto m
business hours (E)	Öffnungzeiten pl	—	heures d'ouverture f pl	orario d'ufficio m	horario de oficina m
businessman (E)	Kaufmann m	—	commerçant m	commerciante m	comerciante m
bussare (I)	klopfen	knock	frapper	—	golpear
busta (I)	Umschlag m	envelope	enveloppe f	—	sobre m
busy (E)	beschäftigt	—	occupé(e)	occupato(a)	ocupado(a)
but[1] (E)	aber	—	mais	ma	pero
but[2] (E)	sondern	—	mais	ma/bensì	sino
but[1] (F)	Zweck m	purpose	—	scopo m	finalidad f
but[2] (F)	Ziel n	goal	—	meta f	intención f
butcher (E)	Metzger m	—	boucher m	macellaio m	carnicero m
butcher's (E)	Metzgerei f	—	boucherie f	macelleria f	carnicería f
Butter (D)	—	butter	beurre m	burro m	mantequilla f
butter (E)	Butter f	—	beurre m	burro m	mantequilla f
butterfly (E)	Schmetterling m	—	papillon m	farfalla f	mariposa f
button (E)	Knopf m	—	bouton m	bottone m	botón m
buy (E)	kaufen	—	acheter	comprare	comprar
buyer (E)	Käufer m	—	acheteur m	acquirente m	comprador m
buzón (Es)	Briefkasten m	letterbox	boîte aux lettres f	cassetta delle lettere f	—
by chance (E)	zufällig	—	par hasard	per caso	por casualidad
bye! (E)	tschüs!	—	salut!	ciao!	¡hasta luego!
by heart (E)	auswendig	—	par cœur	a memoria	de memoria
by the way (E)	übrigens	—	d'ailleurs	del resto	por lo demás
cabalgar (Es)	reiten	ride	monter	cavalcare	—
caballo (Es)	Pferd n	horse	cheval m	cavallo m	—
cabaña (Es)	Hütte f	hut	cabane f	capanna f	—
cabane (F)	Hütte f	hut	—	capanna f	cabaña f
cabbage (E)	Kohl m	—	chou m	cavolo m	col f
cabeza (Es)	Kopf m	head	tête f	testa f	—
cabin (E)	Kabine f	—	cabine f	cabina f	cabina f

	D	E	F	I	Es
cabina (Es)	Kabine *f*	cabin	cabine *f*	cabina *f*	—
cabina (I)	Kabine *f*	cabin	cabine *f*	—	cabina *f*
cabina de teléfono (Es)	Telefonzelle *f*	phone box	cabine téléphonique *f*	cabina telefonica *f*	—
cabina telefonica (I)	Telefonzelle *f*	phone box	cabine téléphonique *f*	—	cabina de teléfono *f*
cabine (F)	Kabine *f*	cabin	—	cabina *f*	cabina *f*
cabine téléphonique (F)	Telefonzelle *f*	phone box	—	cabina telefonica *f*	cabina de teléfono *f*
cabinets (F)	Klosett *n*	lavatory	—	gabinetto *m*	retrete *m*
cable (E)	Kabel *n*	—	câble *m*	cavo *m*	cable *m*
cable (Es)	Kabel *n*	cable	câble *m*	cavo *m*	—
câble (F)	Kabel *n*	cable	—	cavo *m*	cable *m*
cabra (Es)	Ziege *f*	goat	chèvre *f*	capra *f*	—
caccia (I)	Jagd *f*	hunt	chasse *f*	—	caza *f*
cacciare (I)	jagen	hunt	chasser	—	cazar
cacciavite (I)	Schraubenzieher *m*	screwdriver	tournevis *m*	—	destornillador *m*
cacher (F)	verstecken	hide	—	nascondere	ocultar
cada (Es)	jede(r,s)	each/every	chaque	ogni/ognuno	—
cada hora (Es)	stündlich	hourly	toutes les heures	ogni ora	—
cadáver (Es)	Leiche *f*	corpse	cadavre *m*	cadavere *m*	—
cadavere (I)	Leiche *f*	corpse	cadavre *m*	—	cadáver *m*
cada vez (Es)	jedesmal	each time	chaque fois	ogni volta	—
cadavre (F)	Leiche *f*	corpse	—	cadavere *m*	cadáver *m*
cadeau (F)	Geschenk *n*	present	—	regalo *m*	regalo *m*
cadena (Es)	Kette *f*	chain	chaîne *f*	catena *f*	—
cadera (Es)	Hüfte *f*	hip	hanche *f*	fianco *m*	—
cadere¹ (I)	fallen	fall	tomber	—	caer
cadere² (I)	stürzen	fall	tomber	—	caer
cadere³ (I)	umfallen	fall over	tomber	—	caerse
cadre (F)	Rahmen *m*	frame	—	cornice *f*	marco *m*
caducado (Es)	ungültig	invalid	non valable	non valido(a)	—
caduta¹ (I)	Absturz *m*	crash	chute *f*	—	caída *f*
caduta² (I)	Sturz *m*	fall	chute *f*	—	caída *f*
caer¹ (Es)	fallen	fall	tomber	cadere	—
caer² (Es)	stürzen	fall	tomber	cadere	—
caer a tierra (Es)	abstürzen	crash	faire une chute	precipitare	—
caerse (Es)	umfallen	fall over	tomber	cadere	—
Café (D)	—	café	café *m*	caffè *m*	café *m*
café (E)	Café *n*	—	café *m*	caffè *m*	café *m*
café¹ (Es)	Café *n*	café	café *m*	caffè *m*	—
café² (Es)	Kaffee *m*	coffee	café *m*	caffè *m*	—
café¹ (F)	Café *n*	café	—	caffè *m*	café *m*
café² (F)	Kaffee *m*	coffee	—	caffè *m*	café *m*
caffè¹ (I)	Café *n*	café	café *m*	—	café *m*
caffè² (I)	Kaffee *m*	coffee	café *m*	—	café *m*
cage (E)	Käfig *m*	—	cage *f*	gabbia *f*	jaula *f*
cage (F)	Käfig *m*	cage	—	gabbia *f*	jaula *f*
cahier (F)	Heft *n*	exercise book	—	quaderno *m*	cuaderno *m*

	D	E	F	I	Es
caída[1] (Es)	Absturz m	crash	chute f	caduta f	—
caída[2] (Es)	Sturz m	fall	chute f	caduta f	—
caisse[1] (F)	Kasse f	till	—	cassa f	caja f
caisse[2] (F)	Kiste f	box	—	cassetta f	caja f
caisse d'épargne (F)	Sparkasse f	savings bank	—	cassa di risparmio f	caja de ahorros f
caja[1] (Es)	Kasse f	till	caisse f	cassa f	—
caja[2] (Es)	Kiste f	box	caisse f	cassetta f	—
caja[3] (Es)	Schachtel f	box	boîte f	scatola f	—
caja de ahorros (Es)	Sparkasse f	savings bank	caisse d'épargne f	cassa di risparmio f	—
cajón (Es)	Schublade f	drawer	tiroir m	cassetto m	—
cake[1] (E)	Kuchen m	—	gâteau m	dolce m	pastel m
cake[2] (E)	Torte f	—	gâteau m	torta f	tarta f
cake shop (E)	Konditorei f	—	pâtisserie f	pasticceria f	pastelería f
calamar (Es)	Tintenfisch m	cuttlefish	seiche f	seppia f	—
calcetín (Es)	Socke f	sock	chaussette f	calzino m	—
calcolare (I)	berechnen	calculate	calculer	—	calcular
calcular[1] (Es)	berechnen	calculate	calculer	calcolare	—
calcular[2] (Es)	rechnen	calculate	calculer	fare i conti	—
calculate (E)	rechnen	—	calculer	fare i conti	calcular
calculer[1] (F)	berechnen	calculate	—	calcolare	calcular
calculer[2] (F)	rechnen	calculate	—	fare i conti	calcular
caldo (Es)	Brühe f	broth	bouillon m	brodo m	—
caldo[1] (I)	heiß	hot	chaud(e)	—	caliente
caldo[2] (I)	Hitze f	heat	chaleur f	—	calor m
caldo[3] (I)	warm	warm	chaud(e)	—	caliente
calefacción (Es)	Heizung f	heating	chauffage m	riscaldamento m	—
calefacción central (Es)	Zentralheizung f	central heating	chauffage central m	riscaldamento centrale m	—
calendar (E)	Kalender m	—	calendrier m	calendario m	calendario m
calendario (Es)	Kalender m	calendar	calendrier m	calendario m	—
calendario (I)	Kalender m	calendar	calendrier m	—	calendario m
calendrier (F)	Kalender m	calendar	—	calendario m	calendario m
calentar[1] (Es)	heizen	heat	chauffer	riscaldare	—
calentar[2] (Es)	wärmen	warm	chauffer	riscaldare	—
calf (E)	Kalb n	—	veau m	vitello m	ternera f
caliente[1] (Es)	heiß	hot	chaud(e)	caldo(a)	—
caliente[2] (Es)	warm	warm	chaud(e)	caldo(a)	—
calificación (Es)	Note f	mark	note f	voto m	—
call[1] (E)	Anruf m	—	coup de téléphone m	chiamata f	llamada f
call[2] (E)	nennen	—	appeler	chiamare	nombrar
callar (Es)	schweigen	be silent	taire, se	tacere	—
calle (Es)	Straße f	street	rue f	strada f	—
calle central (Es)	Hauptstraße f	main street	grande rue f	strada principale f	—
calle de dirección única (Es)	Einbahnstraße f	one-way street	rue à sens unique f	senso unico m	—
callejear (Es)	bummeln	stroll	flâner	girellare	—
callejón (Es)	Gasse f	lane	ruelle f	vicolo m	—

cambiarsi

	D	E	F	I	Es
call off (E)	abblasen	—	annuler	disdire	anular
calm¹ (E)	beruhigen	—	calmer, se	calmarsi	calmarse
calm² (E)	Ruhe f	—	calme m	silenzio m	quietud f
calmar (Es)	beruhigen	calm down	calmer, se	calmarsi	—
calmare (I)	beruhigen, sich	calm down	calmer, se	—	calmarse
calme¹ (F)	Ruhe f	calm	—	silenzio m	quietud f
calme² (F)	still	quiet	—	calmo(a)	tranquilo(a)
calmer, se (F)	beruhigen	calm down	—	calmare	calmar
calmo¹ (I)	ruhig	quiet	tranquille	—	quieto(a)
calmo² (I)	still	quiet	calme	—	tranquilo(a)
calor¹ (Es)	Hitze f	heat	chaleur f	caldo m	—
calor² (Es)	Wärme f	warmth	chaleur f	calore m	—
calore (I)	Wärme f	warmth	chaleur f	—	calor m
calvo (I)	kahl	bald	chauve	—	calvo(a)
calvo (Es)	kahl	bald	chauve	calvo(a)	—
calza (I)	Strumpf m	stocking	bas m	—	media f
calzada (Es)	Fahrbahn f	roadway	chaussée f	carreggiata f	—
calzamaglia (I)	Strumpfhose f	tights	collants m pl	—	leotardos m pl
calzino (I)	Socke f	sock	chausette f	—	calcetín m
calzolaio (I)	Schuster m	shoemaker	cordonnier m	—	zapatero m
calzoncillos (Es)	Unterhose f	underpants	slip m	mutande f pl	—
cama (Es)	Bett n	bed	lit m	letto m	—
camarada (Es)	Genosse m	comrade	camarade m	compagno m	—
camarade (F)	Genosse m	comrade	—	compagno m	camarada m
camarero (Es)	Kellner m/ Ober m	waiter	garçon m	cameriere m	—
cambiamento¹ (I)	Veränderung f	change	changement m	—	cambio m
cambiamento² (I)	Wechsel m	change	changement m	—	cambio m
cambiar¹ (Es)	ändern	change	changer	cambiare	—
cambiar² (Es)	austauschen	exchange	échanger	scambiare	—
cambiar³ (Es)	tauschen	swap	échanger	scambiare	—
cambiar⁴ (Es)	umtauschen	exchange	échanger	cambiare	—
cambiar⁵ (Es)	umziehen	move	déménager	cambiare casa	—
cambiar⁶ (Es)	umwechseln	change	changer	cambiare	—
cambiar⁷ (Es)	vertauschen	exchange	échanger	scambiare	—
cambiar⁸ (Es)	verändern	change	transformer	mutare	—
cambiar⁹ (Es)	wechseln	change	changer	cambiare	—
cambiare¹ (I)	ändern	change	changer	—	cambiar
cambiare² (I)	umtauschen	exchange	échanger	—	cambiar
cambiare³ (I)	umsteigen	change	changer (de train)	—	transbordar
cambiare⁴ (I)	umwechseln	change	changer	—	cambiar
cambiare⁵ (I)	wechseln	change	changer	—	cambiar
cambiare casa (I)	umziehen	move	déménager	—	cambiar
cambiarse (Es)	umziehen	change	changer, se	cambiarsi	—
cambiarse de ropa (Es)	umkleiden	change	changer de vêtements	cambiarsi	—
cambiarsi¹ (I)	umziehen	change	changer, se	—	cambiarse
cambiarsi² (I)	umkleiden	change	changer de vêtements	—	cambiarse de ropa

cambio

	D	E	F	I	Es
cambio¹ (Es)	Austausch *m*	exchange	échange *m*	scambio *m*	—
cambio² (Es)	Kleingeld *n*	small change	monnaie *f*	spiccioli *m pl*	—
cambio³ (Es)	Umbuchung *f*	alteration	transfert *m*	riporto *m*	—
cambio⁴ (Es)	Veränderung *f*	change	changement *m*	cambiamento *m*	—
cambio⁵ (Es)	Wechsel *m*	change	changement *m*	cambiamento *m*	—
cambrioler (F)	einbrechen	break in	—	fare irruzione	irrumpir
camera (E)	Fotoapparat *m*	—	appareil photo *m*	macchina fotografica *f*	máquina fotográfica *f*
camera (I)	Zimmer *n*	room	chambre *f*	—	habitación *f*
camera da letto (I)	Schlafzimmer *n*	bedroom	chambre à coucher *f*	—	dormitorio *m*
cameriere (I)	Kellner *m*/Ober *m*	waiter	garçon *m*	—	camarero *m*
camicetta (I)	Bluse *f*	blouse	chemisier *m*	—	blusa *f*
camicia (I)	Hemd *n*	shirt	chemise *f*	—	camisa *f*
camilla (Es)	Bahre *f*	stretcher	brancard *m*	barella *f*	—
camino (Es)	Weg *m*	way	chemin *m*	via *f*	—
camión (Es)	Lastwagen *m*	lorry	camion *m*	camion *m*	—
camion (F)	Lastwagen *m*	lorry	—	camion *m*	camión *m*
camion (I)	Lastwagen *m*	lorry	camion *m*	—	camión *m*
camionero (Es)	Fernfahrer *m*	long-distance driver	routier *m*	camionista *m*	—
camión grúa (Es)	Abschleppwagen *m*	breakdown van	dépanneuse *f*	carro attrezzi *m*	—
camionista (I)	Fernfahrer *m*	long-distance driver	routier *m*	—	camionero *m*
camisa (Es)	Hemd *n*	shirt	chemise *f*	camicia *f*	—
camiseta (Es)	Unterhemd *n*	vest	tricot *m*	canottiera *f*	—
camp (E)	zelten	—	camper	campeggiare	acampar
campana (Es)	Glocke *f*	bell	cloche *f*	campana *f*	—
campana (I)	Glocke *f*	bell	cloche *f*	—	campana *f*
campanello (I)	Klingel *f*	bell	sonnette *f*	—	timbre *m*
campeggiare (I)	zelten	camp	camper	—	acampar
campeggio¹ (I)	Camping *n*	camping	camping *m*	—	camping *m*
campeggio² (I)	Campingplatz *m*	campsite	terrain de camping *m*	—	camping *m*
camper (E)	Wohnmobil *n*	—	caravane *f*	camper *m*	caravana *f*
camper (F)	zelten	camp	—	campeggiare	acampar
camper (I)	Wohnmobil *n*	camper	caravane *f*	—	caravana *f*
campesino (Es)	Bauer *m*	farmer	paysan *m*	contadino *m*	—
Camping (D)	—	camping	camping *m*	campeggio *m*	camping *m*
camping (E)	Camping *n*	—	camping *m*	campeggio *m*	camping *m*
camping¹ (Es)	Campingplatz *m*	campsite	terrain de camping *m*	campeggio *m*	—
camping² (Es)	Camping *n*	camping	camping *m*	campeggio *m*	—
camping (F)	Camping *n*	camping	—	campeggio *m*	camping *m*
Campingplatz (D)	—	campsite	terrain de camping *m*	campeggio *m*	camping *m*
campione (I)	Muster *n*	sample	modèle *m*	—	muestra *f*
campo¹ (Es)	Acker *m*	field	champ *m*	campo *m*	—
campo² (Es)	Feld *n*	field	champ *m*	campo *m*	—
campo¹ (I)	Acker *m*	field	champ *m*	—	campo *m*

	D	E	F	I	Es
campo² (I)	Feld n	field	champ m	—	campo m
campo dei giochi (I)	Spielplatz m	playground	terrain de jeux m	—	campo de juego m
campo de juego (Es)	Spielplatz m	playground	terrain de jeux m	campo dei giochi m	—
campsite (E)	Campingplatz m	—	terrain de camping m	campeggio m	camping m
can (E)	können	—	pouvoir	sapere	saber
Canada (E)	Kanada n	—	Canada m	Canada m	Canadá m
Canadá (Es)	Kanada n	Canada	Canada m	Canada m	—
Canada (F)	Kanada n	Canada	—	Canada m	Canadá m
Canada (I)	Kanada n	Canada	Canada m	—	Canadá m
Canal de la Mancha (Es)	Ärmelkanal m	Channel	Manche f	Manica f	—
canapé¹ (F)	Couch f	couch	—	divano m	diván m
canapé² (F)	Sofa n	sofa	—	sofà m	sofá m
canard (F)	Ente f	duck	—	anatra f	pato m
cancel (E)	abbestellen	—	décommander	annullare	anular el pedido de
cancelliere federale (I)	Bundeskanzler m	Federal Chancellor	chancelier fédéral m	—	canciller federal m
cancer (E)	Krebs m	—	cancer m	cancro m	cáncer m
cáncer (Es)	Krebs m	cancer	cancer m	cancro m	—
cancer (F)	Krebs m	cancer	—	cancro m	cáncer m
canciller federal (Es)	Bundeskanzler m	Federal Chancellor	chancelier fédéral m	cancelliere federale m	—
canción (Es)	Lied n	song	chanson f	canzone f	—
cancro (I)	Krebs m	cancer	cancer m	—	cáncer m
candela (I)	Kerze f	candle	bougie f	—	vela f
candidature (F)	Bewerbung f	application	—	domanda d'impiego f	candidatura f
candle (E)	Kerze f	—	bougie f	candela f	vela f
cane (I)	Hund m	dog	chien m	—	perro m
cangrejo (Es)	Krebs m	crayfish	écrevisse f	gambero m	—
cannocchiale (I)	Fernglas n	binoculars	jumelles f pl	—	gemelos m pl
canoa (I)	Paddelboot n	canoe	canoë m	—	piragua f
canoe (E)	Paddelboot n	—	canoë m	canoa f	piragua f
canot pneumatique (F)	Schlauchboot n	(rubber) dinghy	—	canotto pneumatico m	bote neumático m
canottiera (I)	Unterhemd n	vest	tricot m	—	camiseta f
canotto pneumatico (I)	Schlauchboot n	(rubber) dinghy	canot pneumatique m	—	bote neumático m
cansado (Es)	müde	tired	fatigué(e)	stanco(a)	—
cansar¹ (Es)	anstrengen	make an effort	faire des efforts	affaticare	—
cansar² (Es)	ermüden	tire	fatiguer	stancare	—
cantante (Es)	Sänger m	singer	chanteur m	cantante m	—
cantante (I)	Sänger m	singer	chanteur m	—	cantante m
cantar (Es)	singen	sing	chanter	cantare	—
cantare (I)	singen	sing	chanter	—	cantar
cantidad¹ (Es)	Menge f	quantity	quantité f	quantità f	—
cantidad² (Es)	Quantität f	quantity	quantité f	quantità f	—
cantina (I)	Keller m	cellar	cave f	—	sótano m
canto (Es)	Gesang m	singing	chant m	canto m	—

	D	E	F	I	Es
canto (I)	Gesang *m*	singing	chant *m*	—	canto *m*
cantuccio (I)	Winkel *m*	corner	coin *m*	—	rincón *m*
canzone (I)	Lied *n*	song	chanson *f*	—	canción *f*
cap (E)	Mütze *f*	—	casquette *f*	berretto *m*	gorra *f*
capable (E)	fähig	—	capable	capace	hábil
capable[1] (F)	fähig	capable	—	capace	hábil
capable[2] (F)	imstande	able	—	capace	en condiciones
capace[1] (I)	fähig	capable	capable	—	hábil
capace[2] (I)	imstande	able	capable	—	en condiciones
capacidad (Es)	Fähigkeit *f*	ability	capacité *f*	capacità *f*	—
capacità (I)	Fähigkeit *f*	ability	capacité *f*	—	capacidad *f*
capacité (F)	Fähigkeit *f*	ability	—	capacità *f*	capacidad *f*
capanna (I)	Hütte *f*	hut	cabane *f*	—	cabaña *f*
capello (I)	Haar *n*	hair	cheveu *m*	—	pelo *m*
capilla (Es)	Kapelle *f*	chapel	chapelle *f*	cappella *f*	—
capire (I)	verstehen	understand	comprendre	—	entender
capitaine (F)	Kapitän *m*	captain	—	capitano *m*	capitán *m*
capital[1] (E)	Hauptstadt *f*	—	capitale *f*	capitale *f*	capital *f*
capital[2] (E)	Kapital *n*	—	capital *m*	capitale *m*	capital *m*
capital[1] (Es)	Hauptstadt *f*	capital	capitale *f*	capitale *f*	—
capital[2] (Es)	Kapital *n*	capital	capital *m*	capitale *m*	—
capital (F)	Kapital *n*	capital	—	capitale *m*	capital *m*
capitale (F)	Hauptstadt *f*	capital	—	capitale *f*	capital *f*
capitale[1] (I)	Hauptstadt *f*	capital	capitale *f*	—	capital *f*
capitale[2] (I)	Kapital *n*	capital	capital *m*	—	capital *m*
capitán (Es)	Kapitän *m*	captain	capitaine *m*	capitano *m*	—
capitano (I)	Kapitän *m*	captain	capitaine *m*	—	capitán *m*
capitolo (I)	Kapitel *n*	chapter	chapitre *m*	—	capítulo *m*
capítulo (Es)	Kapitel *n*	chapter	chapitre *m*	capitolo *m*	—
capo (I)	Chef *m*	boss	patron *m*	—	jefe *m*
Capodanno (I)	Neujahr *n*	New Year	nouvel an *m*	—	Año Nuevo *m*
capolinea (I)	Endstation *f*	terminus	terminus *m*	—	estación terminal *f*
cappella (I)	Kapelle *f*	chapel	chapelle *f*	—	capilla *f*
cappello (I)	Hut *m*	hat	chapeau *m*	—	sombrero *m*
cappotto (I)	Mantel *m*	coat	manteau *m*	—	abrigo *m*
cappuccio (I)	Kapuze *f*	hood	capuchon *m*	—	capucha *f*
capra (I)	Ziege *f*	goat	chèvre *f*	—	cabra *f*
capriolo (I)	Reh *n*	deer	chevreuil *m*	—	corzo *m*
captain (E)	Kapitän *m*	—	capitaine *m*	capitano *m*	capitán *m*
capucha (Es)	Kapuze *f*	hood	capuchon *m*	cappuccio *m*	—
capuchon (F)	Kapuze *f*	hood	—	cappuccio *m*	capucha *f*
car[1] (E)	Auto *n*	—	voiture *f*	automobile *f* / macchina *f*	coche *m*
car[2] (E)	Wagen *m*	—	voiture *f*	vettura *f*	coche *m*
car (F)	denn	for	—	perché	pues/porque
cara (Es)	Gesicht *n*	face	visage *m*	faccia *f*	—
car accident (E)	Autounfall *m*	—	accident de voiture *m*	incidente stradale *m*	accidente de automóvil *m*
carácter (Es)	Charakter *m*	character	caractère *m*	carattere *m*	—

	D	E	F	I	Es
caractère (F)	Charakter m	character	—	carattere m	carácter m
caramella (I)	Bonbon n	sweet	bonbon m	—	caramelo m
caramelo (Es)	Bonbon n	sweet	bonbon m	caramella f	—
carattere (I)	Charakter m	character	caractère m	—	carácter m
caratteristica (I)	Merkmal n	characteristic	signe m	—	rasgo m
caravan (E)	Wohnwagen m	—	caravane f	roulotte f	rulota f
caravana (Es)	Wohnmobil n	camper	caravane f	camper m	—
caravane[1] (F)	Wohnwagen m	caravan	—	roulotte f	rulota f
caravane[2] (F)	Wohnmobil n	camper	—	camper m	caravana f
carbón (Es)	Kohle f	coal	charbon m	carbone m	—
carbone (I)	Kohle f	coal	charbon m	—	carbón m
cárcel (Es)	Gefängnis n	prison	prison f	prigione f	—
card (E)	Karte f	—	carte f	cartolina f	postal f
cardboard (E)	Pappe f	—	carton m	cartone m	cartón m
cardboard box (E)	Karton m	—	carton m	cartone m	cartón m
cardigan (E)	Strickjacke f	—	veste en tricot f	giacca di maglia f	chaqueta de punto f
care (E)	Pflege f	—	soins m pl	cura f	cuidado m
career (E)	Karriere f	—	carrière f	carriera f	carrera f
careful[1] (E)	sorgfältig	—	soigneux(-euse)	accurato(a)	cuidadoso(a)
careful[2] (E)	vorsichtig	—	prudent(e)	prudente	cauto(a)
careless[1] (E)	leichtsinnig	—	étourdi(e)	spensierato(a)	imprudente
careless[2] (E)	unvorsichtig	—	imprudent(e)	imprudente	descuidado(a)
caretaker (E)	Hausmeister m	—	concierge m	portinaio m	portero m
carga (Es)	Ladung f	cargo	charge f	carico m	—
cargar[1] (Es)	aufladen	load	charger	caricare	—
cargar[2] (Es)	aufbürden	burden	charger	addossare	—
cargar[3] (Es)	verladen	load	charger	caricare	—
cargo (E)	Ladung f	—	charge f	carico m	carga f
caricare[1] (I)	aufladen	load	charger	—	cargar
caricare[2] (I)	verladen	load	charger	—	cargar
carico[1] (I)	Ladung f	cargo	charge f	—	carga f
carico[2] (I)	Last f	load	charge f	—	peso m
cariño (Es)	Zärtlichkeit f	tenderness	tendresse f	tenerezza f	—
carino[1] (I)	hübsch	pretty	joli(e)	—	bonito(a)
carino[2] (I)	nett	nice	joli(e)	—	agradable
carino[3] (I)	niedlich	sweet	mignon(ne)	—	gracioso(a)
carnation (E)	Nelke f	—	œillet m	garofano m	clavel m
carnaval (Es)	Karneval m/ Fasching m	carnival	carnaval m	carnevale m	—
carnaval (F)	Karneval m/ Fasching m	carnival	—	carnevale m	carnaval m
carne (Es)	Fleisch n	meat	viande f	carne f	—
carne (I)	Fleisch n	meat	viande f	—	carne f
carne de cerdo (Es)	Schweinefleisch n	pork	viande de porc f	carne di maiale f	—
carne de vaca (Es)	Rindfleisch n	beef	viande de bœuf f	carne di manzo f	—
carne di maiale (I)	Schweinefleisch n	pork	viande de porc f	—	carne de cerdo f
carne di manzo (I)	Rindfleisch n	beef	viande de bœuf f	—	carne de vaca f
carne picada (Es)	Hackfleisch n	minced meat	viande hachée f	carne tritata f	—

	D	E	F	I	Es
carnet de chèques (F)	Scheckbuch n	cheque book	—	libretto degli assegni m	talonario de cheques m
carne tritata (I)	Hackfleisch n	minced meat	viande hachée f	—	carne picada f
carnevale (I)	Karneval m/ Fasching m	carnival	carnaval m	—	carnaval m
carnicería (Es)	Metzgerei f	butcher's	boucherie f	macelleria f	—
carnicero (Es)	Metzger m	butcher	boucher m	macellaio m	—
carnival (E)	Karneval m/ Fasching m	—	carnaval m	carnevale m	carnaval m
caro¹ (I)	lieb	sweet	gentil(le)	—	amable
caro² (I)	teuer	expensive	cher(-ère)	—	caro(a)
caro (Es)	teuer	expensive	cher(-ère)	caro(a)	—
carota (I)	Karotte f/ Möhre f	carrot	carotte f	—	zanahoria f
carotte (F)	Karotte f/ Möhre f	carrot	—	carota f	zanahoria f
carpenter (E)	Tischler m	—	menuisier m	falegname m	carpintero m
carpet (E)	Teppich m	—	tapis m	tappeto m	alfombra f
carpeta (Es)	Mappe f	folder	serviette f	raccoglitore m	—
carpintero (Es)	Tischler m	carpenter	menuisier m	falegname m	—
carré¹ (F)	Quadrat n	square	—	quadrato m	cuadrado m
carré² (F)	viereckig	square	—	quadrato(a)	cuadrangular
carré³ (F)	quadratisch	square	—	quadrato(a)	cuadrado(a)
carreau (F)	Scheibe f	pane	—	vetro m	cristal m
carreggiata (I)	Fahrbahn f	roadway	chaussée f	—	calzada f
carrera (Es)	Karriere f	career	carrière f	carriera f	—
carretera de circulación rápida (Es)	Schnellstraße f	expressway	voie rapide f	superstrada f	—
carretera nacional¹ (Es)	Bundesstraße f	Federal Highway/ main road	route nationale f	strada statale f	—
carretera nacional² (Es)	Landstraße f	country road	route f	strada provinciale f	—
carriage (E)	Waggon m	—	wagon m	vagone m	vagón m
carrier (E)	Träger m	—	porteur m	facchino m	mozo m
carriera (I)	Karriere f	career	carrière f	—	carrera f
carrière (F)	Karriere f	career	—	carriera f	carrera f
carro attrezzi (I)	Abschlepp- wagen m	breakdown van	dépanneuse f	—	camión grúa m
carrocería (Es)	Karosserie f	body	carrosserie f	carrozzeria f	—
carrosserie (F)	Karosserie f	body	—	carrozzeria f	carrocería f
carrot (E)	Karotte f/ Möhre f	—	carotte f	carota f	zanahoria f
carrozzeria (I)	Karosserie f	body	carrosserie f	—	carrocería f
carry (E)	tragen	—	porter	portare	llevar
carry on (E)	weitermachen	—	continuer	continuare	continuar
carta (Es)	Brief m	letter	lettre f	lettera f	—
carta (I)	Papier n	paper	papier m	—	papel m
carta con acuse de recibo (Es)	Einschreibebrief m	recorded delivery letter	lettre recommandée f	lettera raccomandata f	—
carta de amor (Es)	Liebesbrief m	love letter	lettre d'amour f	lettera d'amore f	—
carta d'identità (I)	Personalausweis m	identity card	carte d'identité f	—	documento de identidad m
carta geografica (I)	Landkarte f	map	carte f	—	mapa m

	D	E	F	I	Es
carte¹ (F)	Karte f	card	—	cartolina f	postal f
carte² (F)	Landkarte f	map	—	carta geografica f	mapa m
carte d'identité (F)	Personalausweis m	identity card	—	carta d'identitá f	documento de identidad m
cartel (Es)	Plakat n	poster	affiche f	affisso m	—
cartella (I)	Aktenmappe f	file	porte-documents m	—	cartera f
carte postale¹ (F)	Ansichtskarte f	postcard	—	cartolina f	tarjeta postal f
carte postale² (F)	Postkarte f	postcard	—	cartolina f	postal f
cartera (Es)	Aktenmappe f	file	porte-documents m	cartella f	—
cartero (Es)	Postbote m	postman	facteur m	postino m	—
cartoleria (I)	Schreibwaren-handlung f	stationery shop	papeterie f	—	papelería f
cartolina¹ (I)	Ansichtskarte f	postcard	carte postale f	—	tarjeta postal f
cartolina² (I)	Karte f	card	carte f	—	postal f
cartolina³ (I)	Postkarte f	postcard	carte postale f	—	postal f
cartón¹ (Es)	Karton m	cardboard box	carton m	cartone m	—
cartón² (Es)	Pappe f	cardboard	carton m	cartone m	—
carton¹ (F)	Karton m	cardboard box	—	cartone m	cartón m
carton² (F)	Pappe f	cardboard	—	cartone m	cartón m
cartone¹ (I)	Karton m	cardboard box	carton m	—	cartón m
cartone² (I)	Pappe f	cardboard	carton m	—	cartón m
casa¹ (Es)	Haus n	house	maison f	casa f	—
casa² (Es)	Haushalt m	household	ménage m	casa f	—
casa¹ (I)	Haus n	house	maison f	—	casa f
casa² (I)	Haushalt m	household	ménage m	—	casa f
casa de cambio (Es)	Wechselstube f	bureau de change	bureau de change m	ufficio di cambio m	—
casado (Es)	verheiratet	married	marié(e)	sposato(a)	—
casalinga (I)	Hausfrau f	housewife	femme de maison f	—	ama de casa f
casarse (Es)	heiraten	marry	marier, se	sposarsi	—
casco (Es)	Helm m	helmet	casque m	casco m	—
casco (I)	Helm m	helmet	casque m	—	casco m
cas d'urgence (F)	Notfall m	emergency	—	caso di emergenza m	caso de urgencia m
cash (E)	Bargeld f	—	espèces f pl	contanti m pl	dinero al contado m
cash on delivery (E)	Nachnahme f	—	remboursement m	pagamento contro assegno m	entrega contro reembolso f
casi¹ (Es)	beinahe	nearly	presque	circa/quasi	—
casi² (Es)	fast	nearly	presque	quasi	—
casino (Es)	Kasino n	casino	casino m	casinò m	—
casino (F)	Kasino n	casino	—	casinò m	casino m
casinò (I)	Kasino n	casino	casino m	—	casino m
caso¹ (I)	Vorfall m	incident	incident m	—	suceso m
caso² (I)	Zufall m	chance	hasard m	—	casualidad f
caso de urgencia (Es)	Notfall m	emergency	cas d'urgence m	caso di emergenza m	—
caso di emergenza (I)	Notfall m	emergency	cas d'urgence m	—	caso de urgencia m
cásquara (Es)	Schale f	peel	peau f	buccia f	—

	D	E	F	I	Es
casque (F)	Helm *m*	helmet	—	casco *m*	casco *m*
casquette (F)	Mütze *f*	cap	—	berretto *m*	gorra *f*
cassa (I)	Kasse *f*	till	caisse *f*	—	caja *f*
cassa di risparmio (I)	Sparkasse *f*	savings bank	caisse d'épargne *f*	—	caja de ahorros *f*
cassé (F)	kaputt	broken	—	rotto(a)	roto(a)
casse-croûte (F)	Imbiß *m*	snack	—	spuntino *m*	refrigerio *m*
casser[1] (F)	brechen/ zerbrechen	break	—	rompere	romper
casser[2] (F)	einschlagen	smash	—	rompere	romper
casserole[1] (F)	Kochtopf *m*	saucepan	—	pentola *f*	olla *f*
casserole[2] (F)	Topf *m*	pot	—	pentola *f*	olla *f*
cassetta[1] (I)	Kiste *f*	box	caisse *f*	—	caja *f*
cassetta[2] (I)	Kassette *f*	cassette	cassette *f*	—	cassette *f*
cassetta delle lettere (I)	Briefkasten *m*	letterbox	boîte aux lettres *f*	—	buzón *m*
cassette (E)	Kassette *f*	—	cassette *f*	cassetta *f*	cassette *f*
cassette (Es)	Kassette *f*	cassette	cassette *f*	cassetta *f*	—
cassette (F)	Kassette *f*	cassette	—	cassetta *f*	cassette *f*
cassetto (I)	Schublade *f*	drawer	tiroir *m*	—	cajón *m*
castello (I)	Schloß *n*	castle	château *m*	—	castillo *m*
castigar (Es)	strafen	punish	punir	punire	—
castigo (Es)	Strafe *f*	punishment	punition *f*	punizione *f*	—
castillo (Es)	Schloß *n*	castle	château *m*	castello *m*	—
castle (E)	Schloß *n*	—	château *m*	castello *m*	castillo *m*
casualidad (Es)	Zufall *m*	chance	hasard *m*	caso *m*	—
cat (E)	Katze *f*	—	chat *m*	gatto *m*	gato *m*
catarro (Es)	Erkältung *f*	cold	refroidissement *m*	raffreddore *m*	—
catch[1] (E)	erwischen	—	attraper	acchiappare	atrapar
catch[2] (E)	fangen	—	attraper	acchiappare	coger
catedral[1] (Es)	Dom *m*	cathedral	cathédrale *f*	duomo *m*	—
catedral[2] (Es)	Kathedrale *f*	cathedral	cathédrale *f*	cattedrale *f*	—
catena (I)	Kette *f*	chain	chaîne *f*	—	cadena *f*
catenaccio (I)	Riegel *m*	bolt	verrou *m*	—	cerrojo *m*
catering (E)	Verpflegung *f*	—	nourriture *f*	vitto *m*	alimentación *f*
cathedral[1] (E)	Dom *m*	—	cathédrale *f*	duomo *m*	catedral *f*
cathedral[2] (E)	Kathedrale *f*	—	cathédrale *f*	cattedrale *f*	catedral *f*
cathédrale[1] (F)	Dom *m*	cathedral	—	duomo *m*	catedral *f*
cathédrale[2] (F)	Kathedrale *f*	cathedral	—	cattedrale *f*	catedral *f*
catholic (E)	katholisch	—	catholique	cattolico(a)	católico(a)
catholique (F)	katholisch	catholic	—	cattolico(a)	católico(a)
católico (Es)	katholisch	catholic	catholique	cattolico(a)	—
catorce (Es)	vierzehn	fourteen	quatorze	quattordici	—
cattedrale (I)	Kathedrale *f*	cathedral	cathédrale *f*	—	catedral *f*
cattivo[1] (I)	böse	wicked	méchant(e)	—	malo(a)
cattivo[2] (I)	schlecht	bad	mauvais(e)	—	malo(a)
cattivo[3] (I)	übel	bad	mauvais(e)	—	malo(a)
cattolico (I)	katholisch	catholic	catholique	—	católico(a)
cauliflower (E)	Blumenkohl *m*	—	chou-fleur *m*	cavolfiore *m*	coliflor *f*
causa[1] (Es)	Anlaß *m*	occasion	occasion *f*	occasione *f*	—

	D	E	F	I	Es
causa² (Es)	Grund *m*	reason	raison *f*	causa *f*	—
causa³ (Es)	Ursache *f*	cause	cause *f*	causa *f*	—
causa¹ (I)	Grund *m*	reason	raison *f*	—	causa *f*
causa² (I)	Ursache *f*	cause	cause *f*	—	causa *f*
causare (I)	verursachen	cause	causer	—	ocasionar
cause¹ (E)	Anlaß *m*	—	occasion *f*	occasione *f*	ocasión *f*
cause² (E)	Ursache *f*	—	cause *f*	causa *f*	causa *f*
cause³ (E)	verursachen	—	causer	causare	ocasionar
cause (F)	Ursache *f*	cause	—	causa *f*	causa *f*
causer¹ (F)	plaudern	chat	—	chiacchierare	conversar
causer² (F)	verursachen	cause	—	causare	ocasionar
caution (E)	Vorsicht *f*	—	prudence *f*	prudenza *f*	cuidado *m*
cauto (Es)	vorsichtig	careful	prudent(e)	prudente	—
cavalcare (I)	reiten	ride	monter	—	cabalgar
cavallo (I)	Pferd *n*	horse	cheval *m*	—	caballo *m*
cavar (Es)	graben	dig	creuser	scavare	—
cavatappi (I)	Korkenzieher *m*	corkscrew	tire-bouchon *m*	—	sacacorchos *m*
cave (E)	Höhle *f*	—	grotte *f*	caverna *f*	cueva *f*
cave (F)	Keller *m*	cellar	—	cantina *f*	sótano *m*
caverna (I)	Höhle *f*	cave	grotte *f*	—	cueva *f*
caviglia (I)	Knöchel *m*	ankle	cheville *f*	—	tobillo *m*
cavo¹ (I)	hohl	hollow	creux(-euse)	—	hueco(a)
cavo² (I)	Kabel *n*	cable	câble *m*	—	cable *m*
cavolfiore (I)	Blumenkohl *m*	cauliflower	chou-fleur *m*	—	coliflor *f*
cavolo (I)	Kohl *m*	cabbage	chou *m*	—	col *f*
caza¹ (Es)	Jagd *f*	hunt	chasse *f*	caccia *f*	—
caza² (Es)	Wild *n*	game	gibier *m*	selvaggina *f*	—
cazar (Es)	jagen	hunt	chasser	cacciare	—
ce¹ (F)	diese(r,s)	this	—	questo(a)	esta, este, esto
ce² (F)	jene(r,s)	that	—	quello(a)	aquella, aquel, aquello
cebolla (Es)	Zwiebel *f*	onion	oignon *m*	cipolla *f*	—
Cecoslovacchia (I)	Tschecho-slowakei *f*	Czechoslovakia	Tchécoslovaquie *f*	—	Checoslovaquia *f*
ceder (Es)	nachgeben	yield	céder	cedere	—
céder¹ (F)	nachgeben	yield	—	cedere	ceder
céder² (F)	überschreiben	make over	—	cedere	transferir
cedere¹ (I)	nachgeben	yield	céder	—	ceder
cedere² (I)	überschreiben	make over	céder	—	transferir
ceinture¹ (F)	Gurt *m*	belt	—	cinghia *f*	cinturón *m*
ceinture² (F)	Gürtel *m*	belt	—	cintura *f*	cinturón *m*
celebrar (Es)	feiern	celebrate	fêter	festeggiare	—
celebrate (E)	feiern	—	fêter	festeggiare	celebrar
célèbre (F)	berühmt	famous	—	famoso(a)	famoso(a)
célibataire¹ (F)	ledig	single	—	celibe *m*/nubile *f*	soltero(a)
célibataire² (F)	Junggeselle *m*	bachelor	—	scapolo *m*	soltero *m*
celibe¹ (I)	ledig	single	célibataire	—	soltero(a)
celibe² (I)	unverheiratet	unmarried	non marié(e)	—	soltero(a)
cellar (E)	Keller *m*	—	cave *f*	cantina *f*	sótano *m*

	D	E	F	I	Es
celos (Es)	Eifersucht *f*	jealousy	jalousie *f*	gelosia *f*	—
cementerio (Es)	Friedhof *m*	cemetery	cimetière *m*	cimitero *m*	—
cemetery (E)	Friedhof *m*	—	cimetière *m*	cimitero *m*	cementerio *m*
cena (Es)	Abendessen *n*	supper	dîner *m*	cena *f*	—
cena (I)	Abendessen *n*	supper	dîner *m*	—	cena *f*
cenar (Es)	speisen	dine	manger	cenare	—
cendre (F)	Asche *f*	ash	—	cenere *f*	ceniza *f*
cendrier (F)	Aschenbecher *m*	ashtray	—	portacenere *m*	cenicero *m*
cenere (I)	Asche *f*	ash	cendre *f*	—	ceniza *f*
cenicero (Es)	Aschenbecher *m*	ashtray	cendrier *m*	portacenere *m*	—
ceniza (Es)	Asche *f*	ash	cendre *f*	cenere *f*	—
cent¹ (F)	einhundert	one hundred	—	cento	cien
cent² (F)	hundert	hundred	—	cento	cien
cento¹ (I)	einhundert	one hundred	cent	—	cien
cento² (I)	hundert	hundred	cent	—	cien
central (E)	zentral	—	central(e)	centrale	céntrico(a)
central (F)	zentral	central	—	centrale	céntrico(a)
centrale (I)	zentral	central	central(e)	—	céntrico(a)
central heating (E)	Zentralheizung *f*	—	chauffage central *m*	riscaldamento centrale *m*	calefacción central *f*
central station (E)	Hauptbahnhof *m*	—	gare centrale *f*	stazione centrale *f*	estación central *f*
centre (E)	Zentrum *n*	—	centre *m*	centro *m*	centro *m*
centre (F)	Zentrum *n*	centre	—	centro *m*	centro *m*
centre ville (F)	Innenstadt *f*	town centre	—	centro città *m*	centro de ciudad *m*
céntrico (Es)	zentral	central	central(e)	centrale	—
centro (Es)	Zentrum *n*	centre	centre *m*	centro *m*	—
centro¹ (I)	Mitte *f*	middle	milieu *m*	—	medio *m*
centro² (I)	Zentrum *n*	centre	centre *m*	—	centro *m*
centro città (I)	Innenstadt *f*	town centre	centre ville *m*	—	centro de ciudad *m*
centro de ciudad (Es)	Innenstadt *f*	town centre	centre ville *m*	centro città *m*	—
century (E)	Jahrhundert *n*	—	siècle *m*	secolo *m*	siglo *m*
cependant¹ (F)	dennoch	nevertheless	—	tuttavia	sin embargo
cependant² (F)	indessen	meanwhile	—	nel frattempo	en eso
cependant³ (F)	jedoch	however	—	tuttavia	sin embargo
cepillo (Es)	Bürste *f*	brush	brosse *f*	spazzola *f*	—
cepillo de dientes (Es)	Zahnbürste *f*	toothbrush	brosse à dents *f*	spazzolino da denti *m*	—
cerca de (Es)	bei	at/near	chez/près de	da/presso	—
cercare (I)	suchen	look for	chercher	—	buscar
cerchio (I)	Kreis *m*	circle	cercle	—	círculo *m*
cercle (F)	Kreis *m*	circle	—	cerchio *m*	círculo *m*
cercueil (F)	Sarg *m*	coffin	—	bara *f*	ataúd *m*
cerdo (Es)	Schwein *n*	pig	cochon *m*	maiale *m*	—
cereal (E)	Getreide *n*	—	céréales *f pl*	cereali *m pl*	cereales *m pl*
cereales (Es)	Getreide *n*	grain	céréales *f pl*	cereali *m pl*	—
céréales (F)	Getreide *n*	grain	—	cereali *m pl*	cereales *m pl*
cereali (I)	Getreide *n*	grain	céréales *f pl*	—	cereales *m pl*
cerebro (Es)	Hirn *n*	brain	cerveau *m*	cervello *m*	—

	D	E	F	I	Es
cereza (Es)	Kirsche f	cherry	cerise f	ciliegia f	—
cerilla (Es)	Streichholz n	match	allumette f	fiammifero m	—
cerise (F)	Kirsche f	cherry	—	ciliegia f	cereza f
cero (Es)	Null f	zero	zéro	zero	—
cerotto (I)	Pflaster n	plaster	emplâtre m	—	esparadrapo m
cerrado (Es)	geschlossen	closed	fermé(e)	chiuso(a)	—
cerradura (Es)	Schloß n	lock	serrure f	serratura f	—
cerrar[1] (Es)	schließen	close	fermer	chiudere	—
cerrar[2] (Es)	zudrehen	turn off	fermer	chiudere	—
cerrar[3] (Es)	zumachen	shut	fermer	chiudere	—
cerrar con llave[1] (Es)	verschließen	lock (up)	fermer à clé	chiudere a chiave	—
cerrar con llave[2] (Es)	zuschließen	lock (up)	fermer à clé	chiudere a chiave	—
cerrojo (Es)	Riegel m	bolt	verrou m	catenaccio m	—
certain (F)	gewiß	certainely	—	certo(a)	cierto(a)
certain (E)	gewiß	—	certain(e)	certo(a)	cierto(a)
certainement (F)	bestimmt	definitely	—	certamente	ciertamente
certamente (I)	bestimmt	definitely	certainement	—	ciertamente
certificado[1] (Es)	Attest n	certificate	certificat m	certificato m	—
certificado[2] (Es)	Bescheinigung f	certificate	attestation f	certificato m	—
certificat (F)	Attest n	certificate	—	certificato m	certificado m
certificate[1] (E)	Attest n	—	certificat m	certificato m	certificado m
certificate[2] (E)	Bescheinigung f	—	attestation f	certificato m	certificado m
certificato[1] (I)	Attest n	certificate	certificat m	—	certificado m
certificato[2] (I)	Bescheinigung f	certificate	attestation f	—	certificado m
certify (E)	bescheinigen	—	attester	attestare	atestiguar
certo (I)	gewiß	certain(ly)	certain(e)	—	cierto
cerveau (F)	Hirn n	brain	—	cervello m	cerebro m
cervello (I)	Hirn n	brain	cerveau m	—	cerebro m
cerveza (Es)	Bier n	beer	bière f	birra f	—
césped (Es)	Rasen m	lawn	pelouse f	prato m	—
cespuglio (I)	Strauch m	bush	buisson m	—	arbusto m
cessare (I)	aufhören	stop	arrêter	—	terminar
cesta (Es)	Korb m	basket	panier m	cesto m	—
cesto (I)	Korb m	basket	panier m	—	cesta f
c'est pourquoi (F)	deshalb	therefore	—	perció	por eso
ceto (I)	Rang m	rank	rang m	—	clase f
cetriolo (I)	Gurke f	cucumber	concombre m	—	pepino m
chagrin (F)	Kummer m	grief	—	dolore m	pena f
chain (E)	Kette f	—	chaîne f	catena f	cadena f
chaîne (F)	Kette f	chain	—	catena f	cadena f
chair (E)	Stuhl m	—	chaise f	sedia f	silla f
chaise (F)	Stuhl m	chair	—	sedia f	silla f
chaise longue (F)	Liegestuhl m	deck chair	—	sedia a sdraio f	tumbona f
chal (Es)	Schal m	scarf	écharpe f	sciarpa f	—
chaleco salvavidas (Es)	Schwimmweste f	life jacket	gilet de sauvetage m	giubbotto di salvataggio m	—
chaleur[1] (F)	Hitze f	heat	—	caldo m	calor m

chaleur

	D	E	F	I	Es
chaleur² (F)	Wärme f	warmth	—	calore m	calor m
chambre (F)	Zimmer n	room	—	camera f	habitación f
chambre à coucher (F)	Schlafzimmer n	bedroom	—	camera da letto f	dormitorio m
champ¹ (F)	Acker m	field	—	campo m	campo m
champ² (F)	Feld n	field	—	campo m	campo m
champagne (E)	Sekt m	—	champagne m	spumante m	champán m
champagne (F)	Sekt m	champagne	—	spumante m	champán m
champán (Es)	Sekt m	champagne	champagne m	spumante m	—
champignon (F)	Pilz m	mushroom	—	fungo m	hongo m
Chance (D)	—	chance	possibilité f	occasione f	oportunidad f
chance¹ (E)	Chance f	—	possibilité f	occasione f	oportunidad f
chance² (E)	Zufall m	—	hasard m	caso m	casualidad f
chance (F)	Glück n	luck	—	fortuna f	suerte f
chanceler (F)	wanken	stagger	—	barcollare	vacilar
chancelier fédéral (F)	Bundeskanzler m	Federal Chancellor	—	cancelliere federale m	canciller federal m
change¹ (E)	ändern	—	changer	cambiare	cambiar
change² (E)	umkleiden	—	changer de vêtements	cambiarsi	cambiarse de ropa
change³ (E)	umsteigen	—	changer (de train)	cambiare	transbordar
change⁴ (E)	umziehen	—	changer, se	cambiarsi	cambiarse
change⁵ (E)	umwechseln	—	changer	cambiare	cambiar
change⁶ (E)	verändern	—	transformer	mutare	cambiar
change⁷ (E)	Veränderung f	—	changement m	cambiamento m	cambio m
change⁸ (E)	wechseln	—	changer	cambiare	cambiar
change⁹ (E)	Wechsel m	—	changement m	cambiamento m	cambio m
changeable (E)	veränderlich	—	variable	variabile	variable
changement¹ (F)	Veränderung f	change	—	cambiamento m	cambio m
changement² (F)	Wechsel m	change	—	cambiamento m	cambio m
changer (de train) (F)	umsteigen	change	—	cambiare	transbordar
changer¹ (F)	ändern	change	—	cambiare	cambiar
changer² (F)	umwechseln	change	—	cambiare	cambiar
changer³ (F)	wechseln	change	—	cambiare	cambiar
changer, se (F)	umziehen	change	—	cambiarsi	cambiarse
changer de vêtements (F)	umkleiden	change	—	cambiarsi	cambiarse de ropa
Channel (E)	Ärmelkanal m	—	Manche f	Manica f	Canal de la Mancha m
chanson (F)	Lied n	song	—	canzone f	canción f
chant (F)	Gesang m	singing	—	canto m	canto m
chantage (F)	Erpressung f	blackmail	—	ricatto m	chantaje m
chantaje (Es)	Erpressung f	blackmail	chantage m	ricatto m	—
chanter (F)	singen	sing	—	cantare	cantar
chanteur (F)	Sänger m	singer	—	cantante m	cantante m
chapa (Es)	Blech n	sheet metal	tôle f	latta f	—
chapeau (F)	Hut m	hat	—	cappello m	sombrero m
chapel (E)	Kapelle f	—	chapelle f	cappella f	capilla f
chapelle (F)	Kapelle f	chapel	—	cappella f	capilla f
chapitre (F)	Kapitel n	chapter	—	capitolo m	capítulo m

	D	E	F	I	Es
chapter (E)	Kapitel *n*	—	chapitre *m*	capitolo *m*	capítulo *m*
chaque (F)	jede(r,s)	each/every	—	ogni/ognuno	cada
chaque fois (F)	jedesmal	each time	—	ogni volta	cada vez
chaqueta (Es)	Jacke *f*	jacket	veste *f*	giacca *f*	—
chaqueta de punto (Es)	Strickjacke *f*	cardigan	veste en tricot *f*	giacca di maglia *f*	—
character (E)	Charakter *m*	—	caractère *m*	carattere *m*	carácter *m*
characteristic (E)	Merkmal *n*	—	signe *m*	caratteristica *f*	rasgo *m*
Charakter (D)	—	character	caractère *m*	carattere *m*	carácter *m*
charbon (F)	Kohle *f*	coal	—	carbone *m*	carbón *m*
charco (Es)	Pfütze *f*	puddle	flaque *f*	pozzanghera *f*	—
charcuterie (F)	Aufschnitt *m*	cold meat	—	affettato *m*	fiambre *m*
charge[1] (E)	anrechnen	—	compter	mettere in conto	poner en cuenta
charge[2] (E)	berechnen	—	calculer	calcolare	calcular
charge (F)	Last *f*	load	—	carico *m*	peso *m*
charge for admission (E)	Eintritt *m*	—	entrée *f*	entrata *f*	entrada *f*
chargement (F)	Ladung *f*	cargo	—	carico *m*	carga *f*
charger[1] (F)	aufladen	load	—	caricare	cargar
charger[2] (F)	verladen	load	—	caricare	cargar
charger[3] (F)	aufbürden	burden	—	addossare	cargar
charger de (F)	beauftragen	instruct	—	incaricare	encargar
charlar (Es)	schwatzen	chatter	bavarder	chiacchierare	—
charmant (D)	—	charming	charmant(e)	affascinante	encantador(a)
charmant (F)	charmant	charming	—	affascinante	encantador(a)
charming (E)	charmant	—	charmant(e)	affascinante	encantador(a)
charwoman (E)	Putzfrau *f*	—	femme de ménage *f*	donna delle pulizie *f*	mujer de la limpieza *f*
chasse (F)	Jagd *f*	hunt	—	caccia *f*	caza *f*
chasser (F)	jagen	hunt	—	cacciare	cazar
chat (E)	plaudern	—	causer	chiacchierare	conversar
chat (F)	Katze *f*	cat	—	gatto *m*	gato *m*
château (F)	Schloß *n*	castle	—	castello *m*	castillo *m*
château fort (F)	Burg *f*	fortress	—	rocca *f*	fortaleza *f*
chatter (E)	schwatzen	—	bavarder	chiacchierare	charlar
chaud[1] (F)	heiß	hot	—	caldo(a)	caliente
chaud[2] (F)	warm	warm	—	caldo(a)	caliente
chauffage (F)	Heizung *f*	heating	—	riscaldamento *m*	calefacción *f*
chauffage central (F)	Zentralheizung *f*	central heating	—	riscaldamento centrale *m*	calefacción central *f*
chauffer[1] (F)	heizen	heat	—	riscaldare	calentar
chauffer[2] (F)	wärmen	warm	—	riscaldare	calentar
Chauffeur (D)	—	chauffeur	chauffeur *m*	autista *m*	chófer *m*
chauffeur (E)	Chauffeur *m*	—	chauffeur *m*	autista *m*	chófer *m*
chauffeur (F)	Chauffeur *m*	chauffeur	—	autista *m*	chófer *m*
chausette (F)	Socke *f*	sock	—	calzino *m*	calcetín *m*
chaussée (F)	Fahrbahn *f*	roadway	—	carreggiata *f*	calzada *f*
chaussure (F)	Schuh *m*	shoe	—	scarpa *f*	zapato *m*
chauve (F)	kahl	bald	—	calvo(a)	calvo(a)
che[1] (I)	daß	that	que	—	que

	D	E	F	I	Es
che[2] (I)	welch	what a	quel(le)	—	¿qué?
che[3] (I)	was	what	quoi/ qu'est-ce que	—	¿qué?
cheap (E)	billig	—	bon marché(e)	a buon mercato	barato(a)
cheat (E)	betrügen	—	tromper	ingannare	engañar
check[1] (E)	nachsehen	—	vérifier	controllare	examinar
check[2] (E)	nachprüfen	—	contrôler	controllare	comprobar
check[3] (E)	überprüfen	—	contrôler	esaminare	examinar
checked (E)	kariert	—	à carreaux	a quadretti	a cuadros
Checoslovaquia (Es)	Tschecho- slowakei f	Czechoslovakia	Tchécoslovaquie f	Cecoslovacchia f	—
cheek (E)	Wange f	—	joue f	guancia f	mejilla f
cheeky (E)	frech	—	insolent(e)	sfacciato(a)	atrevido(a)
cheers! (E)	prost!	—	santé!	salute!	¡salud!
cheese (E)	Käse m	—	fromage m	formaggio m	queso m
Chef (D)	—	boss	patron m	capo m	jefe m
chef d'orchestre (F)	Dirigent m	conductor	—	direttore d'orchestra m	director(de orquesta) m
chemical (E)	chemisch	—	chimique	chimico(a)	químico(a)
chemin (F)	Weg m	way	—	via f	camino m
chemin de fer (F)	Eisenbahn f	railway	—	ferrovia f	ferrocarril m
chemisch (D)	—	chemical	chimique	chimico(a)	químico(a)
chemise (F)	Hemd n	shirt	—	camicia f	camisa f
chemisier (F)	Bluse f	blouse	—	camicetta f	blusa f
chemist's[1] (E)	Apotheke f	—	pharmacie f	farmacia f	farmacia f
chemist's[2] (E)	Drogerie f	—	droguerie f	drogheria f	droguería f
cheque (E)	Scheck m	—	chèque m	assegno m	cheque m
cheque (Es)	Scheck m	cheque	chèque m	assegno m	—
chèque (F)	Scheck m	cheque	—	assegno m	cheque m
cheque book (E)	Scheckbuch n	—	carnet de chèques m	libretto degli assegni m	talonario de cheques m
cheque de viaje (Es)	Reisescheck m	traveller's cheque	cheque de voyage m	assegno turistico m	—
chèque de voyage (F)	Reisescheck m	traveller's cheque	—	assegno turistico m	cheque de viaje m
cher[1] (F)	wert	worth	—	che vale	valioso(a)
cher[2] (F)	teuer	expensive	—	caro(a)	caro(a)
chercher (F)	suchen	look for	—	cercare	buscar
chéri (F)	Liebling m	darling	—	tesoro m	querido m
cherry (E)	Kirsche f	—	cerise f	ciliegia f	cereza f
cheval (F)	Pferd n	horse	—	cavallo m	caballo m
che vale (I)	wert	worth	cher(-ère)	—	valioso(a)
cheveu (F)	Haar n	hair	—	capello m	pelo m
cheville (F)	Knöchel m	ankle	—	caviglia f	tobillo m
chèvre (F)	Ziege f	goat	—	capra f	cabra f
chevreuil (F)	Reh n	deer	—	capriolo m	corzo m
chew (E)	kauen	—	mâcher	masticare	masticar
chez (F)	bei	at/near	—	da/presso	cerca de/junto a
chi (I)	wer	who	qui	—	¿quién?
chiacchierare[1] (I)	plaudern	chat	causer	—	conversar
chiacchierare[2] (I)	schwatzen	chatter	bavarder	—	charlar

	D	E	F	I	Es
chiamare¹ (I)	nennen	call	appeler	—	nombrar
chiamare² (I)	rufen	shout	appeler	—	llamar
chiamare con cenni (I)	winken	wave	faire signe	—	llamar con gestos
chiamarsi (I)	heißen	be called	appeler, se	—	llamarse
chiamata (I)	Anruf *m*	call	coup de téléphone *m*	—	llamada *f*
chiaro¹ (I)	deutlich	clear	clair(e)	—	claro(a)
chiaro² (I)	klar	clear	clair(e)	—	claro(a)
chiaro³ (I)	hell	bright	clair(e)	—	claro(a)
chiasso (I)	Krach *m*	noise	bruit *m*	—	ruido *m*
chiatta (I)	Kahn *m*	barge	barque *f*	—	barcaza *f*
chiave (I)	Schlüssel *m*	key	clé *f*	—	llave *f*
chic (F)	schick	stylish	—	elegante	elegante
chica (Es)	Mädchen *n*	girl	jeune fille *f*	ragazza *f*	—
chicken (E)	Huhn *n*	—	poule *f*	pollo *m*	gallina *f*
chico (Es)	Junge *m*	boy	garçon *m*	ragazzo *m*	—
chien (F)	Hund *m*	dog	—	cane *m*	perro *m*
chiesa (I)	Kirche *f*	church	église *f*	—	iglesia *f*
chiffre (F)	Zahl *f*	number	—	numero *m*	número *m*
child (E)	Kind *n*	—	enfant *m*	bambino *m*	niño *m*
childhood (E)	Kindheit *f*	—	enfance *f*	infanzia *f*	niñez *f*
chilogrammo (I)	Kilogramm *n*	kilogram	kilogramme *m*	—	kilogramo *m*
chilometro (I)	Kilometer *m*	kilometre	kilomètre *m*	—	kilómetro *m*
chimico (I)	chemisch	chemical	chimique	—	químico(a)
chimique (F)	chemisch	chemical	—	chimico(a)	químico(a)
chin (E)	Kinn *n*	—	menton *m*	mento *m*	barbilla *f*
chiodo (I)	Nagel *m*	nail	clou *m*	—	clavo *m*
Chirurg (D)	—	surgeon	chirurgien *m*	chirurgo *m*	cirujano *m*
chirurgien (F)	Chirurg *m*	surgeon	—	chirurgo *m*	cirujano *m*
chirurgo (I)	Chirurg *m*	surgeon	chirurgien *m*	—	cirujano *m*
chiste (Es)	Witz *m*	joke	plaisanterie *f*	barzelletta *f*	—
chitarra (I)	Gitarre *f*	guitar	guitare *f*	—	guitarra *f*
chiudere¹ (I)	schließen	close	fermer	—	cerrar
chiudere² (I)	verschließen	lock (up)	fermer à clé	—	cerrar con llave
chiudere³ (I)	zumachen	shut	fermer	—	cerrar
chiudere⁴ (I)	zudrehen	turn off	fermer	—	cerrar
chiudere a chiave (I)	zuschließen	lock (up)	fermer à clé	—	cerrar con llave
chiuso (I)	geschlossen	closed	fermé(e)	—	cerrado(a)
chiusura (I)	Verschluß *m*	lock	fermeture *f*	—	cierre *m*
chiusura lampo (I)	Reißverschluß *m*	zip	fermeture éclair *f*	—	cremallera *f*
chocolat (F)	Schokolade *f*	chocolate	—	cioccolato *m*	chocolate *m*
chocolate (E)	Schokolade *f*	—	chocolat *m*	cioccolato *m*	chocolate *m*
chocolate (Es)	Schokolade *f*	chocolate	chocolat *m*	cioccolato *m*	—
chœur (F)	Chor *m*	choir	—	coro *m*	coro *m*
chófer (Es)	Chauffeur *m*	chauffeur	chauffeur *m*	autista *m*	—
choice¹ (E)	Auswahl *f*	—	choix *m*	scelta *f*	elección *f*
choice² (E)	Wahl *f*	—	choix *m*	scelta *f*	opción *f*
choir (E)	Chor *m*	—	chœur *m*	coro *m*	coro *m*

	D	E	F	I	Es
choisir[1] (F)	auswählen	choose	—	scegliere	elegir
choisir[2] (F)	aussuchen	select	—	scegliere	escoger
choix[1] (F)	Auswahl *f*	choice	—	scelta *f*	elección *f*
choix[2] (F)	Wahl *f*	choice	—	scelta *f*	opción *f*
chômage (F)	Arbeitslosig-keit *f*	unemployment	—	disoccupazione *f*	desempleo *m*
choose (E)	auswählen	—	choisir	scegliere	elegir
Chor (D)	—	choir	chœur *m*	coro *m*	coro *m*
chose[1] (F)	Ding *n*	thing	—	cosa *f*	cosa *f*
chose[2] (F)	Sache *f*	thing	—	cosa *f*	cosa *f*
chou (F)	Kohl *m*	cabbage	—	cavolo *m*	col *f*
chou-fleur (F)	Blumenkohl *m*	cauliflower	—	cavolfiore *m*	coliflor *f*
chrétien (F)	Christ *m*	Christian	—	cristiano *m*	cristiano *m*
Christ (D)	—	Christian	chrétien *m*	cristiano *m*	cristiano *m*
christian (E)	Christ *m*	—	chrétien *m*	cristiano *m*	cristiano *m*
Christian name (E)	Vorname *m*	—	prénom *m*	nome di battesimo *m*	nombre *m*
Christmas (E)	Weihnachten *n*	—	Noël *m*	Natale *m*	Navidad(es) *f (pl)*
Christmas Eve (E)	Heiligabend *m*	—	nuit de Noël *f*	vigilia di Natale *f*	Nochebuena *f*
chuchoter (F)	flüstern	whisper	—	bisbigliare	cuchichear
chuleta (Es)	Kotelett *n*	cutlet	côtelette *f*	costoletta *f*	—
chupar (Es)	lutschen	suck	sucer	succhiare	—
church (E)	Kirche *f*	—	église *f*	chiesa *f*	iglesia *f*
chute[1] (F)	Absturz *m*	crash	—	caduta *f*	caída *f*
chute[2] (F)	Sturz *m*	fall	—	caduta *f*	caída *f*
ciao! (I)	tschüs!	bye!	salut!	—	¡hasta luego!
cibo[1] (I)	Kost *f*	food	nourriture *f*	—	alimento *m*
cibo[2] (I)	Speise *f*	food	aliment *m*	—	comida *f*
cicatrice (F)	Narbe *f*	scar	—	cicatrice *f*	cicatriz *f*
cicatrice (I)	Narbe *f*	scar	cicatrice *f*	—	cicatriz *f*
cicatriz (Es)	Narbe *f*	scar	cicatrice *f*	cicatrice *f*	—
cieco (I)	blind	blind	aveugle	—	ciego(a)
ciego (Es)	blind	blind	aveugle	cieco(a)	—
ciel (F)	Himmel *m*	sky	—	cielo *m*	cielo *m*
cielo (Es)	Himmel *m*	sky	ciel *m*	cielo *m*	—
cielo (I)	Himmel *m*	sky	ciel *m*	—	cielo *m*
cien[1] (Es)	einhundert	one hundred	cent	cento	—
cien[2] (Es)	hundert	hundred	cent	cento	—
ciencia (Es)	Wissenschaft *f*	science	science *f*	scienza *f*	—
científico (Es)	Wissen-schaftler *m*	scientist	scientifique *m*	scienziato *m*	—
cierre (Es)	Verschluß *m*	lock	fermeture *f*	chiusura *f*	—
ciertamente (Es)	bestimmt	definite	certainement	certamente	—
cierto (Es)	gewiß	certain	certain(e)	certo	—
cigar (E)	Zigarre *f*	—	cigare *m*	sigaro *m*	cigarro *m*
cigare (F)	Zigarre *f*	cigar	—	sigaro *m*	cigarro *m*
cigarette (E)	Zigarette *f*	—	cigarette *f*	sigaretta *f*	cigarrillo *m*
cigarette (F)	Zigarette *f*	cigarette	—	sigaretta *f*	cigarrillo *m*
cigarrillo (Es)	Zigarette *f*	cigarette	cigarette *f*	sigaretta *f*	—

	D	E	F	I	Es
cigarro (Es)	Zigarre *f*	cigar	cigare *m*	sigaro *m*	—
ciglia (I)	Wimper *f*	eyelash	cil *m*	—	pestaña *f*
cil (F)	Wimper *f*	eyelash	—	ciglia *f*	pestaña *f*
ciliegia (I)	Kirsche *f*	cherry	cerise *f*	—	cereza *f*
cima (I)	Gipfel *m*	peak	sommet *m*	—	cumbre *f*
cimetière (F)	Friedhof *m*	cemetery	—	cimitero *m*	cementerio *m*
cimitero (I)	Friedhof *m*	cemetery	cimetière *m*	—	cementerio *m*
cinco (Es)	fünf	five	cinq	cinque	—
cincuenta (Es)	fünfzig	fifty	cinquante	cinquanta	—
cine (Es)	Kino *n*	cinema	cinéma *m*	cinema *m*	—
cinema (E)	Kino *n*	—	cinéma *m*	cinema *m*	cine *m*
cinéma (F)	Kino *n*	cinema	—	cinema *m*	cine *m*
cinema (I)	Kino *n*	cinema	cinéma *m*	—	cine *m*
cinghia[1] (I)	Gurt *m*	belt	ceinture *f*	—	cinturón *m*
cinghia[2] (I)	Riemen *m*	strap	courroie *f*	—	correa *f*
cinq (F)	fünf	five	—	cinque	cinco
cinquanta (I)	fünfzig	fifty	cinquante	—	cincuenta
cinquante (F)	fünfzig	fifty	—	cinquanta	cincuenta
cinque (I)	fünf	five	cinq	—	cinco
cinta (Es)	Band *n*	ribbon	bandeau *m*	nastro *m*	—
cinta magnetofónica (Es)	Tonband *n*	tape	bande magnétique *f*	nastro magnetico *m*	—
cintura (I)	Gürtel *m*	belt	ceinture *f*	—	cinturón *m*
cinturón[1] (Es)	Gurt *m*	belt	ceinture *f*	cinghia *f*	—
cinturón[2] (Es)	Gürtel *m*	girdle	ceinture *f*	cintura *f*	—
cioccolato (I)	Schokolade *f*	chocolate	chocolat *m*	—	chocolate *m*
cioè (I)	nämlich	namely	à savoir	—	a saber
cipolla (I)	Zwiebel *f*	onion	oignon *m*	—	cebolla *f*
cipria (I)	Puder *m*	powder	poudre *f*	—	polvos *m pl*
cirage (F)	Schuhcreme *f*	shoe polish	—	lucido per scarpe *m*	betún *m*
circa (I)	beinahe	nearly	presque	—	casi
circle (E)	Kreis *m*	—	cercle	cerchio *m*	círculo *m*
circo (Es)	Zirkus *m*	circus	cirque *m*	circo *m*	—
circo (I)	Zirkus *m*	circus	cirque *m*	—	circo *m*
circolazione (I)	Kreislauf *m*	circulation	circulation *f*	—	circulación *f*
circondare (I)	umgeben	surround	entourer	—	rodear
circonstances (F)	Umstände *pl*	circumstances	—	circostanze *f pl*	circunstancias *f pl*
circostanze (I)	Umstände *pl*	circumstances	circonstances *f pl*	—	circunstancias *f pl*
circuit (F)	Rundfahrt *f*	round trip	—	giro *m*	gira *f*
circulación (Es)	Kreislauf *m*	circulation	circulation *f*	circolazione *f*	—
circulation (E)	Kreislauf *m*	—	circulation *f*	circolazione *f*	circulación *f*
circulation[1] (F)	Kreislauf *m*	circulation	—	circolazione *f*	circulación *f*
circulation[2] (F)	Verkehr *m*	traffic	—	traffico *m*	tráfico *m*
círculo (Es)	Kreis *m*	circle	cercle	cerchio *m*	—
circumstances (E)	Umstände *m*	—	circonstances *f pl*	circostanze *f pl*	circunstancias *f pl*
circunstancias (Es)	Umstände *m*	circumstances	circonstances *f pl*	circostanze *f pl*	—
circus (E)	Zirkus *m*	—	cirque *m*	circo *m*	circo *m*
cirque (F)	Zirkus *m*	circus	—	circo *m*	circo *m*

	D	E	F	I	Es
ciruela (Es)	Pflaume *f*	plum	prune *f*	prugna *f*	—
cirujano (Es)	Chirurg *m*	surgeon	chirurgien *m*	chirurgo *m*	—
ciseaux (F)	Schere *f*	pair of scissors	—	forbici *f pl*	tijeras *f pl*
cistifellea (I)	Galle *f*	gall	fiel *m*	—	bilis *f*
cita (Es)	Verabredung *f*	date	rendez-vous *m*	appuntamento *m*	—
citar (Es)	vorladen	summon	assigner	citare in giudizio	—
citare in giudizio (I)	vorladen	summon	assigner	—	citar
cité (F)	Siedlung *f*	settlement	—	agglomerato *m*	colonia *f*
citron (F)	Zitrone *f*	lemon	—	limone *m*	limón *m*
città (I)	Stadt *f*	town	ville *f*	—	ciudad *f*
cittadinanza (I)	Staatsangehörig-keit *f*	nationality	nationalité *f*	—	nacionalidad *f*
ciudad (Es)	Stadt *f*	town	ville *f*	città *f*	—
civil (E)	bürgerlich	—	civil(e)	civile	civil
civil (Es)	bürgerlich	civil	civil(e)	civile	—
civil (F)	bürgerlich	civil	—	civile	civil
civile (I)	bürgerlich	civil	civil(e)	—	civil
civilisation (E)	Zivilisation *f*	—	civilisation *f*	civiltà *f*	civilización *f*
civilisation (F)	Zivilisation *f*	civilisation	—	civiltà *f*	civilización *f*
civiltà (I)	Zivilisation *f*	civilisation	civilisation *f*	—	civilización *f*
civilización (Es)	Zivilisation *f*	civilisation	civilisation *f*	civiltà *f*	—
civil servant (E)	Beamter *m*	—	fonctionnaire *m*	impiegato statale *m*	funcionario *m*
clacson (I)	Hupe *f*	horn	claxon *m*	—	bocina *f*
clair[1] (F)	deutlich	clear	—	chiaro(a)	claro(a)
clair[2] (F)	hell	bright	—	chiaro(a)	claro(a)
clair[3] (F)	klar	clear	—	chiaro(a)	claro(a)
claro[1] (Es)	deutlich	clear	clair(e)	chiaro(a)	—
claro[2] (Es)	hell	bright	clair(e)	chiaro(a)	—
claro[3] (Es)	klar	clear	clair(e)	chiaro(a)	—
clase[1] (Es)	Klasse *f*	class	classe *f*	classe *f*	—
clase[2] (Es)	Rang *m*	rank	rang *m*	ceto *m*	—
clase[3] (Es)	Sorte *f*	sort	sorte *f*	specie *f*	—
clase[4] (Es)	Unterrichts-stunde *f*	lesson	leçon *f*	lezione *f*	—
clase[5] (Es)	Vorlesung *f*	lecture	cours magistral *m*	lezione *f*	—
clasificar (Es)	sortieren	sort	trier	assortire	—
class (E)	Klasse *f*	—	classe *f*	classe *f*	clase *f*
classe (F)	Klasse *f*	class	—	classe *f*	clase *f*
classe (I)	Klasse *f*	class	classe *f*	—	clase *f*
clavel (Es)	Nelke *f*	carnation	œillet *m*	garofano *m*	—
clavo (Es)	Nagel *m*	nail	clou *m*	chiodo *m*	—
claxon (F)	Hupe *f*	horn	—	clacson *m*	bocina *f*
clé (F)	Schlüssel *m*	key	—	chiave *f*	llave *f*
clean[1] (E)	putzen	—	nettoyer	pulire	limpiar
clean[2] (E)	reinigen	—	nettoyer	pulire	limpiar
clean[3] (E)	sauber	—	propre	pulito(a)	limpio(a)
cleaning (E)	Reinigung *f*	—	nettoyage *m*	pulitura *f*	limpieza *f*

	D	E	F	I	Es
clear¹ (E)	deutlich	—	clair(e)	chiaro(a)	claro(a)
clear² (E)	klar	—	clair(e)	chiaro(a)	claro(a)
clear away (E)	aufräumen	—	ranger	mettere in ordine	arreglar
clever¹ (E)	clever	—	futé(e)	abile	listo(a)
clever² (E)	klug	—	intelligent(e)	intelligente	inteligente
clever³ (E)	schlau	—	astucieux(-euse)	astuto(a)	astuto(a)
client (F)	Kunde m	customer	—	cliente m	cliente m
cliente (Es)	Kunde m	customer	client m	cliente m	—
cliente (I)	Kunde m	customer	client m	—	cliente m
cliente abituale (I)	Stammgast m	regular	habitué m	—	cliente habitual m
cliente habitual (Es)	Stammgast m	regular	habitué m	cliente abituale m	—
clignoter (F)	blinken	flash	—	lampeggiare	relampaquear
clima (Es)	Klima n	climate	climat m	clima m	—
clima (I)	Klima n	climate	climat m	—	clima m
climat (F)	Klima n	climate	—	clima m	clima m
climate (E)	Klima n	—	climat m	clima m	clima m
climb¹ (E)	hinaufsteigen	—	monter	salire	subir
climb² (E)	klettern	—	grimper	arrampicarsi	escalar
clínica (Es)	Klinik f	hospital	clinique f	clinica f	—
clinica (I)	Klinik f	hospital	clinique f	—	clínica f
clinique (F)	Klinik f	hospital	—	clinica f	clínica f
cloche (F)	Glocke f	bell	—	campana f	campana f
close (E)	schließen	—	fermer	chiudere	cerrar
closed (E)	geschlossen	—	fermé(e)	chiuso(a)	cerrado(a)
closing day (E)	Ruhetag m	—	jour de repos m	giorno di riposo m	día de descanso m
cloth¹ (E)	Stoff m	—	tissu m	stoffa f	tela f
cloth² (E)	Tuch n	—	étoffe f	panno m	paño m
clothing (E)	Kleidung f	—	habits m pl	abbigliamento m	vestuario m
clôture (F)	Zaun m	fence	—	recinto m	valla f
clou (F)	Nagel m	nail	—	chiodo m	clavo m
cloud (E)	Wolke f	—	nuage m	nuvola f	nube f
cloudy (E)	bewölkt	—	couvert(e)	nuvoloso(a)	nublado(a)
club¹ (E)	Kasino n	—	casino m	casinò m	casino m
club² (E)	Verein m	—	association f	associazione f	asociación f
clumsy (E)	ungeschickt	—	maladroit(e)	impacciato(a)	torpe
coal (E)	Kohle f	—	charbon m	carbone m	carbón m
coarse (E)	grob	—	grossier(-ière)	rozzo(a)	tosco(a)
coast (E)	Küste f	—	côte f	costa f	costa f
coat (E)	Mantel m	—	manteau m	cappotto m	abrigo m
cobarde (Es)	feig	cowardly	lâche	vile	—
cobrar¹ (Es)	einkassieren	collect	recouvrer	incassare	—
cobrar² (Es)	kassieren	take	encaisser	incassare	—
coccio (I)	Scherbe f	broken piece	tesson m	—	pedazo m
cocer (Es)	backen	bake	faire cuire	cuocere (al forno)	—
coche¹ (Es)	Auto n	car	voiture f	automobile f/ macchina f	—
coche² (Es)	Wagen m	car	voiture f	vettura f	—
coche cama (Es)	Liegewagen m	couchette	wagon-couchette m	cuccetta f	—

cochon

	D	E	F	I	Es
cochon (F)	Schwein *n*	pig	—	maiale *m*	cerdo *m*
cocina¹ (Es)	Herd *m*	cooker	fourneau *m*	cucina *f*	—
cocina² (Es)	Küche *f*	kitchen	cuisine *f*	cucina *f*	—
cocinar (Es)	kochen	cook	cuire	cucinare	—
cocinera (Es)	Köchin *f*	cook	cuisinière *f*	cuoca *f*	—
cocinero (Es)	Koch *m*	cook	cuisinier *m*	cuoco *m*	—
cock (E)	Hahn *m*	—	coq *m*	gallo *m*	gallo *m*
coda (I)	Schwanz *m*	tail	queue *f*	—	rabo *m*
cœur (F)	Herz *n*	heart	—	cuore *m*	corazón *m*
coffee (E)	Kaffee *m*	—	café *m*	caffè *m*	café *m*
coffin (E)	Sarg *m*	—	cercueil *m*	bara *f*	ataúd *m*
coffre (F)	Kofferraum *m*	boot	—	portabagagli *m*	maletero *m*
coger¹ (Es)	ergreifen	seize	saisir	afferrare	—
coger² (Es)	fassen	grasp	saisir	prendere	—
coger³ (Es)	fangen	catch	attraper	acchiappare	—
coger⁴ (Es)	greifen	seize	saisir	afferrare	—
coger⁵ (Es)	pflücken	pick	cueillir	cogliere	—
cogliere (I)	pflücken	pick	cueillir	—	coger
cognata (I)	Schwägerin *f*	sister-in-law	belle-sœur *f*	—	cuñada *f*
cognato (I)	Schwager *m*	brother-in-law	beau-frère *m*	—	cuñado *m*
cognome (I)	Nachname *m*	surname	nom de famille *m*	—	apellido *m*
coiffeur (F)	Friseur *m*	hairdresser	—	parrucchiere *m*	peluquero *m*
coiffure (F)	Frisur *f*	hairstyle	—	pettinatura *f*	peinado *m*
coin (E)	Münze *f*	—	pièce de monnaie *f*	moneta *f*	moneda *f*
coin¹ (F)	Ecke *f*	corner	—	angolo *m*	esquina *f*
coin² (F)	Winkel *m*	corner	—	cantuccio *m*	rincón *m*
coincidenza (I)	Anschluß *m*	connection	correspondance *f*	—	conexión *f*
cojín (Es)	Kissen *n*	cushion	coussin *m*	cuscino *m*	—
col (Es)	Kohl *m*	cabbage	chou *m*	cavolo *m*	—
col¹ (F)	Kragen *m*	collar	—	colletto *m*	cuello *m*
col² (F)	Paß *m*	pass	—	passo *m*	paso *m*
colador (Es)	Sieb *n*	sieve	tamis *m*	setaccio *m*	—
colazione (I)	Frühstück *n*	breakfast	petit-déjeuner *m*	—	desayuno *m*
colchón (Es)	Matratze *f*	mattress	matelas *m*	materasso *m*	—
colchoneta (Es)	Matte *f*	mat	natte *f*	stuoia *f*	—
cold¹ (E)	Erkältung *f*	—	refroidissement *m*	raffreddore *m*	catarro *m*
cold² (E)	kalt	—	froid(e)	freddo(a)	frío(a)
cold³ (E)	Schnupfen *m*	—	rhume *m*	raffreddore *m*	resfriado *m*
cold meat (E)	Aufschnitt *m*	—	charcuterie *f*	affettato *m*	fiambre *m*
colección (Es)	Sammlung *f*	collection	collection *f*	raccolta *f*	—
coléoptère (F)	Käfer *m*	beetle	—	coleottero *m*	escarabajo *m*
coleottero (I)	Käfer *m*	beetle	coléoptère *m*	—	escarabajo *m*
colère (F)	Wut *f*	anger	—	rabbia *f*	rabia *f*
colgar¹ (Es)	aufhängen	hang up	accrocher	appendere	—
colgar² (Es)	hängen	hang	pendre	pendere	—
coliflor (Es)	Blumenkohl *m*	cauliflower	chou-fleur *m*	cavolfiore *m*	—
colina (Es)	Hügel *m*	hill	colline *f*	collina *f*	—

	D	E	F	I	Es
colla (I)	Klebstoff *m*	glue	colle *f*	—	adhesivo *m*
collants (F)	Strumpfhose *f*	tights	—	calzamaglia *f*	leotardos *m pl*
collapse[1] (E)	einstürzen	—	écrouler, se	crollare	derrumbarse
collapse[2] (E)	zusammenbrechen	—	éffondrer, se	crollare	desmayarse
collar (E)	Kragen *m*	—	col *m*	colletto *m*	cuello *m*
collaudare (I)	testen	test	tester	—	probar
colle (F)	Klebstoff *m*	glue	—	colla *f*	adhesivo *m*
collect[1] (E)	einkassieren	—	recouvrer	incassare	cobrar
collect[2] (E)	sammeln	—	collecter	raccogliere	recolectar
collecter (F)	sammeln	collect	—	raccogliere	recolectar
collection (E)	Sammlung *f*	—	collection *f*	raccolta *f*	colección *f*
collection (F)	Sammlung *f*	collection	—	raccolta *f*	colección *f*
collegio (I)	Internat *n*	boarding school	internat *m*	—	internado *m*
coller (F)	kleben	stick	—	incollare	pegar
colletto (I)	Kragen *m*	collar	col *m*	—	cuello *m*
collina (I)	Hügel *m*	hill	colline *f*	—	colina *f*
colline (F)	Hügel *m*	hill	—	collina *f*	colina *f*
collo (I)	Hals *m*	neck	cou *m*	—	cuello *m*
colloquial language (E)	Umgangs-sprache *f*	—	langue familière *f*	linguaggio familiare *m*	lenguaje coloquial *m*
colloquio (I)	Unterredung *f*	talk	entrevue *f*	—	entrevista *f*
colocar[1] (Es)	anbringen	fasten	fixer	fissare	—
colocar[2] (Es)	legen	lay	mettre	mettere	—
colocar[3] (Es)	stellen	place	mettre	mettere	—
colocar[4] (Es)	unterbringen	stow (away)	ranger	sistemare	—
colonia (Es)	Siedlung *f*	settlement	cité *f*	agglomerato *m*	—
colonna (I)	Säule *f*	pillar	colonne *f*	—	columna *f*
colonna vertebrale (I)	Wirbelsäule *f*	spine	colonne vertébrale *f*	—	columna vertebral *f*
colonne (F)	Säule *f*	pillar	—	colonna *f*	columna *f*
colonne vertébrale (F)	Wirbelsäule *f*	spine	—	colonna vertebrale *f*	columna vertebral *f*
color (Es)	Farbe *f*	colour	couleur *f*	colore *m*	—
colorato (I)	farbig	colourful	coloré(e)	—	de colores
colore (I)	Farbe *f*	colour	couleur *f*	—	color *m*
coloré[1] (F)	bunt	coloured	—	variopinto	de colores
coloré[2] (F)	farbig	colourful	—	colorato(a)	de colores
colorear (Es)	färben	dye	colorer	tingere	—
colorer (F)	färben	dye	—	tingere	colorear
colour (E)	Farbe *f*	—	couleur *f*	colore *m*	color *m*
coloured (E)	bunt	—	coloré(e)	variopinto(a)	de colores
colourful (E)	farbig	—	coloré(e)	colorato(a)	de colores
colpa (I)	Schuld *f*	fault	culpabilité *f*	—	culpa *f*
colpevole (I)	schuldig	guilty	coupable	—	culpable
colpire (I)	treffen	hit	toucher	—	alcanzar
colpo (I)	Schlag *m*	blow	coup *m*	—	golpe *m*
coltello (I)	Messer *n*	knife	couteau *m*	—	cuchillo *m*
coltivare (I)	anbauen	cultivate	cultiver	—	cultivar
columna (Es)	Säule *f*	pillar	colonne *f*	colonna *f*	—

	D	E	F	I	Es
columna vertebral (Es)	Wirbelsäule f	spine	colonne vertébrale f	colonna vertebrale f	—
columpiarse (Es)	schaukeln	swing	balancer, se	dondolare	—
comb[1] (E)	kämmen	—	peigner	pettinare	peinar
comb[2] (E)	Kamm m	—	peigne m	pettine m	peine m
combattere (I)	kämpfen	fight	battre, se	—	luchar
combien[1] (F)	wieviele	how many	—	quanti(e)	¿cuántos(as)?
combien[2] (F)	wieviel	how much	—	quanto	¿cuánto?
combinación (Es)	Unterrock m	slip	jupon m	sottoveste f	—
combustible para la calefacción (Es)	Heizöl n	fuel	mazout m	olio combustibile m	—
come (E)	kommen	—	venir	venire	venir
come (I)	wie	how	comment	—	¿cómo?
come back[1] (E)	wiederkommen	—	revenir	ritornare	venir de nuevo
come back[2] (E)	zurückkommen	—	revenir	ritornare	regresar
comedia (Es)	Komödie f	comedy	comédie f	commedia f	—
comédie (F)	Komödie f	comedy	—	commedia f	comedia f
comedor (Es)	Eßzimmer n	dining room	salle à manger f	sala da pranzo f	—
comedy (E)	Komödie f	—	comédie f	commedia f	comedia f
come mai (I)	wieso	why	pourquoi	—	¿por qué?
com'è noto (I)	bekanntlich	as is well known	comme on sait	—	como es sabido
comer (Es)	essen	eat	manger	mangiare	—
comercial (Es)	geschäftlich	on business	d'affaires	per affari	—
comerciante[1] (Es)	Händler m	dealer	commerçant m	commerciante m	—
comerciante[2] (Es)	Kaufmann m	businessman	commerçant m	commerciante m	—
comestible (Es)	eßbar	eatable	mangeable	commestibile	—
comestibles (Es)	Eßwaren pl	foodstuffs	produits alimentaires m pl	alimentari m pl	—
comfort (E)	trösten	—	consoler	consolare	consolar
comfortable[1] (E)	bequem	—	confortable	comodo(a)	cómodo(a)
comfortable[2] (E)	gemütlich	—	agréable	comodo(a)	cómodo(a)
comico (I)	komisch	funny	drôle	—	cómico(a)
cómico (Es)	komisch	funny	drôle	comico(a)	—
comida[1] (Es)	Essen n	food	repas m	alimentazione f	—
comida[2] (Es)	Mittagessen n	lunch	déjeuner m	pranzo m	—
comida[3] (Es)	Mahlzeit f	meal	repas m	pasto m	—
comida[4] (Es)	Speise f	food	aliment m	cibo m	—
cominciare[1] (I)	anfangen	start	commencer	—	empezar
cominciare[2] (I)	beginnen	begin	commencer	—	empezar
comisión (Es)	Provision f	commission	commission f	provvigione f	—
commander (F)	bestellen	order	—	ordinare	pedir
commedia (I)	Komödie f	comedy	comédie f	—	comedia f
commencement[1] (F)	Anfang m	beginning	—	inizio m	inicio m
commencement[2] (F)	Beginn m	beginning	—	inizio m	principio m
commencer[1] (F)	anfangen	start	—	cominciare	empezar
commencer[2] (F)	beginnen	begin	—	cominciare	empezar
comment (F)	wie	how	—	come	¿cómo?
comme on sait (F)	bekanntlich	as is well known	—	com'è noto	como es sabido
commerçant[1] (F)	Händler m	dealer	—	commerciante m	comerciante m

competente

	D	E	F	I	Es
commerçant² (F)	Kaufmann *m*	businessman	—	commerciante *m*	comerciante *m*
commerciante¹ (I)	Händler *m*	dealer	commerçant *m*	—	comerciante *m*
commerciante² (I)	Kaufmann *m*	businessman	commerçant *m*	—	comerciante *m*
commestibile (I)	eßbar	eatable	mangeable	—	comestible
commission (E)	Provision *f*	—	commission *f*	provvigione *f*	comisión *f*
commission (F)	Provision *f*	commission	—	provvigione *f*	comisión *f*
communication interurbaine (F)	Ferngespräch *n*	long-distance call	—	telefonata interurbana *f*	llamada interurbana *f*
communication téléphonique (F)	Telefongespräch *n*	phone call	—	conversazione telefonica *f*	conversación telefónica *f*
commutare (I)	schalten	switch	connecter	—	conectar
como (Es)	als	when	quand	quando	—
cómo (Es)	wie	how	comment	come	—
comodidad (Es)	Bequemlichkeit *f*	convenience	confort *m*	comodità *f*	—
comodità (I)	Bequemlichkeit *f*	convenience	confort *m*	—	comodidad *f*
comodo¹ (I)	bequem	comfortable	confortable	—	cómodo(a)
comodo² (I)	gemütlich	comfortable	agréable	—	cómodo(a)
cómodo¹ (Es)	bequem	comfortable	confortable	comodo(a)	—
cómodo² (Es)	gemütlich	comfortable	agréable	comodo(a)	—
como es sabido (Es)	bekanntlich	as is well known	comme on sait	com'è noto	—
compadecerse de (Es)	bemitleiden	pity	plaindre	compatire	—
compagno¹ (I)	Genosse *m*	comrade	camarade *m*	—	camarada *m*
compagno² (I)	Lebensgefährte *m*	lifepartner	compagnon *m*	—	compañero en la vida *m*
compagnon (F)	Lebensgefährte *m*	lifepartner	—	compagno *m*	compañero en la vida *m*
compañero en la vida (Es)	Lebensgefährte *m*	lifepartner	compagnon *m*	compagno *m*	
company¹ (E)	Firma *f*	—	firme *f*	ditta *f*	empresa *f*
company² (E)	Unternehmen *n*	—	entreprise *f*	impresa *f*	empresa *f*
comparación (Es)	Vergleich *m*	comparison	comparaison *f*	paragone *m*	—
comparaison (F)	Vergleich *m*	comparison	—	paragone *m*	comparación *f*
comparar (Es)	vergleichen	compare	comparer	paragonare	—
compare (E)	vergleichen	—	comparer	paragonare	comparar
comparer (F)	vergleichen	compare	—	paragonare	comparar
comparison (E)	Vergleich *m*	—	comparaison *f*	paragone *m*	comparación *f*
compartiment¹ (F)	Abteil *n*	compartment	—	scompartimento *m*	compartimiento *m*
compartiment² (F)	Fach *n*	compartment	—	scomparto *m*	compartimiento *m*
compartimiento¹ (Es)	Abteil *n*	compartment	compartiment *m*	scompartimento *m*	—
compartimiento² (Es)	Fach *n*	compartment	compartiment *m*	scomparto *m*	—
compartment¹ (E)	Abteil *n*	—	compartiment *m*	scompartimento *m*	compartimiento *m*
compartment² (E)	Fach *n*	—	compartiment *m*	scomparto *m*	compartimiento *m*
compasión¹ (Es)	Bedauern *n*	regret	regret *m*	dispiacere *m*	—
compasión² (Es)	Mitleid *n*	pity	compassion *f*	compassione *f*	—
compassion (F)	Mitleid *n*	pity	—	compassione *f*	compasión *f*
compassione (I)	Mitleid *n*	pity	compassion *f*	—	compasión *f*
compatire (I)	bemitleiden	pity	plaindre	—	compadecerse de
competent (E)	zuständig	—	compétent(e)	competente	competente
compétent (F)	zuständig	competent	—	competente	competente
competente (Es)	zuständig	competent	compétent(e)	competente	—

	D	E	F	I	Es
competente (I)	zuständig	competent	compétent(e)	—	competente
competition (E)	Wettbewerb *m*	—	concours *m*	concorso *m*	concurso *m*
complain[1] (E)	beschweren, sich	—	plaindre, se	lamentarsi	quejarse
complain[2] (E)	reklamieren	—	plaindre de, se	reclamare	reclamar
complaint[1] (E)	Beschwerde *f*	—	plainte *f*	reclamo *m*	reclamación *f*
complaint[2] (E)	Klage *f*	—	plainte *f*	lamento *m*	lamento *m*
complaint[3] (E)	Reklamation *f*	—	réclamation *f*	reclamo *m*	reclamación *f*
compleanno (I)	Geburtstag *m*	birthday	anniversaire *m*	—	cumpleaños *m*
complement (E)	ergänzen	—	compléter	completare	completar
complessivamente (I)	insgesamt	altogether	dans l'ensemble	—	en suma
complet[1] (F)	ausgebucht	fully booked	—	esaurito(a)	completo(a)
complet[2] (F)	vollständig	complete	—	completo(a)	completo(a)
completamente (Es)	völlig	completely	complètement	completamente	—
completamente (I)	völlig	completely	complètement	—	completamente
completar (Es)	ergänzen	complement	compléter	completare	—
completare (I)	ergänzen	complement	compléter	—	completar
complete (E)	vollständig	—	complet(-ète)	completo(a)	completo(a)
completely[1] (E)	völlig	—	complètement	completamente	completamente
completely[2] (E)	restlos	—	complètement	interamente	totalmente
complètement[1] (F)	restlos	completely	—	interamente	totalmente
complètement[2] (F)	völlig	completely	—	completamente	completamente
compléter (F)	ergänzen	complement	—	completare	completar
completo (I)	vollständig	complete	complet(-ète)	—	completo(a)
completo[1] (Es)	ausgebucht	fully booked	complet(-ète)	esaurito(a)	—
completo[2] (Es)	vollständig	complete	complet(-ète)	completo(a)	—
complicado[1] (Es)	kompliziert	complicated	compliqué(e)	complicato(a)	—
complicado[2] (Es)	umständlich	complicated	compliqué(e)	complicato(a)	—
complicated[1] (E)	kompliziert	—	compliqué(e)	complicato(a)	complicado(a)
complicated[2] (E)	umständlich	—	compliqué(e)	complicato(a)	complicado(a)
complicato[1] (I)	kompliziert	complicated	compliqué(e)	—	complicado(a)
complicato[2] (I)	umständlich	complicated	compliqué(e)	—	complicado(a)
compliqué (F)	kompliziert	complicated	—	complicato(a)	complicado(a)
complique[2] (F)	umständlich	complicated	—	complicato(a)	complicado(a)
comportamento (I)	Benehmen *n*	behaviour	conduite *f*	—	comportamiento *m*
comportamiento (Es)	Benehmen *n*	behaviour	conduite *f*	comportamento *m*	—
comportarse (Es)	benehmen, sich	behave	comporter, se	comportarsi	—
comportarsi (I)	benehmen, sich	behave	comporter, se	—	comportarse
comporter, se (F)	benehmen, sich	behave	—	comportarsi	comportarse
composer (E)	Komponist *m*	—	compositeur *m*	compositore *m*	compositor *m*
compositeur (F)	Komponist *m*	composer	—	compositore *m*	compositor *m*
compositor (Es)	Komponist *m*	composer	compositeur *m*	compositore *m*	compositor *m*
compositore (I)	Komponist *m*	composer	compositeur *m*	—	compositor *m*
compra[1] (Es)	Einkauf *m*	shopping	achat *m*	spesa *f*	—
compra[2] (Es)	Kauf *m*	purchase	achat *m*	acquisto *m*	—
comprador (Es)	Käufer *m*	buyer	acheteur *m*	acquirente *m*	—
comprar (Es)	kaufen	buy	acheter	comprare	—
comprare (I)	kaufen	buy	acheter	—	comprar
comprehend (E)	begreifen	—	comprendre	comprendere	comprender

	D	E	F	I	Es
compréhension (F)	Verständnis n	understanding	—	comprensione f	comprensión f
comprender (Es)	begreifen	comprehend	comprendre	comprendere	—
comprendere (I)	begreifen	comprehend	comprendre	—	comprender
comprendre¹ (F)	begreifen	comprehend	—	comprendere	comprender
comprendre² (F)	verstehen	understand	—	capire	entender
comprensión (Es)	Verständnis n	understanding	compréhension f	comprensione f	—
comprensione (I)	Verständnis n	understanding	compréhension f	—	comprensión f
compreso (I)	inbegriffen	included	compris(e)	—	incluído(a)
compressa (I)	Tablette f	tablet	comprimé m	—	pastilla f
comprimé (F)	Tablette f	tablet	—	compressa f	pastilla f
compris (F)	inbegriffen	included	—	compreso(a)	incluído(a)
comprobar (Es)	nachprüfen	check	contrôler	controllare	—
comptabilité (F)	Buchhaltung f	book-keeping	—	contabilità f	contabilidad f
compte (F)	Konto n	account	—	conto m	cuenta f
compter¹ (F)	anrechnen	charge	—	mettere in conto	poner en cuenta
compter² (F)	zählen	count	—	contare	contar
comptoir (F)	Ladentisch m	counter	—	banco di vendita m	mostrador m
compulsion (E)	Zwang m	—	contrainte f	costrizione f	presión f
comrade (E)	Genosse m	—	camarade m	compagno m	camarada m
comune (I)	gemeinsam	together	ensemble	—	juntos(as)
comunicación¹ (Es)	Anschluß m	connection	correspondance f	coincidenza f	—
comunicación² (Es)	Mitteilung f	message	information f	comunicazione f	—
comunicar¹ (Es)	ausrichten	pass on a message	transmettre	riferire	—
comunicar² (Es)	mitteilen	inform s.o.	informer qn de qch	comunicare	—
comunicare (I)	mitteilen	inform s.o.	informer qn de qch	—	comunicar
comunicazione (I)	Mitteilung f	message	information f	—	comunicación f
con (Es)	mit	with	avec	con	—
con (I)	mit	with	avec	—	con
conceder (Es)	gewähren	grant	accorder	concedere	—
concedere (I)	gewähren	grant	accorder	—	conceder
conseil (F)	Rat m	advice	—	consiglio m	consejo m
concentrar (Es)	konzentrieren	concentrate	concentrer	concentrare	—
concentrare (I)	konzentrieren	concentrate	concentrer	—	concentrar
concentrate (E)	konzentrieren	—	concentrer	concentrare	concentrar
concentrer (F)	konzentrieren	concentrate	—	concentrare	concentrar
concern¹ (E)	betreffen	—	concerner	riguardare	concernir
concern² (E)	Sorge f	—	souci m	preoccupazione f	preocupación f
concerner (F)	betreffen	concern	—	riguardare	concernir
concernir (Es)	betreffen	concern	concerner	riguardare	—
concert (E)	Konzert n	—	concert m	concerto m	concierto m
concert (F)	Konzert n	concert	—	concerto m	concierto m
concertar una cita (Es)	verabreden	arrange to meet	prendre rendez-vous	darsi appuntamento	—
concerto (I)	Konzert n	concert	concert m	—	concierto m
conciencia (Es)	Gewissen n	conscience	conscience f	coscienza f	—
concienzudo (Es)	gewissenhaft	conscientious	consciencieux (-euse)	coscienzioso(a)	—
concierge¹ (F)	Hausmeister m	caretaker	—	portinaio m	portero m
concierge² (F)	Pförtner m	porter	—	portiere m	portero m

	D	E	F	I	Es
concierto (Es)	Konzert *n*	concert	concert *m*	concerto *m*	—
conclusión (Es)	Schluß *m*	end	fin *f*	fine *f*	—
concombre (F)	Gurke *f*	cucumber	—	cetriolo *m*	pepino *m*
concordare (I)	übereinstimmen	agree	être d'accord	—	estar de acuerdo
concorrere (I)	bewerben, sich	apply	poser sa candidature	—	presentarse
concorso (I)	Wettbewerb *m*	competition	concours *m*	—	concurso *m*
concours (F)	Wettbewerb *m*	competition	—	concorso *m*	concurso *m*
concurso (Es)	Wettbewerb *m*	competition	concours *m*	concorso *m*	—
condamner (F)	verurteilen	condemn	—	condannare	sentenciar
condannare (I)	verurteilen	condemn	condamner	—	sentenciar
condecoración (Es)	Orden *m*	decoration	décoration *f*	decorazione *f*	—
condemn (E)	verurteilen	—	condamner	condannare	condenar
condición (Es)	Bedingung *f*	condition	condition *f*	condizione *f*	—
condimentar (Es)	würzen	season	épicer	condire	—
condire (I)	würzen	season	épicer	—	condimentar
condition¹ (E)	Bedingung *f*	—	condition *f*	condizione *f*	condición *f*
condition² (E)	Zustand *m*	—	état *m*	stato *m*	estado *m*
condition (F)	Bedingung *f*	condition	—	condizione *f*	condición *f*
condizione (I)	Bedingung *f*	condition	condition *f*	—	condición *f*
condizioni (I)	Verfassung *f*	constitution	état *m*	—	estado *m*
condoglianza (I)	Beileid *n*	condolence	condoléances *f pl*	—	pésame *m*
condoléances (F)	Beileid *n*	condolence	—	condoglianza *f*	pésame *m*
condolence (E)	Beileid *n*	—	condoléances *f pl*	condoglianza *f*	pésame *m*
conducir (Es)	fahren	drive	conduire	andare	—
conducteur (F)	Fahrer *m*	driver	—	autista *m*	conductor *m*
conductor¹ (E)	Dirigent *m*	—	chef d'orchestre *m*	direttore d'orchestra *m*	director (de orquesta) *m*
conductor² (E)	Schaffner *m*	—	contrôleur *m*	bigliettaio *m*	revisor *m*
conductor (Es)	Fahrer *m*	driver	conducteur *m*	autista *m*	—
conduire¹ (F)	fahren	drive	—	andare	conducir
conduire² (F)	lenken	steer	—	guidare	encauzar
conduite (F)	Benehmen *n*	behaviour	—	comportamento *m*	comportamiento *m*
conduttura (I)	Leitung *f*	pipe	tuyau *m*	—	tubería *f*
conectar¹ (Es)	einschalten	switch on	allumer	accendere	—
conectar² (Es)	schalten	switch	connecter	commutare	—
con ello (Es)	damit	with it	avec cela	con questo	—
conference (E)	Konferenz *f*	—	conférence *f*	conferenza *f*	conferencia *f*
conférence (F)	Konferenz *f*	conference	—	conferenza *f*	conferencia *f*
conferencia (Es)	Konferenz *f*	conference	conférence *f*	conferenza *f*	—
conferenza (I)	Konferenz *f*	conference	conférence *f*	—	conferencia *f*
confermare (I)	bestätigen	confirm	confirmer	—	confirmar
confesar (Es)	gestehen	confess	avouer	confessare	—
confesión (Es)	Bekenntnis *n*	confession	confession *f*	confessione *f*	—
confess (E)	gestehen	—	avouer	confessare	confesar
confessare (I)	gestehen	confess	avouer	—	confesar
confession (E)	Bekenntnis *n*	—	confession *f*	confessione *f*	confesión *f*
confession (F)	Bekenntnis *n*	confession	—	confessione *f*	confesión *f*
confessione (I)	Bekenntnis *n*	confession	confession *f*	—	confesión *f*

	D	E	F	I	Es
confiance (F)	Vertrauen *n*	confidence	—	fiducia *f*	confianza *f*
confianza (Es)	Vertrauen *n*	confidence	confiance *f*	fiducia *f*	—
confiar (Es)	vertrauen	trust	avoir confiance	fidarsi	—
confidence (E)	Vertrauen *n*	—	confiance *f*	fiducia *f*	confianza *f*
confirm (E)	bestätigen	—	confirmer	confermare	confirmar
confirmar (Es)	bestätigen	confirm	confirmer	confermare	—
confirmer (F)	bestätigen	confirm	—	confermare	confirmar
confiture (F)	Marmelade *f*	jam	—	marmellata *f*	mermelada *f*
confondre (F)	verwechseln	confuse	—	scambiare	confundir
confort (F)	Bequemlichkeit *f*	convenience	—	comodità *f*	comodidad *f*
confortable (F)	bequem	comfortable	—	comodo(a)	cómodo(a)
confundido (Es)	verwirrt	confused	confus(e)	confuso(a)	—
confundir (Es)	verwechseln	confuse	confondre	scambiare	—
confus (F)	verwirrt	confused	—	confuso(a)	confundido(a)
confuse (E)	verwechseln	—	confondre	scambiare	confundir
confused (E)	verwirrt	—	confus(e)	confuso(a)	confundido(a)
confusion[1] (E)	Durcheinander *n*	—	désordre *m*	confusione *f*	confusión *f*
confusion[2] (E)	Verwirrung *f*	—	confusion *f*	confusione *f*	confusión *f*
confusión[1] (Es)	Durcheinander *n*	confusion	désordre *m*	confusione *f*	—
confusión[2] (Es)	Verwirrung *f*	confusion	confusion *f*	confusione *f*	—
confusion (F)	Verwirrung *f*	confusion	—	confusione *f*	confusión *f*
confusione[1] (I)	Durcheinander *n*	confusion	désordre *m*	—	confusión *f*
confusione[2] (I)	Verwirrung *f*	confusion	confusion *f*	—	confusión *f*
confuso (I)	verwirrt	confused	confus(e)	—	confundido(a)
congedare (I)	verabschieden	say goodbye to	prendre congé de	—	despedir
congratularsi (I)	gratulieren	congratulate	féliciter	—	felicitar
congratulate (E)	gratulieren	—	féliciter	congratularsi	felicitar
congratulations (E)	Glückwunsch *m*	—	félicitations *f pl*	auguri *m pl*	felicitaciones *f pl*
con gusto (Es)	gern	willingly	avec plaisir	volentieri	—
conifer (E)	Nadelbaum *m*	—	conifère *m*	conifero *m*	conífera *f*
conífera (Es)	Nadelbaum *m*	conifer	conifère *m*	conifero *m*	—
conifère (F)	Nadelbaum *m*	conifer	—	conifero *m*	conífera *f*
conifero (I)	Nadelbaum *m*	conifer	conifère *m*	—	conífera *f*
conmemorar (Es)	gedenken	remember	souvenir de, se	ricordare	—
connaissance[1] (F)	Bekannter *m*	acquaintance	—	conoscente *m*	conocido *m*
connaissance[2] (F)	Kenntnis *f*	knowledge	—	conoscenza *f*	conocimiento *m*
connaître (F)	kennen	know	—	conoscere	conocer
connaître, s'y (F)	auskennen, sich	know one's way about	—	conoscere	conocer a fondo
connect (E)	verbinden	—	relier	unire	unir
connecter (F)	schalten	switch	—	commutare	conectar
connection[1] (E)	Anschluß *m*	—	correspondance *f*	coincidenza *f*	conexión *f*
connection[2] (E)	Verbindung *f*	—	relation *f*	relazione *f*	relación *f*
connu (F)	bekannt	well known	—	conosciuto(a)	conocido(a)
conocer (Es)	kennen	know	connaître	conoscere	—
conocer a fondo (Es)	auskennen, sich	know one's way about	connaître, s'y	conoscere	—
conocido[1] (Es)	Bekannter *m*	acquaintance	ami *m*	conoscente *m*	—

	D	E	F	I	Es
conocido² (Es)	bekannt	well known	connu(e)	conosciuto(a)	—
conocimiento (Es)	Kenntnis f	knowledge	connaissance f	conoscenza f	—
conoscente (I)	Bekannter m	acquaintance	ami m	—	conocido m
conoscenza (I)	Kenntnis f	knowledge	connaissance f	—	conocimiento m
conoscere¹ (I)	auskennen, sich	know one's way about	connaître, s'y	—	conocer a fondo
conoscere² (I)	kennen	know	connaître	—	conocer
conosciuto (I)	bekannt	well known	connu(e)	—	conocido(a)
con paciencia (Es)	geduldig	patient	patient(e)	paziente	—
con questo (I)	damit	with it	avec cela	—	con ello
conscience (E)	Gewissen n	—	conscience f	coscienza f	conciencia f
conscience (F)	Gewissen n	conscience	—	coscienza f	conciencia f
consciencieux (F)	gewissenhaft	conscientious	—	coscienzioso(a)	concienzudo(a)
conscientious (E)	gewissenhaft	—	consciencieux (-euse)	coscienzioso(a)	concienzudo(a)
consegnare¹ (I)	übergeben	hand over	remettre	—	transmitir
consegnare² (I)	überreichen	hand over	présenter	—	entregar
conseguenza (I)	Folge f	consequence	conséquence f	—	consecuencia f
conseguir¹ (Es)	besorgen	acquire	procurer	procurare	—
conseguir² (Es)	gelangen	attain	arriver à	arrivare a	—
conseiller (F)	raten	advise	—	consigliare	aconsejar
consejo (Es)	Rat m	advice	conseil m	consiglio m	—
consentir (Es)	zustimmen	agree	être d'accord	acconsentire	—
consequence (E)	Folge f	—	conséquence f	conseguenza f	consecuencia f
conservare (I)	aufbewahren	keep	garder	—	guardar
consider (E)	überlegen	—	réfléchir à	riflettere	pensar
considerable¹ (E)	beträchtlich	—	considérable	considerevole	notable
considerable² (E)	erheblich	—	considérable	rilevante	considerable
considerable (Es)	erheblich	considerable	considérable	rilevante	—
considérable¹ (F)	beträchtlich	considerable	—	considerevole	notable
considérable² (F)	erheblich	considerable	—	rilevante	considerable
considérer (F)	beachten	take notice of	—	osservare	prestar atención a
considerevole (I)	beträchtlich	considerable	considérable	—	notable
consigliare (I)	raten	advise	conseiller	—	aconsejar
consiglio (I)	Rat m	advice	conseil m	—	consejo m
consolar (Es)	trösten	comfort	consoler	consolare	—
consolare (I)	trösten	comfort	consoler	—	consolar
consolation (E)	Trost m	—	consolation f	consolazione f	consuelo m
consolation (F)	Trost m	consolation	—	consolazione f	consuelo m
consolato (I)	Konsulat n	consulate	consulat m	—	consulado m
consolazione (I)	Trost m	consolation	consolation f	—	consuelo m
consoler (F)	trösten	comfort	—	consolare	consolar
consommation (F)	Verbrauch m	consumption	—	consumo m	consumo m
consommer (F)	verbrauchen	consume	—	consumare	consumir
constitución (Es)	Verfassung f	constitution	constitution f	costituzione f	—
constitution¹ (E)	Verfassung f	—	état m	condizioni f pl	estado m
constitution² (E)	Verfassung f	—	constitution f	costituzione f	constitución f
constitution (F)	Verfassung f	constitution	—	costituzione f	constitución f
construcción (Es)	Bau m	construction	construction f	costruzione f	—

	D	E	F	I	Es
construction (E)	Bau *m*	—	construction *f*	costruzione *f*	construcción *f*
construction¹ (F)	Anlage *f*	plant	—	impianto *m*	establecimiento *m*
construction² (F)	Bau *m*	construction	—	costruzione *f*	construcción *f*
construir (Es)	bauen	build	construire	costruire	—
construire (F)	bauen	build	—	costruire	construir
consuelo (Es)	Trost *m*	consolation	consolation *f*	consolazione *f*	—
consulado (Es)	Konsulat *n*	consulate	consulat *m*	consolato *m*	—
consulat (F)	Konsulat *n*	consulate	—	consolato *m*	consulado *m*
consulate (E)	Konsulat *n*	—	consulat *m*	consolato *m*	consulado *m*
consultation hour (E)	Sprechstunde *f*	—	heures de consultation *f pl*	ora di ricevimento *f*	hora de consulta *f*
consumare¹ (I)	abnutzen	wear out	user	—	desgastar
consumare² (I)	verbrauchen	consume	consommer	—	consumir
consume (E)	verbrauchen	—	consommer	consumare	consumir
consumir (Es)	verbrauchen	consume	consommer	consumare	—
consumo (Es)	Verbrauch *m*	consumption	consommation *f*	consumo *m*	—
consumo (I)	Verbrauch *m*	consumption	consommation *f*	—	consumo *m*
consumption (E)	Verbrauch *m*	—	consommation *f*	consumo *m*	consumo *m*
contabilidad (Es)	Buchhaltung *f*	book-keeping	comptabilité *f*	contabilità *f*	—
contabilità (I)	Buchhaltung *f*	book-keeping	comptabilité *f*	—	contabilidad
contact (E)	Kontakt *m*	—	contact *m*	contatto *m*	contacto *m*
contact (F)	Kontakt *m*	contact	—	contatto *m*	contacto *m*
contacto (Es)	Kontakt *m*	contact	contact *m*	contatto *m*	—
contadino (I)	Bauer *m*	farmer	paysan *m*	—	campesino *m*
contain (E)	enthalten	—	contenir	contenere	contener
container¹ (E)	Behälter *m*	—	récipient *m*	recipiente *m*	recipiente *m*
container² (E)	Gefäß *n*	—	récipient *m*	recipiente *m*	recipiente *m*
contanti (I)	Bargeld *n*	cash	espèces *f pl*	—	dinero al contado *m*
contar¹ (Es)	erzählen	tell	raconter	raccontare	—
contar² (Es)	zählen	count	compter	contare	—
contare (I)	zählen	count	compter	—	contar
contatto (I)	Kontakt *m*	contact	contact *m*	—	contacto *m*
contemporain (F)	zeitgenössisch	contemporary	—	contemporaneo(a)	contemporáneo(a)
contemporaneo¹ (I)	gleichzeitig	simultaneous	en même temps	—	a la vez
contemporaneo² (I)	zeitgenössisch	contemporary	contemporain(e)	—	contemporáneo(a)
contemporáneo (Es)	zeitgenössisch	contemporary	contemporain(e)	contemporaneo(a)	—
contemporary (E)	zeitgenössisch	—	contemporain(e)	contemporaneo(a)	contemporáneo(a)
contener (Es)	enthalten	contain	contenir	contenere	—
contenere (I)	enthalten	contain	contenir	—	contener
contenido (Es)	Inhalt *m*	contents	contenu *m*	contenuto *m*	—
contenir (F)	enthalten	contain	—	contenere	contener
content (F)	zufrieden	satisfied	—	contento(a)	satisfecho(a)
contento (I)	zufrieden	satisfied	content(e)	—	satisfecho(a)
contento¹ (Es)	erfreut	delighted	réjoui(e)	lieto(a)	—
contento² (Es)	froh	glad	content(e)	lieto(a)	—
contents (E)	Inhalt *m*	—	contenu *m*	contenuto *m*	contenido *m*
contenu (F)	Inhalt *m*	contents	—	contenuto *m*	contenido *m*
contenuto (I)	Inhalt *m*	contents	contenu *m*	—	contenido *m*

	D	E	F	I	Es
contiguo (Es)	nahe	near	près de	vicino(a) a	—
continent (E)	Kontinent *m*	—	continent *m*	continente *m*	continente *m*
continent[1] (F)	Festland *n*	mainland	—	terraferma *f*	tierra firme *f*
continent[2] (F)	Kontinent *m*	continent	—	continente *m*	continente *m*
continente (Es)	Kontinent *m*	continent	continent *m*	continente *m*	—
continente (I)	Kontinent *m*	continent	continent *m*	—	continente *m*
continuar (Es)	weitermachen	carry on	continuer	continuare	—
continuare[1] (I)	fortsetzen	continue	continuer	—	proseguir
continuare[2] (I)	weitermachen	carry on	continuer	—	continuar
continuare a dormire (I)	weiterschlafen	sleep on	continuer à dormir	—	seguir durmiendo
continue (E)	fortsetzen	—	continuer	continuare	proseguir
continuer[1] (F)	fortsetzen	continue	—	continuare	proseguir
continuer[2] (F)	weitermachen	carry on	—	continuare	continuar
continuer à dormir (F)	weiterschlafen	sleep on	—	continuare a dormire	seguir durmiendo
conto (I)	Konto n	account	compte m	—	cuenta f
contra[1] (Es)	dagegen	against it	contre cela	contro	—
contra[2] (Es)	gegen	against	contre	contro	—
contract (E)	Vertrag *m*	—	contrat *m*	contratto *m*	contrato *m*
contraddire (I)	widersprechen	contradict	contredire	—	contradecir
contradecir (Es)	widersprechen	contradict	contredire	contraddire	—
contradict (E)	widersprechen	—	contredire	contraddire	contradecir
contrainte (F)	Zwang *m*	compulsion	—	costrizione *f*	presión *f*
contraire (F)	Gegenteil *n*	opposite	—	contrario *m*	opuesto *m*
contrario (I)	Gegenteil *n*	opposite	contraire *m*	—	opuesto *m*
contrario (Es)	umgekehrt	vice versa	vice versa	inverso(a)	—
contrat (F)	Vertrag *m*	contract	—	contratto *m*	contrato *m*
contratiempo (Es)	Verlegenheit *f*	embarrassment	gêne *f*	imbarazzo *m*	—
contrato (Es)	Vertrag *m*	contract	contrat *m*	contratto *m*	—
contratto (I)	Vertrag *m*	contract	contrat *m*	—	contrato *m*
contre (F)	gegen	against	—	contro	contra
contre cela (F)	dagegen	against it	—	contro	contra
contredire (F)	widersprechen	contradict	—	contraddire	contradecir
contribution (E)	Beitrag *m*	—	contribution *f*	contributo *m*	cuota *f*
contribution (F)	Beitrag *m*	contribution	—	contributo *m*	cuota *f*
contributo (I)	Beitrag *m*	contribution	contribution *f*	—	cuota *f*
contro[1] (I)	dagegen	against it	contre cela	—	contra
contro[2] (I)	gegen	against	contre	—	contra
control (E)	Kontrolle *f*	—	contrôle *m*	controllo *m*	control *m*
control (Es)	Kontrolle *f*	control	contrôle *m*	controllo *m*	—
controlador (Es)	Kontrolleur *m*	inspector	contrôleur *m*	controllore *m*	—
control de radar (Es)	Radarkontrolle *f*	speed trap	contrôle radar *m*	controllo radar *m*	—
contrôle (F)	Kontrolle *f*	control	—	controllo *m*	control *m*
contrôler[1] (F)	nachprüfen	check	—	controllare	comprobar
contrôler[2] (F)	überprüfen	check	—	esaminare	examinar
contrôle radar (F)	Radarkontrolle *f*	speed trap	—	controllo radar *m*	control de radar *m*
contrôleur[1] (F)	Kontrolleur *m*	inspector	—	controllore *m*	controlador *m*

	D	E	F	I	Es
contrôleur² (F)	Schaffner *m*	conductor	—	bigliettaio *m*	revisor *m*
controllare¹ (I)	nachprüfen	check	contrôler	—	comprobar
controllare² (I)	nachsehen	check	vérifier	—	examinar
controllo (I)	Kontrolle *f*	control	contrôle *m*	—	control *m*
controllo radar (I)	Radarkontrolle *f*	speed trap	contrôle radar *m*	—	control de radar *m*
controllore (I)	Kontrolleur *m*	inspector	contrôleur *m*	—	controlador *m*
convaincre (F)	überzeugen	convince	—	convincere	convencer
convenable (F)	anständig	decent	—	decente	decente
convencer (Es)	überzeugen	convince	convaincre	convincere	—
convenience (E)	Bequemlich-keit *f*	—	confort *m*	comodità *f*	comodidad *f*
conveniente (I)	preiswert	inexpensive	bon marché	—	económico(a)
convenir¹ (Es)	ausmachen	agree	convenir	stabilire	—
convenir² (Es)	vereinbaren	agree upon	convenir de	fissare	—
convenir (F)	ausmachen	agree	—	stabilire	convenir
convenir de (F)	vereinbaren	agree upon	—	fissare	convenir
convenir pour (F)	taugen	be of use	—	servire	valer
convento (I)	Kloster *n*	monastery	couvent *m*	—	monasterio *m*
conversación¹ (Es)	Gespräch *n*	conversation	conversation *f*	conversazione *f*	—
conversación² (Es)	Unterhaltung *f*	conversation	entretien *m*	conversazione *f*	—
conversación telefónica (Es)	Telefongespräch *n*	phone call	communication téléphonique *f*	conversazione telefonica *f*	—
conversar¹ (Es)	plaudern	chat	causer	chiacchierare	—
conversar² (Es)	unterhalten, sich	talk	entretenir, se	conversare	—
conversare (I)	unterhalten, sich	talk	entretenir, se	—	conversar
conversation¹ (E)	Gespräch *n*	—	conversation *f*	conversazione *f*	conversación *f*
conversation² (E)	Unterhaltung *f*	—	entretien *m*	conversazione *f*	conversación *f*
conversation (F)	Gespräch *n*	conversation	—	conversazione *f*	conversación *f*
conversazione¹ (I)	Gespräch *n*	conversation	conversation *f*	—	conversación *f*
conversazione² (I)	Unterhaltung *f*	conversation	entretien *m*	—	conversación *f*
conversazione telefonica (I)	Telefongespräch *n*	phone call	communication téléphonique *f*	—	conversación telefónica *f*
convert (E)	umrechnen	—	convertir	convertire	convertir
convertir (Es)	umrechnen	convert	convertir	convertire	—
convertir (F)	umrechnen	convert	—	convertire	convertir
convertire (I)	umrechnen	convert	convertir	—	convertir
convey (E)	übermitteln	—	transmettre	trasmettere	transmitir
convince¹ (E)	überreden	—	persuader	persuadere	persuadir
convince² (E)	überzeugen	—	convaincre	convincere	convencer
convincere (I)	überzeugen	convince	convaincre	—	convencer
cook¹ (E)	kochen	—	cuire	cucinare	cocinar
cook² (E)	Koch *m*	—	cuisinier *m*	cuoco *m*	cocinero *m*
cook³ (E)	Köchin *f*	—	cuisinière *f*	cuoca *f*	cocinera *f*
cooker (E)	Herd *m*	—	fourneau *m*	cucina *f*	cocina *f*
cool (E)	kühl	—	frais (fraîche)	fresco(a)	fresco(a)
coperchio (I)	Deckel *m*	lid	couvercle *m*	—	tapa *f*
coperta (I)	Decke *f*	blanket	couverture *f*	—	techo *m*
coperto¹ (I)	bedeckt	covered	couvert(e)	—	cubierto(a)
coperto² (I)	Gedeck *n*	cover	couvert *m*	—	cubierto *m*

	D	E	F	I	Es
copia (Es)	Kopie f	copy	copie f	copia f	—
copia (I)	Kopie f	copy	copie f	—	copia f
copiar (Es)	kopieren	copy	copier	copiare	—
copiare (I)	kopieren	copy	copier	—	copiar
copie (F)	Kopie f	copy	—	copia f	copia f
copier (F)	kopieren	copy	—	copiare	copiar
coprire[1] (I)	bedecken	cover	couvrir	—	cubrir
coprire[2] (I)	zudecken	cover (up)	couvrir	—	tapar
copy[1] (E)	kopieren	—	copier	copiare	copiar
copy[2] (E)	Kopie f	—	copie f	copia f	copia f
coq (F)	Hahn m	cock	—	gallo m	gallo m
coquelicot (F)	Mohn m	poppy	—	papavero m	amapola f
coraggio (I)	Mut m	courage	courage m	—	coraje m
coraggioso (I)	tapfer	brave	courageux (-euse)	—	valiente
coraje (Es)	Mut m	courage	courage m	coraggio m	—
corazón (Es)	Herz n	heart	cœur m	cuore m	—
corbata (Es)	Krawatte f	tie	cravate f	cravatta f	—
corbeau (F)	Rabe m	raven	—	corvo m	cuervo m
corda[1] (I)	Schnur f	string	ficelle f	—	cordel m
corda[2] (I)	Strick m	rope	corde f	—	cuerda f
corde[1] (F)	Seil n	rope	—	fune f	soga f
corde[2] (F)	Strick m	rope	—	corda f	cuerda f
cordel (Es)	Schnur f	string	ficelle f	corda f	—
cordero (Es)	Lamm n	lamb	agneau m	agnello m	—
cordial (E)	herzlich	—	cordial(e)	cordiale	afectuoso(a)
cordial (F)	herzlich	cordial	—	cordiale	afectuoso(a)
cordiale (I)	herzlich	cordial	cordial(e)	—	afectuoso(a)
cordonnier (F)	Schuster m	shoemaker	—	calzolaio m	zapatero m
coriace (F)	zäh	tough	—	duro(a)	duro(a)
corkscrew (E)	Korken-zieher m	—	tire-bouchon m	cavatappi m	sacacorchos m
corn[1] (E)	Korn n	—	grain m	grano m	semilla f
corn[2] (E)	Mais m	—	maïs m	mais m	maíz m
corner[1] (E)	Ecke f	—	coin m	angolo m	esquina f
corner[2] (E)	Winkel m	—	coin m	cantuccio m	rincón m
cornice (I)	Rahmen m	frame	cadre m	—	marco m
coro (Es)	Chor m	choir	chœur m	coro m	—
coro (I)	Chor m	choir	chœur m	—	coro m
corpo (I)	Körper m	body	corps m	—	cuerpo m
corps (F)	Körper m	body	—	corpo m	cuerpo m
corpse (E)	Leiche f	—	cadavre m	cadavere m	cadáver m
correa (Es)	Riemen m	strap	courroie f	cinghia f	—
correct[1] (E)	korrekt	—	correct(e)	corretto(a)	correcto(a)
correct[2] (E)	richtig	—	juste	giusto(a)	correcto(a)
correct (F)	korrekt	correct	—	corretto(a)	correcto(a)
correcto[1] (Es)	korrekt	correct	correct(e)	corretto(a)	—
correcto[2] (Es)	richtig	correct	juste	giusto(a)	—
corredor[1] (Es)	Flur m	hall	entrée f	corridoio m	—

	D	E	F	I	Es
corredor² (Es)	Gang *m*	corridor	couloir *m*	corridoio *m*	—
corrente (I)	Strom *m*	current	courant *m*	—	corriente *f*
corrente d'aria (I)	Luftzug *m*	draught	courant d'air *m*	—	corriente de aire *f*
correo (Es)	Post *f*	post	poste *f*	posta *f*	—
correo aéreo (Es)	Luftpost *f*	air mail	poste aérienne *f*	posta aerea *f*	—
correr¹ (Es)	fließen	flow	couler	scorrere	—
correr² (Es)	laufen	run	courir	correre	—
correr³ (Es)	rennen	run	courir	correre	—
correr⁴ (Es)	vorziehen	draw	tirer	tirare in avanti	—
correre¹ (I)	laufen	run	courir	—	correr
correre² (I)	rennen	run	courir	—	correr
correspond (E)	entsprechen	—	correspondre à	corrispondere	corresponder
correspondance (F)	Anschluß *m*	connection	—	coincidenza *f*	conexión *f*
corresponder (Es)	entsprechen	correspond	correspondre à	corrispondere	—
correspondre à (F)	entsprechen	correspond	—	corrispondere	corresponder
corretto (I)	korrekt	correct	correct(e)	—	correcto(a)
corridoio¹ (I)	Diele *f*	hall	vestibule *m*	—	entrada *f*
corridoio² (I)	Flur *m*	hall	entrée *f*	—	corredor *m*
corridoio³ (I)	Gang *m*	corridor	couloir *m*	—	corredor *m*
corridoio⁴ (I)	Korridor *m*	corridor	corridor *m*	—	pasillo *m*
corridor¹ (E)	Gang *m*	—	couloir *m*	corridoio *m*	corredor *m*
corridor² (E)	Korridor *m*	—	corridor *m*	corridoio *m*	pasillo *m*
corridor (F)	Korridor *m*	corridor	—	corridoio *m*	pasillo *m*
corriente (Es)	Strom *m*	current	courant *m*	corrente *f*	—
corriente de aire (Es)	Luftzug *m*	draught	courant d'air *m*	corrente d'aria *f*	—
corriere (I)	Eilbote *m*	courier	courrier *m*	—	correo urgente *m*
corrispondere (I)	entsprechen	correspond	correspondre à	—	corresponder
corso (I)	Kurs *m*	rate	cours *m*	—	curso *m*
cortante (Es)	scharf	sharp	tranchant(e)	tagliente	—
cortar¹ (Es)	mähen	mow	faucher	falciare	—
cortar² (Es)	schneiden	cut	couper	tagliare	—
corte (Es)	Schnitt *m*	cut	coupe *f*	taglio *m*	—
cortés¹ (Es)	höflich	polite	poli(e)	cortese	—
cortés² (Es)	zuvorkommend	obliging	prévenant(e)	premuroso(a)	—
cortese (I)	höflich	polite	poli(e)	—	cortés
cortesía (Es)	Höflichkeit *f*	politeness	politesse *f*	cortesia *f*	—
cortesia (I)	Höflichkeit *f*	politeness	politesse *f*	—	cortesía *f*
cortile (I)	Hof *m*	yard	cour *f*	—	patio *m*
cortina¹ (Es)	Gardine *f*	curtain	rideau *m*	tenda *f*	—
cortina² (Es)	Vorhang *m*	curtain	rideau *m*	tenda *f*	—
corto (I)	kurz	short	court(e)	—	corto(a)
corto (Es)	kurz	short	court(e)	corto(a)	—
corvo (I)	Rabe *m*	raven	corbeau *m*	—	cuervo *m*
corzo (Es)	Reh *n*	deer	chevreuil *m*	capriolo *m*	—
cosa¹ (Es)	Ding *n*	thing	chose *f*	cosa *f*	—
cosa² (Es)	Sache *f*	thing	chose *f*	cosa *f*	—
cosa³ (Es)	Zeug *n*	stuff	truc *m*	cose *f pl*	—

	D	E	F	I	Es
cosa¹ (I)	Ding *n*	thing	chose *f*	—	cosa *f*
cosa² (I)	Sache *f*	thing	chose *f*	—	cosa *f*
coscienza (I)	Gewissen *n*	conscience	conscience *f*	—	conciencia *f*
coscienzioso (I)	gewissenhaft	conscientious	consciencieux (-euse)	—	concienzudo(a)
cose (I)	Zeug *n*	stuff	truc *m*	—	cosa *f*
cosecha (Es)	Ernte *f*	harvest	moisson *f*	raccolto *m*	—
coser (Es)	nähen	sew	coudre	cucire	—
cosí (I)	so	like this	ainsi	—	así
cost (E)	kosten	—	coûter	costare	costar
costa (Es)	Küste *f*	coast	côte *f*	costa *f*	—
costa (I)	Küste *f*	coast	côte *f*	—	costa *f*
costar (Es)	kosten	cost	coûter	costare	—
costare (I)	kosten	cost	coûter	—	costar
costas (Es)	Kosten *pl*	expenses	coût *m*	spese *f pl*	—
costilla (Es)	Rippe *f*	rib	côte *f*	costola *f*	—
costituzione (I)	Verfassung *f*	constitution	constitution *f*	—	constitución *f*
costola (I)	Rippe *f*	rib	côte *f*	—	costilla *f*
costoletta (I)	Kotelett *n*	cutlet	côtelette *f*	—	chuleta *f*
costoso (I)	kostspielig	expensive	coûteux(-euse)	—	costoso(a)
costoso (Es)	kostspielig	expensive	coûteux(-euse)	costoso(a)	—
costringere (I)	zwingen	force	forcer	—	obligar
costrizione (I)	Zwang *m*	compulsion	contrainte *f*	—	presión *f*
costruire (I)	bauen	build	construire	—	construir
costruzione (I)	Bau *m*	construction	construction *f*	—	construcción *f*
costumbre¹ (Es)	Gewohnheit *f*	habit	habitude *f*	abitudine *f*	—
costumbre² (Es)	Sitte *f*	custom	coutume *f*	usanza *f*	—
costume (E)	Kostüm *n*	—	costume *m*	tailleur *m*	vestido *m*
costume¹ (F)	Anzug *m*	suit	—	vestito *m*	traje *m*
costume² (F)	Kostüm *n*	costume	—	tailleur *m*	vestido *m*
costume da bagno¹ (I)	Badeanzug *m*	swimsuit	maillot de bain *m*	—	traje de baño *m*
costume da bagno² (I)	Badehose *f*	swimming trunks	slip de bain *m*	—	bañador *m*
côte¹ (F)	Küste *f*	coast	—	costa *f*	costa *f*
côte² (F)	Rippe *f*	rib	—	costola *f*	costilla *f*
côtelette (F)	Kotelett *n*	cutlet	—	costoletta *f*	chuleta *f*
cotidiano (Es)	täglich	daily	quotidien(ne)	quotidiano(a)	—
coton (F)	Baumwolle *f*	cotton	—	cotone *m*	algodón *m*
cotone (I)	Baumwolle *f*	cotton	coton *m*	—	algodón *m*
cotto (I)	gar	done	cuit(e)	—	estar a punto
cotton (E)	Baumwolle *f*	—	coton *m*	cotone *m*	algodón *m*
cotton wool (E)	Watte *f*	—	ouate *f*	ovatta *f*	algodón *m*
cou (F)	Hals *m*	neck	—	collo *m*	cuello *m*
Couch (D)	—	couch	canapé *m*	divano *m*	diván *m*
couch (E)	Couch *f*	—	canapé *m*	divano *m*	diván *m*
coucher du soleil (F)	Sonnenuntergang *m*	sunset	—	tramonto del sole *m*	puesta de sol *f*
couchette (E)	Liegewagen *m*	—	wagon-couchette *m*	cuccetta *f*	coche cama *m*

	D	E	F	I	Es
coudre (F)	nähen	sew	—	cucire	coser
cough[1] (E)	husten	—	tousser	tossire	toser
cough[2] (E)	Husten *m*	—	toux *m*	tosse *f*	tos *f*
couler[1] (F)	fließen	flow	—	scorrere	correr
couler[2] (F)	sinken	sink	—	affondare	hundirse
couleur (F)	Farbe *f*	colour	—	colore *m*	color *m*
couloir (F)	Gang *m*	corridor	—	corridoio *m*	corredor *m*
count (E)	zählen	—	compter	contare	contar
counter[1] (E)	Ladentisch *m*	—	comptoir *m*	banco di vendita *m*	mostrador *m*
counter[2] (E)	Schalter *m*	—	guichet *m*	sportello *m*	ventanilla *f*
country road (E)	Landstraße *f*	—	route *f*	strada provinciale *f*	carretera nacional *f*
coup[1] (F)	Stoß *m*	blow	—	spinta *f*	empujón *m*
coup[2] (F)	Schlag *m*	blow	—	colpo *m*	golpe *m*
coup[3] (F)	Schuß *m*	shot	—	sparo *m*	disparo *m*
coupable (F)	schuldig	guilty	—	colpevole	culpable
coup de soleil (F)	Sonnenbrand *m*	sunburn	—	scottatura solare *f*	quemadura solar *f*
coup de téléphone[1] (F)	Anruf *m*	call	—	chiamata *f*	llamada *f*
coup de téléphone[2] (F)	Telefonanruf *m*	phone call	—	telefonata *f*	llamada telefónica *f*
coupe (F)	Schnitt *m*	cut	—	taglio *m*	corte *m*
couper (F)	schneiden	cut	—	tagliare	cortar
cour (F)	Hof *m*	yard	—	cortile *m*	patio *m*
courage (E)	Mut *m*	—	courage *m*	coraggio *m*	coraje *m*
courage (F)	Mut *m*	courage	—	coraggio *m*	coraje *m*
courageux (F)	tapfer	brave	—	coraggioso(a)	valiente
courant (F)	Strom *m*	current	—	corrente *f*	corriente *f*
courant d'air (F)	Luftzug *m*	draught	—	corrente d'aria *f*	corriente de aire *f*
courier (E)	Eilbote *m*	—	courrier *m*	corriere *m*	correo urgente *m*
courir[1] (F)	laufen	run	—	correre	correr
courir[2] (F)	rennen	run	—	correre	correr
courrier (F)	Eilbote *m*	courier	—	corriere *m*	correo urgente *m*
courroie (F)	Riemen *m*	strap	—	cinghia *f*	correa *f*
cours[1] (F)	Kurs *m*	rate	—	corso *m*	curso *m*
cours[2] (F)	Unterricht *m*	lessons	—	lezione *f*	enseñanza *f*
course (E)	Gang *m*	—	plat *m*	portata *f*	plato *m*
cours magistral (F)	Vorlesung *f*	lecture	—	lezione *f*	clase *f*
court (E)	Gericht *n*	—	tribunal *m*	tribunale *m*	tribunal *m*
court (F)	kurz	short	—	corto(a)	corto(a)
cousin[1] (E)	Cousine *f*	—	cousine *f*	cugina *f*	prima *f*
cousin[2] (E)	Vetter *m*	—	cousin *m*	cugino *m*	primo *m*
cousin (F)	Vetter *m*	cousin	—	cugino *m*	primo *m*
Cousine (D)	—	cousin	cousine *f*	cugina *f*	prima *f*
cousine (F)	Cousine *f*	cousin	—	cugina *f*	prima *f*
coussin (F)	Kissen *n*	cushion	—	cuscino *m*	cojín *m*
coût (F)	Kosten *pl*	expenses	—	spese *f pl*	costas *m pl*
couteau (F)	Messer *n*	knife	—	coltello *m*	cuchillo *m*

	D	E	F	I	Es
coûter (F)	kosten	cost	—	costare	costar
coûteux (F)	kostspielig	expensive	—	costoso(a)	costoso(a)
coutume (F)	Sitte *f*	custom	—	usanza *f*	costumbre *f*
couvent (F)	Kloster *n*	monastery	—	convento *m*	monasterio *m*
couvercle (F)	Deckel *m*	lid	—	coperchio *m*	tapa *f*
couvert[1] (F)	bedeckt	covered	—	coperto(a)	cubierto(a)
couvert[2] (F)	Gedeck *n*	cover	—	coperto *m*	cubierto *m*
couvert[3] (F)	bewölkt	cloudy	—	nuvoloso(a)	nublado(a)
couverture (F)	Decke *f*	blanket	—	coperta *f*	techo *m*
couvrir[1] (F)	bedecken	cover	—	coprire	cubrir
couvrir[2] (F)	zudecken	cover (up)	—	coprire	tapar
cover[1] (E)	bedecken	—	couvrir	coprire	cubrir
cover[2] (E)	beziehen	—	recouvrir	ricoprire	tapizar
cover[3] (E)	Gedeck *n*	—	couvert *m*	coperto *m*	cubierto *m*
covered (E)	bedeckt	—	couvert(e)	coperto(a)	cubierto(a)
cover (up) (E)	zudecken	—	couvrir	coprire	tapar
cow[1] (E)	Kuh *f*	—	vache *f*	mucca *f*	vaca *f*
cow[2] (E)	Rind *n*	—	bœuf *m*	manzo *m*	buey *m*
cowardly (E)	feig	—	lâche	vile	cobarde
cozza (I)	Muschel *m*	mussel	moule *f*	—	mejillón *m*
cracher (F)	spucken	spit	—	sputare	escupir
craft (E)	Handwerk *n*	—	métier *m*	artigianato *m*	artesanía *f*
craftsman (E)	Handwerker *m*	—	artisan *m*	artigiano *m*	artesano *m*
craindre[1] (F)	befürchten	fear	—	temere	temer
craindre[2] (F)	fürchten	fear	—	temere	temer
crâne (F)	Schädel *m*	skull	—	cranio *m*	cráneo *m*
cráneo (Es)	Schädel *m*	skull	crâne *m*	cranio *m*	—
cranio (I)	Schädel *m*	skull	crâne *m*	—	cráneo *m*
crash[1] (E)	abstürzen	—	faire une chute	precipitare	caer a tierra
crash[2] (E)	Absturz *m*	—	chute *f*	caduta *f*	caída *f*
cravate (F)	Krawatte *f*	tie	—	cravatta *f*	corbata *f*
cravatta (I)	Krawatte *f*	tie	cravate *f*	—	corbata *f*
crayfish (E)	Krebs *m*	—	écrevisse *f*	gambero *m*	cangrejo *m*
crayon[1] (F)	Bleistift *m*	pencil	—	matita *f*	lápiz *m*
crayon[2] (F)	Stift *m*	pencil	—	penna *f*	lápiz m
cream[1] (E)	Creme *f*	—	crème *f*	crema	crema *f*
cream[2] (E)	Sahne *f*	—	crème *f*	panna *f*	nata *f*
crear (Es)	schaffen	create	réussir à faire	creare	—
creare (I)	schaffen	create	réussir à faire	—	crear
create (E)	schaffen	—	réussir à faire	creare	crear
crecer[1] (Es)	größer werden	grow	grandir	crescere	—
crecer[2] (Es)	wachsen	grow	grandir	crescere	—
credere[1] (I)	glauben	believe	croire	—	creer
credere[2] (I)	meinen	think	penser	—	opinar
credit (E)	Kredit *m*	—	crédit *m*	credito *m*	crédito *m*
crédit (F)	Kredit *m*	credit	—	credito *m*	crédito *m*
crédito (Es)	Kredit *m*	credit	crédit *m*	credito *m*	—
credito (I)	Kredit *m*	credit	crédit *m*	—	crédito *m*

	D	E	F	I	Es
creer (Es)	glauben	believe	croire	credere	—
crema (Es)	Creme f	cream	crème f	crema	—
crema (I)	Creme f	cream	crème f	—	crema f
cremallera (Es)	Reißverschluß m	zip	fermeture éclair f	chiusura lampo f	—
Creme (D)	—	cream	crème f	crema	crema f
crème[1] (F)	Creme f	cream	—	crema	crema f
crème[2] (F)	Sahne f	cream	—	panna f	nata f
crescere[1] (I)	aufwachsen	grow up	grandir	—	criarse
crescere[2] (I)	größer werden	grow	grandir	—	crecer
crescere[3] (I)	wachsen	grow	grandir	—	crecer
creuser (F)	graben	dig	—	scavare	cavar
creux (F)	hohl	hollow	—	cavo(a)	hueco(a)
cri (F)	Schrei m	scream	—	grido m	grito m
criada (Es)	Hausmädchen n	maid	fille de service f	domestica f	—
crianza (Es)	Erziehung f	education	éducation f	educazione f	—
criar[1] (Es)	erziehen	educate	élever	educare	—
criar[2] (Es)	züchten	breed	élever	allevare	—
criarse (Es)	aufwachsen	grow up	grandir	crescere	—
crier[1] (F)	ausrufen	exclaim	—	esclamare	exclamar
crier[2] (F)	schreien	scream	—	gridare	gritar
crime[1] (E)	Untat f	—	méfait m	misfatto m	crimen m
crime[2] (E)	Verbrechen n	—	crime m	delitto m	crimen m
crime (F)	Verbrechen n	crime	—	delitto m	crimen m
crimen[1] (Es)	Untat f	crime	méfait m	misfatto m	—
crimen[2] (Es)	Verbrechen n	crime	crime m	delitto m	—
cristal (Es)	Scheibe f	pane	vitre m	vetro m	—
cristiano (I)	Christ m	Christian	chrétien m	—	cristiano m
cristiano (Es)	Christ m	Christian	chrétien m	cristiano m	—
criticar (Es)	kritisieren	criticize	critiquer	criticare	—
criticare (I)	kritisieren	criticize	critiquer	—	criticar
criticize (E)	kritisieren	—	critiquer	criticare	criticar
critiquer (F)	kritisieren	criticize	—	criticare	criticar
croce (I)	Kreuz n	cross	croix f	—	cruz f
crochet (F)	Haken m	hook	—	gancio m	gancho m
crockery (E)	Geschirr n	—	vaiselle f	stoviglie f pl	vajilla f
croire (F)	glauben	believe	—	credere	creer
croix (F)	Kreuz n	cross	—	croce f	cruz f
crollare[1] (I)	einstürzen	collapse	écrouler, se	—	derrumbarse
crollare[2] (I)	zusammenbrechen	collapse	éffondrer, se	—	desmayarse
crooked (E)	krumm	—	tordu(e)	storto(a)	torcido(a)
cross[1] (E)	Kreuz n	—	croix f	croce f	cruz f
cross[2] (E)	überqueren	—	traverser	attraversare	atravesar
crossing[1] (E)	Kreuzung f	—	intersection f	incrocio m	cruce m
crossing[2] (E)	Übergang m	—	passage m	passaggio m	paso m
crossing[3] (E)	Überfahrt f	—	traversée f	traversata f	travesía f
crowd (E)	Menschenmenge f	—	foule f	folla f	muchedumbre f
crowded (E)	überfüllt	—	bondé(e)	pieno(a) zeppo(a)	abarrotado(a)
cru (F)	roh	raw	—	crudo(a)	crudo(a)

	D	E	F	I	Es
cruce (Es)	Kreuzung *f*	crossing	intersection *f*	incrocio *m*	—
cruche (F)	Krug *m*	jug	—	brocca *f*	jarro(a) *m(f)*
crudele (I)	grausam	cruel	cruel(le)	—	cruel
crudo (I)	roh	raw	cru(e)	—	crudo(a)
crudo (Es)	roh	raw	cru(e)	crudo(a)	—
cruel (E)	grausam	—	cruel(le)	crudele	cruel
cruel (Es)	grausam	cruel	cruel(le)	crudele	—
cruel (F)	grausam	cruel	—	crudele	cruel
cruz (Es)	Kreuz *n*	cross	croix *f*	croce *f*	—
cry (E)	weinen	—	pleurer	piangere	llorar
cuaderno (Es)	Heft *n*	exercise book	cahier *m*	quaderno *m*	—
cuadrado[1] (Es)	Quadrat *n*	square	carré *m*	quadrato *m*	—
cuadrado[2] (Es)	quadratisch	square	carré(e)	quadrato(a)	—
cuadrangular (Es)	viereckig	square	carré(e)	quadrato(a)	—
cuadro[1] (Es)	Bild *n*	picture	image *f*	immagine *f*	—
cuadro[2] (Es)	Gemälde *n*	painting	tableau *m*	quadro *m*	—
¿cuál? (Es)	welche(r,s)	which	qui/que	il(la) quale	—
cualidad (Es)	Qualität *f*	quality	qualité *f*	qualità *f*	—
cualquiera[1] (Es)	irgendein(e)	some/any	quelconque	qualcuno(a)	—
cualquiera[2] (Es)	irgend	at all/some	d'une façon ou d'une autre	in qualche modo	—
cuando[1] (Es)	wenn	when/if	si/quand	se/quando	—
cuando[2] (Es)	wann	when	quand	quando	—
¿cuánto? (Es)	wieviel	how much	combien	quanto	—
¿cuántos? (Es)	wieviele	how many	combien	quanti(e)	—
cuarenta (Es)	vierzig	forty	quarante	quaranta	—
cuarteto (Es)	Quartett *n*	quartet	quatuor *m*	quartetto *m*	—
cuarto (Es)	Viertel *n*	a quarter	quart *m*	quarto *m*	—
cuarto de baño (Es)	Badezimmer *n*	bathroom	salle de bains *f*	stanza da bagno *f*	—
cuatro (Es)	vier	four	quatre	quattro	—
cubic metre (E)	Kubikmeter *m*	—	mètre cube *m*	metro cubo *m*	metro cúbico *m*
cubierta (Es)	Deck *n*	deck	pont *m*	ponte *m*	—
cubierto[1] (Es)	Gedeck *n*	cover	couvert *m*	coperto *m*	—
cubierto[2] (Es)	bedeckt	covered	couvert	coperto(a)	—
cubo (Es)	Eimer m	bucket	seau m	secchio m	—
cubo de la basura[1] (Es)	Abfalleimer *m*	bin	poubelle *f*	pattumiera *f*	—
cubo de la basura[2] (Es)	Mülleimer *m*	dustbin	poubelle *f*	secchio dei rifiuti *m*	—
cubrir (Es)	bedecken	cover	couvrir	coprire	—
cuccetta (I)	Liegewagen *m*	couchette	wagon-couchette *m*	—	coche cama *m*
cucchiaino da tè (I)	Teelöffel *m*	teaspoon	cuiller à thé *f*	—	cucharilla *f*
cucchiaio[1] (I)	Eßlöffel *m*	tablespoon	cuiller *f*	—	cuchara *f*
cucchiaio[2] (I)	Löffel *m*	spoon	cuiller *f*	—	cuchara *f*
cuchara[1] (Es)	Eßlöffel *m*	tablespoon	cuiller *f*	cucchiaio *m*	—
cuchara[2] (Es)	Löffel *m*	spoon	cuiller *f*	cucchiaio *m*	—
cucharilla (Es)	Teelöffel *m*	teaspoon	cuiller à thé *f*	cucchiaino da tè *m*	—
cuchichear (Es)	flüstern	whisper	chuchoter	bisbigliare	—

	D	E	F	I	Es
cuchilla (Es)	Klinge *f*	blade	lame *f*	lama *f*	—
cuchillo (Es)	Messer *n*	knife	couteau *m*	coltello *m*	—
cucina[1] (I)	Küche *f*	kitchen	cuisine *f*	—	cocina *f*
cucina[2] (I)	Herd *m*	cooker	fourneau *m*	—	cocina *f*
cucinare (I)	kochen	cook	cuire	—	cocinar
cucire (I)	nähen	sew	coudre	—	cocer
cucumber (E)	Gurke *f*	—	concombre *m*	cetriolo *m*	pepino *m*
cueillir (F)	pflücken	pick	—	cogliere	coger
cuello[1] (Es)	Hals *m*	neck	cou *m*	collo *m*	—
cuello[2] (Es)	Kragen *m*	collar	col *m*	colletto *m*	—
cuenta (Es)	Konto *n*	account	compte *m*	conto *m*	—
cuerda (Es)	Strick *m*	rope	corde *f*	corda *f*	—
cuero (Es)	Leder *n*	leather	cuir *m*	cuoio *m*	—
cuerpo (Es)	Körper *m*	body	corps *m*	corpo *m*	—
cuerpo de bomberos (Es)	Feuerwehr *f*	fire brigade	sapeurs pompiers *m pl*	vigili del fuoco *m pl*	—
cuervo (Es)	Rabe *m*	raven	corbeau *m*	corvo *m*	—
cuesta abajo (Es)	bergab	downhill	en descendant	in discesa	—
cuesta arriba (Es)	bergauf	uphill	en montant	in salita	—
cueva (Es)	Höhle *f*	cave	grotte *f*	caverna *f*	—
cugina (I)	Cousine *f*	cousin	cousine *f*	—	prima *f*
cugino (I)	Vetter *m*	cousin	cousin *m*	—	primo *m*
cuidado[1] (Es)	Vorsicht *f*	caution	prudence *f*	prudenza *f*	—
cuidado[2] (Es)	gepflegt	looked-after	soigné(e)	curato(a)	—
cuidadoso (Es)	sorgfältig	careful(ly)	soigneux(-euse)	accurato(a)	—
cuidar (Es)	pflegen	look after	soigner	curare	—
cuiller[1] (F)	Eßlöffel *m*	tablespoon	—	cucchiaio *m*	cuchara *f*
cuiller[2] (F)	Löffel *m*	spoon	—	cucchiaio *m*	cuchara *f*
cuiller à thé (F)	Teelöffel *m*	teaspoon	—	cucchiaino da tè *m*	cucharilla *f*
cuir (F)	Leder *n*	leather	—	cuoio *m*	cuero *m*
cuire (F)	kochen	cook	—	cucinare	cocinar
cuisine (F)	Küche *f*	kitchen	—	cucina *f*	cocina *f*
cuisinier (F)	Koch *m*	cook	—	cuoco *m*	cocinero *m*
cuisinière (F)	Köchin *f*	cook	—	cuoca *f*	cocinera *f*
cuit (F)	gar	done	—	cotto(a)	a punto
culpa (Es)	Schuld *f*	fault	culpabilité *f*	colpa *f*	—
culpabilité (F)	Schuld *f*	fault	—	colpa *f*	culpa *f*
culpable (Es)	schuldig	guilty	coupable	colpevole	—
cultivar (Es)	anbauen	cultivate	cultiver	coltivare	—
cultivate (E)	anbauen	—	cultiver	coltivare	cultivar
cultiver (F)	anbauen	cultivate	—	coltivare	cultivar
cultura (Es)	Kultur *f*	culture	culture *f*	cultura *f*	—
cultura (I)	Kultur *f*	culture	culture *f*	—	cultura *f*
culture (E)	Kultur *f*	—	culture *f*	cultura *f*	cultura *f*
culture (F)	Kultur *f*	culture	—	cultura *f*	cultura *f*
cumbre (Es)	Gipfel *m*	peak	sommet *m*	cima *f*	—
cumpleaños (Es)	Geburtstag *m*	birthday	anniversaire *m*	compleanno *m*	—
cuñada (Es)	Schwägerin *f*	sister-in-law	belle-sœur *f*	cognata *f*	—

	D	E	F	I	Es
cuñado (Es)	Schwager *m*	brother-in-law	beau-frère *m*	cognato *m*	—
cuoca (I)	Köchin *f*	cook	cuisinière *f*	—	cocinera *f*
cuocere (al forno) (I)	backen	bake	faire cuire	—	cocer (al horno)
cuoco (I)	Koch *m*	cook	cuisinier *m*	—	cocinero *m*
cuoio (I)	Leder *n*	leather	cuir *m*	—	cuero *m*
cuore (I)	Herz *n*	heart	cœur *m*	—	corazón *m*
cuota (Es)	Beitrag *m*	contribution	contribution *f*	contributo *m*	—
cup (E)	Tasse *f*	—	tasse *f*	tazza *f*	taza *f*
cupboard (E)	Schrank *m*	—	armoire *f*	armadio *m*	armario *m*
cura (Es)	Kur *f*	treatment	cure *f*	cura *f*	—
cura¹ (I)	Kur *f*	treatment	cure *f*	—	cura *f*
cura² (I)	Pflege *f*	care	soins *m pl*	—	aseo *m*
curar (Es)	heilen	heal	guérir	curare	—
curare¹ (I)	heilen	heal	guérir	—	curar
curare² (I)	pflegen	look after	soigner	—	cuidar
curato (I)	gepflegt	looked-after	soigné(e)	—	cuidado(a)
curd cheese (E)	Quark *m*	—	fromage blanc *m*	ricotta *f*	requesón *m*
cure (F)	Kur *f*	treatment	—	cura *f*	cura *f*
curé (F)	Pfarrer *m*	priest	—	parroco *m*	párroco *m*
curieux¹ (F)	merkwürdig	strange	—	curioso(a)	curioso(a)
curieux² (F)	neugierig	curious	—	curioso(a)	curioso(a)
curiosità (I)	Sehenswürdig-keit *f*	sight	curiosité *f*	—	lugares de interés *m pl*
curiosité (F)	Sehenswürdig-keit *f*	sight	—	curiosità *f*	lugares de interés *m pl*
curioso¹ (I)	merkwürdig	strange	curieux(-euse)	—	curioso(a)
curioso² (I)	neugierig	curious	curieux(-euse)	—	curioso(a)
curioso¹ (Es)	merkwürdig	strange	curieux(-euse)	strano(a)	—
curioso² (Es)	neugierig	curious	curieux(-euse)	curioso(a)	—
curious (E)	neugierig	—	curieux(-euse)	curioso(a)	curioso(a)
curl (E)	Locke *f*	—	boucle *f*	riccio *m*	rizo *m*
currant (E)	Johannisbeere *f*	—	groseille *f*	ribes *m*	grosella *f*
currency (E)	Währung *f*	—	monnaie *f*	valuta *f*	moneda *f*
current (E)	Strom *m*	—	courant *m*	corrente *f*	corriente *f*
curriculum vitae (E)	Lebenslauf *m*	—	curriculum vitae *m*	curriculum vitae *m*	curriculum vitae *m*
curriculum vitae (Es)	Lebenslauf *m*	curriculum vitae	curriculum vitae *m*	curriculum vitae *m*	—
curriculum vitae (F)	Lebenslauf *m*	curriculum vitae	—	curriculum vitae *m*	curriculum vitae *m*
curriculum vitae (I)	Lebenslauf *m*	curriculum vitae	curriculum vitae *m*	—	curriculum vitae *m*
curso (Es)	Kurs *m*	rate	cours *m*	corso *m*	—
curtain¹ (E)	Gardine *f*	—	rideau *m*	tenda *f*	cortina *f*
curtain² (E)	Vorhang *m*	—	rideau *m*	tenda *f*	cortina *f*
curva (Es)	Kurve *f*	bend	virage *m*	curva *f*	—
curva (I)	Kurve *f*	bend	virage *m*	—	curva *f*
cuscino (I)	Kissen *n*	cushion	coussin *m*	—	cojín *m*
cushion (E)	Kissen *n*	—	coussin *m*	cuscino *m*	cojín *m*
custode¹ (I)	Aufseher *m*	guard	gardien *m*	—	vigilante *m*

	D	E	F	I	Es
custode[2] (I)	Wärter m	attendant	gardien m	—	guarda m
custom[1] (E)	Gebrauch m	—	usage m	uso m	uso m
custom[2] (E)	Sitte f	—	coutume f	usanza f	costumbre f
customer (E)	Kunde m	—	client m	cliente m	cliente m
customs (E)	Zoll m	—	douane f	dogana f	aduana f
cut[1] (E)	schneiden	—	couper	tagliare	cortar
cut[2] (E)	Schnitt m	—	coupe f	taglio m	corte m
cutlet (E)	Kotelett n	—	côtelette f	costoletta f	chuleta f
cuttlefish (E)	Tintenfisch m	—	seiche f	seppia f	calamar m
Czechoslovakia (E)	Tschecho-slowakei f	—	Tchécoslovaquie f	Cecoslovacchia f	Checoslovaquia f
da (D)	—	there	là/ici	qui/là	allí
da[1] (I)	ab	off	à partir de/dès	—	a partir de/de
da[2] (I)	seit	since/for	depuis	—	de/desde
da[3] (I)	aus	off/from/out of	de/par/hors de	—	de/por
da[4] (I)	zu	to	de/à	—	para
da[5] (I)	bei	at/near	chez/près de	—	cerca de/junto a
d'abord[1] (F)	erst	first	—	dapprima	primero
d'abord[2] (F)	zuerst	at first	—	dapprima	primero
d'accord (F)	einverstanden	agreed	—	d'accordo	de acuerdo
d'accordo (I)	einverstanden	agreed	d'accord	—	de acuerdo
Dach (D)	—	roof	toit m	tetto m	techo m
dado (Es)	Würfel m	dice	dé m	dado m	—
dado (I)	Würfel m	dice	dé m	—	dado m
da dove (I)	woher	where from	d'où	—	¿de dónde?
d'affaires (F)	geschäftlich	on business	—	per affari	comercial
daft (E)	doof	—	bête	scemo(a)	estúpido(a)
dafür[1] (D)	—	for it	pour cela	per questo	para ello
dafür[2] (D)	—	instead	en échange	invece	en su lugar
dagegen (D)	—	against it	contre cela	contro	contra
daheim (D)	—	at home	à la maison	a casa	en casa
dahinter (D)	—	behind it	derrière	dietro	detrás
d'ailleurs (F)	übrigens	by the way	—	del resto	por lo demás
daily (E)	täglich	—	quotidien(ne)	quotidiano(a)	cotidiano(a)
dall'altra parte (I)	drüben	over there	de l'autre côté	—	al otro lado
d'altra parte (I)	andererseits	on the other hand	d'autre part	—	por otra parte
damage[1] (E)	beschädigen	—	endommager	danneggiare	deteriorar
damage[2] (E)	Beschädigung f	—	endommage-ment m	danno m	deterioro m
damage[3] (E)	schaden	—	nuire	nuocere	dañar
damage[4] (E)	Schaden m	—	dommage m	danno m	daño m
damals (D)	—	at that time	alors	allora	entonces
Dame (D)	—	lady	dame f	signora f	señora f
dame (F)	Dame f	lady	—	signora f	señora f
damit (D)	—	with it	avec cela	con questo	con ello
dämmern (D)	—	dawn	poindre	spuntare	amanecer
da molto (I)	längst	a long time ago	depuis bien longtemps	—	hace mucho
damp (E)	feucht	—	humide	umido(a)	húmedo(a)

	D	E	F	I	Es
Dampf (D)	—	steam	vapeur *f*	vapore *m*	vapor *m*
danach (D)	—	afterwards	après	poi/dopo	después
dañar (Es)	schaden	damage	nuire	nuocere	—
dance[1] (E)	tanzen	—	danser	ballare	bailar
dance[2] (E)	Tanz *m*	—	danse *f*	ballo *m*	baile *f*
da nessuna parte (I)	nirgends	nowhere	nulle part	—	en ninguna parte
danger (E)	Gefahr *f*	—	danger *m*	pericolo *m*	peligro *m*
danger (F)	Gefahr *f*	danger	—	pericolo *m*	peligro *m*
dangereux (F)	gefährlich	dangerous	—	pericoloso(a)	peligroso(a)
dangerous (E)	gefährlich	—	dangereux(-euse)	pericoloso(a)	peligroso(a)
Dank (D)	—	thanks	remerciement *m*	ringraziamento *m*	agradecimiento *m*
dankbar (D)	—	grateful	reconnaissant(e)	grato(a)	agradecido(a)
danke (D)	—	thank you	merci	grazie	¡gracias!
danken (D)	—	thank	remercier	ringraziare	agradecer
dann (D)	—	then	ensuite	in seguito	luego
danneggiare (I)	beschädigen	damage	endommager	—	deteriorar
danno[1] (I)	Beschädigung *f*	damage	endommage-ment *m*	—	deterioro *m*
danno[2] (I)	Schaden *m*	damage	dommage *m*	—	daño *m*
daño (Es)	Schaden *m*	damage	dommage *m*	danno *m*	—
dans[1] (F)	hinein	in	—	dentro	dentro
dans[2] (F)	in	in/into	—	in/a/tra/fra	en/a
danse (F)	Tanz *m*	dance	—	ballo *m*	baile *f*
danser (F)	tanzen	dance	—	ballare	bailar
dans l'ensemble (F)	insgesamt	altogether	—	complesivamente	en suma
da piccolo borghese (I)	spießig	bourgeois	bourgeois(e)	—	pequeño(a) burgués(-esa)
dappertutto (I)	überall	everywhere	partout	—	por todas partes
dapprima[1] (I)	erst	first	d'abord	—	primero
dapprima[2] (I)	zunächst	first of all	pour l'instant	—	en primer lugar
dapprima[3] (I)	zuerst	at first	d'abord	—	primero
da questa parte (I)	herüber	over	par ici	—	a este lado
darauf (D)	—	afterwards/on it	dessus/ensuite	dopo/su	después/encima
dare (E)	wagen	—	oser	osare	atreverse
dare (I)	geben	give	donner	—	dar
dare del tu (I)	duzen	use the familiar form	tutoyer	—	tutear
dare in prestito (I)	ausleihen	lend	prêter	—	prestar
dare le dimissioni (I)	zurücktreten	retire	démissionner	—	dimitir
dare nell'occhio (I)	auffallen	be noticeable	faire remarquer, se	—	llamar la atención por algo
d'argent (F)	silbern	silver	—	d'argento	plateado(a)
dar gritos de alegría (Es)	jubeln	rejoice	pousser des cris de joie	giubilare	—
d'argento (I)	silbern	silver	d'argent	—	plateado(a)
dark[1] (E)	dunkel	—	sombre	scuro(a)	oscuro(a)
dark[2] (E)	finster	—	sombre	buio(a)	oscuro(a)
darkness (E)	Finsternis *f*	—	obscurité *f*	buio *m*	oscuridad *f*
darling (E)	Liebling *m*	—	chéri *m*	tesoro *m*	querido *m*
Darm (D)	—	intestine	intestin *m*	intestino *m*	intestino *m*

	D	E	F	I	Es
darse cuenta (Es)	bemerken	notice	remarquer	notare	—
darse prisa[1] (Es)	beeilen, sich	hurry up	dépêcher, se	affrettarsi	—
darse prisa[2] (Es)	eilen	hurry	dépêcher, se	andare in fretta	—
darsi appuntamento (I)	verabreden	arrange to meet	prendre rendez-vous	—	concertar una cita
darstellen (D)	—	represent	représenter	rappresentare	representar
darüber (D)	—	above	au dessus	sopra	por encima
darunter (D)	—	underneath	au dessous	sotto	por debajo
dar vuelta (Es)	herumdrehen	turn around	tourner	girare	—
das (D)	—	that/which	le/la	il/la	lo
Dasein (D)	—	existence	existence *f*	esistenza *f*	existencia *f*
daß (D)	—	that	que	che	que
dasselbe (D)	—	the same	la même chose	lo stesso	lo mismo
data (I)	Datum *n*	date	date *f*	—	fecha *f*
date[1] (E)	Datum *n*	—	date *f*	data *f*	fecha *f*
date[2] (E)	Termin *m*	—	terme *m*	termine *m*	fecha *f*
date[3] (E)	Verabredung *f*	—	rendez-vous *m*	appuntamento *m*	cita *f*
date (F)	Datum *n*	date	—	data *f*	fecha *f*
dated (E)	altertümlich	—	antique	antico(a)	antiguo(a)
Datum (D)	—	date	date *f*	data *f*	fecha *f*
Dauer (D)	—	duration	durée *f*	durata *f*	duración *f*
dauern (D)	—	last	durer	durare	durar
daughter (E)	Tochter *f*	—	fille *f*	figlia *f*	hija *f*
Daumen (D)	—	thumb	pouce *m*	pollice *m*	pulgar *m*
da un lato (I)	einerseits	on one hand	d'une part	—	por un lado
d'autre part (F)	andererseits	on the other hand	—	d'altra parte	por otra parte
davanti (I)	vorn(e)	at the front	devant	—	delante
davanti a (I)	vor	before/ in front of	devant/avant	—	delante de
davon (D)	—	of it	en/de cela	di la/ne	de ello
dawn (E)	dämmern	—	poindre	spuntare	amanecer
day (E)	Tag *m*	—	jour *m*	giorno *m*	día *m*
day after tomorrow (E)	übermorgen	—	après-demain	dopodomani	pasado mañana
day before yesterday (E)	vorgestern	—	avant-hier	l'altro ieri	anteayer
dazio (I)	Zoll *m*	duty	droits de douane *m pl*	—	arbitrio *m*
dazwischen (D)	—	inbetween	entre	in mezzo	entre
de[1] (Es)	aus	off/from/out of	de/par/hors de	da/di	—
de[2] (Es)	seit	since/for	depuis	da	—
de[3] (Es)	von	from/by	de	di/da	—
de[1] (F)	aus	off/from/out of	—	da/di	de/por
de[2] (F)	von	from/by	—	di/da	de
de[3] (F)	zu	to	—	da/di/a	para
dé (F)	Würfel *m*	dice	—	dado *m*	dado *m*
de acuerdo (Es)	einverstanden	agreed	d'accord	d'accordo	—
dead (E)	tot	—	mort(e)	morto(a)	muerto(a)
deaf (E)	taub	—	sourd(e)	sordo(a)	sordo(a)
dealer (E)	Händler *m*	—	commerçant *m*	commerciante *m*	comerciante *m*

	D	E	F	I	Es
de alguna manera (Es)	irgendwie	somehow	n'importe comment	in qualche modo	—
death (E)	Tod *m*	—	mort *f*	morte *f*	muerte *f*
debajo de (Es)	unter	under	sous	al di sotto di	—
deber[1] (Es)	müssen	have to	devoir	dovere	—
deber[2] (Es)	sollen	have to	devoir	dovere	—
deber[3] (Es)	schulden	owe	devoir qch à qn	dovere	—
débil (Es)	schwach	weak	faible	debole	—
debilidad (Es)	Schwäche *f*	weakness	faiblesse *f*	debolezza *f*	—
debiti (I)	Schulden *pl*	debt	dette *f*	—	deudas *f pl*
debole (I)	schwach	weak	faible	—	débil
debolezza (I)	Schwäche *f*	weakness	faiblesse *f*	—	debilidad *f*
debt (E)	Schulden *pl*	—	dette *f*	debiti *m pl*	deudas *f pl*
débutant (F)	Anfänger *m*	beginner	—	principiante *m*	principante *m*
de camino (Es)	unterwegs	on the way	en route	per strada	—
deceive (E)	täuschen	—	tromper	ingannare	engañar
December (E)	Dezember *m*	—	décembre *m*	dicembre *m*	diciembre *m*
décembre (F)	Dezember *m*	December	—	dicembre *m*	diciembre *m*
decent (E)	anständig	—	convenable	decente	decente
decente (Es)	anständig	decent	convenable	decente	—
decente (I)	anständig	decent	convenable	—	decente
décevoir (F)	enttäuschen	disappoint	—	deludere	defraudar
décharger[1] (F)	ausladen	unload	—	scaricare	descargar
décharger[2] (F)	abladen	unload	—	scaricare	descargar
déchets (F)	Abfall *m*	rubbish	—	immondizia *f*	basura *f*
déchirer (F)	zerreißen	rip	—	strappare	romper
déchirer, se (F)	reißen	tear	—	strappare	desgarrarse
decide[1] (E)	beschließen	—	décider	decidere	decidir
decide[2] (E)	entschließen, sich	—	décider, se	decidere	decidirse
decide[3] (E)	entscheiden	—	décider	decidere	decidir
décider[1] (F)	beschließen	decide	—	decidere	decidir
décider[2] (F)	entscheiden	decide	—	decidere	decidir
décider, se (F)	entschließen, sich	decide	—	decidere	decidirse
decidere[1] (I)	beschließen	decide	décider	—	decidir
decidere[2] (I)	entschließen, sich	decide	décider, se	—	decidirse
decidere[3] (I)	entscheiden	decide	décider	—	decidir
decidir[1] (Es)	beschließen	decide	décider	decidere	—
decidir[2] (Es)	entscheiden	decide	décider	decidere	—
decidirse (Es)	entschließen, sich	decide	décider, se	decidere	—
decir (Es)	sagen	say	dire	dire	—
decision[1] (E)	Entschluß *m*	—	décision *f*	decisione *f*	decisión *f*
decision[2] (E)	Entscheidung *f*	—	décision *f*	decisione *f*	decisión *f*
decisión[1] (Es)	Entschluß *m*	decision	décision *f*	decisione *f*	—
decisión[2] (Es)	Entscheidung *f*	decision	décision *f*	decisione *f*	—
décision[1] (F)	Entschluß *m*	decision	—	decisione *f*	decisión *f*
décision[2] (F)	Entscheidung *f*	decision	—	decisione *f*	decisión *f*
decisione[1] (I)	Entschluß *m*	decision	décision *f*	—	decisión *f*

defective

	D	E	F	I	Es
decisione² (I)	Entscheidung f	decision	décision f	—	decisión f
Deck (D)	—	deck	pont m	ponte m	cubierta f
deck (E)	Deck n	—	pont m	ponte m	cubierta f
deck chair (E)	Liegestuhl m	—	chaise longue f	sedia a sdraio f	tumbona f
Decke (D)	—	blanket	couverture f	coperta f	techo m
Deckel (D)	—	lid	couvercle m	coperchio m	tapa f
declarar¹ (Es)	behaupten	assert	affirmer	affermare	—
declarar² (Es)	melden	report	annoncer	annunciare	—
declarar en la aduana (Es)	verzollen	declare	dédouaner	sdoganare	—
déclaration (F)	Aussage f	statement	—	dichiarazione f	afirmación f
declare (E)	verzollen	—	dédouaner	sdoganare	declarar en la aduana
décollage (F)	Abflug m	take-off	—	decollo m	despegue m
de colores¹ (Es)	bunt	coloured	coloré(e)	variopinto(a)	—
de colores² (Es)	farbig	colourful	coloré(e)	colorato(a)	—
decollo (I)	Abflug m	take-off	décollage m	—	despegue m
de color lila (Es)	lila	purple	mauve	lilla	—
de color rosa (Es)	rosa	pink	rose	rosa	—
décombres (F)	Trümmer pl	ruins	—	macerie f pl	escombros m pl
décommander (F)	abbestellen	cancel	—	annullare	anular el pedido de
de confianza (Es)	zuverlässig	reliable	sûr(e)	affidabile	—
de congé (F)	schulfrei	holiday	—	vacanza f	sin colegio
déconseiller (F)	abraten	warn	—	sconsigliare	desaconsejar
decorate (E)	garnieren	—	garnir	guarnire	guarnecer
decoration (E)	Orden m	—	décoration f	decorazione f	condecoración f
décoration (F)	Orden m	decoration	—	decorazione f	condecoración f
decorazione (I)	Orden m	decoration	décoration f	—	condecoración f
découvrir (F)	entdecken	discover	—	scoprire	descubrir
décrire (F)	beschreiben	describe	—	descrivere	describir
décrocher (F)	abnehmen	take away	—	staccare	descolgar
déçu (F)	enttäuscht	disappointed	—	deluso(a)	defraudado(a)
dedicar (Es)	widmen	dedicate	dédier	dedicare	—
dedicare (I)	widmen	dedicate	dédier	—	dedicar
dedicate (E)	widmen	—	dédier	dedicare	dedicar
dédier (F)	widmen	dedicate	—	dedicare	dedicar
dedo (Es)	Finger m	finger	doigt m	dito m	—
dedo del pie (Es)	Zehe f	toe	doigt de pied m	dito del piede m	—
de dónde (Es)	woher	where from	d'où	da dove	—
dédouaner (F)	verzollen	declare	—	sdoganare	declarar en la aduana
deed (E)	Tat f	—	action f	azione f	acción f
de ello (Es)	davon	of it	en/de cela	di la/ne	—
deep (E)	tief	—	profond(e)	profondo(a)	profundo(a)
deer (E)	Reh n	—	chevreuil m	capriolo m	corzo m
défaire (F)	auspacken	unpack	—	disfare	deshacer
défaite (F)	Niederlage f	defeat	—	sconfitta f	derrota f
defeat (E)	Niederlage f	—	défaite f	sconfitta f	derrota f
defective (E)	defekt	—	défectueux(-euse)	guasto(a)	defectuoso(a)

	D	E	F	I	Es
défectueux (F)	defekt	defective	—	guasto(a)	defectuoso(a)
defectuoso (Es)	defekt	defective	défectueux(-euse)	guasto(a)	—
defekt (D)	—	defective	défectueux(-euse)	guasto(a)	defectuoso(a)
defence (E)	Verteidigung *f*	—	défense *f*	difesa *f*	defensa *f*
defend[1] (E)	verteidigen	—	défendre	difendere	defender
defend[2] (E)	wehren, sich	—	défendre, se	difendersi	defenderse
defender (Es)	verteidigen	defend	défendre	difendere	—
defenderse (Es)	wehren, sich	defend	défendre, se	difendersi	—
défendre[1] (F)	verteidigen	defend	—	difendere	defender
défendre[2] (F)	verbieten	forbid	—	proibire	prohibir
défendre, se (F)	wehren, sich	defend	—	difendersi	defenderse
defensa (Es)	Verteidigung *f*	defence	défense *f*	difesa *f*	—
défense[1] (F)	Verteidigung *f*	defence	—	difesa *f*	defensa *f*
défense[2] (F)	Verbot *n*	prohibition	—	divieto *m*	prohibición *f*
défense de stationner (F)	Parkverbot *n*	no parking	—	divieto di parcheggio *m*	estacionamiento prohibido *m*
definitely (E)	bestimmt	—	certainement	certamente	ciertamente
defraudado (Es)	enttäuscht	disappointed	déçu(e)	deluso(a)	—
defraudar (Es)	enttäuschen	disappoint	décevoir	deludere	—
dégoutter (F)	tropfen	drip	—	gocciolare	gotear
degré (F)	Grad *m*	degree	—	grado *m*	grado *m*
degree (E)	Grad *m*	—	degré *m*	grado *m*	grado *m*
dehors[1] (F)	draußen	outside	—	fuori	afuera
dehors[2] (F)	heraus	out	—	fuori	hacia afuera
dehors[3] (F)	hinaus	out	—	fuori	hacia afuera
deinetwegen (D)	—	for your sake	pour toi	per te	por ti
déjà (F)	bereits	already	—	già	ya
dejar[1] (Es)	hinterlassen	leave	laisser	lasciare	—
dejar[2] (Es)	lassen	let	laisser	lasciare	—
dejar[3] (Es)	übriglassen	leave	laisser	lasciare	—
dejar[4] (Es)	verlassen	leave	abandonner	lasciare	—
dejar libre (Es)	loslassen	let go of	lâcher	mollare	—
déjeuner (F)	Mittagessen *n*	lunch	—	pranzo *m*	comida *f*
delante[1] (Es)	hervor	forth	au-dehors	fuori	—
delante[2] (Es)	voraus	ahead	en avant	avanti	—
delante[3] (Es)	vorn(e)	at the front	devant	davanti	—
delante de (Es)	vor	before/ in front of	devant/avant	davanti a	—
de l'autre côté[1] (F)	drüben	over there	—	dall'altra parte	al otro lado
de l'autre côté[2] (F)	hinüber	across	—	di là	hacia el otro lado
de l'autre côté[3] (F)	jenseits	beyond	—	al di là	al otro lado
delay (E)	Verspätung *f*	—	retard *m*	ritardo *m*	retraso *m*
delega (I)	Vollmacht *f*	authority	procuration *f*	—	poder *m*
deleite (Es)	Genuß *m*	pleasure	plaisir *m*	piacere *m*	—
deletrear (Es)	buchstabieren	spell	épeler	sillabare	—
delgado[1] (Es)	dünn	thin	mince	magro(a)	—
delgado[2] (Es)	mager	skinny	maigre	magro(a)	—
delgado[3] (Es)	schlank	slim	mince	snello(a)	—
deliberate (E)	bewußt	—	délibéré(e)	intenzionale	intencionado(a)

	D	E	F	I	Es
délibéré (F)	bewußt	deliberate	—	intenzionale	intencionado(a)
delicious (E)	köstlich	—	savoureux (-euse)	squisito(a)	exquisito(a)
délier (F)	losbinden	free	—	sciogliere	desatar
delight (E)	Lust f	—	plaisir m	piacere m	ganas f pl
delighted[1] (E)	erfreut	—	réjoui(e)	lieto(a)	contento(a)
delighted[2] (E)	entzückt	—	ravi(e)	affascinato(a)	encantado(a)
delightful (E)	entzückend	—	ravissant(e)	affascinante	encantador(a)
delitto (I)	Verbrechen n	crime	crime m	—	crimen m
deliver[1] (E)	liefern	—	livrer	fornire	suministrar
deliver[2] (E)	überbringen	—	remettre	portare	transmitir
delivery (E)	Lieferung f	—	livraison f	fornitura f	suministro m
del norte (Es)	nördlich	northern	du nord	a nord	—
de l'ouest (F)	westlich	western	—	ad ovest	del oeste
del resto (I)	übrigens	by the way	d'ailleurs	—	por lo demás
deludere (I)	enttäuschen	disappoint	décevoir	—	defraudar
de lujo (Es)	luxuriös	luxurious	luxueux(-euse)	lussuoso(a)	—
deluso (I)	enttäuscht	disappointed	déçu(e)	—	defraudado(a)
demain (F)	morgen	tomorrow	—	domani	mañana
de mala gana (Es)	ungern	reluctantly	de mauvaise grâce	malvolentieri	—
demand[1] (E)	fordern	—	exiger	esigere	exigir
demand[2] (E)	Forderung f	—	exigence f	esigenza f	exigencia f
demand[3] (E)	Nachfrage f	—	demande f	domanda f	demanda f
demand[4] (E)	verlangen	—	demander	richiedere	exigir
demanda (Es)	Nachfrage f	demand	demande f	domanda f	—
demande[1] (F)	Antrag m	application	—	domanda f	solicitud f
demande[2] (F)	Bitte f	request	—	domanda f	ruego m
demande[3] (F)	Nachfrage f	demand	—	domanda f	demanda f
demander[1] (F)	anfordern	request	—	esigere	pedir
demander[2] (F)	bitten	request	—	pregare	rogar
demander[3] (F)	fragen	ask	—	domandare	preguntar
demander[4] (F)	verlangen	demand	—	richiedere	exigir
démanger (F)	jucken	itch	—	prudere	picar
démarrer (F)	starten	start	—	partire	partir
demasiado (Es)	zuviel	too much	trop	troppo	—
demasiado poco (Es)	zuwenig	too little	trop peu	troppo poco	—
demasiados (Es)	zuviele	too many	trop	troppi(e)	—
de mauvaise grâce (F)	ungern	reluctantly	—	malvolentieri	de mala gana
de memoria (Es)	auswendig	by heart	par cœur	a memoria	—
déménagement (F)	Umzug m	move	—	trasloco m	mudanza f
déménager[1] (F)	ausziehen	move out	—	sloggiare	mudarse
déménager[2] (F)	umziehen	move	—	cambiare casa	cambiar
démentir (F)	widerrufen	retract	—	revocare	revocación f
demi (F)	halb	half	—	mezzo(a)	medio(a)
demi-pension (F)	Halbpension f	half board	—	mezza pensione f	media pensión f
démissionner (F)	zurücktreten	retire	—	dare le dimissioni	dimitir
demnächst (D)	—	shortly	prochainement	presto	próximamente

	D	E	F	I	Es
democracia (Es)	Demokratie *f*	democracy	démocratie *f*	democrazia *f*	—
democracy (E)	Demokratie *f*	—	démocratie *f*	democrazia *f*	democracia *f*
démocratie (F)	Demokratie *f*	democracy	—	democrazia *f*	democracia *f*
democrazia (I)	Demokratie *f*	democracy	démocratie *f*	—	democracia *f*
démodé (F)	altmodisch	old-fashioned	—	fuori moda	pasado(a) de moda
Demokratie (D)	—	democracy	démocratie *f*	democrazia *f*	democracia *f*
Demonstration (D)	—	demonstration	manifestation *f*	manifestazione *f*	manifestación *f*
demonstration (E)	Demonstration *f*	—	manifestation *f*	manifestazione *f*	manifestación *f*
demostración (Es)	Demonstration *f*	demonstration	manifestation *f*	manifestazione *f*	—
denaro (I)	Geld *n*	money	argent *m*	—	dinero *m*
denaro per le piccole spese (I)	Taschengeld *n*	pocket money	argent de poche *f*	—	dinero de bolsillo *m*
denken (D)	—	think	penser	pensare	pensar
Denkmal (D)	—	monument	monument *m*	monumento *m*	monumento *m*
denn (D)	—	for/than	car	perchè	pues/porque
dennoch (D)	—	nevertheless	cependant	tuttavia	sin embargo
dénonciation (F)	Anzeige *f*	denunciation	—	denuncia *f*	denuncia *f*
de nos jours (F)	heutzutage	nowadays	—	oggigiorno	hoy en día
dénouer (F)	auflösen	dissolve	—	sciogliere	deshacer
de nouveau (F)	wieder	again	—	di nuovo	de nuevo
dense (E)	dicht	—	épais(se)	denso(a)	espeso(a)
denso (I)	dicht	dense	épais(se)	—	espeso(a)
dent (F)	Zahn *m*	tooth	—	dente *m*	diente *m*
dentadura (Es)	Gebiß *n*	teeth	dents *f pl*	denti *m pl*	—
dente (I)	Zahn *m*	tooth	dent *f*	—	diente *m*
denti (I)	Gebiß *n*	teeth	dents *f pl*	—	dentadura *f*
dentifrice (F)	Zahnpasta *f*	toothpaste	—	dentifricio *m*	pasta dentífrica *f*
dentifricio (I)	Zahnpasta *f*	toothpaste	dentifrice *m*	—	pasta dentífrica *f*
dentist (E)	Zahnarzt *m*	—	dentiste *m*	dentista *m*	dentista *m*
dentista (Es)	Zahnarzt *m*	dentist	dentiste *m*	dentista *m*	—
dentista (I)	Zahnarzt *m*	dentist	dentiste *m*	—	dentista *m*
dentiste (F)	Zahnarzt *m*	dentist	—	dentista *m*	dentista *m*
dentro¹ (Es)	hinein	in	dans	dentro	—
dentro² (Es)	innen	inside	à l'intérieur	dentro	—
dentro¹ (I)	hinein	in	dans	—	dentro
dentro² (I)	herein	in	vers l'intérieur	—	adentro
dentro³ (I)	innen	inside	à l'intérieur	—	dentro
dentro de (Es)	innerhalb	within	à l'intérieur de	entro	—
dents (F)	Gebiß *n*	teeth	—	denti *m pl*	dentadura *f*
de nuevo (Es)	wieder	again	de nouveau	di nuovo	—
de nuit (F)	nachts	at nighttime	—	di notte	por la noche
denuncia (Es)	Anzeige *f*	denunciation	dénonciation *f*	denuncia *f*	—
denuncia (I)	Anzeige *f*	denunciation	dénonciation *f*	—	denuncia *f*
denunciation (E)	Anzeige *f*	—	dénonciation *f*	denuncia *f*	denuncia *f*
deny (E)	leugnen	—	nier	negare	negar
de oro (Es)	golden	golden	d'or	d'oro	—
dépanneuse (F)	Abschlepp-wagen *m*	breakdown van	—	carro attrezzi *m*	camión grúa *m*
depart (E)	abfahren	—	partir (de)	partire	salir

	D	E	F	I	Es
départ¹ (F)	Abreise f	departure	—	partenza f	salida f
départ² (F)	Ausreise f	departure	—	partenza f	salida f
départ³ (F)	Abfahrt f	departure	—	partenza f	salida f
départ⁴ (F)	Start m	start	—	partenza f	partida f
departamento (Es)	Abteilung f	department	section f	reparto m	—
department (E)	Abteilung f	—	section f	reparto m	departamento m
department store (E)	Kaufhaus n	—	grand magasin m	grande magazzino m	grandes almacenes m pl
departure¹ (E)	Ausreise f	—	départ m	partenza f	salida f
departure² (E)	Abfahrt f	—	départ m	partenza f	salida f
departure³ (E)	Abreise f	—	départ m	partenza f	salida f
dépêcher, se¹ (F)	beeilen, sich	hurry up	—	affrettarsi	darse prisa
dépêcher, se² (F)	eilen	hurry	—	andare in fretta	darse prisa
depend (E)	abhängen	—	dépendre	dipendere	depender
depender (Es)	abhängen	depend	dépendre	dipendere	—
dépendre (F)	abhängen	depend	—	dipendere	depender
déplacer (F)	rücken	move	—	muovere	mover
dépliant (I)	Prospekt m	brochure	prospectus m	—	prospecto m
deplorare (I)	bedauern	regret	regretter	—	lamentar
deplore (E)	beklagen	—	plaindre de, se	lamentare	quejarse
deporte (Es)	Sport m	sport	sport m	sport m	—
déposer (F)	hinterlegen	deposit	—	depositare	depositar
deposit¹ (E)	Anzahlung f	—	acompte m	acconto m	primer pago m
deposit² (E)	hinterlegen	—	déposer	depositare	depositar
depositar (Es)	hinterlegen	deposit	déposer	depositare	—
depositare (I)	hinterlegen	deposit	déposer	—	depositar
depth (E)	Tiefe f	—	profondeur f	profondità f	profundidad f
depuis (F)	seit	since/for	—	da	de/desde
depuis bien longtemps (F)	längst	a long time ago	—	da molto	hace mucho
de qui (F)	wessen	whose	—	di chi	¿de quién?
de quién (Es)	wessen	whose	de qui	di chi	—
der, die, das (D)	—	the	le, la	il, la	el, la, lo
déranger (F)	stören	disturb	—	disturbare	molestar
derecho¹ (Es)	Jura	law	droit m	giurisprudenza f	—
derecho² (Es)	Recht n	right	droit m	diritto m	—
derecho³ (Es)	aufrecht	upright	droit(e)	diritto(a)	—
derecho⁴ (Es)	gerade	straight	droit(e)	diritto(a)	—
de repente (Es)	plötzlich	suddenly	tout à coup	di colpo	—
de retour (F)	zurück	back	—	indietro	atrás
deridere (I)	auslachen	laugh at	rire de qn	—	reírse de
dernier¹ (F)	vergangene(r,s)	past	—	passato(a)	pasada(o)
dernier² (F)	letzte(r,s)	last	—	ultimo(a)	último(a)
derribar (Es)	umschmeißen	throw over	renverser	rovesciare	—
derrière¹ (F)	dahinter	behind it	—	dietro	detrás
derrière² (F)	hinten	behind	—	dietro	detrás
derrota (Es)	Niederlage f	defeat	défaite f	sconfitta f	—
derrumbarse (Es)	einstürzen	collapse	écrouler, se	crollare	—
derselbe (D)	—	the same	le même	lo stesso	el mismo

	D	E	F	I	Es
desaconsejar (Es)	abraten	warn	déconseiller	sconsigliare	—
desacostumbrado (Es)	ungewöhnlich	unusual	exceptionnel(le)	insolito(a)	—
desagradable[1] (Es)	lästig	troublesome	importun(e)	molesto(a)	—
desagradable[2] (Es)	peinlich	embarrassing	gênant(e)	imbarazzante	—
desagradable[3] (Es)	unangenehm	unpleasant	désagréable	spiacevole	—
desagradecido (Es)	undankbar	ungrateful	ingrat(e)	ingrato(a)	—
désagréable[1] (F)	ungemütlich	uncomfortable	—	poco accogliente	incómodo(a)
désagréable[2] (F)	unangenehm	unpleasant	—	spiacevole	desagradable
desaparecer (Es)	verschwinden	disappear	disparaître	sparire	—
désapprouver (F)	mißbilligen	disapprove	—	disapprovare	desaprobar
desaprobar (Es)	mißbilligen	disapprove	désapprouver	disapprovare	—
desarmar (Es)	abrüsten	disarm	désarmer	disarmare	—
désarmer (F)	abrüsten	disarm	—	disarmare	desarmar
desarrollar (Es)	entwickeln	develop	développer	sviluppare	—
desarrollo (Es)	Entwicklung f	development	développement m	sviluppo m	—
desatar[1] (Es)	losbinden	free	délier	sciogliere	—
desatar[2] (Es)	lösen	solve	résoudre	sciogliere	—
désavantage (F)	Nachteil m	disadvantage	—	svantaggio m	desventaja f
désavantager (F)	benachteiligen	disadvantage	—	svantaggiare	perjudicar
desayuno (Es)	Frühstück n	breakfast	petit-déjeuner m	colazione f	—
descansar[1] (Es)	ausruhen	rest	reposer, se	riposare	—
descansar[2] (Es)	ruhen	rest	reposer, se	riposare	—
descanso[1] (Es)	Erholung f	recovery	repos m	riposo m	—
descanso[2] (Es)	Ruhestand m	retirement	retraite f	pensione f	—
descargar[1] (Es)	ausladen	unload	décharger	scaricare	—
descargar[2] (Es)	abladen	unload	décharger	scaricare	—
descend (E)	hinuntergehen	—	descendre	scendere	bajar
descender[1] (Es)	absteigen	dismount	descendre	scendere	—
descender[2] (Es)	abstammen	be descended	descendre	discendere	—
descendre[1] (F)	aussteigen	get off	—	scendere	bajar
descendre[2] (F)	abstammen	be descended	—	discendere	descender
descendre[3] (F)	absteigen	dismount	—	scendere	descender
descendre[4] (F)	hinuntergehen	descend	—	scendere	bajar
descolgar (Es)	abnehmen	take away	décrocher	staccare	—
desconectar[1] (Es)	abschalten	switch off	éteindre	spegnere	—
desconectar[2] (Es)	ausschalten	switch off	arrêter	spegnere	—
desconectar[3] (Es)	abstellen	turn off	arrêter	spegnere	—
desconfianza (Es)	Mißtrauen n	distrust	méfiance f	sfiducia f	—
desconfiar (Es)	mißtrauen	mistrust	méfier, se	non fidarsi	—
desconocido (Es)	unbekannt	unknown	inconnu(e)	sconosciuto(a)	—
descontento (Es)	unzufrieden	dissatisfied	mécontent(e)	scontento(a)	—
descortés[1] (Es)	unhöflich	impolite	impoli(e)	scortese	—
descortés[2] (Es)	unfreundlich	unfriendly	peu aimable	sgarbato(a)	—
describe (E)	beschreiben	—	décrire	descrivere	describir
describir (Es)	beschreiben	describe	décrire	descrivere	—
descrivere (I)	beschreiben	describe	décrire	—	describir
descubrir (Es)	entdecken	discover	découvrir	scoprire	—

	D	E	F	I	Es
descuidado (Es)	unvorsichtig	careless	imprudent(e)	imprudente	—
descuidar (Es)	vernachlässigen	neglect	négliger	trascurare	—
desear (Es)	wünschen	wish	souhaiter	desiderare	—
desembocadura (Es)	Mündung f	mouth	embouchure f	sbocco m	—
desempleado (Es)	arbeitslos	unemployed	en chômage	disoccupato(a)	—
desempleo (Es)	Arbeitslosigkeit f	unemployment	chômage m	disoccupazione f	—
deseo (Es)	Wunsch m	wish	souhait m	desiderio m	—
desert (E)	Wüste f	—	désert m	deserto m	desierto m
désert[1] (F)	öde	waste	—	deserto(a)	desierto(a)
désert[2] (F)	Wüste f	desert	—	deserto m	desierto m
desert (I)	Nachtisch m	dessert	dessert m	—	postre m
deserto[1] (I)	öde	waste	désert(e)	—	desierto(a)
deserto[2] (I)	Wüste f	desert	désert m	—	desierto m
desesperado (Es)	verzweifelt	desperate	désespéré(e)	disperato(a)	—
désespéré (F)	verzweifelt	desperate	—	disperato(a)	desesperado(a)
desgarrarse (Es)	reißen	tear	déchirer, se	strappare	—
desgastar (Es)	abnutzen	wear out	user	consumare	—
desgracia (Es)	Unglück n	misfortune	malheur m	disgrazia f	—
desgraciadamente (Es)	leider	unfortunately	malheureusement	purtroppo	—
desgraciado (Es)	unglücklich	unhappy	malheureux (-euse)	sfortunato(a)	—
deshacer[1] (Es)	auspacken	unpack	défaire	disfare	—
deshacer[2] (Es)	auflösen	dissolve	dénouer	sciogliere	—
deshalb (D)	—	therefore	c'est pourquoi	perció	por eso
deshelar (Es)	tauen	thaw	fondre	sciogliersi	—
deshonra (Es)	Schande f	disgrace	honte f	vergogna f	—
desiderare (I)	wünschen	wish	souhaiter	—	desear
desiderio (I)	Wunsch m	wish	souhait m	—	deseo m
desierto[1] (Es)	Wüste f	desert	désert m	deserto m	—
desierto[2] (Es)	öde	waste	désert(e)	deserto(a)	—
desmayarse (Es)	zusammenbrechen	collapse	s'éffondrer	crollare	—
desmayo (Es)	Ohnmacht f	faint	évanouissement m	svenimento m	—
desnudo (Es)	nackt	naked	nu(e)	nudo(a)	—
desocupado (Es)	unbesetzt	unoccupied	vacant(e)	libero(a)	—
desorden (Es)	Unordnung f	mess	désordre m	disordine m	—
desordenado (Es)	unordentlich	untidy	désordonné(e)	disordinato(a)	—
désordonné (F)	unordentlich	untidy	—	disordinato(a)	desordenado(a)
désordre[1] (F)	Durcheinander n	confusion	—	confusione f	confusión f
désordre[2] (F)	Unordnung f	mess	—	disordine m	desorden m
despacio (Es)	langsam	slow	lent(e)	lento(a)	—
despedida (Es)	Abschied m	parting	adieux m pl	addio m	—
despedir[1] (Es)	entlassen	release	renvoyer	licenziare	—
despedir[2] (Es)	kündigen	sack	résilier	licenziare	—
despedir[3] (Es)	verabschieden	say goodbye to	prendre congé de	congedare	—
despegue (Es)	Abflug m	take-off	décollage m	decollo m	—
desperate (E)	verzweifelt	—	désespéré(e)	disperato(a)	desesperado(a)
desperdiciar (Es)	verschwenden	waste	gaspiller	sprecare	—
despertador (Es)	Wecker m	alarm clock	réveil m	sveglia f	—

	D	E	F	I	Es
despertar¹ (Es)	aufwecken	wake up	réveiller	svegliare	—
despertar² (Es)	erwachen	wake up	réveiller, se	svegliarsi	—
despertar³ (Es)	wecken	wake (up)	réveiller	svegliare	—
despertarse (Es)	aufwachen	wake up	réveiller, se	svegliarsi	—
despierto (Es)	wach	awake	réveillé(e)	sveglio(a)	—
despite (E)	trotz	—	malgré	nonostante	a pesar de
después¹ (Es)	danach	afterwards	après	poi/dopo	—
después² (Es)	darauf	afterwards	dessus/ensuite	dopo	—
después³ (Es)	nachher	afterwards	ensuite	dopo	—
después que (Es)	nachdem	after	après que	dopo que (di)	—
dès que (F)	sobald	as soon as	—	appena	tan pronto como
desserré (F)	locker	loose	—	lento(a)	flojo(a)
dessert (E)	Nachtisch m	—	dessert m	desert m	postre m
dessert (F)	Nachtisch m	dessert	—	desert m	postre m
dessin (F)	Zeichnung f	drawing	—	disegno m	dibujo m
dessiner (F)	zeichnen	draw	—	disegnare	dibujar
dessous (F)	unten	downstairs	—	sotto/giù	abajo
dessus (F)	darauf	afterwards/on it	—	dopo/su	encima
d'est (F)	östlich	eastern	—	ad est	al este
destin (F)	Schicksal n	fate	—	destino m	destino m
destinataire (F)	Empfänger m	receiver	—	destinatario m	destinatario m
destinatario (Es)	Empfänger m	receiver	destinataire f	destinatario m	—
destinatario (I)	Empfänger m	receiver	destinataire f	—	destinatario m
destino (Es)	Schicksal n	fate	destin m	destino m	—
destino (I)	Schicksal n	fate	destin m	—	destino m
destornillador (Es)	Schrauben-zieher m	screwdriver	tournevis m	cacciavite m	—
destroy¹ (E)	vernichten	—	détruire	distruggere	destruir
destroy² (E)	zerstören	—	détruire	distruggere	destruir
destruir¹ (Es)	vernichten	destroy	détruire	distruggere	—
destruir² (Es)	zerstören	destroy	détruire	distruggere	—
desvalijar (Es)	plündern	loot	piller	saccheggiare	—
desventaja (Es)	Nachteil m	disadvantage	désavantage m	svantaggio m	—
desviación (Es)	Umleitung f	diversion	déviation f	deviazione f	—
desviar (Es)	ablenken	distract	distraire	distrarre	—
detail (E)	Einzelheit f	—	détail m	dettaglio m	detalle f
détail (F)	Einzelheit f	detail	—	dettaglio m	detalle f
detailed (E)	ausführlich	—	détaillé(e)	dettagliato(a)	detallado(a)
détaillé (F)	ausführlich	detailed	—	dettagliato(a)	detallado(a)
detallado (Es)	ausführlich	detailed	détaillé(e)	dettagliato(a)	—
detalle (Es)	Einzelheit f	detail	détail m	dettaglio m	—
detener (Es)	verhaften	arrest	arrêter	arrestare	—
detergent (E)	Waschmittel n	—	lessive f	detersivo m	detergente m
detergente (Es)	Waschmittel n	detergent	lessive f	detersivo m	—
deteriorar (Es)	beschädigen	damage	endommager	danneggiare	—
deterioro (Es)	Beschädigung f	damage	endommage-ment m	danno m	—
detersivo (I)	Waschmittel n	detergent	lessive f	—	detergente m
détester (F)	hassen	hate	—	odiare	odiar

	D	E	F	I	Es
detour (E)	Umweg *m*	—	détour *m*	deviazione *f*	rodeo *m*
détour (F)	Umweg *m*	detour	—	deviazione *f*	rodeo *m*
detrás¹ (Es)	dahinter	behind it	derrière	dietro	—
detrás² (Es)	hinten	behind	derrière	dietro	—
détresse (F)	Not *f*	trouble	—	miseria *f*	necesidad *f*
détruire¹ (F)	vernichten	destroy	—	distruggere	destruir
détruire² (F)	verderben	ruin	—	rovinare	arrruinar
détruire³ (F)	zerstören	destroy	—	distruggere	destruir
dettagliato (I)	ausführlich	detailed	détaillé(e)	—	detallado(a)
dettaglio (I)	Einzelheit *f*	detail	détail *m*	—	detalle *f*
dette (F)	Schulden *pl*	debt	—	debiti *m pl*	deudas *f pl*
deudas (Es)	Schulden *pl*	debt	dette *f*	debiti *m pl*	—
de un solo color (Es)	einfarbig	all one colour	uni(e)	monocolore	—
deutlich (D)	—	clear	clair(e)	chiaro(a)	claro(a)
deutsch (D)	—	German	allemand(e)	tedesco(a)	alemán(-ana)
Deutscher (D)	—	German	Allemand *m*	tedesco	alemán *m*
Deutschland (D)	—	Germany	Allemagne *f*	Germania *f*	Alemania *f*
deux (F)	zwei	two	—	due	dos
deux fois (F)	zweimal	twice	—	due volte	dos veces
devant¹ (F)	vorn(e)	at the front	—	davanti	delante
devant² (F)	vor	before/in front of	—	davanti a	delante de
develop (E)	entwickeln	—	développer	sviluppare	desarrollar
development (E)	Entwicklung *f*	—	développement *m*	sviluppo *m*	desarrollo *m*
développement (F)	Entwicklung *f*	development	—	sviluppo *m*	desarrollo *m*
développer (F)	entwickeln	develop	—	sviluppare	desarrollar
devenir (F)	werden	become	—	diventare	llegar
déviation (F)	Umleitung *f*	diversion	—	deviazione *f*	desviación *f*
deviazione¹ (I)	Umleitung *f*	diversion	déviation *f*	—	desviación *f*
deviazione² (I)	Umweg *m*	detour	détour *m*	—	rodeo *m*
devil (E)	Teufel *m*	—	diable *m*	diavolo *m*	diablo *m*
deviner (F)	raten	guess	—	indovinare	adivinar
devinette (F)	Rätsel *n*	riddle	—	enigma *m*	adivinanza *f*
devoir¹ (F)	müssen	have to	—	dovere	deber
devoir² (F)	Pflicht *f*	duty	—	dovere *m*	obligación *f*
devoir³ (F)	sollen	have to	—	dovere	deber
devoir⁴ (F)	schulden	owe	—	dovere	deber
devolver¹ (Es)	wiedergeben	return	rendre	restituire	—
devolver² (Es)	zurückbringen	bring back	rapporter	riportare	—
devolver³ (Es)	zurückzahlen	pay back	rembourser	rimborsare	—
devolver⁴ (Es)	zurückgeben	give back	rendre	restituire	—
devorar (Es)	fressen	eat	bouffer	mangiare	—
devoto (I)	fromm	pious	pieux(-euse)	—	religioso(a)
Dezember (D)	—	December	décembre *m*	dicembre *m*	diciembre *m*
di (I)	von	from/by	de	—	de
Dia (D)	—	slide	diapositive *f*	diapositiva *f*	diapositiva *f*
día (Es)	Tag *m*	day	jour *m*	giorno *m*	—
diable (F)	Teufel *m*	devil	—	diavolo *m*	diablo *m*
diablo (Es)	Teufel *m*	devil	diable *m*	diavolo *m*	—

	D	E	F	I	Es
día de descanso (Es)	Ruhetag *m*	closing day	jour de repos *m*	giorno di riposo *m*	—
día de fiesta (Es)	Feiertag *m*	holiday	jour férié *m*	giorno festivo *m*	—
día laborable (Es)	Werktag *m*	working day	jour ouvrable *m*	giorno feriale *m*	—
dialling code (E)	Vorwahl *f*	—	indicatif téléphonique *m*	prefisso *m*	prefijo *m*
diapositiva (Es)	Dia *n*	slide	diapositive *f*	diapositiva *f*	—
diapositiva (I)	Dia *n*	slide	diapositive *f*	—	diapositiva *f*
diapositive (F)	Dia *n*	slide	—	diapositiva *f*	diapositiva *f*
Diät (D)	—	diet	diète *f*	dieta *f*	dieta *f*
diavolo (I)	Teufel *m*	devil	diable *m*	—	diablo *m*
dibujar (Es)	zeichnen	draw	dessiner	disegnare	—
dibujo (Es)	Zeichnung *f*	drawing	dessin *m*	disegno *m*	—
diccionario¹ (Es)	Lexikon *n*	encyclopaedia	encyclopédie *f*	enciclopedia *f*	—
diccionario² (Es)	Wörterbuch *n*	dictionary	dictionnaire *m*	dizionario *m*	—
dice (E)	Würfel *m*	—	dé *m*	dado *m*	dado *m*
dicembre (I)	Dezember *m*	December	décembre *m*	—	diciembre *m*
dichi (I)	wessen	whose	de qui	—	¿de quién?
dichiarazione (I)	Aussage *f*	statement	déclaration *f*	—	declaración *f*
dicht (D)	—	dense	épais(se)	denso(a)	espeso(a)
Dichter (D)	—	poet	poète *m*	poeta *m*	poeta *m*
diciannove (I)	neunzehn	nineteen	dix-neuf	—	diecinueve
diciassette (I)	siebzehn	seventeen	dix-sept	—	diecisiete
diciembre (Es)	Dezember *m*	December	décembre *m*	dicembre *m*	—
diciotto (I)	achtzehn	eighteen	dix-huit	—	dieciocho
dick (D)	—	fat	gros(se)	grasso(a)	grueso(a)
di colpo (I)	plötzlich	suddenly	tout à coup	—	de repente
dictionary (E)	Wörterbuch *n*	—	dictionnaire *m*	dizionario *m*	diccionario *m*
dictionnaire (F)	Wörterbuch *n*	dictionary	—	dizionario *m*	diccionario *m*
die (E)	sterben	—	mourir	morire	morir
Dieb (D)	—	thief	voleur *m*	ladro *m*	ladrón *m*
dieci (I)	zehn	ten	dix	—	diez
diecinueve (Es)	neunzehn	nineteen	dix-neuf	diciannove	—
dieciocho (Es)	achtzehn	eighteen	dix-huit	diciotto	—
dieciseis (Es)	sechzehn	sixteen	seize	sedici	—
diecisiete (Es)	siebzehn	seventeen	dix-sept	diciassette	—
Diele (D)	—	hall	vestibule *m*	corridoio *m*	entrada *f*
dienen (D)	—	serve	servir	servire	servir
Dienst (D)	—	service	service *m*	servizio *m*	servicio *m*
Dienstag (D)	—	Tuesday	mardi *m*	martedì *m*	martes *m*
diente (Es)	Zahn *m*	tooth	dent *f*	dente *m*	—
diese (D)	—	this	ce, cette	questo(a)	esta, este, esto
diet (E)	Diät *f*	—	diète *f*	dieta *f*	dieta *f*
dieta (Es)	Diät *f*	diet	diète *f*	dieta *f*	—
dieta (I)	Diät *f*	diet	diète *f*	—	dieta *f*
diète (F)	Diät *f*	diet	—	dieta *f*	dieta *f*
dietro¹ (I)	dahinter	behind it	derrière	—	detrás
dietro² (I)	hinten	behind	derrière	—	detrás
Dieu (F)	Gott *m*	God	—	Dio *m*	Dios *m*

dimenticare

	D	E	F	I	Es
diez (Es)	zehn	ten	dix	dieci	—
difendere (I)	verteidigen	defend	défendre	—	defender
difendersi (I)	wehren, sich	defend	défendre, se	—	defenderse
diferencia (Es)	Unterschied m	difference	différence f	differenza f	—
diferente[1] (Es)	anders	different	différent(e)	differente	—
diferente[2] (Es)	verschieden	different	différent(e)	diverso(a)	—
difesa[3] (I)	Verteidigung f	defence	défense f	—	defensa f
difference (E)	Unterschied m	—	différence f	differenza f	diferencia f
différence (F)	Unterschied m	difference	—	differenza f	diferencia f
different[1] (E)	anders	—	différent(e)	differente	diferente
different[2] (E)	unterschiedlich	—	différent(e)	diverso(a)	distinto(a)
different[3] (E)	verschieden	—	différent(e)	diverso(a)	diferente
différent[1] (F)	anders	different	—	differente	diferente
différent[2] (F)	unterschiedlich	different	—	diverso(a)	distinto(a)
différent[3] (F)	verschieden	different	—	diverso(a)	diferente
differente (I)	anders	different	différent(e)	—	diferente
differenza (I)	Unterschied m	difference	différence f	—	diferencia f
difficile (F)	schwierig	difficult	—	difficile	dificil
difficile (I)	schwierig	difficult	difficile	—	dificil
difficoltà (I)	Schwierigkeit f	difficulty	difficulté f	—	dificultad f
difficult (E)	schwierig	—	difficile	difficile	dificil
difficulté (F)	Schwierigkeit f	difficulty	—	difficoltà f	dificultad f
difficulty (E)	Schwierigkeit f	—	difficulté f	difficoltà f	dificultad f
diffondere (I)	verbreiten	spread	propager	—	difundir
diffusion (F)	Sendung f	transmission	—	trasmissione f	emisión f
dificil (Es)	schwierig	difficult	difficile	difficile	—
dificultad (Es)	Schwierigkeit f	difficulty	difficulté f	difficoltà f	—
di fronte (I)	gegenüber	opposite	en face de	—	en frente
difundir (Es)	verbreiten	spread	propager	diffondere	—
dig (E)	graben	—	creuser	scavare	cavar
¡diga! (Es)	hallo!	hello!	allô!	pronto!	—
digérer (F)	verdauen	digest	—	digerire	digerir
digerir (Es)	verdauen	digest	digérer	digerire	—
digerire (I)	verdauen	digest	digérer	—	digerir
digest (E)	verdauen	—	digérer	digerire	digerir
digiunare (I)	fasten	fast	jeûner	—	ayunar
di là[1] (I)	hinüber	across	de l'autre côté	—	hacia el otro lado
di la[2] (I)	davon	of it	en/de cela	—	de ello
diligent (E)	fleißig	—	travailleur (-euse)	diligente	activo(a)
diligente (Es)	eifrig	keen	zélé(e)	diligente	—
diligente[1] (I)	eifrig	keen	zélé(e)	—	diligente
diligente[2] (I)	fleißig	diligent	travailleur (-euse)	—	activo(a)
dimagrire (I)	abnehmen	lose weight	maigrir	—	adelgazar
dimanche (F)	Sonntag m	Sunday	—	domenica f	domingo m
di mattina (I)	vormittags	in the morning	le matin	—	por la mañana
di meno (I)	weniger	less	moins	—	menos
dimenticare (I)	vergessen	forget	oublier	—	olvidar

	D	E	F	I	Es
dimezzare (I)	halbieren	halve	partager en deux	—	dividir por la mitad
diminuer (F)	verringern	reduce	—	diminuire	disminuir
diminuire¹ (I)	herabsetzen	lower	baisser	—	rebajar
diminuire² (I)	verringern	reduce	diminuer	—	disminuir
dimitir (Es)	zurücktreten	retire	démissionner	dare le dimissioni	—
dindon (F)	Truthahn m	turkey	—	tacchino m	pavo m
dine (E)	speisen	—	manger	mangiare	comer
dîner (F)	Abendessen n	supper	—	cena f	cena f
dinero (Es)	Geld n	money	argent m	denaro m	—
dinero al contado (Es)	Bargeld n	cash	espèces f pl	contanti m	—
dinero de bolsillo (Es)	Taschengeld n	pocket money	argent de poche f	denaro per le piccole spese m	—
Ding (D)	—	thing	chose f	cosa f	cosa f
dining car (E)	Speisewagen m	—	wagon-restaurant m	vagone ristorante m	vagón restaurante m
dining room (E)	Eßzimmer n	—	salle à manger f	sala da pranzo f	comedor m
di notte (I)	nachts	at nighttime	la nuit	—	por la noche
dintorni (I)	Umgebung f	surroundings	environs m pl	—	alrededores m pl
di nuovo¹ (I)	nochmals	again	encore une fois	—	otra vez
di nuovo² (I)	wieder	again	de nouveau	—	de nuevo
Dio (I)	Gott m	God	Dieu m	—	Dios m
Dios (Es)	Gott m	God	Dieu m	Dio m	—
dipendere da (I)	abhängen	depend	dépendre	—	dejar atrás
dipingere (I)	malen	paint	peindre	—	pintar
di pomeriggio (I)	nachmittags	in the afternoon	l'aprés-midi	—	por la tarde
dire (F)	sagen	say	—	dire	decir
dire (I)	sagen	say	dire	—	decir
dirección¹ (Es)	Anschrift f / Adresse f	address	adresse f	indirizzo m	—
dirección² (Es)	Leitung f	direction	direction f	direzione f	—
dirección³ (Es)	Richtung f	direction	direction f	direzione f	—
direct (F)	direkt	direct	—	diretto(a)	directo(a)
direct (E)	direkt	—	direct(e)	diretto(a)	directo(a)
directeur (F)	Direktor m	director	—	direttore m	director m
direction¹ (E)	Leitung f	—	direction f	direzione f	dirección f
direction² (E)	Richtung f	—	direction f	direzione f	dirección f
direction¹ (F)	Leitung f	direction	—	direzione f	dirección f
direction² (F)	Richtung f	direction	—	direzione f	dirección f
directo¹ (Es)	direkt	direct	direct(e)	diretto(a)	—
directo² (Es)	unmittelbar	immediate	immédiat(e)	immediato(a)	—
director¹ (E)	Direktor m	—	directeur m	direttore m	director m
director² (E)	Regisseur m	—	réalisateur m	regista m	director m
director¹ (Es)	Direktor m	director	directeur m	direttore m	—
director² (Es)	Regisseur m	director	réalisateur m	regista m	—
director (de orquesta) (Es)	Dirigent m	conductor	chef d'orchestre m	direttore d'orchestra m	—
direct to (E)	richten	—	diriger	dirigere	dirigir
direkt (D)	—	direct	direct(e)	diretto(a)	directo(a)
Direktor (D)	—	director	directeur m	direttore m	director m

	D	E	F	I	Es
direttissimo (I)	D-Zug *m*	through train	express *m*	—	tren expreso *m*
diretto (I)	direkt	direct	direct(e)	—	directo(a)
direttore (I)	Direktor *m*	director	directeur *m*	—	director *m*
direttore d'orchestra (I)	Dirigent *m*	conductor	chef d'orchestre *m*	—	director (de orquesta) *m*
direzione[1] (I)	Leitung *f*	direction	direction *f*	—	dirección *f*
direzione[2] (I)	Richtung *f*	direction	direction *f*	—	dirección *f*
Dirigent (D)	—	conductor	chef d'orchestre *m*	direttore d'orchestra *m*	director (de orquesta) *m*
diriger (F)	richten	direct to	—	dirigere	dirigir
dirigere (I)	richten	direct to	diriger	—	dirigir
dirigir[1] (Es)	führen	lead	guider	guidare	—
dirigir[2] (Es)	regeln	regulate	régler	regolare	—
dirigir[3] (Es)	richten	direct to	diriger	dirigere	—
diritto[1] (I)	aufrecht	upright	droit(e)	—	derecho(a)
diritto[2] (I)	Recht *n*	right	droit *m*	—	derecho *m*
diritto[3] (I)	gerade	straight	droit(e)	—	derecho(a)
dirt (E)	Schmutz *m*	—	saleté *f*	sporcizia *f*	suciedad *f*
dirty[1] (E)	dreckig	—	sale	sporco(a)	sucio(a)
dirty[2] (E)	schmutzig	—	sale	sporco(a)	sucio(a)
disadvantage[1] (E)	benachteiligen	—	désavantager	svantaggiare	perjudicar
disadvantage[2] (E)	Nachteil *m*	—	désavantage *m*	svantaggio *m*	desventaja *f*
disappear (E)	verschwinden	—	disparaître	sparire	desaparecer
disappoint (E)	enttäuschen	—	décevoir	deludere	defraudar
disappointed (E)	enttäuscht	—	déçu(e)	deluso(a)	defraudado(a)
disapprovare (I)	mißbilligen	disapprove	désapprouver	—	desaprobar
disapprove (E)	mißbilligen	—	désapprouver	disapprovare	desaprobar
disarm (E)	abrüsten	—	désarmer	disarmare	desarmar
disarmare (I)	abrüsten	disarm	désarmer	—	desarmar
disc (E)	Scheibe *f*	—	disque *m*	disco *m*	disco *m*
discendere (I)	abstammen	be descended	descendre	—	descender
disco[1] (Es)	Platte *f*	record	disque *m*	disco *m*	—
disco[2] (Es)	Scheibe *f*	disc	disque *m*	disco *m*	—
disco[3] (Es)	Schallplatte *f*	record	disque *m*	disco *m*	—
disco[1] (I)	Platte *f*	record	disque *m*	—	disco *m*
disco[2] (I)	Schallplatte *f*	record	disque *m*	—	disco *m*
disco[3] (I)	Scheibe *f*	disc	disque *m*	—	disco *m*
discorso (I)	Rede *f*	speech	discours *m*	—	discurso *m*
discoteca (Es)	Diskothek *f*	discotheque	discothèque *f*	discoteca *f*	—
discoteca (I)	Diskothek *f*	discotheque	discothèque *f*	—	discoteca *f*
discotheque (E)	Diskothek *f*	—	discothèque *f*	discoteca *f*	discoteca *f*
discothèque (F)	Diskothek *f*	discotheque	—	discoteca *f*	discoteca *f*
discount (E)	Rabatt *m*	—	rabais *m*	sconto *m*	rebaja *f*
discours (F)	Rede *f*	speech	—	discorso *m*	discurso *m*
discover (E)	entdecken	—	découvrir	scoprire	descubrir
disculpa (Es)	Entschuldigung *f*	apology	excuse *f*	scusa *f*	—
disculparse (Es)	entschuldigen, sich	apologize	excuser, se	scusarsi	—
discurso (Es)	Rede *f*	speech	discours *m*	discorso *m*	—
discusión (Es)	Aussprache *f*	discussion	discussion *f*	discussione *f*	—

	D	E	F	I	Es
discuss (E)	besprechen	—	discuter	discutere	discutir
discussion (E)	Aussprache f	—	discussion f	discussione f	discusión f
discussion (F)	Aussprache f	discussion	—	discussione f	discusión f
discussione (I)	Aussprache f	discussion	discussion f	—	discusión f
discuter (F)	besprechen	discuss	—	discutere	discutir
discutere (I)	besprechen	discuss	discuter	—	discutir
discutir[1] (Es)	besprechen	discuss	discuter	discutere	—
discutir[2] (Es)	streiten	quarrel	disputer, se	litigare	—
disdire (I)	abblasen	call off	souffler	—	anular
disegnare (I)	zeichnen	draw	dessiner	—	dibujar
disegno (I)	Zeichnung f	drawing	dessin m	—	dibujo m
di sera (I)	abends	in the evening	le soir	—	por la tarde
disfare (I)	auspacken	unpack	défaire	—	deshacer
disfrutar (Es)	genießen	enjoy	jouir	godere	—
disgrace (E)	Schande f	—	honte f	vergogna f	deshonra f
disgrazia (I)	Unglück n	misfortune	malheur m	—	desgracia f
disgusting (E)	widerlich	—	repoussant(e)	ripugnante	repugnante
disgustoso (I)	abscheulich	abominable	affreux(-euse)	—	horrible
dish (E)	Gericht n	—	plat m	piatto m	comida f
Diskothek (D)	—	discotheque	discothèque f	discoteca f	discoteca f
disminuir (Es)	verringern	reduce	diminuer	diminuire	—
dismount (E)	absteigen	—	descendre	scendere	descender
disoccupato (I)	arbeitslos	unemployed	en chômage	—	desempleado(a)
disoccupazione (I)	Arbeitslosigkeit f	unemployment	chômage m	—	desempleo m
di solito (I)	meistens	generally	généralement	—	por lo común
disordinato (I)	unordentlich	untidy	désordonné(e)	—	desordenado(a)
disordine (I)	Unordnung f	mess	désordre m	—	desorden m
disparaître (F)	verschwinden	disappear	—	sparire	desaparecer
disparar (Es)	schießen	shoot	tirer	sparare	—
dispari (I)	ungerade	uneven	impair(e)	—	impar
disparo (Es)	Schuß m	shot	coup m	sparo m	—
disperato (I)	verzweifelt	desperate	désespéré(e)	—	desesperado(a)
dispersé (F)	zerstreut	scattered	—	disperso(a)	disperso(a)
disperso (Es)	zerstreut	scattered	dispersé(e)	disperso(a)	—
disperso (I)	zerstreut	scattered	dispersé(e)	—	disperso(a)
dispiacere (I)	Bedauern n	regret	regret m	—	compasión f
disponer (Es)	verfügen	order	disposer de	disporre	—
disponibile (I)	vorhanden	available	présent(e)	—	presente
disporre (I)	verfügen	order	disposer de	—	disponer
disposer de (F)	verfügen	order	—	disporre	disponer
disposition (E)	Gemüt n	—	disposition f	animo m	ánimo m
disposition (F)	Gemüt n	disposition	—	animo m	ánimo m
dispuesto (Es)	bereit	ready	prêt(e)	pronto(a)	—
disputa (Es)	Streit m	argument	dispute f	lite f	—
dispute (F)	Streit m	argument	—	lite f	disputa f
disputer, se (F)	streiten	quarrel	—	litigare	discutir
disque[1] (F)	Platte f	record	—	disco m	disco m
disque[2] (F)	Schallplatte f	record	—	disco m	disco m

distruggere

	D	E	F	I	Es
disque³ (F)	Scheibe f	disc	—	disco m	disco m
dissatisfied (E)	unzufrieden	—	mécontent(e)	scontento(a)	descontento(a)
dissimuler (F)	verbergen	hide	—	nascondere	esconder
dissolve (E)	auflösen	—	dénouer	sciogliere	deshacer
distance¹ (E)	Abstand m	—	distance f	distanza f	distancia f
distance² (E)	Entfernung f	—	distance f	distanza f	distancia f
distance³ (E)	Ferne f	—	lointain m	distanza f	lejanía f
distance¹ (F)	Abstand m	distance	—	distanza f	distancia f
distance² (F)	Entfernung f	distance	—	distanza f	distancia f
distancia¹ (Es)	Abstand m	distance	distance f	distanza f	—
distancia² (Es)	Entfernung f	distance	distance f	distanza f	—
distant (E)	entfernt	—	éloigné(e)	distante	distante
distante (Es)	entfernt	distant	éloigné(e)	distante	—
distante (I)	entfernt	distant	éloigné(e)	—	distante
distanza¹ (I)	Abstand m	distance	distance f	—	distancia f
distanza² (I)	Entfernung f	distance	distance f	—	distancia f
distanza³ (I)	Ferne f	distance	lointain m	—	lejanía f
distingué (F)	vornehm	distinguished	—	distinto(a)	distinguido(a)
distinguer (F)	unterscheiden	distinguish	—	distinguere	distinguir
distinguere (I)	unterscheiden	distinguish	distinguer	—	distinguir
distinguido (Es)	vornehm	distinguished	distingué(e)	distinto(a)	—
distinguir (Es)	unterscheiden	distinguish	distinguer	distinguere	—
distinguish (E)	unterscheiden	—	distinguer	distinguere	distinguir
distinguished (E)	vornehm	—	distingué(e)	distinto(a)	distinguido(a)
distinto (Es)	unterschiedlich	different	différent(e)	diverso(a)	—
distinto (I)	vornehm	distinguished	distingué(e)	—	distinguido(a)
distract (E)	ablenken	—	distraire	distrarre	desviar
distraire (F)	ablenken	distract	—	distrarre	desviar
distrarre (I)	ablenken	distract	distraire	—	desviar
distretto (I)	Revier n	district	district m	—	distrito m
distribuer¹ (F)	austeilen	distribute	—	distribuire	distribuir
distribuer² (F)	verteilen	distribute	—	distribuire	repartir
distribuidor automático (Es)	Automat m	vending machine	distributeur automatique m	distributore automatico m	—
distribuir (Es)	austeilen	distribute	distribuer	distribuire	—
distribuire¹ (I)	austeilen	distribute	distribuer	—	distribuir
distribuire² (I)	verteilen	distribute	distribuer	—	repartir
distribute¹ (E)	austeilen	—	distribuer	distribuire	distribuir
distribute² (E)	verteilen	—	distribuer	distribuire	repartir
distributeur automatique (F)	Automat m	vending machine	—	distributore m	distribuidor automático m
distributore automatico (I)	Automat m	vending machine	distributeur automatique m	—	distribuidor automático m
distributore di benzina (I)	Tankstelle f	filling station	station-service f	—	gasolinera f
district (E)	Revier n	—	district m	distretto m	distrito m
district (F)	Revier n	district	—	distretto m	distrito m
distrito (Es)	Revier n	district	district m	distretto m	—
distruggere¹ (I)	vernichten	destroy	détruire	—	destruir
distruggere² (I)	zerstören	destroy	détruire	—	destruir

	D	E	F	I	Es
distrust (E)	Mißtrauen *n*	—	méfiance *f*	sfiducia *f*	desconfianza *f*
disturb¹ (E)	beunruhigen	—	inquiéter	preoccupare	inquietar
disturb² (E)	stören	—	déranger	disturbare	molestar
disturbare (I)	stören	disturb	déranger	—	molestar
disturbo (I)	Störung *f*	interference	trouble *m*	—	molestia *f*
dito (I)	Finger *m*	finger	doigt *m*	—	dedo *m*
dito del piede (I)	Zehe *f*	toe	doigt de pied *m*	—	dedo del pie *m*
di trasverso¹ (I)	quer	across	en travers	—	al través
di trasverso² (I)	Transport *m*	transport	transport *m*	—	transporte *m*
ditta (I)	Firma *f*	company	firme *f*	—	empresa *f*
diván (Es)	Couch *f*	couch	canapé *m*	divano *m*	—
divano (I)	Couch *f*	couch	canapé *m*	—	diván *m*
dive (E)	tauchen	—	plonger	immergere	bucear
diventare (I)	werden	become	devenir	—	llegar
diversion (E)	Umleitung *f*	—	déviation *f*	deviazione *f*	desviación *f*
diverso¹ (I)	unterschiedlich	different	différent(e)	—	distinto(a)
diverso² (I)	verschieden	different	différent(e)	—	diferente
divertido (Es)	lustig	funny	marrant(e)	allegro(a)	—
divertimento (I)	Vergnügen *n*	pleasure	plaisir *m*	—	placer *m*
divertire (I)	unterhalten	entertain	entretenir	—	entretener
divertirse (Es)	amüsieren, sich	enjoy o.s.	amuser, se	divertirsi	—
divertirsi (I)	amüsieren, sich	enjoy o.s.	amuser, se	—	divertirse
dividere (I)	teilen	share	partager	—	partir
dividir por la mitad (Es)	halbieren	halve	partager en deux	dimezzare	—
divieto (I)	Verbot *n*	prohibition	défense *f*	—	prohibición *f*
divieto di parcheggio (I)	Parkverbot *n*	no parking	défense de stationner *f*	—	estacionamiento prohibido *m*
divisa (I)	Uniform *f*	uniform	uniforme *m*	—	uniforme *m*
dix (F)	zehn	ten	—	dieci	diez
dix-huit (F)	achtzehn	eighteen	—	diciotto	dieciocho
dix-neuf (F)	neunzehn	nineteen	—	diciannove	diecinueve
dix-sept (F)	siebzehn	seventeen	—	diciassette	diecisiete
dizionario (I)	Wörterbuch *n*	dictionary	dictionnaire *m*	—	diccionario *m*
do (E)	tun	—	faire	fare	hacer
doblar¹ (Es)	biegen	bend	plier	piegare	—
doblar² (Es)	einbiegen	turn	tourner	svoltare	—
doble¹ (Es)	doppelt	double	double	doppio(a)	—
doble² (Es)	zweifach	double	double	duplice	—
d'occasion (F)	gebraucht	used	—	usato(a)	usado(a)
doccia (I)	Dusche *f*	shower	douche *f*	—	ducha *f*
doce (Es)	zwölf	twelve	douze	dodici	—
docena (Es)	Dutzend *n*	dozen	douzaine *f*	dozzina *f*	—
doch (D)	—	still	si	si	sin embargo
docteur (F)	Doktor *m*	doctor	—	dottore *m*	doctor *m*
doctor¹ (E)	Arzt *m*	—	médecin *m*	medico *m*	médico(a) *m(f)*
doctor² (E)	Doktor *m*	—	docteur *m*	dottore *m*	doctor *m*
doctor (Es)	Doktor *m*	doctor	docteur *m*	dottore *m*	—
document (E)	Urkunde *f*	—	document *m*	documento *m*	documento *m*
document (F)	Urkunde *f*	document	—	documento *m*	documento *m*

	D	E	F	I	Es
documento (Es)	Urkunde *f*	document	document *m*	documento *m*	—
documento (I)	Urkunde *f*	document	document *m*	—	documento *m*
documento de identidad (Es)	Personalausweis *m*	identity card	carte d'identité *f*	carta d'identitá *f*	—
documento d'identità (I)	Ausweis *m*	passport	pièce d'identité *f*	—	documento de identidad *m*
dodici (I)	zwölf	twelve	douze	—	doce
dog (E)	Hund *m*	—	chien *m*	cane *m*	perro *m*
dogana (I)	Zoll *m*	customs	douane *f*	—	aduana *f*
do gymnastic exercises (E)	turnen	—	faire de la gymnastique	fare ginnastica	hacer gimnasia
doigt (F)	Finger *m*	finger	—	dito *m*	dedo *m*
doigt de pied (F)	Zehe *f*	toe	—	dito del piede *m*	dedo del pie *m*
Doktor (D)	—	doctor	docteur *m*	dottore *m*	doctor *m*
dolce¹ (I)	Kuchen *m*	cake	gâteau *m*	—	pastel *m*
dolce² (I)	süß	sweet	sucré(e)	—	dulce
dolce³ (I)	sanft	gentle	doux(douce)	—	dulce
dolente (I)	weh	hurt	douloureux (-euse)	—	doloroso(a)
doll (E)	Puppe *f*	—	poupée *f*	bambola *f*	muñeca *f*
Dolmetscher (D)	—	interpreter	interprète *m/f*	interprete *m*	intérprete *m(f)*
dolor (Es)	Schmerz *m*	pain	douleur *f*	dolore *m*	—
dolor de cabeza (Es)	Kopfschmerzen *pl*	headache	mal de tête *m*	mal di testa *m*	—
dolor de estómago (Es)	Magenschmerzen *pl*	stomach-ache	mal d'estomac *m*	mal di stomaco *m*	—
dolor de garganta (Es)	Halsschmerzen *pl*	sore throat	mal de gorge *m*	mal di gola *m*	—
dolor de muelas (Es)	Zahnschmerzen *pl*	toothache	mal de dents *m*	mal di denti *m*	—
dolor de oídos (Es)	Ohrenschmerzen *pl*	earache	mal d'oreilles *m*	mal d'orecchi *m*	—
dolore¹ (I)	Kummer *m*	grief	chagrin *m*	—	pesar *m*
dolore² (I)	Schmerz *m*	pain	douleur *f*	—	dolor *m*
doloroso (I)	schmerzhaft	painful	douloureux (-euse)	—	doloroso(a)
doloroso¹ (Es)	schmerzhaft	painful	douloureux (-euse)	doloroso(a)	—
doloroso² (Es)	weh	hurt	douloureux (-euse)	dolente	—
Dom (D)	—	cathedral	cathédrale *f*	duomo *m*	catedral *f*
domaine (F)	Anwesen *n*	premises	—	podere *m*	posesión *f*
domanda¹ (I)	Antrag *m*	application	demande *f*	—	solicitud *f*
domanda² (I)	Bitte *f*	request	demande *f*	—	ruego *m*
domanda³ (I)	Frage *f*	question	question *f*	—	pregunta *f*
domanda⁴ (I)	Nachfrage *f*	demand	demande *f*	—	demanda *f*
domanda d'impiego (I)	Bewerbung *f*	application	candidature *f*	—	solicitud *f*
domandare (I)	fragen	ask	demander	—	preguntar
domani (I)	morgen	tomorrow	demain	—	mañana
domenica (I)	Sonntag *m*	Sunday	dimanche *m*	—	domingo *m*
domestica (I)	Hausmädchen *n*	maid	fille de service *f*	—	criada *f*
domicile (E)	Wohnort *m*	—	domicile *m*	residenza *f*	residencia *f*
domicile (F)	Wohnort *m*	domicile	—	residenza *f*	residencia *f*

	D	E	F	I	Es
dominare (I)	herrschen	rule	régner	—	mandar
domingo (Es)	Sonntag *m*	Sunday	dimanche *m*	domenica *f*	—
dommage (F)	Schaden *m*	damage	—	danno *m*	daño *m*
don (F)	Spende *f*	donation	—	donazione *f*	donativo *m*
donation (E)	Spende *f*	—	don *m*	donazione *f*	donativo *m*
donativo (Es)	Spende *f*	donation	don *m*	donazione *f*	—
donazione (I)	Spende *f*	donation	don *m*	—	donativo *m*
donc (F)	also	therefore	—	dunque/ quindi	así
¿dónde? (Es)	wo	where	où	dove	—
dondolare (I)	schaukeln	swing	balancer, se	—	columpiarse
done (E)	gar	—	cuit(e)	cotto(a)	estar a punto
donkey (E)	Esel *m*	—	âne *m*	asino *m*	burro *m*
donna (I)	Frau *f*	woman	femme *f*	—	mujer *f*
donna delle pulizie (I)	Putzfrau *f*	charwoman	femme de ménage *f*	—	mujer de la limpieza *f*
Donner (D)	—	thunder	tonnerre *m*	tuono *m*	trueno *m*
donner (F)	geben	give	—	dare	andar
Donnerstag (D)	—	Thursday	jeudi *m*	giovedì *m*	jueves *m*
doof (D)	—	daft	bête	scemo(a)	estúpido(a)
door (E)	Tür *f*	—	porte *f*	porta *f*	puerta *f*
dopo[1] (I)	darauf	afterwards	dessus/ensuite	—	encima
dopo[2] (I)	nachher	afterwards	ensuite	—	después
dopo[3] (I)	nachdem	after	après que	—	después que
dopodomani (I)	übermorgen	day after tomorrow	après-demain	—	pasado mañana
doppelt (D)	—	double	double	doppio(a)	doble
doppio (I)	doppelt	double	double	—	doble
d'or (F)	golden	golden	—	d'oro	de oro
Dorf (D)	—	village	village *m*	paese *m*	pueblo *m*
dormir (Es)	schlafen	sleep	dormir	dormire	—
dormir (F)	schlafen	sleep	—	dormire	dormir
dormire (I)	schlafen	sleep	dormir	—	dormir
dormitorio (Es)	Schlafzimmer *n*	bedroom	chambre à coucher *f*	camera da letto *f*	—
d'oro (I)	golden	golden	d'or	—	de oro
dort (D)	—	there	là/y	là	allí
dos (Es)	zwei	two	deux	due	—
dos (F)	Rücken *m*	back	—	schiena *f*	espalda *m*
Dose (D)	—	tin	boîte *f*	scatola *f*	lata *f*
dos veces (Es)	zweimal	twice	deux fois	due volte	—
dotado (Es)	begabt	gifted	doué(e)	dotato(a)	—
dotato (I)	begabt	gifted	doué(e)	—	dotado(a)
dottore (I)	Doktor *m*	doctor	docteur *m*	—	doctor *m*
douane (F)	Zoll *m*	customs	—	dogana *f*	aduana *f*
d'où (F)	woher	where from	—	da dove	¿de dónde?
double[1] (E)	doppelt	—	double	doppio(a)	doble
double[2] (E)	zweifach	—	double	duplice	doble
double[1] (F)	doppelt	double	—	doppio(a)	doble
double[2] (F)	zweifach	double	—	duplice	doble

drehen

	D	E	F	I	Es
doubler (F)	überholen	overtake	—	sorpassare	adelantar
doubt[1] (E)	zweifeln	—	douter	dubitare	dudar
doubt[2] (E)	Zweifel *m*	—	doute *m*	dubbio *m*	duda *f*
doubtful (E)	zweifelhaft	—	douteux(-euse)	dubbioso(a)	dudoso(a)
doubtless (E)	zweifellos	—	sans doute	senza dubbio	sin duda
douche (F)	Dusche *f*	shower	—	doccia *f*	ducha *f*
doué (F)	begabt	gifted	—	dotato(a)	dotado(a)
dough (E)	Teig *m*	—	pâte *f*	pasta *f*	masa *f*
douleur (F)	Schmerz *m*	pain	—	dolore *m*	dolor *m*
douloureux[1] (F)	schmerzhaft	painful	—	doloroso(a)	doloroso(a)
douloureux[2] (F)	weh	hurt	—	dolente	doloroso(a)
doute (F)	Zweifel *m*	doubt	—	dubbio *m*	duda *f*
douter (F)	zweifeln	doubt	—	dubitare	dudar
douter, se (F)	ahnen	suspect	—	supporre	suponer
douteux (F)	zweifelhaft	doubtful	—	dubbioso(a)	dudoso(a)
doux[1] (F)	zart	soft	—	tenero(a)	suave
doux[2] (F)	mild	mild	—	mite	agradable
doux[3] (F)	sanft	gentle	—	dolce	dulce
doux[4] (F)	weich	soft	—	morbido(a)	tierno(a)
douzaine (F)	Dutzend *n*	dozen	—	dozzina *f*	docena *f*
douze (F)	zwölf	twelve	—	dodici	doce
dove[1] (I)	wo	where	où	—	¿dónde?
dove[2] (I)	wohin	where to	où	—	a dónde
dovere[1] (I)	müssen	have to	devoir	—	deber
dovere[2] (I)	Pflicht *f*	duty	devoir *m*	—	obligación *f*
dovere[3] (I)	schulden	owe	devoir qch à qn	—	deber
dovere[4] (I)	sollen	have to	devoir	—	deber
do without (E)	entbehren	—	passer de, se	fare a meno di	pasarse sin
down[1] (E)	herunter	—	en bas	giù	abajo
down[2] (E)	herab/hinab	—	vers le bas	giù	hacia abajo
downhill (E)	bergab	—	en descendant	in discesa	cuesta abajo
downstairs (E)	unten	—	dessous	sotto/giù	abajo
downwards (E)	abwärts	—	en bas	in giù	hacia abajo
dozen (E)	Dutzend *n*	—	douzaine *f*	dozzina *f*	docena *f*
dozzina (I)	Dutzend *n*	dozen	douzaine *f*	—	docena *f*
Draht (D)	—	wire	fil de fer *m*	filo metallico *m*	alambre *m*
drap (F)	Laken *n*	sheet	—	lenzuolo *m*	sábana *f*
drapeau (F)	Fahne *f*	flag	—	bandiera *f*	bandera *f*
draught (E)	Luftzug *m*	—	courant d'air *m*	corrente d'aria *f*	corriente de aire *f*
draußen (D)	—	outside	dehors	fuori	afuera
draw[1] (E)	vorziehen	—	tirer	tirare in avanti	correr
draw[2] (E)	zeichnen	—	dessiner	disegnare	dibujar
drawer (E)	Schublade *f*	—	tiroir *m*	cassetto *m*	cajón *m*
drawing (E)	Zeichnung *f*	—	dessin *m*	disegno *m*	dibujo *m*
dream[1] (E)	träumen	—	rêver	sognare	soñar
dream[2] (E)	Traum *m*	—	rêve *m*	sogno *m*	sueño *m*
dreckig (D)	—	dirty	sale	sporco(a)	sucio(a)
drehen (D)	—	turn	tourner	girare	girar

	D	E	F	I	Es
drei (D)	—	three	trois	tre	tres
dreißig (D)	—	thirty	trente	trenta	treinta
dreizehn (D)	—	thirteen	treize	tredici	trece
dress[1] (E)	kleiden	—	habiller	vestire	vestir
dress[2] (E)	Kleid *n*	—	robe *f*	vestito *m*	vestido *m*
dringend (D)	—	urgent	urgent(e)	urgente	urgente
drink[1] (E)	Getränk *n*	—	boisson *f*	bevanda *f*	bebida *f*
drink[2] (E)	trinken	—	boire	bere	beber
drinkable (E)	trinkbar	—	potable	potabile	potable
drinking water (E)	Trinkwasser *n*	—	eau potable *f*	acqua potabile *f*	agua potable *f*
drinnen (D)	—	inside	à l'intérieur	dentro	dentro
drip (E)	tropfen	—	dégoutter	gocciolare	gotear
dritte (D)	—	third	troisième	terzo(a)	tercera(o)
Drittel (D)	—	a third	tiers *m*	terzo *m*	tercio *m*
dritto (I)	geradeaus	straight ahead	tout droit	—	todo derecho
drive[1] (E)	Auffahrt *f*	—	allée *f*	salita d'ingresso *f*	entrada *f*
drive[2] (E)	fahren	—	conduire	andare	conducir
drive[3] (E)	treiben	—	mener	spingere	estimular
drive back (E)	zurückfahren	—	retourner	tornare indietro	retroceder
driver (E)	Fahrer *m*	—	conducteur *m*	autista *m*	conductor *m*
driving licence (E)	Führerschein *m*	—	permis de conduire *m*	patente *f*	permiso de conducir *m*
droga (Es)	Droge *f*	drug	drogue *f*	droga *f*	—
droga (I)	Droge *f*	drug	drogue *f*	—	droga *f*
Droge (D)	—	drug	drogue *f*	droga *f*	droga *f*
Drogerie (D)	—	chemist's	droguerie *f*	drogheria *f*	droguería *f*
drogheria (I)	Drogerie *f*	chemist's	droguerie *f*	—	droguería *f*
drogue (F)	Droge *f*	drug	—	droga *f*	droga *f*
droguería (Es)	Drogerie *f*	chemist's	droguerie *f*	drogheria *f*	—
droguerie (F)	Drogerie *f*	chemist's	—	drogheria *f*	droguería *f*
drohen (D)	—	threaten	menacer	minacciare	amenazar (a alguien)
droit[1] (F)	Gebühr *f*	fee	—	tassa *f*	tarifa *f*
droit[2] (F)	Jura	law	—	giurisprudenza *f*	derecho *m*
droit[3] (F)	Recht *n*	right	—	diritto *m*	derecho *m*
droit[4] (F)	aufrecht	upright	—	diritto(a)	derecho(a)
droit[5] (F)	gerade	straight	—	diritto(a)	derecho(a)
droits de douane (F)	Zoll *m*	duty	—	dazio *m*	arbitrio *m*
drôle (F)	komisch	funny	—	comico(a)	cómico(a)
drop (E)	Tropfen *m*	—	goutte *f*	goccia *f*	gota *f*
drown (E)	ertrinken	—	noyer, se	annegare	ahogarse
drüben (D)	—	over there	de l'autre côté	dall'altra parte	al otro lado
drücken (D)	—	press	presser	premere	apretar
drug (E)	Droge *f*	—	drogue *f*	droga *f*	droga *f*
drunk (E)	betrunken	—	soûl(e)	ubriaco(a)	borracho(a)
dry[1] (E)	trocknen	—	sécher	asciugare	secar
dry[2] (E)	trocken	—	sec(sèche)	asciutto(a)	seco(a)
du (D)	—	you	tu/toi	tu	tú

	D	E	F	I	Es
dubbio (I)	Zweifel *m*	doubt	doute *m*	—	duda *f*
dubbioso (I)	zweifelhaft	doubtful	douteux (-euse)	—	dudoso(a)
dubitare (I)	zweifeln	doubt	douter	—	dudar
ducha (Es)	Dusche *f*	shower	douche *f*	doccia *f*	—
duck (E)	Ente *f*	—	canard *m*	anatra *f*	pato *m*
duda (Es)	Zweifel *m*	doubt	doute *m*	dubbio *m*	—
dudar (Es)	zweifeln	doubt	douter	dubitare	—
dudoso (Es)	zweifelhaft	doubtful	douteux (-euse)	dubbioso(a)	—
due (I)	zwei	two	deux	—	dos
dueño (Es)	Wirt *m*	landlord	patron *m*	oste *m*	—
due volte (I)	zweimal	twice	deux fois	—	dos veces
Duft (D)	—	scent	odeur *f*	profumo *m*	aroma *m*
dulce[1] (Es)	süß	sweet	sucré(e)	dolce	—
dulce[2] (Es)	sanft	gentle	doux(douce)	dolce	—
dull[1] (E)	fade	—	fade	insipido(a)	soso(a)
dull[2] (E)	trüb	—	trouble	torbido(a)	turbio(a)
dumb (E)	stumm	—	muet(te)	muto(a)	mudo(a)
dumm (D)	—	stupid	bête	stupido(a)	tonto(a)
d'une façon ou d'une autre (F)	irgend	at all/some	—	in qualche modo	cualquiera
d'une part (F)	einerseits	on one hand	—	da un lato	por un lado
dunkel (D)	—	dark	sombre	scuro(a)	oscuro(a)
dünn (D)	—	thin	mince	magro(a)	delgado(a)
du nord (F)	nördlich	northern	—	a nord	del norte
dunque (I)	also	therefore	donc	—	así
duomo (I)	Dom *m*	cathedral	cathédrale *f*	—	catedral *f*
duplice (I)	zweifach	double	double	—	doble
dur (F)	hart	hard	—	duro(a)	duro(a)
durable (E)	haltbar	—	résistant(e)	durevole	duradero
duración (Es)	Dauer *f*	duration	durée *f*	durata *f*	—
duradero (Es)	haltbar	durable	résistant(e)	durevole	—
durante (Es)	während	during	pendant	durante	—
durante (I)	während	during	pendant	—	durante
durar (Es)	dauern	last	durer	durare	—
durare (I)	dauern	last	durer	—	durar
durata (I)	Dauer *f*	duration	durée *f*	—	duración *f*
duration (E)	Dauer *f*	—	durée *f*	durata *f*	duración *f*
durch (D)	—	through	par	per	por
durcheinander (D)	—	in a muddle	pêle-mêle	sottosopra	en desorden
Durcheinander (D)	—	confusion	désordre *m*	confusione *f*	confusión *f*
Durchfahrt (D)	—	transit	passage *m*	passaggio *m*	paso *m*
Durchgang (D)	—	passage	passage *m*	passaggio *m*	paso *m*
durchgehen (D)	—	go through	passer à travers	passare	pasar
Durchreise (D)	—	passing through	passage *m*	transito *m*	paso *m*
durchschnittlich (D)	—	average	moyen(ne)	medio(a)	medio(a)
durée (F)	Dauer *f*	duration	—	durata *f*	duración *f*
durer (F)	dauern	last	—	durare	durar

	D	E	F	I	Es
durevole (I)	haltbar	durable	résistant(e)	—	duradero
dürfen (D)	—	be allowed	avoir le droit	potere	poder
dürftig (D)	—	needy	nécessiteux	misero(a)	escaso(a)
during (E)	während	—	pendant	durante	durante
during the week (E)	wochentags	—	en semaine	nei giorni feriali	entre semana
duro[1] (Es)	hart	hard	dur(e)	duro(a)	—
duro[2] (Es)	zäh	tough	coriace	duro(a)	—
duro[1] (I)	hart	hard	dur(e)	—	duro(a)
duro[2] (I)	zäh	tough	coriace	—	duro(a)
dürr (D)	—	skinny	maigre	secco(a)	árido(a)
Durst (D)	—	thirst	soif f	sete f	sed f
durstig (D)	—	thirsty	assoiffé(e)	assetato(a)	sediento(a)
Dusche (D)	—	shower	douche f	doccia f	ducha f
dust (E)	Staub m	—	poussière f	polvere f	polvo m
dustbin (E)	Mülleimer m	—	poubelle f	secchio dei rifiuti m	cubo de la basura m
dusty (E)	staubig	—	poussiéreux (-euse)	polveroso(a)	polvoriento(a)
du sud (F)	südlich	southern	—	a sud	al sur
duty[1] (E)	Pflicht f	—	devoir m	dovere m	obligación f
duty[2] (E)	Zoll m	—	droits de douane m pl	dazio m	arbitrio m
Dutzend (D)	—	dozen	douzaine f	dozzina f	docena f
duzen (D)	—	use the familiar form	tutoyer	dare del tu	tutear
dye (E)	färben	—	colorer	tingere	colorear
D-Zug (D)	—	through train	express m	direttissimo m	tren expreso m
e (I)	und	and	et	—	y
each (E)	jede(r,s)	—	chaque	ogni/ognuno	cada
each time (E)	jedesmal	—	chaque fois	ogni volta	cada vez
eagle (E)	Adler m	—	aigle m	aquila f	águila f
ear (E)	Ohr n	—	oreille f	orecchio m	oreja f
earache (E)	Ohren-schmerzen pl	—	mal d'oreilles m	mal d'orecchi m	dolor de oídos m
earlier (E)	früher	—	autrefois	prima	antes
early (E)	früh	—	tôt	presto	temprano(a)
earn (E)	verdienen	—	gagner	guadagnare	ganar
ear specialist (E)	Ohrenarzt m	—	spécialiste de l'oreille m	otoiatra m	médico del oído m
earth (E)	Erde f	—	terre f	terra f	tierra f
earthquake (E)	Erdbeben n	—	tremblement de terre m	terremoto m	terremoto m
east (E)	Osten m	—	est m	est m	este m
Easter (E)	Ostern n	—	Pâques f pl	Pasqua f	Pascua f
eastern (E)	östlich	—	d'est	ad est	al este
easy (E)	leicht	—	facile	semplice	ligero(a)
eat[1] (E)	essen	—	manger	mangiare	comer
eat[2] (E)	fressen	—	bouffer	mangiare	devorar
eatable (E)	eßbar	—	mangeable	commestibile	comestible
eau (F)	Wasser n	water	—	acqua f	agua f
eau-de-vie (F)	Schnaps m	spirits	—	acquavite f	aguardiente m

	D	E	F	I	Es
eau minérale (F)	Mineralwasser n	mineral water	—	acqua minerale f	agua mineral f
eau potable (F)	Trinkwasser n	drinking water	—	acqua potabile f	agua potable f
eaux (F)	Gewässer n	waters	—	acque f pl	aguas f pl
Ebbe (D)	—	low tide	marée basse f	bassa marea f	marea baja f
eben (D)	—	even	plan(e)	piano(a)	plano(a)
Ebene (D)	—	plain	plaine f	pianura f	llanura f
ebenfalls (D)	—	likewise	aussi	altrettanto	también
ebreo (I)	Jude m	Jew	juif m	—	judío m
eccellente[1] (I)	ausgezeichnet	excellent	excellent(e)	—	excelente
eccellente[2] (I)	hervorragend	excellent	excellent(e)	—	extraordinario(a)
eccetto[1] (I)	ausgenommen	except	exepté	—	excepto
eccetto[2] (I)	außer	except	hors de	—	salvo
eccezione (I)	Ausnahme f	exception	exeption f	—	excepción f
eccitante (I)	aufregend	exciting	énervant(e)	—	emocionante
eccitato (I)	aufgeregt	excited	agité(e)	—	excitado(a)
échange (F)	Austausch m	exchange	—	scambio m	cambio m
échanger[1] (F)	austauschen	exchange	—	scambiare	cambiar
échanger[2] (F)	tauschen	swap	—	scambiare	cambiar
échanger[3] (F)	umtauschen	exchange	—	cambiare	cambiar
échanger[4] (F)	vertauschen	exchange	—	scambiare	cambiar
échapper (F)	entkommen	escape	—	scappare	escapar
échapper, se (F)	entfliehen	escape	—	scappare	huir
echar[1] (Es)	einwerfen	post	poster	imbucare	—
echar[2] (Es)	eingießen	pour	verser	versare	—
echar de menos (Es)	vermissen	miss	manquer	sentire la mancanza	—
echar en cara (Es)	vorwerfen	blame	reprocher	rimproverare	—
écharpe[1] (F)	Halstuch n	scarf	—	sciarpa f	pañuelo para el cuello m
écharpe[2] (F)	Schal m	scarf	—	sciarpa f	chal m
échec (F)	Mißerfolg m	failure	—	insuccesso m	fracaco m
échelle (F)	Leiter f	ladder	—	scala f	escalera f
echt (D)	—	genuine	vrai(e)	vero(a)	verdadero(a)
Ecke (D)	—	corner	coin m	angolo m	esquina f
éclair (F)	Blitz m	lightning	—	lampo m	rayo m
éclairage (F)	Beleuchtung f	lighting	—	illuminazione f	iluminación f
éclairer (F)	beleuchten	illuminate	—	illuminare	iluminar
éclater (F)	platzen	burst	—	scoppiare	reventar
école (F)	Schule f	school	—	scuola f	escuela f
économe (F)	sparsam	economical	—	parsimonioso(a)	económico(a)
economical (E)	sparsam	—	économe	parsimonioso(a)	económico(a)
económico[1] (Es)	preiswert	inexpensive	bon marché	conveniente	—
económico[2] (Es)	sparsam	economical	économe	parsimonioso(a)	—
économiser (F)	sparen	save	—	risparmiare	ahorrar
écouter (F)	zuhören	listen	—	ascoltare	escuchar
écraser[1] (F)	überfahren	run over	—	investire	atropellar
écraser[2] (F)	zerdrücken	squash	—	sgualcire	aplastar
écrevisse (F)	Krebs m	crayfish	—	gambero m	cangrejo m
écrire (F)	schreiben	write	—	scrivere	escribir

	D	E	F	I	Es
écrit (F)	schriftlich	written	—	scritto(a)	por escrito
écriture (F)	Schrift f	writing	—	scrittura f	escritura f
écrivain (F)	Schriftsteller m	writer	—	scrittore m	escritor m
écrouler, se (F)	einstürzen	collapse	—	crollare	derrumbarse
écume (F)	Schaum m	foam	—	schiuma f	espuma f
edad (Es)	Alter n	age	âge m	età f	—
edificio (Es)	Gebäude n	building	bâtiment m	edificio m	—
edificio (I)	Gebäude n	building	bâtiment m	—	edificio m
editar (Es)	herausgeben	publish	éditer	pubblicare	—
éditer (F)	herausgeben	publish	—	pubblicare	editar
educación (Es)	Bildung f	education	éducation f	educazione f	—
educare (I)	erziehen	educate	élever	—	educar
educate[1] (E)	ausbilden	—	former	addestrare	instruir
educate[2] (E)	erziehen	—	élever	educare	educar
education[1] (E)	Ausbildung f	—	formation f	addestramento m	formación f
education[2] (E)	Bildung f	—	éducation f	istruzione f	educación f
education[3] (E)	Erziehung f	—	éducation f	educazione f	crianza f
éducation[1] (F)	Bildung f	education	—	istruzione f	educación f
éducation[2] (F)	Erziehung f	education	—	educazione f	crianza f
educazione (I)	Erziehung f	education	éducation f	—	crianza f
efecto (Es)	Wirkung f	effect	effet m	effetto m	—
effacer (F)	tilgen	erase	—	estinguere	anular
effect (E)	Wirkung f	—	effet m	effetto m	efecto m
effective (E)	wirksam	—	efficace	efficace	eficaz
effet (F)	Wirkung f	effect	—	effetto m	efecto m
effetto (I)	Wirkung f	effect	effet m	—	efecto m
efficace (F)	wirksam	effective	—	efficace	eficaz
efficace (I)	wirksam	effective	efficace	—	eficaz
éffondrer, se (F)	zusammen-brechen	collapse	—	crollare	desmayarse
efforcer, se (F)	bemühen, sich	make an effort	—	sforzarsi	esforzarse
effort[1] (E)	Bemühung f	—	effort m	sforzo m	esfuerzo m
effort[2] (E)	Mühe f	—	peine f	fatica f	esfuerzo m
effort[1] (F)	Anstrengung f	strain	—	fatica f	esfuerzo m
effort[2] (F)	Bemühung f	effort	—	sforzo m	esfuerzo m
effrayer (F)	erschrecken	frighten	—	spaventare	asustar
eficaz (Es)	wirksam	effective	efficace	efficace	—
egal (D)	—	all the same	égal(e)	uguale	igual
égal[1] (F)	egal	all the same	—	uguale	igual
égal[2] (F)	gleich	same	—	identico(a)	idéntico(a)
égarer (F)	verlegen	mislay	—	perdere	extraviar
egg (E)	Ei n	—	œuf m	uovo m	huevo m
église (F)	Kirche f	church	—	chiesa f	iglesia f
égoïsme (F)	Selbstsucht f	selfishness	—	egoismo m	egoísmo m
egoísmo (Es)	Selbstsucht f	selfishness	égoïsme m	egoismo m	—
egoismo (I)	Selbstsucht f	selfishness	égoïsme m	—	egoísmo m
ehe (D)	—	before	avant que	prima che	antes que
Ehe (D)	—	marriage	mariage m	matrimonio m	matrimonio m

	D	E	F	I	Es
Ehefrau (D)	—	wife	épouse *f*	moglie *f*	mujer *f*
Ehemann (D)	—	husband	mari *m*	marito *m*	marido *m*
eher (D)	—	sooner	plus tôt	prima	antes
Ehre (D)	—	honour	honneur *m*	onore *m*	honor *m*
ehrlich (D)	—	honest	honnête	onesto(a)	honesto(a)
Ei (D)	—	egg	œuf *m*	uovo *m*	huevo *m*
Eifersucht (D)	—	jealousy	jalousie *f*	gelosia *f*	celos *m pl*
eifrig (D)	—	keen	zélé(e)	diligente	diligente
eigen (D)	—	own	propre	proprio(a)	propio(a)
eigenartig (D)	—	strange	singulier(-ère)	strano(a)	extraño(a)
Eigenschaft (D)	—	quality	qualité *f*	qualità *f*	atributo *m*
eigentlich (D)	—	actually	en fait	in fondo	en realidad
Eigentümer (D)	—	owner	propriétaire *m*	proprietario *m*	propietario *m*
eight (E)	acht	—	huit	otto	ocho
eighteen (E)	achtzehn	—	dix-huit	diciotto	dieciocho
eighty (E)	achtzig	—	quatre-vingts	ottanta	ochenta
Eilbote (D)	—	courier	courrier *m*	corriere *m*	correo urgente *m*
Eile (D)	—	haste	hâte *f*	fretta *f*	prisa *f*
eilen (D)	—	hurry	dépêcher, se	andare in fretta	darse prisa
eilig (D)	—	hurried	pressé(e)	frettoloso(a)	rápido(a)
Eilzug (D)	—	limited stop train	express *m*	treno diretto *m*	tren expreso *m*
Eimer (D)	—	bucket	seau *m*	secchio *m*	cubo *m*
Einbahnstraße (D)	—	one-way street	rue à sens unique *f*	senso unico *m*	calle de dirección única *f*
einbehalten (D)	—	keep	retenir	trattenere	retener
einbiegen (D)	—	turn	tourner	svoltare	doblar
einbilden, sich (D)	—	imagine	imaginer, se	immaginarsi	imaginarse
einbrechen (D)	—	break in	cambrioler	rubare	robar
einbüßen (D)	—	lose	perdre	perdere	perder
eindeutig (D)	—	unequivocal	incontestable	univoco(a)	evidente
Eindruck (D)	—	impression	impression *f*	impressione *f*	impresión *f*
eine (D)	—	one	un(e)	un(a)	una/un/uno
einerseits (D)	—	on one hand	d'une part	da un lato	por un lado
einfach (D)	—	simple	simple	semplice	sencillo(a)
Einfahrt (D)	—	entrance	entrée *f*	ingresso *m*	entrada *f*
einfarbig (D)	—	all one colour	uni(e)	monocolore	de un solo color
Einfluß (D)	—	influence	influence *f*	influenza *f*	influencia *f*
Einfuhr (D)	—	import	importation *f*	importazione *f*	importación *f*
Eingang (D)	—	entrance	entrée *f*	entrata *f*	entrada *f*
eingießen (D)	—	pour	verser	versare	echar
eingreifen (D)	—	intervene	intervenir	intervenire	intervenir
einheimisch (D)	—	native	indigène	indigeno(a)	nativo
einhundert (D)	—	one hundred	cent	cento	cien
einige (D)	—	some	quelques	alcuni(e)	algunos(as)
einigen, sich (D)	—	agree	mettre d'accord, se	accordarsi	ponerse de acuerdo
einkassieren (D)	—	call in	recouvrer	incassare	cobrar
Einkauf (D)	—	shopping	achat *m*	spesa *f*	compra *f*
einkaufen gehen (D)	—	go shopping	faire les courses	fare la spesa	ir de compras

	D	E	F	I	Es
Einkaufstasche (D)	—	shopping bag	sac à provision *m*	borsa della spesa *f*	bolsa de compra *f*
Einkommen (D)	—	income	revenu *m*	entrate *f pl*	ingresos *m pl*
einladen (D)	—	invite	inviter	invitare	invitar
Einladung (D)	—	invitation	invitation *f*	invito *m*	invitación *f*
einleben, sich (D)	—	settle down	acclimater, se	ambientarsi	familiarizarse
Einleitung (D)	—	introduction	introduction *f*	introduzione *f*	introducción *f*
einmal (D)	—	once	une fois	una volta	una vez
einreisen (D)	—	enter	entrer dans un pays	entrare (in un paese)	entrar(en un país)
einrichten (D)	—	fit out	aménager	arredare	equipar
Einrichtung (D)	—	furnishing	ameublement *m*	arredamento *m*	mobiliario *m*
eins (D)	—	one	un	uno	uno(a)
einsam (D)	—	lonely	solitaire	solitario(a)	solitario(a)
einschalten (D)	—	switch on	allumer	accendere	conectar
einschlafen (D)	—	falling asleep	endormir, se	addormentarsi	adormecerse
einschlagen (D)	—	smash	casser	rompere	romper
einschließen (D)	—	lock up	renfermer	rinchiudere	encerrar
einschließlich (D)	—	including	y compris	incluso(a)	incluso
Einschreibebrief (D)	—	recorded delivery letter	lettre recommandée *f*	lettera raccomandata *f*	carta con acuse de recibo *f*
einschreiben (D)	—	enrol	inscrire	iscrivere	inscribir
einseitig (D)	—	one-sided	partial(e)	unilaterale	unilateral
einsteigen (D)	—	get in	monter	salire	subir a
einstellen[1] (D)	—	adjust	régler	regolare	ajustar
einstellen[2] (D)	—	employ	recruter	assumere	emplear
Einstellung (D)	—	attitude	attitude *f*	atteggiamento *m*	actitud *f*
einstürzen (D)	—	collapse	écrouler, se	crollare	derrumbarse
eintreffen (D)	—	arrive	arriver	arrivare	llegar
eintreten (D)	—	enter	entrer	entrare	entrar
Eintritt (D)	—	charge for admission	entrée *f*	entrata *f*	entrada *f*
einverstanden (D)	—	agreed	d'accord	d'accordo	de acuerdo
einwerfen (D)	—	post	poster	imbucare	echar
einwickeln (D)	—	wrap up	envelopper	avvolgere	envolver
Einwohner (D)	—	inhabitant	habitant *m*	abitante *m*	habitante *m*
Einzelheit (D)	—	detail	détail *m*	dettaglio *m*	detalle *f*
einzeln (D)	—	single	seul(e)	singolo(a)	singular
einziehen (D)	—	move in	emménager	prendere alloggio	instalarse
einzig (D)	—	only	seul(e)	unico(a)	único(a)
Eis (D)	—	ice	glace *f*	gelato *m*	hielo *m*
Eisen (D)	—	iron	fer *m*	ferro *m*	hierro *m*
Eisenbahn (D)	—	railway	chemin de fer *m*	ferrovia *f*	ferrocarril *m*
Eisschrank (D)	—	freezer	réfrigérateur *m*	frigorifero *m*	refrigerador *m*
eitel (D)	—	vain	vaniteux(-euse)	vanitoso(a)	vanidoso(a)
either...or (E)	entweder...oder	—	ou....ou	o...o	o...o
ejemplo (Es)	Beispiel *n*	example	exemple *m*	esempio *m*	—
ejercer (Es)	ausüben	practise	exercer	esercitare	—
ejercicio (Es)	Übung *f*	exercise	exercice *m*	esercizio *f*	—
él (Es)	er	he	il	lui/egli/esso	—

	D	E	F	I	Es
el, la, lo (Es)	der, die, das	the	le, la	il, la	—
elder (E)	ältere(r,s)	—	aîné(e)	maggiore	mayor
elección[1] (Es)	Auswahl *f*	choice	choix *m*	scelta *f*	—
elección[2] (Es)	Wahl *f*	election	élection *f*	elezioni *f pl*	—
elect (E)	wählen	—	élire	eleggere	elegir
election (E)	Wahl *f*	—	élection *f*	elezioni *f pl*	elección *f*
élection (F)	Wahl *f*	election	—	elezioni *f pl*	elección *f*
electric (E)	elektrisch	—	électrique	elettrico(a)	eléctrico(a)
electrician (E)	Elektriker *m*	—	électricien *m*	elettricista *m*	electricista *m*
electricidad (Es)	Elektrizität *f*	electricity	électricité *f*	elettricità *f*	—
électricien (F)	Elektriker *m*	electrician	—	elettricista *m*	electricista *m*
electricista (Es)	Elektriker *m*	electrician	électricien *m*	elettricista *m*	—
électricité (F)	Elektrizität *f*	electricity	—	elettricità *f*	electricidad *f*
electricity (E)	Elektrizität *f*	—	électricité *f*	elettricità *f*	electricidad *f*
eléctrico (Es)	elektrisch	electric	électrique	elettrico(a)	—
électrique (F)	elektrisch	electric	—	elettrico(a)	eléctrico(a)
Elefant (D)	—	elephant	éléphant *m*	elefante *m*	elefante *m*
elefante (Es)	Elefant *m*	elephant	éléphant *m*	elefante *m*	—
elefante (I)	Elefant *m*	elephant	éléphant *m*	—	elefante *m*
elegant (D)	—	elegant	élégant(e)	elegante	elegante
elegant (E)	elegant	—	élégant(e)	elegante	elegante
élégant (F)	elegant	elegant	—	elegante	elegante
elegante[1] (Es)	elegant	elegant	élégant(e)	elegante	—
elegante[2] (Es)	schick	stylish	chic	elegante	—
elegante[1] (I)	elegant	elegant	élégant(e)	—	elegante
elegante[2] (I)	schick	stylish	chic	—	elegante
eleggere (I)	wählen	elect	élire	—	elegir
elegir (Es)	wählen	elect	élire	eleggere	—
Elektriker (D)	—	electrician	électricien *m*	elettricista *m*	electricista *m*
elektrisch (D)	—	electric	électrique	elettrico(a)	eléctrico(a)
Elektrizität (D)	—	electricity	électricité *f*	elettricità *f*	electricidad *f*
elemosina (I)	Almosen *n*	alms	aumône *f*	—	limosna *f*
elenco (I)	Verzeichnis *n*	list	registre *m*	—	lista *f*
elenco telefonico (I)	Telefonbuch *n*	phone book	annuaire du téléphone *m*	—	guía telefónica *f*
Elend (D)	—	misery	misère *f*	miseria *f*	miseria *f*
elephant (E)	Elefant *m*	—	éléphant *m*	elefante *m*	elefante *m*
éléphant (F)	Elefant *m*	elephant	—	elefante *m*	elefante *m*
elettricista (I)	Elektriker *m*	electrician	électricien *m*	—	electricista *m*
elettricità (I)	Elektrizität *f*	electricity	électricité *f*	—	electricidad *f*
elettrico (I)	elektrisch	electric	électrique	—	eléctrico(a)
elevar[1] (Es)	erhöhen	raise	augmenter	innalzare	—
elevar[2] (Es)	erheben	raise	lever	alzare	—
elevator (E)	Fahrstuhl *m*/ Lift *m*	—	ascenseur *m*	ascensore *m*	ascensor *m*
élève (F)	Schüler *m*	pupil	—	scolaro *m*	alumno *m*
eleven (E)	elf	—	onze	undici	once
élever[1] (F)	erziehen	educate	—	educare	criar
élever[2] (F)	züchten	breed	—	allevare	criar

	D	E	F	I	Es
elezioni (I)	Wahl f	election	élection f	—	elección f
elf (D)	—	eleven	onze	undici	once
elegir (Es)	auswählen	choose	choisir	scegliere	—
élire (F)	wählen	elect	—	eleggere	elegir
ella (Es)	sie	she	elle	lei	—
elle (F)	sie	she	—	lei	ella
ellos, ellas (Es)	sie pl	they	ils/elles	loro	—
el mismo (Es)	derselbe	the same	le même	lo stesso	—
elogiar (Es)	loben	praise	louer	lodare	—
éloigné[1] (F)	entfernt	distant	—	distante	distante
éloigné[2] (F)	fern	far away	—	lontano(a)	lejos
éloigné[3] (F)	weit	far	—	largo(a)	ancho(a)
éloigner (F)	entfernen	remove	—	allontanare	quitar
elsewhere (E)	woanders	—	ailleurs	altrove	en otra parte
Eltern (D)	—	parents	parents m pl	genitori m pl	padres m pl
embajada (Es)	Botschaft f	embassy	ambassade f	ambasciata f	—
emballer (F)	verpacken	pack	—	impacchettare	empaquetar
embarazada (Es)	schwanger	pregnant	enceinte	incinta	—
embarrassing (E)	peinlich	—	gênant(e)	imbarazzante	desagradable
embarrassment (E)	Verlegenheit f	—	gêne f	imbarazzo m	contratiempo m
embassy (E)	Botschaft f	—	ambassade f	ambasciata f	embajada f
embezzle (E)	unterschlagen	—	soustraire	sottrarre	sustraer
emborracharse (Es)	betrinken, sich	get drunk	enivrer, se	ubriacarsi	—
embotella-miento (Es)	Stau m	traffic jam	embouteillage m	ingorgo m	—
embouchure (F)	Mündung f	mouth	—	sbocco m	desembocadura f
embouteillage (F)	Stau m	traffic jam	—	ingorgo m	embotella-miento m
embrace (E)	umarmen	—	embrasser	abbracciare	abrazar
embrasser[1] (F)	küssen	kiss	—	baciare	besar
embrasser[2] (F)	umarmen	embrace	—	abbracciare	abrazar
embutido (Es)	Wurst f	sausage	saucisse f	salsiccia f	—
emerald (E)	Smaragd m	—	émeraude f	smeraldo m	esmeralda f
émeraude (F)	Smaragd m	emerald	—	smeraldo m	esmeralda f
emergency (E)	Notfall m	—	cas d'urgence m	caso di emergenza m	caso de urgencia m
emergency exit (E)	Notausgang m	—	sortie de secours f	uscita di sicurezza f	salida de emergencia f
émetteur (F)	Sender m	station	—	trasmettitore m	emisora f
emicrania (I)	Migräne f	migraine	migraine f	—	jaqueca f
emigrar (Es)	auswandern	emigrate	émigrer	emigrare	—
emigrare (I)	auswandern	emigrate	émigrer	emigrare	emigrar
emigrate (E)	auswandern	—	émigrer	emigrare	emigrar
émigrer[1] (F)	auswandern	emigrate	—	emigrare	emigrar
émigrer[2] (F)	übersiedeln	move	—	trasferirsi	transladarse
emisión (Es)	Sendung f	transmission	diffusion f	trasmissione f	—
emisora (Es)	Sender m	station	émetteur m	trasmettitore m	—
emitir reflejos (Es)	blinken	flash	clignoter	lampeggiare	—
emménager (F)	einziehen	move in	—	prendere alloggio	instalarse
emmener (F)	mitnehmen	take along	—	prendere con sé	llevar consigo

	D	E	F	I	Es
emocionante (Es)	aufregend	exciting	énervant(e)	eccitante	—
empanada (Es)	Pastete f	pie	pâté m	vol-au-vent m	—
empaquetar (Es)	verpacken	pack	emballer	impacchettare	—
emparentado (Es)	verwandt	related	parent(e)	imparentato(a)	—
empêché (F)	verhindert	unable to make it	—	impedito(a)	impedido(a)
empêcher[1] (F)	hindern	hinder	—	impedire	impedir
empêcher[2] (F)	verhindern	prevent	—	impedire	evitar
emperador (Es)	Kaiser m	emperor	empereur m	imperatore m	—
empereur (F)	Kaiser m	emperor	—	imperatore m	emperador m
emperor (E)	Kaiser m	—	empereur m	imperatore m	emperador m
empezar[1] (Es)	anfangen	start	commencer	cominciare	—
empezar[2] (Es)	beginnen	begin	commencer	cominciare	—
Empfang (D)	—	reception	réception f	ricezione f	recepción f
empfangen (D)	—	receive	recevoir	ricevere	recibir
Empfänger (D)	—	receiver	destinataire f	destinatario m	destinatario m
empfehlen (D)	—	recommend	recommander	raccomandare	recomendar
Empfehlung (D)	—	recommendation	recommandation f	raccomandazione f	recomendación f
empfindlich (D)	—	sensitive	sensible	sensibile	sensible
emplâtre (F)	Pflaster n	plaster	—	cerotto m	esparadrapo m
empleado (Es)	Angestellter m	employee	employé m	impiegato m	—
emplear (Es)	einstellen	employ	recruter	assumere	—
emploi (F)	Verwendung f	use	—	uso m	utilización f
employ (E)	einstellen	—	recruter	assumere	emplear
employé (F)	Angestellter m	employee	—	impiegato m	empleado(a) m(f)
employee (E)	Angestellter m	—	employé m	impiegato m	empleado(a) m(f)
employer[1] (F)	anwenden	apply	—	impiegare	usar
employer[2] (F)	verwenden	use	—	usare	utilizar
empört (D)	—	indignant	révolté(e)	indignato(a)	indignado(a)
emprender (Es)	unternehmen	undertake	entreprendre	intraprendere	—
empresa[1] (Es)	Firma f	company	firme f	ditta f	—
empresa[2] (Es)	Unternehmen n	company	entreprise f	impresa f	—
empty (E)	leer	—	vide	vuoto(a)	vacío(a)
empujar[1] (Es)	anstoßen	bump	heurter	urtare	—
empujar[2] (Es)	stoßen	push	pousser	spingere	—
empujar[3] (Es)	schieben	push	pousser	spingere	—
empujón (Es)	Stoß m	blow	coup m	spinta f	—
en (Es)	in	in/into	dans/à/en	in/a/tra/fra	—
en (F)	davon	of it	—	di la/ne	de ello
en alguna parte (Es)	irgendwo	somewhere	n'importe où	in qualche posto	—
enamorado (Es)	verliebt	in love	amoureux(-euse)	innamorato(a)	—
enamorarse (Es)	verlieben	fall in love	tomber amoureux(-euse)	innamorarsi	—
en arrière (F)	rückwärts	backwards	—	in dietro	marcha atrás
en avant[1] (F)	voraus	ahead	—	avanti	delante
en avant[2] (F)	vorwärts	forward(s)	—	avanti	adelante
en bas[1] (F)	abwärts	downwards	—	in giù	hacia abajo
en bas[2] (F)	herunter	down	—	giù	abajo
encaisser (F)	kassieren	take	—	incassare	cobrar

	D	E	F	I	Es
encantado (Es)	entzückt	delighted	ravi(e)	affascinato(a)	—
encantador¹ (Es)	entzückend	delightful	ravissant(e)	affascinante	—
encantador² (Es)	charmant	charming	charmant(e)	affascinante	—
encargar (Es)	beauftragen	instruct	charger de	incaricare	—
en casa (Es)	daheim	at home	à la maison	a casa	—
en caso de que (Es)	falls	in case	au cas où	qualora	—
encauzar (Es)	lenken	steer	conduire	guidare	—
enceinte (F)	schwanger	pregnant	—	incinta	embarazada
encender¹ (Es)	anzünden	light	allumer	accendere	—
encender² (Es)	anmachen	put on	allumer	accendere	—
encender³ (Es)	zünden	ignite	allumer, se	accendersi	—
encerrar (Es)	einschließen	lock up	renfermer	rinchiudere	—
en chômage (F)	arbeitslos	unemployed	—	disoccupato(a)	desempleado(a)
enchufe (Es)	Steckdose f	socket	prise électrique f	presa f	—
enciclopedia (I)	Lexikon n	encyclopaedia	encyclopédie f	—	diccionario m
en condiciones (Es)	imstande	able	capable	capace	—
encontrar¹ (Es)	begegnen	meet	rencontrer	incontrare	—
encontrar² (Es)	finden	find	trouver	trovare	—
encontrar³ (Es)	treffen	meet	rencontrer	incontrare	—
encontrarse (Es)	befinden, sich	be situated	trouver, se	trovarsi	—
encore (F)	noch	still	—	ancora	aún/todavía
encore une fois (F)	nochmals	again	—	di nuovo	otra vez
en cualquier caso (Es)	jedenfalls	in any case	en tout cas	in ogni caso	—
encuentro (Es)	Treffen n	meeting	rencontre f	incontro m	—
encuesta (Es)	Umfrage f	poll	enquête f	inchiesta f	—
encyclopaedia (E)	Lexikon n	—	encyclopédie f	enciclopedia f	diccionario m
encyclopédie (F)	Lexikon n	encyclopaedia	—	enciclopedia f	diccionario m
end¹ (E)	enden	—	finir	finire	acabar
end² (E)	Ende n	—	fin f	fine f	fin m
end³ (E)	Schluß m	—	fin f	fine f	conclusión f
Ende (D)	—	end	fin f	fine f	fin m
enden (D)	—	end	finir	finire	acabar
en descendant (F)	bergab	downhill	—	in discesa	cuesta abajo
en desorden (Es)	durcheinander	in a muddle	pêle-mêle	sottosopra	—
en dessous (F)	darunter	underneath	—	sotto	por debajo
en dessus (F)	darüber	above	—	sopra	por encima
endlich (D)	—	at last	enfin	finalmente	finalmente
endommage- ment (F)	Beschädigung f	damage	—	danno m	deterioro m
endommager (F)	beschädigen	damage	—	danneggiare	deteriorar
endormir, se (F)	einschlafen	fall asleep	—	addormentarsi	adormecerse
endroit (F)	Ort m	place	—	luogo m	lugar m
Endstation (D)	—	terminus	terminus m	capolinea m	estación terminal f
en échange (F)	dafür	instead	—	invece	en su lugar
en el futuro (Es)	zukünftig	future	futur(e)	futuro(a)	—
enemigo (Es)	Feind m	enemy	ennemi m	nemico m	—
enemy (E)	Feind m	—	ennemi m	nemico m	enemigo m
enero (Es)	Januar m	January	janvier m	gennaio m	—

enlever

	D	E	F	I	Es
énervant (F)	aufregend	exciting	—	eccitante	emocionante
énerver (F)	aufregen	excite	—	agitare	agitar
en eso (Es)	indessen	meanwhile	cependant	nel frattempo	—
en face de (F)	gegenüber	opposite	—	di fronte (a)	en frente
enfadado (Es)	ärgerlich	angry	fâché(e)	arrabbiato(a)	—
enfadarse (Es)	ärgern	annoy	fâcher	arrabbiare	—
en fait (F)	eigentlich	actually	—	in fondo	en realidad
enfance (F)	Kindheit f	childhood	—	infanzia f	niñez f
enfant (F)	Kind n	child	—	bambino m	niño m
enfer (F)	Hölle f	hell	—	inferno m	infierno m
enfermar (Es)	erkranken	get ill	tomber malade	ammalarsi	—
enfermedad (Es)	Krankheit f	illness	maladie f	malattia f	—
enfermera (Es)	Krankenschwester f	nurse	infirmière f	infermiera f	—
enfermero (Es)	Krankenpfleger m	nursing orderly	infirmier m	infermiere m	—
enfermizo (Es)	ungesund	unhealthy	malsain(e)	malsano(a)	—
enfermo (Es)	krank	ill	malade	malato(a)	—
enfin (F)	endlich	at last	—	finalmente	finalmente
enflé (F)	geschwollen	swollen	—	gonfio(a)	hinchado(a)
enfoncer (F)	stecken	insert	—	inserire	introducir
enfoncer, se (F)	versinken	sink	—	affondare	hundirse
en frente (Es)	gegenüber	opposite	en face de	di fronte(a)	—
eng (D)	—	narrow	étroit(e)	stretto(a)	estrecho(a)
engaged (E)	besetzt	—	occupé(e)	occupato(a)	ocupado(a)
engañar[1] (Es)	betrügen	cheat	tromper	ingannare	—
engañar[2] (Es)	täuschen	deceive	tromper	ingannare	—
engañar[3] (Es)	verführen	seduce	séduire	sedurre	—
engaño (Es)	Betrug m	fraud	tromperie f	inganno m	—
Engel (D)	—	angel	ange m	angelo m	ángel m
en general (Es)	überhaupt	at all	en général	in genere	—
en général (F)	überhaupt	at all	—	in genere	en general
engineer (E)	Mechaniker m	—	mécanicien m	meccanico m	mecánico m
England (D)	—	England	Angleterre f	Inghilterra f	Inglaterra f
England (E)	England n	—	Angleterre f	Inghilterra f	Inglaterra f
Engländer (D)	—	Englishman	Anglais m	inglese m	inglés m
englisch (D)	—	English	anglais(e)	inglese	inglés(-esa)
English (E)	englisch	—	anglais(e)	inglese	inglés(a)
Englishman (E)	Engländer m	—	Anglais m	inglese m	inglés m
en haut (F)	oben	above	—	sopra	arriba
enigma (I)	Rätsel n	riddle	devinette f	—	adivinanza f
enivrer, se (F)	betrinken, sich	get drunk	—	ubriacarsi	emborracharse
enjoy (E)	genießen	—	jouir	godere	disfrutar
enjoy o.s. (E)	amüsieren, sich	—	amuser, se	divertirsi	divertirse
Enkel (D)	—	grandson	petit-fils m	nipote m	nieto m
Enkelin (D)	—	granddaughter	petite-fille f	nipote f	nieta f
Enkelkind (D)	—	grandchild	petit-enfant m	nipote m/f	nieto m
enlarge (E)	vergrößern	—	agrandir	ingrandire	agrandar
enlever[1] (F)	ausziehen	take off	—	levare	quitarse

	D	E	F	I	Es
enlever² (F)	wegnehmen	take away	—	togliere	quitar
en medio (Es)	mitten	in the middle	au milieu	in mezzo(a)	—
en medio de (Es)	inmitten	in the middle of	au milieu de	in mezza	—
en même temps (F)	gleichzeitig	simultaneous	—	contemporaneo(a)	a la vez
en modo alguno (Es)	keineswegs	not at all	pas du tout	non affatto	—
en montant (F)	bergauf	uphill	—	in salita	cuesta arriba
ennemi (F)	Feind m	enemy	—	nemico m	enemigo m
en ninguna parte (Es)	nirgends	nowhere	nulle part	da nessuna parte	—
ennuyer, se (F)	langweilen, sich	get bored	—	annoiarsi	aburrirse
ennuyeux (F)	langweilig	boring	—	noioso(a)	aburrido(a)
enorme (Es)	riesig	huge	énorme	enorme	—
énorme¹ (F)	gewaltig	tremendous	—	enorme	formidable
énorme² (F)	riesig	huge	—	enorme	enorme
enorme¹ (I)	gewaltig	tremendous	énorme	—	formidable
enorme² (I)	riesig	huge	énorme	—	enorme
en otra parte (Es)	woanders	elsewhere	ailleurs	altrove	—
enough (E)	genug	—	assez	abbastanza	bastante
en outre (F)	außerdem	besides	—	inoltre	además
en parte (Es)	teilweise	partly	en partie	in parte	—
en partie (F)	teilweise	partly	—	in parte	en parte
en persona (Es)	persönlich	personal	personnel(le)	personale	—
en primer lugar (Es)	zunächst	first of all	pour l'instant	dapprima	—
en principio (Es)	grundsätzlich	fundamental	par principe	basilare	—
enquête (F)	Umfrage f	poll	—	inchiesta f	encuesta f
en realidad (Es)	eigentlich	actually	en fait	in fondo	—
enregistrement des bagages (F)	Gepäckannahme f	luggage desk	—	accettazione bagagli f	recepción de equipajes f
enregistrer (F)	verzeichnen	list	—	registrare	hacer una lista
enrol (E)	einschreiben	—	inscrire	iscrivere	inscribir
enrouler (F)	wickeln	wind	—	avvolgere	envolver
en route (F)	unterwegs	on the way	—	per strada	en camino
ensalada (Es)	Salat m	salad	salade f	insalata f	—
en seguida (Es)	sofort	immediately	immédiatement	subito	—
enseigner (F)	lehren	teach	—	insegnare	enseñar
en semaine (F)	wochentags	during the week	—	nei giorni feriali	entre semana
ensemble¹ (F)	miteinander	together	—	insieme	juntos
ensemble² (F)	zusammen	together	—	insieme	juntos
ensemble³ (F)	gemeinsam	together	—	comune	juntos
enseñanza (Es)	Unterricht m	lessons	cours m	lezione f	—
enseñar (Es)	lehren	teach	enseigner	insegnare	—
ensoleillé (F)	sonnig	sunny	—	sereno(a)	soleado(a)
ensuite¹ (F)	dann	then	—	in seguito	luego
ensuite² (F)	nachher	afterwards	—	dopo	después
en su lugar (Es)	dafür	instead	en échange	invece	—
en suma (Es)	insgesamt	altogether	dans l'ensemble	complessivamente	—
en tanto que (Es)	solange	as long	tant que	finché	—

	D	E	F	I	Es
entarimado (Es)	Parkett *n*	stalls	parquet *m*	parquet *m*	—
entbehren (D)	—	do without	passer de, se	fare a meno di	pasarse sin
entdecken (D)	—	discover	découvrir	scoprire	descubrir
Ente (D)	—	duck	canard *m*	anatra *f*	pato *m*
entender (Es)	verstehen	understand	comprendre	capire	—
entendre (F)	hören	hear	—	sentire	oír
enter[1] (E)	betreten	—	entrer dans	entrare in	entrar en
enter[2] (E)	eintreten	—	entrer	entrare	entrar
enter[3] (E)	einreisen	—	entrer dans un pays	entrare (in un paese)	entrar (en un país)
enterarse (Es)	erfahren	learn	apprendre	venire a sapere	—
entero[1] (Es)	ganz	whole	tout(e)	intero(a)	—
entero[2] (Es)	gesamt	entire	tout(e)	totale	—
enterrement (F)	Beerdigung *f*	funeral	—	funerale *m*	entierro *m*
entertain (E)	unterhalten	—	entretenir	divertire	entretener
entfernen (D)	—	remove	éloigner	allontanare	quitar
entfernt (D)	—	distant	éloigné(e)	distante	distante
Entfernung (D)	—	distance	distance *f*	distanza *f*	distancia *f*
entfliehen (D)	—	escape	échapper, se	scappare	huir
entgegengesetzt (D)	—	opposite	opposé(e)	opposto(a)	opuesto(a)
entgegen-kommen (D)	—	approach	venir à la rencontre	venire incontro	venir al encuentro
enthalten (D)	—	contain	contenir	contenere	contener
enthousiasmer (F)	begeistern	inspire	—	entusiasmare	entusiasmar
enthousiaste (F)	begeistert	inspired	—	entusiasta	entusiasta
entierro (Es)	Beerdigung *f*	funeral	enterrement *m*	funerale *m*	—
entire (E)	gesamt	—	tout(e)	totale	entero(a)
entkommen (D)	—	escape	échapper	scappare	escapar
entlang (D)	—	along	le long de	lungo	a lo largo de
entlassen (D)	—	release	renvoyer	licenziare	despedir
entonces (Es)	damals	at that time	alors	allora	—
entourer (F)	umgeben	surround	—	circondare	rodear
en tout cas (F)	jedenfalls	in any case	—	in ogni caso	en cualquier caso
entrada[1] (Es)	Eingang *m*	entrance	entrée *f*	entrata *f*	—
entrada[2] (Es)	Eintritt *m*	charge for admission	entrée *f*	entrata *f*	—
entrada[3] (Es)	Einfahrt *f*	entrance	entrée *f*	ingresso *m*	—
entrada[4] (Es)	Zugang *m*	access	accès *m*	entrata *f*	—
entrambi (I)	beide	both	tous/ toutes les deux	—	ambos(as)
entrance[1] (E)	Eingang *m*	—	entrée *f*	entrata *f*	entrada *f*
entrance[2] (E)	Einfahrt *f*	—	entrée *f*	ingresso *m*	entrada *f*
entrar (Es)	eintreten	enter	entrer	entrare	—
entrar en (Es)	betreten	enter	entrer dans	entrare in	—
entrare[1] (I)	betreten	enter	entrer dans	—	entrar
entrare[2] (I)	eintreten	enter	entrer	—	entrar
entrare (in un paese) (I)	einreisen	enter	entrer dans un pays	—	entrar (en un país)
entrar (en un país) (Es)	einreisen	enter	entrer dans un pays	entrare (in un paese)	—
entrata[1] (I)	Auffahrt *f*	slip road	bretelle d'accès *f*	—	vía de acceso *f*

	D	E	F	I	Es
entrata² (I)	Eingang m	entrance	entrée f	—	entrada f
entrata³ (I)	Eintritt m	charge for admission	entrée f	—	entrada f
entrata⁴ (I)	Zugang m	access	accès m	—	entrada f
entrate (I)	Einkommen n	income	revenu m	—	ingresos m pl
en travers (F)	quer	across	—	di trasverso	al través
entre¹ (Es)	dazwischen	in between	entre	in mezzo	—
entre² (Es)	zwischen	between	entre	tra/fra	—
entre¹ (F)	dazwischen	in between	—	in mezzo	entre
entre² (F)	zwischen	between	—	tra/fra	entre
entrée¹ (F)	Eingang m	entrance	—	entrata f	entrada f
entrée² (F)	Eintritt m	charge for admission	—	entrata f	entrada f .
entrée³ (F)	Einfahrt f	entrance	—	ingresso m	entrada f
entrée⁴ (F)	Flur m	hall	—	corridoio m	corredor m
entregar (Es)	überreichen	hand over	présenter	consegnare	—
entreprendre (F)	unternehmen	undertake	—	intraprendere	emprender
entreprise (F)	Unternehmen n	company	—	impresa f	empresa f
entrer (F)	eintreten	enter	—	entrare	entrar
entrer dans (F)	betreten	enter	—	entrare	entrar
entrer dans un pays (F)	einreisen	enter	—	entrare (in un paese)	entrar (en un país)
entre semana (Es)	wochentags	during the week	en semaine	nei giorni feriali	—
entretemps (F)	inzwischen	meanwhile	—	frattanto	mientras tanto
entretener (Es)	unterhalten	entertain	entretenir	divertire	—
entretenir (F)	unterhalten	entertain	—	divertire	entretener
entretenir, se (F)	unterhalten, sich	talk	—	conversare	conversar
entretien (F)	Unterhaltung f	conversation	—	conversazione f	conversación f
entrevista¹ (Es)	Interview n	interview	interview f	intervista f	—
entrevista² (Es)	Unterredung f	talk	entrevue f	colloquio m	—
entrevue (F)	Unterredung f	talk	—	colloquio m	entrevista f
entro (I)	innerhalb	within	à l'intérieur de	—	dentro de
entscheiden (D)	—	decide	décider	decidere	decidir
Entscheidung (D)	—	decision	décision f	decisione f	decisión f
entschließen, sich (D)	—	decide	décider, se	decidere	decidirse
Entschluß (D)	—	decision	décision f	decisione f	decisión f
entschuldigen, sich (D)	—	apologize	excuser, se	scusarsi	disculparse
Entschuldigung (D)	—	apology	excuse f	scusa f	disculpa f
entsprechen (D)	—	correspond	correspondre à	corrispondere	corresponder
entstehen (D)	—	arise	naître	nascere	surgir
enttäuschen (D)	—	disappoint	décevoir	deludere	defraudar
enttäuscht (D)	—	disappointed	déçu(e)	deluso(a)	defraudado(a)
entusiasmar (Es)	begeistern	inspire	enthousiasmer	entusiasmare	—
entusiasmare (I)	begeistern	inspire	enthousiasmer	—	entusiasmar
entusiasta (Es)	begeistert	inspired	enthousiaste	entusiasta	—
entusiasta (I)	begeistert	inspired	enthousiaste	entusiasta	—
entweder...oder (D)	—	either...or	ou...ou	o...o	o...o
entwickeln (D)	—	develop	développer	sviluppare	desarrollar

	D	E	F	I	Es
Entwicklung (D)	—	development	développement *m*	sviluppo *m*	desarrollo *m*
Entwurf (D)	—	outline	esquisse *f*	abbozzo *m*	proyecto *m*
entzückend (D)	—	delightful	ravissant(e)	affascinante	encantador(a)
entzückt (D)	—	delighted	ravi(e)	affascinato(a)	encantado(a)
Entzündung (D)	—	inflammation	inflammation *f*	infiammazione *f*	inflamación *f*
en vain (F)	umsonst	for nothing	—	per niente	en vano
en valoir la peine (F)	lohnen	be worth while	—	valere la pena	valer la pena
en vano (Es)	umsonst	for nothing	en vain	per niente	—
envelope (E)	Umschlag *m*	—	enveloppe *f*	busta *f*	sobre *m*
enveloppe (F)	Umschlag *m*	envelope	—	busta *f*	sobre *m*
envelopper (F)	einwickeln	wrap up	—	avvolgere	envolver
en vente (F)	erhältlich	available	—	acquistabile	que puede adquirirse
en vez de[1] (Es)	anstatt	instead of	au lieu de	invece di	—
en vez de[2] (Es)	statt	instead	au lieu de	invece di	—
enviar (Es)	übersenden	send	envoyer	spedire	—
enviar a la nueva dirección (Es)	nachsenden	send on	faire suivre	inoltrare	—
envidia (Es)	Neid *m*	envy	jalousie *f*	invidia *f*	—
envidiar (Es)	beneiden	envy	envier	invidiare	—
envidioso (Es)	neidisch	envious	envieux(-euse)	invidioso(a)	—
envier (F)	beneiden	envy	—	invidiare	envidiar
envieux (F)	neidisch	envious	—	invidioso(a)	envidioso(a)
envious (E)	neidisch	—	envieux(-euse)	invidioso(a)	envidioso(a)
environ[1] (F)	etwa	about	—	pressappoco	unos
environ[2] (F)	ungefähr	about	—	pressappoco	aproximadamente
environment (E)	Umwelt *f*	—	environnement *m*	ambiente *m*	medioambiente *m*
environnement (F)	Umwelt *f*	environment	—	ambiente *m*	medioambiente *m*
environs[1] (F)	Nähe *f*	proximity	—	vicinanza *f*	proximidad *f*
environs[2] (F)	Umgebung *f*	surroundings	—	dintorni *m pl*	alrededores *m pl*
envolver[1] (Es)	einwickeln	wrap up	envelopper	avvolgere	—
envolver[2] (Es)	wickeln	wind	enrouler	avvolgere	—
envoyer[1] (F)	schicken	send	—	inviare	mandar
envoyer[2] (F)	übersenden	send	—	spedire	enviar
envy[1] (E)	beneiden	—	envier	invidiare	envidiar
envy[2] (E)	Neid *m*	—	jalousie *f*	invidia *f*	envidia *f*
épais (F)	dicht	dense	—	denso(a)	espeso(a)
épaule (F)	Schulter *f*	shoulder	—	spalla *f*	hombro *m*
épeler (F)	buchstabieren	spell	—	sillabare	deletrear
épice (F)	Gewürz *n*	spice	—	spezia *f*	especia *f*
épicé[1] (F)	scharf	hot	—	piccante	picante
épicé[2] (F)	würzig	spicy	—	aromatico(a)	aromático(a)
épicer (F)	würzen	season	—	condire	condimentar
épinard (F)	Spinat *m*	spinach	—	spinaci *m pl*	espinacas *f pl*
éplucher (F)	schälen	peel	—	sbucciare	pelar
éponge (F)	Schwamm *m*	sponge	—	spugna *f*	esponja *f*
épouse (F)	Ehefrau *f*	wife	—	moglie *f*	mujer *f*
épuisé[1] (F)	ausverkauft	sold out	—	esaurito(a)	vendido(a)

	D	E	F	I	Es
épuisé[2] (F)	erschöpft	exhausted	—	esausto(a)	agotado(a)
equipaje (Es)	Gepäck n	luggage	bagages m pl	bagaglio m	—
equipaje de mano (Es)	Handgepäck n	hand-luggage	bagage à main m	bagaglio a mano m	—
equipar (Es)	einrichten	fit out	aménager	arredare	—
équipe (F)	Mannschaft f	team	—	squadra f	equipo m
equipo (Es)	Mannschaft f	team	équipe f	squadra f	—
equivocado (Es)	verkehrt	wrong	faux(fausse)	sbagliato(a)	—
equivocarse (Es)	irren	be mistaken	tromper, se	sbagliare	—
equivoco (I)	Mißverständnis n	misunderstanding	malentendu m	—	malentendido m
er (D)	—	he	il	lui/egli/esso	él
erase (E)	tilgen	—	effacer	estinguere	anular
erba (I)	Gras n	grass	herbe f	—	hierba f
erben (D)	—	inherit	hériter	ereditare	heredar
Erbse (D)	—	pea	pois m	pisello m	guisante m
Erdbeben (D)	—	earthquake	tremblement de terre m	terremoto m	terremoto m
Erdbeere (D)	—	strawberry	fraise f	fragola f	fresa f
Erde (D)	—	earth	terre f	terra f	tierra f
Erdgeschoß (D)	—	ground floor	rez-de-chaussée m	pianterreno m	planta baja f
Erdöl (D)	—	oil	pétrole m	petrolio m	petróleo m
ereditare[1] (I)	beerben	inherit from	hériter	—	heredar
ereditare[2] (I)	erben	inherit	hériter	—	heredar
Ereignis (D)	—	event	événement m	avvenimento m	suceso m
erfahren (D)	—	learn	apprendre	venire a sapere	enterarse
Erfahrung (D)	—	experience	expérience f	esperienza f	experiencia f
erfinden (D)	—	invent	inventer	inventare	inventar
Erfolg (D)	—	success	succès m	successo m	éxito m
erfolgreich (D)	—	successful	avec succès	pieno(a) di successi	afortunado(a)
erforderlich (D)	—	necessary	nécessaire	necessario(a)	necesario(a)
erfreut (D)	—	delighted	réjoui(e)	lieto(a)	contento(a)
erfrieren (D)	—	freeze to death	mourir de froid	morire di freddo	morirse de frío
Erfrischung (D)	—	refreshment	rafraîchissement m	rinfresco m	refresco m
erfüllen (D)	—	fulfil	remplir	esaudire	conceder
ergänzen (D)	—	supplement	compléter	completare	completar
Ergebnis (D)	—	result	résultat m	risultato m	resultado m
ergreifen (D)	—	seize	saisir	afferrare	coger
erhalten (D)	—	receive	recevoir	ricevere	obtener
erhältlich (D)	—	available	en vente	acquistabile	que puede adquirirse
erheben (D)	—	raise	lever	alzare	elevar
erheblich (D)	—	considerable	considérable	rilevante	considerable
erhöhen (D)	—	raise	augmenter	innalzare	elevar
erholen, sich (D)	—	recover	reposer, se	rimettersi	recuperarse
Erholung (D)	—	recovery	repos m	riposo m	descanso m
erinnern (D)	—	remember	souvenir	ricordare	recordar
Erinnerung (D)	—	memory	souvenir m	ricordo m	memoria f

	D	E	F	I	Es
erkältet (D)	—	have a cold	avoir un rhume	essere raffreddato(a)	estar acatarrado(a)
Erkältung (D)	—	cold	refroidissement m	raffreddore m	catarro m
erkennen (D)	—	recognize	reconnaître	riconoscere	reconocer
erklären (D)	—	explain	expliquer	spiegare	explicar
erkranken (D)	—	get ill	tomber malade	ammalarsi	enfermar
erkundigen, sich (D)	—	inquire	renseigner, se	informarsi	informarse
erlauben (D)	—	allow	permettre	permettere	permitir
Erlaubnis (D)	—	permission	permission f	permesso m	permiso m
erleben (D)	—	experience	être témoin de	vivere	experimentar
erledigen (D)	—	take care of	régler	sbrigare	acabar
Ermäßigung (D)	—	reduction	réduction f	riduzione f	rebaja f
ermöglichen (D)	—	make possible	rendre possible	rendere possibile	facilitar
ermüden (D)	—	tire	fatiguer	stancarsi	cansar
ernähren (D)	—	feed	nourrir	nutrire	alimentar
Ernährung (D)	—	nourishment	nourriture f	alimentazione f	alimentación f
erneuern (D)	—	renew	rénover	rinnovare	renovar
ernst (D)	—	serious	sérieux(-ieuse)	serio(a)	serio(a)
Ernst (D)	—	seriousness	sérieux m	serietà f	seriedad f
Ernte (D)	—	harvest	moisson f	raccolto m	cosecha f
eroe (I)	Held m	hero	héros m	—	héroe m
Eröffnung (D)	—	opening	ouverture f	apertura f	abertura f
Erpressung (D)	—	blackmail	chantage m	ricatto m	chantaje m
erreichen (D)	—	reach	atteindre	raggiungere	alcanzar
erreur (F)	Irrtum m	mistake	—	errore m	error m
error (Es)	Irrtum m	mistake	erreur f	errore m	—
errore (I)	Irrtum m	mistake	erreur f	—	error m
Ersatz (D)	—	substitute	remplacement m	sostituzione f	sustitución f
erscheinen (D)	—	appear	apparaître	apparire	aparecer
erschöpft (D)	—	exhausted	épuisé(e)	esausto(a)	agotado(a)
erschrecken (D)	—	frighten	effrayer	spaventare	asustar
ersetzen (D)	—	replace	remplacer	sostituire	sustituir
erst (D)	—	first	d'abord	dapprima	primero
erste (D)	—	first	premier(-ière)	primo(a)	primero(a)
ertragen (D)	—	bear	supporter	sopportare	soportar
ertrinken (D)	—	drown	noyer, se	annegare	ahogarse
erwachen (D)	—	wake up	réveiller, se	svegliarsi	despertar
erwachsen (D)	—	grown up	adulte	adulto(a)	adulto(a)
Erwachsener (D)	—	adult	adulte m	adulto m	adulto m
erwähnen (D)	—	mention	mentionner	menzionare	mencionar
erwarten (D)	—	expect	attendre	aspettare	esperar
erwerben (D)	—	acquire	acquérir	acquistare	adquirir
erwischen (D)	—	catch	attraper	acchiappare	atrapar
erzählen (D)	—	tell	raconter	raccontare	contar
erzeugen (D)	—	produce	produire	fabbricare	generar
Erzeugnis (D)	—	product	produit m	prodotto m	producto m
erziehen (D)	—	educate	élever	educare	educar
Erziehung (D)	—	education	éducation f	educazione f	crianza f

	D	E	F	I	Es
erzwingen (D)	—	obtain by force	forcer	ottenere con la forza	forzar
esagerare (I)	übertreiben	exaggerate	exagérer	—	exagerar
esagerato (I)	übertrieben	exaggerated	exagéré(e)	—	exagerado(a)
esagerazione (I)	Übertreibung f	exaggeration	exagération f	—	exageración f
esame (I)	Prüfung f	examination	examen m	—	examen m
esaminare[1] (I)	prüfen	test	tester	—	examinar
esaminare[2] (I)	untersuchen	examine	examiner	—	examinar
esaminare[3] (I)	überprüfen	check	contrôler	—	examinar
esaudire (I)	erfüllen	fulfil	remplir	—	conceder
esaurito[1] (I)	ausverkauft	sold out	épuisé(e)	—	vendido(a)
esaurito[2] (I)	ausgebucht	fully booked	complet(-ète)	—	completo(a)
esausto (I)	erschöpft	exhausted	épuisé(e)	—	agotado(a)
escala (Es)	Zwischen-landung f	intermediate landing	escale f	scalo intermedio m	—
escalar (Es)	klettern	climb	grimper	arrampicarsi	—
escalator (E)	Rolltreppe f	—	escalier roulant m	scala mobile f	escalera mecánica f
escale (F)	Zwischen-landung f	intermediate landing	—	scalo intermedio m	escala f
escalera[1] (Es)	Leiter f	ladder	échelle f	scala f	—
escalera[2] (Es)	Treppe f	stairs	escalier m	scala f	—
escalera mecánica (Es)	Rolltreppe f	escalator	escalier roulant m	scala mobile f	—
escalier (F)	Treppe f	stairs	—	scala f	escalera f
escalier roulant (F)	Rolltreppe f	escalator	—	scala mobile f	escalera mecánica f
escalón (Es)	Stufe f	step	marche f	gradino m	—
escándalo (Es)	Skandal m	scandal	scandale m	scandalo m	—
Escandinavia (Es)	Skandinavien	Scandinavia	Scandinavie f	Scandinavia f	—
escapar (Es)	entkommen	escape	échapper	scappare	—
escaparate (Es)	Schaufenster n	shop window	vitrine f	vetrina f	—
escape[1] (E)	entkommen	—	échapper	scappare	escapar
escape[2] (E)	entfliehen	—	échapper, se	scappare	huir
escarabajo (Es)	Käfer m	beetle	coléoptère m	coleottero m	—
escasez (Es)	Mangel m	lack	manque m	mancanza f	—
escaso (Es)	dürftig	needy	nécessiteux	misero(a)	—
escenario (Es)	Bühne f	stage	scène f	palcoscenico m	—
escenificar (Es)	inszenieren	stage	mettre en scène	mettere in scena	—
esclamare (I)	ausrufen	exclaim	crier	—	exclamar
esclave (F)	Sklave m	slave	—	schiavo m	esclavo m
esclavo (Es)	Sklave m	slave	esclave m	schiavo m	—
escluso (I)	ausgeschlossen	impossible	hors de question	—	imposible
escoba (Es)	Besen m	broom	balai m	scopa f	—
escoger (Es)	aussuchen	select	choisir	scegliere	—
escombros (Es)	Trümmer pl	ruins	décombres m pl	macerie f pl	—
esconder (Es)	verbergen	hide	dissimuler	nascondere	—
escorpión (Es)	Skorpion m	scorpion	scorpion m	scorpione m	—
escribir (Es)	schreiben	write	écrire	scrivere	—
escribir a máquina (Es)	tippen	type	taper (à la machine)	battere a macchina	—

	D	E	F	I	Es
escritor (Es)	Schriftsteller *m*	writer	écrivain *m*	scrittore *m*	—
escritura (Es)	Schrift *f*	writing	écriture *f*	scrittura *f*	—
escuchar (Es)	zuhören	listen	écouter	ascoltare	—
escudo (Es)	Schild *n*	shield	bouclier *m*	scudo *m*	—
escuela (Es)	Schule *f*	school	école *f*	scuola *f*	—
escuela superior (Es)	Hochschule *f*	university	université *f*	istituto superiore *m*	—
escultor (Es)	Bildhauer *m*	sculptor	sculpteur *m*	scultore *m*	—
escultura (Es)	Skulptur *f*	sculpture	sculpture *f*	scultura *f*	—
escupir (Es)	spucken	spit	cracher	sputare	—
Esel (D)	—	donkey	âne *m*	asino *m*	burro *m*
esempio (I)	Beispiel *n*	example	exemple *m*	—	ejemplo *m*
esencial (Es)	wesentlich	essential	essentiel(-le)	essenziale	—
esercitare (I)	ausüben	practise	exercer	—	ejercer
esercitare la magia (I)	zaubern	practise magic	faire de la magie	—	hacer magia
esercitarsi (I)	üben	practise	étudier	—	practicar
esercizio (I)	Übung *f*	exercise	exercice *m*	—	ejercicio *m*
esforzarse (Es)	bemühen, sich	make an effort	efforcer, se	sforzarsi	—
esfuerzo¹ (Es)	Anstrengung *f*	strain	effort *m*	fatica *f*	—
esfuerzo² (Es)	Bemühung *f*	effort	effort *m*	sforzo *m*	—
esfuerzo³ (Es)	Mühe *f*	effort	peine *f*	fatica *f*	—
esibire (I)	vorzeigen	show	montrer	—	presentar
esigenza (I)	Forderung *f*	demand	exigence *f*	—	exigencia *f*
esigere¹ (I)	anfordern	request	demander	—	pedir
esigere² (I)	fordern	demand	exiger	—	exigir
esistenza (I)	Dasein *n*	existence	existence *f*	—	existencia *f*
esistere (I)	existieren	exist	exister	—	existir
esitare (I)	zögern	hesitate	hésiter	—	vacilar
esmeralda (Es)	Smaragd *m*	emerald	émeraude *f*	smeraldo *m*	—
espacio (Es)	Lücke *f*	gap	lacune *f*	lacuna *f*	—
espace (F)	Zwischenraum *m*	space	—	spazio *m*	espacio intermedio *m*
espacio intermedio (Es)	Zwischenraum *m*	space	espace *m*	spazio *m*	—
espacioso (Es)	geräumig	spacious	spacieux(-euse)	spazioso(a)	—
Espagne (F)	Spanien *n*	Spain	—	Spagna *f*	España *f*
Espagnol (F)	Spanier *m*	Spaniard	—	spagnolo *m*	español *m*
espagnol (F)	spanisch	Spanish	—	spagnolo(a)	español(a)
espalda (Es)	Rücken *m*	back	dos *m*	schiena *f*	—
España (Es)	Spanien *n*	Spain	Espagne *f*	Spagna *f*	—
español¹ (Es)	Spanier *m*	Spaniard	Espagnol *m*	spagnolo *m*	—
español² (Es)	spanisch	Spanish	espagnol(e)	spagnolo(a)	—
espantoso (Es)	schauderhaft	horrible	horrible	spaventoso(a)	—
esparadrapo (Es)	Pflaster *n*	plaster	emplâtre *m*	cerotto *m*	—
espatrio (I)	Ausreise *f*	departure	départ *m*	—	salida *f*
espèce (F)	Art *f*	species	—	specie *f*	especie *f*
espèces (F)	Bargeld *n*	cash	—	contanti *m pl*	dinero al contado *m*
especia (Es)	Gewürz *n*	spice	épice *f*	spezia *f*	—

	D	E	F	I	Es
especial (Es)	speziell	special	spécial(e)	speciale	—
especially (E)	besonders	—	surtout	particolarmente	sobre todo
especie (Es)	Art *f*	species	espèce *f*	specie *f*	—
espectáculo (Es)	Schauspiel *n*	play	spectacle *m*	spettacolo *m*	—
espectador (Es)	Zuschauer *m*	spectator	spectateur *m*	spettatore *m*	—
espejo (Es)	Spiegel *m*	mirror	miroir *m*	specchio *m*	—
esperar[1] (Es)	erwarten	expect	attendre	aspettare	—
esperar[2] (Es)	hoffen	hope	espérer	sperare	—
esperar[3] (Es)	warten	wait	attendre	aspettare	—
espérer (F)	hoffen	hope	—	sperare	esperar
esperienza (I)	Erfahrung *f*	experience	expérience *f*	—	experiencia *f*
espérons (F)	hoffentlich	hopefully	—	speriamo que	espero que
espero que (Es)	hoffentlich	hopefully	espérons	speriamo que	—
espeso (Es)	dicht	dense	épais(se)	denso(a)	—
espinacas (Es)	Spinat *m*	spinach	épinard *m*	spinaci *m pl*	—
espíritu (Es)	Geist *m*	spirit	esprit *m*	spirito *m*	—
esponja (Es)	Schwamm *m*	sponge	éponge *f*	spugna *f*	—
esporre (I)	ausstellen	exhibit	exposer	—	exponer
esportare (I)	ausführen	export	exporter	—	exportar
esportazione[1] (I)	Ausfuhr *f*	export	exportation *f*	—	exportación *f*
esportazione[2] (I)	Export *m*	export	exportation *f*	—	exportación *f*
esposizione (I)	Ausstellung *f*	exhibition	exposition *f*	—	exposición *f*
espressione (I)	Ausdruck *m*	expression	expression *f*	—	término *m*
espresso (I)	ausdrücklich	explicit	exprès(-esse)	—	explícito(a)
esprit (F)	Geist *m*	spirit	—	spirito *m*	espíritu *m*
espuma (Es)	Schaum *m*	foam	écume *f*	schiuma *f*	—
esquí (Es)	Ski *m*	ski	ski *m*	sci *m*	—
esquina (Es)	Ecke *f*	corner	coin *m*	angolo *m*	—
esquisse[1] (F)	Entwurf *m*	outline	—	abbozzo *m*	proyecto *m*
esquisse[2] (F)	Skizze *f*	sketch	—	schizzo *m*	boceto *m*
essai[1] (F)	Probe *f*	test	—	prova *f*	prueba *f*
essai[2] (F)	Versuch *m*	try	—	tentativo *m*	intento *m*
essayer[1] (F)	anprobieren	try on	—	provare	probar
essayer[2] (F)	probieren	try	—	assaggiare	probar
essayer[3] (F)	versuchen	try	—	provare	probar
eßbar (D)	—	eatable	mangeable	commestibile	comestible
essen (D)	—	eat	manger	mangiare	comer
Essen (D)	—	food	repas *m*	alimentazione *f*	comida *f*
essence (F)	Benzin *n*	petrol	—	benzina	gasolina *f*
essential (E)	wesentlich	—	essentiel(-le)	essenziale	esencial
essentiale (I)	wesentlich	essential	essentiel(-le)	—	esencial
essentiel (F)	wesentlich	essential	—	essenziale	esencial
essere[1] (I)	sein	be	être	—	ser/estar
essere[2] (I)	Wesen *n*	being	être *m*	—	ser *m*
essere portato (I)	taugen	be of use	convenir pour	—	valer
essere raffreddato (I)	erkältet	have a cold	avoir un rhume	—	estar acatarrado(a)
essere umano (I)	Mensch *m*	human being	homme *m*	—	persona *f*
Essig (D)	—	vinegar	vinaigre *m*	aceto *m*	vinagre *m*

	D	E	F	I	Es
Eßlöffel (D)	—	tablespoon	cuiller *f*	cucchiaio *m*	cuchara *f*
essuyer (F)	wischen	wipe	—	pulire	fregar
Eßwaren (D)	—	victuals	produits alimentaires *m pl*	alimentari *m pl*	comestibles *m pl*
Eßzimmer (D)	—	dining room	salle à manger *f*	sala da pranzo *f*	comedor *m*
est (F)	Osten *m*	east	—	est *m*	este *m*
est (I)	Osten *m*	east	est *m*	—	este *m*
esta (Es)	diese(r,s)	this	ce, cette	questo(a)	—
establecimiento (Es)	Anlage *f*	plant	édifices *m pl*	impianto *m*	—
estación[1] (Es)	Bahnhof *m*	station	gare *f*	stazione *f*	—
estación[2] (Es)	Station *f*	station	station *f*	stazione *f*	—
estacionamiento prohibido (Es)	Parkverbot *n*	no parking	défense de stationner	divieto di parcheggio	—
estación central (Es)	Hauptbahnhof *m*	central station	gare centrale *f*	stazione centrale *f*	—
estación del año (Es)	Jahreszeit *f*	time of year	saison *f*	stagione *f*	—
estación terminal (Es)	Endstation *f*	terminus	terminus *m*	capolinea *m*	—
estado[1] (Es)	Stand *m*	position	état *m*	stato *m*	—
estado[2] (Es)	Staat *m*	state	état *m*	stato *m*	—
estado[3] (Es)	Verfassung *f*	constitution	état *m*	condizioni *f pl*	—
estado[4] (Es)	Zustand *m*	condition	état *m*	stato *m*	—
Estados Unidos (Es)	Vereinigte Staaten *pl*	United States	Etats-Unis *m pl*	Stati Uniti *m pl*	—
estancia (Es)	Aufenthalt *m*	stay	séjour *m*	soggiorno *m*	—
estanque (Es)	Teich *m*	pond	étang *m*	stagno *m*	—
estantería (Es)	Regal *n*	shelves	étagère *f*	scaffale *m*	—
estar acatarrado (Es)	erkältet sein	have a cold	avoir un rhume	essere raffreddato(a)	—
estar a punto (Es)	gar	done	cuit(e)	cotto(a)	—
estar de acuerdo (Es)	übereinstimmen	agree	être d'accord	concordare	—
estar de pie (Es)	stehen	stand	être debout	stare in piedi	—
estar sentado (Es)	sitzen	sit	être assis(e)	stare seduto(a)	—
estar tumbado (Es)	liegen	lie	trouver, se	giacere	—
estate (I)	Sommer *m*	summer	été *m*	—	verano *m*
este (Es)	Osten *m*	east	est *m*	est *m*	—
esterno (I)	äußerlich	external	externe	—	superficial
estero (I)	Ausland *n*	abroad	étranger *m*	—	extranjero *m*
estimado (Es)	beliebt	popular	populaire	popolare	—
estimar (Es)	schätzen	estimate	estimer	stimare	—
estimate (E)	schätzen	—	estimer	stimare	estimar
estimer (F)	schätzen	estimate	—	stimare	estimar
estimular (Es)	treiben	drive	mener	spingere	—
estinguere[1] (I)	auslöschen	extinguish	éteindre	—	apagar
estinguere[2] (I)	tilgen	erase	effacer	—	anular
estomac (F)	Magen *m*	stomach	—	stomaco *m*	estómago *m*
estómago (Es)	Magen *m*	stomach	estomac *m*	stomaco *m*	—
estornudar (Es)	niesen	sneeze	éternuer	starnutire	—
estraneo (I)	fremd	foreign	étranger(-ère)	—	extranjero(a)

	D	E	F	I	Es
estrecho¹ (Es)	eng	narrow	étroit(e)	stretto(a)	—
estrecho² (Es)	knapp	tight	étroit(e)	scarso(a)	—
estrella (Es)	Stern *m*	star	étoile *f*	stella *f*	—
estudiante (Es)	Student *m*	student	étudiant *m*	studente *m*	—
estudiar (Es)	studieren	study	étudier	studiare	—
estudio (Es)	Studium *n*	studies	études *f pl*	studi *m pl*	—
estufa (Es)	Ofen *m*	oven	poêle *m*	stufa *f*	—
estúpido (Es)	doof	daft	bête	scemo(a)	—
et (F)	und	and	—	e	y
età (I)	Alter *n*	age	âge *m*	—	edad *f*
Etage (D)	—	floor	étage *m*	piano *m*	piso *m*
étage (F)	Etage *f*	floor	—	piano *m*	piso *m*
étagère (F)	Regal *n*	shelves	—	scaffale *m*	estantería *f*
étang (F)	Teich *m*	pond	—	stagno *m*	estanque *m*
état¹ (F)	Stand *m*	position	—	stato *m*	estado *m*
état² (F)	Staat *m*	state	—	stato *m*	estado *m*
état³ (F)	Verfassung *f*	constitution	—	condizioni *f pl*	estado *m*
état⁴ (F)	Zustand *m*	condition	—	stato *m*	estado *m*
Etats-Unis (F)	Vereinigte Staaten *pl*	United States	—	Stati Uniti *m pl*	Estados Unidos *m pl*
été (F)	Sommer *m*	summer	—	estate *f*	verano *m*
éteindre¹ (F)	ausmachen	switch off	—	spegnere	apagar
éteindre² (F)	abschalten	switch off	—	spegnere	desconectar
éteindre³ (F)	auslöschen	extinguish	—	estinguere	apagar
éteindre⁴ (F)	löschen	extinguish	—	spengere	apagar
eternal (E)	ewig	—	éternel(le)	eterno(a)	eterno(a)
éternel (F)	ewig	eternal	—	eterno(a)	eterno(a)
eterno (I)	ewig	eternal	éternel(le)	—	eterno(a)
eterno (Es)	ewig	eternal	éternel(le)	eterno(a)	—
éternuer (F)	niesen	sneeze	—	starnutire	estornudar
etliche (D)	—	several	quelques	alcuni(e)	algunos(as)
étoffe (F)	Tuch *n*	cloth	—	panno *m*	paño *m*
étoile (F)	Stern *m*	star	—	stella *f*	estrella *f*
étonner (F)	wundern	wonder	—	stupire	asombrar
étonner, se (F)	staunen	be astonished	—	stupirsi	asombrarse
étourdi (F)	leichtsinnig	careless	—	spensierato(a)	imprudente
étranger¹ (F)	ausländisch	foreign	—	straniero(a)	extranjero(a)
étranger² (F)	Ausland *n*	abroad	—	estero *m*	extranjero *m*
étranger³ (F)	Ausländer *m*	foreigner	—	straniero *m*	extranjero *m*
étranger⁴ (F)	fremd	foreign	—	estraneo(a)	extranjero(a)
étranger⁵ (F)	Fremder *m*	foreigner	—	straniero *m*	extranjero *m*
être¹ (F)	sein	be	—	essere	ser/estar
être² (F)	Wesen *n*	being	—	essere *m*	ser *m*
être assis (F)	sitzen	sit	—	stare seduto(a)	estar sentado(a)
être d'accord¹ (F)	übereinstimmen	agree	—	concordare	estar de acuerdo
être d'accord² (F)	zustimmen	agree	—	acconsentire	consentir
être debout (F)	stehen	stand	—	stare in piedi	estar en pie
être en retard (F)	verspäten	be late	—	ritardare	llevar retraso

	D	E	F	I	Es
être heureux (F)	freuen, sich	be glad	—	rallegrarsi	alegrarse
être témoin de (F)	erleben	experience	—	vivere	experimentar
être vaincu par qn (F)	unterliegen	be defeated	—	soccombere	sucumbir
étroit[1] (F)	eng	narrow	—	stretto(a)	estrecho(a)
étroit[2] (F)	knapp	tight	—	scarso(a)	estrecho(a)
études (F)	Studium *n*	studies	—	studi *m pl*	estudio *m*
étudiant (F)	Student *m*	student	—	studente *m*	estudiante *m(f)*
étudier[1] (F)	studieren	study	—	studiare	estudiar
étudier[2] (F)	üben	practise	—	esercitarsi	practicar
etwa (D)	—	about	environ	pressappoco	unos
etwas (D)	—	something	quelque chose	qualcosa	algo
Europa (D)	—	Europe	Europe *f*	Europa *f*	Europa *f*
Europa (Es)	Europa *n*	Europe	Europe *f*	Europa *f*	—
Europa (I)	Europa *n*	Europe	Europe *f*	—	Europa *f*
Europäer (D)	—	European	Européen *m*	europeo *m*	europeo *m*
europäisch (D)	—	European	européen(ne)	europeo(a)	europeo(a)
Europe (E)	Europa *n*	—	Europe *f*	Europa *f*	Europa *f*
Europe (F)	Europa *n*	Europe	—	Europa *f*	Europa *f*
European[1] (E)	europäisch	—	européen(ne)	europeo(a)	europeo(a)
European[2] (E)	Europäer *m*	—	Européen *m*	europeo *m*	europeo *m*
européen (F)	europäisch	European	—	europeo(a)	europeo(a)
Européen (F)	Europäer *m*	European	—	europeo *m*	europeo *m*
europeo[1] (I)	europäisch	European	européen(ne)	—	europeo(a)
europeo[2] (I)	Europäer *m*	European	Européen *m*	—	europeo *m*
europeo[1] (Es)	europäisch	European	européen(ne)	europeo(a)	—
europeo[2] (Es)	Europäer *m*	European	Européen *m*	europeo *m*	—
evangelisch (D)	—	Protestant	protestant(e)	protestante	protestante
évanouissement (F)	Ohnmacht *f*	faint	—	svenimento *m*	desmayo *m*
éveillé (F)	munter	lively	—	vivace	alegre
even[1] (E)	eben	—	plan(e)	piano(a)	plano(a)
even[2] (E)	gerade	—	pair(e)	pari	par
even[3] (E)	sogar	—	même	perfino	incluso
événement (F)	Ereignis *n*	event	—	avvenimento *m*	suceso *m*
evening (E)	Abend *m*	—	soir *m*	sera *f*	noche *f*
evening before (E)	Vorabend *m*	—	veille *f*	vigilia *f*	víspera *f*
event[1] (E)	Ereignis *n*	—	événement *m*	avvenimento *m*	suceso *m*
event[2] (E)	Veranstaltung *f*	—	manifestation *f*	manifestazione *f*	manifestación *f*
éventé (F)	windig	windy	—	ventoso(a)	ventoso(a)
eventual (Es)	eventuell	possible	éventuel(le)	eventuale	—
eventuale (I)	eventuell	possible	éventuel(le)	—	eventual
éventuel (F)	eventuell	possible	—	eventuale	eventual
eventuell (D)	—	possible	éventuel(le)	eventuale	eventual
ever (E)	jemals	—	jamais	mai	jamás
everyday life (E)	Alltag *m*	—	vie quotidienne *f*	vita quotidiana *f*	vida cotidiana *f*
everything (E)	alles	—	tout	tutto	todo
everywhere (E)	überall	—	partout	dappertutto	por todas partes
évidemment (F)	selbstverständlich	of course	—	naturalmente	por supuesto

	D	E	F	I	Es
evidente[1] (Es)	eindeutig	unequivocal	incontestable	univoco(a)	—
evidente[2] (Es)	offensichtlich	obvious	manifeste	evidente	—
evidente (I)	offensichtlich	obvious	manifeste	—	evidente
evitar[1] (Es)	meiden/ vermeiden	avoid	éviter	evitare	—
evitar[2] (Es)	verhindern	prevent	empêcher	impedire	—
evitare (I)	meiden/ vermeiden	avoid	éviter	—	evitar
éviter (F)	meiden/ vermeiden	avoid	—	evitare	evitar
ewig (D)	—	eternal	éternel(le)	eterno(a)	eterno(a)
exact (F)	genau	exact	—	preciso(a)	exacto(a)
exact (E)	genau	—	exact(e)	preciso(a)	exacto(a)
exactitud (Es)	Genauigkeit f	accuracy	exactitude f	precisione f	—
exactitude (F)	Genauigkeit f	accuracy	—	precisione f	exactitud f
exacto (Es)	genau	exact	exact(e)	preciso(a)	—
exageración (Es)	Übertreibung f	exaggeration	exagération f	esagerazione f	—
exagerado (Es)	übertrieben	exaggerated	exagéré(e)	esagerato(a)	—
exagerar (Es)	übertreiben	exaggerate	exagérer	esagerare	—
exagération (F)	Übertreibung f	exaggeration	—	esagerazione f	exageración f
exagéré (F)	übertrieben	exaggerated	—	esagerato(a)	exagerado(a)
exagérer (F)	übertreiben	exaggerate	—	esagerare	exagerar
exaggerate (E)	übertreiben	—	exagérer	esagerare	exagerar
exaggerated (E)	übertrieben	—	exagéré(e)	esagerato(a)	exagerado(a)
exaggeration (E)	Übertreibung f	—	exagération f	esagerazione f	exageración f
examen (Es)	Prüfung f	examination	examen m	esame m	—
examen (F)	Prüfung f	examination	—	esame m	examen m
examinar[1] (Es)	nachsehen	check	vérifier	controllare	—
examinar[2] (Es)	prüfen	test	tester	esaminare	—
examinar[3] (Es)	untersuchen	examine	examiner	esaminare	—
examinar[4] (Es)	überprüfen	check	contrôler	esaminare	—
examination (E)	Prüfung f	—	examen m	esame m	examen m
examine (E)	untersuchen	—	examiner	esaminare	examinar
examiner (F)	untersuchen	examine	—	esaminare	examinar
example (E)	Beispiel n	—	exemple m	esempio m	ejemplo m
excelente (Es)	ausgezeichnet	excellent	excellent(e)	eccellente	—
excellent[1] (E)	ausgezeichnet	—	excellent(e)	eccellente	excelente
excellent[2] (E)	hervorragend	—	excellent(e)	eccellente	extraordinario(a)
excellent[1] (F)	ausgezeichnet	excellent	—	eccellente	excelente
excellent[2] (F)	hervorragend	excellent	—	eccellente	extraordinario(a)
excepción (Es)	Ausnahme f	exception	exception f	eccezione f	—
excepcional (Es)	außergewöhnlich	exceptional	exceptionnel(le)	straordinario(a)	—
except[1] (E)	außer	—	hors de	eccetto	salvo
except[2] (E)	ausgenommen	—	excepté	eccetto	excepto
excepté (F)	ausgenommen	except	—	eccetto	excepto
exception (E)	Ausnahme f	—	exception f	eccezione f	excepción f
exception (F)	Ausnahme f	exception	—	eccezione f	excepción f
exceptional (E)	außergewöhnlich	—	exceptionnel(le)	straordinario(a)	excepcional

	D	E	F	I	Es
exceptionnel (F)	ungewöhnlich	unusual	—	insolito(a)	desacostumbrado(a)
excepto (Es)	ausgenommen	except	excepté	eccetto	—
exchange[1] (E)	austauschen	—	échanger	scambiare	cambiar
exchange[2] (E)	Austausch m	—	échange m	scambio m	cambio m
exchange[3] (E)	umtauschen	—	échanger	cambiare	cambiar
exchange[4] (E)	vertauschen	—	échanger	scambiare	cambiar
excitado (Es)	aufgeregt	excited	agité(e)	eccitato(a)	—
excite (E)	aufregen	—	énerver	agitare	agitar
excited (E)	aufgeregt	—	agité(e)	eccitato(a)	excitado(a)
exciting (E)	aufregend	—	énervant(e)	eccitante	emocionante
exclaim (E)	ausrufen	—	crier	esclamare	exclamar
exclamar (Es)	ausrufen	exclaim	crier	esclamare	—
excursión[1] (Es)	Ausflug m	outing	excursion f	gita f	—
excursión[2] (Es)	Tour f	tour	excursion f	giro m	—
excursion[1] (F)	Ausflug m	outing	—	gita f	excursión f
excursion[2] (F)	Tour f	tour	—	giro m	excursión f
excuse (F)	Entschuldigung f	apology	—	scusa f	disculpar
excuser, se (F)	entschuldigen, sich	apologize	—	scusarsi	disculparse
exemple (F)	Beispiel n	example	—	esempio m	ejemplo m
exercer (F)	ausüben	exercise	—	esercitare	ejercer
exercice (F)	Übung f	exercise	—	esercizio f	ejercicio m
exercise (E)	Übung f	—	exercice m	esercizio f	ejercicio m
exercise book (E)	Heft n	—	cahier m	quaderno m	cuaderno m
exhausted (E)	erschöpft	—	épuisé(e)	esausto(a)	agotado(a)
exhibit (E)	ausstellen	—	exposer	esporre	exponer
exhibition (E)	Ausstellung f	—	exposition f	esposizione f	exposición f
exhorter (F)	mahnen	warn	—	ammonire	notificar
exigence (F)	Forderung f	demand	—	esigenza f	exigencia f
exigencia (Es)	Forderung f	demand	exigence f	esigenza f	—
exiger[1] (F)	fordern	demand	—	esigere	exigir
exiger[2] (F)	zumuten	expect	—	pretendere	exigir
exigir[1] (Es)	auffordern	ask	inviter	invitare	—
exigir[2] (Es)	fordern	demand	exiger	esigere	—
exigir[3] (Es)	verlangen	demand	demander	richiedere	—
exigir[4] (Es)	zumuten	expect	exiger	pretendere	—
exist (E)	existieren	—	exister	esistere	existir
existence (E)	Dasein n	—	existence f	esistenza f	existencia f
existence (F)	Dasein n	existence	—	esistenza f	existencia f
existencia (Es)	Dasein n	existence	existence f	esistenza f	—
exister[1] (F)	existieren	exist	—	esistere	existir
exister[2] (F)	vorkommen	occur	—	accadere	suceder
existieren (D)	—	exist	exister	esistere	existir
existir (Es)	existieren	exist	exister	esistere	—
exit (E)	Ausgang m	—	sortie f	uscita f	salida f
éxito (Es)	Erfolg m	success	succès m	successo m	—
expect[1] (E)	erwarten	—	attendre	aspettare	esperar
expect[2] (E)	zumuten	—	exiger	pretendere	exigir

	D	E	F	I	Es
expéditeur (F)	Absender *m*	sender	—	mittente *m*	remitente *m*
expenses[1] (E)	Kosten *pl*	—	coûts *m pl*	spese *f pl*	costas *m pl*
expenses[2] (E)	Spesen *pl*	—	frais *m pl*	spese *f pl*	gastos *m pl*
expenses[3] (E)	Unkosten *pl*	—	frais *m pl*	spese *f pl*	gastos *m pl*
expensive[1] (E)	kostspielig	—	coûteux(-euse)	costoso(a)	costoso(a)
expensive[2] (E)	teuer	—	cher(-ère)	caro(a)	caro(a)
experience[1] (E)	erleben	—	être témoin de	vivere	experimentar
experience[2] (E)	Erfahrung *f*	—	expérience *f*	esperienza *f*	experiencia *f*
expérience (F)	Erfahrung *f*	experience	—	esperienza *f*	experiencia *f*
experiencia (Es)	Erfahrung *f*	experience	expérience *f*	esperienza *f*	—
experimentar (Es)	erleben	experience	être témoin de	vivere	—
explain (E)	erklären	—	expliquer	spiegare	explicar
explicar (Es)	erklären	explain	expliquer	spiegare	—
explicit (E)	ausdrücklich	—	exprès(-esse)	espresso(a)	explícito(a)
explícito (Es)	ausdrücklich	explicit	exprès(-esse)	espresso(a)	—
expliquer (F)	erklären	explain	—	spiegare	explicar
exponer (Es)	ausstellen	exhibit	exposer	esporre	—
Export (D)	—	export	exportation *f*	esportazione *f*	exportación *f*
export[1] (E)	ausführen	—	exporter	esportare	exportar
export[2] (E)	Ausfuhr *f*	—	exportation *f*	esportazione *f*	exportación *f*
export[3] (E)	Export *m*	—	exportation *f*	esportazione *f*	exportación *f*
exportación[1] (Es)	Ausfuhr *f*	export	exportation *f*	esportazione *f*	—
exportación[2] (Es)	Export *m*	export	exportation *f*	esportazione *f*	—
exportar (Es)	ausführen	export	exporter	esportare	—
exportation[1] (F)	Ausfuhr *f*	export	—	esportazione *f*	exportación *f*
exportation[2] (F)	Export *m*	export	—	esportazione *f*	exportación *f*
exporter (F)	ausführen	export	—	esportare	exportar
exposer (F)	ausstellen	exhibit	—	esporre	exponer
exposición (Es)	Ausstellung *f*	exhibition	exposition *f*	esposizione *f*	—
exposition (F)	Ausstellung *f*	exhibition	—	esposizione *f*	exposición *f*
exprès[1] (F)	absichtlich	intentionally	—	apposta	adrede
exprès[2] (F)	ausdrücklich	explicit	—	espresso(a)	explícito(a)
express[1] (F)	D-Zug *m*	through train	—	direttissimo *m*	tren expreso *m*
express[2] (F)	Eilzug *m*	limited stop train	—	treno diretto *m*	tren expreso *m*
expression[1] (E)	Ausdruck *m*	—	expression *f*	espressione *f*	término *m*
expression[2] (E)	Miene *f*	—	mine *f*	aspetto *m*	expresión *f*
expression (F)	Ausdruck *m*	expression	—	espressione *f*	término *m*
express train (E)	Schnellzug *m*	—	rapide *m*	treno direttissimo *m*	tren expreso *m*
expressway (E)	Schnellstraße *f*	—	voie rapide *f*	superstrada *f*	carretera de circulación rápida *f*
exquisito (Es)	köstlich	delicious	savoureux(-euse)	squisito(a)	—
extend (E)	verlängern	—	prolonger	allungare	alargar
extensión (Es)	Breite *f*	width	largeur *f*	larghezza *f*	—
external (E)	äußerlich	—	externe	esterno(a)	superficial
externe (F)	äußerlich	external	—	esterno(a)	superficial
extinguish[1] (E)	auslöschen	—	éteindre	estinguere	apagar
extinguish[2] (E)	löschen	—	éteindre	spegnere	apagar
extra (D)	—	extra	à part	a parte	separado(a)

	D	E	F	I	Es
extra (E)	extra	—	à part	a parte	separado(a)
extra charge (E)	Zuschlag m	—	supplément m	supplemento m	suplemento m
extranjero¹ (Es)	Ausland n	abroad	étranger m	estero m	—
extranjero² (Es)	Fremder m	foreigner	étranger m	straniero m	—
extranjero³ (Es)	ausländisch	foreign	étranger(-ère)	straniero(a)	—
extranjero⁴ (Es)	Ausländer m	foreigner	étranger m	straniero m	—
extranjero⁵ (Es)	fremd	foreign	étranger(-ère)	estraneo(a)	—
extraño¹ (Es)	eigenartig	strange	singulier(-ère)	strano(a)	—
extraño² (Es)	seltsam	strange	bizarre	strano(a)	—
extraordinaire¹ (F)	außergewöhnlich	exceptional	—	straordinario(a)	excepcional
extraordinaire² (F)	außerordentlich	extraordinary	—	straordinario(a)	extraordinario(a)
extraordinario¹ (Es)	außerordentlich	extraordinary	extraordinaire	straordinario(a)	—
extraordinario² (Es)	besondere(r,s)	special	spécial(e)	straordinario(a)	—
extraordinario³ (Es)	hervorragend	excellent	excellent(e)	eccellente	—
extraordinary (E)	außerordentlich	—	exceptionnel(le)	straordinario(a)	extraordinario(a)
extraviar (Es)	verlegen	mislay	égarer	perdere	—
eye (E)	Auge n	—	œil m (yeux pl)	occhio m	ojo m
eyelash (E)	Wimper f	—	cil m	ciglia f	pestaña f
eye specialist (E)	Augenarzt m	—	oculiste m	oculista m	oculista m
fabbrica (I)	Fabrik f	factory	usine f	—	fábrica f
fabbricare¹ (I)	erzeugen	produce	produire	—	producir
fabbricare² (I)	herstellen	manufacture	produire	—	producir
fabric (E)	Gewebe n	—	tissu m	tessuto m	tela f
fábrica (Es)	Fabrik f	factory	usine f	fabbrica f	—
Fabrik (D)	—	factory	usine f	fabbrica f	fábrica f
façade (E)	Fassade f	—	façade f	facciata f	fachada f
façade (F)	Fassade f	façade	—	facciata f	fachada f
facchino (I)	Träger m	carrier	porteur m	—	mozo m
faccia (I)	Gesicht n	face	visage m	—	cara f
facciata (I)	Fassade f	façade	façade f	—	fachada f
face (E)	Gesicht n	—	visage m	faccia f	cara f
Fach¹ (D)	—	compartment	compartiment m	scomparto m	compartimiento m
Fach² (D)	—	subject	matière f	materia f	materia f
fachada (Es)	Fassade f	façade	façade f	facciata f	—
fâché (F)	ärgerlich	angry	—	arrabbiato(a)	enfadado(a)
fâcher (F)	ärgern	annoy	—	arrabbiare	enfadar
facile (F)	leicht	easy	—	semplice	ligero(a)
facilitar (Es)	ermöglichen	make possible	rendre possible	rendere possibile	—
fact (E)	Tatsache f	—	fait m	fatto m	hecho m
facteur (F)	Postbote m	postman	—	postino m	cartero m
factory (E)	Fabrik f	—	usine f	fabbrica f	fábrica f
factura (Es)	Rechnung f	bill	facture f	fattura f	—
facture (F)	Rechnung f	bill	—	fattura f	factura f
fade (D)	—	dull	fade	insipido(a)	soso(a)
fade (F)	fade	dull	—	insipido(a)	soso(a)
Faden (D)	—	thread	fil m	filo m	hilo m
fagiolo (I)	Bohne f	bean	haricot m	—	judía f
fähig (D)	—	capable	capable	capace	hábil

	D	E	F	I	Es
Fähigkeit (D)	—	ability	capacité f	capacità f	capacidad f
Fahne (D)	—	flag	drapeau m	bandiera f	bandera f
Fahrbahn (D)	—	carriageway	chaussée f	corsia f	calzada f
Fähre (D)	—	ferry	bac m	traghetto m	transbordador m
fahren (D)	—	drive	conduire	andare	conducir
Fahrer (D)	—	driver	conducteur m	autista m	conductor m
Fahrgast (D)	—	passenger	passager m	passeggero m	pasajero m
Fahrkarte (D)	—	ticket	billet m	biglietto m	billete m
Fahrplan (D)	—	timetable	horaire m	orario m	horario m
Fahrrad (D)	—	bicycle	bicyclette f	bicicletta f	bicicleta f
Fahrschein (D)	—	ticket	ticket m	biglietto m	billete m
Fahrstuhl (D)	—	elevator	ascenseur m	ascensore m	ascensor m
Fahrt (D)	—	journey	voyage f	viaggio m	viaje m
Fahrzeug (D)	—	vehicle	véhicule m	veicolo m	vehículo m
faible (F)	schwach	weak	—	debole	débil
faiblesse (F)	Schwäche f	weakness	—	debolezza f	debilidad f
failure (E)	Mißerfolg m	—	échec m	insuccesso m	fracaso m
faim (F)	Hunger m	hunger	—	fame f	hambre m
faint (E)	Ohnmacht f	—	évanouissement m	svenimento m	desmayo m
fair¹ (E)	Jahrmarkt m	—	foire f	fiera f	feria f
fair² (E)	Messe f	—	foire f	fiera f	feria f
faire¹ (F)	machen	make/do	—	fare	hacer
faire² (F)	tun	do	—	fare	hacer
faire attention¹ (F)	aufpassen	pay attention	—	fare attenzione	prestar atención
faire attention² (F)	achtgeben	take care	—	badare	atender
faire cuire (F)	backen	bake	—	cuocere (al forno)	cocer (al horno)
faire de la gymnastique (F)	turnen	do gymnastic exercises	—	fare ginnastica	hacer gimnasia
faire de la magie (F)	zaubern	practise magic	—	esercitare la magia	hacer magia
faire de la publicité (F)	werben	advertise	—	fare propaganda	hacer propaganda
faire de la voile (F)	segeln	sail	—	andare a vela	navegar a vela
faire des efforts (F)	anstrengen	make an effort	—	affaticare	cansar
faire grève (F)	streiken	be on strike	—	scioperare	hacer huelga
faire la vaisselle (F)	abspülen	wash up	—	sciacquare	lavar
faire les malles (F)	packen	pack	—	fare le valigie	hacer la maleta
faire les courses (F)	einkaufen gehen	go shopping	—	fare la spesa	ir de compras
faire passer (F)	herumreichen	pass around	—	far circolare	pasar de mano en mano
faire remarquer, se (F)	auffallen	be noticeable	—	dare nell'occhio	llamar la atención por algo
faire signe (F)	winken	wave	—	chiamare con cenni	llamar con gestos
faire suivre (F)	nachsenden	send on	—	inoltrare	enviar a la nueva dirección
faire une chute (F)	abstürzen	crash	—	precipitare	caer a tierra
faire un rapport (F)	berichten	report	—	riferire	informar
faire un signe de tête (F)	nicken	nod	—	annuire	inclinar la cabeza
fait (F)	Tatsache f	fact	—	fatto m	hecho m

	D	E	F	I	Es
faithful (E)	treu	—	fidèle	fedele	fiel
faja (Es)	Binde *f*	bandage	bandage *m*	fascia *f*	—
fake (E)	unecht	—	imité(e)	falso(a)	falso(a)
falciare (I)	mähen	mow	faucher	—	cortar
falda (Es)	Rock *m*	skirt	jupe *f*	gonna *f*	—
falegname (I)	Tischler *m*	carpenter	menuisier *m*	—	carpintero *m*
fall[1] (E)	fallen	—	tomber	cadere	caer
fall[2] (E)	stürzen	—	tomber	cadere	caer
fall[3] (E)	Sturz *m*	—	chute *f*	caduta *f*	caída *f*
fall asleep (E)	einschlafen	—	endormir, se	addormentarsi	adormecerse
fallen (D)	—	fall	tomber	cadere	caer
fall in love (E)	verlieben	—	tomber amoureux(-euse)	innamorarsi	enamorarse
fallito (I)	pleite	penniless	fauché(e)	—	sin dinero
fall over (E)	umfallen	—	tomber	cadere	caerse
falls (D)	—	in case	au cas où	qualora	en caso de que
falsch (D)	—	wrong	faux(fausse)	falso(a)	falso(a)
falso[1] (I)	falsch	wrong	faux(fausse)	—	falso(a)
falso[2] (I)	unecht	fake	imité(e)	—	falso(a)
falso[1] (Es)	falsch	wrong	faux(fausse)	falso(a)	—
falso[2] (Es)	unecht	fake	imité(e)	falso(a)	—
falta (Es)	Fehler *m*	mistake	faute *f*	sbaglio *m*	—
faltar (Es)	fehlen	miss	manquer	mancare	—
fame (I)	Hunger *m*	hunger	faim *f*	—	hambre *m*
famiglia (I)	Familie *f*	family	famille *f*	—	familia *f*
familia (Es)	Familie *f*	family	famille *f*	famiglia *f*	—
familiarizarse (Es)	einleben, sich	settle down	acclimater, se	ambientarsi	—
Familie (D)	—	family	famille *f*	famiglia *f*	familia *f*
famille (F)	Familie *f*	family	—	famiglia *f*	familia *f*
family (E)	Familie *f*	—	famille *f*	famiglia *f*	familia *f*
famoso (I)	berühmt	famous	célèbre	—	famoso(a)
famoso (Es)	berühmt	famous	célèbre	famoso(a)	—
famous (E)	berühmt	—	célèbre	famoso(a)	famoso(a)
faner, se (F)	welken	wither	—	appassire	marchitarse
fangen (D)	—	catch	attraper	acchiappare	coger
fango (I)	Schlamm *m*	mud	boue *f*	—	barro *m*
far (E)	weit	—	éloigné(e)	largo(a)	ancho(a)
far away (E)	fern	—	éloigné(e)	lontano(a)	lejos
Farbe (D)	—	colour	couleur *f*	colore *m*	color *m*
färben (D)	—	dye	colorer	tingere	colorear
farbig (D)	—	colourful	coloré(e)	colorato(a)	de colores
far circolare (I)	herumreichen	pass around	faire passer	—	pasar de mano en mano
fare[1] (I)	machen	make/do	faire	—	hacer
fare[2] (I)	tun	do	faire	—	hacer
fare a meno di (I)	entbehren	do without	passer de, se	—	pasarse sin
fare attenzione (I)	aufpassen	pay attention	faire attention	—	prestar atención
fare benzina (I)	tanken	fill up with petrol	prendre de l'essence	—	llenar de gasolina

	D	E	F	I	Es
fare escursioni a piedi (I)	wandern	hike	marcher	—	hacer excursiones
fare ginnastica (I)	turnen	do gymnastic exercises	faire de la gymnastique	—	hacer gimnasia
fare i conti (I)	rechnen	calculate	calculer	—	calcular
fare il bagno (I)	baden	bathe	baigner, se	—	bañarse
fare la barba (I)	rasieren	shave	raser	—	afeitar
fare la spesa (I)	einkaufen gehen	go shopping	faire les courses	—	ir de compras
fare la valigie (I)	packen	pack	faire les malles	—	hacer la maleta
fare propaganda (I)	werben	advertise	faire de la publicité	—	hacer propaganda
fare una radiografia (I)	röntgen	X-ray	radiographier	—	radiografiar
farfalla (I)	Schmetterling *m*	butterfly	papillon *m*	—	mariposa *f*
farina (I)	Mehl *n*	flour	farine *f*	—	harina *f*
farine (F)	Mehl *n*	flour	—	farina *f*	harina *f*
faringe (I)	Rachen *m*	throat	gorge *f*	—	garganta *f*
farmacia (Es)	Apotheke *f*	chemist's	pharmacie *f*	farmacia *f*	—
farmacia (I)	Apotheke *f*	chemist's	pharmacie *f*	—	farmacia *f*
farmer[1] (E)	Bauer *m*	—	paysan *m*	contadino *m*	campesino *m*
farmer[2] (E)	Landwirt *m*	—	agriculteur *m*	agricoltore *m*	agricultor *m*
farmhouse (E)	Bauernhof *m*	—	ferme *f*	fattoria *f*	granja *f*
farola (Es)	Laterne *f*	street light	réverbère *m*	lampione *m*	—
Fasching (D)	—	carnival	carnaval *m*	carnevale *m*	carnaval *m*
fascia (I)	Binde *f*	bandage	bandage *m*	—	faja *f*
fashion (E)	Mode *f*	—	mode *f*	moda *f*	moda *f*
Fassade (D)	—	façade	façade *f*	facciata *f*	fachada *f*
fassen (D)	—	grasp	saisir	prendere	coger
fast (D)	—	nearly	presque	quasi	casi
fast[1] (E)	fasten	—	jeûner	digiunare	ayunar
fast[2] (E)	schnell	—	rapide	veloce	rápido(a)
fasten (D)	—	fast	jeûner	digiunare	ayunar
fasten[1] (E)	anbringen	—	fixer	fissare	colocar
fasten[2] (E)	befestigen	—	fixer	fissare	sujetar
fat[1] (E)	dick	—	gros(se)	grasso(a)	grueso(a)
fat[2] (E)	fett	—	gras(se)	grasso(a)	graso(a)
fat[3] (E)	Fett *n*	—	graisse *f*	grasso *m*	grasa *f*
fate (E)	Schicksal *n*	—	destin *m*	destino *m*	destino *m*
father (E)	Vater *m*	—	père *m*	padre *m*	padre *m*
fatica[1] (I)	Anstrengung *f*	strain	effort *m*	—	esfuerzo *m*
fatica[2] (I)	Mühe *f*	effort	peine *f*	—	esfuerzo *m*
faticoso (I)	anstrengend	tiring	fatigant(e)	—	fatigoso(a)
fatigant (F)	anstrengend	tiring	—	faticoso(a)	fatigoso(a)
fatigoso (Es)	anstrengend	tiring	fatigant(e)	faticoso(a)	—
fatigué (F)	müde	tired	—	stanco(a)	cansado(a)
fatiguer (F)	ermüden	tire	—	stancarsi	cansar
fatto (I)	Tatsache *f*	fact	fait *m*	—	hecho *m*
fattoria (I)	Bauernhof *m*	farmhouse	ferme *f*	—	granja *f*
fattura (I)	Rechnung *f*	bill	facture *f*	—	factura *f*
faubourg (F)	Vorort *m*	suburb	—	sobborgo *m*	suburbio *m*

	D	E	F	I	Es
fauché (F)	pleite	penniless	—	fallito(a)	sin dinero
faucher (F)	mähen	mow	—	falciare	cortar
faul (D)	—	lazy	paresseux(-euse)	pigro(a)	perezoso(a)
fault (E)	Schuld *f*	—	culpabilité *f*	colpa *f*	culpa *f*
Faust (D)	—	fist	poing *m*	pugno *m*	puño *m*
faute (F)	Fehler *m*	mistake	—	sbaglio *m*	falta *f*
fauteuil (F)	Sessel *m*	armchair	—	poltrona *f*	sillón *m*
faux[1] (F)	falsch	wrong	—	falso(a)	falso(a)
faux[2] (F)	verkehrt	wrong	—	sbagliato(a)	equivocado(a)
favor[1] (Es)	Gefallen *m*	favour	service *m*	favore *m*	—
favor[2] (Es)	Gefälligkeit *f*	favour	obligeance *f*	favore *m*	—
favorable (Es)	günstig	favourable	favorable	favorevole	—
favorable (F)	günstig	favourable	—	favorevole	favorable
favore[1] (I)	Gefälligkeit *f*	favour	obligeance *f*	—	favor *m*
favore[2] (I)	Gefallen *m*	favour	service *m*	—	favor *m*
favorevole (I)	günstig	favourable	favorable	—	favorable
favour[1] (E)	Gefälligkeit *f*	—	obligeance *f*	favore *m*	favor *m*
favour[2] (E)	Gefallen *m*	—	service *m*	favore *m*	favor *m*
favourable (E)	günstig	—	favorable	favorevole	favorable
fazzoletto (I)	Taschentuch *n*	handkerchief	mouchoir *m*	—	pañuelo *m*
fear[1] (E)	Angst *f*	—	peur *f*	paura *f*	miedo *m*
fear[2] (E)	befürchten	—	craindre	temere	temer
fear[3] (E)	fürchten	—	craindre	temere	temer
fearful (E)	ängstlich	—	peureux(-euse)	pauroso(a)	miedoso(a)
feather (E)	Feder *f*	—	plume *f*	piuma *f*	pluma *f*
febbraio (I)	Februar *m*	February	février *m*	—	febrero *m*
febbre (I)	Fieber *n*	fever	fièvre *f*	—	fiebre *m*
febrero (Es)	Februar *m*	February	février *m*	febbraio *m*	—
fébrile (F)	hektisch	hectic	—	nervoso(a)	inquieto(a)
Februar (D)	—	February	février *m*	febbraio *m*	febrero *m*
February (E)	Februar *m*	—	février *m*	febbraio *m*	febrero *m*
fecha[1] (Es)	Datum *n*	date	date *f*	data *f*	—
fecha[2] (Es)	Termin *m*	date	terme *m*	termine *m*	—
fedele (I)	treu	faithful	fidèle	—	fiel
Feder[1] (D)	—	pen nib	plume *f*	penna *f*	pluma *f*
Feder[2] (D)	—	feather	plume *f*	piuma *f*	pluma *f*
Federal Chancellor (E)	Bundeskanzler *m*	—	chancelier fédéral *m*	cancelliere federale *m*	canciller federal *m*
Federal Highway (E)	Bundesstraße *f*	—	route nationale *f*	strada statale *f*	carretera nacional *f*
fee (E)	Gebühr *f*	—	droit *m*	tassa *f*	tarifa *f*
feed (E)	ernähren	—	nourrir	nutrire	alimentar
feel[1] (E)	befinden, sich	—	trouver, se	trovarsi	encontrarse
feel[2] (E)	fühlen	—	sentir	sentire	sentir
feeling (E)	Gefühl *n*	—	sentiment *m*	sensazione *f*	sentimiento *m*
fegato (I)	Leber *f*	liver	foie *m*	—	hígado *m*
fegen (D)	—	sweep	balayer	scopare	barrer
fehlen (D)	—	miss	manquer	mancare	faltar
Fehler (D)	—	mistake	faute *f*	sbaglio *m*	falta *f*

	D	E	F	I	Es
feiern (D)	—	celebrate	fêter	festeggiare	celebrar
Feiertag (D)	—	holiday	jour férié *m*	giorno festivo *m*	día de fiesta *m*
feig (D)	—	cowardly	lâche	vile	cobarde
Feige (D)	—	fig	figue *f*	fico *m*	higo *m*
fein (D)	—	fine	fin(e)	sottile	fino(a)
Feind (D)	—	enemy	ennemi *m*	nemico *m*	enemigo *m*
Feld (D)	—	field	champ *m*	campo *m*	campo *m*
felice (I)	glücklich	happy	heureux(-euse)	—	feliz
felicitaciónes (Es)	Glückwunsch *m*	congratulations	félicitations *f pl*	auguri *m pl*	—
felicitar (Es)	gratulieren	congratulate	féliciter	congratularsi	—
félicitations (F)	Glückwunsch *m*	congratulations	—	auguri *m pl*	felicitaciónes *f pl*
féliciter (F)	gratulieren	congratulate	—	congratularsi	felicitar
feliz (Es)	glücklich	happy	heureux(-euse)	felice	—
fellow (E)	Bursche *m*	—	garçon *m*	ragazzo *m*	chico *m*
femenino (Es)	weiblich	feminine	féminin(e)	femminile	—
féminin (F)	weiblich	feminine	—	femminile	femenino(a)
feminine (E)	weiblich	—	féminin(e)	femminile	femenino(a)
femme (F)	Frau *f*	woman	—	donna *f*	mujer *f*
femme de maison (F)	Hausfrau *f*	housewife	—	casalinga *f*	ama de casa *f*
femme de ménage (F)	Putzfrau *f*	charwoman	—	donna delle pulizie *f*	mujer de la limpieza *f*
femminile (I)	weiblich	feminine	féminin(e)	—	femenino(a)
fence (E)	Zaun *m*	—	clôture *f*	recinto *m*	valla *f*
fenêtre (F)	Fenster *n*	window	—	finestra *f*	ventana *f*
Fenster (D)	—	window	fenêtre *f*	finestra *f*	ventana *f*
feo (Es)	häßlich	ugly	laid(e)	brutto(a)	—
fer (F)	Eisen *n*	iron	—	ferro *m*	hierro *m*
fer à repasser (F)	Bügeleisen *n*	iron	—	ferro da stiro *m*	plancha *f*
feria¹ (Es)	Jahrmarkt *m*	fair	foire *f*	fiera *f*	—
feria² (Es)	Messe *f*	fair	foire *f*	fiera *f*	—
Ferien (D)	—	holidays	vacances *f pl*	vacanze *f pl*	vacaciones *f pl*
ferire¹ (I)	verwunden	wound	blesser	—	herir
ferire² (I)	verletzen	injure	blesser	—	herir
ferita¹ (I)	Verletzung *f*	injury	blessure *f*	—	herida *f*
ferita² (I)	Wunde *f*	wound	blessure *f*	—	herida *f*
fermare (I)	anhalten	stop	arrêter	—	parar
fermata (I)	Haltestelle *f*	stop	arrêt *m*	—	parada *f*
ferme (F)	Bauernhof *m*	farmhouse	—	fattoria *f*	granja *f*
fermé (F)	geschlossen	closed	—	chiuso	cerrado(a)
fermer¹ (F)	schließen	close	—	chiudere	cerrar
fermer² (F)	zumachen	shut	—	chiudere	cerrar
fermer³ (F)	zudrehen	turn off	—	chiudere girando	cerrar
fermer à clé¹ (F)	verschließen	lock (up)	—	chiudere a chiave	cerrar con llave
fermer à clé² (F)	zuschließen	lock (up)	—	chiudere a chiave	cerrar con llave
fermeture (F)	Verschluß *m*	lock	—	chiusura *f*	cierre *m*
fermeture éclair (F)	Reißverschluß *m*	zip	—	chiusura lampo *f*	cremallera *f*
fern (D)	—	far away	éloigné(e)	lontano(a)	lejos
Ferne (D)	—	distance	lointain *m*	distanza *f*	lejanía *f*

fiamma

	D	E	F	I	Es
Fernfahrer (D)	—	long-distance driver	routier *m*	camionista *m*	camionero *m*
Ferngespräch (D)	—	long-distance call	communication interurbaine *f*	telefonata interurbana *f*	llamada interurbana *f*
Fernglas (D)	—	binoculars	jumelles *f pl*	cannocchiale *m*	gemelos *m pl*
fernsehen (D)	—	watch television	regarder la télévision	guardare la TV	ver la televisión
Fernsehen (D)	—	television	télévision *f*	televisione *f*	televisión *f*
Fernseher (D)	—	television set	poste de télévision *m*	televisore *m*	televisor *m*
ferro (I)	Eisen *n*	iron	fer *m*	—	hierro *m*
ferrocarril (Es)	Eisenbahn *f*	railway	chemin de fer *m*	ferrovia *f*	—
ferro da stiro (I)	Bügeleisen *n*	iron	fer à repasser *m*	—	plancha *f*
ferrovia (I)	Eisenbahn *f*	railway	chemin de fer *m*	—	ferrocarril *m*
ferry (E)	Fähre *f*	—	bac *m*	traghetto *m*	transbordador *m*
fertig (D)	—	ready	prêt(e)	pronto(a)	listo(a)
fest (D)	—	solid	solide	solido(a)	firme
Fest (D)	—	party	fête *f*	festa *f*	fiesta *f*
festa¹ (I)	Fest *n*	party	fête *f*	—	fiesta *f*
festa² (I)	Party *f*	party	fête *f*	—	fiesta *f*
festeggiare (I)	feiern	celebrate	fêter	—	celebrar
festhalten (D)	—	seize	tenir ferme	tener fermo	sujetar
Festland (D)	—	mainland	continent *m*	terraferma *f*	tierra firme *f*
festsetzen (D)	—	fix	fixer	stabilire	fijar
fetch¹ (E)	bringen	—	porter	portare	llevar
fetch² (E)	holen	—	aller chercher	andare a prendere	traer
fête¹ (F)	Fest *n*	party	—	festa *f*	fiesta *f*
fête² (F)	Party *f*	party	—	festa *f*	fiesta *f*
fêter (F)	feiern	celebrate	—	festeggiare	celebrar
fett (D)	—	fat	gras(se)	grasso(a)	graso(a)
Fett (D)	—	fat	graisse *f*	grasso *m*	grasa *f*
fette biscottate (I)	Zwieback *m*	rusk	biscotte *f*	—	bizcocho *m*
feu (F)	Feuer *n*	fire	—	fuoco *m*	fuego *m*
feucht (D)	—	damp	humide	umido(a)	húmedo(a)
feu d'artifice (F)	Feuerwerk *n*	fireworks	—	fuoco d'artificio *m*	fuegos artificiales *m pl*
Feuer (D)	—	fire	feu *m*	fuoco *m*	fuego *m*
feuergefährlich (D)	—	inflammable	inflammable	infiammabile	inflamable
Feuerwehr (D)	—	fire brigade	sapeurs pompiers *m pl*	vigili del fuoco *m pl*	cuerpo de bomberos *m*
Feuerwerk (D)	—	fireworks	feu d'artifice *m*	fuoco d'artificio *m*	fuegos artificiales *m pl*
Feuerzeug (D)	—	lighter	briquet *m*	accendino *m*	mechero *m*
feuille (F)	Blatt *n*	leaf	—	foglia *m*	hoja *f*
feux (F)	Ampel *f*	traffic lights	—	semaforo *m*	semáforo *m*
fever (E)	Fieber *n*	—	fièvre *f*	febbre *f*	fiebre *m*
février (F)	Februar *m*	February	—	febbraio *m*	febrero *m*
few (E)	wenige	—	peu	pochi	pocos(as)
fiambre (Es)	Aufschnitt *m*	cold meat	charcuterie *f*	affettato *m*	—
fiamma (I)	Flamme *f*	flame	flamme *f*	—	llama *f*

	D	E	F	I	Es
fiammifero (I)	Streichholz *n*	match	allumette *f*	—	cerilla *f*
fiancé (E)	Verlobter *m*	—	fiancé *m*	fidanzato *m*	prometido *m*
fiancé (F)	Verlobter *m*	fiancé	—	fidanzato *m*	prometido *m*
fiancer, se (F)	verloben	get engaged	—	fidanzarsi	prometerse
fianco (I)	Hüfte *f*	hip	hanche *f*	—	cadera *f*
fiato (I)	Atem *m*	breath	respiration *f*	—	respiro *m*
ficelle (F)	Schnur *f*	string	—	corda *f*	cordel *m*
fico (I)	Feige *f*	fig	figue *f*	—	higo *m*
fidanzarsi (I)	verloben	get engaged	fiancer, se	—	prometerse
fidanzato (I)	Verlobter *m*	fiancé	fiancé *m*	—	prometido *m*
fidarsi (I)	vertrauen	trust	avoir confiance	—	confiar
fidèle (F)	treu	faithful	—	fedele	fiel
fiducia (I)	Vertrauen *n*	confidence	confiance *f*	—	confianza *f*
Fieber (D)	—	fever	fièvre *f*	febbre *f*	fiebre *m*
fiebre (Es)	Fieber *n*	fever	fièvre *f*	febbre *f*	—
fiel (Es)	treu	faithful	fidèle	fedele	—
fiel (F)	Galle *f*	gall	—	cistifellea *f*	bilis *f*
field[1] (E)	Acker *m*	—	champ *m*	campo *m*	campo *m*
field[2] (E)	Feld *n*	—	champ *m*	campo *m*	campo *m*
fier (F)	stolz	proud	—	orgoglioso(a)	orgulloso(a)
fiera[1] (I)	Messe *f*	fair	foire *f*	—	feria *f*
fiera[2] (I)	Jahrmarkt *m*	fair	foire *f*	—	feria *f*
fierce (E)	heftig	—	violent(e)	violento(a)	fuerte
fiesta[1] (Es)	Fest *n*	party	fête *f*	festa *f*	—
fiesta[2] (Es)	Party *f*	party	fête *f*	festa *f*	—
fièvre (F)	Fieber *n*	fever	—	febbre *f*	fiebre *m*
fifteen (E)	fünfzehn	—	quinze	quindici	quince
fifty (E)	fünfzig	—	cinquante	cinquanta	cincuenta
fig (E)	Feige *f*	—	figue *f*	fico *m*	higo *m*
fight (E)	kämpfen	—	battre, se	combattere	luchar
figlia (I)	Tochter *f*	daughter	fille *f*	—	hija *f*
figlio (I)	Sohn *m*	son	fils *m*	—	hijo *m*
figue (F)	Feige *f*	fig	—	fico *m*	higo *m*
fijar (Es)	festsetzen	fix	fixer	stabilire	—
fijo (Es)	starr	rigid	rigide	rigido(a)	—
fil (F)	Faden *m*	thread	—	filo *m*	hilo *m*
fila (Es)	Reihe *f*	row	rangée *f*	fila *f*	—
fila (I)	Reihe *f*	row	rangée *f*	—	fila *f*
fil de fer (F)	Draht *m*	wire	—	filo metallico *m*	alambre *m*
file (E)	Aktenmappe *f*	—	porte-documents *m*	cartella *f*	cartera *f*
filet (F)	Netz *n*	net	—	rete *f*	red *f*
Filiale (D)	—	branch	succursale *f*	filiale *f*	sucursal *f*
filiale (I)	Filiale *f*	branch	succursale *f*	—	sucursal *f*
fill (E)	füllen	—	remplir	riempire	llenar
fille (F)	Tochter *f*	daughter	—	figlia *f*	hija *f*
fille de service (F)	Hausmädchen *n*	maid	—	domestica *f*	criada *f*
fill in (E)	ausfüllen	—	remplir	riempire	llenar

fire

	D	E	F	I	Es
filling station (E)	Tankstelle *f*	—	station-service *f*	distributore di benzina *m*	gasolinera *f*
fill up with petrol (E)	tanken	—	prendre de l'essence	fare benzina	llenar de gasolina
Film (D)	—	film	film *m*	film *m*	película *f*
film (E)	Film *m*	—	film *m*	film *m*	película *f*
film (F)	Film *m*	film	—	film *m*	película *f*
film (I)	Film *m*	film	film *m*	—	película *f*
filo (I)	Faden *m*	thread	fil *m*	—	hilo *m*
filo metallico (I)	Draht *m*	wire	fil de fer *m*	—	alambre *m*
fils (F)	Sohn *m*	son	—	figlio *m*	hijo *m*
fin (Es)	Ende *n*	end	fin *f*	fine *f*	—
fin¹ (F)	Ende *n*	end	—	fine *f*	fin *m*
fin² (F)	fein	fine	—	sottile	fino(a)
fin³ (F)	Schluß *m*	end	—	fine *f*	conclusión *f*
finalement¹ (F)	schließlich	finally	—	finalmente	finalmente
finalement² (F)	zuletzt	finally	—	infine	por último
finalidad (Es)	Zweck *m*	purpose	but *m*	scopo *m*	—
finally¹ (E)	schließlich	—	finalement	finalmente	finalmente
finally² (E)	zuletzt	—	finalement	infine	por último
finalmente¹ (Es)	endlich	at last	enfin	finalmente	—
finalmente² (Es)	schließlich	finally	finalement	finalmente	—
finalmente¹ (I)	endlich	at last	enfin	—	finalmente
finalmente² (I)	schließlich	finally	finalement	—	finalmente
finché (I)	solange	as long	tant que	—	en tanto que
find (E)	finden	—	trouver	trovare	encontrar
finden (D)	—	find	trouver	trovare	encontrar
fin de semana (Es)	Wochenende *n*	weekend	week-end *m*	fine settimana *m*	—
find one's way (E)	zurechtfinden, sich	—	retrouver, se	orientarsi	orientarse
fin dove (I)	soweit	as far as	autant que	—	hasta tanto
fine (E)	fein	—	fin(e)	sottile	fino(a)
fine¹ (I)	Ende *n*	end	fin *f*	—	fin *m*
fine² (I)	Schluß *m*	end	fin *f*	—	conclusión *f*
fine settimana (I)	Wochenende *n*	weekend	week-end *m*	—	fin de semana *m*
finestra (I)	Fenster *n*	window	fenêtre *f*	—	ventana *f*
Finger (D)	—	finger	doigt *m*	dito *m*	dedo *m*
finger (E)	Finger *m*	—	doigt *m*	dito *m*	dedo *m*
finir (F)	enden	end	—	finire	acabar
finir de payer (F)	abbezahlen	pay off	—	saldare	saldar
finire (I)	enden	end	finir	—	acabar
fino (Es)	fein	fine	fin(e)	sottile	—
fino a (I)	bis	until	jusqu'à	—	hasta
finora (I)	bisher	so far	jusqu'à présent	—	hasta ahora
finster (D)	—	dark	sombre	buio(a)	oscuro(a)
Finsternis (D)	—	darkness	obscurité *f*	buio *m*	oscuridad *f*
fiore (I)	Blume *f*	flower	fleur *f*	—	flor *f*
fiorire (I)	blühen	bloom	fleurir	—	florecer
fire¹ (E)	Brand *m*	—	incendie *m*	incendio *m*	incendio *m*

	D	E	F	I	Es
fire² (E)	Feuer *n*	—	feu *m*	fuoco *m*	fuego *m*
fire brigade (E)	Feuerwehr *f*	—	sapeurs pompiers *m pl*	vigili del fuoco *m pl*	cuerpo de bomberos *m*
fireworks (E)	Feuerwerk *n*	—	feu d'artifice *m*	fuoco d'artificio *m*	fuegos artificiales *m pl*
Firma (D)	—	company	firme *f*	ditta *f*	empresa *f*
firma (Es)	Unterschrift *f*	signature	signature *f*	firma *f*	—
firma (I)	Unterschrift *f*	signature	signature *f*	—	firma *f*
firmar (Es)	unterschreiben	sign	signer	firmare	—
firmare (I)	unterschreiben	sign	signer	—	firmar
firme (Es)	fest	solid	solide	solido(a)	—
firme (F)	Firma *f*	company	—	ditta *f*	empresa *f*
first¹ (E)	erst	—	d'abord	dapprima	primero
first² (E)	erste(r,s)	—	premier(-ière)	primo(a)	primero(a)
first of all (E)	zunächst	—	pour l'instant	dapprima	en primer lugar
Fisch (D)	—	fish	poisson *m*	pesce *m*	pez *m*
fischen (D)	—	fish	pêcher	pescare	pescar
Fischer (D)	—	fisher	pêcheur *m*	pescatore *m*	pescador *m*
fischietto (I)	Pfeife *f*	whistle	sifflet *m*	—	silbato *m*
fish¹ (E)	fischen	—	pêcher	pescare	pescar
fish² (E)	Fisch *m*	—	poisson *m*	pesce *m*	pez *m*
fish³ (E)	angeln	—	pêcher	pescare	pescar con caña
fisher (E)	Fischer *m*	—	pêcheur *m*	pescatore *m*	pescador *m*
fissare¹ (I)	anbringen	fasten	fixer	—	colocar
fissare² (I)	befestigen	fasten	fixer	—	sujetar
fissare³ (I)	vereinbaren	agree upon	convenir de	—	convenir
fisso (I)	ständig	permanent	permanent(e)	—	permanente
fist (E)	Faust *f*	––	poing *m*	pugno *m*	puño *m*
fit out (E)	einrichten	—	aménager	arredare	equipar
fiume (I)	Fluß *m*	river	fleuve *m*	—	rio *m*
five (E)	fünf	—	cinq	cinque	cinco
fix (E)	festsetzen	—	fixer	stabilire	fijar
fixer¹ (F)	anbringen	fasten	—	fissare	colocar
fixer² (F)	befestigen	fasten	—	fissare	sujetar
fixer³ (F)	festsetzen	fix	—	stabilire	fijar
flach (D)	—	flat	plat(e)	piatto(a)	llano(a)
Fläche (D)	—	area	surface *f*	area *f*	área *f*
flag¹ (E)	Fahne *f*	—	drapeau *m*	bandiera *f*	bandera *f*
flag² (E)	Flagge *f*	—	pavillon *m*	bandiera *f*	bandera *f*
Flagge (D)	—	flag	pavillon *m*	bandiera *f*	bandera *f*
flame (E)	Flamme *f*	—	flamme *f*	fiamma *f*	llama *f*
Flamme (D)	—	flame	flamme *f*	fiamma *f*	llama *f*
flamme (F)	Flamme *f*	flame	—	fiamma *f*	llama *f*
flan (Es)	Pudding *m*	pudding	flan *m*	budino *m*	—
flan (F)	Pudding *m*	pudding	—	budino *m*	flan *m*
flâner (F)	bummeln	stroll	—	girellare	callejear
flaque (F)	Pfütze *f*	puddle	—	pozzanghera *f*	charco *m*
Flasche (D)	—	bottle	bouteille *f*	bottiglia *f*	botella *f*

	D	E	F	I	Es
Flaschenöffner (D)	—	bottle opener	ouvre-bouteilles *m*	apribottiglie *m*	abrebotellas *m*
flash (E)	blinken	—	clignoter	lampeggiare	emitir reflejos
flat[1] (E)	flach	—	plat(e)	piatto(a)	llano(a)
flat[2] (E)	Wohnung *f*	—	appartement *m*	abitazione *f*	piso *m*
flauta (Es)	Flöte *f*	flute	flûte *f*	flauto *m*	—
flauto (I)	Flöte *f*	flute	flûte *f*	—	flauta *f*
flea (E)	Floh *m*	—	puce *f*	pulce *f*	pulga *f*
fleamarket (E)	Flohmarkt *m*	—	marché aux puces *m*	mercato delle pulci *m*	rastro *m*
flecha (Es)	Pfeil *m*	arrow	flèche *f*	freccia *f*	—
flèche (F)	Pfeil *m*	arrow	—	freccia *f*	flecha *f*
Fleck (D)	—	stain	tache *f*	macchia *f*	mancha *f*
Fleisch (D)	—	meat	viande *f*	carne *f*	carne *f*
fleißig (D)	—	diligent	travailleur(-euse)	diligente	activo(a)
fleur (F)	Blume *f*	flower	—	fiore *m*	flor *f*
fleurir (F)	blühen	bloom	—	fiorire	florecer
fleuve (F)	Fluß *m*	river	—	fiume *m*	rio *m*
Fliege (D)	—	fly	mouche *f*	mosca *f*	mosca *f*
fliegen (D)	—	fly	voler	volare	volar
fließen (D)	—	flow	couler	scorrere	correr
flight[1] (E)	Flug *m*	—	vol *m*	volo *m*	vuelo *m*
flight[2] (E)	Flucht *f*	—	fuite *f*	fuga *f*	fuga *f*
Flitterwochen (D)	—	honeymoon	lune de miel *f*	luna di miele *f*	luna de miel *f*
Floh (D)	—	flea	puce *f*	pulce *f*	pulga *f*
Flohmarkt (D)	—	fleamarket	marché aux puces *m*	mercato delle pulci *m*	rastro *m*
flojo (Es)	locker	loose	desserré(e)	lento(a)	—
flood (E)	Über-schwemmung *f*	—	inondation *f*	inondazione *f*	inundación *f*
floor[1] (E)	Boden *m*	—	terre *f*	terra *f*	suelo *m*
floor[2] (E)	Etage *f*	—	étage *m*	piano *m*	piso *m*
floor[3] (E)	Fußboden *m*	—	sol *m*	pavimento *m*	suelo *m*
flor (Es)	Blume *f*	flower	fleur *f*	fiore *m*	—
florecer (Es)	blühen	bloom	fleurir	fiorire	—
florero (Es)	Vase *f*	vase	vase *m*	vaso *m*	—
Flöte (D)	—	flute	flûte *f*	flauto *m*	flauta *f*
flour (E)	Mehl *n*	—	farine *f*	farina *f*	harina *f*
flow (E)	fließen	—	couler	scorrere	correr
flower (E)	Blume *f*	—	fleur *f*	fiore *m*	flor *f*
flu (E)	Grippe *f*	—	grippe *f*	influenza *f*	gripe *f*
Flucht (D)	—	flight	fuite *f*	fuga *f*	fuga *f*
Flug (D)	—	flight	vol *m*	volo *m*	vuelo *m*
Flügel (D)	—	wing	aile *f*	ala *f*	ala *f*
Flughafen (D)	—	airport	aéroport *m*	aeroporto *m*	aeropuerto *m*
Flugzeug (D)	—	aeroplane	avion *m*	aereo *m*	avión *m*
fluid (E)	flüssig	—	liquide	liquido(a)	líquido(a)
Flur (D)	—	hall	entrée *f*	corridoio *m*	corredor *m*
Fluß (D)	—	river	fleuve *m*	fiume *m*	rio *m*
flüssig (D)	—	fluid	liquide	liquido(a)	líquido(a)

	D	E	F	I	Es
flüstern (D)	—	whisper	chuchoter	bisbigliare	cuchichear
Flut (D)	—	high tide	marée haute f	alta marea f	marea alta f
flute (E)	Flöte f	—	flûte f	flauto m	flauta f
flûte (F)	Flöte f	flute	—	flauto m	flauta f
fly[1] (E)	fliegen	—	voler	volare	volar
fly[2] (E)	Fliege f	—	mouche f	mosca f	mosca f
foam (E)	Schaum m	—	écume f	schiuma f	espuma f
foca (Es)	Robbe f	seal	phoque m	foca f	—
foca (I)	Robbe f	seal	phoque m	—	foca f
fog (E)	Nebel m	—	brouillard m	nebbia f	niebla f
foglia (I)	Blatt n	leaf	feuille f	—	hoja f
foie (F)	Leber f	liver	—	fegato m	hígado m
foire[1] (F)	Jahrmarkt m	fair	—	fiera f	feria f
foire[2] (F)	Messe f	fair	—	fiera f	feria f
folder (E)	Mappe f	—	serviette f	raccoglitore m	carpeta f
Folge (D)	—	consequence	suite f	conseguenza f	serie f
folgen (D)	—	follow	suivre	seguire	seguir
folgend (D)	—	following	suivant(e)	seguente	siguiente
folla (I)	Menschen-menge f	crowd	foule f	—	muchedumbre f
follow (E)	folgen	—	suivre	seguire	seguir
following (E)	folgend	—	suivant(e)	seguente	siguiente
fonctionnaire (F)	Beamter m	civil servant	—	impiegato statale m	funcionario m
fonctionner (F)	funktionieren	work	—	funzionare	funcionar
fondare (I)	gründen	found	fonder	—	fundar
fonder (F)	gründen	found	—	fondare	fundar
fondre (F)	tauen	thaw	—	sciogliersi	deshelar
fontaine (F)	Brunnen m	fountain	—	fontana f	fuente f
fontana (I)	Brunnen m	fountain	fontaine f	—	fuente f
food[1] (E)	Essen n	—	repas m	alimentazione f	comida f
food[2] (E)	Kost f	—	nourriture f	cibo m	alimento m
food[3] (E)	Lebensmittel n	—	alimentation f	alimentari m pl	alimentos m pl
food[4] (E)	Nahrung f	—	nourriture f	alimentazione f	nutrición f
food[5] (E)	Speise f	—	aliment m	cibo m	comida f
fool (E)	Narr m	—	fou m	pazzo m	loco m
foolish (E)	albern	—	sot(te)	sciocco(a)	tonto(a)
foot (E)	Fuß m	—	pied m	piede m	pie m
football (E)	Fußball m	—	football m	pallone m	fútbol m
football (F)	Fußball m	football	—	pallone m	fútbol m
for[1] (E)	für	—	pour	per	por/para
for[2] (E)	denn	—	car	perché	pues/porque
forbici (I)	Schere f	pair of scissors	ciseaux m pl	—	tijeras f pl
forbid[1] (E)	untersagen	—	interdire qch à qn	proibire	prohibir
forbid[2] (E)	verbieten	—	défendre	proibire	prohibir
forbidden (E)	verboten	—	interdit(e)	vietato(a)	prohibido(a)
force[1] (E)	Gewalt f	—	force f	forza f	poder m
force[2] (E)	zwingen	—	forcer	costringere	obligar
force[1] (F)	Gewalt f	force	—	forza f	poder m

	D	E	F	I	Es
force² (F)	Kraft *f*	strength	—	forza *f*	fuerza *f*
forcer¹ (F)	erzwingen	obtain by force	—	ottenere con la forza	forzar
forcer² (F)	zwingen	force	—	costringere	obligar
forchetta (I)	Gabel *f*	fork	fourchette *f*	—	tenedor *m*
fordern (D)	—	demand	exiger	esigere	exigir
Forderung (D)	—	demand	exigence *f*	esigenza *f*	exigencia *f*
forehead (E)	Stirn *f*	—	front *m*	fronte *f*	frente *f*
foreign¹ (E)	ausländisch	—	étranger(-ère)	straniero(a)	extranjero(a)
foreign² (E)	fremd	—	étranger(-ère)	estraneo(a)	extranjero(a)
foreigner¹ (E)	Ausländer *m*	—	étranger *m*	straniero *m*	extranjero *m*
foreigner² (E)	Fremder *m*	—	étranger *m*	straniero *m*	extranjero *m*
foreign language (E)	Fremdsprache *f*	—	langue étrangère *f*	lingua straniera *f*	idioma extranjero *m*
Forelle (D)	—	trout	truite *f*	trota *f*	trucha *f*
forest¹ (E)	Forst *m*	—	forêt *f*	foresta *f*	bosque *m*
forest² (E)	Wald *m*	—	forêt *f*	bosco *m*	bosque *m*
foresta (I)	Forst *m*	forest	forêt *f*	—	bosque *m*
forêt¹ (F)	Forst *m*	forest	—	foresta *f*	bosque *m*
forêt² (F)	Wald *m*	forest	—	bosco *m*	bosque *m*
forget (E)	vergessen	—	oublier	dimenticare	olvidar
forgive (E)	verzeihen	—	pardonner	perdonare	perdonar
forgiveness (E)	Verzeihung *f*	—	pardon *m*	perdono *m*	perdón *m*
forgo (E)	verzichten	—	renoncer	rinunciare	renunciar
for it (E)	dafür	—	pour cela	per questo	para ello
fork (E)	Gabel *f*	—	fourchette *f*	forchetta *f*	tenedor *m*
Form (D)	—	form	forme *f*	forma *f*	forma *f*
form¹ (E)	bilden	—	former	formare	formar
form² (E)	Formular *n*	—	formulaire *m*	modulo *m*	formulario *m*
form³ (E)	Form *f*	—	forme *f*	forma *f*	forma *f*
forma (Es)	Form *f*	form	forme *f*	forma *f*	—
forma (I)	Form *f*	form	forme *f*	—	forma *f*
formación¹ (Es)	Ausbildung *f*	education	formation *f*	addestramento *m*	—
formación² (Es)	Bildung *f*	formation	formation *f*	formazione *f*	—
formaggio (I)	Käse *m*	cheese	fromage *m*	—	queso *m*
formal (E)	formell	—	formel(le)	formale	formal
formal (Es)	formell	formal	formel(le)	formale	—
formale (I)	formell	formal	formel(le)	—	formal
formar (Es)	bilden	form	former	formare	—
formare (I)	bilden	form	former	—	formar
formation (E)	Bildung *f*	—	formation *f*	formazione *f*	formación *f*
formation¹ (F)	Ausbildung *f*	education	—	addestramento *m*	formación *f*
formation² (F)	Bildung *f*	formation	—	formazione *f*	formación *f*
formazione (I)	Bildung *f*	formation	formation *f*	—	formación *f*
forme (F)	Form *f*	form	—	forma *f*	forma *f*
formel (F)	formell	formal	—	formale	formal
formell (D)	—	formal	formel(le)	formale	formal
former¹ (F)	ausbilden	educate	—	addestrare	instruir
former² (F)	bilden	form	—	formare	formar

	D	E	F	I	Es
formidable (Es)	gewaltig	tremendous	énorme	enorme	—
formidable (F)	großartig	magnificent	—	grandioso(a)	magnífico(a)
formulaire (F)	Formular *n*	form	—	modulo *m*	formulario *m*
Formular (D)	—	form	formulaire *m*	modulo *m*	formulario *m*
formulario (Es)	Formular *n*	form	formulaire *m*	modulo *m*	—
fornire (I)	liefern	deliver	fournir	—	suministrar
fornitura (I)	Lieferung *f*	delivery	livraison *f*	—	suministro *m*
for nothing (E)	umsonst	—	en vain	per niente	en vano
forschen (D)	—	research	rechercher	ricercare	investigar
forse (I)	vielleicht	maybe	peut-être	—	tal vez
Forst (D)	—	forest	forêt *f*	foresta *f*	bosque *m*
fort (D)	—	away	parti	via	lejos
fort¹ (F)	kräftig	strong	—	forte	fuerte
fort² (F)	laut	loud	—	rumoroso(a)	fuerte
fort³ (F)	stark	strong	—	forte	fuerte
fortaleza (Es)	Burg *f*	fortress	château fort *m*	rocca *f*	—
forte¹ (I)	kräftig	strong	fort(e)	—	fuerte
forte² (I)	stark	strong	fort(e)	—	fuerte
forth (E)	hervor	—	au-dehors	fuori	delante
fortress (E)	Burg *f*	—	château fort *m*	rocca *f*	fortaleza *f*
Fortschritt (D)	—	progress	progrès *m*	progresso *m*	progreso *m*
fortsetzen (D)	—	continue	continuer	continuare	proseguir
fortuna (I)	Glück *n*	luck	chance *f*	—	suerte *f*
forty (E)	vierzig	—	quarante	quaranta	cuarenta
forward (E)	vorwärts	—	en avant	avanti	adelante
for your sake (E)	deinetwegen	—	pour toi	per te	por ti
forza¹ (I)	Gewalt *f*	force	force *f*	—	poder *m*
forza² (I)	Kraft *f*	strength	force *f*	—	fuerza *f*
forza³ (I)	Stärke *f*	strength	puissance *f*	—	fuerza *f*
forzar (Es)	erzwingen	obtain by force	forcer	ottenere con la forza	—
Foto (D)	—	photo	photo *f*	foto *f*	foto *f*
foto (Es)	Foto *n*	photo	photo *f*	foto *f*	—
foto (I)	Foto *n*	photo	photo *f*	—	foto *f*
Fotoapparat (D)	—	camera	appareil photo *m*	macchina fotografica *f*	máquina fotográfica *f*
fotocopia (Es)	Fotokopie *f*	photocopy	photocopie *f*	fotocopia *f*	—
fotocopia (I)	Fotokopie *f*	photocopy	photocopie *f*	—	fotocopia *f*
fotografare¹ (I)	aufnehmen	photograph	photographier	—	fotografiar
fotografare² (I)	fotografieren	take pictures	photographier	—	fotografiar
fotografía (Es)	Aufnahme *f*	photograph	photographie *f*	fotografia *f*	—
fotografia (I)	Aufnahme *f*	photograph	photographie *f*	—	fotografía *f*
fotografiar¹ (Es)	aufnehmen	photograph	photographier	fotografare	—
fotografiar² (Es)	fotografieren	take pictures	photographier	fotografare	—
fotografieren (D)	—	take pictures	photographier	fotografare	fotografiar
Fotokopie (D)	—	photocopy	photocopie *f*	fotocopia *f*	fotocopia *f*
fou¹ (F)	Narr *m*	fool	—	pazzo *m*	loco *m*
fou² (F)	verrückt	mad	—	pazzo(a)	loco(a)
fouiller (F)	wühlen	scrabble	—	rovistare	revolver

	D	E	F	I	Es
foule (F)	Menschen-menge f	crowd	—	folla f	muchedumbre f
found (E)	gründen	—	fonder	fondare	fundar
fountain (E)	Brunnen m	—	fontaine f	fontana f	fuente f
fountain pen (E)	Füller m	—	stylo m	penna stilografica f	pluma f
four (E)	vier	—	quatre	quattro	cuatro
fourchette (F)	Gabel f	fork	—	forchetta f	tenedor m
fourneau (F)	Herd m	cooker	—	cucina f	cocina f
fournir en (F)	versorgen	provide	—	approvvigionare	proveer
fourrure (F)	Pelz m	fur	—	pelliccia f	piel f
fourteen (E)	vierzehn	—	quatorze	quattordici	catorce
fox (E)	Fuchs m	—	renard m	volpe f	zorro m
fracaso¹ (Es)	Mißerfolg m	failure	échec m	insuccesso m	—
fracaso² (Es)	Niete f	blank	mauvais numéro m	biglietto non vincente m	—
Frage (D)	—	question	question f	domanda f	pregunta f
fragen (D)	—	ask	demander	domandare	preguntar
frágil (Es)	zerbrechlich	fragile	fragile	fragile	—
fragile (E)	zerbrechlich	—	fragile	fragile	frágil
fragile (F)	zerbrechlich	fragile	—	fragile	frágil
fragile (I)	zerbrechlich	fragile	fragile	—	frágil
fragola (I)	Erdbeere f	strawberry	fraise f	—	fresa f
frais¹ (F)	frisch	fresh	—	fresco(a)	fresco(a)
frais² (F)	Spesen pl	expenses	—	spese f pl	gastos m pl
frais³ (F)	Unkosten pl	expenses	—	spese f pl	gastos m pl
frais⁴ (F)	kühl	cool	—	fresco(a)	fresco(a)
fraise (F)	Erdbeere f	strawberry	—	fragola f	fresa f
framboise (F)	Himbeere f	raspberry	—	lampone m	frambuesa f
frambuesa (Es)	Himbeere f	raspberry	framboise f	lampone m	—
frame (E)	Rahmen m	—	cadre m	cornice f	marco m
français (F)	französisch	French	—	francese	francés(-esa)
Français (F)	Franzose m	Frenchman	—	francese m	francés m
France (E)	Frankreich n	—	France f	Francia f	Francia f
France (F)	Frankreich n	France	—	Francia f	Francia f
francés¹ (Es)	Franzose m	Frenchman	Français	francese m	—
francés² (Es)	französisch	French	français(e)	francese	—
francese¹ (I)	französisch	French	français(e)	—	francés(-esa)
francese² (I)	Franzose m	Frenchman	Français	—	francés m
Francia (Es)	Frankreich n	France	France f	Francia f	—
Francia (I)	Frankreich n	France	France f	—	Francia f
francobollo (I)	Briefmarke f	stamp	timbre m	—	sello m
frankieren (D)	—	stamp	affranchir	affrancare	franquear
Frankreich (D)	—	France	France f	Francia f	Francia f
franquear (Es)	frankieren	stamp	affranchir	affrancare	—
franqueo (Es)	Porto n	postage	port m	affrancatura f	—
Franzose (D)	—	Frenchman	Français	francese m	francés m
französisch (D)	—	French	français(e)	francese	francés(-esa)
frapper¹ (F)	klopfen	knock	—	bussare	golpear
frapper² (F)	pochen	knock	—	battere	golpear

	D	E	F	I	Es
frase (I)	Satz *m*	sentence	phrase *f*	—	oración *f*
fratelli (I)	Geschwister *pl*	brothers and sisters	frère(s) et sœur(s) *pl*	—	hermanos *m pl*
fratello (I)	Bruder *m*	brother	frère *m*	—	hermano *m*
frattanto (I)	inzwischen	meanwhile	entretemps	—	mientras tanto
Frau (D)	—	woman	femme *f*	donna *f*	mujer *f*
fraud (E)	Betrug *m*	—	tromperie *f*	inganno *m*	engaño *m*
Fräulein (D)	—	Miss	mademoiselle *f*	signorina *f*	señorita *f*
freccia (I)	Pfeil *m*	arrow	flèche *f*	—	flecha *f*
frech (D)	—	cheeky	insolent(e)	sfacciato(a)	atrevido(a)
frecuente (Es)	häufig	frequent	fréquent(e)	frequente	—
freddo (I)	kalt	cold	froid(e)	—	frío(a)
free¹ (E)	frei	—	libre	libero(a)	libre
free² (E)	kostenlos	—	gratuit(e)	gratuito(a)	gratis
free³ (E)	losbinden	—	délier	sciogliere	desatar
freedom (E)	Freiheit *f*	—	liberté *f*	libertà *f*	libertad *f*
free of charge (E)	gratis	—	gratuit(e)	gratuito(a)	gratis
free time (E)	Freizeit *f*	—	loisirs *m pl*	tempo libero	tiempo libre *m*
freezer (E)	Eisschrank *m*	—	réfrigérateur *m*	frigorifero *m*	refrigerador *m*
freeze to death (E)	erfrieren	—	mourir de froid	morire di freddo	morirse de frío
fregar (Es)	wischen	wipe	essuyer	pulire	—
frei (D)	—	free	libre	libero(a)	libre
Freibad (D)	—	open-air swimming pool	piscine en plein air *f*	piscina all'aperto *f*	piscina al aire libre *f*
Freiheit (D)	—	freedom	liberté *f*	libertà *f*	libertad *f*
freilassen (D)	—	release	libérer	mettere in libertà	poner en libertad
frein (F)	Bremse *f*	brake	—	freno *m*	freno *m*
freiner (F)	bremsen	brake	—	frenare	frenar
Freitag (D)	—	Friday	vendredi *m*	venerdì *m*	viernes *m*
freiwillig (D)	—	voluntary	volontaire	volontario(a)	voluntario(a)
Freizeit (D)	—	free time	loisirs *m pl*	tempo libero	tiempo libre *m*
fremd (D)	—	foreign	étranger(-ère)	estraneo(a)	extranjero(a)
Fremder (D)	—	foreigner	étranger(-ère) *m(f)*	straniero *m*	extranjero *m*
Fremdsprache (D)	—	foreign-language	langue étrangère *f*	lingua straniera *f*	idioma extranjero *m*
frenar (Es)	bremsen	brake	freiner	frenare	—
frenare (I)	bremsen	brake	freiner	—	frenar
French (E)	französisch	—	français(e)	francese	francés(-esa)
french fries (E)	Pommes frites *pl*	—	frites *f pl*	patate fritte *f pl*	patatas fritas *f pl*
Frenchman (E)	Franzose *m*	—	Français	francese *m*	francés *m*
freno (Es)	Bremse *f*	brake	frein *m*	freno *m*	—
freno (I)	Bremse *f*	brake	frein *m*	—	freno *m*
frente (Es)	Stirn *f*	forehead	front *m*	fronte *f*	—
frequent (E)	häufig	—	fréquent(e)	frequente	frecuente
fréquent (F)	häufig	frequent	—	frequente	frecuente
frequente (I)	häufig	frequent	fréquent(e)	—	frecuente
frère (F)	Bruder *m*	brother	—	fratello *m*	hermano *m*
frère(s) et sœur(s) (F)	Geschwister *pl*	brothers and sisters	—	fratelli *m pl*	hermanos *m pl*

	D	E	F	I	Es
fresa (Es)	Erdbeere f	strawberry	fraise f	fragola f	—
fresco[1] (I)	frisch	fresh	frais(fraîche)	—	fresco(a)
fresco[2] (I)	kühl	cool	frais(fraîche)	—	fresco(a)
fresco[1] (Es)	frisch	fresh	frais(fraîche)	fresco(a)	—
fresco[2] (Es)	kühl	cool	frais(fraîche)	fresco(a)	—
fresh (E)	frisch	—	frais(fraîche)	fresco(a)	fresco(a)
fressen (D)	—	eat	bouffer	mangiare	devorar
fretta (I)	Eile f	haste	hâte f	—	prisa f
frettoloso (I)	eilig	hurried	pressé(e)	—	rápido(a)
Freude (D)	—	joy	joie f	gioia f	alegría f
freuen, sich (D)	—	be glad	être heureux(-euse)	rallegrarsi	alegrarse
Freund (D)	—	friend	ami m	amico m	amigo m
freundlich (D)	—	friendly	aimable	gentile	amistoso(a)
Freundschaft (D)	—	friendship	amitié f	amicizia f	amistad f
Friday (E)	Freitag m	—	vendredi m	venerdì m	viernes m
fridge (E)	Kühlschrank m	—	réfrigérateur m	frigorifero m	nevera f
fried (E)	gebraten	—	rôti(e)	arrostito(a)	asado(a)
Friede (D)	—	peace	paix f	pace f	paz f
Friedhof (D)	—	cemetery	cimetière m	cimitero m	cementerio m
friedlich (D)	—	peaceful	paisible	pacifico(a)	pacifico(a)
friend (E)	Freund m	—	ami m	amico m	amigo m
friendly[1] (E)	befreundet	—	ami(e) de	amico(a)	amigo(a) de
friendly[2] (E)	freundlich	—	aimable	gentile	amistoso(a)
friendship (E)	Freundschaft f	—	amitié f	amicizia f	amistad f
frieren (D)	—	be cold	avoir froid	avere freddo	tener frío
frighten (E)	erschrecken	—	effrayer	spaventare	asustar
frigorifero[1] (I)	Eisschrank m	freezer	réfrigérateur m	—	refrigerador m
frigorifero[2] (I)	Kühlschrank m	fridge	réfrigérateur m	—	nevera f
frío (Es)	kalt	cold	froid(e)	freddo(a)	—
frisch (D)	—	fresh	frais(fraîche)	fresco(a)	fresco(a)
Friseur (D)	—	hairdresser	coiffeur m	parrucchiere m	peluquero m
Frisur (D)	—	hairstyle	coiffure f	pettinatura f	peinado m
frites (F)	Pommes frites pl	french fries	—	patate fritte f pl	patatas fritas f pl
frittata (I)	Omelett n	omelette	omelette f	—	tortilla f
frog (E)	Frosch m	—	grenouille f	rana f	rana f
froh (D)	—	glad	content(e)	lieto(a)	contento(a)
froid (F)	kalt	cold	—	freddo(a)	frío(a)
from (E)	von	—	de	di/da	de
fromage (F)	Käse m	cheese	—	formaggio m	queso m
fromage blanc (F)	Quark m	curd cheese	—	ricotta f	requesón m
fromm (D)	—	pious	pieux(-euse)	devoto(a)	religioso(a)
front (F)	Stirn f	forehead	—	fronte f	frente f
fronte (I)	Stirn f	forehead	front m	—	frente f
frontera (Es)	Grenze f	frontier	frontière f	frontiera f	—
frontier (E)	Grenze f	—	frontière f	frontiera f	frontera f
frontiera (I)	Grenze f	frontier	frontière f	—	frontera f
frontière (F)	Grenze f	frontier	—	frontiera f	frontera f

	D	E	F	I	Es
Frosch (D)	—	frog	grenouille f	rana f	rana f
Frost (D)	—	frost	gelée f	gelo m	helada f
frost (E)	Frost m	—	gelée f	gelo m	helada f
frotar (Es)	reiben	rub	frotter	sfregare	—
frotter (F)	reiben	rub	—	sfregare	frotar
Frucht (D)	—	fruit	fruit m	frutto m	fruto m
früh (D)	—	early	tôt	presto	temprano(a)
früher (D)	—	earlier	autrefois	prima	antes
Frühjahr (D)	—	spring	printemps m	primavera f	primavera f
Frühstück (D)	—	breakfast	petit-déjeuner m	colazione f	desayuno m
fruit[1] (E)	Frucht f	—	fruit m	frutto m	fruto m
fruit[2] (E)	Obst n	—	fruits m pl	frutta f	fruta f
fruit (F)	Frucht f	fruit	—	frutto m	fruto m
fruits (F)	Obst n	fruit	—	frutta f	fruta f
fruta (Es)	Obst n	fruit	fruits m pl	frutta f	—
frumento (I)	Weizen m	wheat	blé m	—	trigo m
fruto (Es)	Frucht f	fruit	fruit m	frutto m	—
frutta (I)	Obst n	fruit	fruits m pl	—	fruta f
frutto (I)	Frucht f	fruit	fruit m	—	fruto m
Fuchs (D)	—	fox	renard m	volpe f	zorro m
fuego (Es)	Feuer n	fire	feu m	fuoco m	—
fuegos artificiales (Es)	Feuerwerk n	fireworks	feu d'artifice m	fuoco d'artificio m	
fuel (E)	Heizöl n	—	mazout m	olio combustibile m	combustible para la calefacción m
fuente[1] (Es)	Brunnen m	well	fontaine f	fontana f	—
fuente[2] (Es)	Quelle f	spring	source f	sorgente f	—
fuente[3] (Es)	Schüssel m	bowl	jatte f	scodella f	—
fuera[1] (Es)	auswärts	outwards	à l'extérieur	fuori	—
fuera[2] (Es)	weg	away	pas là	via	—
fuera de (Es)	außerhalb	out of	hors de	fuori di	—
fuerte[1] (Es)	heftig	fierce	violent(e)	violento(a)	—
fuerte[2] (Es)	kräftig	strong	fort(e)	forte	—
fuerte[3] (Es)	laut	loud	fort(e)	rumoroso(a)	—
fuerte[4] (Es)	stark	strong	fort(e)	forte	—
fuerza[1] (Es)	Kraft f	strength	force f	forza f	—
fuerza[2] (Es)	Stärke f	strength	puissance f	forza f	—
fuga (Es)	Flucht f	flight	fuite f	fuga f	—
fuga (I)	Flucht f	flight	fuite f	—	fuga f
fühlen (D)	—	feel	sentir	sentire	sentir
führen (D)	—	lead	guider	guidare	dirigir
Führer (D)	—	leader	guide m	guida f	guía m
Führerschein (D)	—	driving licence	permis de conduire m	patente f	permiso de conducir m
Führung (D)	—	guided tour	visite guidée f	visita guidata f	visita guiada f
fuite (F)	Flucht f	flight	—	fuga f	fuga f
fulfil (E)	erfüllen	—	remplir	esaudire	conceder
full[1] (E)	satt	—	rassasié(e)	sazio(a)	satisfecho(a)
full[2] (E)	voll	—	plein(e)	pieno(a)	lleno(a)

	D	E	F	I	Es
full board (E)	Vollpension f	—	pension complète f	pensione completa f	pensión completa f
füllen (D)	—	fill	remplir	riempire	llenar
Füller (D)	—	fountain pen	stylo m	penna stilografica f	pluma f
fully booked (E)	ausgebucht	—	complet(-ète)	esaurito(a)	completo(a)
fumador (Es)	Raucher m	smoker	fumeur m	fumatore m	—
fumar (Es)	rauchen	smoke	fumer	fumare	—
fumare (I)	rauchen	smoke	fumer	—	fumar
fumatore (I)	Raucher m	smoker	fumeur m	—	fumador m
fumée (F)	Rauch m	smoke	—	fumo m	humo m
fumer (F)	rauchen	smoke	—	fumare	fumar
fumeur (F)	Raucher m	smoker	—	fumatore m	fumador m
fumo (I)	Rauch m	smoke	fumée f	—	humo m
fun (E)	Spaß m	—	plaisir m	scherzo m	broma f
funcionar (Es)	funktionieren	work	fonctionner	funzionare	—
funcionario (Es)	Beamter m	civil servant	fonctionnaire m	impiegato statale m	—
fundamental (E)	grundsätzlich	—	par principe	basilare	por principio
fundar (Es)	gründen	found	fonder	fondare	—
Fundbüro (D)	—	lost property office	bureau des objets trouvés m	ufficio oggetti smarriti m	oficina de objetos perdidos f
fune (I)	Seil n	rope	corde f	—	soga f
funeral (E)	Beerdigung f	—	enterrement m	funerale m	entierro m
funerale (I)	Beerdigung f	funeral	enterrement m	—	entierro m
fünf (D)	—	five	cinq	cinque	cinco
fünfzehn (D)	—	fifteen	quinze	quindici	quince
fünfzig (D)	—	fifty	cinquante	cinquanta	cincuenta
fungo (I)	Pilz m	mushroom	champignon m	—	hongo m
funktionieren (D)	—	work	fonctionner	funzionare	funcionar
funny[1] (E)	komisch	—	drôle	comico(a)	cómico(a)
funny[2] (E)	lustig	—	marrant(e)	allegro(a)	divertido(a)
funzionare (I)	funktionieren	work	fonctionner	—	funcionar
fuoco (I)	Feuer n	fire	feu m	—	fuego m
fuoco d'artificio (I)	Feuerwerk n	fireworks	feu d'artifice m		fuegos artificiales m pl
fuori[1] (I)	auswärts	out(wards)	à l'extérieur	—	fuera
fuori[2] (I)	außen	outside	au dehors	—	afuera
fuori[3] (I)	draußen	outside	dehors	—	afuera
fuori[4] (I)	hervor	forth	au-dehors	—	delante
fuori[5] (I)	hinaus	out	dehors	—	hacia afuera
fuori[6] (I)	heraus	out	dehors	—	hacia afuera
fuori di (I)	außerhalb	out of	hors de	—	fuera de
fuori moda (I)	altmodisch	old-fashioned	démodé	—	pasado(a) de moda
für (D)	—	for	pour	per	por/para
fur (E)	Pelz m	—	fourrure f	pelliccia f	piel f
furieux (F)	wütend	furious	—	arrabbiato(a)	furioso(a)
fürchten (D)	—	fear	craindre	temere	temer
fürchterlich (D)	—	terrible	terrible	terribile	terrible
furioso (Es)	wütend	furious	furieux(-euse)	arrabbiato(a)	—

	D	E	F	I	Es
furious (E)	wütend	—	furieux(-euse)	arrabbiato(a)	furioso(a)
furnish (E)	möblieren	—	meubler	ammobiliare	amueblar
furnished (E)	möbliert	—	meublé(e)	ammobiliato(a)	amueblado(a)
furnishing (E)	Einrichtung *f*	—	ameublement *m*	arredamento *m*	mobiliario *m*
furniture (E)	Möbel *n*	—	meuble *m*	mobile *m*	mueble *m*
Fürst (D)	—	prince	prince *m*	principe *m*	príncipe *m*
further (E)	weiter	—	plus éloigné(e)	più ampio(a)	adelante
Fuß (D)	—	foot	pied *m*	piede *m*	pie *m*
Fußball (D)	—	football	football *m*	pallone *m*	fútbol *m*
Fußboden (D)	—	floor	sol *m*	pavimento *m*	suelo *m*
Fußgänger (D)	—	pedestrian	piéton *m*	pedone *m*	peatón *m*
fútbol (Es)	Fußball *m*	football	football *m*	pallone *m*	—
futé (F)	clever	clever	—	abile	listo(a)
futur (F)	zukünftig	future	—	futuro(a)	en el futuro
future[1] (E)	zukünftig	—	futur(e)	futuro(a)	en el futuro
future[2] (E)	Zukunft *f*	—	avenir *m*	futuro *m*	futuro *m*
futuro (Es)	Zukunft *f*	future	avenir *m*	futuro *m*	—
futuro[1] (I)	zukünftig	future	futur(e)	—	en el futuro
futuro[2] (I)	Zukunft *f*	future	avenir *m*	—	futuro *m*
gabbia (I)	Käfig *m*	cage	cage *f*	—	jaula *f*
gabbiano (I)	Möwe *f*	seagull	mouette *f*	—	gaviota *f*
Gabel (D)	—	fork	fourchette *f*	forchetta *f*	tenedor *m*
gabinetto (I)	Klosett *n*	lavatory	cabinets *m pl*	—	retrete *m*
gafas (Es)	Brille *f*	glasses	lunettes *f pl*	occhiali *m pl*	—
gafas de sol (Es)	Sonnenbrille *f*	sunglasses	lunettes de soleil *f pl*	occhiali da sole *m pl*	—
gage (F)	Pfand *n*	piedge	—	pegno *m*	prenda *f*
gagner[1] (F)	gewinnen	win	—	vincere	ganar
gagner[2] (F)	siegen	win	—	vincere	vencer
gagner[3] (F)	verdienen	earn	—	guadagnare	ganar
gain (F)	Gewinn *m*	profit	—	guadagno *m*	ganancia *f*
gall (E)	Galle *f*	—	fiel *m*	cistifellea *f*	bilis *f*
Galle (D)	—	gall	fiel *m*	cistifellea *f*	bilis *f*
galleria (I)	Tunnel *m*	tunnel	tunnel *m*	—	túnel *m*
galleta (Es)	Keks *m*	biscuit	biscuit *m*	biscotto *m*	—
gallina[1] (Es)	Henne *f*	hen	poule *f*	gallina *f*	—
gallina[2] (Es)	Huhn *n*	chicken	poule *f*	pollo *m*	—
gallina (I)	Henne *f*	hen	poule *f*	—	gallina *f*
gallo (Es)	Hahn *m*	cock	coq *m*	gallo *m*	—
gallo (I)	Hahn *m*	cock	coq *m*	—	gallo *m*
gamba (I)	Bein *n*	leg	jambe *f*	—	pierna *f*
gambero (I)	Krebs *m*	crayfish	écrevisse *f*	—	cangrejo *m*
game[1] (E)	Spiel *n*	—	jeu *m*	gioco *m*	juego *m*
game[2] (E)	Wild *n*	—	gibier *m*	selvaggina *f*	caza *f*
ganancia[1] (Es)	Gewinn *m*	profit	gain *m*	guadagno *m*	—
ganancia[2] (Es)	Verdienst *m*	income	revenus *m pl*	guadagno *m*	—
ganar[1] (Es)	gewinnen	win	gagner	vincere	—
ganar[2] (Es)	verdienen	earn	gagner	guadagnare	—

	D	E	F	I	Es
ganas (Es)	Lust *f*	delight	plaisir *m*	piacere *m*	—
gancho (Es)	Haken *m*	hook	crochet *m*	gancio *m*	—
gancio (I)	Haken *m*	hook	crochet *m*	—	gancho *m*
Gang[1] (D)	—	course	plat *m*	portata *f*	plato *m*
Gang[2] (D)	—	corridor	couloir *m*	corridoio *m*	corredor *m*
Gang[3] (D)	—	gear	vitesse *f*	marcia *f*	marcha *f*
Gans (D)	—	goose	oie *f*	oca *f*	ganso *m*
ganso (Es)	Gans *f*	goose	oie *f*	oca *f*	—
gant (F)	Handschuh *m*	glove	—	guanto *m*	guante *m*
ganz (D)	—	whole	tout(e)	intero(a)	entero(a)
Ganze (D)	—	lot	le tout	insieme *m*	todo *m*
gap (E)	Lücke *f*	—	lacune *f*	lacuna *f*	espacio *m*
gar (D)	—	done	cuit(e)	cotto(a)	estar a punto
Garage (D)	—	garage	garage *m*	garage *m*	garaje *m*
garage (E)	Garage *f*	—	garage *m*	garage *m*	garaje *m*
garage (F)	Garage *f*	garage	—	garage *m*	garaje *m*
garage (I)	Garage *f*	garage	garage *m*	—	garaje *m*
garaje (Es)	Garage *f*	garage	garage *m*	garage *m*	—
garantía[1] (Es)	Garantie *f*	guarantee	garantie *f*	garanzia *f*	—
garantía[2] (Es)	Gewähr *f*	guarantee	garantie *f*	garanzia *f*	—
Garantie (D)	—	guarantee	garantie *f*	garanzia *f*	garantía *f*
garantie[1] (F)	Garantie *f*	guarantee	—	garanzia *f*	garantía *f*
garantie[2] (F)	Gewähr *f*	guarantee	—	garanzia *f*	garantía *f*
garanzia[1] (I)	Gewähr *f*	guarantee	garantie *f*	—	garantía *f*
garanzia[2] (I)	Garantie *f*	guarantee	garantie *f*	—	garantía *f*
garçon[1] (F)	Bursche *m*	fellow	—	ragazzo *m*	chico *m*
garçon[2] (F)	Junge *m*	boy	—	ragazzo *m*	chico *m*
garçon[3] (F)	Kellner *m*/ Ober *m*	waiter	—	cameriere *m*	camarero *m*
garden (E)	Garten *m*	—	jardin *m*	giardino *m*	jardín *m*
gardener (E)	Gärtner *m*	—	jardinier *m*	giardiniere *m*	jardinero *m*
garder[1] (F)	aufbewahren	keep	—	conservare	guardar
garder[2] (F)	bewachen	guard	—	sorvegliare	vigilar
garder[3] (F)	behalten	keep	—	tenere	retener
Garderobe (D)	—	wardrobe	vestiaire *m*	guardaroba *m*	guardaropa *m*
garderobe (F)	Kleiderschrank *m*	wardrobe	—	armadio *m*	armario ropero *m*
gardien[1] (F)	Aufseher *m*	guard	—	custode *m*	vigilante *m*
gardien[2] (F)	Wärter *m*	attendant	—	custode *m*	guarda *m*
Gardine (D)	—	curtain	rideau *m*	tenda *f*	cortina *f*
gare (F)	Bahnhof *m*	station	—	stazione *f*	estación *f*
gare centrale (F)	Hauptbahnhof *m*	central station	—	stazione centrale *f*	estación central *f*
garer (F)	parken	park	—	parcheggiare	aparcar
garganta (Es)	Rachen *m*	throat	gorge *f*	faringe *m*	—
garlic (E)	Knoblauch *m*	—	ail *m*	aglio *m*	ajo *m*
garnieren (D)	—	decorate	garnir	guarnire	guarnecer
garnir (F)	garnieren	decorate	—	guarnire	guarnecer
garofano (I)	Nelke *f*	carnation	œillet *m*	—	clavel *m*
Garten (D)	—	garden	jardin *m*	giardino *m*	jardín *m*

	D	E	F	I	Es
Gärtner (D)	—	gardener	jardinier *m*	giardiniere *m*	jardinero *m*
gaseosa (Es)	Limonade *f*	lemonade	limonade *f*	limonata *f*	—
gasolina (Es)	Benzin *n*	petrol	essence *f*	benzina	—
gasolinera (Es)	Tankstelle *f*	filling station	station-service *f*	distributore di benzina *m*	—
gaspiller (F)	verschwenden	waste	—	sprecare	desperdiciar
Gasse (D)	—	lane	ruelle *f*	vicolo *m*	callejón *m*
Gast (D)	—	guest	hôte *m/f*	ospite *m*	invitado *m*
gastfreundlich (D)	—	hospitable	hospitalier(-ière)	ospitale	hospitalario(a)
Gastfreund- schaft (D)	—	hospitality	hospitalité *f*	ospitalità *f*	hospitalidad *f*
Gastgeber (D)	—	host	hôte *m*	ospite *m*	anfitrión *m*
Gasthaus (D)	—	hotel	auberge *f*	osteria *m*	posada *f*
gastos[1] (Es)	Spesen *pl*	expenses	frais *m pl*	spese *f pl*	—
gastos[2] (Es)	Unkosten *pl*	expenses	frais *m pl*	spese *f pl*	—
gate (E)	Tor *n*	—	porte *f*	porta *f*	puerta *f*
gâteau[1] (F)	Kuchen *m*	cake	—	dolce *m*	pastel *m*
gâteau[2] (F)	Torte *f*	cake	—	torta *f*	tarta *f*
gâter (F)	verwöhnen	spoil	—	viziare	mimar
gato (Es)	Katze *f*	cat	chat *m*	gatto *m*	—
gatto (I)	Katze *f*	cat	chat *m*	—	gato *m*
gaviota (Es)	Möwe *f*	seagull	mouette *f*	gabbiano *m*	—
gear (E)	Gang *m*	—	vitesse *f*	marcia *f*	marcha *f*
Gebäck (D)	—	pastry	pâtisserie *f*	biscotti *m pl*	pastas *f pl*
gebären (D)	—	give birth to	mettre au monde	partorire	parir
Gebäude (D)	—	building	bâtiment *m*	edificio *m*	edificio *m*
geben (D)	—	give	donner	dare	andar
Gebet (D)	—	prayer	prière *f*	preghiera *f*	oración *f*
Gebiet (D)	—	region	région *f*	regione *f*	zona *f*
Gebirge (D)	—	mountain chain	montagne *f*	montagna *f*	montañas *f pl*
Gebiß (D)	—	teeth	dents *f pl*	denti *m pl*	dentadura *f*
geboren (D)	—	born	né(e)	nato(a)	nacido(a)
gebraten (D)	—	fried	rôti(e)	arrostito(a)	asado(a)
Gebrauch (D)	—	custom	usage *m*	uso *m*	uso *m*
gebrauchen (D)	—	use	utiliser	usare	usar
gebraucht (D)	—	used	d'occasion	usato(a)	usado(a)
Gebühr (D)	—	fee	droit *m*	tassa *f*	tarifa *f*
Geburt (D)	—	birth	naissance *f*	nascita *f*	nacimiento *m*
Geburtstag (D)	—	birthday	anniversaire *m*	compleanno *m*	cumpleaños *m*
Gedächtnis (D)	—	memory	mémoire *f*	memoria *f*	memoria *f*
Gedanke (D)	—	thought	pensée *f*	pensiero *m*	pensamiento *m*
Gedeck (D)	—	cover	couvert *m*	coperto *m*	cubierto *m*
gedenken (D)	—	remember	souvenir de, se	ricordare	conmemorar
Gedicht (D)	—	poem	poème *m*	poesia *f*	poema *m*
Geduld (D)	—	patience	patience *f*	pazienza *f*	paciencia *f*
geduldig (D)	—	patient	patient(e)	paziente	con paciencia
geeignet (D)	—	suitable	approprié(e)	adatto(a)	indicado(a)
Gefahr (D)	—	danger	danger *m*	pericolo *m*	peligro *m*
gefährlich (D)	—	dangerous	dangereux(-euse)	pericoloso(a)	peligroso(a)

	D	E	F	I	Es
gefallen (D)	—	please	plaire	piacere	gustar
Gefallen (D)	—	favour	service *m*	favore *m*	favor *m*
Gefälligkeit (D)	—	favour	obligeance *f*	favore *m*	favor *m*
Gefängnis (D)	—	prison	prison *f*	prigione *f*	cárcel *f*
Gefäß (D)	—	container	récipient *m*	recipiente *m*	recipiente *m*
Geflügel (D)	—	poultry	volaille *f*	pollame *m*	aves *f pl*
Gefühl (D)	—	feeling	sentiment *m*	sensazione *f*	sentimiento *m*
gegen (D)	—	against	contre	contro	contra
Gegend (D)	—	region	région *f*	regione *f*	región *f*
Gegenstand (D)	—	object	objet *m*	oggetto *m*	objeto *m*
Gegenteil (D)	—	opposite	contraire *m*	contrario *m*	opuesto *m*
gegenüber (D)	—	opposite	en face de	di fronte(a)	en frente
Gegenwart (D)	—	present	présent *m*	presente *m*	presente *m*
Gegner (D)	—	opponent	adversaire *m*	avversario *m*	adversario *m*
Gehalt (D)	—	salary	salaire *m*	stipendio *m*	sueldo *m*
geheim (D)	—	secret	secret(-ète)	segreto(a)	secreto(a)
Geheimnis (D)	—	secret	secret *m*	segreto *m*	secreto *m*
gehen (D)	—	go	aller	andare	andar
Gehör (D)	—	hearing	ouïe *f*	udito *m*	oreja *f*
gehorchen (D)	—	obey	obéir	ubbidire	obedecer
gehören (D)	—	belong	appartenir	appartenere	pertenecer
gehorsam (D)	—	obedient	obéissant(e)	ubbidiente	obediente
Gehweg (D)	—	pavement	trottoir *m*	marciapiede *m*	acera *f*
Geige (D)	—	violin	violon *m*	violino *m*	violín *m*
Geist (D)	—	spirit	esprit *m*	spirito *m*	espíritu *m*
geizig (D)	—	mean	avare	avaro(a)	avaro(a)
Gelächter (D)	—	laughter	rires *m pl*	risata *f*	risa *f*
gelähmt (D)	—	paralysed	paralysé(e)	paralizzato(a)	paralítico(a)
Gelände (D)	—	terrain	terrain	terreno *m*	terreno *m*
gelangen (D)	—	attain	arriver à	arrivare a	conseguir
gelato (I)	Eis *n*	ice	glace *f*	—	hielo *m*
gelb (D)	—	yellow	jaune	giallo(a)	amarillo(a)
Geld (D)	—	money	argent *m*	denaro *m*	dinero *m*
gelée (F)	Frost *m*	frost	—	gelo *m*	helada *f*
Gelegenheit (D)	—	occasion	occasion *f*	occasione *f*	oportunidad *f*
gelegentlich (D)	—	occasional	occasionnel(le)	occasionale	ocasional
gelingen (D)	—	succeed	réussir	riuscire	acertar
gelo (I)	Frost *m*	frost	gelée *f*	—	helada *f*
gelosia (I)	Eifersucht *f*	jealousy	jalousie *f*	—	celos *m pl*
gelten (D)	—	be worth	valoir	valere	valer
Gemälde (D)	—	painting	tableau *m*	quadro *m*	cuadro *m*
gemein (D)	—	mean	méchant(e)	volgare	vulgar
gemeinsam (D)	—	together	ensemble	comune	juntos(as)
gemelli (I)	Zwillinge *pl*	twins	jumeaux *m pl*	—	gemelos *m pl*
gemelos[1] (Es)	Fernglas *n*	binoculars	jumelles *f pl*	cannocchiale *m*	—

	D	E	F	I	Es
gemelos² (Es)	Zwillinge pl	twins	jumeaux m pl	gemelli m pl	—
Gemüse (D)	—	vegetables	légumes m pl	verdura f	legumbres f pl
Gemüt (D)	—	disposition	disposition f	animo m	ánimo m
gemütlich (D)	—	comfortable	agréable	comodo(a)	cómodo(a)
gênant (F)	peinlich	embarrassing	—	imbarazzante	desagradable
genau (D)	—	exact	exact(e)	preciso(a)	exacto(a)
Genauigkeit (D)	—	accuracy	exactitude f	precisione f	exactitud f
gêne (F)	Verlegenheit f	embarrassment	—	imbarazzo m	contratiempo m
genehmigen (D)	—	approve	autoriser	approvare	permitir
Genehmigung (D)	—	authorization	autorisation f	permesso m	permiso m
General (D)	—	General	général m	generale m	general m
general (E)	allgemein	—	général(e)	generale	general
General (E)	General m	—	général m	generale m	general m
general¹ (Es)	allgemein	general	général(e)	generale	—
general² (Es)	General m	General	général m	generale m	—
général¹ (F)	General m	General	—	generale m	general m
général² (F)	allgemein	general	—	generale	general
generale¹ (I)	allgemein	general	général(e)	—	general
generale² (I)	General m	General	général m	—	general m
généralement (F)	meistens	generally	—	di solito	por lo común
generally (E)	meistens	—	généralement	di solito	por lo común
généreux (F)	großzügig	generous	—	generoso(a)	generoso(a)
generoso (I)	großzügig	generous	généreux(-euse)	—	generoso(a)
generoso (Es)	großzügig	generous	généreux(-euse)	generoso(a)	—
generous (E)	großzügig	—	généreux(-euse)	generoso(a)	generoso(a)
genießen (D)	—	enjoy	jouir	godere	disfrutar
genitori (I)	Eltern pl	parents	parents m pl	—	padres m pl
gennaio (I)	Januar m	January	janvier m	—	enero m
Genosse (D)	—	comrade	camarade m	compagno m	camarada m
genou (F)	Knie n	knee	—	ginocchio m	rodilla f
gens (F)	Leute f	people	—	gente f	gente f
gente (Es)	Leute f	people	gens m pl	gente f	—
gente (I)	Leute f	people	gens m pl	—	gente f
gentil (Es)	liebenswürdig	kind	aimable	gentile	—
gentil¹ (F)	lieb	sweet	—	caro(a)	amable
gentil² (F)	brav	good	—	bravo(a)	bueno(a)
gentile¹ (I)	freundlich	friendly	aimable	—	amistoso(a)
gentile² (I)	liebenswürdig	kind	aimable	—	gentil
gentle (E)	sanft	—	doux(douce)	dolce	dulce
gentleman (E)	Herr m	—	monsieur m	signore m	señor m
genug (D)	—	enough	assez	abbastanza	bastante
genügen (D)	—	suffice	suffire	bastare	bastar
genuine (E)	echt	—	vrai(e)	vero(a)	verdadero(a)
Genuß (D)	—	pleasure	plaisir m	piacere m	deleite m

Gesellschaft

	D	E	F	I	Es
geöffnet (D)	—	open	ouvert(e)	aperto(a)	abierto(a)
Gepäck (D)	—	luggage	bagages *m pl*	bagaglio *m*	equipaje *m*
Gepäckannahme (D)	—	luggage desk	enregistrement des bagages *m*	accettazione bagagli *f*	recepción de equipajes *f*
gepflegt (D)	—	looked-after	soigné(e)	curato(a)	cuidado(a)
gerade[1] (D)	—	even	pair(e)	pari	par
gerade[2] (D)	—	straight	droit(e)	diritto(a)	derecho(a)
geradeaus (D)	—	straight ahead	tout droit	dritto	todo derecho
gérant (F)	Geschäftsführer *m*	manager	—	gerente *m*	gerente *m*
Gerät (D)	—	appliance	appareil *m*	apparecchio *m*	utensilio *m*
geräumig (D)	—	spacious	spacieux(-euse)	spazioso(a)	espacioso(a)
Geräusch (D)	—	sound	bruit *m*	rumore *m*	ruido *m*
gerecht (D)	—	just	juste	giusto(a)	justo(a)
gerente (Es)	Geschäftsführer *m*	manager	gérant *m*	gerente *m*	—
gerente (I)	Geschäftsführer *m*	manager	gérant *m*	—	gerente *m*
Gericht[1] (D)	—	court	tribunal *m*	tribunale *m*	tribunal *m*
Gericht[2] (D)	—	dish	plat *m*	piatto *m*	comida *f*
gering (D)	—	slight	minime	poco(a)	pequeño(-ana)
German[1] (E)	deutsch	—	allemand	tedesco(a)	alemán(-ana)
German[2] (E)	Deutscher *m*	—	Allemand *m*	tedesco(a)	alemán *m*
Germania (I)	Deutschland *n*	Germany	Allemagne *f*	—	Alemania *f*
German school leaving examinations (E)	Abitur *n*	—	baccalauréat *m*	maturità *f*	bachillerato *m*
Germany (E)	Deutschland *n*	—	Allemagne *f*	Germania *f*	Alemania *f*
gern (D)	—	willingly	avec plaisir	volentieri	con gusto
Geruch (D)	—	smell	odeur *f*	odore *m*	olor *m*
Gerücht (D)	—	rumour	rumeur *f*	voce *f*	rumor *m*
gesamt (D)	—	entire	tout(e)	totale	entero(a)
Gesang (D)	—	singing	chant *m*	canto *m*	canto *m*
Geschäft (D)	—	shop	magasin *m*	negozio *m*	tienda *f*
geschäftlich (D)	—	on business	d'affaires	per affari	comercial
Geschäftsführer (D)	—	manager	gérant *m*	gerente *m*	gerente *m*
geschehen (D)	—	happen	arriver	accadere	ocurrir
Geschenk (D)	—	present	cadeau *m*	regalo *m*	regalo *m*
Geschichte (D)	—	history	histoire *f*	storia *f*	historia *f*
geschickt (D)	—	skilful	habile	abile	mañoso(a)
Geschirr (D)	—	crockery	vaiselle *f*	stoviglie *f pl*	vajilla *f*
Geschlecht (D)	—	sex	sexe *m*	sesso *m*	sexo *m*
geschlossen (D)	—	closed	fermé(e)	chiuso(a)	cerrado(a)
Geschmack (D)	—	taste	goût *m*	gusto *m*	sabor *m*
Geschwindigkeit (D)	—	speed	vitesse *f*	velocità *f*	velocidad *f*
Geschwister (D)	—	brothers and sisters	frère(s) et sœur(s) *pl*	fratelli *m pl*	hermanos *m pl*
geschwollen (D)	—	swollen	enflé(e)	gonfio(a)	hinchado(a)
Gesellschaft (D)	—	society	société *f*	società *f*	sociedad *f*

	D	E	F	I	Es
Gesetz (D)	—	law	loi *f*	legge *f*	ley *f*
gesetzlich (D)	—	legal	légal(e)	legale	legal
gesetzwidrig (D)	—	illegal	illégal(e)	illegale	ilegal
Gesicht (D)	—	face	visage *m*	faccia *f*	cara *f*
gespannt (D)	—	tense	tendu(e)	teso(a)	tenso(a)
Gespräch (D)	—	conversation	conversation *f*	conversazione *f*	conversación *f*
gestatten (D)	—	allow	permettre	permettere	permitir
gestehen (D)	—	confess	avouer	confessare	confesar
gestern (D)	—	yesterday	hier	ieri	ayer
gesund (D)	—	healthy	sain(e)	sano(a)	sano(a)
Gesundheit (D)	—	health	santé *f*	salute *f*	salud *f*
get[1] (E)	beschaffen	—	procurer	procurare	proporcionar
get[2] (E)	bekommen	—	recevoir	ricevere	recibir
get bored (E)	langweilen, sich	—	ennuyer, se	annoiarsi	aburrirse
get drunk (E)	betrinken, sich	—	enivrer, se	ubriacarsi	emborracharse
get engaged (E)	verloben	—	fiancer, se	fidanzarsi	prometerse
get ill (E)	erkranken	—	tomber malade	ammalarsi	enfermar
get in (E)	einsteigen	—	monter	salire	subir a
get lost (E)	verlaufen	—	perdre, se	perdersi	perderse
get off (E)	aussteigen	—	descendre	scendere	bajar
Getränk (D)	—	drink	boisson *f*	bevanda *f*	bebida *f*
Getreide (D)	—	cereals	céréales *f pl*	cereali *m pl*	cereales *m pl*
getrennt (D)	—	separate	séparé(e)	separato(a)	separado(a)
get up (E)	aufstehen	—	lever, se	alzarsi	levantarse
get used to (E)	gewöhnen, sich	—	habituer, se	abituare	acostumbrarse
Gewähr (D)	—	guarantee	garantie *f*	garanzia *f*	garantía *f*
gewähren (D)	—	grant	accorder	concedere	conceder
Gewalt (D)	—	force	force *f*	forza *f*	poder *m*
gewaltig (D)	—	tremendous	énorme	enorme	formidable
Gewässer (D)	—	waters	eaux *f pl*	acque *f pl*	aguas *f pl*
Gewebe (D)	—	fabric	tissu *m*	tessuto *m*	tela *f*
Gewerkschaft (D)	—	trade union	syndicat *m*	sindacato *m*	sindicato *m*
Gewicht (D)	—	weight	poids *m*	peso *m*	peso *m*
Gewinn (D)	—	profit	gain *m*	guadagno *m*	ganancia *f*
gewinnen (D)	—	win	gagner	guadagnare	ganar
gewiß (D)	—	certain	certain(e)	certo(a)	cierto
Gewissen (D)	—	conscience	conscience *f*	coscienza *f*	conciencia *f*
gewissenhaft (D)	—	conscientious	consciencieux (-euse)	coscienzioso(a)	concienzudo(a)
Gewitter (D)	—	thunderstorm	orage *m*	temporale *m*	tormenta *f*
gewöhnen, sich (D)	—	get used to	habituer	abituare	acostumbrarse
Gewohnheit (D)	—	habit	habitude *f*	abitudine *f*	costumbre *f*
gewöhnlich (D)	—	usual	habituel(le)	abituale	habitual
Gewürz (D)	—	spice	épice *f*	spezia *f*	especia *f*

	D	E	F	I	Es
già (I)	bereits, schon	already	déjà	—	ya
giacca (I)	Jacke f	jacket	veste f	—	chaqueta f
giacca di maglia (I)	Strickjacke f	cardigan	veste en tricot f	—	chaqueta de punto f
giacere (I)	liegen	lie	trouver, se	—	estar tumbado(a)
giallo (I)	gelb	yellow	jaune	—	amarillo(a)
giardiniere (I)	Gärtner m	gardener	jardinier m	—	jardinero m
giardino (I)	Garten m	garden	jardin m	—	jardín m
gibier (F)	Wild n	game	—	selvaggina f	caza f
gießen (D)	—	water	arroser	annaffiare	regar
Gift (D)	—	poison	poison m	veleno m	veneno m
gifted (E)	begabt	—	doué(e)	dotato(a)	dotado(a)
giftig (D)	—	poisonous	toxique	velenoso(a)	venenoso(a)
gilet de sauvetage (F)	Schwimmweste f	life jacket	—	giubbotto di salvataggio m	chaleco salvavidas m
ginocchio (I)	Knie n	knee	genou m	—	rodilla f
giocare (I)	spielen	play	jouer	—	jugar
giocatore (I)	Spieler m	player	joueur m	—	jugador m
gioco (I)	Spiel n	game	jeu m	—	juego m
gioia (I)	Freude f	joy	joie f	—	alegría f
gioielli (I)	Schmuck m	jewellery	bijoux m pl	—	joyas f pl
gioielliere (I)	Juwelier m	jeweller	bijoutier m	—	joyero m
gioiello (I)	Juwel n	jewel	joyau m	—	joya f
giornale (I)	Zeitung f	newspaper	journal m	—	periódico m
giornale radio (I)	Nachrichten pl	news	informations f pl	—	noticiario m
giornalista (I)	Journalist m	journalist	journaliste m	—	periodista m
giorno (I)	Tag m	day	jour m	—	día m
giorno di riposo (I)	Ruhetag m	closing day	jour de repos m	—	día de descanso m
giorno feriale (I)	Werktag m	working day	jour ouvrable m	—	día laborable m
giorno festivo (I)	Feiertag m	holiday	jour férié m	—	día de fiesta m
giostra (I)	Karussell n	roundabout	manège m	—	tíovivo m
giovane (I)	jung	young	jeune	—	joven
giovedì (I)	Donnerstag m	Thursday	jeudi m	—	jueves m
gioventù (I)	Jugend f	youth	jeunesse f	—	juventud f
Gipfel (D)	—	peak	sommet m	cima f	cumbre f
gira (Es)	Rundfahrt f	round trip	circuit m	giro m	—
giradischi (I)	Plattenspieler m	record player	tourne-disque m	—	tocadiscos m
girar (Es)	drehen	turn	tourner	girare	—
girare[1] (I)	drehen	turn	tourner	—	girar
girare[2] (I)	herumdrehen	turn around	tourner	—	dar vuelta
girare[3] (I)	umdrehen	turn around	tourner	—	volver
girellare (I)	bummeln	stroll	flâner	—	callejear
girl (E)	Mädchen n	—	jeune fille f	ragazza f	chica f
giro[1] (I)	Rundfahrt f	round trip	circuit m	—	circuito m
giro[2] (I)	Tour f	tour	excursion f	—	excursión f

	D	E	F	I	Es
gita (I)	Ausflug *m*	outing	excursion *f*	—	excursión *f*
Gitarre (D)	—	guitar	guitare *f*	chitarra *f*	guitarra *f*
giù[1] (I)	herab/hinab	down	vers le bas	—	hacia abajo
giù[2] (I)	herunter	down	en bas	—	abajo
giubbotto di salvataggio (I)	Schwimmweste *f*	life jacket	gilet de sauvetage *m*	—	chaleco salvavidas *m*
giubilare (I)	jubeln	rejoice	pousser des cris de joie	—	dar gritos de alegría
giudicare[1] (I)	beurteilen	judge	juger	—	juzgar
giudicare[2] (I)	urteilen	judge	juger	—	juzgar
giudice (I)	Richter *m*	judge	juge *m*	—	juez *m*
giudizio (I)	Urteil *n*	judgement	jugement *m*	—	juicio *m*
giugno (I)	Juni *m*	June	juin *m*	—	junio *m*
giurare (I)	schwören	swear	jurer	—	jurar
giurisprudenza (I)	Jura	law	droit *m*	—	derecho *m*
giusto[1] (I)	gerecht	just	juste	—	justo(a)
giusto[2] (I)	richtig	correct	juste	—	correcto(a)
give[1] (E)	geben	—	donner	dare	dar
give[2] (E)	schenken	—	offrir	regalare	regalar
give back (E)	zurückgeben	—	rendre	restituire	devolver
give birth to (E)	gebären	—	mettre au monde	partorire	parir
give in one's notice (E)	kündigen	—	résilier	licenziare	despedir
give up (E)	aufgeben	—	abandonner	rinunciare	renunciar
glace (F)	Eis *n*	ice	—	gelato *m*	hielo *m*
glad (E)	froh	—	content(e)	lieto(a)	contento(a)
glänzen (D)	—	shine	briller	splendere	brillar
Glas (D)	—	glass	verre *m*	bicchiere *m*	vaso *m*
glass (E)	Glas *n*	—	verre *m*	bicchiere *m*	vaso *m*
glasses (E)	Brille *f*	—	lunettes *f pl*	occhiali *m pl*	gafas *f pl*
glatt (D)	—	smooth	lisse	liscio(a)	liso(a)
glauben (D)	—	believe	croire	credere	creer
gleich (D)	—	same	égal(e)	identico(a)	idéntico(a)
gleichzeitig (D)	—	simultaneous	en même temps	contemporaneo (a)	a la vez
Gleis (D)	—	track	voie *f*	binario *m*	vía *f*
glisser (F)	rutschen	slide	—	scivolare	resbalar
Glocke (D)	—	bell	cloche *f*	campana *f*	campana *f*
glove (E)	Handschuh *m*	—	gant *m*	guanto *m*	guante *m*
Glück (D)	—	luck	chance *f*	fortuna *f*	suerte *f*
glücklich (D)	—	happy	heureux(-euse)	felice	feliz
Glückwunsch (D)	—	congratulations	félicitations *f pl*	auguri *m pl*	felicitaciones *f pl*
glue (E)	Klebstoff *m*	—	colle *f*	colla *f*	adhesivo *m*
Glühbirne (D)	—	light bulb	ampoule *f*	lampadina *f*	lámpara *f*
go (E)	gehen	—	aller	andare	andar
go ahead (E)	vorangehen	—	marcher devant	andare avanti	pasar adelante

	D	E	F	I	Es
goal (E)	Ziel *n*	—	but *m*	meta *f*	intención *f*
go along with (E)	mitgehen	—	accompagner	accompagnare	acompañar
goat (E)	Ziege *f*	—	chèvre *f*	capra *f*	cabra *f*
go away[1] (E)	verreisen	—	partir en voyage	partire in viaggio	irse de viaje
go away[2] (E)	weggehen	—	s'en aller	andare via	marcharse
gobierno (Es)	Regierung *f*	government	gouvernement *m*	governo *m*	—
goccia (I)	Tropfen *m*	drop	goutte *f*	—	gota *f*
gocciolare (I)	tropfen	drip	dégoutter	—	gotear
God (E)	Gott *m*	—	Dieu *m*	Dio *m*	Dios *m*
godere (I)	genießen	enjoy	jouir	—	disfrutar
godfather (E)	Pate *m*	—	parrain *m*	padrino *m*	padrino *m*
godmother (E)	Patin *f*	—	marraine *f*	madrina *f*	madrina *f*
go for a walk (E)	spazierengehen	—	promener, se	passeggiare	ir de paseo
Gold (D)	—	gold	or *m*	oro *m*	oro *m*
gold (E)	Gold *n*	—	or *m*	oro *m*	oro *m*
golden (D)	—	golden	d'or	d'oro	de oro
golden (E)	golden	—	d'or	d'oro	de oro
golpe (Es)	Schlag *m*	blow	coup *m*	colpo *m*	—
golpear[1] (Es)	klopfen	knock	frapper	bussare	—
golpear[2] (Es)	pochen	knock	frapper	battere	—
golpear[3] (Es)	schlagen	hit	battre	battere	—
goma (Es)	Gummi *m*	rubber	gomme *f*	gomma *f*	—
gomma (I)	Gummi *m*	rubber	gomme *f*	—	goma *f*
gomme (F)	Gummi *m*	rubber	—	gomma *f*	goma *f*
gonfio (I)	geschwollen	swollen	enflé(e)	—	hinchado(a)
gonna (I)	Rock *m*	skirt	jupe *f*	—	falda *f*
good[1] (E)	brav	—	gentil(-le)	bravo(a)	bueno(a)
good[2] (E)	gut	—	bon(ne)/bien	buono(a)/bene	bueno(a)/bien
good-bye![1] (E)	wiederhören!	—	au revoir!	a risentirci!	¡adiós!
good-bye![2] (E)	wiedersehen!	—	au revoir!	arrivederci!	¡adiós!
goods[1] (E)	Güter *pl*	—	marchandises *f pl*	beni *m pl*	bienes *f pl*
goods[2] (E)	Ware *f*	—	marchandise *f*	merce *f*	mercancía *f*
go on (E)	weitergehen	—	aller plus loin	proseguire	proseguir
goose (E)	Gans *f*	—	oie *f*	oca *f*	ganso *m*
go out[1] (E)	ausgehen	—	sortir	uscire	salir
go out[2] (E)	hinausgehen	—	sortir	uscire	salir afuera
gorge (F)	Rachen *m*	throat	—	faringe *m*	garganta *f*
gorra (Es)	Mütze *f*	cap	casquette *f*	berretto *m*	—
go shopping (E)	einkaufen gehen	—	faire les courses	fare la spesa	ir de compras
gota (Es)	Tropfen *m*	drop	goutte *f*	goccia *f*	—
gotear (Es)	tropfen	drip	dégoutter	gocciolare	—
go through (E)	durchgehen	—	passer à travers	passare	pasar
Gott (D)	—	God	Dieu *m*	Dio *m*	Dios *m*
Gottesdienst (D)	—	service	office divin *m*	messa *f*	servicio religioso *m*

	D	E	F	I	Es
go up (E)	steigen	—	monter	salire	subir
goût (F)	Geschmack m	taste	—	gusto m	sabor m
goutte (F)	Tropfen m	drop	—	goccia f	gota f
gouvernement (F)	Regierung f	government	—	governo m	gobierno m
government (E)	Regierung f	—	gouvernement m	governo m	gobierno m
governo (I)	Regierung f	government	gouvernement m	—	gobierno m
Grab (D)	—	grave	tombe f	tomba f	tumba f
graben (D)	—	dig	creuser	scavare	cavar
gracias (Es)	danke	thank you	merci	grazie	—
gracioso (Es)	niedlich	sweet	mignon(ne)	carino(a)	—
Grad[1] (D)	—	degree	degré m	grado m	grado m
Grad[2] (D)	—	rank	grade m	rango m	título m
grade (F)	Grad m	rank	—	rango m	título m
gradevole (I)	angenehm	pleasant	agréable	—	agradable
gradino (I)	Stufe f	step	marche f	—	escalón m
grado (Es)	Grad m	degree	degré m	grado m	—
grado (I)	Grad m	degree	degré m	—	grado m
gradual (E)	allmählich	—	graduel(le)	graduale	gradual
gradual (Es)	allmählich	gradual	graduel(le)	graduale	—
graduale (I)	allmählich	gradual	graduel(le)	—	gradual
graduel (F)	allmählich	gradual	—	graduale	gradual
grain (F)	Korn n	corn	—	grano m	semilla f
graisse (F)	Fett n	fat	—	grasso m	grasa f
gram (E)	Gramm n	—	gramme m	grammo m	gramo m
Gramm (D)	—	gram	gramme m	grammo m	gramo m
grammar school (E)	Gymnasium n	—	lycée m	liceo m	instituto de enseñanza media m
gramme (F)	Gramm n	gram	—	grammo m	gramo m
grammo (I)	Gramm n	gram	gramme m	—	gramo m
gramo (Es)	Gramm n	gram	gramme m	grammo m	—
grand (F)	groß	big/large	—	grande	grande
grandchild (E)	Enkelkind n	—	petit-enfant m	nipote m	nieto m
granddaughter (E)	Enkelin f	—	petite-fille f	nipote f	nieta f
grande (Es)	groß	big/large	grand(e)	grande	—
grande (I)	groß	big/large	grand(e)	—	grande
grande città (I)	Großstadt f	large town	grande ville f	—	gran ciudad f
grande magazzino (I)	Kaufhaus n	department store	grand magasin m	—	grandes almacenes m pl
grandes almacenes (Es)	Kaufhaus n	department store	grand magasin m	grande magazzino m	—
grandeur (F)	Größe f	greatness	—	grandezza f	grandeza f
grande ville (F)	Großstadt f	large town	—	grande città f	gran ciudad f
grandeza (Es)	Größe f	greatness	grandeur f	grandezza f	—
grandezza (I)	Größe f	greatness	grandeur f	—	grandeza f
grandfather (E)	Großvater m	—	grand-père m	nonno m	abuelo m

gratulieren

	D	E	F	I	Es
grandinare (I)	hageln	hail	grêler	—	granizar
grandine (I)	Hagel *m*	hail	grêle *f*	—	granizo *m*
grandioso (I)	großartig	magnificent	formidable	—	magnífico(a)
grandir[1] (F)	aufwachsen	grow up	—	crescere	criarse
grandir[2] (F)	größer werden	grow	—	crescere	crecer
grandir[3] (F)	wachsen	grow	—	crescere	crecer
grand magasin (F)	Kaufhaus *n*	department store	—	grande magazzino *m*	grandes almacenes *m pl*
grand-mère (F)	Großmutter *f*	grandmother	—	nonna *f*	abuela *f*
grandmother (E)	Großmutter *f*	—	grand-mère *f*	nonna *f*	abuela *f*
grandparents (E)	Großeltern *pl*	—	grands-parents *m pl*	nonni *m pl*	abuelos *m pl*
grand-père (F)	Großvater *m*	grandfather	—	nonno *m*	abuelo *m*
grand propriétaire (F)	Großgrund-besitzer *m*	landowner	—	latifondista *m*	latifundista *m*
grand-rue (F)	Hauptstraße *f*	main street	—	strada principale *f*	calle central *f*
grandson (E)	Enkel *m*	—	petit-fils *m*	nipote *m*	nieto *m*
grands-parents (F)	Großeltern *pl*	grandparents	—	nonni *m pl*	abuelos *m pl*
granizar (Es)	hageln	hail	grêler	grandinare	—
granizo (Es)	Hagel *m*	hail	grêle *f*	grandine *f*	—
granja (Es)	Bauernhof *m*	farmhouse	ferme *f*	fattoria *f*	—
grano (I)	Korn *n*	corn	grain *m*	—	semilla *f*
grant (E)	gewähren	—	accorder	concedere	conceder
grape (E)	Traube *f*	—	grappe *f*	uva *f*	uva *f*
grapefruit (E)	Pampelmuse *f*	—	pamplemousse *m*	pompelmo *m*	pomelo *m*
grappe (F)	Traube *f*	grape	—	uva *f*	uva *f*
Gras (D)	—	grass	herbe *f*	erba *f*	hierba *f*
gras (F)	fett	fat	—	grasso(a)	graso(a)
grasa (Es)	Fett *n*	fat	graisse *f*	grasso *m*	—
graso (Es)	fett	fat	gras(se)	grasso(a)	—
grasp (E)	fassen	—	saisir	prendere	coger
grass (E)	Gras *n*	—	herbe *f*	erba *f*	hierba *f*
grasso[1] (I)	dick	fat	gros(se)	—	grueso(a)
grasso[2] (I)	fett	fat	gras(se)	—	graso(a)
grasso[3] (I)	Fett *n*	fat	graisse *f*	—	grasa *f*
grateful (E)	dankbar	—	reconnaissant(e)	grato(a)	agradecido(a)
gratis (D)	—	free of charge	gratuit(e)	gratuito(a)	gratis
gratis[1] (Es)	gratis	free of charge	gratuit(e)	gratuito(a)	—
gratis[2] (Es)	kostenlos	free	gratuit(e)	gratuito(a)	—
grato (I)	dankbar	grateful	reconnaissant(e)	—	agradecido(a)
gratuit[1] (F)	gratis	free of charge	—	gratuito(a)	gratis
gratuit[2] (F)	kostenlos	free	—	gratuito(a)	gratis
gratuito[1] (I)	gratis	free of charge	gratuit(e)	—	gratis
gratuito[2] (I)	kostenlos	free	gratuit(e)	—	gratis
gratulieren (D)	—	congratulate	féliciter	congratularsi	felicitar

	D	E	F	I	Es
grau (D)	—	grey	gris(e)	grigio(a)	gris
grausam (D)	—	cruel	cruel(le)	crudele	cruel
grave (E)	Grab *n*	—	tombe *f*	tomba *f*	tumba *f*
grazie (I)	danke	thank you	merci	—	¡gracias!
great-grandparents (E)	Urgroßeltern *pl*	—	arrière-grands-parents *m pl*	bisnonni *m pl*	bisabuelos *m pl*
greatness (E)	Größe *f*	—	grandeur *f*	grandezza *f*	grandeza *f*
Grèce (F)	Griechenland *n*	Greece	—	Grecia *f*	Grecia *f*
Grecia (Es)	Griechenland *n*	Greece	Grèce *f*	Grecia *f*	—
Grecia (I)	Griechenland *n*	Greece	Grèce *f*	—	Grecia *f*
Greece (E)	Griechenland *n*	—	Grèce *f*	Grecia *f*	Grecia *f*
green (E)	grün	—	vert(e)	verde	verde
greet[1] (E)	begrüßen	—	saluer	salutare	saludar
greet[2] (E)	grüßen	—	saluer	salutare	saludar
greeting (E)	Gruß *m*	—	salut *m*	saluto *m*	saludo *m*
greifen (D)	—	seize	saisir	afferrare	coger
grêle (F)	Hagel *m*	hail	—	grandine *f*	granizo *m*
grêler (F)	hageln	hail	—	grandinare	granizar
grenouille (F)	Frosch *m*	frog	—	rana *f*	rana *f*
Grenze (D)	—	frontier	frontière *f*	frontiera *f*	frontera *f*
grève (F)	Streik *m*	strike	—	sciopero *m*	huelga *f*
grey (E)	grau	—	gris(e)	grigio(a)	gris
gridare (I)	schreien	scream	crier	—	gritar
grido (I)	Schrei *m*	scream	cri *m*	—	grito *m*
Griechenland (D)	—	Greece	Grèce *f*	Grecia *f*	Grecia *f*
grief (E)	Kummer *m*	—	chagrin *m*	dolore *m*	pesar *m*
Griff (D)	—	handle	poignée *f*	maniglia *f*	asidero *m*
grigio (I)	grau	grey	gris	—	gris
griller (F)	rösten	roast	—	abbrustolire	tostar
grimper (F)	klettern	climb	—	arrampicarsi	escalar
gripe (Es)	Grippe *f*	flu	grippe *f*	influenza *f*	—
Grippe (D)	—	flu	grippe *f*	influenza *f*	gripe *f*
grippe (F)	Grippe *f*	flu	—	influenza *f*	gripe *f*
gris (Es)	grau	grey	gris(e)	grigio(a)	—
gris (F)	grau	grey	—	grigio(a)	gris
gritar (Es)	schreien	scream	crier	gridare	—
grito (Es)	Schrei *m*	scream	cri *m*	grido *m*	—
grob (D)	—	coarse	grossier(-ière)	rozzo(a)	tosco(a)
grocer's (E)	Lebensmittel-geschäft *n*	—	magasin d'alimentation *m*	negozio di alimentari *m*	tienda de comestibles *f*
gronder (F)	schimpfen	scold	—	imprecare	insultar
gros (F)	dick	fat	—	grasso(a)	grueso(a)
groseille (F)	Johannisbeere *f*	currant	—	ribes *m*	grosella *f*
grosella (Es)	Johannisbeere *f*	currant	groseille *f*	ribes *m*	—
groß (D)	—	big/large	grand(e)	grande	grande

	D	E	F	I	Es
großartig (D)	—	magnificent	formidable	grandioso(a)	magnifico(a)
Größe[1] (D)	—	`	greatness	grandeur *f*	grandezza *f*	grandeza *f*
Größe[2] (D)	—	size	taille *f*	taglia *f*	talla *f*
Großeltern (D)	—	grandparents	grands-parents *m pl*	nonni *m pl*	abuelos *m pl*
größer werden (D)	—	grow	grandir	crescere	crecer
Großgrund-besitzer (D)	—	landowner	grand propriétaire *m*	latifondista *m*	latifundista *m*
grossier (F)	grob	coarse	—	rozzo(a)	tosco(a)
Großmutter (D)	—	grandmother	grand-mère *f*	nonna *f*	abuela *f*
Großstadt (D)	—	large town	grande ville *f*	grande città *f*	gran ciudad *f*
Großvater (D)	—	grandfather	grand-père *m*	nonno *m*	abuelo *m*
großzügig (D)	—	generous	généreux(-euse)	generoso(a)	generoso(a)
grotte (F)	Höhle *f*	cave	—	caverna *f*	cueva *f*
ground floor[1] (E)	Erdgeschoß *n*	—	rez-de-chaussée *m*	pianterreno *m*	planta baja *f*
ground floor[2] (E)	Parterre *n*	—	rez-de chaussée *m*	pianterreno *m*	planta baja *f*
group (E)	Gruppe *f*	—	groupe *m*	gruppo *m*	grupo *m*
groupe (F)	Gruppe *f*	group	—	gruppo *m*	grupo *m*
grow[1] (E)	größer werden	—	grandir	crescere	crecer
grow[2] (E)	wachsen	—	grandir	crescere	crecer
grown up (E)	erwachsen	—	adulte	adulto(a)	adulto(a)
grow up (E)	aufwachsen	—	grandir	crescere	criarse
grueso (Es)	dick	fat	gros(se)	grasso(a)	—
grün (D)	—	green	vert(e)	verde	verde
Grund (D)	—	reason	raison *f*	causa *f*	causa *f*
gründen (D)	—	found	fonder	fondare	fundar
Grundfläche (D)	—	base	base *f*	base *f*	base *f*
gründlich (D)	—	thorough	à fond	a fondo	a fondo
grundsätzlich (D)	—	fundamental	par principe	basilare	en principio
grupo[1] (Es)	Gruppe *f*	group	groupe *m*	gruppo *m*	—
grupo[2] (Es)	Schar *f*	band	bande *f*	schiera *f*	—
Gruppe (D)	—	group	groupe *m*	gruppo *m*	grupo *m*
gruppo (I)	Gruppe *f*	group	groupe *m*	—	grupo *m*
Gruß (D)	—	greeting	salut *m*	saluto *m*	saludo *m*
grüßen (D)	—	greet	saluer	salutare	saludar
guadagnare (I)	verdienen	earn	gagner	—	ganar
guadagno[1] (I)	Gewinn *m*	profit	gain *m*	—	ganancia *f*
guadagno[2] (I)	Verdienst *m*	income	revenus *m pl*	—	ganancia *f*
guancia (I)	Wange *f*	cheek	joue *f*	—	mejilla *f*
guanciale (I)	Kopfkissen *n*	pillow	oreiller *m*	—	almohada *f*
guante (Es)	Handschuh *m*	glove	gant *m*	guanto *m*	—
guanto (I)	Handschuh *m*	glove	gant *m*	—	guante *m*
guarantee[1] (E)	Gewähr *f*	—	garantie *f*	garanzia *f*	garantía *f*
guarantee[2] (E)	Garantie *f*	—	garantie *f*	garanzia *f*	garantía *f*
guard[1] (E)	Aufseher *m*	—	gardien *m*	custode *m*	vigilante *m*

	D	E	F	I	Es
guard² (E)	bewachen	—	garder	sorvegliare	vigilar
guarda (Es)	Wärter *m*	attendant	gardien *m*	custode *m*	—
guardar (Es)	aufbewahren	keep	garder	conservare	—
guardare¹ (I)	anschauen	look at	regarder	—	mirar
guardare² (I)	ansehen	look at	regarder	—	mirar
guardare³ (I)	blicken	look	regarder	—	mirar
guardare⁴ (I)	schauen	look	regarder	—	mirar
guardare la TV (I)	fernsehen	watch television	regarder la télévision	—	ver la televisión
guardaroba (I)	Garderobe *f*	wardrobe	vestiaire *m*	—	guardaropa *m*
guardaropa (Es)	Garderobe *f*	wardrobe	vestiaire *m*	guardaroba *m*	—
guardia notturna (I)	Nachtwächter *m*	night-watchman	veilleur de nuit *m*	—	sereno *m*
guarnecer (Es)	garnieren	decorate	garnir	guarnire	—
guarnire (I)	garnieren	decorate	garnir	—	guarnecer
guasto (I)	defekt	defect	défectueux (-euse)	—	defecto(a)
guêpe (F)	Wespe *f*	wasp	—	vespa *f*	avispa *f*
guérir (F)	heilen	heal	—	curare	curar
guerra (Es)	Krieg *m*	war	guerre *f*	guerra *f*	—
guerra (I)	Krieg *m*	war	guerre *f*	—	guerra *f*
guerre (F)	Krieg *m*	war	—	guerra *f*	guerra *f*
guess (E)	raten	—	deviner	indovinare	adivinar
guest (E)	Gast *m*	—	hôte *m/f*	ospite *m*	invitado *m*
gueule (F)	Maul *n*	mouth	—	muso *m*	hocico *m*
guía¹ (Es)	Führer *m*	leader	guide *m*	guida *f*	—
guía² (Es)	Reiseführer *m*	guide	guide *m*	guida *f*	—
guía telefónica (Es)	Telefonbuch *n*	phone book	annuaire du téléphone *m*	elenco telefonico *m*	—
guichet (F)	Schalter *m*	counter	—	sportello *m*	ventanilla *f*
guida¹ (I)	Führer *m*	leader	guide *m*	—	guía *m*
guida² (I)	Reiseführer *m*	guide	guide *m*	—	guía *m*
guidare¹ (I)	führen	lead	guider	—	dirigir
guidare² (I)	lenken	steer	conduire	—	encauzar
guide (E)	Reiseführer *m*	—	guide *m*	guida *f*	guía *m*
guide¹ (F)	Führer *m*	leader	—	guida *f*	guía *m*
guide² (F)	Reiseführer *m*	guide	—	guida *f*	guía *m*
guided tour (E)	Führung *f*	—	visite guidée *f*	visita guidata *f*	visita guiada *f*
guider (F)	führen	lead	—	guidare	dirigir
guilty (E)	schuldig	—	coupable	colpevole	culpable
guisante (Es)	Erbse *f*	pea	pois *m*	pisello *m*	—
guitar (E)	Gitarre *f*	—	guitare *f*	chitarra *f*	guitarra *f*
guitare (F)	Gitarre *f*	guitar	—	chitarra *f*	guitarra *f*
guitarra (Es)	Gitarre *f*	guitar	guitare *f*	chitarra *f*	—
gültig (D)	—	valid	valable	valido(a)	válido(a)
Gültigkeit (D)	—	validity	validité *f*	validità *f*	validez *f*
Gummi (D)	—	rubber	gomme *f*	gomma *f*	goma *f*

	D	E	F	I	Es
günstig (D)	—	favourable	favorable	favorevole	favorable
Gurke (D)	—	cucumber	concombre *m*	cetriolo *m*	pepino *m*
Gurt (D)	—	belt	ceinture *f*	cinghia *f*	cinturón *m*
Gürtel (D)	—	belt	ceinture *f*	cintura *f*	cinturón *m*
gustar[1] (Es)	gefallen	please	plaire	piacere	—
gustar[2] (Es)	schmecken	taste	sentir	piacere	—
gusto (I)	Geschmack *m*	taste	goût *m*	—	sabor *m*
gut (D)	—	good/well	bon(ne)/bien	buono(a)/bene	bueno(a)/bien
Güter (D)	—	goods	marchandises *f pl*	beni *m pl*	bienes *f pl*
Gutschein (D)	—	voucher	bon *m*	buono *m*	vale *m*
Gymnasium (D)	—	grammar school	lycée *m*	liceo *m*	instituto de enseñanza media *m*
Haar (D)	—	hair	cheveu *m*	capello *m*	pelo *m*
haben (D)	—	have	avoir	avere	tener
hábil (Es)	fähig	capable	capable	capace	—
habile (F)	geschickt	skilful	—	abile	mañoso(a)
habiller (F)	kleiden	dress	—	vestire	vestir
habit (E)	Gewohnheit *f*	—	habitude *f*	abitudine *f*	costumbre *f*
habitación[1] (Es)	Raum *m*	room	pièce *f*	stanza *f*	—
habitación[2] (Es)	Zimmer *n*	room	chambre *f*	camera *f*	—
habitant[1] (F)	Bewohner *m*	inhabitant	—	abitante *m*	habitante *m(f)*
habitant[2] (F)	Einwohner *m*	inhabitant	—	abitante *m*	habitante *m*
habitante[1] (Es)	Bewohner *m*	inhabitant	habitant *m*	abitante *m*	—
habitante[2] (Es)	Einwohner *m*	inhabitant	habitant *m*	abitante *m*	—
habiter (F)	wohnen	live	—	abitare	vivir
habits (F)	Kleidung *f*	clothing	—	abbigliamento *m*	vestuario *m*
habitual (Es)	gewöhnlich	usual	habituel(le)	abituale	—
habitude (F)	Gewohnheit *f*	habit	—	abitudine *f*	costumbre *f*
habitué (F)	Stammgast *m*	regular	—	cliente abituale *m*	cliente habitual *m*
habituel[1] (F)	gewöhnlich	usual	—	abituale	habitual
habituel[2] (F)	üblich	usual	—	solito(a)	usual
habituer, se (F)	gewöhnen, sich	get used to	—	abituare	acostumbrarse
hablar[1] (Es)	reden	talk	parler	parlare	—
hablar[2] (Es)	sprechen	speak	parler	parlare	—
hace mucho (Es)	längst	a long time ago	depuis bien longtemps	da molto	—
hacer[1] (Es)	machen	make/do	faire	fare	—
hacer[2] (Es)	tun	do	faire	fare	—
hacer excursiones (Es)	wandern	hike	marcher	fare escursioni a piedi	—
hacer gimnasia (Es)	turnen	do gymnastic exercises	faire de la gymnastique	fare ginnastica	—
hacer huelga (Es)	streiken	be on strike	faire grève	scioperare	—
hacer la maleta (Es)	packen	pack	faire les malles	fare le valigie	—
hacer magia (Es)	zaubern	practise magic	faire de la magie	esercitare la magia	—

	D	E	F	I	Es
hacer propaganda (Es)	werben	advertise	faire de la publicité	fare propaganda	—
hacer punto (Es)	stricken	knit	tricoter	lavorare a maglia	—
hacer reservar (Es)	vorbestellen	book	réserver	prenotare	—
hacer una foto (Es)	knipsen	take a snap	photographier	scattare	—
hacer una lista (Es)	verzeichnen	list	enregistrer	registrare	—
hacia abajo[1] (Es)	abwärts	downwards	en bas	in giù	—
hacia abajo[2] (Es)	herab/hinab	down	vers le bas	giù	—
hacia afuera[1] (Es)	heraus	out	dehors	fuori	—
hacia afuera[2] (Es)	hinaus	out	dehors	fuori	—
hacia allá (Es)	hin	there	jusqu'à/vers	là	—
hacia arriba[1] (Es)	aufwärts	upwards	vers le haut	in su	—
hacia arriba[2] (Es)	hinauf	up	montez	su	—
hacia arriba[3] (Es)	herauf	up	vers le haut	su	—
hacia el otro lado (Es)	hinüber	across	de l'autre côté	di là	—
Hackfleisch (D)	—	minced meat	viande hachée f	carne tritata f	carne picada f
Hafen (D)	—	port	port m	porto m	puerto m
Hagel (D)	—	hail	grêle f	grandine f	granizo m
hageln (D)	—	hail	grêler	grandinare	granizar
Hahn (D)	—	cock	coq m	gallo m	gallo m
Hai (D)	—	shark	requin m	pescecane m	tiburón m
hail[1] (E)	hageln	—	grêler	grandinare	granizar
hail[2] (E)	Hagel m	—	grêle f	grandine f	granizo m
haine (F)	Haß m	hate	—	odio m	odio m
hair (E)	Haar n	—	cheveu m	capello m	pelo m
hairdresser (E)	Friseur m	—	coiffeur m	parrucchiere m	peluquero m
hairstyle (E)	Frisur f	—	coiffure f	pettinatura f	peinado m
Haken (D)	—	hook	crochet m	gancio m	gancho m
halb (D)	—	half	demi(e)	mezzo(a)	medio(a)
halbieren (D)	—	halve	partager en deux	dimezzare	dividir por la mitad
Halbinsel (D)	—	peninsula	presqu'île f	penisola f	península f
Halbpension (D)	—	half board	demi-pension f	mezza pensione f	media pensión f
half[1] (E)	halb	—	demi(e)	mezzo(a)	medio(a)
half[2] (E)	Hälfte f	—	moitié f	metà f	mitad f
half board (E)	Halbpension f	—	demi-pension f	mezza pensione f	media pensión f
halfcaste (E)	Mischling m	—	métis m	sangue misto m	mestizo m
Hälfte (D)	—	half	moitié f	metà f	mitad f
hall[1] (E)	Diele f	—	vestibule m	corridoio m	tabla f
hall[2] (E)	Flur m	—	entrée f	corridoio m	corredor m
hall[3] (E)	Saal m	—	salle f	sala f	sala f
Hallenbad (D)	—	indoor swimming pool	piscine f	piscina coperta f	piscina cubierta f
hallo! (D)	—	hello!	allô!	pronto!	¡diga!
Hals (D)	—	neck	cou m	collo m	cuello m

	D	E	F	I	Es
Halsschmerzen (D)	—	sore throat	mal de gorge *m*	mal di gola *m*	dolor de garganta *m*
Halstuch (D)	—	scarf	écharpe *f*	sciarpa *f*	pañuelo para el cuello *m*
halt! (D)	—	stop!	stop!	alt!	¡alto!
haltbar (D)	—	durable	résistant(e)	durevole	duradero
halten (D)	—	hold	tenir	tenere	sujetar
Haltestelle (D)	—	stop	arrêt *m*	fermata *f*	parada *f*
halve (E)	halbieren	—	partager en deux	dimezzare	dividir por la mitad
ham (E)	Schinken *m*	—	jambon *m*	prosciutto *m*	jamón *m*
hambre (Es)	Hunger *m*	hunger	faim *f*	fame *f*	—
hambriento (Es)	hungrig	hungry	affamé(e)	affamato(a)	—
Hammer (D)	—	hammer	marteau *m*	martello *m*	martillo *m*
hammer (E)	Hammer *m*	—	marteau *m*	martello *m*	martillo *m*
hanche (F)	Hüfte *f*	hip	—	fianco *m*	cadera *f*
Hand (D)	—	hand	main *f*	mano *f*	mano *f*
hand (E)	Hand *f*	—	main *f*	mano *f*	mano *f*
handbag (E)	Handtasche *f*	—	sac à main *m*	borsetta *f*	bolso *m*
handeln (D)	—	act	agir	agire	obrar
Handgepäck (D)	—	hand-luggage	bagage à main	bagaglio a mano *m*	equipaje de mano *m*
handkerchief (E)	Taschentuch *n*	—	mouchoir *m*	fazzoletto *m*	pañuelo *m*
handle (E)	Griff *m*	—	poignée *f*	maniglia *f*	asidero *m*
Händler (D)	—	dealer	commerçant *m*	commerciante *m*	comerciante *m*
hand-luggage (E)	Handgepäck *n*	—	bagage à main *m*	bagaglio a mano *m*	equipaje de mano *m*
hand over[1] (E)	übergeben	—	remettre	consegnare	transmitir
hand over[2] (E)	überreichen	—	présenter	consegnare	entregar
Handschuh (D)	—	glove	gant *m*	guanto *m*	guante *m*
Handtasche (D)	—	handbag	sac à main *m*	borsetta *f*	bolso *m*
Handtuch (D)	—	towel	serviette *f*	asciugamano *m*	pañuelo *m*
Handwerk (D)	—	craft	métier *m*	artigianato *m*	artesanía *f*
Handwerker (D)	—	craftsman	artisan *m*	artigiano *m*	artesano *m*
Hang (D)	—	slope	versant *m*	pendio *m*	pendiente *m*
hang (E)	hängen	—	pendre	pendere	colgar
hängen (D)	—	hang	pendre	pendere	colgar
hang up (E)	aufhängen	—	accrocher	appendere	colgar
happen[1] (E)	geschehen	—	arriver	accadere	ocurrir
happen[2] (E)	passieren	—	arriver	succedere	pasar
happy (E)	glücklich	—	heureux(-euse)	felice	feliz
hard (E)	hart	—	dur(e)	duro(a)	duro(a)
hardly (E)	kaum	—	à peine	appena	apenas
hare (E)	Hase *m*	—	lièvre *m*	lepre *f*	liebre *m*
haricot (F)	Bohne *f*	bean	—	fagiolo *m*	judía *f*
harina (Es)	Mehl *n*	flour	farine *f*	farina *f*	—
harmful (E)	schädlich	—	nuisible	nocivo(a)	nocivo(a)

	D	E	F	I	Es
harmless (E)	harmlos	—	inoffensif(-ive)	inoffensivo(a)	inofensivo(a)
harmlos (D)	—	harmless	inoffensif(-ive)	inoffensivo(a)	inofensivo(a)
Harn (D)	—	urine	urine *f*	urina *f*	orina *f*
hart (D)	—	hard	dur(e)	duro(a)	duro(a)
harvest (E)	Ernte *f*	—	moisson *f*	raccolto *m*	cosecha *f*
hasard (F)	Zufall *m*	chance	—	caso *m*	casualidad *f*
Hase (D)	—	hare	lièvre *m*	lepre *f*	liebre *m*
Haß (D)	—	hate	haine *f*	odio *m*	odio *m*
hassen (D)	—	hate	détester	odiare	odiar
häßlich (D)	—	ugly	laid(e)	brutto(a)	feo(a)
hasta (Es)	bis	until	jusqu'à	fino a	—
hasta ahora (Es)	bisher	so far	jusqu'à présent	finora	—
¡hasta luego! (Es)	tschüs	bye	salut	ciao	—
hasta tanto (Es)	soweit	as far as	autant que	fin dove	—
haste (E)	Eile *f*	—	hâte *f*	fretta *f*	prisa *f*
hat (E)	Hut *m*	—	chapeau *m*	cappello *m*	sombrero *m*
hate¹ (E)	hassen	—	détester	odiare	odiar
hate² (E)	Haß *m*	—	haine *f*	odio *m*	odio *m*
hâte (F)	Eile *f*	haste	—	fretta *f*	prisa *f*
Haufen (D)	—	heap	tas *m*	mucchio *m*	montón *m*
häufig (D)	—	frequent	fréquent(e)	frequente	frecuente
Hauptbahnhof (D)	—	central station	gare centrale *f*	stazione centrale *f*	estación central *f*
hauptsächlich (D)	—	mainly	surtout	principalmente	principalmente
Hauptstadt (D)	—	capital	capitale *f*	capitale *f*	capital *f*
Hauptstraße (D)	—	main street	grand-rue *f*	strada principale *f*	calle central *f*
Haus (D)	—	house	maison *f*	casa *f*	casa *f*
Hausfrau (D)	—	housewife	femme de maison *f*	casalinga *f*	ama de casa *f*
Haushalt (D)	—	household	ménage *m*	casa *f*	casa *f*
Hausmädchen (D)	—	maid	fille de service *f*	domestica *f*	criada *f*
Hausmeister (D)	—	caretaker	concierge *m*	portinaio *m*	portero *m*
Haut (D)	—	skin	peau *f*	pelle *f*	piel *f*
haut (F)	hoch	up/high	—	alto(a)	alto(a)
haute montage (F)	Hochgebirge *n*	high mountain-chain	—	alta montagna *f*	montañas elevadas *f pl*
hauteur (F)	Höhe *f*	height	—	altezza *f*	altura *f*
haut-parleur (F)	Lautsprecher *m*	loudspeaker	—	altoparlante *m*	altavoz *m*
have (E)	haben	—	avoir	avere	tener
have a cold (E)	erkältet sein	—	avoir un rhume	essere raffreddato(a)	estar acatarrado(a)
have a look at (E)	besichtigen	—	visiter	visitare	visitar
have on (E)	anhaben	—	porter	indossare	llevar
have to¹ (E)	müssen	—	devoir	dovere	deber
have to² (E)	sollen	—	devoir	dovere	deber
he (E)	er	—	il	lui/egli/esso	él
head (E)	Kopf *m*	—	tête *f*	testa *f*	cabeza *f*

	D	E	F	I	Es
headache (E)	Kopfschmerzen *pl*	—	mal de tête *m*	mal di testa *m*	dolor de cabeza *m*
heading (E)	Überschrift *f*	—	titre *m*	titolo *m*	título *m*
headline (E)	Schlagzeile *f*	—	manchette *f*	titolo *m*	titular *m*
heal (E)	heilen	—	guérir	curare	curar
health (E)	Gesundheit *f*	—	santé *f*	salute *f*	salud *f*
health food shop (E)	Reformhaus *n*	—	magasin diététique *m*	negozio di prodotti dietetici *m*	tienda de productos dietéticos *f*
healthy (E)	gesund	—	sain(e)	sano(a)	sano(a)
heap (E)	Haufen *m*	—	tas *m*	mucchio *m*	montón *m*
hear (E)	hören	—	entendre	sentire	oír
hearing (E)	Gehör *n*	—	ouïe *f*	udito *m*	oído *m*
heart (E)	Herz *n*	—	cœur *m*	cuore *m*	corazón *m*
heat¹ (E)	heizen	—	chauffer	riscaldare	calentar
heat² (E)	Hitze *f*	—	chaleur *f*	caldo *m*	calor *m*
heating (E)	Heizung *f*	—	chauffage *m*	riscaldamento *m*	calefacción *f*
heavy (E)	schwer	—	lourd(e)	pesante	pesado(a)
hebdomadaire (F)	wöchentlich	weekly	—	settimanale	semanal
heben (D)	—	lift	soulever	alzare	levantar
hecho (Es)	Tatsache *f*	fact	fait *m*	fatto *m*	—
hectic (E)	hektisch	—	fébrile	nervoso(a)	inquieto(a)
Heft (D)	—	exercise book	cahier *m*	quaderno *m*	cuaderno *m*
heftig (D)	—	fierce	violent(e)	violento(a)	fuerte
height (E)	Höhe *f*	—	hauteur	altezza *f*	altura *f*
heilen (D)	—	heal	guérir	curare	curar
heilig (D)	—	holy	saint(e)	santo(a)	santo(a)
Heiligabend (D)	—	Christmas Eve	nuit de Noël *f*	vigilia di Natale *f*	Nochebuena *f*
Heimat (D)	—	home	patrie *f*	patria *f*	patria *f*
heimlich (D)	—	secret	secret(-ète)	segreto(a)	oculto(a)
Heimweh (D)	—	homesickness	mal du pays *m*	nostalgia *f*	nostalgia *f*
Heirat (D)	—	marriage	mariage *m*	matrimonio *m*	boda *f*
heiraten (D)	—	marry	marier	sposarsi	casarse
heiß (D)	—	hot	chaud(e)	caldo(a)	caliente
heißen (D)	—	be called	appeler, se	chiamarsi	llamarse
heizen (D)	—	heat	chauffer	riscaldare	calentar
Heizöl (D)	—	fuel	mazout *m*	olio combustibile *m*	combustible para la calefacción *m*
Heizung (D)	—	heating	chauffage *m*	riscaldamento *m*	calefacción *f*
hektisch (D)	—	hectic	fébrile	nervoso(a)	inquieto(a)
helada (Es)	Frost *m*	frost	gelée *f*	gelo *m*	—
Held (D)	—	hero	héros *m*	eroe *m*	héroe *m*
helfen (D)	—	help	aider	aiutare	ayudar
hell (D)	—	bright	clair(e)	chiaro(a)	claro(a)
hell (E)	Hölle *f*	—	enfer *m*	inferno *m*	infierno *m*
hello! (E)	hallo!	—	allô!	pronto!	¡diga!

	D	E	F	I	Es
Helm (D)	—	helmet	casque *m*	casco *m*	casco *m*
helmet (E)	Helm *m*	—	casque *m*	casco *m*	casco *m*
help¹ (E)	helfen	—	aider	aiutare	ayudar
help² (E)	Hilfe *f*	—	aide *f*	aiuto *m*	ayuda *f*
help s.b. (E)	behilflich sein	—	aider qn	aiutare	ayudar a alguien
Hemd (D)	—	shirt	chemise *f*	camicia *f*	camisa *f*
hen (E)	Henne *f*	—	poule *f*	gallina *f*	gallina *f*
Henne (D)	—	hen	poule *f*	gallina *f*	gallina *f*
her (D)	—	here/ago	ici	qua/qui/da	aquí
herab (D)	—	down	vers le bas	giù	hacia abajo
herabsetzen (D)	—	lower	baisser	diminuire	rebajar
herauf (D)	—	up	vers le haut	su	hacia arriba
heraus (D)	—	out	dehors	fuori	hacia afuera
herausgeben (D)	—	publish	éditer	pubblicare	editar
heraustreten (D)	—	step out	sortir	uscire fuori	salir
herb (D)	—	bitter	amer(-ère)	amaro(a)	amargo(a)
herbe (F)	Gras *n*	grass	—	erba *f*	hierba *f*
Herbst (D)	—	autumn	automne *m*	autunno *m*	otoño *m*
Herd (D)	—	cooker	fourneau *m*	cucina *f*	cocina *f*
here¹ (E)	hier	—	ici	qui	aquí
here² (E)	her	—	ici	qua/qui/da	aquí
heredar¹ (Es)	beerben	inherit from	hériter	ereditare	—
heredar² (Es)	erben	inherit	hériter	ereditare	—
herein (D)	—	in	vers l'intérieur	dentro	adentro
herida¹ (Es)	Verletzung *f*	injury	blessure *f*	ferita *f*	—
herida² (Es)	Wunde *f*	wound	blessure *f*	ferita *f*	—
herir¹ (Es)	verwunden	wound	blesser	ferire	—
herir² (Es)	verletzen	injure	blesser	ferire	—
hériter¹ (F)	beerben	inherit from	—	ereditare	heredar
hériter² (F)	erben	inherit	—	ereditare	heredar
hermana (Es)	Schwester *f*	sister	sœur *f*	sorella *f*	—
hermano (Es)	Bruder *m*	brother	frère *m*	fratello *m*	—
hermanos (Es)	Geschwister *pl*	brothers and sisters	frère(s) et sœur(s) *pl*	fratelli *m pl*	—
hermoso (Es)	schön	beautiful	beau, bel, belle	bello(a)	—
hero (E)	Held *m*	—	héros *m*	eroe *m*	héroe *m*
héroe (Es)	Held *m*	hero	héros *m*	eroe *m*	—
héros (F)	Held *m*	hero	—	eroe *m*	héroe *m*
Herr (D)	—	gentleman	monsieur *m*	signore *m*	señor *m*
herramienta (Es)	Werkzeug *n*	tool	outil *m*	utensile *m*	—
herrlich (D)	—	marvellous	magnifique	stupendo(a)	maravilloso(a)
herrschen (D)	—	rule	régner	dominare	mandar
herstellen (D)	—	manufacture	produire	fabbricare	producir
Hersteller (D)	—	manufacturer	producteur *m*	produttore *m*	productor *m*
herüber (D)	—	over	par ici	da questa parte	a este lado

	D	E	F	I	Es
herum (D)	—	around	autour	intorno	alrededor
herumdrehen (D)	—	turn around	tourner	girare	dar vuelta
herumreichen (D)	—	pass around	faire passer	far circolare	pasar de mano en mano
herunter (D)	—	down	en bas	giù	abajo
hervor (D)	—	forth	au-dehors	fuori	delante
hervorragend (D)	—	excellent	excellent(e)	eccellente	extraordinario(a)
Herz (D)	—	heart	cœur m	cuore m	corazón m
herzlich (D)	—	cordial	cordial(e)	cordiale	afectuoso(a)
hesitate (E)	zögern	—	hésiter	esitare	vacilar
hésiter (F)	zögern	hesitate	—	esitare	vacilar
heure (F)	Stunde f	hour	—	ora f	hora f
heure d'été (F)	Sommerzeit f	summertime	—	ora legale f	temporada de verano f
heures de consultation (F)	Sprechstunde f	consultation hour	—	ora di ricevimento f	hora de consulta f
heures d'ouverture (F)	Öffnungszeiten pl	business hours	—	orario di apertura m pl	horario de abertura m
heureux (F)	glücklich	happy	—	felice	feliz
heurter (F)	anstoßen	bump	—	urtare	empujar
heute (D)	—	today	aujourd'hui	oggi	hoy
heutzutage (D)	—	nowadays	de nos jours	oggigiorno	hoy en día
Hexe (D)	—	witch	sorcière f	strega f	bruja f
hide¹ (E)	verstecken	—	cacher	nascondere	ocultar
hide² (E)	verbergen	—	dissimuler	nascondere	esconder
hielo (Es)	Eis n	ice	glace f	gelato m	—
hier (D)	—	here	ici	qui	aquí
hier (F)	gestern	yesterday	—	ieri	ayer
hierba (Es)	Gras n	grass	herbe f	erba f	—
hierbleiben (D)	—	stay here	rester	restare qui	quedarse aquí
hierher (D)	—	over here	par ici	qua	para acá
hierro (Es)	Eisen n	iron	fer m	ferro m	—
hígado (Es)	Leber f	liver	foie m	fegato m	—
high mountain-chain (E)	Hochgebirge n	—	haute montage f	alta montagna f	montañas elevadas f pl
high season (E)	Hochsaison f	—	pleine saison f	alta stagione f	temporada alta f
high tide (E)	Flut f	—	marée haute f	altamarea f	marea alta f
higo (Es)	Feige f	fig	figue f	fico m	—
hija (Es)	Tochter f	daughter	fille f	figlia f	—
hijo (Es)	Sohn m	son	fils m	figlio m	—
hike (E)	wandern	—	marcher	fare escursioni a piedi	hacer excursiones
Hilfe (D)	—	help	aide f	aiuto m	ayuda f
hill (E)	Hügel m	—	colline f	collina f	colina f
hilo (Es)	Faden m	thread	fil m	filo m	—
Himbeere (D)	—	raspberry	framboise f	lampone m	frambuesa f

	D	E	F	I	Es
Himmel (D)	—	sky	ciel *m*	cielo *m*	cielo *m*
hin (D)	—	there	jusqu'à/vers	là	hacia allá/hasta
hinab (D)	—	down	vers le bas	giù	hacia abajo
hinauf (D)	—	up	montez	su	hacia arriba
hinaufsteigen (D)	—	climb	monter	salire	subir
hinaus (D)	—	out	dehors	fuori	hacia afuera
hinausgehen (D)	—	go out	sortir	uscire	salir afuera
hinchado (Es)	geschwollen	swollen	enflé(e)	gonfio(a)	—
hinder (E)	hindern	—	empêcher	impedire	impedir
hindern (D)	—	hinder	empêcher	impedire	impedir
hindurch (D)	—	through	à travers	attraverso	a través de
hinein (D)	—	in	dans	dentro	dentro
hinlegen (D)	—	put down	poser	posare	poner
hinsetzen (D)	—	sit down	asseoir, se	sedersi	sentarse
hint (E)	Hinweis *m*	—	indication *f*	indicazione *f*	indicación *f*
hinten (D)	—	behind	derrière	dietro	detrás
hintereinander (D)	—	one after the other	l'un derrière l'autre	uno dopo l'altro	uno detras de otro
hinterlassen (D)	—	leave	laisser	lasciare	dejar
hinterlegen (D)	—	deposit	déposer	depositare	depositar
hinüber (D)	—	across	de l'autre côté	di là	hacia el otro lado
hinunter (D)	—	down	vers le bas	giù	hacia abajo
hinuntergehen (D)	—	descend	descendre	scendere	bajar
Hinweis (D)	—	hint	indication *f*	indicazione *f*	indicación *f*
hinzufügen (D)	—	add	ajouter	aggiungere	añadir
hip (E)	Hüfte *f*	—	hanche *f*	fianco *m*	cadera *f*
Hirn (D)	—	brain	cerveau *m*	cervello *m*	cerebro *m*
histoire (F)	Geschichte *f*	history	—	storia *f*	historia *f*
historia (Es)	Geschichte *f*	history	histoire *f*	storia *f*	—
history (E)	Geschichte *f*	—	histoire *f*	storia *f*	historia *f*
hit[1] (E)	schlagen	—	battre	battere	golpear
hit[2] (E)	treffen	—	toucher	colpire	alcanzar
hitch-hiker (E)	Anhalter *m*	—	auto-stoppeur *m*	autostoppista *m*	autoestopista *m*
Hitze (D)	—	heat	chaleur *f*	caldo *m*	calor *m*
hiver (F)	Winter *m*	winter	—	inverno *m*	invierno *m*
hoch (D)	—	up/high	haut(e)	alto(a)	alto(a)
Hochgebirge (D)	—	high mountain-chain	haute montage *f*	alta montagna *f*	montañas elevadas *f pl*
Hochsaison (D)	—	high season	pleine saison *f*	alta stagione *f*	temporada alta *f*
Hochschule (D)	—	university	université *f*	istituto supériore *m*	escuela superior *f*
höchstens (D)	—	at the most	tout au plus	al massimo	a lo sumo
Höchst-geschwindigkeit (D)	—	maximum speed	vitesse maximum *f*	velocità massima *f*	velocidad máxima *f*
Höchstpreis (D)	—	maximum price	prix plafond *m*	prezzo massimo *m*	precio máximo *m*
Hochzeit (D)	—	wedding	mariage *m*	nozze *f pl*	boda *f*

	D	E	F	I	Es
hocico (Es)	Maul n	mouth	gueule f	muso m	—
Hof (D)	—	yard	cour f	cortile m	patio m
hoffen (D)	—	hope	espérer	sperare	esperar
hoffentlich (D)	—	hopefully	espérons	speriamo que	espero que
höflich (D)	—	polite	poli(e)	cortese	cortés
Höflichkeit (D)	—	politeness	politesse f	cortesia f	cortesía f
Höhe (D)	—	height	hauteur	altezza f	altura f
hohl (D)	—	hollow	creux(-euse)	cavo	hueco(a)
Höhle (D)	—	cave	grotte f	caverna f	cueva f
hoja (Es)	Blatt n	leaf	feuille f	foglia f	—
hold (E)	halten	—	tenir	tenere	sujetar
hole (E)	Loch n	—	trou m	buco m	agujero m
holen (D)	—	fetch	aller chercher	andare a prendere	traer
holiday¹ (E)	Feiertag m	—	jour férié m	giorno festivo m	día de fiesta m
holiday² (E)	schulfrei	—	de congé	vacanza f	sin colegio
holidays (E)	Ferien pl	—	vacances f pl	vacanze f pl	vacaciones f pl
Hölle (D)	—	hell	enfer m	inferno m	infierno m
hollow (E)	hohl	—	creux(-euse)	cavo(a)	hueco(a)
holy (E)	heilig	—	saint(e)	santo(a)	santo(a)
Holy week (E)	Osterwoche f	—	semaine sainte f	settimana santa f	Semana Santa f
Holz (D)	—	wood	bois m	legno m	madera f
hombre (Es)	Mann m	man	homme m	uomo m	—
hombro (Es)	Schulter f	shoulder	épaule f	spalla f	—
home¹ (E)	Heimat f	—	patrie f	patria f	patria f
home² (E)	nach Hause	—	à la maison	a casa	a casa
homesickness (E)	Heimweh n	—	mal du pays m	nostalgia f	nostalgia f
homme¹ (F)	Mensch m	human being	—	essere umano m	persona f
homme² (F)	Mann m	man	—	uomo m	hombre m
honest¹ (E)	aufrichtig	—	sincère	onesto(a)	sincero(a)
honest² (E)	ehrlich	—	honnête	onesto(a)	honesto(a)
honesto (Es)	ehrlich	honest	honnête	onesto(a)	—
honey (E)	Honig m	—	miel m	miele m	miel f
honeymoon (E)	Flitterwochen pl	—	lune de miel f	luna di miele f	luna de miel f
hongo (Es)	Pilz m	mushroom	champignon m	fungo m	—
Honig (D)	—	honey	miel m	miele m	miel f
honnête (F)	ehrlich	honest	—	onesto(a)	honesto(a)
honneur (F)	Ehre f	honour	—	onore m	honor m
honor (Es)	Ehre f	honour	honneur m	onore m	—
honour (E)	Ehre f	—	honneur m	onore m	honor m
honte (F)	Schande f	disgrace	—	vergogna f	deshonra f
hood (E)	Kapuze f	—	capuchon m	cappuccio m	capucha f
hook (E)	Haken m	—	crochet m	gancio m	gancho m
hope (E)	hoffen	—	espérer	sperare	esperar
hopefully (E)	hoffentlich	—	espérons	speriamo que	espero que

	D	E	F	I	Es
hôpital (F)	Krankenhaus *n*	hospital	—	ospedale *m*	hospital *m*
hora (Es)	Stunde *f*	hour	heure *f*	ora *f*	—
horación (Es)	Gebet *n*	prayer	prière *f*	preghiera *f*	—
hora de consulta (Es)	Sprechstunde *f*	consultation hour	heures de consultation *f pl*	ora di ricevimento *f*	—
horaire (F)	Fahrplan *m*	timetable	—	orario *m*	horario *m*
horario (Es)	Fahrplan *m*	timetable	horaire *m*	orario *m*	—
horario de abertura (Es)	Öffnungszeiten *pl*	opening times	heures d'ouverture *f pl*	orario di apertura *m pl*	—
hören (D)	—	hear	entendre	sentire	oír
Hörer[1] (D)	—	listener	auditeur *m*	ascoltatore *m*	oyente *m*
Hörer[2] (D)	—	receiver	récepteur *m*	ricevitore *m*	auricular *m*
horizontal (E)	waagrecht	—	horizontal(e)	orizzontale	horizontal
horizontal (Es)	waagrecht	horizontal	horizontal(e)	orizzontale	—
horizontal (F)	waagrecht	horizontal	—	orizzontale	horizontal
horn (E)	Hupe *f*	—	claxon *m*	clacson *m*	bocina *f*
horrible (E)	schauderhaft	—	horrible	spaventoso(a)	espantoso(a)
horrible[1] (Es)	abscheulich	abominable	affreux(-euse)	disgustoso(a)	—
horrible[2] (Es)	schrecklich	terrible	terrible	spaventoso(a)	—
horrible (F)	schauderhaft	horrible	—	spaventoso(a)	espantoso(a)
hors de[1] (F)	außerhalb	out of	—	fuori di	fuera de
hors de[2] (F)	außer	except	—	eccetto	salvo
hors de question (F)	ausgeschlossen	impossible	—	escluso	imposible
hors-d'œuvre (F)	Vorspeise *f*	appetizer	—	antipasto *m*	primer plato *m*
horse (E)	Pferd *n*	—	cheval *m*	cavallo *m*	caballo *m*
Hose (D)	—	trousers	pantalon *m*	pantaloni *m pl*	pantalón *m*
hospedaje (Es)	Unterkunft *f*	accommodation	logement *m*	alloggio *m*	—
hospitable (E)	gastfreundlich	—	hospitalier(-ière)	ospitale	hospitalario(a)
hospital[1] (E)	Krankenhaus *n*	—	hôpital *m*	ospedale *m*	hospital *m*
hospital[2] (E)	Klinik *f*	—	clinique *f*	clinica *f*	clínica *f*
hospital (Es)	Krankenhaus *n*	hospital	hôpital *m*	ospedale *m*	—
hospitalario (Es)	gastfreundlich	hospitable	hospitalier(-ière)	ospitale	—
hospitalidad (Es)	Gastfreundschaft *f*	hospitality	hospitalité *f*	ospitalità *f*	—
hospitalier (F)	gastfreundlich	hospitable	—	ospitale	hospitalario(a)
hospitalité (F)	Gastfreundschaft *f*	hospitality	—	ospitalità *f*	hospitalidad *f*
hospitality (E)	Gastfreundschaft *f*	—	hospitalité *f*	ospitalità *f*	hospitalidad *f*
host (E)	Gastgeber *m*	—	hôte *m*	ospite *m*	anfitrión *m*
hostess (I)	Stewardeß *f*	stewardess	hôtesse de l'air *f*	—	azafata *f*
hot[1] (E)	heiß		chaud(e)	caldo	caliente
hot[2] (E)	scharf	—	épicé(e)	piccante	picante
hôte[1] (F)	Gast *m*	guest	—	ospite *m*	invitado *m*
hôte[2] (F)	Gastgeber *m*	host	—	ospit *m*	anfitrión *m*
Hotel (D)	—	hotel	hôtel *m*	albergo *m*	hotel *m*
hotel[1] (E)	Gasthaus *n*	—	auberge *f*	osteria *f*	posada *f*
hotel[2] (E)	Hotel *n*	—	hôtel *m*	albergo *m*	hotel *m*

	D	E	F	I	Es
hotel (Es)	Hotel *n*	hotel	hôtel *m*	albergo *m*	—
hôtel (F)	Hotel *n*	hotel	—	albergo *m*	hotel *m*
hôtesse de l'air (F)	Stewardeß *f*	stewardess	—	hostess *f*	azafata *f*
hour (E)	Stunde *f*	—	heure *f*	ora *f*	hora *f*
hourly (E)	stündlich	—	toutes les heures	ogni ora	cada hora
house (E)	Haus *n*	—	maison *f*	casa *f*	casa *f*
household (E)	Haushalt *m*	—	ménage *m*	casa *f*	casa *f*
housewife (E)	Hausfrau *f*	—	femme de maison *f*	casalinga *f*	ama de casa *f*
how (E)	wie	—	comment	come	cómo
however (E)	jedoch	—	cependant	tutta via	sin embargo
how many (E)	wieviele	—	combien	quanti(e)	cuántos(as)
how much (E)	wieviel	—	combien	quanto	cuánto
hoy (Es)	heute	today	aujourd'hui	oggi	—
hoy en día (Es)	heutzutage	nowadays	de nos jour	oggigiorno	—
hübsch (D)	—	pretty	joli(e)	carino(a)	bonito(a)
hueco (Es)	hohl	hollow	creux(-euse)	cavo(a)	—
huelga (Es)	Streik *m*	strike	grève *f*	sciopero *m*	—
huérfano (Es)	Waise *f*	orphan	orphelin *m*	orfano *m*	—
hueso[1] (Es)	Kern *m*	pip	noyau *m*	nocciolo *m*	—
hueso[2] (Es)	Knochen *m*	bone	os *m*	osso *m*	—
huevo (Es)	Ei *n*	egg	œuf *m*	uovo *m*	—
Hüfte (D)	—	hip	hanche *f*	fianco *m*	cadera *f*
huge (E)	riesig	—	énorme	enorme	enorme
Hügel (D)	—	hill	colline *f*	collina *f*	colina *f*
Huhn (D)	—	chicken	poule *f*	pollo *m*	gallina *f*
huile (F)	Öl *n*	oil	—	olio *m*	aceite *m*
huir (Es)	entfliehen	escape	échapper, se	scappare	—
huit (F)	acht	eight	—	otto	ocho
huître (F)	Auster *f*	oyster	—	ostrica *f*	ostra *f*
humain (F)	menschlich	human	—	umano(a)	humano(a)
human (E)	menschlich	—	humain(e)	umano(a)	humano(a)
human being (E)	Mensch *m*	—	homme *m*	essere umano *m*	persona *f*
humano (Es)	menschlich	human	humain(e)	umano(a)	—
húmedo[1] (Es)	feucht	damp	humide	umido(a)	—
húmedo[2] (Es)	naß	wet	mouillé(e)	bagnato(a)	—
humeur (F)	Laune *f*	mood	—	umore *m*	humor *m*
humide (F)	feucht	damp	—	umido(a)	húmedo(a)
humo (Es)	Rauch *m*	smoke	fumée *f*	fumo *m*	—
humor (Es)	Laune *f*	mood	humeur *f*	umore *m*	—
Hund (D)	—	dog	chien *m*	cane *m*	perro *m*
hundert (D)	—	hundred	cent	cento	cien
hundirse[1] (Es)	sinken	sink	couler	affondare	—
hundirse[2] (Es)	versinken	sink	enfoncer, se	affondare	—
hundred (E)	hundert	—	cent	cento	cien

	D	E	F	I	Es
Hunger (D)	—	hunger	faim *f*	fame *f*	hambre *m*
hunger (E)	Hunger *m*	—	faim *f*	fame *f*	hambre *m*
hungrig (D)	—	hungry	affamé(e)	affamato(a)	hambriento(a)
hungry (E)	hungrig	—	affamé(e)	affamato(a)	hambriento(a)
hunt¹ (E)	jagen	—	chasser	cacciare	cazar
hunt² (E)	Jagd *f*	—	chasse *f*	caccia *f*	caza *f*
Hupe (D)	—	horn	claxon *m*	clacson *m*	bocina *f*
hüpfen (D)	—	jump	sautiller	saltellare	saltar
hurried (E)	eilig	—	pressé(e)	frettoloso(a)	rápido(a)
hurry (E)	eilen	—	dépêcher, se	andare in fretta	darse prisa
hurry up (E)	beeilen, sich	—	dépêcher, se	affrettarsi	darse prisa
hurt (E)	weh	—	douloureux(-euse)	dolente	doloroso(a)
husband (E)	Ehemann *m*	—	mari *m*	marito *m*	marido *m*
husten (D)	—	cough	tousser	tossire	toser
Husten (D)	—	cough	toux *m*	tosse *f*	tos *f*
Hut (D)	—	hat	chapeau *m*	cappello *m*	sombrero *m*
hut (E)	Hütte *f*	—	cabane *f*	capanna *f*	cabaña *f*
Hütte (D)	—	hut	cabane *f*	capanna *f*	cabaña *f*
I (E)	ich	—	je/moi	io	yo
ice (E)	Eis *n*	—	glace *f*	gelato *m*	hielo *m*
ich (D)	—	I	je/moi	io	yo
ici¹ (F)	her	here	—	qua/qui/da	aquí
ici² (F)	hier	here	—	qui	aquí
idea¹ (E)	Idee *f*	—	idée *f*	idea *f*	idea *f*
idea² (E)	Vorstellung *f*	—	idée *f*	idea *f*	idea *f*
idea¹ (Es)	Idee *f*	idea	idée *f*	idea *f*	—
idea² (Es)	Vorstellung *f*	idea	idée *f*	idea *f*	—
idea¹ (I)	Idee *f*	idea	idée *f*	—	idea *f*
idea² (I)	Vorstellung *f*	idea	idée *f*	—	idea *f*
ideal (D)	—	ideal	idéal(e)	ideale	ideal
ideal¹ (E)	ideal	—	idéal(e)	ideale	ideal
ideal² (E)	Vorbild *n*	—	modèle *m*	modello *m*	modelo *m*
ideal (Es)	ideal	ideal	idéal(e)	ideale	—
idéal (F)	ideal	ideal	—	ideale	ideal
ideale (I)	ideal	ideal	idéal(e)	—	ideal
Idee (D)	—	idea	idée *f*	idea *f*	idea *f*
idée (F)	Idee *f*	idea	—	idea *f*	idea *f*
idéntico (Es)	gleich	same	égal(e)	identico(a)	—
identico (I)	gleich	same	égal(e)	—	idéntico(a)
identity card (E)	Personalausweis *m*	—	carte d'identité *f*	carta d'identitá *f*	documento de identidad *m*
idioma extranjero (Es)	Fremdsprache *f*	foreign language	langue étrangère *f*	lingua straniera *f*	—
ieri (I)	gestern	yesterday	hier	—	ayer
if (E)	ob	—	si	se	si

	D	E	F	I	Es
iglesia (Es)	Kirche *f*	church	église *f*	chiesa *f*	—
ignite (E)	zünden	—	allumer, se	accendersi	encender
ignorar (Es)	ignorieren	ignore	ignorer	ignorare	—
ignorare (I)	ignorieren	ignore	ignorer	—	ignorar
ignore[1] (E)	ignorieren	—	ignorer	ignorare	ignorar
ignore[2] (E)	übersehen	—	ignorer	non vedere	no ver
ignorer[1] (F)	ignorieren	ignore	—	ignorare	ignorar
ignorer[2] (F)	übersehen	ignore	—	non vedere	no ver
ignorieren (D)	—	ignore	ignorer	ignorare	ignorar
igual (Es)	egal	all the same	égal(e)	uguale	—
ihr (D)	—	you	vous	voi	vosotros
il (F)	er	he	—	lui/egli/esso	él
il, la[1] (I)	der, die, das	the	le, la	—	el, la, lo
il, la[2] (I)	das	that/which	le, la	—	lo
île (F)	Insel *f*	island	—	isola *f*	isla *f*
ilegal (Es)	gesetzwidrig	illegal	illégal(e)	illegale	—
ilegítimo (Es)	unrechtmäßig	unlawful	illégitime	illegale	—
ilimitado (Es)	unbegrenzt	unlimited	illimité(e)	illimitato(a)	—
ill (E)	krank	—	malade	malato(a)	enfermo(a)
illegal (E)	gesetzwidrig	—	illégal(e)	illegale	ilegal
illégal (F)	gesetzwidrig	illegal	—	illegale	ilegal
illegale[1] (I)	gesetzwidrig	illegal	illégal(e)	—	ilegal
illegale[2] (I)	unrechtmäßig	unlawful	illégitime	—	ilegítimo(a)
illégitime (F)	unrechtmäßig	unlawful	—	illegale	ilegítimo(a)
illimitato (I)	unbegrenzt	unlimited	illimité(e)	—	ilimitado(a)
illimité (F)	unbegrenzt	unlimited	—	illimitato(a)	ilimitado(a)
illness (E)	Krankheit *f*	—	maladie *f*	malattia *f*	enfermedad *f*
illuminare (I)	beleuchten	illuminate	éclairer	—	iluminar
illuminate (E)	beleuchten	—	éclairer	illuminare	iluminar
illuminazione (I)	Beleuchtung *f*	lighting	éclairage *m*	—	iluminación *f*
il lunedì (I)	montags	Mondays	le lundi	—	los lunes
illustré (F)	Illustrierte *f*	illustrated magazine	—	rivista *f*	revista
Illustrierte (D)	—	illustrated magazine	illustré *m*	rivista *f*	revista
il quale (I)	welche(r,s)	which	qui/que	—	¿cual?
ils (F)	sie	they	—	loro	ellos, ellas
iluminación (Es)	Beleuchtung *f*	lighting	éclairage *m*	illuminazione *f*	—
iluminar (Es)	beleuchten	illuminate	éclairer	illuminare	—
image (F)	Bild *n*	picture	—	immagine *f*	cuadro *m*
imaginarse (Es)	einbilden, sich	imagine	imaginer, se	immaginarsi	—
imagine (E)	einbilden, sich	—	imaginer, se	immaginarsi	imaginarse
imaginer, se (F)	einbilden, sich	imagine	—	immaginarsi	imaginarse
imbarazzante (I)	peinlich	embarrassing	gênant(e)	—	desagradable
imbarazzo (I)	Verlegenheit *f*	embarrassment	gêne *f*	—	contratiempo *m*

	D	E	F	I	Es
Imbiß (D)	—	snack	casse-croûte *m*	spuntino *m*	refrigerio *m*
imbucare (I)	einwerfen	post	poster	—	echar
imitar (Es)	nachahmen	imitate	imiter	imitare	—
imitare (I)	nachahmen	imitate	imiter	—	imitar
imitate (E)	nachahmen	—	imiter	imitare	imitar
imité (F)	unecht	fake	—	falso(a)	falso(a)
imiter (F)	nachahmen	imitate	—	imitare	imitar
immaginarsi (I)	einbilden, sich	imagine	imaginer, se	—	imaginarse
immagine (I)	Bild *n*	picture	image *f*	—	cuadro *m*
immédiat (F)	unmittelbar	immediate	—	inmediato(a)	directo(a)
immediate (E)	unmittelbar	—	immédiat(e)	inmediato(a)	directo(a)
immediately (E)	sofort	—	immédiatement	subito	en seguida
immédiatement (F)	sofort	immediately	—	subito	en seguida
immediato (I)	unmittelbar	immediate	immédiat(e)	—	directo(a)
immer (D)	—	always	toujours	sempre	siempre
immergere (I)	tauchen	dive	plonger	—	bucear
immobile (F)	bewegungslos	motionless	—	immobile	inmóvil
immobile (I)	bewegungslos	motionless	immobile	—	inmóvil
immondizia (I)	Abfall *m*	rubbish	déchets *m pl*	—	basura *f*
impacchettare (I)	verpacken	pack	emballer	—	empaquetar
impacciato (I)	ungeschickt	clumsy	maladroit(e)	—	torpe
impair (F)	ungerade	uneven	—	dispari	impar
impar (Es)	ungerade	uneven	impair(e)	dispari	—
imparare (I)	lernen	learn	apprendre	—	aprender
imparentato (I)	verwandt	related	parent(e)	—	emparentado(a)
impatient (E)	ungeduldig	—	impatient(e)	impaziente	impaciente
impatient (F)	ungeduldig	impatient	—	impaziente	impaciente
impaziente (I)	ungeduldig	impatient	impatient(e)	—	impaciente
impedido (Es)	verhindert	unable to make it	empêché(e)	impedito(a)	—
impedir (Es)	hindern	hinder	empêcher	impedire	—
impedire¹ (I)	hindern	hinder	empêcher	—	impedir
impedire² (I)	verhindern	prevent	empêcher	—	evitar
impedito (I)	verhindert	unable to make it	empêché(e)	—	impedido(a)
imperatore (I)	Kaiser *m*	emperor	empereur *m*	—	emperador *m*
impermeabile (I)	Regenmantel *m*	raincoat	imperméable *m*	—	impermeable *m*
impermeable (Es)	Regenmantel *m*	raincoat	imperméable *m*	impermeabile *m*	—
imperméable (F)	Regenmantel *m*	raincoat	—	impermeabile *m*	impermeable *m*
impfen (D)	—	vaccinate	vacciner	vaccinare	vacunar
Impfung (D)	—	vaccination	vaccination *f*	vaccinazione *f*	vacunación *f*
impianto (I)	Anlage *f*	plant	construction *f*	—	establecimiento *m*
impiegare (I)	anwenden	apply	employer	—	usar
impiegato (I)	Angestellter *m*	employee	employé *m*	—	empleado *m*
impiegato statale (I)	Beamter *m*	civil servant	fonctionnaire *m*	—	funcionario *m*
impoli (F)	unhöflich	impolite	—	scortese	descortés

	D	E	F	I	Es
impolite (E)	unhöflich	—	impoli(e)	scortese	descortés
Import (D)	—	import	importation *f*	importazione *f*	importación *f*
import[1] (E)	Einfuhr *f*	—	importation *f*	importazione *f*	importación *f*
import[2] (E)	Import *m*	—	importation *f*	importazione *f*	importación *f*
importación[1] (Es)	Einfuhr *f*	import	importation *f*	importazione *f*	—
importación[2] (Es)	Import *m*	import	importation *f*	importazione *f*	—
important (E)	wichtig	—	important(e)	importante	importante
important[1] (F)	bedeutend	significant	—	importante	importante
important[2] (F)	wichtig	important	—	importante	importante
importante[1] (Es)	bedeutend	significant	important(e)	importante	—
importante[2] (Es)	wichtig	important	important(e)	importante	—
importante[1] (I)	bedeutend	significant	important(e)	—	importante
importante[2] (I)	wichtig	important	important(e)	—	importante
importation[1] (F)	Einfuhr *f*	import	—	importazione *f*	importación *f*
importation[2] (F)	Import *m*	import	—	importazione *f*	importación *f*
importazione[1] (I)	Einfuhr *f*	import	importation *f*	—	importación *f*
importazione[2] (I)	Import *m*	import	importation *f*	—	importación *f*
importe (Es)	Betrag *m*	amount	montant *m*	somma *f*	—
importun (F)	lästig	troublesome	—	molesto(a)	desagradable
importunare (I)	belästigen	annoy	importuner	—	molestar
importuner (F)	belästigen	annoy	—	importunare	molestar
imposible[1] (Es)	ausgeschlossen	impossible	hors de question	escluso(a)	—
imposible[2] (Es)	unmöglich	impossible	impossible	impossibile	—
impossibile (I)	unmöglich	impossible	impossible	—	imposible
impossible[1] (E)	ausgeschlossen	—	hors de question	escluso(a)	imposible
impossible[2] (E)	unmöglich	—	impossible	impossibile	imposible
impossible (F)	unmöglich	impossible	—	impossibile	imposible
imposta sul'valore aggiunto (I)	Mehrwertsteuer *f*	value added tax	taxe sur la valeur ajoutée *f*	—	impuesto sobre el valor añadido *m*
imposte (I)	Steuern *pl*	tax	impôt *m*	—	impuesto *m*
impôt (F)	Steuern *pl*	tax	—	imposte *f pl*	impuesto *m*
imprecare (I)	schimpfen	scold	gronder	—	insultar
impreciso (I)	ungenau	inaccurate	inexact(e)	—	inexacto(a)
impresa (I)	Unternehmen *n*	company	entreprise *f*	—	empresa *f*
impresión (Es)	Eindruck *m*	impression	impression *f*	impressione *f*	—
impression (E)	Eindruck *m*	—	impression *f*	impressione *f*	impresión *f*
impression (F)	Eindruck *m*	impression	—	impressione *f*	impresión *f*
impressione (I)	Eindruck *m*	impression	impression *f*	—	impresión *f*
improbabile (I)	unwahrscheinlich	unlikely	invraisemblable	—	improbable
improbable (Es)	unwahrscheinlich	unlikely	invraisemblable	improbabile	—
improve (E)	verbessern	—	améliorer	migliorare	mejorar
improvement (E)	Besserung *f*	—	amélioration *f*	miglioramento *m*	restablecimiento *m*
improvviso (I)	abrupt	abrupt	subit(e)	—	súbito(a)
imprudent (F)	unvorsichtig	careless	—	imprudente	descuidado(a)
imprudente (Es)	leichtsinnig	careless	étourdi(e)	spensierato(a)	—

	D	E	F	I	Es
imprudente (I)	unvorsichtig	careless	imprudent(e)	—	descuidado(a)
impuesto (Es)	Steuern *pl*	tax	impôt *m*	imposte *f pl*	—
impuesto sobre el valor añadido (Es)	Mehrwertsteuer *f*	value added tax	taxe sur la valeur ajoutée *f*	imposta sul'valore aggiunto *f*	—
impulsivo (Es)	rasch	quick	rapide	rapido(a)	—
imstande (D)	—	able	capable	capace	en condiciones
in (D)	—	in/into	dans/à/en	in/a/tra/fra	en/a
in[1] (E)	herein	—	vers l'intérieur	dentro	adentro
in[2] (E)	hinein	—	dans	dentro	dentro
in[3] (E)	in	—	dans/à/en	in/a/tra/fra	en/a
in (I)	in	in/into	dans/à/en	—	en/a
inaccurate (E)	ungenau	—	inexact(e)	impreciso(a)	inexacto(a)
in addition (E)	zusätzlich	—	supplémentaire	supplementare	adicional
inadecuado (Es)	unpassend	inappropriate	mal à propos	sconveniente	—
inaguantable (Es)	unerträglich	unbearable	insupportable	insopportabile	—
in a muddle (E)	durcheinander	—	pêle-mêle	sottosopra	en desorden
in any case (E)	jedenfalls	—	en tout cas	in ogni caso	en cualquier caso
inappropriate (E)	unpassend	—	mal à propos	sconveniente	inadecuado(a)
inatteso (I)	unerwartet	unexpected	inattendu(e)	—	inesperado(a)
in basso (I)	nieder	inferior	bas(se)	—	abajo
inbegriffen (D)	—	included	compris	compreso(a)	incluído(a)
inbetween (E)	dazwischen	—	entre	in mezzo	entre
inborn (E)	angeboren	—	inné(e)	innato(a)	innato(a)
incapable (E)	unfähig	—	incapable	incapace	incapaz
incapable[1] (F)	untauglich	unfit	—	incapace	inútil
incapable[2] (F)	unfähig	incapable	—	incapace	incapaz
incapace[1] (I)	untauglich	unfit	incapable	—	inútil
incapace[2] (I)	unfähig	incapable	incapable	—	incapaz
incapaz (Es)	unfähig	incapable	incapable	incapace	—
incaricare (I)	beauftragen	instruct	charger de	—	encargar
incarico (I)	Aufgabe *f*	task	tâche *f*	—	tarea *f*
in case (E)	falls	—	au cas où	qualora	en caso de que
incassare[1] (I)	einkassieren	collect	recouvrer	—	cobrar
incassare[2] (I)	kassieren	take	encaisser	—	cobrar
incendie (F)	Brand *m*	fire	—	incendio *m*	incendio *m*
incendio (Es)	Brand *m*	fire	incendie *m*	incendio *m*	—
incendio (I)	Brand *m*	fire	incendie *m*	—	incendio *m*
incertain[1] (F)	unsicher	uncertain	—	incerto(a)	inseguro(a)
incertain[2] (F)	ungewiß	uncertain	—	incerto(a)	incierto(a)
incerto[1] (I)	ungewiß	uncertain	incertain(e)	—	incierto(a)
incerto[2] (I)	unsicher	uncertain	incertain(e)	—	inseguro(a)
incerto[3] (I)	unbestimmt	uncertain	indéfini(e)	—	indeterminado(a)
inchiesta (I)	Umfrage *f*	poll	enquête *f*	—	encuesta *f*
inciampare (I)	stolpern	stumble	trébucher	—	tropezar
incident (E)	Vorfall *m*	—	incident *m*	caso *m*	suceso *m*

	D	E	F	I	Es
incident (F)	Vorfall *m*	incident	—	caso *m*	suceso *m*
incidente (I)	Unfall *m*	accident	accident *m*	—	accidente *m*
incidente stradale (I)	Autounfall *m*	car accident	accident de voiture *m*	—	accidente de automóvil *m*
incierto (Es)	ungewiß	uncertain	incertain(e)	incerto(a)	—
incinta (I)	schwanger	pregnant	enceinte	—	embarazada
inclinado (Es)	steil	steep	raide	ripido(a)	—
inclinar (Es)	nicken	nod	faire un signe de tête	annuire	—
included (E)	inbegriffen	—	compris	compreso(a)	incluído(a)
including (E)	einschließlich	—	y compris	incluso(a)	incluído
incluído (Es)	inbegriffen	included	compris	compreso(a)	—
incluso¹ (Es)	einschließlich	including	y compris	incluso(a)	—
incluso² (Es)	sogar	even	même	perfino	—
incluso (I)	einschließlich	including	y compris	—	incluído
incollare (I)	kleben	stick	coller	—	pegar
income¹ (E)	Einkommen *n*	—	revenu *m*	entrate *f pl*	ingresos *m pl*
income² (E)	Verdienst *m*	—	revenus *m pl*	guadagno *m*	ganancia *f*
incómodo¹ (Es)	ungemütlich	uncomfortable	désagréable	poco accogliente	—
incómodo² (Es)	unbequem	uncomfortable	inconfortable	scomodo(a)	—
incomplet (F)	unvollständig	incomplete	—	incompleto(a)	incompleto(a)
incomplete (E)	unvollständig	—	incomplet(-ète)	incompleto(a)	incompleto(a)
incompleto (I)	unvollständig	incomplete	incomplet(-ète)	—	incompleto(a)
incompleto (Es)	unvollständig	incomplete	incomplet(-ète)	incompleto(a)	—
inconfortable (F)	unbequem	uncomfortable	—	scomodo(a)	incómodo(a)
inconnu (F)	unbekannt	unknown	—	sconosciuto(a)	desconocido(a)
incontestable (F)	eindeutig	unequivocal	—	univoco(a)	evidente
incontrare¹ (I)	begegnen	meet	rencontrer	—	encontrar
incontrare² (I)	treffen	meet	rencontrer	—	encontrar
incontro (I)	Treffen *n*	meeting	rencontre *f*	—	encuentro *m*
increase¹ (E)	vermehren	—	augmenter	aumentare	aumentar
increase² (E)	zunehmen	—	augmenter	aumentare	aumentar
incredibile (I)	unglaublich	incredible	incroyable	—	increíble
incredible (E)	unglaublich	—	incroyable	incredibile	increíble
increíble (Es)	unglaublich	incredible	incroyable	incredibile	—
incrocio (I)	Kreuzung *f*	crossing	intersection *f*	—	cruce *m*
incroyable (F)	unglaublich	incredible	—	incredibile	increíble
indecent (E)	unanständig	—	indécent(e)	indecente	inmoral
indécent (F)	unanständig	indecent	—	indecente	inmoral
indecente (I)	unanständig	indecent	indécent(e)	—	inmoral
indeciso (I)	unentschlossen	undecided	irrésolu(e)	—	irresoluto(a)
indéfini (F)	unbestimmt	uncertain	—	incerto(a)	indeterminado(a)
indépendant¹ (F)	selbständig	independent	—	indipendente	independiente
indépendant² (F)	unabhängig	independent	—	indipendente	independiente
independent¹ (E)	selbständig	—	indépendant(e)	indipendente	independiente

	D	E	F	I	Es
independent² (E)	unabhängig	—	indépendant(e)	indipendente	independiente
independiente¹ (Es)	selbständig	independent	indépendant(e)	indipendente	—
independiente² (Es)	unabhängig	independent	indépendant(e)	indipendente	—
indeseado (Es)	unerwünscht	unwelcome	inopportun(e)	indesiderato(a)	—
indesiderato (I)	unerwünscht	unwelcome	inopportun(e)	—	indeseado(a)
indessen (D)	—	meanwhile	cependant	nel frattempo	en eso
indeterminado (Es)	unbestimmt	uncertain	indéfini(e)	incerto(a)	—
Indianer (D)	—	Red Indian	Indien m	indiano m	indio m
indiano (I)	Indianer m	Red Indian	Indien m	—	indio m
indicación (Es)	Hinweis m	hint	indication f	indicazione f	—
indicado (Es)	geeignet	suitable	approprié(e)	adatto(a)	—
indicar (Es)	zeigen	show	montrer	mostrare	—
indicatif téléphonique (F)	Vorwahl f	dialling code	—	prefisso m	prefijo m
indicazione¹ (I)	Angabe f	information	information f	—	información f
indicazione² (I)	Hinweis m	hint	indication f	—	indicación f
índice (Es)	Inhalts- verzeichnis n	table of contents	table des matières f	indice m	—
indice (I)	Inhalts- verzeichnis n	table of contents	table des matières f	—	índice m
Indien (F)	Indianer m	Red Indian	—	indiano m	indio m
in dietro (I)	rückwärts	backwards	en arrière	—	marcha atrás
indietro (I)	zurück	back	de retour	—	atrás
indigène (F)	einheimisch	native	—	indigeno(a)	nativo
indigeno (I)	einheimisch	native	indigène	—	nativo
indignado (Es)	empört	indignant	révolté(e)	indignato(a)	—
indignant (E)	empört	—	révolté(e)	indignato(a)	indignado(a)
indignato (I)	empört	indignant	révolté(e)	—	indignado(a)
indio (Es)	Indianer m	Red Indian	Indien m	indiano m	—
indipendente¹ (I)	selbständig	independent	indépendant(e)	—	independiente
indipendente² (I)	unabhängig	independent	indépendant(e)	—	independiente
indirizzare (I)	adressieren	address	adresser	—	poner las señas en
indirizzo (I)	Anschrift f / Adresse f	address	adresse f	—	dirección f
in discesa (I)	bergab	downhill	en descendant	—	cuesta abajo
indispensabile (I)	unentbehrlich	indispensable	indispensable	—	indispensable
indispensable (E)	unentbehrlich	—	indispensable	indispensabile	indispensable
indispensable (Es)	unentbehrlich	indispensable	indispensable	indispensabile	—
indispensable (F)	unentbehrlich	indispensable	—	indispensabile	indispensable
indisposé (F)	unwohl	unwell	—	indisposto(a)	indispuesto(a)
indisposto (I)	unwohl	unwell	indisposé(e)	—	indispuesto(a)
indispuesto (Es)	unwohl	unwell	indisposé(e)	indisposto(a)	—
indoor swimming pool (E)	Hallenbad n	—	piscine f	piscina coperta f	piscina cubierta f
indossare¹ (I)	anhaben	have on	porter	—	llevar
indossare² (I)	anziehen	dress	mettre	—	ponerse

influence

	D	E	F	I	Es
indovinare (I)	raten	guess	deviner	—	adivinar
industria (Es)	Industrie f	industry	industrie f	industria f	—
industria (I)	Industrie f	industry	industrie f	—	industria f
Industrie (D)	—	industry	industrie f	industria f	industria f
industrie (F)	Industrie f	industry	—	industria f	industria f
industry (E)	Industrie f	—	industrie f	industria f	industria f
ineinander (D)	—	into one another	l'un dans l'autre	l'uno nell'altro	uno en otro
inesperado (Es)	unerwartet	unexpected	inattendu(e)	inatteso(a)	—
inesperto (I)	unerfahren	inexperienced	inexpérimenté(e)	—	inexperto(a)
inevitabile (I)	unvermeidlich	inevitable	inévitable	—	inevitable
inevitable (E)	unvermeidlich	—	inévitable	inevitabile	inevitable
inevitable (Es)	unvermeidlich	inevitable	inévitable	inevitabile	—
inévitable (F)	unvermeidlich	inevitable	—	inevitabile	inevitable
inexact (F)	ungenau	inaccurate	—	impreciso(a)	inexacto(a)
inexacto (Es)	ungenau	inaccurate	inexact(e)	impreciso(a)	—
inexpensive (E)	preiswert	—	bon marché	conveniente	económico(a)
inexperienced (E)	unerfahren	—	inexpérimenté(e)	inesperto(a)	inexperto(a)
inexpérimenté (F)	unerfahren	inexperienced	—	inesperto(a)	inexperto(a)
inexperto (Es)	unerfahren	inexperienced	inexpérimenté(e)	inesperto(a)	—
infanzia (I)	Kindheit f	childhood	enfance f	—	niñez f
inférieur (F)	unterste(r,s)	lowest	—	inferiore	inferior(a)
inferior (E)	nieder	—	bas(se)	in basso	abajo
inferior (Es)	unterste(r,s)	lowest	inférieur(e)	inferiore	—
inferiore (I)	unterste(r,s)	lowest	inférieur(e)	—	inferior(a)
infermiera (I)	Kranken-schwester f	nurse	infirmière f	—	enfermera f
infermiere (I)	Kranken-pfleger m	nursing orderly	infirmier m	—	enfermero m
inferno (I)	Hölle f	hell	enfer m	—	infierno m
infiammabile (I)	feuergefährlich	inflammable	inflammable	—	inflamable
infiammazione (I)	Entzündung f	inflammation	inflammation f	—	inflamación f
infierno (Es)	Hölle f	hell	enfer m	inferno m	—
infine (I)	zuletzt	finally	finalement	—	por último
infirmier (F)	Kranken-pfleger m	nursing orderly	—	infermiere m	enfermero m
infirmière (F)	Kranken-schwester f	nurse	—	infermiera f	enfermera f
inflamable (Es)	feuergefährlich	inflammable	inflammable	infiammabile	—
inflamación (Es)	Entzündung f	inflammation	inflammation f	infiammazione f	—
inflammable (E)	feuergefährlich	—	inflammable	infiammabile	inflamable
inflammable (F)	feuergefährlich	inflammable	—	infiammabile	inflamable
inflammation (E)	Entzündung f	—	inflammation f	infiammazione f	inflamación f
inflammation (F)	Entzündung f	inflammation	—	infiammazione f	inflamación f
influence[1] (E)	beeinflussen	—	influencer	influenzare	influir
influence[2] (E)	Einfluß m	—	influence f	influenza f	influencia f
influence (F)	Einfluß m	influence	—	influenza f	influencia f

	D	E	F	I	Es
influencer (F)	beeinflussen	influence	—	influenzare	influir
influencia (Es)	Einfluß m	influence	influence f	influenza f	—
influenza[1] (I)	Einfluß m	influence	influence f	—	influencia f
influenza[2] (I)	Grippe f	flu	grippe f	—	gripe f
influenzare (I)	beeinflussen	influence	influencer	—	influir
influir (Es)	beeinflussen	influence	influencer	influenzare	—
infolge (D)	—	as a result of	par suite de	in seguito a	por
in fondo (I)	eigentlich	actually	en fait	—	en realidad
inform[1] (E)	benachrichtigen	—	informer	informare	avisar
inform[2] (E)	informieren	—	informer	informare	informar
inform[3] (E)	verständigen	—	prévenir	informare	informar
inform s.o. (E)	mitteilen	—	informer qn de qch	comunicare	comunicar
información[1] (Es)	Auskunft f	information	renseigne- ment m	informazione f	—
información[2] (Es)	Angabe f	information	information f	indicazione f	—
informar[1] (Es)	berichten	report	faire un rapport	riferire	—
informar[2] (Es)	informieren	inform	informer	informare	—
informar[3] (Es)	verständigen	inform	prévenir	informare	—
informare[1] (I)	benachrichtigen	inform	informer	—	avisar
informare[2] (I)	informieren	inform	informer	—	informar
informare[3] (I)	verständigen	inform	prévenir	—	informar
informarse (Es)	erkundigen, sich	inquire	renseigner, se	informarsi	—
informarsi (I)	erkundigen, sich	inquire	renseigner, se	—	informarse
information[1] (E)	Angabe f	—	information f	indicazione f	información f
information[2] (E)	Auskunft f	—	renseignement m	informazione f	información f
information[1] (F)	Angabe f	information	—	indicazione f	información f
information[2] (F)	Mitteilung f	message	—	comunicazione f	comunicación f
informations (F)	Nachrichten pl	news	—	giornale radio m	noticiario m
informazione (I)	Auskunft f	information	renseignement m	—	información f
informe (Es)	Zeugnis n	report	bulletin m	pagella f	—
informe metereológico (Es)	Wetterbericht m	weather report	bulletin météorologique m	bollettino metereologico m	—
informer[1] (F)	benachrichtigen	inform	—	informare	avisar
informer[2] (F)	informieren	inform	—	informare	informar
informer qn de qch (F)	mitteilen	inform s.o.	—	comunicare	comunicar
informieren (D)	—	inform	informer	informare	informar
ingannare[1] (I)	betrügen	cheat	tromper	—	engañar
ingannare[2] (I)	täuschen	deceive	tromper	—	engañar
inganno (I)	Betrug m	fraud	tromperie f	—	engaño m
in genere (I)	überhaupt	at all	en général	—	en general
Inghilterra (I)	England n	England	Angleterre f	—	Inglaterra f
inghiottire (I)	schlucken	swallow	avaler	—	tragar
in giù (I)	abwärts	downwards	en bas	—	hacia abajo
ingiustizia (I)	Ungerechtigkeit f	injustice	injustice f	—	injusticia f

	D	E	F	I	Es
ingiusto (I)	ungerecht	unjust	injuste	—	injusto(a)
Inglaterra (Es)	England n	England	Angleterre f	Inghilterra f	—
inglés[1] (Es)	englisch	English	anglais(e)	inglese	—
inglés[2] (Es)	Engländer m	Englishman	Anglais m	inglese m	—
inglese[1] (I)	englisch	English	anglais(e)	—	inglés(-esa)
inglese[2] (I)	Engländer m	Englishman	Anglais m	—	inglés m
ingorgo (I)	Stau m	traffic jam	embouteillage m	—	embotella-miento m
ingrandire (I)	vergrößern	enlarge	agrandir	—	agrandar
ingrat (F)	undankbar	ungrateful	—	ingrato(a)	desagradecido(a)
ingrato (I)	undankbar	ungrateful	ingrat(e)	—	desagradecido(a)
ingraziamento (I)	Dank m	thanks	remerciement m	—	agradecimiento m
ingresos (Es)	Einkommen n	income	revenu m	entrate f pl	—
ingresso (I)	Einfahrt f	entrance	entrée f	—	entrada f
Inhaber (D)	—	owner	propriétaire m	proprietario m	propietario m
inhabitant[1] (E)	Bewohner m	—	habitant m	abitante m	habitante m
inhabitant[2] (E)	Einwohner m	—	habitant m	abitante m	habitante m
Inhalt (D)	—	contents	contenu m	contenuto m	contenido m
Inhalts-verzeichnis (D)	—	table of contents	table des matières f	indice m	índice m
inherit (E)	erben	—	hériter	ereditare	heredar
inherit from (E)	beerben	—	hériter	ereditare	heredar
inicio (Es)	Anfang m	beginning	commencement m	inizio m	—
iniezione (I)	Spritze f	injection	piqûre f	—	inyección f
inizio[1] (I)	Anfang m	beginning	commencement m	—	inicio m
inizio[2] (I)	Beginn m	beginning	commencement m	—	principio m
injection (E)	Spritze f	—	piqûre f	iniezione f	inyección f
injure (E)	verletzen	—	blesser	ferire	herir
injury (E)	Verletzung f	—	blessure f	ferita f	herida f
injuste (F)	ungerecht	unjust	—	ingiusto(a)	injusto(a)
injustice (E)	Ungerechtigkeit f	—	injustice f	ingiustizia f	injusticia f
injustice[1] (F)	Ungerechtigkeit f	injustice	—	ingiustizia f	injusticia f
injustice[2] (F)	Unrecht n	wrong	—	torto m	injusticia f
injusticia[1] (Es)	Unrecht n	wrong	injustice f	torto m	—
injusticia[2] (Es)	Ungerechtigkeit f	injustice	injustice f	ingiustizia f	—
injusto (Es)	ungerecht	unjust	injuste	ingiusto(a)	—
Inland (D)	—	inland	intérieur m	territorio nazionale m	territorio nacional m
inland (E)	Inland n	—	intérieur m	territorio nazionale m	territorio nacional m
in love (E)	verliebt	—	amoureux(-euse)	innamorato(a)	enamorado(a)
in mezzo[1] (I)	dazwischen	in between	entre	—	entre
in mezzo[2] (I)	mitten	in the middle	au milieu	—	en medio
in mezzo a (I)	inmitten	in the middle of	au milieu de	—	en medio de
inmitten (D)	—	in the middle of	au milieu de	in mezzo a	en medio de
inmoral (Es)	unanständig	indecent	indécent(e)	indecente	—

	D	E	F	I	Es
inmóvil (Es)	bewegungslos	motionless	immobile	immobile	—
inn (E)	Wirtshaus *n*	—	auberge *f*	osteria *f*	restaurante *m*
innalzare (I)	erhöhen	raise	augmenter	—	elevar
innamorarsi (I)	verlieben	fall in love	tomber amoureux(-euse)	—	enamorarse
innamorato (I)	verliebt	in love	amoureux(-euse)	—	enamorado(a)
innato (I)	angeboren	inborn	inné(e)	—	innato(a)
innato (Es)	angeboren	inborn	inné(e)	innato(a)	—
innattendu (F)	unerwartet	unexpected	—	inatteso(a)	inesperado(a)
inné (F)	angeboren	inborn	—	innato(a)	innato(a)
innen (D)	—	inside	à l'intérieur	dentro	dentro
Innenstadt (D)	—	town centre	centre ville *m*	centro città *m*	centro de la ciudad *m*
innere (D)	—	internal	intérieur(e)	interno(a)	interior
innerhalb (D)	—	within	à l'intérieur de	entro	dentro de
innocent (E)	unschuldig	—	innocent(e)	innocente	inocente/puro(a)
innocent (F)	unschuldig	innocent	—	innocente	inocente/puro(a)
innocente (I)	unschuldig	innocent	innocent(e)	—	inocente/puro(a)
inocente (Es)	unschuldig	innocent	innocent(e)	innocente	—
inofensivo (Es)	harmlos	harmless	inoffensif(-ive)	inoffensivo(a)	—
inoffensif (F)	harmlos	harmless	—	inoffensivo(a)	inofensivo(a)
inoffensivo (I)	harmlos	harmless	inoffensif(-ive)	—	inofensivo(a)
in ogni caso (I)	jedenfalls	in any case	en tout cas	—	en cualquier caso
inoltrare (I)	nachsenden	send on	faire suivre	—	enviar a la nueva dirección
inoltre (I)	außerdem	besides	en outre	—	además
inondation (F)	Überschwemmung *f*	flood	—	inondazione *f*	inundación *f*
inondazione (I)	Überschwemmung *f*	flood	inondation *f*	—	inundación *f*
inopportun (F)	unerwünscht	unwelcome	—	indesiderato(a)	indeseado(a)
inpaciente (Es)	ungeduldig	impatient	impatient(e)	impaziente	—
in parte (I)	teilweise	partly	en partie	—	en parte
in qualche modo[1] (I)	irgendwie	somehow	n'importe comment	—	de alguna manera
in qualche modo[2] (I)	irgend	at all/some	d'une façon ou d'une autre	—	cualquiera
in qualche posto (I)	irgendwo	somewhere	n'importe où	—	en alguna parte
inquiet (F)	unruhig	restless	—	inquieto(a)	intranquilo(a)
inquietar (Es)	beunruhigen	disturb	inquiéter	preoccupare	—
inquiéter (F)	beunruhigen	disturb	—	preoccupare	inquietar
inquieto (I)	unruhig	restless	inquiet(-ète)	—	intranquilo(a)
inquieto (Es)	hektisch	hectic	fébrile	nervoso(a)	—
inquilino (Es)	Mieter *m*	tenant	locataire *m*	inquilino *m*	—
inquilino (I)	Mieter *m*	tenant	locataire *m*	—	inquilino *m*
inquire (E)	erkundigen, sich	—	renseigner, se	informarsi	informarse
insalata (I)	Salat *m*	salad	salade *f*	—	ensalada *f*

	D	E	F	I	Es
in salita (I)	bergauf	uphill	en montant	—	cuesta arriba
inscribir (Es)	einschreiben	enrol	inscrire	iscrivere	—
inscrire (F)	einschreiben	enrol	—	iscrivere	inscribir
insect (E)	Insekt *n*	—	insecte *m*	insetto *m*	insecto *m*
insecte (F)	Insekt *n*	insect	—	insetto *m*	insecto *m*
insecto (Es)	Insekt *n*	insect	insecte *m*	insetto *m*	—
insegnare (I)	lehren	teach	enseigner	—	enseñar
inseguire (I)	verfolgen	pursue	poursuivre	—	perseguir
in seguito (I)	dann	then	ensuite	—	luego
in seguito a (I)	infolge	as a result of	par suite de	—	por
inseguro (Es)	unsicher	uncertain	incertain(e)	incerto(a)	—
Insekt (D)	—	insect	insecte *m*	insetto *m*	insecto *m*
Insel (D)	—	island	île *f*	isola *f*	isla *f*
insensato (I)	unsinnig	nonsensical	insensé(e)	—	absurdo(a)
insensé[1] (F)	unsinnig	nonsensical	—	insensato(a)	absurdo(a)
insensé[2] (F)	sinnlos	senseless	—	assurdo(a)	inútil
Inserat (D)	—	advertisement	annonce *f*	inserzione *f*	anuncio *m*
inserire (I)	stecken	insert	enfoncer	—	introducir
insert (E)	stecken	—	enfoncer	inserire	introducir
inserzione (I)	Inserat *n*	advertisement	annonce *f*	—	anuncio *m*
insetto (I)	Insekt *n*	insect	insecte *m*	—	insecto *m*
insgesamt (D)	—	altogether	dans l'ensemble	complessiva-mente	en suma
inside (E)	innen	—	à l'intérieur	dentro	dentro
insieme[1] (I)	Ganze(s) *n*	lot	le tout	—	todo *m*
insieme[2] (I)	miteinander	together	ensemble	—	juntos
insieme[3] (I)	zusammen	together	ensemble	—	juntos
insipido (I)	fade	dull	fade	—	soso(a)
insolent (F)	frech	cheeky	—	sfacciato(a)	atrevido(a)
insolito (I)	ungewöhnlich	unusual	exceptionnel(le)	—	desacostum-brado(a)
insopportabile (I)	unerträglich	unbearable	insupportable	—	inaguantable
inspector (E)	Kontrolleur *m*	—	contrôleur *m*	controllore *m*	controlador *m*
inspire (E)	begeistern	—	enthousiasmer	entusiasmare	entusiasmar
inspired (E)	begeistert	—	enthousiaste	entusiasta	entusiasta
instalarse[1] (Es)	einziehen	move in	emménager	prendere alloggio	—
instalarse[2] (Es)	niederlassen	settle down	installer, se	stabilirsi	—
installer, se (F)	niederlassen	settle down	—	stabilirsi	instalarse
instalment (E)	Rate *f*	—	quote-part *f*	rata *f*	plazo *m*
instant (F)	Augenblick *m*	moment	—	attimo *m*	momento *m*
instantané (F)	augenblicklich	instantaneous	—	instantaneo(a)	instantáneo(a)
instantaneo (I)	augenblicklich	immediately	instantané(e)	—	inmediato(a)
instantáneo (Es)	augenblicklich	at the moment	instantané(e)	immediato(a)	—
instantaneous (E)	augenblicklich	—	instantané(e)	instantaneo(a)	instantáneo(a)
instead[1] (E)	dafür	—	en échange	invece	en su lugar

	D	E	F	I	Es
instead² (E)	statt	—	au lieu de	invece di	en vez de
instead of (E)	anstatt	—	au lieu de	invece di	en vez de
instituto de enseñanza media (Es)	Gymnasium n	grammar school	lycée m	liceo m	—
instruct (E)	beauftragen	—	charger de	incaricare	encargar
instruir (Es)	ausbilden	educate	former	addestrare	—
Instrument (D)	—	instrument	instrument m	strumento m	instrumento m
instrument (E)	Instrument n	—	instrument m	strumento m	instrumento m
instrument (F)	Instrument n	instrument	—	strumento m	instrumento m
instrumento (Es)	Instrument n	instrument	instrument m	strumento m	—
in su (I)	aufwärts	upwards	vers le haut	—	hacia arriba
insuccesso (I)	Mißerfolg m	failure	échec m	—	fracaso m
insufficient (E)	ungenügend	—	insuffisant(e)	insufficiente	insuficiente
insufficiente (I)	ungenügend	insufficient	insuffisant(e)	—	insuficiente
insuffisant (F)	ungenügend	insufficient	—	insufficiente	insuficiente
insuficiente (Es)	ungenügend	insufficient	insuffisant(e)	insufficiente	—
insult¹ (E)	beleidigen	—	offenser	offendere	ofender
insult² (E)	Beleidigung f	—	offense f	offesa f	ofensa f
insultar (Es)	schimpfen	scold	gronder	imprecare	—
insupportable (F)	unerträglich	unbearable	—	insopportabile	inaguantable
insurance (E)	Versicherung f	—	assurance f	assicurazione f	seguro m
insurrezione (I)	Aufstand m	rebellion	soulèvement m	—	revuelta f
inszenieren (D)	—	stage	mettre en scène	mettere in scena	escenificar
inteligente¹ (Es)	intelligent	intelligent	intelligent(e)	intelligente	—
inteligente² (Es)	klug	clever	intelligent(e)	intelligente	—
intelligence (E)	Verstand m	—	intelligence f	intelligenza f	razón f
intelligence (F)	Verstand m	intelligence	—	intelligenza f	razón f
intelligent (D)	—	intelligent	intelligent(e)	intelligente	inteligente
intelligent (E)	intelligent	—	intelligent(e)	intelligente	inteligente
intelligent¹ (F)	intelligent	intelligent	—	intelligente	inteligente
intelligent² (F)	klug	clever	—	intelligente	inteligente
intelligente¹ (I)	intelligent	intelligent	intelligent(e)	—	inteligente
intelligente² (I)	klug	clever	intelligent(e)	—	inteligente
intelligenza (I)	Verstand m	intelligence	intelligence f	—	razón f
in tempo (I)	rechtzeitig	in time	à temps	—	a tiempo
intención¹ (Es)	Absicht f	intention	intention f	intenzione f	—
intención² (Es)	Ziel n	goal	but m	meta f	—
intencionado (Es)	bewußt	deliberate	délibéré(e)	intenzionale	—
intend¹ (E)	beabsichtigen	—	avoir l'intention de	avere (l')intenzione di	proyectar
intend² (E)	vorhaben	—	avoir l'intention de	avere intenzione di	tener la intención de
intention (E)	Absicht f	—	intention f	intenzione f	intención f
intention (F)	Absicht f	intention	—	intenzione f	intención f

	D	E	F	I	Es
intentionally (E)	absichtlich	—	exprès	apposta	adrede
intento (Es)	Versuch *m*	try	essai *m*	tentativo *m*	—
intenzionale (I)	bewußt	deliberate	délibéré(e)	—	intencionado(a)
intenzione (I)	Absicht *f*	intention	intention *f*	—	intención *f*
interamente (I)	restlos	completely	complètement	—	totalmente
interdire (F)	untersagen	forbid	—	proibire	prohibir
interdit (F)	verboten	forbidden	—	vietato(a)	prohibido(a)
interés (Es)	Interesse *n*	interest	intérêt *m*	interesse *m*	—
interesante (Es)	interessant	interesting	intéressant(e)	interessante	—
interesar (Es)	interessieren	interest	intéresser	interessare	—
interessant (D)	—	interesting	intéressant(e)	interessante	interesante
intéressant (F)	interessant	interesting	—	interessante	interesante
interessante (I)	interessant	interesting	intéressant(e)	—	interesante
interessare (I)	interessieren	interest	intéresser	—	interesar
interessarsi di (I)	kümmern, sich	look after	›occuper de, se	—	ocuparse de
Interesse (D)	—	interest	intérêt *m*	interesse *m*	interés *m*
interesse (I)	Interesse *n*	interest	intérêt *m*	—	interés *m*
intéresser (F)	interessieren	interest	—	interessare	interesar
interessieren (D)	—	interest	intéresser	interessare	interesar
interest[1] (E)	interessieren	—	intéresser	interessare	interesar
interest[2] (E)	Interesse *n*	—	intérêt *m*	interesse *m*	interés *m*
interesting (E)	interessant	—	intéressant(e)	interessante	interesante
intérêt (F)	Interesse *n*	interest	—	interesse *m*	interés *m*
interference (E)	Störung *f*	—	trouble *m*	disturbo *m*	molestia *f*
intérieur[1] (F)	innere	internal	—	interno(a)	interior
intérieur[2] (F)	Inland *n*	inland	—	territorio nazionale *m*	territorio nacional *m*
interior (Es)	innere	internal	intérieur(e)	interno(a)	—
intermediate landing (E)	Zwischenlandung *f*	—	escale *f*	scalo intermedio *m*	escala *f*
internacional (Es)	international	international	international(e)	internazionale	—
internado (Es)	Internat *n*	boarding school	internat *m*	collegio *m*	—
internal (E)	innere	—	intérieur(e)	interno(a)	interior
Internat (D)	—	boarding school	internat *m*	collegio *m*	internado *m*
internat (F)	Internat *n*	boarding school	—	collegio *m*	internado *m*
international (D)	—	international	international(e)	internazionale	internacional
international (E)	international	—	international(e)	internazionale	internacional
international (F)	international	international	—	internazionale	internacional
internazionale (I)	international	international	international(e)	—	internacional
interno (I)	innere	internal	intérieur(e)	—	interior
intero (I)	ganz	whole	tout(e)	—	entero(a)
intérprete (Es)	Dolmetscher *m*	interpreter	interprète *m*	interprete *m*	—
interprete (I)	Dolmetscher *m*	interpreter	interprète *m*	—	intérprete *m(f)*
interprète (F)	Dolmetscher *m*	interpreter	—	interprete *m*	intérprete *m(f)*
interpreter (E)	Dolmetscher *m*	—	interprète *m*	interprete *m*	intérprete *m*

	D	E	F	I	Es
interrompere (I)	unterbrechen	interrupt	interrompre	—	interrumpir
interrompre (F)	unterbrechen	interrupt	—	interrompere	interrumpir
interrumpir (Es)	unterbrechen	interrupt	interrompre	interrompere	—
interrupción (Es)	Unterbrechung f	interruption	interruption f	interruzione f	—
interrupt (E)	unterbrechen	—	interrompre	interrompere	interrumpir
interrupteur (F)	Lichtschalter m	light switch	—	inerruttore m	interruptor m
interruption (E)	Unterbrechung f	—	interruption f	interruzione f	interrupción f
interruption (F)	Unterbrechung f	interruption	—	interruzione f	interrupción f
interruptor (Es)	Lichtschalter m	light switch	interrupteur m	interruttore m	—
interruttore (I)	Lichtschalter m	light switch	interrupteur m	—	interruptor m
interruzione (I)	Unterbrechung f	interruption	interruption f	—	interrupción f
intersecting road (E)	Querstraße f	—	rue transversale f	traversa f	travesía f
intersection (F)	Kreuzung f	crossing	—	incrocio m	cruce m
intervene (E)	eingreifen	—	intervenir	intervenire	intervenir
intervenir (Es)	eingreifen	intervene	intervenir	intervenire	—
intervenir (F)	eingreifen	intervene	—	intervenire	intervenir
intervenire (I)	eingreifen	intervene	intervenir	—	intervenir
Interview (D)	—	interview	interview f	intervista f	entrevista f
interview (E)	Interview n	—	interview f	intervista f	entrevista f
interview (F)	Interview n	interview	—	intervista f	entrevista f
intervista (I)	Interview n	interview	interview f	—	entrevista f
intestin (F)	Darm m	intestine	—	intestino m	intestino m
intestine (E)	Darm m	—	intestin m	intestino m	intestino m
intestino (Es)	Darm m	intestine	intestin m	intestino m	—
intestino (I)	Darm m	intestine	intestin m	—	intestino m
in the afternoon (E)	nachmittags	—	l'après-midi	di pomeriggio	por la tarde
in the evening (E)	abends	—	le soir m	di sera	por la tarde
in the middle (E)	mitten	—	au milieu	in mezzo	en medio
in the middle of (E)	inmitten	—	au milieu de	in mezzo a	en medio de
in the morning (E)	vormittags	—	le matin	di mattina	por la mañana
in time (E)	rechtzeitig	—	à temps	in tempo	a tiempo
into one another (E)	ineinander	—	l'un dans l'autre	l'uno nell'altro	uno en otro
intorno (I)	herum	around	autour	—	alrededor
intorno a (I)	um	at/around	autour de/à	—	alrededor de/a las
intranquilo (Es)	unruhig	restless	inquiet(-ète)	inquieto(a)	—
intraprendere (I)	unternehmen	undertake	entreprendre	—	emprender
introducción (Es)	Einleitung f	introduction	introduction f	introduzione f	—
introduce (E)	vorstellen	—	présenter	presentare	presentar
introducir (Es)	stecken	insert	enfoncer	inserire	—
introduction (E)	Einleitung f	—	introduction f	introduzione f	introducción f
introduction (F)	Einleitung f	introduction	—	introduzione f	introducción f
introduzione (I)	Einleitung f	introduction	introduction f	—	introducción f
inundación (Es)	Überschwemmung f	flood	inondation f	inondazione f	—

	D	E	F	I	Es
inútil[1] (Es)	nutzlos	useless	inutile	inutile	—
inútil[2] (Es)	sinnlos	senseless	insensé(e)	assurdo(a)	—
inútil[3] (Es)	unnötig	unnecessary	inutile	inutile	—
inútil[4] (Es)	untauglich	unfit	incapable	incapace	—
inútil[5] (Es)	zwecklos	pointless	inutile	inutile	—
inutile[1] (F)	nutzlos	useless	—	inutile	inútil
inutile[2] (F)	unnötig	unnecessary	—	inutile	inútil
inutile[3] (F)	zwecklos	pointless	—	inutile	inútil
inutile[3] (I)	zwecklos	pointless	inutile	—	inútil
inutile[2] (I)	nutzlos	useless	inutile	—	inútil
inutile[3] (I)	unnötig	unnecessary	inutile	—	inútil
invalid (E)	ungültig	—	non valable	non valido(a)	caducado(a)
invece (I)	dafür	instead	en échange	—	en su lugar
invece di[1] (I)	anstatt	instead of	au lieu de	—	en vez de
invece di[2] (I)	statt	instead	au lieu de	—	en vez de
invent (E)	erfinden	—	inventer	inventare	inventar
inventar (Es)	erfinden	invent	inventer	inventare	—
inventare (I)	erfinden	invent	inventer	—	inventar
inventer (F)	erfinden	invent	—	inventare	inventar
inverno (I)	Winter m	winter	hiver m	—	invierno m
inverso (I)	umgekehrt	vice versa	vice versa	—	contrario(a)
investigar (Es)	forschen	research	rechercher	ricercare	—
investire (I)	überfahren	run over	écraser	—	atropellar
inviare (I)	schicken	send	envoyer	—	mandar
invidia (I)	Neid m	envy	jalousie f	—	envidia f
invidiare (I)	beneiden	envy	envier	—	envidiar
invidioso (I)	neidisch	envious	envieux(-euse)	—	envidioso(a)
invierno (Es)	Winter m	winter	hiver m	inverno m	—
invitación (Es)	Einladung f	invitation	invitation f	invito m	—
invitado (Es)	Gast m	guest	hôte m	ospite m	—
invitar (Es)	einladen	invite	inviter	invitare	—
invitare[1] (I)	auffordern	ask	inviter	—	exigir
invitare[2] (I)	einladen	invite	inviter	—	invitar
invitation (E)	Einladung f	—	invitation f	invito m	invitación f
invitation (F)	Einladung f	invitation	—	invito m	invitación f
invite (E)	einladen	—	inviter	invitare	invitar
inviter[1] (F)	auffordern	ask	—	invitare	exigir
inviter[2] (F)	einladen	invite	—	invitare	invitar
invito (I)	Einladung f	invitation	invitation f	—	invitación f
invraisemblable (F)	unwahrscheinlich	unlikely	—	improbabile	improbable
inyección (Es)	Spritze f	injection	piqûre f	iniezione f	—
inzwischen (D)	—	meanwhile	entretemps	frattanto	mientras tanto
io (I)	ich	I	je/moi	—	yo
ir de compras (Es)	einkaufen gehen	go shopping	faire les courses	fare la spesa	—

	D	E	F	I	Es
ir de paseo (Es)	spazierengehen	go for a walk	promener, se	passeggiare	—
irgend (D)	—	at all/some	d'une façon ou d'une autre	in qualche modo	cualquiera
irgendein (D)	—	some/any	quelconque	qualcuno(a)	cualquiera
irgend etwas (D)	—	something	n'importe quoi	qualsiasi cosa	algo
irgend jemand (D)	—	somebody	n'importe qui	qualcuno	alguno(a)
irgendwie (D)	—	somehow	n'importe comment	in qualche modo	de alguna manera
irgendwo (D)	—	somewhere	n'importe où	in qualche posto	en alguna parte
iron¹ (E)	bügeln	—	repasser	stirare	planchar
iron² (E)	Bügeleisen *n*	—	fer à repasser *m*	ferro da stiro *m*	plancha *f*
iron³ (E)	Eisen *n*	—	fer *m*	ferro *m*	hierro *m*
irregolare (I)	unregelmäßig	irregular	irrégulier(-ère)	—	irregular
irregular (E)	unregelmäßig	—	irrégulier(-ère)	irregolare	irregular
irregular (Es)	unregelmäßig	irregular	irrégulier(-ère)	irregolare	—
irrégulier (F)	unregelmäßig	irregular	—	irregolare	irregular
irren (D)	—	be mistaken	tromper, se	sbagliare	equivocarse
irrésolu (F)	unentschlossen	undecided	—	indeciso(a)	irresoluto(a)
irresoluto (Es)	unentschlossen	undecided	irrésolu(e)	indeciso(a)	—
Irrtum (D)	—	mistake	erreur *f*	errore *m*	error *m*
irse de viaje (Es)	verreisen	go away	partir en voyage	partire in viaggio	—
iscrivere (I)	einschreiben	enrol	inscrire	—	inscribir
isla (Es)	Insel *f*	island	île *f*	isola *f*	—
island (E)	Insel *f*	—	île *f*	isola *f*	isla *f*
isola (I)	Insel *f*	island	île *f*	—	isla *f*
istituto superiore (I)	Hochschule *f*	university	université *f*	—	escuela superior *f*
istruzione (I)	Bildung *f*	education	éducation *f*	—	educación *f*
Italia (Es)	Italien *n*	Italy	Italie *f*	Italia *f*	—
Italia (I)	Italien *n*	Italy	Italie *f*	—	Italia *f*
Italian¹ (E)	italienisch	—	italien(ne)	italiano(a)	italiano(a)
Italian² (E)	Italiener *m*	—	Italien *m*	italiano *m*	italiano *m*
italiano¹ (Es)	Italiener *m*	Italian	Italien *m*	italiano *m*	—
italiano² (Es)	italienisch	Italian	italien(ne)	italiano(a)	—
italiano¹ (I)	italienisch	Italian	italien(ne)	—	italiano(a)
italiano² (I)	Italiener *m*	Italian	Italien *m*	—	italiano *m*
Italie (F)	Italien *n*	Italy	—	Italia *f*	Italia *f*
Italien (D)	—	Italy	Italie *f*	Italia *f*	Italia *f*
italien¹ (F)	italienisch	Italian	—	italiano(a)	italiano(a)
Italien² (F)	Italiener *m*	Italian	—	italiano *m*	italiano *m*
Italiener (D)	—	Italian	Italien *m*	italiano *m*	italiano *m*
italienisch (D)	—	Italian	italien(ne)	italiano(a)	italiano(a)
Italy (E)	Italien *n*	—	Italie *f*	Italia *f*	Italia *f*
itch (E)	jucken	—	démanger	prudere	picar
itinéraire (F)	Reiseroute *f*	route	—	itinerario *m*	itinerario *m*
itinerario (Es)	Reiseroute *f*	route	itinéraire *m*	itinerario *m*	—

	D	E	F	I	Es
itinerario (I)	Reiseroute f	route	itinéraire m	—	itinerario m
ja (D)	—	yes	oui	sì	sí
jabón (Es)	Seife f	soap	savon m	sapone m	—
Jacht (D)	—	yacht	yacht m	panfilo m	yate m
Jacke (D)	—	jacket	veste f	giacca f	chaqueta f
jacket (E)	Jacke f	—	veste f	giacca f	chaqueta f
Jagd (D)	—	hunt	chasse f	caccia f	caza f
jagen (D)	—	hunt	chasser	cacciare	cazar
Jahr (D)	—	year	année f	anno m	año m
Jahreszeit (D)	—	time of year	saison f	stagione f	estación del año f
Jahrhundert (D)	—	century	siècle m	secolo m	siglo m
jährlich (D)	—	annual	annuel(le)	annuale	anualmente
Jahrmarkt (D)	—	fair	foire f	fiera f	feria f
jalousie¹ (F)	Eifersucht f	jealousy	—	gelosia f	celos m pl
jalousie² (F)	Neid m	envy	—	invidia f	envidia f
jam (E)	Marmelade f	—	confiture f	marmellata f	mermelada f
jamais (F)	jemals	ever	—	mai	jamás
jamás¹ (Es)	jemals	ever	jamais	mai	—
jamás² (Es)	niemals	never	ne...jamais	mai	—
jambe (F)	Bein n	leg	—	gamba f	pierna f
jambon (F)	Schinken m	ham	—	prosciutto m	jamón m
jamón (Es)	Schinken m	ham	jambon m	prosciutto m	—
Januar (D)	—	January	janvier m	gennaio m	enero m
January (E)	Januar m	—	janvier m	gennaio m	enero m
janvier (F)	Januar m	January	—	gennaio m	enero m
jaqueca (Es)	Migräne f	migraine	migraine f	emicrania f	—
jardín (Es)	Garten m	garden	jardin m	giardino m	—
jardin (F)	Garten m	garden	—	giardino m	jardín m
jardín de infancia (Es)	Kindergarten m	nursery school	jardin d'enfants m	asilo (infantile) m	—
jardin d'enfants (F)	Kindergarten m	nursery school	—	asilo (infantile) m	jardín de infancia m
jardinero (Es)	Gärtner m	gardener	jardinier m	giardiniere m	—
jardinier (F)	Gärtner m	gardener	—	giardiniere m	jardinero m
jarro (Es)	Krug m	jug	cruche f	brocca f	—
jatte (F)	Schüssel f	bowl	—	scodella f	fuente f
jaula (Es)	Käfig m	cage	cage f	gabbia f	—
jaune (F)	gelb	yellow	—	giallo(a)	amarillo(a)
je (F)	ich	I	—	io	yo
jealousy (E)	Eifersucht f	—	jalousie f	gelosia f	celos m pl
jede (D)	—	each/every	chaque	ogni, ognuno	cada
jedenfalls (D)	—	in any case	en tout cas	in ogni caso	en cualquier caso
jedesmal (D)	—	each time	chaque fois	ogni volta	cada vez
jedoch (D)	—	however	cependant	tuttavia	sin embargo
jefe (Es)	Chef m	boss	patron m	capo m	—

	D	E	F	I	Es
jemals (D)	—	ever	jamais	mai	jamás
jemand (D)	—	somebody	quelqu'un	qualcuno	alguien
jene (D)	—	that	ce, cette	quello(a)	aquella, aquel, aquello
jenseits (D)	—	beyond	de l'autre côté	al di là	al otro lado
jersey (Es)	Pullover *m*	pullover	pull-over *m*	pullover *m*	—
jetzt (D)	—	now	maintenant	adesso	ahora
jeu (F)	Spiel *n*	game	—	gioco *m*	juego *m*
jeudi (F)	Donnerstag *m*	Thursday	—	giovedì *m*	jueves *m*
jeune (F)	jung	young	—	giovane	joven
jeune fille (F)	Mädchen *n*	girl	—	ragazza *f*	chica *f*
jeûner (F)	fasten	fast	—	digiunare	ayunar
jeunesse (F)	Jugend *f*	youth	—	gioventù *f*	juventud *f*
jeux olympiques (F)	Olympische Spiele *pl*	Olympic Games	—	Olimpiadi *f pl*	Juegos Olímpicos *m pl*
Jew (E)	Jude *m*	—	juif *m*	ebreo *m*	judío *m*
jewel (E)	Juwel *n*	—	joyau *m*	gioiello *m*	joya *f*
jeweller (E)	Juwelier *m*	—	bijoutier *m*	gioielliere *m*	joyero *m*
jewellery (E)	Schmuck *m*	—	bijoux *m pl*	gioielli *m pl*	joyas *f pl*
Joghurt (D)	—	yogurt	yaourt *m*	yoghurt *m*	yogur(t) *m*
Johannisbeere (D)	—	currant	groseille *f*	ribes *m*	grosella *f*
joie (F)	Freude *f*	joy	—	gioia *f*	alegría *f*
joke[1] (E)	spaßen	—	plaisanter	scherzare	bromear
joke[2] (E)	Scherz *m*	—	plaisanterie *f*	scherzo *m*	broma *f*
joke[3] (E)	Witz *m*	—	plaisanterie *f*	barzelletta *f*	chiste *m*
joli[1] (F)	hübsch	pretty	—	carino(a)	bonito(a)
joli[2] (F)	nett	nice	—	carino(a)	agradable
joue (F)	Wange *f*	cheek	—	guancia *f*	mejilla *f*
jouer (F)	spielen	play	—	giocare	jugar
joueur (F)	Spieler *m*	player	—	giocatore *m*	jugador *m*
jouir (F)	genießen	enjoy	—	godere	disfrutar
jour (F)	Tag *m*	day	—	giorno *m*	día *m*
jour de repos (F)	Ruhetag *m*	closing day	—	giorno di riposo *m*	día de descanso *m*
jour férié (F)	Feiertag *m*	holiday	—	giorno festivo *m*	día de fiesta *m*
journal (F)	Zeitung *f*	newspaper	—	giornale *m*	periódico *m*
Journalist (D)	—	journalist	journaliste *m*	giornalista *m*	periodista *m*
journalist (E)	Journalist *m*	—	journaliste *m*	giornalista *m*	periodista *m*
journaliste (F)	Journalist *m*	journalist	—	giornalista *m*	periodista *m*
journey[1] (E)	Fahrt *f*	—	voyage *m*	viaggio *m*	viaje *m*
journey[2] (E)	Reise *f*	—	voyage *m*	viaggio *m*	viaje *m*
jour ouvrable (F)	Werktag *m*	working day	—	giorno feriale *m*	día laborable *m*
joven (Es)	jung	young	jeune	giovane	—
joy (E)	Freude *f*	—	joie *f*	gioia *f*	alegría *f*
joya (Es)	Juwel *n*	jewel	joyau *m*	gioiello *m*	—
joyas (Es)	Schmuck *m*	jewellery	bijoux *m pl*	gioielli *m pl*	—

	D	E	F	I	Es
joyau (F)	Juwel *n*	jewel	—	gioiello *m*	joya *f*
joyero (Es)	Juwelier *m*	jeweller	bijoutier *m*	gioielliere *m*	—
joyeux (F)	froh	glad	—	lieto(a)	contento(a)
jubeln (D)	—	rejoice	pousser des cris de joie	giubilare	dar gritos de alegría
jucken (D)	—	itch	démanger	prudere	picar
Jude (D)	—	Jew	juif *m*	ebreo *m*	judío *m*
judge[1] (E)	beurteilen	—	juger	giudicare	juzgar
judge[2] (E)	Richter *m*	—	juge *m*	giudice *m*	juez *m*
judge[3] (E)	urteilen	—	juger	giudicare	juzgar
judgement (E)	Urteil *n*	—	jugement *m*	giudizio *m*	juicio *m*
judía (Es)	Bohne *f*	bean	haricot *m*	fagiolo *m*	—
judío (Es)	Jude *m*	Jew	juif *m*	ebreo *m*	—
juego (Es)	Spiel *n*	game	jeu *m*	gioco *m*	—
Juegos Olímpicos (Es)	Olympische Spiele *pl*	Olympic Games	jeux olympiques *m pl*	Olimpiadi *f pl*	—
jueves (Es)	Donnerstag *m*	Thursday	jeudi *m*	giovedì *m*	—
juez (Es)	Richter *m*	judge	juge *m*	giudice *m*	—
jug (E)	Krug *m*	—	cruche *f*	brocca *f*	jarro *m*
jugador (Es)	Spieler *m*	player	joueur *m*	giocatore *m*	—
jugar (Es)	spielen	play	jouer	giocare	—
juge (F)	Richter *m*	judge	—	giudice *m*	juez *m*
jugement (F)	Urteil *n*	judgement	—	giudizio *m*	juicio *m*
Jugend (D)	—	youth	jeunesse *f*	gioventù *f*	juventud *f*
juger[1] (F)	beurteilen	judge	—	giudicare	juzgar
juger[2] (F)	urteilen	judge	—	giudicare	juzgar
juice (E)	Saft *m*	—	jus *m*	succo *m*	zumo *m*
juicio (Es)	Urteil *n*	judgement	jugement *m*	giudizio *m*	—
juif (F)	Jude *m*	Jew	—	ebreo *m*	judío *m*
juillet (F)	Juli *m*	July	—	luglio *m*	julio *m*
juin (F)	Juni *m*	June	—	giugno *m*	junio *m*
Juli (D)	—	July	juillet *m*	luglio *m*	julio *m*
julio (Es)	Juli *m*	July	juillet *m*	luglio *m*	—
July (E)	Juli *m*	—	juillet *m*	luglio *m*	julio *m*
jumeaux (F)	Zwillinge *pl*	twins	—	gemelli *m pl*	gemelos *m pl*
jumelles (F)	Fernglas *n*	binoculars	—	cannocchiale *m*	gemelos *m pl*
jump[1] (E)	hüpfen	—	sautiller	saltellare	saltar
jump[2] (E)	springen	—	sauter	saltare	saltar
jump[3] (E)	Sprung *m*	—	saut *m*	salto *m*	salto *m*
June (E)	Juni *m*	—	juin *m*	giugno *m*	junio *m*
jung (D)	—	young	jeune	giovane	joven
Junge (D)	—	boy	garçon *m*	ragazzo *m*	chico *m*
Jungfrau (D)	—	virgin	vierge *f*	vergine *f*	virgen *f*
Junggeselle (D)	—	bachelor	célibataire *m*	scapolo *m*	soltero *m*
Juni (D)	—	June	juin *m*	giugno *m*	junio *m*

	D	E	F	I	Es
junio (Es)	Juni *m*	June	juin *m*	giugno *m*	—
junto (Es)	an	at/on/by	à/près de	a/in/su	—
juntos¹ (Es)	gemeinsam	together	ensemble	comune	—
juntos² (Es)	miteinander	together	ensemble	insieme	—
juntos³ (Es)	zusammen	together	ensemble	insieme	—
jupe (F)	Rock *m*	skirt	—	gonna *f*	falda *f*
jupon (F)	Unterrock *m*	slip	—	sottoveste *f*	combinación *f*
Jura (D)	—	law	droit *m*	giurisprudenza *f*	derecho *m*
jurar (Es)	schwören	swear	jurer	giurare	—
jurer (F)	schwören	swear	—	giurare	jurar
jus (F)	Saft *m*	juice	—	succo *m*	zumo *m*
jusqu'à¹ (F)	bis	until	—	fino a	hasta
jusqu'à² (F)	hin	there	—	là	hacia allá/hasta
jusqu'à présent (F)	bisher	so far	—	finora	hasta ahora
just (E)	gerecht	—	juste	giusto(a)	justo(a)
juste (F)	gerecht	just	—	giusto(a)	justo(a)
juste (F)	richtig	correct	—	giusto(a)	correcto(a)
just now (E)	soeben	—	à l'instant même	poco fa	ahora mismo
justo (Es)	gerecht	just	juste	giusto(a)	—
juventud (Es)	Jugend *f*	youth	jeunesse *f*	gioventù *f*	—
Juwel (D)	—	jewel	joyau *m*	gioiello *m*	joya *f*
Juwelier (D)	—	jeweller	bijoutier *m*	gioielliere *m*	joyero *m*
juzgar¹ (Es)	beurteilen	judge	juger	giudicare	—
juzgar² (Es)	urteilen	judge	juger	giudicare	—
Kabel (D)	—	cable	câble *m*	cavo *m*	cable *m*
Kabine (D)	—	cabin	cabine *f*	cabina *f*	cabina *f*
Käfer (D)	—	beetle	coléoptère *m*	coleottero *m*	escarabajo *m*
Kaffee (D)	—	coffee	café *m*	caffè *m*	café *m*
Käfig (D)	—	cage	cage *f*	gabbia *f*	jaula *f*
kahl (D)	—	bald	chauve	calvo(a)	calvo(a)
Kahn (D)	—	barge	barque *f*	chiatta *f*	barcaza *f*
Kaiser (D)	—	emperor	empereur *m*	imperatore *m*	emperador *m*
Kalb (D)	—	calf	veau *m*	vitello *m*	ternera *f*
Kalender (D)	—	calendar	calendrier *m*	calendario *m*	calendario *m*
kalt (D)	—	cold	froid(e)	freddo(a)	frío(a)
Kamm (D)	—	comb	peigne *m*	pettine *m*	peine *m*
kämmen (D)	—	comb	peigner	pettinare	peinar
kämpfen (D)	—	fight	battre, se	combattere	luchar
Kanada (D)	—	Canada	Canada *m*	Canada *m*	Canadá *m*
Kapelle¹ (D)	—	chapel	chapelle *f*	cappella *f*	capilla *f*
Kapelle² (D)	—	band	orchestre *m*	banda *f*	banda *f*
Kapital (D)	—	capital	capital *m*	capitale *m*	capital *m*
Kapitän (D)	—	captain	capitaine *m*	capitano *m*	capitán *m*
Kapitel (D)	—	chapter	chapitre *m*	capitolo *m*	capítulo *m*

	D	E	F	I	Es
kaputt (D)	—	broken	cassé(e)	rotto(a)	roto(a)
Kapuze (D)	—	hood	capuchon *m*	cappuccio *m*	capucha *f*
kariert (D)	—	checked	à carreaux	a quadretti	a cuadros
Karneval (D)	—	carnival	carnaval *m*	carnevale *m*	carnaval *m*
Karosserie (D)	—	body	carrosserie *f*	carrozzeria *f*	carrocería *f*
Karotte (D)	—	carrot	carotte *f*	carota *f*	zanahoria *f*
Karriere (D)	—	career	carrière *f*	carriera *f*	carrera *f*
Karte (D)	—	card	carte *f*	cartolina *f*	postal *f*
Kartoffel (D)	—	potato	pomme de terre *f*	patata *f*	patata *f*
Karton (D)	—	cardboard box	carton *m*	cartone *m*	cartón *m*
Karussell (D)	—	roundabout	manège *m*	giostra *f*	tíovivo *m*
Käse (D)	—	cheese	fromage *m*	formaggio *m*	queso *m*
Kasino (D)	—	club	casino *m*	casinò *m*	casino *m*
Kasse (D)	—	till	caisse *f*	cassa *f*	caja *f*
Kassette (D)	—	cassette	cassette *f*	cassetta *f*	cassette *f*
kassieren (D)	—	take	encaisser	incassare	cobrar
Kathedrale (D)	—	cathedral	cathédrale *f*	cattedrale *f*	catedral *f*
katholisch (D)	—	catholic	catholique	cattolico(a)	católico(a)
Katze (D)	—	cat	chat *m*	gatto *m*	gato *m*
kauen (D)	—	chew	mâcher	masticare	masticar
Kauf (D)	—	purchase	achat *m*	acquisto *m*	compra *f*
kaufen (D)	—	buy	acheter	comprare	comprar
Käufer (D)	—	buyer	acheteur *m*	acquirente *m*	comprador *m*
Kaufhaus (D)	—	department store	grand magasin *m*	grande magazzino *m*	grandes almacenes *m pl*
Kaufmann (D)	—	businessman	commerçant *m*	commerciante *m*	comerciante *m*
kaum (D)	—	hardly	à peine	appena	apenas
keen (E)	eifrig	—	zélé(e)	diligente	diligente
keep[1] (E)	aufbewahren	—	garder	conservare	guardar
keep[2] (E)	behalten	—	garder	tenere	retener
keep[3] (E)	einbehalten	—	retenir	trattenere	retener
kehren (D)	—	sweep	balayer	scopare	barrer
keine (D)	—	none	aucun(e)	nessuno(a)	ninguno(a)
keineswegs (D)	—	not at all	pas du tout	non affatto	en modo alguno
Keks (D)	—	biscuit	biscuit *m*	biscotto *m*	galleta *f*
Keller (D)	—	cellar	cave *f*	cantina *f*	sótano *m*
Kellner (D)	—	waiter	garçon *m*	cameriere *m*	camarero *m*
kennen (D)	—	know	connaître	conoscere	conocer
Kenntnis (D)	—	knowledge	connaissance *f*	conoscenza *f*	conocimiento *m*
Kern (D)	—	pip	noyau *m*	nocciolo *m*	hueso *m*
Kerze (D)	—	candle	bougie *f*	candela *f*	vela *f*
Kette (D)	—	chain	chaîne *f*	catena *f*	cadena *f*
key (E)	Schlüssel *m*	—	clé *f*	chiave *f*	llave *f*

	D	E	F	I	Es
keyhole (E)	Schlüsselloch *n*	—	trou de la serrure *m*	buco della chiave *m*	ojo de la cerradura *m*
kidney (E)	Niere *f*	—	rein *m*	rene *m*	riñón *m*
kill[1] (E)	töten	—	tuer	uccidere	matar
kill[2] (E)	umbringen	—	tuer	uccidere	matar
kilogram (E)	Kilogramm *n*	—	kilogramme *m*	chilogrammo *m*	kilógramo *m*
Kilogramm (D)	—	kilogram	kilogramme *m*	chilogrammo *m*	kilógramo *m*
kilogramme (F)	Kilogramm *n*	kilogram	—	chilogrammo *m*	kilógramo *m*
kilogramo (Es)	Kilogramm *n*	kilogram	kilogramme *m*	chilogrammo *m*	—
Kilometer (D)	—	kilometre	kilomètre *m*	chilometro *m*	kilómetro *m*
kilometre (E)	Kilometer *m*	—	kilomètre *m*	chilometro *m*	kilómetro *m*
kilomètre (F)	Kilometer *m*	kilometre	—	chilometro *m*	kilómetro *m*
kilómetro (Es)	Kilometer *m*	kilometre	kilomètre *m*	chilometro *m*	—
Kind (D)	—	child	enfant *m*	bambino *m*	niño *m*
kind (E)	liebenswürdig	—	aimable	gentile	gentil
Kindergarten (D)	—	nursery school	jardin d'enfants *m*	asilo (infantile) *m*	jardín de infancia *m*
Kindheit (D)	—	childhood	enfance *f*	infanzia *f*	niñez *f*
king (E)	König *m*	—	roi *m*	re *m*	rey *m*
Kinn (D)	—	chin	menton *m*	mento *m*	barbilla *f*
Kino (D)	—	cinema	cinéma *m*	cinema *m*	cine *m*
Kirche (D)	—	church	église *f*	chiesa *f*	iglesia *f*
Kirsche (D)	—	cherry	cerise *f*	ciliegia *f*	cereza *f*
kiss[1] (E)	küssen	—	embrasser	baciare	besar
kiss[2] (E)	Kuß *m*	—	baiser *m*	bacio *m*	beso *m*
Kissen (D)	—	cushion	coussin *m*	cuscino *m*	cojín *m*
Kiste (D)	—	box	caisse *f*	cassetta *f*	caja *f*
kitchen (E)	Küche *f*	—	cuisine *f*	cucina *f*	cocina *f*
Klage (D)	—	complaint	plainte *f*	lamento *m*	lamento *m*
Klang (D)	—	sound	son *m*	suono *m*	sonido *m*
klar (D)	—	clear	clair(e)	chiaro(a)	claro(a)
Klasse (D)	—	class	classe *f*	classe *f*	clase *f*
klatschen (D)	—	applaud	applaudir	battere le mani	aplaudir
Klavier (D)	—	piano	piano *m*	pianoforte *m*	piano *m*
kleben (D)	—	stick	coller	incollare	pegar
Klebstoff (D)	—	glue	colle *f*	colla *f*	adhesivo *m*
Kleid (D)	—	dress	robe *f*	vestito *m*	vestido *m*
kleiden (D)	—	dress	habiller	vestire	vestir
Kleiderschrank (D)	—	wardrobe	garde-robe *f*	armadio *m*	armario ropero *m*
Kleidung (D)	—	clothing	habits *m pl*	abbigliamento *m*	vestuario *m*
klein (D)	—	small/little	petit(e)	piccolo(a)	pequeño(a)
Kleingeld (D)	—	small change	monnaie *f*	spiccioli *m pl*	cambio *m*
klettern (D)	—	climb	grimper	arrampicarsi	escalar
Klima (D)	—	climate	climat *m*	clima *m*	clima *m*
Klinge (D)	—	blade	lame *f*	lama *f*	cuchilla *f*

	D	E	F	I	Es
Klingel (D)	—	bell	sonnette *f*	campanello *m*	timbre *m*
klingeln (D)	—	ring the bell	sonner	suonare	tocar el timbre
Klinik (D)	—	hospital	clinique *f*	clinica *f*	clínica *f*
klopfen (D)	—	knock	frapper	bussare	golpear
Klosett (D)	—	lavatory	cabinets *m pl*	gabinetto *m*	retrete *m*
Kloster (D)	—	monastery	couvent *m*	convento *m*	monasterio *m*
klug (D)	—	clever	intelligent(e)	intelligente	inteligente
knapp (D)	—	tight	étroit(e)	scarso(a)	escaso(a)
knee (E)	Knie *n*	—	genou *m*	ginocchio *m*	rodilla *f*
Kneipe (D)	—	pub	bistro *m*	osteria *f*	tasca *f*
Knie (D)	—	knee	genou *m*	ginocchio *m*	rodilla *f*
knife (E)	Messer *n*	—	couteau *m*	coltello *m*	cuchillo *m*
knipsen (D)	—	take a snap	photographier	scattare una foto	hacer una foto
knit (E)	stricken	—	tricoter	lavorare a maglia	hacer punto
Knoblauch (D)	—	garlic	ail *m*	aglio *m*	ajo *m*
Knöchel (D)	—	ankle	cheville *f*	caviglia *f*	tobillo *m*
Knochen (D)	—	bone	os *m*	osso *m*	hueso *m*
knock[1] (E)	klopfen	—	frapper	bussare	golpear
knock[2] (E)	pochen	—	frapper	battere	golpear
Knopf (D)	—	button	bouton *m*	bottone *m*	botón *m*
Knospe (D)	—	bud	bourgeon *m*	bocciolo *m*	yema *f*
knot (E)	Knoten *m*	—	nœud *m*	nodo *m*	nudo *m*
Knoten (D)	—	knot	nœud *m*	nodo *m*	nudo *m*
know[1] (E)	kennen	—	connaître	conoscere	conocer
know[2] (E)	wissen	—	savoir	sapere	saber
knowledge[1] (E)	Kenntnis *f*	—	connaissance *f*	conoscenza *f*	conocimiento *m*
knowledge[2] (E)	Wissen *n*	—	savoir *m*	sapere *m*	saber *m*
know one's way about (E)	auskennen, sich	—	connaître, s'y	conoscere	conocer a fondo
Koch (D)	—	cook	cuisinier *m*	cuoco *m*	cocinero *m*
kochen (D)	—	cook	cuire	cucinare	cocinar
Köchin (D)	—	cook	cuisinière *f*	cuoca *f*	cocinera *f*
Kochtopf (D)	—	saucepan	casserole *f*	pentola *f*	olla *f*
Koffer (D)	—	suitcase	valise *f*	valigia *f*	maleta *f*
Kofferraum (D)	—	boot	coffre *m*	portabagagli *m*	maletero *m*
Kohl (D)	—	cabbage	chou *m*	cavolo *m*	col *f*
Kohle (D)	—	coal	charbon *m*	carbone *m*	carbón *m*
komisch (D)	—	funny	drôle	comico(a)	cómico(a)
kommen (D)	—	come	venir	venire	venir
Komödie (D)	—	comedy	comédie *f*	commedia *f*	comedia *f*
kompliziert (D)	—	complicated	compliqué(e)	complicato(a)	complicado(a)
Komponist (D)	—	composer	compositeur *m*	compositore *m*	compositor *m*
Konditorei (D)	—	cake shop	pâtisserie *f*	pasticceria *f*	pastelería *f*
Konferenz (D)	—	conference	conférence *f*	conferenza *f*	conferencia *f*

	D	E	F	I	Es
König (D)	—	king	roi *m*	re *m*	rey *m*
Königin (D)	—	queen	reine *f*	regina *f*	reina *f*
können (D)	—	can	pouvoir	sapere	saber
Konsulat (D)	—	consulate	consulat *m*	consolato *m*	consulado *m*
Kontakt (D)	—	contact	contact *m*	contatto *m*	contacto *m*
Kontinent (D)	—	continent	continent *m*	continente *m*	continente *m*
Konto (D)	—	account	compte *m*	conto *m*	cuenta *f*
Kontrolle (D)	—	control	contrôle *m*	controllo *m*	control *m*
Kontrolleur (D)	—	inspector	contrôleur *m*	controllore *m*	controlador *m*
konzentrieren (D)	—	concentrate	concentrer	concentrare	concentrar
Konzert (D)	—	concert	concert *m*	concerto *m*	concierto *m*
Kopf (D)	—	head	tête *f*	testa *f*	cabeza *f*
Kopfkissen (D)	—	pillow	oreiller *m*	guanciale *m*	almohada *f*
Kopfschmerzen (D)	—	headache	mal de tête *m*	mal di testa *m*	dolor de cabeza *m*
Kopie (D)	—	copy	copie *f*	copia *f*	copia *f*
kopieren (D)	—	copy	copier	copiare	copiar
Korb (D)	—	basket	panier *m*	cesto *m*	cesta *f*
Korkenzieher (D)	—	corkscrew	tire-bouchon *m*	cavatappi *m*	sacacorchos *m*
Korn (D)	—	corn	grain *m*	grano *m*	semilla *f*
Körper (D)	—	body	corps *m*	corpo *m*	cuerpo *m*
korrekt (D)	—	correct	correct(e)	corretto(a)	correcto(a)
Korridor (D)	—	corridor	corridor *m*	corridoio *m*	pasillo *m*
Kost (D)	—	food	nourriture *f*	cibo *m*	alimento *m*
kostbar (D)	—	precious	précieux(-euse)	prezioso(a)	valioso(a)
kosten (D)	—	cost	coûter	costare	costar
Kosten (D)	—	expenses	coûts *m pl*	spese *f pl*	costas *f pl*
kostenlos (D)	—	free	gratuit(e)	gratuito(a)	gratis
köstlich (D)	—	delicious	savoureux(-euse)	squisito(a)	exquisito(a)
kostspielig (D)	—	expensive	coûteux(-euse)	costoso(a)	costoso(a)
Kostüm (D)	—	costume	costume *m*	tailleur *m*	vestido *m*
Kotelett (D)	—	cutlet	côtelette *f*	costoletta *f*	chuleta *f*
Krach (D)	—	noise	bruit *m*	chiasso *m*	ruido *m*
kräftig (D)	—	strong	fort(e)	forte	fuerte
Kraft (D)	—	strength	force *f*	forza *f*	fuerza *f*
Kragen (D)	—	collar	col *m*	colletto *m*	cuello *m*
krank (D)	—	ill	malade	malato(a)	enfermo(a)
Krankenhaus (D)	—	hospital	hôpital *m*	ospedale *m*	hospital *m*
Krankenpfleger (D)	—	nursing orderly	infirmier *m*	infermiere *m*	enfermero *m*
Kranken-schwester (D)	—	nurse	infirmière *f*	infermiera *f*	enfermera *f*
Krankenwagen (D)	—	ambulance	ambulance *f*	ambulanza *f*	ambulancia *f*
Krankheit (D)	—	illness	maladie *f*	malattia *f*	enfermedad *f*
Krawatte (D)	—	tie	cravate *f*	cravatta *f*	corbata *f*
Krebs[1] (D)	—	crayfish	écrevisse *f*	gambero *m*	cangrejo *m*

	D	E	F	I	Es
Krebs² (D)	—	cancer	cancer *m*	cancro *m*	cáncer *m*
Kredit (D)	—	credit	crédit *m*	credito *m*	crédito *m*
Kreis (D)	—	circle	cercle	cerchio *m*	círculo *m*
Kreislauf (D)	—	circulation	circulation *f*	circolazione *f*	circulación *f*
Kreuz (D)	—	cross	croix *f*	croce *f*	cruz *f*
Kreuzung (D)	—	crossing	intersection *f*	incrocio *m*	cruce *m*
Krieg (D)	—	war	guerre *f*	guerra *f*	guerra *f*
kritisieren (D)	—	criticize	critiquer	criticare	criticar
Krug (D)	—	jug	cruche *f*	brocca *f*	jarro *m*
krumm (D)	—	crooked	tordu(e)	storto(a)	torcido(a)
Kubikmeter (D)	—	cubic metre	mètre cube	metro cubo *m*	metro cúbico *m*
Küche (D)	—	kitchen	cuisine *f*	cucina *f*	cocina *f*
Kuchen (D)	—	cake	gâteau *m*	dolce *m*	pastel *m*
Kugelschreiber (D)	—	biro	stylo à bille *m*	biro *f*	bolígrafo *m*
Kuh (D)	—	cow	vache *f*	mucca *f*	vaca *f*
kühl (D)	—	cool	frais (fraîche)	fresco(a)	fresco(a)
Kühlschrank (D)	—	fridge	réfrigérateur *m*	frigorifero *m*	nevera *f*
Kultur (D)	—	culture	culture *f*	cultura *f*	cultura *f*
Kummer (D)	—	grief	chagrin *m*	dolore *m*	pesar *m*
kümmern, sich (D)	—	look after	occuper de, se	interessarsi di	ocuparse de
Kunde (D)	—	customer	client *m*	cliente *m*	cliente *m*
kündigen (D)	—	sack	résilier	licenziare	despedir
Kunst (D)	—	art	art *m*	arte *f*	arte *m*
Künstler (D)	—	artist	artiste *m*	artista *m*	artista *m*
künstlich (D)	—	artificial	artificiel(le)	artificiale	artificial
Kur (D)	—	treatment	cure *f*	cura *f*	cura *f*
Kurs (D)	—	rate	cours *m*	corso *m*	curso *m*
Kurve (D)	—	bend	virage *m*	curva *f*	curva *f*
kurz (D)	—	short	court(e)	corto(a)	corto(a)
kürzlich (D)	—	lately	récemment	recente	reciente
Kuß (D)	—	kiss	baiser *m*	bacio *m*	beso *m*
küssen (D)	—	kiss	embrasser	baciare	besar
Küste (D)	—	coast	côte *f*	costa *f*	costa *f*
la¹ (I)	dort	there	là/y	—	allí
là² (I)	hin	there	jusqu'à/ vers	—	hacia allá/ hasta
là¹ (F)	da	there	—	qui/là	allí
là² (F)	dort	there	—	là	allí
labbro (I)	Lippe *f*	lip	lèvre *f*	—	labio *m*
labio (Es)	Lippe *f*	lip	lèvre *f*	labbro *m*	—
lac (F)	See *m*	lake	—	lago *m*	lago *m*
lâche (F)	feig	cowardly	—	vile	cobarde
lächeln (D)	—	smile	sourire	sorridere	sonreír
Lächeln (D)	—	smile	sourire *m*	sorriso *m*	sonrisa *f*

	D	E	F	I	Es
lachen (D)	—	laugh	rire	ridere	reír
Lachen (D)	—	laughter	rire *m*	riso *m*	risa *f*
lâcher (F)	loslassen	let go of	—	mollare	dejar libre
lächerlich (D)	—	ridiculous	ridicule	ridicolo(a)	ridículo(a)
Lachs (D)	—	salmon	saumon *m*	salmone *m*	salmón *m*
lack (E)	Mangel *m*	—	manque *m*	mancanza *f*	escasez *f*
lacrima (I)	Träne *f*	tear	larme *f*	—	lágrima *f*
lacuna (I)	Lücke *f*	gap	lacune *f*	—	espacio *m*
lacune (F)	Lücke *f*	gap	—	lacuna *f*	espacio *m*
ladder (E)	Leiter *f*	—	échelle *f*	scala *f*	escalera *f*
Laden (D)	—	shop	magasin *m*	negozio *m*	tienda *f*
Ladentisch (D)	—	counter	comptoir *m*	banco di vendita *m*	mostrador *m*
ladrillo (Es)	Ziegel *m*	brick	brique *f*	mattone *m*	—
ladro (I)	Dieb *m*	thief	voleur *m*	—	ladrón *m*
ladrón (Es)	Dieb *m*	thief	voleur *m*	ladro *m*	—
Ladung (D)	—	cargo	charge *f*	carico *m*	carga *f*
lady (E)	Dame *f*	—	dame *f*	signora *f*	señora *f*
Lage (D)	—	situation	situation *f*	situazione *f*	situación *f*
Lager (D)	—	store	magasin *m*	magazzino *m*	almacén *m*
lago (Es)	See *m*	lake	lac *m*	lago *m*	—
lago (I)	See *m*	lake	lac *m*	—	lago *m*
lágrima (Es)	Träne *f*	tear	larme *f*	lacrima *f*	—
laid (F)	häßlich	ugly	—	brutto(a)	feo(a)
laine (F)	Wolle *f*	wool	—	lana *f*	lana *f*
laisser[1] (F)	hinterlassen	leave	—	lasciare	dejar
laisser[2] (F)	lassen	let	—	lasciare	dejar
laisser[3] (F)	übriglassen	leave	—	lasciare	dejar
lait (F)	Milch *f*	milk	—	latte *m*	leche *f*
lake (E)	See *m*	—	lac *m*	lago *m*	lago *m*
Laken (D)	—	sheet	drap *m*	lenzuolo *m*	sábana *f*
l'altro ieri (I)	vorgestern	day before yesterday	avant-hier	—	anteayer
lama (I)	Klinge *f*	blade	lame *f*	—	cuchilla *f*
la mayor parte de (Es)	meist	most	la plupart de	nella maggior parte di	—
lamb (E)	Lamm *n*	—	agneau *m*	agnello *m*	cordero *m*
lame (F)	Klinge *f*	blade	—	lama *f*	cuchilla *f*
la même chose (F)	dasselbe	the same	—	lo stesso	lo mismo
lamentar (Es)	bedauern	regret	regretter	deplorare	—
lamentare (I)	beklagen	deplore	plaindre de, se	—	quejarse
lamentarsi (I)	beschweren, sich	complain	plaindre, se	—	quejarse
lamento (Es)	Klage *f*	complaint	plainte *f*	lamento *m*	—
lamento (I)	Klage *f*	complaint	plainte *f*	—	lamento *m*
Lamm (D)	—	lamb	agneau *m*	agnello *m*	cordero *m*
lamp (E)	Lampe *f*	—	lampe *f*	lampada *f*	lámpara *f*

	D	E	F	I	Es
lampada (I)	Lampe *f*	lamp	lampe *f*	—	lámpara *f*
lampadina (I)	Glühbirne *f*	light bulb	ampoule *f*	—	lámpara *f*
lampadina tascabile (I)	Taschenlampe *f*	torch	lampe de poche *f*	—	linterna *f*
lámpara[1] (Es)	Glühbirne *f*	light bulb	ampoule *f*	lampadina *f*	—
lámpara[2] (Es)	Lampe *f*	lamp	lampe *f*	lampada *f*	—
Lampe (D)	—	lamp	lampe *f*	lampada *f*	lámpara *f*
lampe (F)	Lampe *f*	lamp	—	lampada *f*	lámpara *f*
lampe de poche (F)	Taschenlampe *f*	torch	—	lampadina tascabile *f*	linterna *f*
lampeggiare (I)	blinken	flash	clignoter	—	relampagnear
lampione (I)	Laterne *f*	street light	réverbère *f*	—	farola *f*
lampo (I)	Blitz *m*	lightning	éclair *m*	—	rayo *m*
lampone (I)	Himbeere *f*	raspberry	framboise *f*	—	frambuesa *f*
lana (Es)	Wolle *f*	wool	laine *f*	lana *f*	—
lana (I)	Wolle *f*	wool	laine *f*	—	lana *f*
lancer (F)	werfen	throw	—	lanciare	tirar
lanciare (I)	werfen	throw	lancer	—	tirar
Land (D)	—	land	pays *m*	paese *m*	país *m*
land[1] (E)	landen	—	atterrir	atterrare	aterrizar
land[2] (E)	Land *n*	—	pays *m*	paese *m*	país *m*
landen (D)	—	land	atterrir	atterrare	aterrizar
landing (E)	Landung *f*	—	atterrissage *m*	atterraggio *m*	aterrizaje *m*
Landkarte (D)	—	map	carte *f*	carta geografica *f*	mapa *m*
landlord (E)	Wirt *m*	—	patron *m*	oste *m*	dueño *m*
landowner (E)	Großgrund- besitzer *m*	—	grand propriétaire *m*	latifondista *m*	latifundio *m*
landscape (E)	Landschaft *f*	—	paysage *m*	paesaggio *m*	paisaje *m*
Landschaft (D)	—	landscape	paysage *m*	paesaggio *m*	paisaje *m*
Landstraße (D)	—	country road	route *f*	strada provinciale *f*	carretera nacional *f*
Landung (D)	—	landing	atterrissage *m*	atterraggio *m*	aterrizaje *m*
Landwirt (D)	—	farmer	agriculteur *m*	agricoltore *m*	agricultor *m*
lane (E)	Gasse *f*	—	ruelle *f*	vicolo *m*	callejón *m*
lang (D)	—	long	long(ue)	lungo(a)	largo(a)
langage (F)	Sprache *f*	language	—	lingua *f*	lengua *f*
lange (D)	—	long time	longtemps	molto tempo	mucho tiempo
Länge (D)	—	length	longueur *f*	lunghezza *f*	longitud *f*
lange (F)	Windel *f*	nappy	—	pannolino *m*	pañal *m*
langsam (D)	—	slow	lent(e)	lento(a)	despacio(a)
längst (D)	—	a long time ago	depuis bien longtemps	da molto	hace mucho
language (E)	Sprache *f*	—	langage *m*	lingua *f*	lengua *f*
langue (F)	Zunge *f*	tongue	—	lingua *f*	lengua *f*
langue étrangère (F)	Fremdsprache *f*	foreign-language	—	lingua straniera *f*	idioma extranjero *m*

	D	E	F	I	Es
langue familière (F)	Umgangssprache f	colloquial language	—	linguaggio corrente	lenguaje coloquial m
langue internationale (F)	Weltsprache f	world language	—	lingua mondiale f	lengua universal f
langue maternelle (F)	Muttersprache f	native language	—	lingua madre f	lengua materna f
langweilen, sich (D)	—	get bored	ennuyer, se	annoiarsi	aburrirse
langweilig (D)	—	boring	ennuyeux (-euse)	noioso(a)	aburrido(a)
lápiz[1] (Es)	Bleistift m	pencil	crayon m	matita f	—
lápiz[2] (Es)	Stift m	pencil	crayon m	penna f	—
la plupart de (F)	meist	most	—	nella maggior parte di	la mayor parte de
l'après-midi (F)	nachmittags	in the afternoon	—	di pomeriggio	por la tarde
lard (F)	Speck m	bacon	—	lardo m	tocino m
lardo (I)	Speck m	bacon	lard m	—	tocino m
large (F)	breit	broad	—	largo(a)	amplio(a)
large town (E)	Großstadt f	—	grande ville f	grande città f	gran ciudad f
largeur (F)	Breite f	width	—	larghezza f	extensión f
larghezza (I)	Breite f	width	largeur f	—	extensión f
largo (I)	breit	broad	large	—	amplio(a)
largo (Es)	lang	long	long(ue)	lungo(a)	—
Lärm (D)	—	noise	bruit m	rumore m	ruido m
larme (F)	Träne f	tear	—	lacrima f	lágrima f
lasciare[1] (I)	hinterlassen	leave	laisser	—	dejar
lasciare[2] (I)	lassen	let	laisser	—	dejar
lasciare[3] (I)	übriglassen	leave	laisser	—	dejar
lasciare[4] (I)	verlassen	leave	abandonner	—	dejar
lasciare in eredità (I)	vererben	bequeath	léguer	—	transmitir hereditariamente
lassen (D)	—	let	laisser	lasciare	dejar
Last (D)	—	load	charge f	carico m	peso m
last[1] (E)	dauern	—	durer	durare	durar
last[2] (E)	letzte(r,s)	—	dernier(-ière)	ultimo(a)	última(o)
lästig (D)	—	troublesome	importun(e)	molesto(a)	desagradable
lastricato (I)	Pflaster n	pavement	pavé m	—	adoquinado m
Lastwagen (D)	—	lorry	camion m	camion m	camión m
lata (Es)	Dose f	tin	boîte f	scatola f	—
late (E)	spät	—	tard	tardi	tarde
lately (E)	kürzlich	—	récemment	recente	reciente
later (E)	später	—	plus tard	piú tardi	más tarde
Laterne (D)	—	street light	réverbère f	lampione m	farola f
latifondista (I)	Großgrund-besitzer m	landowner	grand propriétaire m	—	latifundista m
latifundista (Es)	Großgrund-besitzer m	landowner	grand propriétaire m	latifondista m	—
latta (I)	Blech n	sheet metal	tôle f	—	chapa f
latte (I)	Milch f	milk	lait m	—	leche f

leader

	D	E	F	I	Es
laufen (D)	—	run	courir	correre	correr
laugh (E)	lachen	—	rire	ridere	reír
laugh at (E)	auslachen	—	rire de qn	deridere	reírse de
laughter[1] (E)	Gelächter n	—	rires m pl	risata f	risa f
laughter[2] (E)	Lachen n	—	rire m	riso m	risa f
laundry (E)	Wäscherei f	—	blanchisserie f	lavanderia f	lavandería f
Laune (D)	—	mood	humeur f	umore m	humor m
laut (D)	—	loud	fort(e)	rumoroso(a)	fuerte
läuten (D)	—	ring	sonner	suonare	tocar
l'autre jour (F)	neulich	recently	—	recentemente	recientemente
Lautsprecher (D)	—	loudspeaker	haut-parleur m	altoparlante m	altavoz m
lauwarm (D)	—	lukewarm	tiède	tiepido(a)	templado(a)
lavabile (I)	waschbar	washable	lavable	—	lavable
lavable (Es)	waschbar	washable	lavable	lavabile	—
lavable (F)	waschbar	washable	—	lavabile	lavable
lavabo[1] (Es)	Toilette f	toilet	toilette f	toilette f	—
lavabo[2] (Es)	Waschbecken n	wash-basin	lavabo m	lavandino m	—
lavabo (F)	Waschbecken n	wash-basin	—	lavandino m	lavabo m
lavadora (Es)	Waschmaschine f	washing machine	machine à laver f	lavatrice f	—
lavandería (Es)	Wäscherei f	laundry	blanchisserie f	lavanderia f	—
lavanderia (I)	Wäscherei f	laundry	blanchisserie f	—	lavandería f
lavandino (I)	Waschbecken n	wash-basin	lavabo m	—	lavabo m
lavar[1] (Es)	abwaschen	wash off	laver	lavar via	—
lavar[2] (Es)	abspülen	wash up	faire la vaisselle	sciacquare	—
lavar[3] (Es)	waschen	wash	laver	lavare	—
lavare (I)	waschen	wash	laver	—	lavar
lavar via (I)	abwaschen	wash off	laver	—	lavar
lavatory (E)	Klosett n	—	cabinets m pl	gabinetto m	retrete m
lavatrice (I)	Waschmaschine f	washing machine	machine à laver f	—	lavadora f
laver[1] (F)	abwaschen	wash off	—	lavar via	lavar
laver[2] (F)	waschen	wash	—	lavare	lavar
lavorare (I)	arbeiten	work	travailler	—	trabajar
lavorare a maglia (I)	stricken	knit	tricoter	—	hacer punto
lavoro (I)	Arbeit f	work	travail m	—	trabajo m
law[1] (E)	Gesetz n	—	loi f	legge f	ley f
law[2] (E)	Jura	—	droit m	giurisprudenza f	derecho m
lawn (E)	Rasen m	—	pelouse f	prato m	césped m
lawyer (E)	Rechtsanwalt m	—	avocat m	avvocato m	abogado m
lay (E)	legen	—	mettre	mettere	colocar
lazy (E)	faul	—	paresseux(-euse)	pigro(a)	perezoso(a)
le, la (F)	der, die, das	the	—	il, la	el, la, lo
lead (E)	führen	—	guider	guidare	dirigir
leader (E)	Führer m	—	guide m	guida f	guía m

	D	E	F	I	Es
leaf (E)	Blatt *n*	—	feuille *f*	foglia *f*	hoja *f*
learn[1] (E)	erfahren	—	apprendre	venire a sapere	enterarse
learn[2] (E)	lernen	—	apprendre	imparare	aprender
lease out (E)	verpachten	—	affermer	affittare	arrendar
leather (E)	Leder *n*	—	cuir *m*	cuoio *m*	cuero *m*
leave[1] (E)	abreisen	—	partir	partire	salir
leave[2] (E)	hinterlassen	—	laisser	lasciare	dejar
leave[3] (E)	verlassen	—	abandonner	lasciare	dejar
leave[4] (E)	übriglassen	—	laisser	lasciare	dejar
leben (D)	—	live	vivre	vivere	vivir
Leben (D)	—	life	vie *f*	vita *f*	vida *f*
lebendig (D)	—	alive	vivant(e)	vivo(a)	vivo(a)
Lebensgefährte (D)	—	life partner	compagnon *m*	compagno *m*	compañero en la vida *m*
Lebenslauf (D)	—	curriculum vitae	curriculum vitae *m*	curriculum vitae *m*	curriculum vitae *m*
Lebensmittel (D)	—	food	alimentation *f*	alimentari *m pl*	alimentos *m pl*
Lebensmittel-geschäft (D)	—	grocer's	magasin d'alimentation *m*	negozio di alimentari *m*	tienda de comestibles *f*
Leber (D)	—	liver	foie *m*	fegato *m*	hígado *m*
lebhaft (D)	—	lively	vif(vive)	vivace	vivaz
leche (Es)	Milch *f*	milk	lait *m*	latte *m*	—
leçon (F)	Unterrichts-stunde *f*	lesson	—	lezione *f*	clase *f*
lecture (E)	Vorlesung *f*	—	cours magistral *m*	lezione *f*	clase *f*
Leder (D)	—	leather	cuir *m*	cuoio *m*	cuero *m*
ledig (D)	—	single	célibataire	celibe m/nubile *f*	soltero(a)
leer (D)	—	empty	vide	vuoto(a)	vacío(a)
leer (Es)	lesen	read	lire	leggere	—
left[1] (E)	links	—	à gauche	a sinistra	a la izquierda
left[2] (E)	übrig	—	restant(e)	restante	restante
leg (E)	Bein *n*	—	jambe *f*	gamba *f*	pierna *f*
legal (E)	gesetzlich	—	légal(e)	legale	legal
legal (Es)	gesetzlich	legal	légal(e)	legale	—
légal (F)	gesetzlich	legal	—	legale	legal
legale (I)	gesetzlich	legal	légal(e)	—	legal
legare (I)	binden	bind	attacher	—	atar
legen (D)	—	lay	mettre	mettere	colocar
léger (F)	leicht	light	—	leggero(a)	sencillo(a)
legge (I)	Gesetz *n*	law	loi *f*	—	ley *f*
leggere (I)	lesen	read	lire	—	leer
leggero (I)	leicht	light	léger(-ère)	—	sencillo(a)
legno (I)	Holz *n*	wood	bois *m*	—	madera *f*
léguer (F)	vererben	bequeath	—	lasciare in eredità	transmitir hereditariamente
legumbres (Es)	Gemüse *n*	vegetables	légumes *m pl*	verdura *f*	—
légumes (F)	Gemüse *n*	vegetables	—	verdura *f*	legumbres *f pl*

lento

	D	E	F	I	Es
lehren (D)	—	teach	enseigner	insegnare	enseñar
Lehrer (D)	—	teacher	professeur *m*	maestro *m*	profesor *m*
Lehrling (D)	—	apprentice	apprenti *m*	apprendista *m*	aprendiz *m*
lei (I)	sie	she	elle	—	ella
Leiche (D)	—	corpse	cadavre *m*	cadavere *m*	cadáver *m*
leicht[1] (D)	—	easy	facile	semplice	ligero(a)
leicht[2] (D)	—	light	léger(-ère)	leggero(a)	sencillo(a)
leichtsinnig (D)	—	careless	étourdi(e)	spensierato(a)	imprudente
leiden (D)	—	suffer	souffrir	soffrire	sufrir
Leidenschaft (D)	—	passion	passion *f*	passione *f*	pasión *f*
leider (D)	—	unfortunately	malheureuse-ment	purtroppo	desgraciadamente
leihen (D)	—	lend	prêter	prestare	prestar
leise (D)	—	quietly	à voix basse	a bassa voce	sin ruido
Leiter (D)	—	ladder	échelle *f*	scala *f*	escalera *f*
Leitung[1] (D)	—	direction	direction *f*	direzione *f*	dirección *f*
Leitung[2] (D)	—	pipe	tuyau *m*	conduttura *f*	tubería *f*
lejanía (Es)	Ferne *f*	distance	lointain *m*	distanza *f*	—
lejos[1] (Es)	fort	away	parti	via	—
lejos[2] (Es)	fern	far away	éloigné(e)	lontano(a)	—
lejos[3] (Es)	auseinander	apart	séparé(e)	separato(a)	—
le long de (F)	entlang	along	—	lungo	a lo largo de
le lundi (F)	montags	Mondays	—	il lunedì	los lunes
le matin (F)	vormittags	in the morning	—	di mattina	por la mañana
le même (F)	derselbe	the same	—	lo stesso	el mismo
le mien (F)	meine(r,s)	mine/my	—	mio(a)	mío(a)
lemon (E)	Zitrone *f*	—	citron *m*	limone *m*	limón *m*
lemonade (E)	Limonade *f*	—	limonade *f*	limonata *f*	gaseosa *f*
lend[1] (E)	ausleihen	—	prêter	dare in prestito	prestar
lend[2] (E)	leihen	—	prêter	prestare	prestar
lend[2] (E)	verleihen	—	prêter	prestare	prestar
lend[4] (E)	borgen	—	prêter	prestare	prestar
length (E)	Länge *f*	—	longueur *f*	lunghezza *f*	longitud *f*
lengua[1] (Es)	Sprache *f*	language	langage *m*	lingua *f*	—
lengua[2] (Es)	Zunge *f*	tongue	langue *f*	lingua *f*	—
lenguado (Es)	Seezunge *f*	sole	sole *f*	sogliola *f*	—
lenguaje coloquial (Es)	Umgangssprache *f*	colloquial language	langue familière *f*	linguaggio corrente *m*	—
lengua materna (Es)	Muttersprache *f*	native language	langue maternelle *f*	lingua madre *f*	—
lengua universal (Es)	Weltsprache *f*	world language	langue internationale *f*	lingua mondiale *f*	—
lenken (D)	—	steer	conduire	guidare	encauzar
Lenkrad (D)	—	steering wheel	volant *m*	volante *m*	volante *m*
lent (F)	langsam	slow	—	lento(a)	despacio(a)
lento[1] (I)	langsam	slow	lent(e)	—	despacio(a)

	D	E	F	I	Es
lento² (I)	locker	loose	desserré(e)	—	flojo(a)
lenzuolo (I)	Laken *n*	sheet	drap *m*	—	sábana *f*
león (Es)	Löwe *m*	lion	lion *m*	leone *m*	—
leone (I)	Löwe *m*	lion	lion *m*	—	león *m*
Leopard (D)	—	leopard	léopard *m*	leopardo *m*	leopardo *m*
leopard (E)	Leopard *m*	—	léopard *m*	leopardo *m*	leopardo *m*
léopard (F)	Leopard *m*	leopard	—	leopardo *m*	leopardo *m*
leopardo (Es)	Leopard *m*	leopard	léopard *m*	leopardo *m*	—
leopardo (I)	Leopard *m*	leopard	léopard *m*	—	leopardo *m*
leotardos (Es)	Strumpfhose *f*	tights	collants *m pl*	calzamaglia *f*	—
lepre (I)	Hase *m*	hare	lièvre *m*	—	liebre *m*
lernen (D)	—	learn	apprendre	imparare	aprender
lesen (D)	—	read	lire	leggere	leer
les jours ouvrables (F)	werktags	on working days	—	nei giorni feriali	los días laborables
le soir (F)	abends	in the evening	—	di sera	por la tarde
less (E)	weniger	—	moins	di meno	menos
lessive (F)	Waschmittel *n*	detergent	—	detersivo *m*	detergente *m*
lesson (E)	Unterrichts-stunde *f*	—	leçon *f*	lezione *f*	clase *f*
lessons (E)	Unterricht *m*	—	cours	lezione *f*	enseñanza *f*
let (E)	lassen	—	laisser	lasciare	dejar
let go of (E)	loslassen	—	lâcher	mollare	dejar libre
le tout (F)	Ganze(s) *n*	lot	—	insieme *m*	todo *m*
letra (Es)	Buchstabe *m*	letter	lettre *f*	lettera *f*	—
letter¹ (E)	Buchstabe *m*	—	lettre *f*	lettera *f*	letra *f*
letter² (E)	Brief *m*	—	lettre *f*	lettera *f*	carta *f*
lettera¹ (I)	Buchstabe *m*	letter	lettre *f*	—	letra *f*
lettera² (I)	Brief *m*	letter	lettre *f*	—	carta *f*
lettera d'amore (I)	Liebesbrief *m*	love letter	lettre d'amour *f*	—	carta de amor *f*
lettera raccomandata (I)	Einschreibe-brief *m*	recorded delivery letter	lettre recommandée *f*	—	carta con acuse de recibo *f*
letterbox (E)	Briefkasten *m*	—	boîte aux lettres *f*	cassetta postale *f*	buzón *m*
letto (I)	Bett *n*	bed	lit *m*	—	cama *f*
lettre¹ (F)	Brief *m*	letter	—	lettera *f*	carta *f*
lettre² (F)	Buchstabe *m*	letter	—	lettera *f*	letra *f*
lettre d'amour (F)	Liebesbrief *m*	love letter	—	lettera d'amore *f*	carta de amor *f*
lettre recommandée (F)	Einschreibe-brief *m*	recorded delivery letter	—	lettera raccomandata *f*	carta con acuse de recibo *f*
letzte (D)	—	last	dernier(-ière)	ultimo(a)	último(a)
leugnen (D)	—	deny	nier	negare	negar
Leute (D)	—	people	gens *m pl*	gente *f*	gente *f*
levantar (Es)	heben	lift	soulever	alzare	—
levantarse (Es)	aufstehen	get up	lever, se	alzarsi	—
levare (I)	ausziehen	take off	enlever	—	quitarse
lever (F)	erheben	raise	—	alzare	elevar

	D	E	F	I	Es
lever, se (F)	aufstehen	get up	—	alzarsi	levantarse
lever du soleil (F)	Sonnenaufgang *m*	sunrise	—	sorgere del sole *m*	salida del sol *f*
lèvre (F)	Lippe *f*	lip	—	labbro *m*	labio *m*
Lexikon (D)	—	dictionary	encyclopédie *f*	enciclopedia *f*	diccionario *m*
ley (Es)	Gesetz *n*	law	loi *f*	legge *f*	—
lezione¹ (I)	Unterrichts-stunde *f*	lesson	leçon *f*	—	clase *f*
lezione² (I)	Unterricht *m*	lessons	cours *m*	—	enseñanza *f*
lezione (I)	Vorlesung *f*	lecture	cours magistral *m*	—	clase *f*
libérer (F)	freilassen	release	—	mettere in libertà	poner en libertad
libero¹ (I)	frei	free	libre	—	libre
libero² (I)	unbesetzt	unoccupied	vacant(e)	—	desocupado(a)
libertà (I)	Freiheit *f*	freedom	liberté *f*	—	libertad *f*
libertad (Es)	Freiheit *f*	freedom	liberté *f*	libertà *f*	—
liberté (F)	Freiheit *f*	freedom	—	libertà *f*	libertad *f*
libra (Es)	Pfund *n*	pound	livre *f*	mezzo chilo *m*	—
librairie (F)	Buchhandlung *f*	bookshop	—	libreria *f*	librería *f*
libre (Es)	frei	free	libre	libero(a)	—
libre (F)	frei	free	—	libero(a)	libre
librería (Es)	Buchhandlung *f*	bookshop	librairie *f*	libreria *f*	—
libreria (I)	Buchhandlung *f*	bookshop	librairie *f*	—	librería *f*
libre-service (F)	Selbstbedienung *f*	self service	—	self-service *m*	autoservicio *m*
libreta de ahorro (Es)	Sparbuch *n*	savings book	livret de caisse d'épargne *m*	libretto di risparmio *m*	—
libretto degli assegni (I)	Scheckbuch *n*	cheque book	carnet de chèques *m*	—	talonario de cheques *m*
libretto di risparmio (I)	Sparbuch *n*	savings book	livret de caisse d'épargne *m*	—	libreta de ahorro *f*
libro (Es)	Buch *n*	book	livre *m*	libro *m*	—
libro (I)	Buch *n*	book	livre *m*	—	libro *m*
licenziare¹ (I)	entlassen	release	renvoyer	—	despedir
licenziare² (I)	kündigen	sack	résilier	—	despedir
liceo (I)	Gymnasium *n*	grammar school	lycée *m*	—	instituto de enseñanza media *m*
Licht (D)	—	light	lumière *f*	luce *f*	luz *f*
Lichtschalter (D)	—	light switch	interrupteur *m*	interruttore *m*	interruptor *m*
licor (Es)	Likör *m*	liqueur	liqueur *f*	liquore *m*	—
lid (E)	Deckel *m*	—	couvercle *m*	coperchio *m*	tapa *f*
lie¹ (E)	lügen	—	mentir	mentire	mentir
lie² (E)	liegen	—	trouver, se	giacere	estar tumbado(a)
lieb (D)	—	sweet	gentil(le)	caro(a)	amable
Liebe (D)	—	love	amour *m*	amore *m*	amor *m*
lieben (D)	—	love	aimer	amare	amar
liebenswürdig (D)	—	kind	aimable	gentile	gentil
lieber (D)	—	rather	mieux	piuttosto	más bien
Liebesbrief (D)	—	love letter	lettre d'amour *f*	lettera d'amore *f*	carta de amor *f*

	D	E	F	I	Es
Liebling (D)	—	darling	chéri *m*	tesoro *m*	querido *m*
liebre (Es)	Hase *m*	hare	lièvre *m*	lepre *f*	—
Lied (D)	—	song	chanson *f*	canzone *f*	canción *f*
liefern (D)	—	deliver	livrer	fornire	suministrar
Lieferung (D)	—	delivery	livraison *f*	fornitura *f*	suministro *m*
liegen (D)	—	lie	trouver, se	giacere	estar tumbado(a)
Liegestuhl (D)	—	deck chair	chaise longue *f*	sedia a sdraio *f*	tumbona *f*
Liegewagen (D)	—	couchette	wagon-couchette *m*	cuccetta *f*	coche cama *m*
lieto¹ (I)	erfreut	delighted	réjoui(e)	—	contento(a)
lieto² (I)	froh	glad	content(e)	—	contento(a)
lièvre (F)	Hase *m*	hare	—	lepre *f*	liebre *m*
life (E)	Leben *n*	—	vie *f*	vita *f*	vida *f*
lifebelt (E)	Rettungsring *m*	—	bouée de sauvetage *f*	salvagente *m*	salvavidas *m*
life jacket (E)	Schwimmweste *f*	—	gilet de sauvetage *m*	giubbetto di salvataggio *m*	chaleco salvavidas *m*
life partner (E)	Lebensgefährte *m*	—	compagnon *m*	compagno *m*	compañero en la vida *m*
Lift (D)	—	elevator	ascenseur *m*	ascensore *m*	ascensor *m*
lift (E)	heben	—	soulever	alzare	levantar
ligero (Es)	leicht	easy	facile	semplice	—
light¹ (E)	anzünden	—	allumer	accendere	encender
light² (E)	leicht	—	léger(-ère)	leggero(a)	sencillo(a)
light³ (E)	Licht *n*	—	lumière *f*	luce *f*	luz *f*
light⁴ (E)	Schein *m*	—	lumière *f*	luce *f*	luz *f*
light bulb (E)	Glühbirne *f*	—	ampoule *f*	lampadina *f*	lámpara *f*
lighter (E)	Feuerzeug *n*	—	briquet *m*	accendino *m*	mechero *m*
lighting (E)	Beleuchtung *f*	—	éclairage *m*	illuminazione *f*	iluminación *f*
lightning (E)	Blitz *m*	—	éclair *m*	lampo *m*	rayo *m*
light switch (E)	Lichtschalter *m*	—	interrupteur *m*	interruttore *m*	interruptor *m*
ligne¹ (F)	Linie *f*	line	—	linea *f*	línea *f*
ligne² (F)	Zeile *f*	line	—	riga *f*	línea *f*
like (E)	mögen	—	aimer	piacere	querer
likeable (E)	sympathisch	—	sympathique	simpatico(a)	simpático(a)
like this (E)	so	—	ainsi	così	así
likewise (E)	ebenfalls	—	aussi	altrettanto	también
Likör (D)	—	liqueur	liqueur *f*	liquore *m*	licor *m*
lila (D)	—	purple	mauve	lilla	de color lila
lilla (I)	lila	purple	mauve	—	de color lila
limit (E)	begrenzen	—	limiter	limitare	limitar
limitar (Es)	begrenzen	limit	limiter	limitare	—
limitare (I)	begrenzen	limit	limiter	—	limitar
limited stop train (E)	Eilzug *m*	—	express *m*	treno diretto *m*	tren expreso *m*
limiter (F)	begrenzen	limit	—	limitare	limitar
limón (Es)	Zitrone *f*	lemon	citron *m*	limone *m*	—

	D	E	F	I	Es
Limonade (D)	—	lemonade	limonade f	limonata f	gaseosa f
limonade (F)	Limonade f	lemonade	—	limonata f	gaseosa f
limonata (I)	Limonade f	lemonade	limonade f	—	gaseosa f
limone (I)	Zitrone f	lemon	citron m	—	limón m
limosna (Es)	Almosen n	alms	aumône f	elemosina f	—
limpiar[1] (Es)	putzen	clean	nettoyer	pulire	—
limpiar[2] (Es)	reinigen	clean	nettoyer	pulire	—
limpieza (Es)	Reinigung f	cleaning	nettoyage m	pulitura f	—
limpio (Es)	sauber	clean	propre	pulito(a)	—
line[1] (E)	Linie f	—	ligne f	linea f	línea f
line[2] (E)	Strich m	—	trait m	linea f	línea f
line[3] (E)	Zeile f	—	ligne f	riga f	línea f
línea[1] (Es)	Linie f	line	ligne f	linea f	—
línea[2] (Es)	Strich m	line	trait m	linea f	—
línea[3] (Es)	Zeile f	line	ligne f	riga f	—
linea[1] (I)	Linie f	line	ligne f	—	línea f
linea[2] (I)	Strich m	line	trait m	—	línea f
Lineal (D)	—	ruler	règle f	riga f	regla f
linge (F)	Wäsche f	washing	—	biancheria f	ropa f
lingua[1] (I)	Sprache f	language	langage m	—	lengua f
lingua[2] (I)	Zunge f	tongue	langue f	—	lengua f
linguaggio corrente (I)	Umgangssprache f	colloquial language	langue familière f	—	lenguaje coloquial m
lingua madre (I)	Muttersprache f	native language	langue maternelle f	—	lengua materna f
lingua mondiale (I)	Weltsprache f	world language	langue internationale f	—	lengua universal f
lingua straniera (I)	Fremdsprache f	foreign language	langue étrangère f	—	idioma extranjero m
Linie (D)	—	line	ligne f	linea f	línea f
links (D)	—	left	à gauche	a sinistra	a la izquierda
linterna (Es)	Taschenlampe f	torch	lampe de poche f	lampadina tascabile f	—
lion (E)	Löwe m	—	lion m	leone m	león m
lion (F)	Löwe m	lion	—	leone m	león m
lip (E)	Lippe f	—	lèvre f	labbro m	labio m
Lippe (D)	—	lip	lèvre f	labbro m	labio m
liqueur (E)	Likör m	—	liqueur f	liquore m	licor m
liqueur (F)	Likör m	liqueur	—	liquore m	licor m
liquidación (Es)	Ausverkauf m	sale	soldes m pl	saldi m pl	—
liquide (F)	flüssig	fluid	—	liquido(a)	líquido(a)
liquido (I)	flüssig	fluid	liquide	—	líquido(a)
líquido (Es)	flüssig	fluid	liquide	liquido(a)	—
liquore (I)	Likör m	liqueur	liqueur f	—	licor m
lire (F)	lesen	read	—	leggere	leer
liscio (I)	glatt	smooth	lisse	—	liso(a)
liso (Es)	glatt	smooth	lisse	liscio	—

	D	E	F	I	Es
lisse (F)	glatt	smooth	—	liscio(a)	liso(a)
list¹ (E)	Liste *f*	—	liste *f*	lista *f*	lista *f*
list² (E)	verzeichnen	—	enregistrer	registrare	hacer una lista
list³ (E)	Verzeichnis *n*	—	registre *m*	elenco *m*	lista *f*
lista¹ (Es)	Liste *f*	list	liste *f*	lista *f*	—
lista² (Es)	Verzeichnis *n*	list	registre *m*	elenco *m*	—
lista (I)	Liste *f*	list	liste *f*	—	lista *f*
lista de platos (Es)	Speisekarte *f*	menu	menu *m*	menu *m*	—
Liste (D)	—	list	liste *f*	lista *f*	lista *f*
liste (F)	Liste *f*	list	—	lista *f*	lista *f*
listen (E)	zuhören	—	écouter	ascoltare	escuchar
listener (E)	Hörer *m*	—	auditeur *m*	ascoltatore *m*	oyente *m*
listo¹ (Es)	clever	clever	futé(e)	abile	—
listo² (Es)	fertig	ready	prêt(e)	pronto(a)	—
lit (F)	Bett *n*	bed	—	letto *m*	cama *f*
lite (I)	Streit *m*	argument	dispute *f*	—	disputa *f*
Liter (D)	—	litre	litre *m*	litro *m*	litro *m*
litigare (I)	streiten	quarrel	disputer, se	—	discutir
litre (E)	Liter *n*	—	litre *m*	litro *m*	litro *m*
litre (F)	Liter *n*	litre	—	litro *m*	litro *m*
litro (Es)	Liter *n*	litre	litre *m*	litro *m*	—
litro (I)	Liter *n*	litre	litre *m*	—	litro *m*
little (E)	wenig	—	peu de	poco(a)	poco(a)
live¹ (E)	leben	—	vivre	vivere	vivir
live² (E)	wohnen	—	habiter	abitare	vivir
livello del mare (I)	Meeresspiegel *m*	sea level	niveau de la mer *m*	—	nivel del mar *m*
lively¹ (E)	lebhaft	—	vif(vive)	vivace	vivaz
lively² (E)	munter	—	éveillé(e)	vivace	alegre
lively³ (E)	belebt	—	animé(e)	animato(a)	animado(a)
liver (E)	Leber *f*	—	foie *m*	fegato *m*	hígado *m*
living room (E)	Wohnzimmer *n*	—	salle de séjour *f*	salotto *m*	sala de estar *f*
livraison (F)	Lieferung *f*	delivery	—	fornitura *f*	suministro *m*
livre¹ (F)	Buch *n*	book	—	libro *m*	libro *m*
livre² (F)	Pfund *n*	pound	—	mezzo chilo *m*	libra *f*
livrer (F)	liefern	deliver	—	fornire	suministrar
livret de caisse d'épargne (F)	Sparbuch *n*	savings book	—	libretto di risparmio *m*	libreta de ahorro *f*
llama (Es)	Flamme *f*	flame	flamme *f*	fiamma *f*	—
llamada (Es)	Anruf *m*	call	coup de téléphone *m*	chiamata *f*	—
llamada interurbana (Es)	Ferngespräch *n*	long-distance call	communication interurbaine *f*	telefonata interurbana *f*	—
llamada telefónica (Es)	Telefonanruf *m*	phone call	coup de téléphone *m*	telefonata *f*	—
llamar (Es)	rufen	shout	appeler	chiamare	—
llamar con gestos (Es)	winken	wave	faire signe	chiamare con cenni	—

	D	E	F	I	Es
llamar la atención por algo (Es)	auffallen	be noticeable	faire remarquer, se	dare nell'occhio	—
llamar por teléfono[1] (Es)	anrufen	ring up	téléphoner	telefonare	—
llamar por teléfono[2] (Es)	telefonieren	telephone	téléphoner	telefonare	—
llamarse (Es)	heißen	be called	appeler, se	chiamarsi	—
llano (Es)	flach	flat	plat(e)	piatto(a)	—
llanura[1] (Es)	Ebene f	plain	plaine f	pianura f	—
llanura[2] (Es)	Fläche f	area	surface f	area f	—
llave (Es)	Schlüssel m	key	clé f	chiave f	—
llegada (Es)	Ankunft f	arrival	arrivée f	arrivo m	—
llegar[1] (Es)	ankommen	arrive	arriver	arrivare	—
llegar[2] (Es)	eintreffen	arrive	arriver	arrivare	—
llegar a ser (Es)	werden	become	devenir	diventare	—
llenar[1] (Es)	ausfüllen	fill in	remplir	riempire	—
llenar[2] (Es)	erfüllen	fulfil	remplir	esaudire	—
llenar[3] (Es)	füllen	fill	remplir	riempire	—
llenar de gasolina (Es)	tanken	fill up with petrol	prendre de l'essence	fare benzina	—
lleno (Es)	voll	full	plein(e)	pieno(a)	—
llevar[1] (Es)	anhaben	have on	porter	indossare	—
llevar[2] (Es)	bringen	fetch	porter	portare	—
llevar[3] (Es)	tragen	carry	porter	portare	—
llevar a cabo (Es)	verwirklichen	realize	réaliser	realizzare	—
llevar consigo (Es)	mitnehmen	take along	emmener	prendere con sè	—
llevar retraso (Es)	verspäten	be late	être en retard	ritardare	—
llorar (Es)	weinen	cry	pleurer	piangere	—
llover (Es)	regnen	rain	pleuvoir	piovere	—
lluvia (Es)	Regen m	rain	pluie f	pioggia f	—
lo (Es)	das	that/which	le/la	il/la	—
load[1] (E)	aufladen	—	charger	caricare	cargar
load[2] (E)	Last f	—	charge f	carico m	peso m
load[3] (E)	verladen	—	charger	caricare	cargar
loben (D)	—	praise	louer	lodare	elogiar
local (E)	örtlich	—	local(e)	locale	local
local[1] (Es)	Lokal n	pub	restaurant m	locale m	—
local[2] (Es)	örtlich	local	local(e)	locale	—
local (F)	örtlich	local	—	locale	local
locale[1] (I)	Lokal n	pub	restaurant m	—	local m
locale[2] (I)	örtlich	local	local(e)	—	local
local nocturno (Es)	Nachtlokal n	(night) club	boîte de nuit f	night m	—
locataire (F)	Mieter m	tenant	—	inquilino m	inquilino m
location (F)	Vorverkauf m	advance booking	—	prevendita f	venta anticipada f
Loch (D)	—	hole	trou m	buco m	agujero m
lock[1] (E)	Schloß n	—	serrure f	serratura f	cerradura f

	D	E	F	I	Es
lock² (E)	Verschluß m	—	fermeture f	chiusura f	cierre m
Locke (D)	—	curl	boucle f	riccio m	rizo m
locken (D)	—	attract	attirer	attirare	atraer
locker (D)	—	loose	desserré(e)	lento(a)	flojo(a)
lock (up)¹ (E)	verschließen	—	fermer à clé	chiudere a chiave	cerrar con llave
lock (up)² (E)	zuschließen	—	fermer à clé	chiudere a chiave	cerrar con llave
lock up³ (E)	einschließen	—	renfermer	rinchiudere	encerrar
loco¹ (Es)	Narr m	fool	fou m	pazzo m	—
loco² (Es)	verrückt	mad	fou (folle)	pazzo(a)	—
lodare (I)	loben	praise	louer	—	elogiar
Löffel (D)	—	spoon	cuiller f	cucchiaio m	cuchara f
Loge (D)	—	box	loge f	palco m	palco m
loge (F)	Loge f	box	—	palco m	palco m
logement (F)	Unterkunft f	accommodation	—	alloggio m	hospedaje m
logement pour une nuit (F)	Übernachtung f	overnight stay	—	pernottamento m	pernoctación f
Lohn (D)	—	wages	salaire m	salario m	salario m
lohnen (D)	—	be worth while	en valoir la peine	valere la pena	valer la pena
loi (F)	Gesetz n	law	—	legge f	ley f
lointain (F)	Ferne f	distance	—	distanza f	lejanía f
loisirs (F)	Freizeit f	free time	—	tempo libero m	tiempo libre m
Lokal (D)	—	pub	restaurant m	locale m	local m
lo mismo (Es)	dasselbe	the same	la même chose	lo stesso	—
lonely (E)	einsam	—	solitaire	solitario(a)	solitario(a)
long (E)	lang	—	long(ue)	lungo(a)	largo(a)
long (F)	lang	long	—	lungo(a)	largo(a)
long-distance call (E)	Ferngespräch n	—	communication interurbaine f	telefonata interurbana f	llamada interurbana f
long-distance driver (E)	Fernfahrer m	—	routier m	camionista m	camionero m
longitud (Es)	Länge f	length	longueur f	lunghezza f	—
longtemps (F)	lange	long time	—	molto tempo	mucho tiempo
long time (E)	lange	—	longtemps	molto tempo	mucho tiempo
longueur (F)	Länge f	length	—	lunghezza f	longitud f
lontano (I)	fern	far away	éloigné(e)	—	lejos
look¹ (E)	aussehen	—	avoir l'air	avere l'aspetto	parecer
look² (E)	blicken	—	regarder	guardare	mirar
look³ (E)	Blick m	—	regard m	sguardo m	vista f
look⁴ (E)	schauen	—	regarder	guardare	mirar
look after¹ (E)	kümmern, sich	—	occuper de, se	interessarsi di	ocuparse de
look after² (E)	pflegen	—	soigner	curare	cuidar
look at¹ (E)	ansehen	—	regarder	guardare	mirar
look at² (E)	anschauen	—	regarder	guardare	mirar
looked-after (E)	gepflegt	—	soigné(e)	curato(a)	cuidado(a)
look for (E)	suchen	—	chercher	cercare	buscar

lucidare

	D	E	F	I	Es
loose (E)	locker	—	desserré(e)	lento(a)	flojo(a)
loot (E)	plündern	—	piller	saccheggiare	desvalijar
loro (I)	sie	they	ils/elles	—	ellos, ellas
lorry (E)	Lastwagen *m*	—	camion *m*	camion *m*	camión *m*
los! (D)	—	off!	allons-y!	avanti!	¡adelante!
losbinden (D)	—	free	délier	sciogliere	desatar
löschen (D)	—	extinguish	éteindre	spegnere	apagar
los días laborables (Es)	werktags	on working days	les jours ouvrables	nei giorni feriali	—
lösen (D)	—	solve	résoudre	sciogliere	desatar
lose[1] (E)	einbüßen	—	perdre	perdere	perder
lose[2] (E)	verlieren	—	perdre	perdere	perder
lose weight (E)	abnehmen	—	maigrir	dimagrire	adelgazar
loslassen (D)	—	let go of	lâcher	mollare	dejar libre
los lunes (Es)	montags	Mondays	le lundi	il lunedì	—
los Países Bajos (Es)	Niederlande *f*	Netherlands	Pays-Bas *m pl*	Paesi Bassi *m pl*	—
loss (E)	Verlust *m*	—	perte *f*	perdita *f*	pérdida *f*
lo stesso[1] (I)	dasselbe	the same	la même chose	—	lo mismo
lo stesso[2] (I)	derselbe	the same	le même	—	el mismo
lost property office (E)	Fundbüro *n*	—	bureau des objets trouvés *m*	ufficio oggetti smarriti *m*	oficina de objetos perdidos *f*
Lösung (D)	—	solution	solution *f*	soluzione *f*	solución *f*
lot (E)	Ganze(s) *n*	—	le tout	insieme *m*	todo *m*
loud (E)	laut	—	fort(e)	rumoroso(a)	fuerte
loudspeaker (E)	Lautsprecher *m*	—	haut-parleur *m*	altoparlante *m*	altavoz *m*
louer[1] (F)	loben	praise	—	lodare	elogiar
louer[2] (F)	mieten	rent	—	affittare	alquilar
louer[3] (F)	vermieten	rent	—	affittare	alquilar
lourd[1] (F)	schwül	sultry	—	afoso(a)	sofocante
lourd[2] (F)	schwer	heavy	—	pesante	pesado(a)
love[1] (E)	lieben	—	aimer	amare	amar
love[2] (E)	Liebe *f*	—	amour *m*	amore *m*	amor *m*
love letter (E)	Liebesbrief *m*	—	lettre d'amour *f*	lettera d'amore *f*	carta de amor *f*
low (E)	niedrig	—	bas(se)	basso(a)	bajo
Löwe (D)	—	lion	lion *m*	leone *m*	león *m*
lower[1] (E)	herabsetzen	—	baisser	diminuire	rebajar
lower[2] (E)	senken	—	baisser	abbassare	bajar
lowest (E)	unterste(r,s)	—	inférieur(e)	inferiore	inferior(a)
low season (E)	Vorsaison *f*	—	basse saison *f*	bassa stagione *f*	pretemporada *f*
low tide (E)	Ebbe *f*	—	marée basse *f*	bassa marea *f*	marea baja *f*
loyer (F)	Miete *f*	rent	—	affitto *m*	alquiler *m*
luce[1] (I)	Licht *n*	light	lumière *f*	—	luz *f*
luce[2] (I)	Schein *m*	light	lumière *f*	—	luz *f*
luchar (Es)	kämpfen	fight	battre, se	combattere	—
lucidare (I)	polieren	polish	astiquer	—	pulir

	D	E	F	I	Es
lucido per scarpe (I)	Schuhcreme f	shoe polish	cirage m	—	betún m
luck (E)	Glück n	—	chance f	fortuna f	suerte f
Lücke (D)	—	gap	lacune f	lacuna f	espacio m
luego (Es)	dann	then	ensuite	in seguito	—
Luft (D)	—	air	air m	aria f	aire m
lüften (D)	—	air	aérer	arieggiare	ventilar
Luftpost (D)	—	air mail	poste aérienne f	posta aerea f	correo aéreo m
Luftzug (D)	—	draught	courant d'air m	corrente d'aria f	corriente de aire f
lugar (Es)	Ort m	place	endroit m	luogo m	—
lugares de interés (Es)	Sehenswürdig- keit f	sight	curiosité f	curiosità f	—
lügen (D)	—	lie	mentir	mentire	mentir
luggage (E)	Gepäck n	—	bagages m pl	bagaglio m	equipaje m
luggage desk (E)	Gepäckannahme f	—	enregistrement des bagages m	accettazione bagagli f	recepción de equipajes f
luglio (I)	Juli m	July	juillet m	—	julio m
lui/egli/esso (I)	er	he	il	—	él
lujo (Es)	Luxus m	luxury	luxe m	lusso m	—
lukewarm (E)	lauwarm	—	tiède	tiepido(a)	templado(a)
lumière[1] (F)	Licht n	light	—	luce f	luz f
lumière[2] (F)	Schein m	light	—	luce f	luz f
luna (Es)	Mond m	moon	lune f	luna f	—
luna (I)	Mond m	moon	lune f	—	luna f
luna de miel (Es)	Flitterwochen pl	honeymoon	lune de miel f	luna di miele f	—
luna di miele (I)	Flitterwochen pl	honeymoon	lune de miel f	—	luna de miel f
lunch (E)	Mittagessen n	—	déjeuner m	pranzo m	comida f
l'un dans l'autre (F)	ineinander	into one another	—	l'uno nell'altro	uno en otro
l'un derrière l'autre (F)	hintereinander	one after the other	—	uno dopo l'altro	uno detrás de otro
lundi (F)	Montag m	Monday	—	lunedì m	lunes m
lune (F)	Mond m	moon	—	luna f	luna f
lune de miel (F)	Flitterwochen pl	honeymoon	—	luna di miele f	luna de miel f
lunedì (I)	Montag m	Monday	lundi m	—	lunes m
lunes (Es)	Montag m	Monday	lundi m	lunedì m	—
l'un(e) sur l'autre (F)	übereinander	one upon the other	—	uno sopra l'altro	uno sobre otro
lunettes (F)	Brille f	glasses	—	occhiali m pl	gafas f pl
lunettes de soleil (F)	Sonnenbrille f	sunglasses	—	occhiali da sole m pl	gafas de sol f pl
lung (E)	Lunge f	—	poumon m	polmone m	pulmón m
Lunge (D)	—	lung	poumon m	polmone m	pulmón m
lunghezza (I)	Länge f	length	longueur f	—	longitud f
lungo[1] (I)	entlang	along	le long de	—	a lo largo de
lungo[2] (I)	lang	long	long(ue)	—	largo(a)
l'uno nell'altro (I)	ineinander	into one another	l'un dans l'autre	—	uno en otro
luogo[3] (I)	Ort m	place	endroit m	—	lugar m
lusso (I)	Luxus m	luxury	luxe m	—	lujo m

	D	E	F	I	Es
lussuoso (I)	luxuriös	luxurious	luxueux(-euse)	—	de lujo
Lust (D)	—	delight	plaisir *m*	piacere *m*	ganas *f pl*
lustig (D)	—	funny	marrant(e)	allegro(a)	divertido(a)
lutschen (D)	—	suck	sucer	succhiare	chupar
luxe (F)	Luxus *m*	luxury	—	lusso *m*	lujo *m*
luxueux (F)	luxuriös	luxurious	—	lussuoso(a)	de lujo
luxuriös (D)	—	luxurious	luxueux(-euse)	lussuoso(a)	de lujo
luxurious (E)	luxuriös	—	luxueux(-euse)	lussuoso(a)	de lujo
luxury (E)	Luxus *m*	—	luxe *m*	lusso *m*	lujo *m*
Luxus (D)	—	luxury	luxe *m*	lusso *m*	lujo *m*
luz[1] (Es)	Licht *n*	light	lumière *f*	luce *f*	—
luz[2] (Es)	Schein *m*	light	lumière *f*	luce *f*	—
lycée (F)	Gymnasium *n*	grammar school	—	liceo *m*	instituto de enseñanza media *m*
ma[1] (I)	aber	but	mais	—	pero
ma[2] (I)	sondern	but	mais	—	sino
macchia (I)	Fleck *m*	stain	tache *f*	—	mancha *f*
macchina[1] (I)	Auto *n*	car	voiture *f*	—	coche *m*
macchina[2] (I)	Maschine *f*	machine	machine *f*	—	máquina *f*
macchina da scrivere (I)	Schreibmaschine *f*	typewriter	machine à écrire *f*	—	máquina de escribir *f*
macchina fotografica (I)	Fotoapparat *m*	camera	appareil-photo *m*	—	máquina fotográfica *f*
macellaio (I)	Metzger *m*	butcher	boucher *m*	—	carnicero *m*
macelleria (I)	Metzgerei *f*	butcher's	boucherie *f*	—	carnicería *f*
macerie (I)	Trümmer *pl*	ruins	décombres *m pl*	—	escombros *m pl*
machen (D)	—	make/do	faire	fare	hacer
mâcher (F)	kauen	chew	—	masticare	masticar
machine (E)	Maschine *f*	—	machine *f*	macchina *f*	máquina *f*
machine (F)	Maschine *f*	machine	—	macchina *f*	máquina *f*
machine à écrire (F)	Schreibmaschine *f*	typewriter	—	macchina da scrivere *f*	máquina de escribir *f*
machine à laver (F)	Waschmaschine *f*	washing machine	—	lavatrice *f*	lavadora *f*
machitarse (Es)	welken	wither	faner, se	appassire	—
Macht (D)	—	power	pouvoir *m*	potere *m*	poder *m*
mad (E)	verrückt	—	fou (folle)	pazzo	loco(a)
Mädchen (D)	—	girl	jeune fille *f*	ragazza *f*	chica *f*
mademoiselle (F)	Fräulein *n*	Miss	—	signorina *f*	señorita *f*
madera (Es)	Holz *n*	wood	bois *m*	legno *m*	—
madre (Es)	Mutter *f*	mother	mère *f*	madre *f*	—
madre (I)	Mutter *f*	mother	mère *f*	—	madre *f*
madrina (Es)	Patin *f*	godmother	marraine *f*	madrina *f*	—
madrina (I)	Patin *f*	godmother	marraine *f*	—	madrina *f*
maduro (Es)	reif	ripe	mûr(e)	maturo(a)	—
maestro (Es)	Meister *m*	master	maître *m*	maestro *m*	—

	D	E	F	I	Es
maestro¹ (I)	Lehrer m	teacher	professeur m	—	profesor m
maestro² (I)	Meister m	master	maître m	—	maestro m
magasin¹ (F)	Geschäft n	shop	—	negozio m	tienda f
magasin² (F)	Laden m	shop	—	negozio m	tienda f
magasin³ (F)	Lager n	store	—	magazzino m	almacén m
magasin d'alimentation (F)	Lebensmittel-geschäft n	grocer's	—	negozio di alimentari m	tienda de comestibles f
magasin de chaussures (F)	Schuhgeschäft n	shoeshop	—	negozio di scarpe m	zapatería f
magasin diététique (F)	Reformhaus n	health food shop	—	negozio di prodotti dietetici m	tienda de productos dietéticos f
magazine (E)	Zeitschrift f	—	revue f	rivista f	revista f
magazzino (I)	Lager n	store	magasin m	—	almacén m
Magen (D)	—	stomach	estomac m	stomaco m	estómago m
Magen-schmerzen (D)	—	stomach-ache	mal d'estomac m	mal di stomaco m	dolor de estómago
mager (D)	—	skinny	maigre	magro(a)	delgado(a)
maggio (I)	Mai m	May	mai m	—	mayo m
maggioranza (I)	Mehrheit f	majority	majorité f	—	mayoría f
maggiorenne (I)	volljährig	of age	majeur(e)	—	mayor de edad
magician (E)	Zauberer m	—	magicien m	mago m	mago m
magicien (F)	Zauberer m	magician	—	mago m	mago m
magnificent (E)	großartig	—	formidable	grandioso(a)	magnífico(a)
magnífico¹ (Es)	großartig	magnificent	formidable	grandioso(a)	—
magnífico² (Es)	prächtig	splendid	magnifique	meraviglioso(a)	—
magnifique¹ (F)	herrlich	marvellous	—	stupendo(a)	maravilloso(a)
magnifique² (F)	prächtig	splendid	—	meraviglioso(a)	magnífico(a)
mago (Es)	Zauberer m	magician	magicien m	mago m	—
mago (I)	Zauberer m	magician	magicien m	—	mago m
magro¹ (I)	dünn	thin	mince	—	delgado(a)
magro² (I)	mager	skinny	maigre	—	delgado(a)
mähen (D)	—	mow	faucher	falciare	cortar
Mahlzeit (D)	—	meal	repas m	pasto m	comida f
mahnen (D)	—	warn	exhorter	ammonire	notificar
Mai (D)	—	May	mai m	maggio m	mayo m
mai (F)	Mai m	May	—	maggio m	mayo m
mai¹ (I)	jemals	ever	jamais	—	jamás
mai² (I)	niemals	never	ne…jamais	—	jamás
maiale (I)	Schwein n	pig	cochon m	—	cerdo m
maid (E)	Hausmädchen n	—	fille de service f	domestica f	criada f
maigre¹ (F)	dürr	skinny	—	secco(a)	árido(a)
maigre² (F)	mager	skinny	—	magro(a)	delgado(a)
maigrir (F)	abnehmen	lose weight	—	dimagrire	adelgazar
maillot de bain (F)	Badeanzug m	swimsuit	—	costume da bagno m	traje de baño m
main (F)	Hand f	hand	—	mano f	mano f

	D	E	F	I	Es
mainland (E)	Festland *n*	—	continent *m*	terraferma *f*	tierra firme *f*
mainly (E)	hauptsächlich	—	surtout	principalmente	principalmente
main street (E)	Hauptstraße *f*	—	grand-rue *f*	strada principale *f*	calle central *f*
maintenant[1] (F)	jetzt	now	—	adesso	ahora
maintenant[2] (F)	nun	now	—	adesso	actualmente
maire (F)	Bürgermeister *m*	mayor	—	sindaco *m*	alcalde *m*
mairie (F)	Rathaus *n*	town hall	—	municipio *m*	ayuntamiento *m*
Mais (D)	—	corn	maïs *m*	mais *m*	maíz *m*
mais[1] (F)	aber	but	—	ma	pero
mais[2] (F)	sondern	but	—	ma/bensì	sino
maïs (F)	Mais *m*	corn	—	mais *m*	maíz *m*
mais (I)	Mais *m*	corn	maïs *m*	—	maíz *m*
maison (F)	Haus *n*	house	—	casa *f*	casa *f*
maître (F)	Meister *m*	master	—	maestro *m*	maestro *m*
maître baigneur (F)	Bademeister *m*	baths attendant	—	bagnino *m*	bañero *m*
maíz (Es)	Mais *m*	corn	maïs *m*	mais *m*	—
majeur (F)	volljährig	of age	—	maggiorenne	mayor de edad
majorité (F)	Mehrheit *f*	majority	—	maggioranza *f*	mayoría *f*
majority (E)	Mehrheit *f*	—	majorité *f*	maggioranza *f*	mayoría *f*
make (E)	machen	—	faire	fare	hacer
make an effort[1] (E)	anstrengen	—	faire des efforts	affaticare	cansar
make an effort[2] (E)	bemühen, sich	—	efforcer, se	sforzarsi	esforzarse
make over (E)	überschreiben	—	céder	cedere	transferir
make possible (E)	ermöglichen	—	rendre possible	rendere possibile	facilitar
make smaller (E)	verkleinern	—	réduire	ridurre	reducir
make-up (E)	Schminke *f*	—	maquillage *m*	trucco *m*	maquillaje *m*
make up for (E)	wiedergut-machen	—	réparer	riparare	subsanar
Mal (D)	—	mark	marque *f*	segno *m*	marca *f*
malade (F)	krank	ill	—	malato(a)	enfermo(a)
maladie (F)	Krankheit *f*	illness	—	malattia *f*	enfermedad *f*
maladroit (F)	ungeschickt	clumsy	—	impacciato(a)	torpe
mal à propos (F)	unpassend	inappropriate	—	sconveniente	inadecuado(a)
mala suerte (Es)	Pech *n*	bad luck	malchance *f*	sfortuna *f*	—
malato (I)	krank	ill	malade	—	enfermo(a)
malattia (I)	Krankheit *f*	illness	maladie *f*	—	enfermedad *f*
malchance (F)	Pech *n*	bad luck	—	sfortuna *f*	mala suerte *f*
mal de dents (F)	Zahn-schmerzen *pl*	toothache	—	mal di denti *m*	dolor de muelas *m*
mal de gorge (F)	Hals-schmerzen *pl*	sore throat	—	mal di gola *m*	dolor de garganta *m*
mal d'estomac (F)	Magen-schmerzen *pl*	stomach-ache	—	mal di stomaco *m*	dolor de estómago
mal de tête (F)	Kopfschmerzen *pl*	headache	—	mal di testa *m*	dolor de cabeza *m*
mal di denti (I)	Zahn-schmerzen *pl*	toothache	mal de dents *m*	—	dolor de muelas *m*

	D	E	F	I	Es
mal di gola (I)	Halsschmerzen *pl*	sore throat	mal de gorge *m*	—	dolor de garganta *m*
mal di stomaco (I)	Magenschmerzen *pl*	stomach-ache	mal d'estomac *m*	—	dolor de estómago
mal di testa (I)	Kopfschmerzen *pl*	headache	mal de tête *m*	—	dolor de cabeza *m*
mal d'orecchi (I)	Ohrenschmerzen *pl*	earache	mal d'oreilles *m*	—	dolor de oídos
mal d'oreilles (F)	Ohrenschmerzen *pl*	earache	—	mal d'orecchi *m*	dolor de oídos
mal du pays (F)	Heimweh *n*	homesickness	—	nostalgia *f*	nostalgía *f*
malen (D)	—	paint	peindre	dipingere	pintar
malentendido (Es)	Mißverständnis *n*	misunderstanding	malentendu *m*	equivoco *m*	—
malentendu (F)	Mißverständnis *n*	misunderstanding	—	equivoco *m*	malentendido *m*
Maler (D)	—	painter	peintre *m*	pittore *m*	pintor *m*
Malerei (D)	—	painting	peinture *f*	pittura *f*	pintura *f*
malerisch (D)	—	picturesque	pittoresque	pittoresco(a)	pintoresco(a)
maleta (Es)	Koffer *m*	suitcase	valise *f*	valigia *f*	—
maletero (Es)	Kofferraum *m*	boot	coffre *m*	portabagagli *m*	—
malgré (F)	trotz	despite	—	nonostante	a pesar de
malgré tout (F)	trotzdem	nevertheless	—	tuttavia	no obstante
malheur (F)	Unglück *n*	misfortune	—	disgrazia *f*	desgracia *f*
malheureusement (F)	leider	unfortunately	—	purtroppo	desgraciadamente
malheureux (F)	unglücklich	unhappy	—	sfortunato(a)	desgraciado(a)
malo[1] (Es)	böse	wicked	méchant(e)	cattivo(a)	—
malo[2] (Es)	schlecht	bad	mauvais(e)	cattivo(a)	—
malo[3] (Es)	übel	bad	mauvais(e)	cattivo(a)	—
malsain (F)	ungesund	unhealthy	—	malsano(a)	enfermizo(a)
malsano (I)	ungesund	unhealthy	malsain(e)	—	enfermizo(a)
maltempo (I)	Unwetter *n*	thunderstorm	tempête *f*	—	tormenta *f*
malvolentieri (I)	ungern	reluctantly	de mauvaise grâce	—	de mala gana
man (E)	Mann *m*	—	homme *m*	uomo *m*	hombre *m*
manager (E)	Geschäftsführer *m*	—	gérant *m*	gerente *m*	gerente *m*
mañana[1] (Es)	morgen	tomorrow	demain	domani	—
mañana[2] (Es)	Morgen *m*	morning	matin *m*	mattino *m*	—
mañana[3] (Es)	Vormittag *m*	before noon	matinée *f*	mattina *f*	—
mancanza (I)	Mangel *m*	lack	manque *m*	—	escasez *f*
mancare (I)	fehlen	miss	manquer	—	faltar
mancha (Es)	Fleck *m*	stain	tache *f*	macchia *f*	—
manche (F)	Ärmel *m*	sleeve	—	manica *f*	manga *f*
Manche (F)	Ärmelkanal *m*	Channel	—	Manica *f*	Canal de la Mancha *m*
manchette (F)	Schlagzeile *f*	headline	—	titolo *m*	titular *m*
manchmal (D)	—	sometimes	quelquefois	talvolta	a veces
mancia (I)	Trinkgeld *n*	tip	pourboire *m*	—	propina *f*
mandar[1] (Es)	herrschen	rule	régner	dominare	—
mandar[2] (Es)	schicken	send	envoyer	inviare	—
mandarin (E)	Mandarine *f*	—	mandarine *f*	mandarino *m*	mandarina *f*
mandarina (Es)	Mandarine *f*	mandarin	mandarine *f*	mandarino *m*	—
Mandarine (D)	—	mandarin	mandarine *f*	mandarino *m*	mandarina *f*

	D	E	F	I	Es
mandarine (F)	Mandarine f	mandarin	—	mandarino m	mandarina f
mandarino (I)	Mandarine f	mandarin	mandarine f	—	mandarina f
Mandel (D)	—	almond	amande f	mandorla f	almendra f
mando¹ (Es)	Befehl m	order	ordre m	ordine m	—
mando² (Es)	Führung f	leadership	visite guidée f	visita guidata f	—
mandorla (I)	Mandel f	almond	amande f	—	almendra f
manège (F)	Karussell n	roundabout	—	giostra f	tíovivo m
manera¹ (Es)	Art f	way	manière f	modo m	—
manera² (Es)	Weise f	way	manière f	maniera f	—
manga (Es)	Ärmel m	sleeve	manche f	manica f	—
mangeable (F)	eßbar	eatable	—	commestibile	comestible
Mangel (D)	—	lack	manque m	mancanza f	escasez f
manger¹ (F)	essen	eat	—	mangiare	comer
manger² (F)	speisen	dine	—	mangiare	comer
mangiare¹ (I)	essen	eat	manger	—	comer
mangiare² (I)	fressen	eat	bouffer	—	devorar
mangiare³ (I)	speisen	dine	manger	—	comer
Manica (I)	Ärmel m	sleeve	manche f	—	manga f
manica (I)	Ärmelkanal m	Channel	Manche f	—	Canal de la Mancha m
maniera (I)	Weise f	way	manière f	—	manera f
manière¹ (F)	Art f	way	—	modo m	manera f
manière² (F)	Weise f	way	—	maniera f	manera f
manifestation¹ (F)	Demonstration f	demonstration	—	manifestazione f	manifestación f
manifestation² (F)	Veranstaltung f	event	—	manifestazione f	representación f
manifestazione¹ (I)	Demonstration f	demonstration	manifestation f	—	manifestación f
manifestazione² (I)	Veranstaltung f	event	manifestation f	—	representación f
manifeste (F)	offensichtlich	obvious	—	evidente	evidente
maniglia (I)	Griff m	handle	poignée f	—	asidero m
Mann (D)	—	man	homme m	uomo m	hombre m
männlich (D)	—	masculine	masculin(e)	maschile	masculino m
Mannschaft (D)	—	team	équipe f	squadra f	equipo m
mano (Es)	Hand f	hand	main f	mano f	—
mano (I)	Hand f	hand	main f	—	mano f
mañoso (Es)	geschickt	skilful	habile	abile	—
manque (F)	Mangel m	lack	—	mancanza f	escasez f
manquer¹ (F)	fehlen	miss	—	mancare	faltar
manquer² (F)	versäumen	miss	—	perdere	perder
manquer³ (F)	vermissen	miss	—	sentire la mancanza	echar de menos
manteau (F)	Mantel m	coat	—	cappotto m	abrigo m
Mantel (D)	—	coat	manteau m	cappotto m	abrigo m
mantequilla (Es)	Butter f	butter	beurre m	burro m	—
manufacture (E)	herstellen	—	produire	fabbricare	producir
manufacturer (E)	Hersteller m	—	producteur m	produttore m	productor m
many (E)	viele	—	beaucoup de	molti(e)	muchos(as)
manzana (Es)	Apfel m	apple	pomme f	mela f	—
manzo (I)	Rind n	cow	bœuf m	—	buey m
map (E)	Landkarte f	—	carte f	carta geografica f	mapa m

	D	E	F	I	Es
mapa (Es)	Landkarte *f*	map	carte *f*	carta geografica *f*	—
Mappe (D)	—	folder	serviette *f*	raccoglitore *m*	carpeta *f*
maquillage (F)	Schminke *f*	make-up	—	trucco *m*	maquillaje *m*
maquillaje (Es)	Schminke *f*	make-up	maquillage *m*	trucco *m*	—
máquina (Es)	Maschine *f*	machine	machine *f*	macchina *f*	—
máquina de afeitar (Es)	Rasierapparat *m*	shaver	rasoir *m*	rasoio *m*	—
máquina de escribir (Es)	Schreibmaschine *f*	typewriter	machine à écrire *f*	macchina da scrivere *f*	—
máquina fotográfica (Es)	Fotoapparat *m*	camera	appareil-photo *m*	macchina fotografica *f*	—
mar (Es)	Meer *n*	sea	mer *f*	mare *m*	—
maravilloso¹ (Es)	herrlich	marvellous	magnifique	stupendo(a)	—
maravilloso² (Es)	wunderbar	wonderful	miraculeux(-euse)	meraviglioso(a)	—
marca¹ (Es)	Marke *f*	brand	marque *f*	marca *f*	—
marca² (Es)	Mal *n*	mark	marque *f*	segno *m*	—
marca (I)	Marke *f*	brand	marque *f*	—	marca *f*
March (E)	März *m*	—	mars *m*	marzo *m*	marzo *m*
marcha (Es)	Gang *m*	gear	vitesse *f*	marcia *f*	—
marcha atrás (Es)	rückwärts	backwards	en arrière	in dietro	—
marchandise (F)	Ware *f*	goods	—	merce *f*	mercancía *f*
marchandises (F)	Güter *pl*	goods	—	beni *m pl*	bienes *f pl*
marcharse (Es)	weggehen	go away	s'en aller	andare via	—
marché (F)	Markt *m*	market	—	mercato *m*	mercado *m*
marche (F)	Stufe *f*	step	—	gradino *m*	escalón *m*
marché aux puces (F)	Flohmarkt *m*	fleamarket	—	mercato delle pulci *m*	rastro *m*
marcher (F)	wandern	hike	—	fare escursioni a piedi	hacer excursiones
marcher devant (F)	vorangehen	go ahead	—	andare avanti	pasar adelante
marcia (I)	Gang *m*	gear	vitesse *f*	—	marcha *f*
marciapiede (I)	Gehweg *m*	pavement	trottoir *m*	—	acera *f*
marco¹ (Es)	Mark *f*	mark	mark *m*	marco *m*	—
marco² (Es)	Rahmen *m*	frame	cadre *m*	cornice *f*	—
marco (I)	Mark *f*	mark	mark *m*	—	marco *m*
mar del norte (Es)	Nordsee *f*	North Sea	mer du Nord *f*	Mare del Nord *m*	—
mardi (F)	Dienstag *m*	Tuesday	—	martedì *m*	martes *m*
mare (I)	Meer *n*	sea	mer *f*	—	mar *m*
marea alta (Es)	Flut *f*	high tide	marée haute *f*	alta marea *f*	—
marea baja (Es)	Ebbe *f*	low tide	marée basse *f*	bassa marea *f*	—
Mare del Nord (I)	Nordsee *f*	North Sea	mer du Nord *f*	—	mar del norte *m*
marée basse (F)	Ebbe *f*	low tide	—	bassa marea *f*	marea baja *f*
marée haute (F)	Flut *f*	high tide	—	alta marea *f*	marea alta *f*
margine (I)	Rand *m*	brim	bord *m*	—	borde *m*
mari (F)	Ehemann *m*	husband	—	marito *m*	marido *m*
mariage¹ (F)	Ehe *f*	marriage	—	matrimonio *m*	matrimonio *m*
mariage² (F)	Hochzeit *f*	wedding	—	nozze *f pl*	boda *f*
mariage³ (F)	Heirat *f*	marriage	—	matrimonio *m*	boda *f*
marido (Es)	Ehemann *m*	husband	mari *m*	marito *m*	—
marié (F)	verheiratet	married	—	sposato(a)	casado(a)

	D	E	F	I	Es
mariée (F)	Braut f	bride	—	sposa f	novia f
marier, se (F)	heiraten	marry	—	sposarsi	casarse
marinaio (I)	Matrose m	sailor	matelot m	—	marinero m
marinero (Es)	Matrose m	sailor	matelot m	marinaio m	—
mariposa (Es)	Schmetterling m	butterfly	papillon m	farfalla f	—
marito (I)	Ehemann m	husband	mari m	—	marido m
Mark (D)	—	mark	mark m	marco m	marco m
mark[1] (E)	Mark f	—	mark m	marco m	marco m
mark[2] (E)	Mal n	—	marque f	segno m	marca f
mark[3] (E)	Note f	—	note f	voto m	calificación f
mark (F)	Mark f	mark	—	marco m	marco m
Marke (D)	—	brand	marque f	marca f	marca f
market (E)	Markt m	—	marché m	mercato m	mercado m
Markt (D)	—	market	marché m	mercato m	mercado m
mar mediterráneo (Es)	Mittelmeer n	Mediterranean	Méditerranée f	Mediterraneo m	—
Marmelade (D)	—	jam	confiture f	marmellata f	mermelada f
marmelade (E)	Orangen-marmelade f	—	marmelade d'oranges f	marmellata d'arancia f	mermelada de naranja f
marmellata (I)	Marmelade f	jam	confiture f	—	mermelada f
marque[1] (F)	Mal n	mark	—	segno m	marca f
marque[2] (F)	Marke f	brand	—	marca f	marca f
marraine (F)	Patin f	godmother	—	madrina f	madrina f
marrant (F)	lustig	funny	—	allegro(a)	divertido(a)
marriage[1] (E)	Ehe f	—	mariage m	matrimonio m	matrimonio m
marriage[2] (E)	Heirat f	—	mariage m	matrimonio m	boda f
married (E)	verheiratet	—	marié(e)	sposato(a)	casado(a)
marrón (Es)	braun	brown	marron	marrone	—
marron (F)	braun	brown	—	marrone	marrón
marrone (I)	braun	brown	marron	—	marrón
marry (E)	heiraten	—	marier, se	sposarsi	casarse
mars (F)	März m	March	—	marzo m	marzo m
marteau (F)	Hammer m	hammer	—	martello m	martillo m
martedì (I)	Dienstag m	Tuesday	mardi m	—	martes m
martello (I)	Hammer m	hammer	marteau m	—	martillo m
martes (Es)	Dienstag m	Tuesday	mardi m	martedì m	—
martillo (Es)	Hammer m	hammer	marteau m	martello m	—
marvellous (E)	herrlich	—	magnifique	stupendo(a)	maravilloso(a)
März (D)	—	March	mars m	marzo m	marzo m
marzo (Es)	März m	March	mars m	marzo m	—
marzo (I)	März m	March	mars m	—	marzo m
más[1] (Es)	mehr	more	plus	più	—
más[2] (Es)	plus	plus	plus	più	—
masa (Es)	Teig m	dough	pâte f	pasta f	—
masaje (Es)	Massage f	massage	massage m	massaggio m	—
más bien (Es)	lieber	rather	mieux	piuttosto	—
máscara (Es)	Maske f	mask	masque m	maschera f	—
maschera (I)	Maske f	mask	masque m	—	másquera f
maschile (I)	männlich	masculine	masculin(e)	—	masculino m

	D	E	F	I	Es
Maschine (D)	—	machine	machine *f*	macchina *f*	máquina *f*
masculin (F)	männlich	masculine	—	maschile	masculino *m*
masculine (E)	männlich	—	masculin(e)	maschile	masculino *m*
masculino (Es)	männlich	masculine	masculin(e)	maschile	—
Masern (D)	—	measles	rougeole *f*	morbillo *m*	sarampión *m*
mask (E)	Maske *f*	—	masque *m*	maschera *f*	másquera *f*
Maske (D)	—	mask	masque *m*	maschera *f*	másquera *f*
masque (F)	Maske *f*	mask	—	maschera *f*	másquera *f*
Maß (D)	—	measure	mesure *f*	misura *f*	medida *f*
Massage (D)	—	massage	massage *m*	massaggio *m*	masaje *m*
massage (E)	Massage *f*	—	massage *m*	massaggio *m*	masaje *m*
massage (F)	Massage *f*	massage	—	massaggio *m*	masaje *m*
massaggio (I)	Massage *f*	massage	massage *m*	—	masaje *m*
mäßig (D)	—	moderate	modéré(e)	moderato(a)	moderado(a)
massimo (I)	Maximum *n*	maximum	maximum *m*	—	máximo *m*
más tarde (Es)	später	later	plus tard	piú tardi	—
master (E)	Meister *m*	—	maître *m*	maestro *m*	maestro *m*
masticar (Es)	kauen	chew	mâcher	masticare	—
masticare (I)	kauen	chew	mâcher	—	mastigar
mat (E)	Matte *f*	—	natte *f*	stuoia *f*	colchoneta *f*
matar[1] (Es)	töten	kill	tuer	uccidere	—
matar[2] (Es)	umbringen	kill	tuer	uccidere	—
match (E)	Streichholz *n*	—	allumette *f*	fiammifero *m*	cerilla *f*
matelas (F)	Matratze *f*	mattress	—	materasso *m*	colchón *m*
matelot (F)	Matrose *m*	sailor	—	marinaio *m*	marinero *m*
materasso (I)	Matratze *f*	mattress	matelas *m*	—	colchón *m*
materia (Es)	Fach *n*	subject	matière *f*	materia *f*	—
materia (I)	Fach *n*	subject	matière *f*	—	materia *f*
Material (D)	—	material	matériel *m*	materiale *m*	material *m*
material (E)	Material *n*	—	matériel *m*	materiale *m*	material *m*
material (Es)	Material *n*	material	matériel *m*	materiale *m*	—
materiale (I)	Material *n*	material	matériel *m*	—	material *m*
matériel (F)	Material *n*	material	—	materiale *m*	material *m*
matière (F)	Fach *n*	subject	—	materia *f*	materia *f*
matin (F)	Morgen *m*	morning	—	mattino *m*	mañana *f*
matinée (F)	Vormittag *m*	before noon	—	mattina *f*	mañana *f*
matita (I)	Bleistift *m*	pencil	crayon *m*	—	lápiz *m*
Matratze (D)	—	mattress	matelas *m*	materasso *m*	colchón *m*
matrícula (Es)	Nummernschild *n*	number plate	plaque d'immatriculation *f*	targa *f*	—
matrimonio (Es)	Ehe *f*	marriage	mariage *m*	matrimonio *m*	—
matrimonio[1] (I)	Ehe *f*	marriage	mariage *m*	—	matrimonio *m*
matrimonio[2] (I)	Heirat *f*	marriage	mariage *m*	—	boda *f*
Matrose (D)	—	sailor	matelot *m*	marinaio *m*	marinero *m*
Matte (D)	—	mat	natte *f*	stuoia *f*	colchoneta *f*
mattina (I)	Vormittag *m*	before noon	matinée *f*	—	mañana *f*
mattino (I)	Morgen *m*	morning	matin *m*	—	mañana *f*
mattone (I)	Ziegel *m*	brick	brique *f*	—	ladrillo *m*

	D	E	F	I	Es
mattress (E)	Matratze f	—	matelas m	materasso m	colchón m
maturità (I)	Abitur n	German school leaving examinations	baccalauréat m	—	bachillerato m
maturo (I)	reif	ripe	mûr(e)	—	maduro(a)
Mauer (D)	—	wall	mur m	muro m	muro m
Maul (D)	—	mouth	gueule f	muso m	hocico m
Maus (D)	—	mouse	souris f	topo m	ratón m
mauvais¹ (F)	schlecht	bad	—	cattivo(a)	malo(a)
mauvais² (F)	übel	bad	—	cattivo(a)	malo(a)
mauvais numéro (F)	Niete f	blanc	—	biglietto non vincente m	número sin premio m
mauve (F)	lila	purple	—	lilla	de color lila
máximo (Es)	Maximum n	maximum	maximum m	massimo m	—
Maximum (D)	—	maximum	maximum m	massimo m	máximo m
maximum (E)	Maximum n	—	maximum m	massimo m	máximo m
maximum (F)	Maximum n	maximum	—	massimo m	máximo m
maximum price (E)	Höchstpreis m	—	prix plafond m	prezzo massimo m	precio máximo m
maximum speed (E)	Höchst-geschwindigkeit f	—	vitesse maximum f	velocità massima f	velocidad máxima f
May (E)	Mai m	—	mai m	maggio m	mayo m
maybe (E)	vielleicht	—	peut-être	forse	tal vez
mayo (Es)	Mai m	May	mai m	maggio m	—
mayor (E)	Bürgermeister m	—	maire m	sindaco m	alcalde m
mayor (Es)	ältere(r,s)	elder	aîné(e)	maggiore	—
mayor de edad (Es)	volljährig	of age	majeur(e)	maggiorenne	—
mayoría (Es)	Mehrheit f	majority	majorité f	maggioranza f	—
mazout (F)	Heizöl n	fuel	—	olio combustibile m	combustible para la calefacción m
mazzo (I)	Strauß m	bunch	bouquet m	—	ramo m
meadow (E)	Wiese f	—	pré m	prato m	prado m
meal (E)	Mahlzeit f	—	repas m	pasto m	comida f
mean¹ (E)	bedeuten	—	signifier	significare	significar
mean² (E)	geizig	—	avare	avaro(a)	avaro(a)
mean³ (E)	gemein	—	méchant(e)	volgare	vulgar
meaning (E)	Bedeutung f	—	signification f	significato m	significado m
means (E)	Mittel n	—	moyen m	mezzo m	medio m
meanwhile¹ (E)	inzwischen	—	entretemps	frattanto	mientras tanto
meanwhile² (E)	indessen	—	cependant	nel frattempo	en eso
measles (E)	Masern pl	—	rougeole f	morbillo m	sarampión m
measurable (E)	meßbar	—	mesurable	misurabile	mensurable
measure¹ (E)	messen	—	mesurer	misurare	medir
measure² (E)	Maß n	—	mesure f	misura f	medida f
meat (E)	Fleisch n	—	viande f	carne f	carne f
mécanicien (F)	Mechaniker m	engineer	—	meccanico m	mecánico m
mecánico (Es)	Mechaniker m	engineer	mécanicien m	meccanico m	—
meccanico (I)	Mechaniker m	engineer	mécanicien m	—	mecánico m
Mechaniker (D)	—	engineer	mécanicien m	meccanico m	mecánico m
méchant¹ (F)	böse	wicked	—	cattivo(a)	malo(a)
méchant² (F)	gemein	mean	—	volgare	vulgar

	D	E	F	I	Es
mechero (Es)	Feuerzeug n	lighter	briquet m	accendino m	—
mécontent (F)	unzufrieden	dissatisfied	—	scontento(a)	descontento(a)
médecin (F)	Arzt m	doctor	—	medico m	médico m
médecine (F)	Medizin f	medicine	—	medicina f	medicina f
media (Es)	Strumpf m	stocking	bas m	calza f	—
medianoche (Es)	Mitternacht f	midnight	minuit m	mezzanotte f	—
media pensión (Es)	Halbpension f	half board	demi-pension f	mezza pensione f	—
medicament (E)	Medikament n	—	médicament m	medicamento m	medicamento m
médicament¹ (F)	Arznei f	medicine	—	medicina f	medicina f
médicament² (F)	Medikament n	medicament	—	medicamento m	medicamento m
medicamento (Es)	Medikament n	medicament	médicament m	medicamento m	—
medicamento (I)	Medikament n	medicament	médicament m	—	medicamento m
medicina¹ (Es)	Arznei f	medicine	médicament m	medicina f	—
medicina² (Es)	Medizin f	medicine	médecine f	medicina f	—
medicina¹ (I)	Arznei f	medicine	médicament m	—	medicina f
medicina² (I)	Medizin f	medicine	médecine f	—	medicina f
medicine¹ (E)	Arznei f	—	médicament m	medicina f	medicina f
medicine² (E)	Medizin f	—	médecine f	medicina f	medicina f
medico (I)	Arzt m	doctor	médecin m	—	médico m
médico (Es)	Arzt m	doctor	médecin m	medico m	—
médico del oído (Es)	Ohrenarzt m	ear specialist	spécialiste de l'oreille m	otoiatra m	—
medida (Es)	Maß n	measure	mesure f	misura f	—
Medikament (D)	—	medicament	médicament m	medicamento m	medicamento m
medio¹ (Es)	Mitte f	middle	milieu m	centro m	—
medio² (Es)	Mittel n	means	moyen m	mezzo m	—
medio³ (Es)	halb	half	demi(e)	mezzo(a)	—
medio (I)	durchschnittlich	average	moyen(ne)	—	medio(a)
medio ambiente (Es)	Umwelt f	environment	environnement m	ambiente m	—
mediodía¹ (Es)	mittags	midday	à midi	a mezzogiorno	—
mediodía² (Es)	Mittag m	midday	midi m	mezzogiorno m	—
medir (Es)	messen	measure	mesurer	misurare	—
Mediterranean (E)	Mittelmeer n ~	—	Méditerranée f	Mediterraneo m	mar mediterráneo m
Méditerranée (F)	Mittelmeer n	Mediterranean	—	Mediterraneo m	mar mediterráneo m
Mediterraneo (I)	Mittelmeer n	Mediterranean	Méditerranée f	—	mar mediterráneo m
Medizin (D)	—	medicine	médecine f	medicina f	medicina f
Meer (D)	—	sea	mer m	mare m	mar m
Meeresspiegel (D)	—	sea level	niveau de la mer m	livello del mare m	nivel del mar m
meet¹ (E)	begegnen	—	rencontrer	incontrare	encontrar
meet² (E)	treffen	—	rencontrer	incontrare	encontrar
meeting¹ (E)	Sitzung f	—	séance f	seduta f	reunión f
meeting² (E)	Treffen n	—	rencontre f	incontro m	encuentro m
méfait (F)	Untat f	crime	—	misfatto m	crimen m
méfiance (F)	Mißtrauen n	distrust	—	sfiducia f	desconfianza f
méfier, se (F)	mißtrauen	mistrust	—	non fidarsi	desconfiar
meglio (I)	besser	better	meilleur(e)	—	mejor

	D	E	F	I	Es
Mehl (D)	—	flour	farine *f*	farina *f*	harina *f*
mehr (D)	—	more	plus	più	más
mehrere (D)	—	several	plusieurs	parecchi	muchos(as)
Mehrheit (D)	—	majority	majorité *f*	maggioranza *f*	mayoría *f*
Mehrwertsteuer (D)	—	value added tax	taxe sur la valeur ajoutée *f*	imposta sul'valore aggiunto *f*	impuesto sobre el valor añadido *m*
Mehrzahl (D)	—	plural	pluriel *m*	plurale *m*	plural *m*
meiden (D)	—	avoid	éviter	evitare	evitar
Meile (D)	—	mile	mille *m*	miglio *m*	milla *f*
meilleur[1] (F)	beste(r,s)	best	—	migliore	óptimo(a)
meilleur[2] (F)	besser	better	—	meglio	mejor
meine (D)	—	my/mine	le(la) mien(ne)	mio(a)	mío(a)
meinen (D)	—	think	penser	credere	opinar
Meinung (D)	—	opinion	opinion *f*	opinione *f*	opinión *f*
meist (D)	—	most	la plupart de	nella maggior parte di	la mayor parte de
meistens (D)	—	generally	généralement	di solito	por lo común
Meister (D)	—	master	maître *m*	maestro *m*	maestro *m*
Méjico (Es)	Mexiko	Mexico	Mexique *m*	Messico *m*	—
mejilla (Es)	Wange *f*	cheek	joue *f*	guancia *f*	—
mejillón (Es)	Muschel *f*	mussel	moule *f*	cozza *f*	—
mejor (Es)	besser	better	meilleur(e)	meglio	—
mejorar (Es)	verbessern	improve	améliorer	migliorare	—
mela (I)	Apfel *m*	apple	pomme *f*	—	manzana *f*
mélanger (F)	mischen	mix	—	mescolare	mezclar
melden (D)	—	report	annoncer	annunciare	declarar
Meldung (D)	—	report	annonce *f*	annuncio *m*	aviso *m*
melocotón (Es)	Pfirsich *m*	peach	pêche *f*	pesca *f*	—
melodía (Es)	Melodie *f*	melody	mélodie *f*	melodia *f*	—
melodia (I)	Melodie *f*	melody	mélodie *f*	—	melodía *f*
Melodie (D)	—	melody	mélodie *f*	melodia *f*	melodía *f*
mélodie (F)	Melodie *f*	melody	—	melodia *f*	melodía *f*
melody (E)	Melodie *f*	—	mélodie *f*	melodia *f*	melodía *f*
melon (E)	Melone *f*	—	melon *m*	melone *m*	melón *m*
melón (Es)	Melone *f*	melon	melon *m*	melone *m*	—
melon (F)	Melone *f*	melon	—	melone *m*	melón *m*
Melone (D)	—	melon	melon *m*	melone *m*	melón *m*
melone (I)	Melone *f*	melon	melon *m*	—	melón *m*
member (E)	Mitglied *n*	—	membre *m*	membro *m*	miembro *m*
membre (F)	Mitglied *n*	member	—	membro *m*	miembro *m*
membro (I)	Mitglied *n*	member	membre *m*	—	miembro *m*
même (F)	sogar	even	—	perfino	incluso
mémoire (F)	Gedächtnis *n*	memory	—	memoria *f*	memoria *f*
memoria[1] (Es)	Andenken *n*	souvenir	souvenir *m*	ricordo *m*	—
memoria[2] (Es)	Erinnerung *f*	memory	souvenir *m*	ricordo *m*	—
memoria[3] (Es)	Gedächtnis *n*	memory	mémoire *f*	memoria *f*	—
memoria (I)	Gedächtnis *n*	memory	mémoire *f*	—	memoria *f*
memory[1] (E)	Erinnerung *f*	—	souvenir *m*	ricordo *m*	recuerdo *m*
memory[2] (E)	Gedächtnis *n*	—	mémoire *f*	memoria *f*	memoria *f*

	D	E	F	I	Es
menacer¹ (F)	androhen	threaten s.b.	—	minacciare	amenazar
menacer² (F)	bedrohen	threaten	—	minacciare	amenazar
menacer³ (F)	drohen	threaten	—	minacciare	amenazar (a alguien)
ménage (F)	Haushalt m	household	—	casa f	casa f
mencionar (Es)	erwähnen	mention	mentionner	menzionare	—
mener (F)	treiben	drive	—	spingere	estimular
Menge (D)	—	quantity	quantité f	quantità f	cantidad f
meno (I)	minus	minus	moins	—	menos
menos¹ (Es)	minus	minus	moins	meno	—
menos² (Es)	weniger	less	moins	di meno	—
mensaje (Es)	Botschaft f	message	message m	messaggio m	—
mensajero (Es)	Eilbote m	courier	courrier m	corriere m	—
Mensch (D)	—	human being	homme m	essere umano m	persona f
Menschen-menge (D)	—	crowd	foule f	folla f	muchedumbre f
menschlich (D)	—	human	humain(e)	umano(a)	humano(a)
mensile (I)	monatlich	monthly	mensuel(le)	—	mensual
mensual (Es)	monatlich	monthly	mensuel(le)	mensile	—
mensuel (F)	monatlich	monthly	—	mensile	mensual
mensurable (Es)	meßbar	measurable	mesurable	misurabile	—
mention (E)	erwähnen	—	mentionner	menzionare	mencionar
mentionner (F)	erwähnen	mention	—	menzionare	mencionar
mentir (Es)	lügen	lie	mentir	mentire	—
mentir (F)	lügen	lie	—	mentire	mentir
mentire (I)	lügen	lie	mentir	—	mentir
mento (I)	Kinn n	chin	menton m	—	barbilla f
menton (F)	Kinn n	chin	—	mento m	barbilla f
menu (E)	Speisekarte f	—	menu m	menu m	lista de platos f
menu (F)	Speisekarte f	menu	—	menu m	lista de platos f
menu (I)	Speisekarte f	menu	menu m	—	lista de platos f
menuisier (F)	Tischler m	carpenter	—	falegname m	carpintero m
menzionare (I)	erwähnen	mention	mentionner	—	mencionar
mer (F)	Meer n	sea	—	mare m	mar m
meraviglioso¹ (I)	prächtig	splendid	magnifique	—	magnífico(a)
meraviglioso² (I)	wunderbar	wonderful	miraculeux (-euse)	—	maravilloso(a)
mercado (Es)	Markt m	market	marché m	mercato m	—
mercancía (Es)	Ware f	goods	marchandise f	merce f	—
mercato (I)	Markt m	market	marché m	—	mercado m
mercato delle pulci (I)	Flohmarkt m	fleamarket	marché aux puces m	—	rastro m
merce (I)	Ware f	goods	marchandise f	—	mercancía f
merci (F)	danke	thank you	—	grazie	¡gracias!
mercoledì (I)	Mittwoch m	Wednesday	mercredi m	—	miércoles m
mercredi (F)	Mittwoch m	Wednesday	—	mercoledì m	miércoles m
mercure (F)	Quecksilber n	mercury	—	mercurio m	mercurio m
mercurio (Es)	Quecksilber n	mercury	mercure m	mercurio m	—
mercurio (I)	Quecksilber n	mercury	mercure m	—	mercurio m
mercury (E)	Quecksilber n	—	mercure m	mercurio m	mercurio m

	D	E	F	I	Es
mer du Nord (F)	Nordsee *f*	North Sea	—	mare del Nord *m*	mar del norte *m*
mère (F)	Mutter *f*	mother	—	madre *f*	madre *f*
merit (E)	Verdienst *n*	—	mérite *m*	merito *m*	mérito *m*
mérite (F)	Verdienst *n*	merit	—	merit *m*	mérito *m*
mérito (Es)	Verdienst *n*	merit	mérite *m*	merito *m*	—
merito (I)	Verdienst *n*	merit	mérite *m*	—	mérito *m*
merken (D)	—	notice	remarquer	accorgersi di	notar
Merkmal (D)	—	characteristic	signe *m*	caratteristica *f*	rasgo *m*
merkwürdig (D)	—	strange	curieux(-euse)	curioso(a)	curioso(a)
mermelada (Es)	Marmelade *f*	jam	confiture *f*	marmellata *f*	—
mero (Es)	pur	pure	pur(e)	puro(a)	—
mes (Es)	Monat *m*	month	mois *m*	mese *m*	—
mesa (Es)	Tisch *m*	table	table *f*	tavolo *m*	—
mescolare (I)	mischen	mix	mélanger	—	mezclar
mese (I)	Monat *m*	month	mois *m*	—	mes *m*
mess (E)	Unordnung *f*	—	désordre *m*	disordine *m*	desorden *m*
messa (I)	Gottesdienst *m*	service	office divin *m*	—	servicio religioso *m*
message[1] (E)	Botschaft *f*	—	message *m*	messaggio *m*	mensaje *m*
message[2] (E)	Mitteilung *f*	—	information *f*	comunicazione *f*	comunicación *f*
message[3] (E)	Nachricht *f*	—	nouvelle *f*	notizia *f*	noticia *f*
message (F)	Botschaft *f*	message	—	messaggio *m*	mensaje *m*
messaggio (I)	Botschaft *f*	message	message *m*	—	mensaje *m*
meßbar (D)	—	measurable	mesurable	misurabile	mesurable
Messe (D)	—	fair	foire *f*	fiera *f*	feria *f*
messen (D)	—	measure	mesurer	misurare	medir
Messer (D)	—	knife	couteau *m*	coltello *m*	cuchillo *m*
Messico (I)	Mexiko	Mexico	Mexique *m*	—	Méjico *m*
mestizo (Es)	Mischling *m*	halfcaste	métis *m*	sangue misto *m*	—
mesurable (F)	meßbar	measurable	—	misurabile	mesurable
mesure (F)	Maß *n*	measure	—	misura *f*	medida *f*
mesurer (F)	messen	measure	—	misurare	medir
meta (I)	Ziel *n*	goal	but *m*	—	intención *f*
metà (I)	Hälfte *f*	half	moitié *f*	—	mitad *f*
metal (E)	Metall *n*	—	métal *m*	metallo *m*	metal *m*
metal (Es)	Metall *n*	metal	métal *m*	metallo *m*	—
métal (F)	Metall *n*	metal	—	metallo *m*	metal *m*
Metall (D)	—	metal	métal *m*	metallo *m*	metal *m*
metallo (I)	Metall *n*	metal	métal *m*	—	metal *m*
Meter (D)	—	metre	mètre *m*	metro *m*	metro *m*
method (E)	Methode *f*	—	méthode *f*	metodo *m*	método *m*
Methode (D)	—	method	méthode *f*	metodo *m*	método *m*
méthode (F)	Methode *f*	method	—	metodo *m*	método *m*
métier (F)	Handwerk *n*	craft	—	artigianato *m*	artesanía *f*
métis (F)	Mischling *m*	halfcaste	—	sangue misto *m*	mestizo *m*
método (Es)	Methode *f*	method	méthode *f*	metodo *m*	—
metodo (I)	Methode *f*	method	méthode *f*	—	método *m*
metre (E)	Meter *m*	—	mètre *m*	metro *m*	metro *m*
mètre (F)	Meter *m*	metre	—	metro *m*	metro *m*

	D	E	F	I	Es
mètre carré (F)	Quadratmeter *n*	square metre	—	metro quadrato *m*	metro cuadrado *m*
mètre cube (F)	Kubikmeter *m*	cubic metre	—	metro cubo *m*	metro cúbico *m*
metro[1] (Es)	Meter *m*	metre	mètre *m*	metro *m*	—
metro[2] (Es)	U-Bahn *f*	underground	métro *m*	metropolitana *f*	—
métro (F)	U-Bahn *f*	underground	—	metropolitana *f*	metro *m*
metro (I)	Meter *m*	metre	mètre *m*	—	metro *m*
metro cuadrado (Es)	Quadratmeter *m*	square metre	mètre carré *m*	metro quadrato *m*	—
metro cúbico (Es)	Kubikmeter *m*	cubic metre	mètre cube *m*	metro cubo *m*	—
metro cubo (I)	Kubikmeter *m*	cubic metre	mètre cube *m*	—	metro cúbico *m*
metropolitana (I)	U-Bahn *f*	underground	métro *m*	—	metro *m*
metro quadrato (I)	Quadratmeter *m*	square metre	mètre carré *m*	—	metro cuadrado *m*
mettere[1] (I)	legen	lay	mettre	—	colocar
mettere[2] (I)	stellen	place	mettre	—	colocar
mettere[3] (I)	setzen	put	mettre	—	poner
mettere in conto (I)	anrechnen	charge	compter	—	poner en cuenta
mettere in libertà (I)	freilassen	release	libérer	—	poner en libertad
mettere in ordine (I)	aufräumen	clear away	ranger	—	arreglar
mettere in scena (I)	inszenieren	stage	mettre en scène	—	escenificar
mettre[1] (F)	anziehen	dress	—	indossare	ponerse
mettre[2] (F)	legen	lay	—	mettere	colocar
mettre[3] (F)	setzen	put	—	mettere	poner
mettre[4] (F)	stellen	place	—	mettere	colocar
mettre au monde (F)	gebären	give birth to	—	partorire	parir
mettre d'accord, se (F)	einigen, sich	agree	—	accordarsi	ponerse de acuerdo
mettre en marche (F)	anstellen	turn on	—	accendere	poner
mettre en scène (F)	inszenieren	stage	—	mettere in scena	escenificar
mettre le pied sur (F)	treten	step	—	pestare	pisar
Metzger (D)	—	butcher	boucher *m*	macellaio *m*	carnicero *m*
Metzgerei (D)	—	butcher's	boucherie *f*	macelleria *f*	carnicería *f*
meuble (F)	Möbel *n*	furniture	—	mobile *m*	mueble *m*
meublé (F)	möbliert	furnished	—	ammobiliato(a)	amueblado(a)
meubler (F)	möblieren	furnish	—	ammobiliare	amueblar
meurtre (F)	Mord *m*	murder	—	assassinio *m*	asesinato *m*
Mexico (E)	Mexiko	—	Mexique *m*	Messico *m*	Méjico *m*
Mexiko (D)	—	Mexico	Mexique *m*	Messico *m*	Méjico *m*
Mexique (F)	Mexiko	Mexico	—	Messico *m*	Méjico *m*
mezclar (Es)	mischen	mix	mélanger	mescolare	—
mezzanotte (I)	Mitternacht *f*	midnight	minuit *m*	—	medianoche *f*
mezza pensione (I)	Halbpension *f*	half board	demi-pension *f*	—	media pensión *f*
mezzo[1] (I)	halb	half	demi(e)	—	medio(a)
mezzo[2] (I)	Mittel *n*	means	moyen *m*	—	medio *m*
mezzo chilo (I)	Pfund *n*	pound	livre *f*	—	libra *f*
mezzogiorno (I)	Mittag *m*	midday	midi *m*	—	mediodía *m*
mío (Es)	meine(r,s)	mine	le(la) mien(ne)	mio(a)	—
midday (E)	Mittag *m*	—	midi *m*	mezzogiorno *m*	mediodía *m*
middle (E)	Mitte *f*	—	milieu *m*	centro *m*	medio *m*

	D	E	F	I	Es
midi (F)	Mittag *m*	midday	—	mezzogiorno *m*	mediodía *m*
midnight (E)	Mitternacht *f*	—	minuit *m*	mezzanotte *f*	medianoche *f*
miedo (Es)	Angst *f*	fear	peur *f*	paura *f*	—
miedoso (Es)	ängstlich	fearful	peureux(-euse)	pauroso(a)	—
miel (Es)	Honig *m*	honey	miel *m*	miele *m*	—
miel (F)	Honig *m*	honey	—	miele *m*	miel *f*
miele (I)	Honig *m*	honey	miel *m*	—	miel *f*
miembro (Es)	Mitglied *n*	member	membre *m*	membro *m*	—
Miene (D)	—	expression	mine *f*	aspetto *m*	expresión *f*
mientras tanto (Es)	inzwischen	meanwhile	entretemps	frattanto	—
miércoles (Es)	Mittwoch *m*	Wednesday	mercredi *m*	mercoledì *m*	—
Miete (D)	—	rent	loyer *m*	affitto *m*	alquiler *m*
mieten (D)	—	rent	louer	affittare	alquilar
Mieter (D)	—	tenant	locataire *m*	inquilino *m*	inquilino *m*
mieux (F)	lieber	rather	—	piuttosto	más bien
miglio (I)	Meile *f*	mile	mille *m*	—	milla *f*
miglioramento (I)	Besserung *f*	improvement	amélioration *f*	—	restablecimiento *m*
migliorare (I)	verbessern	improve	améliorer	—	mejorar
migliore (I)	beste(r,s)	best	meilleur(e)	—	óptimo(a)
mignon (F)	niedlich	sweet	—	carino(a)	gracioso(a)
migraine (E)	Migräne *f*	—	migraine *f*	emicrania *f*	jaqueca *f*
migraine (F)	Migräne *f*	migraine	—	emicrania *f*	jaqueca *f*
Migräne (D)	—	migraine	migraine *f*	emicrania *f*	jaqueca *f*
mil (Es)	tausend	thousand	mille	mille	—
milagro (Es)	Wunder *n*	miracle	miracle *m*	miracolo *m*	—
Milch (D)	—	milk	lait *m*	latte *m*	leche *f*
mild (D)	—	mild	doux(douce)	mite	agradable
mild (E)	mild	—	doux(douce)	mite	agradable
mile (E)	Meile *f*	—	mille *m*	miglio *m*	milla *f*
miliardo (I)	Milliarde *f*	billion	milliard *m*	—	mil millones *m*
milieu (F)	Mitte *f*	middle	—	centro *m*	medio *m*
milione (I)	Million *f*	million	million *m*	—	millón *m*
militaires (F)	Militär *n*	military	—	militari *m pl*	militar *m*
Militär (D)	—	military	militaires *m pl*	militari *m pl*	militar *m*
militar (Es)	Militär *n*	military	militaires *m pl*	militari *m pl*	—
militari (I)	Militär *n*	military	militaires *m pl*	—	militar *m*
military (E)	Militär *n*	—	militaires *m pl*	militari *m pl*	militar *m*
milk (E)	Milch *f*	—	lait *m*	latte *m*	leche *f*
milla (Es)	Meile *f*	mile	mille *m*	miglio *m*	—
mille[1] (F)	Meile *f*	mile	—	miglio *m*	milla *f*
mille[2] (F)	tausend	thousand	—	mille	mil
mille (I)	tausend	thousand	mille	—	mil
milliard (F)	Milliarde *f*	billion	—	miliardo *m*	mil millones *m*
Milliarde (D)	—	billion	milliard *m*	miliardo *m*	mil millones *m*
Million (D)	—	million	million *m*	milione *m*	millón *m*
million (E)	Million *f*	—	million *m*	milione *m*	millón *m*
million (F)	Million *f*	million	—	milione *m*	millón *m*
millón (Es)	Million *f*	million	million *m*	milione *m*	—

	D	E	F	I	Es
mil millones (Es)	Milliarde *f*	billion	milliard *m*	miliardo *m*	—
mimar (Es)	verwöhnen	spoil	gâter	viziare	—
minacciare[1] (I)	androhen	threaten s.b.	menacer	—	amenazar
minacciare[2] (I)	drohen	threaten	menacer	—	amenazar (a alguien)
minacciare[3] (I)	bedrohen	threaten	menacer	—	amenazar
mince[1] (F)	dünn	thin	—	magro(a)	delgado(a)
mince[2] (F)	schlank	slim	—	snello(a)	delgado(a)
minced meat (E)	Hackfleisch *n*	—	viande hachée *f*	carne tritata *f*	carne picada *f*
Minderheit (D)	—	minority	minorité *f*	minoranza *f*	minoría *f*
mindestens (D)	—	at least	au moins	almeno	por lo menos
mine (E)	meine(r,s)	—	le(la) mien(ne)	mio(a)	mío(a)
mine (F)	Miene *f*	expression	—	aspetto *m*	expresión *f*
Mineralwasser (D)	—	mineral water	eau minérale *f*	acqua minerale *f*	agua mineral *f*
mineral water (E)	Mineralwasser *n*	—	eau minérale *f*	acqua minerale *f*	agua mineral *f*
minime (F)	gering	slight	—	poco(a)	pequeño(a)
mínimo (Es)	Minimum *n*	minimum	minimum *m*	minimo *m*	—
minimo (I)	Minimum *n*	minimum	minimum *m*	—	mínimo *m*
Minimum (D)	—	minimum	minimum *m*	minimo *m*	mínimo *m*
minimum (E)	Minimum *n*	—	minimum *m*	minimo *m*	mínimo *m*
minimum (F)	Minimum *n*	minimum	—	minimo *m*	mínimo *m*
Minister (D)	—	minister	ministre *m*	ministro *m*	ministro *m*
minister (E)	Minister *m*	—	ministre *m*	ministro *m*	ministro *m*
ministre (F)	Minister *m*	minister	—	ministro *m*	ministro *m*
ministro (Es)	Minister *m*	minister	ministre *m*	ministro *m*	—
ministro (I)	Minister *m*	minister	ministre *m*	—	ministro *m*
minoranza[1] (I)	Minorität *f*	minority	minorité *f*	—	minoría *f*
minoranza[2] (I)	Minderheit *f*	minority	minorité *f*	—	minoría *f*
minoría[1] (Es)	Minorität *f*	minority	minorité *f*	minoranza *f*	—
minoría[2] (Es)	Minderheit *f*	minority	minorité *f*	minoranza *f*	—
Minorität (D)	—	minority	minorité *f*	minoranza *f*	minoría *f*
minorité[1] (F)	Minorität *f*	minority	—	minoranza *f*	minoría *f*
minorité[2] (F)	Minderheit *f*	minority	—	minoranza *f*	minoría *f*
minority[1] (E)	Minorität *f*	—	minorité *f*	minoranza *f*	minoría *f*
minority[2] (E)	Minderheit *f*	—	minorité *f*	minoranza *f*	minoría *f*
minuit (F)	Mitternacht *f*	midnight	—	mezzanotte *f*	medianoche *f*
minus (D)	—	minus	moins	meno	menos
minus (E)	minus	—	moins	meno	menos
Minute (D)	—	minute	minute *f*	minuto *m*	minuto *m*
minute (E)	Minute *f*	—	minute *f*	minuto *m*	minuto *m*
minute (F)	Minute *f*	minute	—	minuto *m*	minuto *m*
minuto (Es)	Minute *f*	minute	minute *f*	minuto *m*	—
minuto (I)	Minute *f*	minute	minute *f*	—	minuto *m*
mio (I)	meine(r,s)	mine	le(la) mien(ne)	—	mía(o)
miracle (E)	Wunder *n*	—	miracle *m*	miracolo *m*	milagro *m*
miracle (F)	Wunder *n*	miracle	—	miracolo *m*	milagro *m*
miracolo (I)	Wunder *n*	miracle	miracle *m*	—	milagro *m*
miraculeux (F)	wunderbar	wonderful	—	meraviglioso(a)	maravilloso(a)

	D	E	F	I	Es
mirar¹ (Es)	ansehen	look at	regarder	guardare	—
mirar² (Es)	anschauen	look at	regarder	guardare	—
mirar³ (Es)	blicken	look	regarder	guardare	—
mirar⁴ (Es)	schauen	look	regarder	guardare	—
mirar⁵ (Es)	zusehen	watch	regarder	stare a guardare	—
mirar⁶ (Es)	zuschauen	watch	regarder	stare a guardare	—
miroir (F)	Spiegel *m*	mirror	—	specchio *m*	espejo *m*
mirror (E)	Spiegel *m*	—	miroir *m*	specchio *m*	espejo *m*
mischen (D)	—	mix	mélanger	mescolare	mezclar
Mischling (D)	—	halfcaste	métis *m*	sangue misto *m*	mestizo *m*
misère (F)	Elend *n*	misery	—	miseria *f*	miseria *f*
miseria (Es)	Elend *n*	misery	misère *f*	miseria *f*	—
miseria¹ (I)	Elend *n*	misery	misère *f*	—	miseria *f*
miseria² (I)	Not *f*	trouble	détresse *f*	—	necesidad *f*
misero (I)	dürftig	needy	nécessiteux	—	escaso(a)
misery (E)	Elend *n*	—	misère *f*	miseria *f*	miseria *f*
misfatto (I)	Untat *f*	crime	méfait *m*	—	crimen *m*
misfortune (E)	Unglück *n*	—	malheur *m*	disgrazia *f*	desgracia *f*
mislay (E)	verlegen	—	égarer	perdere	extraviar
miss¹ (E)	fehlen	—	manquer	mancare	faltar
miss² (E)	versäumen	—	manquer	perdere	perder
miss³ (E)	vermissen	—	manquer	sentire la mancanza	echar de menos
Miss (E)	Fräulein *n*	—	mademoiselle *f*	signorina *f*	señorita *f*
mißbilligen (D)	—	disapprove	désapprouver	disapprovare	desaprobar
Mißbrauch (D)	—	abuse	abus *m*	abuso *m*	abuso *m*
mißbrauchen (D)	—	abuse	abuser de	abusare	abusar
Mißerfolg (D)	—	failure	échec *m*	insuccesso *m*	fracaso *m*
mißtrauen (D)	—	mistrust	méfier, se	non fidarsi	desconfiar
Mißtrauen (D)	—	distrust	méfiance *f*	sfiducia *f*	desconfianza *f*
Mißverständnis (D)	—	misunderstanding	malentendu *m*	equivoco *m*	malentendido *m*
mistake¹ (E)	Fehler *m*	—	faute *f*	sbaglio *m*	falta *f*
mistake² (E)	Irrtum *m*	—	erreur *f*	errore *m*	error *m*
mistrust (E)	mißtrauen	—	méfier, se	non fidarsi	desconfiar
misunder-standing (E)	Mißverständnis *n*	—	malentendu *m*	equivoco *m*	malentendido *m*
misura (I)	Maß *n*	measure	mesure *f*	—	medida *f*
misurabile (I)	meßbar	measurable	mesurable	—	mensurable
misurare (I)	messen	measure	mesurer	—	medir
mit (D)	—	with	avec	con	con
mitad (Es)	Hälfte *f*	half	moitié *f*	metà *f*	—
mitbringen (D)	—	bring (along)	apporter	portare con sè	traer
mite (I)	mild	mild	doux(douce)	—	agradable
miteinander (D)	—	together	ensemble	insieme	juntos
mitgehen (D)	—	go along with	accompagner	accompagnare	acompañar
Mitglied (D)	—	member	membre *m*	membro *m*	miembro *m*
Mitleid (D)	—	pity	compassion *f*	compassione *f*	compasión *f*
mitnehmen (D)	—	take along	emmener	prendere con sè	llevar consigo
Mittag (D)	—	at midday	midi *m*	mezzogiorno *m*	a mediodía *m*

	D	E	F	I	Es
Mittagessen (D)	—	lunch	déjeuner *m*	pranzo *m*	comida *f*
mittags (D)	—	at midday	à midi	a mezzogiorno	a mediodía
Mitte (D)	—	middle	milieu *m*	centro *m*	medio *m*
mitteilen (D)	—	inform s.o.	informer qn de qch	comunicare	comunicar
Mitteilung (D)	—	message	information *f*	comunicazione *f*	comunicación *f*
Mittel (D)	—	means	moyen *m*	mezzo *m*	medio *m*
Mittelmeer (D)	—	Mediterranean	Méditerranée *f*	Mediterraneo *m*	mar mediterráneo *m*
mitten (D)	—	in the middle	au milieu	in mezzo	en medio
mittente (I)	Absender *m*	sender	expéditeur *m*	—	remitente *m*
Mitternacht (D)	—	midnight	minuit *m*	mezzanotte *f*	medianoche *f*
Mittwoch (D)	—	Wednesday	mercredi *m*	mercoledì *m*	miércoles *m*
mix (E)	mischen	—	mélanger	mescolare	mezclar
Möbel (D)	—	furniture	meuble *m*	mobile *m*	mueble *m*
mobile (I)	Möbel *n*	furniture	meuble *m*	—	mueble *m*
mobiliario (Es)	Einrichtung *f*	furnishing	ameublement *m*	arredamento *m*	—
möblieren (D)	—	furnish	meubler	ammobiliare	amueblar
möbliert (D)	—	furnished	meublé(e)	ammobiliato(a)	amueblado(a)
mochila (Es)	Rucksack *m*	rucksack	sac à dos *m*	zaino *m*	—
moda (Es)	Mode *f*	fashion	mode *f*	moda *f*	—
moda (I)	Mode *f*	fashion	mode *f*	—	moda *f*
Mode (D)	—	fashion	mode *f*	moda *f*	moda *f*
mode (F)	Mode *f*	fashion	—	moda *f*	moda *f*
model (E)	Modell *n*	—	modèle *m*	modello *m*	modelo *m*
modèle[1] (F)	Muster *n*	sample	—	campione *m*	modelo *m*
modèle[2] (F)	Modell *n*	model	—	modello *m*	modelo *m*
modèle[3] (F)	Vorbild *n*	ideal	—	modello *m*	modelo *m*
Modell (D)	—	model	modèle *m*	modello *m*	modelo *m*
modello[1] (I)	Modell *n*	model	modèle *m*	—	modelo *m*
modello[2] (I)	Vorbild *n*	ideal	modèle *m*	—	modelo *m*
modelo[1] (Es)	Muster *n*	sample	modèle *m*	campione *m*	—
modelo[2] (Es)	Modell *n*	model	modèle *m*	modello *m*	—
modelo[3] (Es)	Vorbild *n*	ideal	modèle *m*	modello *m*	—
moderado[1] (Es)	bescheiden	modest	modeste	modesto(a)	—
moderado[2] (Es)	mäßig	moderate	modéré(e)	moderato(a)	—
moderate (E)	mäßig	—	modéré(e)	moderato(a)	moderado(a)
moderato (I)	mäßig	moderate	modéré(e)	—	moderado(a)
modéré (F)	mäßig	moderate	—	moderato(a)	moderado(a)
modern (D)	—	modern	moderne	moderno(a)	moderno(a)
modern (E)	modern	—	moderne	moderno(a)	moderno(a)
moderne (F)	modern	modern	—	moderno(a)	moderno(a)
moderno (I)	modern	modern	moderne	—	moderno(a)
moderno (Es)	modern	modern	moderne	moderno(a)	—
modest (E)	bescheiden	—	modeste	modesto(a)	moderado(a)
modeste (F)	bescheiden	modest	—	modesto(a)	moderado(a)
modesto (I)	bescheiden	modest	modeste	—	moderado(a)
modo (I)	Art *f*	way	manière *f*	—	manera *f*
modulo (I)	Formular *n*	form	formulaire *m*	—	formulario *m*

	D	E	F	I	Es
mögen (D)	—	like	aimer	piacere	querer
möglich (D)	—	possible	possible	possibile	posible
Möglichkeit (D)	—	possibility	possibilité f	possibilità f	posibilidad f
moglie (I)	Ehefrau f	wife	épouse f	—	mujer f
Mohn (D)	—	poppy	coquelicot m	papavero m	amapola f
Möhre (D)	—	carrot	carotte f	carota f	zanahoria f
moine (F)	Mönch m	monk	—	monaco m	monje m
moins[1] (F)	minus	minus	—	meno	menos
moins[2] (F)	weniger	less	—	di meno	menos
mois (F)	Monat m	month	—	mese m	mes m
moisson (F)	Ernte f	harvest	—	raccolto m	cosecha f
moitié (F)	Hälfte f	half	—	metà f	mitad f
molestar[1] (Es)	belästigen	annoy	importuner	importunare	—
molestar[2] (Es)	stören	disturb	déranger	disturbare	—
molestia (Es)	Störung f	interference	trouble m	disturbo m	—
molesto (I)	lästig	troublesome	importun(e)	—	desagradable
mollare (I)	loslassen	let go of	lâcher	—	dejar libre
molti (I)	viele	many/a lot of	beaucoup de	—	muchos(as)
molto[1] (I)	sehr	very	très	—	mucho/muy
molto[2] (I)	viel	a lot of	beaucoup de	—	mucho(a)
molto tempo (I)	lange	long time	longtemps	—	mucho tiempo
Moment (D)	—	moment	moment m	momento m	momento m
moment[1] (E)	Augenblick m	—	instant m	attimo m	momento m
moment[2] (E)	Moment m	—	moment m	momento m	momento m
moment[1] (F)	Moment m	moment	—	momento m	momento m
moment[2] (F)	Weile f	while	—	momento m	rato m
momento[1] (Es)	Augenblick m	moment	instant m	attimo m	—
momento[2] (Es)	Moment m	moment	moment m	momento m	—
momento[1] (I)	Moment m	moment	moment m	—	momento m
momento[2] (I)	Weile f	while	moment m	—	rato m
monaco (I)	Mönch m	monk	moine m	—	monje m
monasterio (Es)	Kloster n	monastery	couvent m	convento m	—
monastery (E)	Kloster n	—	couvent m	convento m	monasterio m
Monat (D)	—	month	mois m	mese m	mes m
monatlich (D)	—	monthly	mensuel(le)	mensile	mensual
Mönch (D)	—	monk	moine m	monaco m	monje m
Mond (D)	—	moon	lune f	luna f	luna f
Monday (E)	Montag m	—	lundi m	lunedì m	lunes m
Mondays (E)	montags	—	le lundi	il lunedì	los lunes
monde (F)	Welt f	world	—	mondo m	mundo m
mondo (I)	Welt f	world	monde m	—	mundo m
moneda[1] (Es)	Münze f	coin	pièce de monnaie f	moneta f	—
moneda[2] (Es)	Währung f	currency	monnaie f	valuta f	—
moneta (I)	Münze f	coin	pièce de monnaie f	—	moneda f
money (E)	Geld n	—	argent m	denaro m	dinero m
monja (Es)	Nonne f	nun	religieuse f	suora f	—
monje (Es)	Mönch m	monk	moine m	monaco m	—

	D	E	F	I	Es
monk (E)	Mönch *m*	—	moine *m*	monaco *m*	monje *m*
monnaie[1] (F)	Kleingeld *n*	small change	—	spiccioli *m pl*	cambio *m*
monnaie[2] (F)	Währung *f*	currency	—	valuta *f*	moneda *f*
mono (Es)	Affe *m*	ape	singe *m*	scimmia *f*	—
monocolore (I)	einfarbig	all one colour	uni(e)	—	de un solo color
monsieur (F)	Herr *m*	gentleman	—	signore *m*	señor *m*
mont (F)	Berg *m*	mountain	—	monte *m*	montaña *f*
Montag (D)	—	Monday	lundi *m*	lunedì *m*	lunes *m*
montagna (I)	Gebirge *n*	mountain chain	montagne *f*	—	montañas *f pl*
montagne (F)	Gebirge *n*	mountain chain	—	montagna *f*	montañas *f pl*
montags (D)	—	Mondays	le lundi	il lunedì	los lunes
montaña (Es)	Berg *m*	mountain	mont *m*	monte *m*	—
montañas (Es)	Gebirge *n*	mountain chain	montagne *f*	montagna *f*	—
montañas elevadas (Es)	Hochgebirge *n*	high mountain-chain	haute montage *f*	alta montagna *f*	—
montant (F)	Betrag *m*	amount	—	somma *f*	importe *m*
monte (I)	Berg *m*	mountain	mont *m*	—	montaña *f*
montée (F)	Aufgang *m*	staircase	—	scala *f*	subida *f*
monter[1] (F)	aufsteigen	ascend	—	salire	subir
monter[2] (F)	einsteigen	get in	—	salire	subir a
monter[3] (F)	hinaufsteigen	climb	—	salire	subir
monter[4] (F)	reiten	ride	—	cavalcare	cabalgar
monter[5] (F)	steigen	go up	—	salire	subir
month (E)	Monat *m*	—	mois *m*	mese *m*	mes *m*
monthly (E)	monatlich	—	mensuel(le)	mensile	mensual
montón (Es)	Haufen *m*	heap	tas *m*	mucchio *m*	—
montre (F)	Uhr *f*	watch	—	orologio *m*	reloj *m*
montrer[1] (F)	vorzeigen	show	—	esibire	presentar
montrer[2] (F)	zeigen	show	—	mostrare	indicar
monument (E)	Denkmal *n*	—	monument *m*	monumento *m*	monumento *m*
monument (F)	Denkmal *n*	monument	—	monumento *m*	monumento *m*
monumento (Es)	Denkmal *n*	monument	monument *m*	monumento *m*	—
monumento (I)	Denkmal *n*	monument	monument *m*	—	monumento *m*
mood (E)	Laune *f*	—	humeur *f*	umore *m*	humor *m*
moon (E)	Mond *m*	—	lune *f*	luna *f*	luna *f*
mora (I)	Brombeere *f*	blackberry	mûre *f*	—	zarzamora *f*
Moral (D)	—	morality	morale *f*	morale *f*	moral *f*
moral (E)	sittlich	—	moral(e)	morale	moral
moral[1] (Es)	Moral *f*	morality	morale *f*	morale *f*	—
moral[2] (Es)	sittlich	moral	moral(e)	morale	—
moral (F)	sittlich	moral	—	morale	moral
morale (F)	Moral *f*	morality	—	morale *f*	moral *f*
morale[1] (I)	Moral *f*	morality	morale *f*	—	moral *f*
morale[2] (I)	sittlich	moral	moral(e)	—	moral
morality (E)	Moral *f*	—	morale *f*	morale *f*	moral *f*
morbido (I)	weich	soft	doux(douce)	—	tierno(a)
morbillo (I)	Masern *pl*	measles	rougeole *f*	—	sarampión *m*
morceau (F)	Stück *n*	piece	—	pezzo *m*	parte *f*

	D	E	F	I	Es
Mord (D)	—	murder	meurtre *m*	assassinio *m*	asesinato *m*
morder (Es)	beißen	bite	mordre	mordere	—
mordere (I)	beißen	bite	mordre	—	morder
mordre (F)	beißen	bite	—	mordere	morder
more (E)	mehr	—	plus	più	más
morgen (D)	—	tomorrow	demain	domani	mañana
Morgen (D)	—	morning	matin *m*	mattino *m*	mañana *f*
morir (Es)	sterben	die	mourir	morire	—
morir de hambre (Es)	verhungern	starve	mourir de faim	morire di fame	—
morire (I)	sterben	die	mourir	—	morir
morire di fame (I)	verhungern	starve	mourir de faim	—	morir de hambre
morire di freddo (I)	erfrieren	freeze to death	mourir de froid	—	morirse de frío
morirse de frío (Es)	erfrieren	freeze to death	mourir de froid	morire di freddo	—
mormorare (I)	rauschen	rush	bruire	—	susurrar
morning (E)	Morgen *m*	—	matin *m*	mattino *m*	mañana *f*
mort[1] (F)	Tod *m*	death	—	morte *f*	muerte *f*
mort[2] (F)	tot	dead	—	morto(a)	muerto(a)
morte (I)	Tod *m*	death	mort *f*	—	muerte *f*
morto (I)	tot	dead	mort(e)	—	muerto(a)
mosca (Es)	Fliege *f*	fly	mouche *f*	mosca *f*	—
mosca (I)	Fliege *f*	fly	mouche *f*	—	mosca *f*
mosquito (E)	Mücke *f*	—	moustique *m*	zanzara *f*	mosquito *m*
mosquito (Es)	Mücke *f*	mosquito	moustique *m*	zanzara *f*	—
most (E)	meist	—	la plupart de	nella maggior parte di	la mayor parte de
mostaza (Es)	Senf *m*	mustard	moutarde *f*	senape *f*	—
mostrador (Es)	Ladentisch *m*	counter	comptoir *m*	banco di vendita *m*	—
mostrare (I)	zeigen	show	montrer	—	indicar
mot (F)	Wort *n*	word	—	parola *f*	palabra *f*
moteur (F)	Motor *m*	motor	—	motore *m*	motor *m*
mother (E)	Mutter *f*	—	mère *f*	madre *f*	madre *f*
mother-in-law (E)	Schwieger-mutter *f*	—	belle-mère *f*	suocera *f*	suegra *f*
motionless (E)	bewegungslos	—	immobile	immobile	inmóvil
moto (F)	Motorrad *n*	motorbike	—	motocicletta *f*	motocicleta *f*
motocicleta (Es)	Motorrad *n*	motorbike	moto *f*	motocicletta *f*	—
motocicletta (I)	Motorrad *n*	motorbike	moto *f*	—	motocicleta *f*
Motor (D)	—	motor	moteur *m*	motore *m*	motor *m*
motor (E)	Motor *m*	—	moteur *m*	motore *m*	motor *m*
motor (Es)	Motor *m*	motor	moteur *m*	motore *m*	—
motorbike (E)	Motorrad *n*	—	moto *f*	motocicletta *f*	motocicleta *f*
motore (I)	Motor *m*	motor	moteur *m*	—	motor *m*
Motorrad (D)	—	motorbike	moto *f*	motocicletta *f*	motocicleta *f*
motorway (E)	Autobahn *f*	—	autoroute *f*	autostrada *f*	autopista *f*

	D	E	F	I	Es
mouche (F)	Fliege *f*	fly	—	mosca *f*	mosca *f*
mouchoir (F)	Taschentuch *n*	handkerchief	—	fazzoletto *m*	pañuelo *m*
mouette (F)	Möwe *f*	seagull	—	gabbiano *m*	gaviota *f*
mouillé (F)	naß	wet	—	bagnato(a)	húmedo(a)
moule (F)	Muschel *f*	mussel	—	cozza *f*	mejillón *m*
mountain (E)	Berg *m*	—	mont *m*	monte *m*	montaña *f*
mountain chain (E)	Gebirge *n*	—	montagne *f*	montagna *f*	montañas *f pl*
mountaineer (E)	Bergsteiger *m*	—	alpiniste *m*	alpinista *m*	alpinista *m*
mourir (F)	sterben	die	—	morire	morir
mourir de faim (F)	verhungern	starve	—	morire di fame	morir de hambre
mourir de froid (F)	erfrieren	freeze to death	—	morire di freddo	morirse de frío
mouse (E)	Maus *f*	—	souris *f*	topo *m*	ratón *m*
moustache (E)	Schnurrbart *m*	—	moustache *f*	baffi *m pl*	bigote *m*
moustache (F)	Schnurrbart *m*	moustache	—	baffi *m pl*	bigote *m*
moustique (F)	Mücke *f*	mosquito	—	zanzara *f*	mosquito *m*
moutarde (F)	Senf *m*	mustard	—	senape *f*	mostaza *f*
mouth[1] (E)	Maul *n*	—	gueule *f*	muso *m*	hocico *m*
mouth[2] (E)	Mündung *f*	—	embouchure *f*	sbocco *m*	desembocadura *f*
mouth[3] (E)	Mund *m*	—	bouche *f*	bocca *f*	boca *f*
mouton (F)	Schaf *n*	sheep	—	pecora *f*	oveja *f*
mouvement (F)	Bewegung *f*	movement	—	movimento *m*	movimiento *m*
move[1] (E)	bewegen	—	bouger	muovere	mover
move[2] (E)	rücken	—	déplacer	muovere	mover
move[3] (E)	übersiedeln	—	émigrer	trasferirsi	transladarse
move[4] (E)	umziehen	—	déménager	cambiare casa	cambiar
move[5] (E)	Umzug *m*	—	déménagement *m*	trasloco *m*	mudanza *f*
move in (E)	einziehen	—	emménager	prendere alloggio	instalarse
movement (E)	Bewegung *f*	—	mouvement *m*	movimento *m*	movimiento *m*
move out (E)	ausziehen	—	déménager	sloggiare	mudarse
mover[1] (Es)	bewegen	move	bouger	muovere	—
mover[2] (Es)	rücken	move	déplacer	muovere	—
movimento (I)	Bewegung *f*	movement	mouvement *m*	—	movimiento *m*
movimiento (Es)	Bewegung *f*	movement	mouvement *m*	movimento *m*	—
mow (E)	mähen	—	faucher	falciare	cortar
Möwe (D)	—	seagull	mouette *f*	gabbiano *m*	gaviota *f*
moyen[1] (F)	Mittel *n*	means	—	mezzo *m*	medio *m*
moyen[2] (F)	durchschnittlich	average	—	medio(a)	medio(a)
mozo[1] (Es)	Bursche *m*	fellow	garçon *m*	ragazzo *m*	—
mozo[2] (Es)	Träger *m*	carrier	porteur *m*	facchino *m*	—
mucca (I)	Kuh *f*	cow	vache *f*	—	vaca *f*
mucchio (I)	Haufen *m*	heap	tas *m*	—	montón *m*
muchedumbre (Es)	Menschenmenge *f*	crowd	foule *f*	folla *f*	—
mucho[1] (Es)	sehr	very	très	molto(a)	—
mucho[2] (Es)	viel	a lot of	beaucoup de	molto(a)	—

museo

	D	E	F	I	Es
muchos[1] (Es)	mehrere	several	plusieurs	parecchi	—
muchos[2] (Es)	viele	many/a lot of	beaucoup de	molti(e)	—
mucho tiempo (Es)	lange	long time	longtemps	molto tempo	—
Mücke (D)	—	mosquito	moustique *m*	zanzara *f*	mosquito *m*
mud (E)	Schlamm *m*	—	boue *f*	fango *m*	barro *m*
mudanza (Es)	Umzug *m*	move	déménagement *m*	trasloco *m*	—
mudarse (Es)	ausziehen	move out	déménager	sloggiare	—
müde (D)	—	tired	fatigué(e)	stanco(a)	cansado(a)
mudo (Es)	stumm	dumb	muet(te)	muto(a)	—
mueble (Es)	Möbel *n*	furniture	meuble *m*	mobile *m*	—
muerte (Es)	Tod *m*	death	mort *f*	morte *f*	—
muerto (Es)	tot	dead	mort(e)	morto(a)	—
muet (F)	stumm	dumb	—	muto(a)	mudo(a)
Mühe (D)	—	effort	peine *f*	fatica *f*	esfuerzo *m*
mujer[1] (Es)	Ehefrau *f*	wife	épouse *f*	moglie *f*	—
mujer[2] (Es)	Frau *f*	woman	femme *f*	donna *f*	—
mujer de la limpieza (Es)	Putzfrau *f*	charwoman	femme de ménage *f*	donna delle pulizie *f*	—
Mülleimer (D)	—	dustbin	poubelle *f*	secchio dei rifiuti *m*	cubo de la basura *m*
Mund (D)	—	mouth	bouche *f*	bocca *f*	boca *f*
mündlich (D)	—	oral	oral(e)	orale	oral
mundo (Es)	Welt *f*	world	monde *m*	mondo *m*	—
Mündung (D)	—	mouth	embouchure *f*	sbocco *m*	desembocadura *f*
muñeca (Es)	Puppe *f*	doll	poupée *f*	bambola *f*	—
municipio (I)	Rathaus *n*	town hall	mairie *f*	—	ayuntamiento *m*
munter (D)	—	lively	éveillé(e)	vivace	alegre
Münze (D)	—	coin	pièce de monnaie *f*	moneta *f*	moneda *f*
muovere[1] (I)	bewegen	move	bouger	—	mover
muovere[2] (I)	rücken	move	déplacer	—	mover
mur[1] (F)	Mauer *f*	wall	—	muro *m*	muro *m*
mur[2] (F)	Wand *f*	wall	—	parete *f*	pared *f*
mûr (F)	reif	ripe	—	maturo(a)	maduro(a)
murder (E)	Mord *m*	—	meurtre *m*	assassinio *m*	asesinato *m*
mûre (F)	Brombeere *f*	blackberry	—	mora *f*	zarzamora *f*
muro (Es)	Mauer *f*	wall	mur *m*	muro *m*	—
muro (I)	Mauer *f*	wall	mur *m*	—	muro *m*
Muschel (D)	—	mussel	moule *f*	cozza *f*	mejillón *m*
muscle (E)	Muskel *m*	—	muscle *m*	muscolo *m*	músculo *m*
muscle (F)	Muskel *m*	muscle	—	muscolo *m*	músculo *m*
muscolo (I)	Muskel *m*	muscle	muscle *m*	—	músculo *m*
músculo (Es)	Muskel *m*	muscle	muscle *m*	muscolo *m*	—
musée (F)	Museum *n*	museum	—	museo *m*	museo *m*
museo (Es)	Museum *n*	museum	musée *m*	museo *m*	—
museo (I)	Museum *n*	museum	musée *m*	—	museo *m*

	D	E	F	I	Es
Museum (D)	—	museum	musée *m*	museo *m*	museo *m*
museum (E)	Museum *n*	—	musée *m*	museo *m*	museo *m*
mushroom (E)	Pilz *m*	—	champignon *m*	fungo *m*	hongo *m*
music (E)	Musik *f*	—	musique *f*	musica *f*	música *f*
música (Es)	Musik *f*	music	musique *f*	musica *f*	—
musica (I)	Musik *f*	music	musique *f*	—	música *f*
Musik (D)	—	music	musique *f*	musica *f*	música *f*
musique (F)	Musik *f*	music	—	musica *f*	música *f*
Muskel (D)	—	muscle	muscle *m*	muscolo *m*	músculo *m*
muso (I)	Maul *n*	mouth	gueule *f*	—	hocico *m*
mussel (E)	Muschel *f*	—	moule *f*	conchiglia *f*	concha *f*
müssen (D)	—	have to	devoir	dovere	deber
mustard (E)	Senf *m*	—	moutarde *f*	senape *f*	mostaza *f*
Muster (D)	—	sample	modèle *m*	campione *m*	modelo *m*
Mut (D)	—	courage	courage *m*	coraggio *m*	coraje *m*
mutande (I)	Unterhose *f*	underpants	slip *m*	—	calzoncillos *m pl*/ bragas *f pl*
mutare (I)	verändern	change	transformer	—	cambiar
muto (I)	stumm	dumb	muet(te)	—	mudo(a)
Mutter (D)	—	mother	mère *f*	madre *f*	madre *f*
Muttersprache (D)	—	native language	langue maternelle *f*	lingua madre *f*	lengua materna *f*
Mütze (D)	—	cap	casquette *f*	berretto *m*	gorra *f*
Nabel (D)	—	navel	nombril *m*	ombelico *m*	ombligo *m*
nach (D)	—	after/to	après/selon	a/in/verso/dopo	a/hacia/después
nachahmen (D)	—	imitate	imiter	imitare	imitar
Nachbar (D)	—	neighbour	voisin *m*	vicino *m*	vecino *m*
nachdem (D)	—	after	après que	dopo	después que
nachdenken (D)	—	think	réfléchir	riflettere	reflexionar
Nachfrage (D)	—	demand	demande *f*	domanda *f*	demanda *f*
nachgeben (D)	—	yield	céder	cedere	ceder
nach Hause (D)	—	home	à la maison	a casa	a casa
nachher (D)	—	afterwards	ensuite	dopo	después
nachlassen (D)	—	slacken	apaiser, se	allentare	aflojar
Nachmittag (D)	—	afternoon	après-midi *m*	pomeriggio *m*	tarde *f*
nachmittags (D)	—	in the afternoon	l'aprés-midi	di pomeriggio	por la tarde
Nachnahme (D)	—	cash on delivery	remboursement *m*	contro assegno *m*	reembolso *m*
Nachname (D)	—	surname	nom de famille *m*	cognome *m*	apellido *m*
nachprüfen (D)	—	check	contrôler	controllare	comprobar
Nachricht (D)	—	message	nouvelle *f*	notizia *f*	noticia *f*
Nachrichten (D)	—	news	informations *f pl*	giornale radio *m*	noticiario *m*
nachsehen (D)	—	check	vérifier	controllare	examinar
nachsenden (D)	—	send on	faire suivre	inoltrare	enviar a la nueva dirección
nächste (D)	—	next	suivant(e)	prossimo(a)	siguiente

	D	E	F	I	Es
Nacht (D)	—	night	nuit f	notte f	noche m
Nachteil (D)	—	disadvantage	désavantage m	svantaggio m	desventaja f
Nachtisch (D)	—	dessert	dessert m	desert m	postre m
Nachtlokal (D)	—	club	boîte de nuit f	night m	local nocturno m
nachts (D)	—	at nighttime	de nuit	di notte	por la noche
Nachtwächter (D)	—	night-watchman	veilleur de nuit m	guardia notturna f	sereno m
nacido (Es)	geboren	born	né(e)	nato(a)	—
nacimiento (Es)	Geburt f	birth	naissance f	nascita f	—
nacional (Es)	national	national	national(e)	nazionale	—
nacionalidad[1] (Es)	Nationalität f	nationality	nationalité f	nazionalità f	—
nacionalidad[2] (Es)	Staatsangehörigkeit f	nationality	nationalité f	cittadinanza f	—
nackt (D)	—	naked	nu(e)	nudo(a)	desnudo(a)
nada (Es)	nichts	nothing	rien	niente	—
nadar (Es)	schwimmen	swim	nager	nuotare	—
Nadel (D)	—	needle	aiguille f	ago m	aguja f
Nadelbaum (D)	—	conifer	conifère m	conifero m	conífera f
nadie (Es)	niemand	nobody	personne	nessuno(a)	—
Nagel[1] (D)	—	nail	clou m	chiodo m	clavo m
Nagel[2] (D)	—	nail	ongle m	unghia f	uña f
nager (F)	schwimmen	swim	—	nuotare	nadar
nahe (D)	—	near	près de	vicino(a)	contiguo(a)
Nähe (D)	—	proximity	environs m pl	vicinanza f	proximidad f
nähen (D)	—	sew	coudre	cucire	coser
nähern, sich (D)	—	approach	approcher, se	avvicinarsi	acercarse
Nahrung (D)	—	food	nourriture f	alimentazione f	nutrición f
nail[1] (E)	Nagel m	—	ongle m	unghia m	uña f
nail[2] (E)	Nagel m	—	clou m	chiodo m	clavo m
naissance (F)	Geburt f	birth	—	nascita f	nacimiento m
naître (F)	entstehen	arise	—	nascere	surgir
naked (E)	nackt	—	nu(e)	nudo(a)	desnudo(a)
Name (D)	—	name	nom m	nome m	nombre m
name (E)	Name m	—	nom m	nome m	nombre m
namely (E)	nämlich	—	à savoir	cioè	a saber
nämlich (D)	—	namely	à savoir	cioè	a saber
nappy (E)	Windel f	—	lange m	pannolino m	pañal m
naranja[1] (Es)	Apfelsine f	orange	orange f	arancia f	—
naranja[2] (Es)	Orange f	orange	orange f	arancia f	—
Narbe (D)	—	scar	cicatrice f	cicatrice f	cicatriz f
nariz (Es)	Nase f	nose	nez m	naso m	—
Narr (D)	—	fool	fou m	pazzo m	loco m
narrow (E)	eng	—	étroit(e)	stretto(a)	estrecho(a)
nascere (I)	entstehen	arise	naître	—	surgir
nascita (I)	Geburt f	birth	naissance f	—	nacimiento m

	D	E	F	I	Es
nascondere[1] (I)	verstecken	hide	cacher	—	ocultar
nascondere[2] (I)	verbergen	hide	dissimuler	—	esconder
Nase (D)	—	nose	nez *m*	naso *m*	nariz *f*
naso (I)	Nase *f*	nose	nez *m*	—	nariz *f*
naß (D)	—	wet	mouillé(e)	bagnato(a)	húmedo(a)
nastro (I)	Band *n*	ribbon	bandeau *m*	—	cinta *f*
nastro magnetico (I)	Tonband *n*	tape	bande magnétique *f*	—	cinta magnetofónica *f*
nata (Es)	Sahne *f*	cream	crème *f*	panna *f*	—
Natale (I)	Weihnachten *n*	Christmas	Noël *m*	—	Navidad(es) *f (pl)*
national (D)	—	national	national(e)	nazionale	nacional
national (E)	national	—	national(e)	nazionale	nacional
national (F)	national	national	—	nazionale	nacional
Nationalität (D)	—	nationality	nationalité *f*	nazionalità *f*	nacionalidad *f*
nationalité[1] (F)	Nationalität *f*	nationality	—	nazionalità *f*	nacionalidad *f*
nationalité[2] (F)	Staats- angehörigkeit *f*	nationality	—	cittadinanza *f*	nacionalidad *f*
nationality[1] (E)	Nationalität *f*	—	nationalité *f*	nazionalità *f*	nacionalidad *f*
nationality[2] (E)	Staats- angehörigkeit *f*	—	nationalité *f*	cittadinanza *f*	nacionalidad *f*
native (E)	einheimisch	—	indigène	indigeno(a)	nativo(a)
native language (E)	Muttersprache *f*	—	langue maternelle *f*	lingua madre *f*	lengua materna *f*
nativo (Es)	einheimisch	native	indigène	indigeno(a)	—
nato (I)	geboren	born	né(e)	—	nacido(a)
natte[1] (F)	Matte *f*	mat	—	stuoia *f*	colchoneta *f*
natte[2] (F)	Zopf *m*	plait	—	treccia *f*	trenza *f*
Natur (D)	—	nature	nature *f*	natura *f*	naturaleza *f*
natura (I)	Natur *f*	nature	nature *f*	—	naturaleza *f*
natural (E)	natürlich	—	naturel(le)	naturale	natural
natural (Es)	natürlich	natural	naturel(le)	naturale	—
naturale (I)	natürlich	natural	naturel(le)	—	natural
naturaleza (Es)	Natur *f*	nature	nature *f*	natura *f*	—
naturalmente (I)	selbstverständlich	of course	évidemment	—	por su puesto
nature (E)	Natur *f*	—	nature *f*	natura *f*	naturaleza *f*
nature (F)	Natur *f*	nature	—	natura *f*	naturaleza *f*
naturel (F)	natürlich	natural	—	naturale	natural
natürlich (D)	—	natural	naturel(le)	naturale	natural
nausea (E)	Übelkeit *f*	—	nausée *f*	nausea *f*	náuseas *f pl*
nausea (I)	Übelkeit *f*	nausea	nausée *f*	—	náuseas *f pl*
náuseas (Es)	Übelkeit *f*	nausea	nausée *f*	nausea *f*	—
nausée (F)	Übelkeit *f*	nausea	—	nausea *f*	náuseas *f pl*
nave (I)	Schiff *n*	ship	navire *m*	—	barco *m*
navegar a vela (Es)	segeln	sail	faire de la voile	andare a vela	—
navel (E)	Nabel *m*	—	nombril *m*	ombelico *m*	ombligo *m*
Navidad(es) (Es)	Weihnachten *n*	Christmas	Noël *m*	Natale *m*	—
navire (F)	Schiff *n*	ship	—	nave *f*	barco *m*
nazionale (I)	national	national	national(e)	—	nacional
nazionalità (I)	Nationalität *f*	nationality	nationalité *f*	—	nacionalidad *f*
né (F)	geboren	born	—	nato(a)	nacido(a)

	D	E	F	I	Es
near (E)	nahe	—	près de	vicino(a)	contiguo(a)
nearly[1] (E)	beinahe	—	presque	circa/quasi	casi
nearly[2] (E)	fast	—	presque	quasi	casi
nebbia (I)	Nebel *m*	fog	brouillard *m*	—	niebla *f*
Nebel (D)	—	fog	brouillard *m*	nebbia *f*	niebla *f*
neben (D)	—	beside	près de	accanto a	al lado de
necesario[1] (Es)	erforderlich	necessary	nécessaire	necessario(a)	—
necesario[2] (Es)	notwendig	necessary	nécessaire	necessario(a)	—
necesario[3] (Es)	nötig	necessary	nécessaire	necessario(a)	—
necesidad[1] (Es)	Bedürfnis *n*	need	besoin *m*	bisogno *m*	—
necesidad[2] (Es)	Notwendigkeit *f*	necessity	nécessité *f*	necessità *f*	—
necesidad[3] (Es)	Not *f*	trouble	détresse *f*	miseria *f*	—
necesitar[1] (Es)	benötigen/ brauchen	need	avoir besoin de	aver bisogno di	—
necesitar[2] (Es)	bedürfen	need	nécessiter	aver bisogno di	—
nécessaire[1] (F)	erforderlich	necessary	—	necessario(a)	necesario(a)
nécessaire[2] (F)	notwendig	necessary	—	necessario(a)	necesario(a)
nécessaire[3] (F)	nötig	necessary	—	necessario(a)	necesario(a)
necessario[1] (I)	erforderlich	necessary	nécessaire	—	necesario(a)
necessario[2] (I)	notwendig	necessary	nécessaire	—	necesario(a)
necessario[3] (I)	nötig	necessary	nécessaire	—	necesario(a)
necessary[1] (E)	erforderlich	—	nécessaire	necessario(a)	necesario(a)
necessary[2] (E)	nötig	—	nécessaire	necessario(a)	necesario(a)
necessary[3] (E)	notwendig	—	nécessaire	necessario(a)	necesario(a)
necessità (I)	Notwendigkeit *f*	necessity	nécessité *f*	—	necesidad *f*
nécessité (F)	Notwendigkeit *f*	necessity	—	necessità *f*	necesidad *f*
nécessiter (F)	bedürfen	need	—	aver bisogno di	necesitar
nécessiteux (F)	dürftig	needy	—	misero(a)	escaso(a)
necessity (E)	Notwendigkeit *f*	—	nécessité *f*	necessità *f*	necesidad *f*
neck (E)	Hals *m*	—	cou *m*	collo *m*	cuello *m*
need[1] (E)	bedürfen	—	nécessiter	aver bisogno di	necesitar
need[2] (E)	benötigen/ brauchen	—	avoir besoin de	aver bisogno di	necesitar
need[3] (E)	Bedürfnis *n*	—	besoin *m*	bisogno *m*	necesidad *f*
needle (E)	Nadel *f*	—	aiguille *f*	ago *m*	aguja *f*
needy (E)	dürftig	—	nécessiteux	misero(a)	escaso(a)
Neffe (D)	—	nephew	neveu *m*	nipote *m*	sobrino *m*
negar[1] (Es)	leugnen	deny	nier	negare	—
negar[2] (Es)	verweigern	refuse	refuser	rifiutare	—
negare (I)	leugnen	deny	nier	—	negar
negativa (Es)	Absage *f*	refusal	refus *m*	risposta negativa *f*	—
neglect (E)	vernachlässigen	—	négliger	trascurare	descuidar
négliger (F)	vernachlässigen	neglect	—	trascurare	descuidar
negozio[1] (I)	Geschäft *n*	shop	magasin *m*	—	tienda *f*
negozio[2] (I)	Laden *m*	shop	magasin *m*	—	tienda *f*
negozio di alimentari (I)	Lebensmittel- geschäft *n*	grocer's	magasin d'alimentation *m*	—	tienda de comestibles *f*
negozio di prodotti dietetici (I)	Reformhaus *n*	health food shop	magasin diététique *m*	—	tienda de productos dietéticos *f*

	D	E	F	I	Es
negozio di scarpe (I)	Schuhgeschäft *n*	shoeshop	magasin de chaussures *m*	—	zapatería *f*
negro (Es)	schwarz	black	noir(e)	nero(a)	—
nehmen (D)	—	take	prendre	prendere	tomar
Neid (D)	—	envy	jalousie *f*	invidia *f*	envidia *f*
neidisch (D)	—	envious	envieux(-euse)	invidioso(a)	envidioso(a)
neige (F)	Schnee *m*	snow	—	neve *f*	nieve *f*
neiger (F)	schneien	snow	—	nevicare	nevar
neighbour (E)	Nachbar *m*	—	voisin *m*	vicino *m*	vecino *m*
neighbouring (E)	benachbart	—	avoisinant(e)	vicino(a)	vecino(a)
nei giorni feriali[1] (I)	wochentags	during the week	en semaine	—	entre semana
nei giorni feriali[2] (I)	werktags	on working days	les jours ouvrables	—	los días laborables
nein (D)	—	no	non	no	no
neither (E)	weder	—	ni	né...né	ni
ne...jamais (F)	niemals	never	—	mai	jamás
nel frattempo (I)	indessen	meanwhile	cependant	—	en eso
Nelke (D)	—	carnation	œillet *m*	garofano *m*	clavel *m*
nella maggior parte di (I)	meist	most	la plupart de	—	la mayor parte de
nemico (I)	Feind *m*	enemy	ennemi *m*	—	enemigo *m*
né...né (I)	weder	neither	ni	—	ni
nennen (D)	—	call	appeler	chiamare	nombrar
ne...pas (F)	nicht	not	—	non	no
ne personne (F)	niemand	nobody	—	nessuno(a)	nadie
nephew (E)	Neffe *m*	—	neveu *m*	nipote *m*	sobrino *m*
nero (I)	schwarz	black	noir(e)	—	negro(a)
nerveux (F)	nervös	nervous	—	nervoso(a)	nervioso(a)
nervioso (Es)	nervös	nervous	nerveux(-euse)	nervoso(a)	—
nervös (D)	—	nervous	nerveux(-euse)	nervoso(a)	nervioso(a)
nervoso[1] (I)	hektisch	hectic	fébrile	—	inquieto(a)
nervoso[2] (I)	nervös	nervous	nerveux(-euse)	—	nervioso(a)
nervous (E)	nervös	—	nerveux(-euse)	nervoso(a)	nervioso(a)
nessuno[1] (I)	niemand	nobody	personne	—	nadie
nessuno[2] (I)	keine(r,s)	none	aucun(e)	—	ninguno(a)
Nest (D)	—	nest	nid *m*	nido *m*	nido *m*
nest (E)	Nest *n*	—	nid *m*	nido *m*	nido *m*
net (E)	Netz *n*	—	filet *m*	rete *f*	red *f*
Netherlands (E)	Niederlande *f*	—	Pays-Bas *m pl*	Paesi Bassi *m pl*	los Países Bajos *m pl*
nett (D)	—	nice	joli(e)	carino(a)	agradable
nettoyage (F)	Reinigung *f*	cleaning	—	pulitura *f*	limpieza *f*
nettoyer[1] (F)	putzen	clean	—	pulire	limpiar
nettoyer[2] (F)	reinigen	clean	—	pulire	limpiar
Netz (D)	—	net	filet *m*	rete *f*	red *f*
neu (D)	—	new	nouveau, nouvel, nouvelle	nuovo(a)	nuevo(a)
neuf (F)	neun	nine	—	nove	nueve
neugierig (D)	—	curious	curieux(-euse)	curioso(a)	curioso(a)
Neuheit (D)	—	novelty	nouveauté *f*	novità *f*	originalidad *f*
Neuigkeit (D)	—	news	nouvelle *f*	novità *f*	novedad *f*

niedrig

	D	E	F	I	Es
Neujahr (D)	—	New Year	nouvel an *m*	Capodanno *m*	Año Nuevo *m*
neulich (D)	—	recently	l'autre jour	recentemente	recientemente
neumático (Es)	Reifen *m*	tyre	pneu *m*	pneumatico *m*	—
neun (D)	—	nine	neuf	nove	nueve
neunzehn (D)	—	nineteen	dix-neuf	diciannove	diecinueve
neunzig (D)	—	ninety	quatre-vingt-dix	novanta	noventa
neutral (D)	—	neutral	neutre	neutro(a)	neutral
neutral (E)	neutral	—	neutre	neutro(a)	neutral
neutral (Es)	neutral	neutral	neutre	neutro(a)	—
neutre (F)	neutral	neutral	—	neutro(a)	neutral
neutro (I)	neutral	neutral	neutre	—	neutral
nevar (Es)	schneien	snow	neiger	nevicare	—
neve (I)	Schnee *m*	snow	neige *f*	—	nieve *f*
never (E)	niemals	—	ne…jamais	mai	jamás
nevera (Es)	Kühlschrank *m*	fridge	réfrigérateur *m*	frigorifero *m*	—
nevertheless[1] (E)	dennoch	—	cependant	tuttavia	sin embargo
nevertheless[2] (E)	trotzdem	—	malgré tout	tuttavia	no obstante
neveu (F)	Neffe *m*	nephew	—	nipote *m*	sobrino *m*
nevicare (I)	schneien	snow	neiger	—	nevar
new (E)	neu	—	nouveau, nouvel, nouvelle	nuovo(a)	nuevo(a)
news[1] (E)	Neuigkeit *f*	—	nouvelle *f*	novità *f*	novedad *f*
news[2] (E)	Nachrichten *pl*	—	informations *f pl*	giornale radio *m*	noticiario *m*
newspaper (E)	Zeitung *f*	—	journal *m*	giornale *m*	periódico *m*
New Year (E)	Neujahr *n*	—	nouvel an *m*	Capodanno *m*	Año Nuevo *m*
New Year's Eve (E)	Silvester *n*	—	Saint Sylvestre *m*	San Silvestro *m*	Noche Vieja *f*
next (E)	nächste(r,s)	—	suivant(e)	prossimo(a)	siguiente
nez (F)	Nase *f*	nose	—	naso *m*	nariz *f*
ni (Es)	weder	neither	ni	né…né	—
ni (F)	weder	neither	—	né…né	ni
nice (E)	nett	—	joli(e)	carino(a)	agradable
nicht (D)	—	not	ne…pas	non	no
Nichte (D)	—	niece	nièce *f*	nipote *f*	sobrina *f*
nichts (D)	—	nothing	rien	niente	nada
nicken (D)	—	nod	faire un signe de tête	annuire	inclinar la cabeza
nid (F)	Nest *n*	nest	—	nido *m*	nido *m*
nido (Es)	Nest *n*	nest	nid *m*	nido *m*	—
nido (I)	Nest *n*	nest	nid *m*	—	nido *m*
niebla (Es)	Nebel *m*	fog	brouillard *m*	nebbia *f*	—
niece (E)	Nichte *f*	—	nièce *f*	nipote *f*	sobrina *f*
nièce (F)	Nichte *f*	niece	—	nipote *f*	sobrina *f*
nieder (D)	—	inferior	bas(se)	in basso	abajo
Niederlage (D)	—	defeat	défaite *f*	sconfitta *f*	derrota *f*
Niederlande (D)	—	Netherlands	Pays-Bas *m pl*	Paesi Bassi *m pl*	los Países Bajos *m pl*
niederlassen (D)	—	settle down	s'installer	stabilirsi	instalarse
niedlich (D)	—	sweet	mignon(ne)	carino(a)	gracioso(a)
niedrig (D)	—	low	bas(se)	basso(a)	bajo

	D	E	F	I	Es
niemals (D)	—	never	ne...jamais	mai	jamás
niemand (D)	—	nobody	personne	nessuno(a)	nadie
niente (I)	nichts	nothing	rien	—	nada
nier (F)	leugnen	deny	—	negare	negar
Niere (D)	—	kidney	rein *m*	rene *m*	riñón *m*
niesen (D)	—	sneeze	éternuer	starnutire	estornudar
nieta (Es)	Enkelin *f*	granddaughter	petite-fille *f*	nipote *f*	—
Niete (D)	—	blank	mauvais numéro *m*	biglietto non vincente *m*	número sin premio *m*
nieto¹ (Es)	Enkel *m*	grandson	petit-fils *m*	nipote *m*	—
nieto² (Es)	Enkelkind *n*	grandchild	petit-enfant *m*	nipote *m/f*	—
nieve (Es)	Schnee *m*	snow	neige *f*	neve *f*	—
night (E)	Nacht *f*	—	nuit *f*	notte *f*	noche *m*
night (I)	Nachtlokal *n*	(night) club	boîte de nuit *f*	—	local nocturno *m*
night club (E)	Nachtlokal *n*	—	boîte de nuit *f*	night *m*	local nocturno *m*
night-watchman (E)	Nachtwächter *m*	—	veilleur de nuit *m*	guardia notturna *f*	sereno *m*
n'importe comment (F)	irgendwie	somehow	—	in qualche modo	de alguna manera
n'importe où (F)	irgendwo	somewhere	—	in qualche posto	en alguna parte
n'importe quel (F)	beliebig	any	—	qualsiasi	a voluntad
n'importe qui (F)	irgend jemand	somebody	—	qualcuno	alguno(a)
n'importe quoi (F)	irgend etwas	something	—	qualsiasi cosa	algo
nine (E)	neun	—	neuf	nove	nueve
nineteen (E)	neunzehn	—	dix-neuf	diciannove	diecinueve
ninety (E)	neunzig	—	quatre-vingt-dix	novanta	noventa
niñez (Es)	Kindheit *f*	childhood	enfance *f*	infanzia *f*	—
ninguno (Es)	keine(r,s)	none	aucun(e)	nessuno(a)	—
niño (Es)	Kind *n*	child	enfant *m*	bambino *m*	—
nipote¹ (I)	Enkelin *f*	granddaughter	petite-fille *f*	—	nieta *f*
nipote² (I)	Enkel *m*	grandson	petit-fils *m*	—	nieto *m*
nipote³ (I)	Nichte *f*	niece	nièce *f*	—	sobrina *f*
nipote⁴ (I)	Neffe *m*	nephew	neveu *m*	—	sobrino *m*
nipote⁵ (I)	Enkelkind *n*	grandchild	petit-enfant *m*	—	nieto *m*
nirgends (D)	—	nowhere	nulle part	da nessuna parte	en ninguna parte
niveau de la mer (F)	Meeresspiegel *m*	sea level	—	livello del mare *m*	nivel del mar *m*
nivel del mar (Es)	Meeresspiegel *m*	sea level	niveau de la mer *m*	livello del mare *m*	—
no (E)	nein	—	non	no	no
no¹ (Es)	nein	no	non	no	—
no² (Es)	nicht	not	ne...pas	non	—
no (I)	nein	no	non	—	no
no autorizado (Es)	unbefugt	unauthorized	non autorisé(e)	non autorizzato(a)	—
nobody (E)	niemand	—	personne	nessuno(a)	nadie
nocciolo (I)	Kern *m*	pip	noyau *m*	—	hueso *m*
noce (I)	Nuß *f*	nut	noix *f*	—	nuez *f*
noch (D)	—	still	encore	ancora	aún/todavía
noche¹ (Es)	Nacht *f*	night	nuit *f*	notte *f*	—
noche² (Es)	Abend *m*	evening	soir *m*	sera *f*	—
Nochebuena (Es)	Heiligabend *m*	Christmas Eve	nuit de Noël *f*	vigilia di Natale *f*	—

no obstante

	D	E	F	I	Es
Noche Vieja (Es)	Silvester *n*	New Year's Eve	Saint Sylvestre *m*	San Silvestro *m*	—
nochmals (D)	—	again	encore une fois	di nuovo	otra vez
nocivo (I)	schädlich	harmful	nuisible	—	nocivo(a)
nocivo (Es)	schädlich	harmful	nuisible	nocivo(a)	—
nod (E)	nicken	—	faire un signe de la tête	annuire	inclinar la cabeza
nodo (I)	Knoten *m*	knot	nœud *m*	—	nudo *m*
Noël (F)	Weihnachten *n*	Christmas	—	Natale *m*	Navidad(es) *f (pl)*
nœud (F)	Knoten *m*	knot	—	nodo *m*	nudo *m*
noi (I)	wir	we	nous	—	nosotros(as)
noioso (I)	langweilig	boring	ennuyeux(-euse)	—	aburrido(a)
noir (F)	schwarz	black	—	nero(a)	negro(a)
noise[1] (E)	Krach *m*	—	bruit *m*	chiasso *m*	ruido *m*
noise[2] (E)	Lärm *m*	—	bruit *m*	rumore *m*	ruido *m*
noix (F)	Nuß *f*	nut	—	noce *f*	nuez *f*
nom (F)	Name *m*	name	—	nome *m*	nombre *m*
nombrar (Es)	nennen	call	appeler	chiamare	—
nombre (Es)	Name *m*	name	nom *m*	nome *m*	—
nombre (F)	Anzahl *f*	number	—	numero *m*	número *m*
nombre de pila (Es)	Vorname *m*	Christian name	prénom *m*	nome di battesimo *m*	—
nombreux (F)	zahlreich	numerous	—	numeroso(a)	numeroso(a)
nombril (F)	Nabel *m*	navel	—	ombelico *m*	ombligo *m*
nom de famille (F)	Nachname *m*	surname	—	cognome *m*	apellido *m*
nome (I)	Name *m*	name	nom *m*	—	nombre *m*
nome di battesimo (I)	Vorname *m*	Christian name	prénom *m*	—	nombre de pila *m*
non (F)	nein	no	—	no	no
non (I)	nicht	not	ne...pas	—	no
non affatto (I)	keineswegs	not at all	pas du tout	—	en modo alguno
non autorisé (F)	unbefugt	unauthorized	—	non autorizzato(a)	no autorizado(a)
non autorizzato (I)	unbefugt	unauthorized	non autorisé(e)	—	no autorizado(a)
none (E)	keine(r,s)	—	aucun(e)	nessuno(a)	ninguno(a)
non fidarsi (I)	mißtrauen	mistrust	méfier, se	—	desconfiar
non impegnativo (I)	unverbindlich	not binding	sans engagement	—	sin compromiso
non importante (I)	unwichtig	unimportant	sans importance	—	sin importancia
non marié (F)	unverheiratet	unmarried	—	celibe *m*/nubile *f*	soltero(a)
nonna (I)	Großmutter *f*	grandmother	grand-mère *f*	—	abuela *f*
Nonne (D)	—	nun	religieuse *f*	suora *f*	monja *f*
nonni (I)	Großeltern *pl*	grandparents	grands-parents *m pl*	—	abuelos *m pl*
nonno (I)	Großvater *m*	grandfather	grand-père *m*	—	abuelo *m*
nonostante (I)	trotz	despite	malgré	—	a pesar de
nonsense (E)	Unsinn *m*	—	bêtises *f pl*	nonsenso *m*	absurdo *m*
nonsensical (E)	unsinnig	—	insensé(e)	insensato(a)	absurdo(a)
nonsenso (I)	Unsinn *m*	nonsense	bêtises *f pl*	—	absurdo *m*
non valable (F)	ungültig	invalid	—	non valido(a)	caducado(a)
non valido (I)	ungültig	invalid	non valable	—	caducado(a)
non vedere (I)	übersehen	ignore	ignorer	—	no ver
no obstante (Es)	trotzdem	nevertheless	malgré tout	tuttavia	—

	D	E	F	I	Es
noodles (E)	Nudeln *pl*	—	nouilles *f pl*	pasta *f*	pastas *f pl*
no parking (E)	Parkverbot *n*	—	défense de stationner *f*	divieto di parcheggio *m*	estacionamiento prohibido *m*
nord (F)	Norden *m*	north	—	nord *m*	norte *m*
nord (I)	Norden *m*	north	nord *m*	—	norte *m*
Nordamerika (D)	—	North America	Amérique du Nord *f*	America del Nord *f*	América del Norte *f*
Norden (D)	—	north	nord *m*	nord *m*	norte *m*
nördlich (D)	—	northern	du nord	a nord	del norte
Nordsee (D)	—	North Sea	mer du Nord *f*	Mare del Nord *m*	mar del norte *m*
norma (I)	Vorschrift *f*	regulation	règle *f*	—	reglamento *m*
normal (D)	—	normal	normal(e)	normale	normal
normal (E)	normal	—	normal(e)	normale	normal
normal (Es)	normal	normal	normal(e)	normale	—
normal (F)	normal	normal	—	normale	normal
normale (I)	normal	normal	normal(e)	—	normal
normalement (F)	normalerweise	normally	—	normalmente	normalmente
normaler- weise (D)	—	normally	normalement	normalmente	normalmente
normally (E)	normalerweise	—	normalement	normalmente	normalmente
normalmente (Es)	normalerweise	normally	normalement	normalmente	—
normalmente (I)	normalerweise	normally	normalement	—	normalmente
norte (Es)	Norden *m*	north	nord *m*	nord *m*	—
north (E)	Norden *m*	—	nord *m*	nord *m*	norte *m*
North America (E)	Nordamerika *n*	—	Amérique du Nord *f*	America del Nord *f*	América del Norte *f*
northern (E)	nördlich	—	du nord	a nord	del norte
North Sea (E)	Nordsee *f*	—	mer du Nord *f*	Mare del Nord *m*	mar del norte *m*
Noruega (Es)	Norwegen *n*	Norway	Norvège *f*	Norvegia *f*	—
Norvège (F)	Norwegen *n*	Norway	—	Norvegia *f*	Noruega *f*
Norvegia (I)	Norwegen *n*	Norway	Norvège *f*	—	Noruega *f*
Norway (E)	Norwegen *n*	—	Norvège *f*	Norvegia *f*	Noruega *f*
Norwegen (D)	—	Norway	Norvège *f*	Norvegia *f*	Noruega *f*
nose (E)	Nase *f*	—	nez *m*	naso *m*	nariz *f*
nosotros (Es)	wir	we	nous	noi	—
nostalgia (Es)	Heimweh *n*	homesickness	mal du pays *m*	nostalgia *f*	—
nostalgia (I)	Heimweh *n*	homesickness	mal du pays *m*	—	nostalgia *f*
Not (D)	—	trouble	détresse *f*	miseria *f*	necesidad *f*
not (E)	nicht	—	ne...pas	non	no
nota (Es)	Note *f*	note	note *f*	nota *f*	—
nota (I)	Note *f*	note	note *f*	—	nota *f*
notable (Es)	beträchtlich	considerable	considérable	considerevole	—
notaio (I)	Notar *m*	notary	notaire *m*	—	notario *m*
notaire (F)	Notar *m*	notary	—	notaio *m*	notario *m*
Notar (D)	—	notary	notaire *m*	notaio *m*	notario *m*
notar (Es)	merken	notice	remarquer	accorgersi di	—
notare (I)	bemerken	notice	remarquer	—	darse cuenta
notario (Es)	Notar *m*	notary	notaire *m*	notaio *m*	—
notary (E)	Notar *m*	—	notaire *m*	notaio *m*	notario *m*
not at all (E)	keineswegs	—	pas du tout	non affatto	en modo alguno

	D	E	F	I	Es
Notausgang (D)	—	emergency exit	sortie de secours *f*	uscita di sicurezza *f*	salida de emergencia *f*
not binding (E)	unverbindlich	—	sans engagement	non impegnativo(a)	sin compromiso
Note[1] (D)	—	mark	note *f*	voto *m*	calificación *f*
Note[2] (D)	—	note	note *f*	nota *f*	nota *f*
note[1] (E)	Note *f*	—	note *f*	nota *f*	nota *f*
note[2] (E)	Schein *m*	—	billet *m*	banconota *f*	billete *m*
note[1] (F)	Note *f*	note	—	nota *f*	nota *f*
note[2] (F)	Note *f*	mark	—	voto *m*	calificación *f*
note down (E)	notieren	—	noter	annotare	anotar
noter (F)	notieren	note down	—	annotare	anotar
Notfall (D)	—	emergency	cas d'urgence *m*	caso di emergenza *m*	caso de urgencia *m*
nothing (E)	nichts	—	rien	niente	nada
notice[1] (E)	bemerken	—	remarquer	notare	darse cuenta
notice[2] (E)	merken	—	remarquer	accorgersi di	notar
noticia (Es)	Nachricht *f*	message	nouvelle *f*	notizia *f*	—
noticiario (Es)	Nachrichten *pl*	news	informations *f pl*	giornale radio *m*	—
notieren (D)	—	note down	noter	annotare	anotar
notificar (Es)	mahnen	warn	exhorter	ammonire	—
nötig (D)	—	necessary	nécessaire	necessario(a)	necesario(a)
notizia (I)	Nachricht *f*	message	nouvelle *f*	—	noticia *f*
notte (I)	Nacht *f*	night	nuit *f*	—	noche *m*
notwendig (D)	—	necessary	nécessaire	necessario(a)	necesario(a)
Notwendigkeit (D)	—	necessity	nécessité *f*	necessità *f*	necesidad *f*
nouilles (F)	Nudeln *pl*	noodles	—	pasta *f*	pastas *f pl*
nourishment (E)	Ernährung *f*	—	nourriture *f*	alimentazione *f*	alimentación *f*
nourrir (F)	ernähren	feed	—	nutrire	alimentar
nourriture[1] (F)	Ernährung *f*	nourishment	—	alimentazione *f*	alimentación *f*
nourriture[2] (F)	Kost *f*	food	—	cibo *m*	alimento *m*
nourriture[3] (F)	Nahrung *f*	food	—	alimentazione *f*	nutrición *f*
nourriture[4] (F)	Verpflegung *f*	catering	—	vitto *m*	alimentación *f*
nous (F)	wir	we	—	noi	nosotros(as)
nouveau (F)	neu	new	—	nuovo(a)	nuevo(a)
nouveauté (F)	Neuheit *f*	novelty	—	novità *f*	originalidad *f*
nouvel an (F)	Neujahr *n*	New Year	—	Capodanno *m*	Año Nuevo *m*
nouvelle[1] (F)	Neuigkeit *f*	news	—	novità *f*	novedad *f*
nouvelle[2] (F)	Nachricht *f*	message	—	notizia *f*	noticia *f*
novanta (I)	neunzig	ninety	quatre-vingt-dix	—	noventa
nove (I)	neun	nine	neuf	—	nueve
novedad (Es)	Neuigkeit *f*	news	nouvelle *f*	novità *f*	—
novel (E)	Roman *m*	—	roman *m*	romanzo *m*	novela *f*
novela (Es)	Roman *m*	novel	roman *m*	romanzo *m*	—
novelty (E)	Neuheit *f*	—	nouveauté *f*	novità *f*	originalidad *f*
November (D)	—	November	novembre *m*	novembre *m*	noviembre *m*
November (E)	November *m*	—	novembre *m*	novembre *m*	noviembre *m*
novembre (F)	November *m*	November	—	novembre *m*	noviembre *m*
novembre (I)	November *m*	November	novembre *m*	—	noviembre *m*

	D	E	F	I	Es
noventa (Es)	neunzig	ninety	quatre-vingt-dix	novanta	—
no ver (Es)	übersehen	ignore	ignorer	non vedere	—
novia (Es)	Braut *f*	bride	mariée *f*	sposa *f*	—
noviembre (Es)	November *m*	November	novembre *m*	novembre *m*	—
novità[1] (I)	Neuigkeit *f*	news	nouvelle *f*	—	novedad *f*
novità[2] (I)	Neuheit *f*	novelty	nouveauté *f*	—	originalidad *f*
now[1] (E)	jetzt	—	maintenant	adesso	ahora
now[2] (E)	nun	—	maintenant	adesso	actualmente
nowadays (E)	heutzutage	—	de nos jours	oggigiorno	hoy en día
nowhere (E)	nirgends	—	nulle part	da nessuna parte	en ninguna parte
noyau (F)	Kern *m*	pip	—	nocciolo *m*	hueso *m*
noyer, se (F)	ertrinken	drown	—	annegare	ahogarse
nozze (I)	Hochzeit *f*	wedding	mariage *m*	—	boda *f*
nu (F)	nackt	naked	—	nudo(a)	desnudo(a)
nuage (F)	Wolke *f*	cloud	—	nuvola *f*	nube *f*
nube (Es)	Wolke *f*	cloud	nuage *m*	nuvola *f*	—
nublado (Es)	bewölkt	cloudy	couvert(e)	nuvoloso(a)	—
nüchtern (D)	—	sober	sobre	sobrio(a)	sobrio(a)
Nudeln (D)	—	noodles	nouilles *f pl*	pasta *f*	pastas *f pl*
nudo (Es)	Knoten *m*	knot	nœud *m*	nodo *m*	—
nudo (I)	nackt	naked	nu(e)	—	desnudo(a)
nueve (Es)	neun	nine	neuf	nove	—
nuevo (Es)	neu	new	nouveau, nouvel, nouvelle	nuovo(a)	—
nuez (Es)	Nuß *f*	nut	noix *f*	noce *f*	—
nuire (F)	schaden	damage	—	nuocere	dañar
nuisible (F)	schädlich	harmful	—	nocivo(a)	nocivo(a)
nuit (F)	Nacht *f*	night	—	notte *f*	noche *m*
nuit de Noël (F)	Heiligabend *m*	Christmas Eve	—	vigilia di Natale *f*	Nochebuena *f*
Null (D)	—	zero	zéro	zero	cero
nulle part (F)	nirgends	nowhere	—	da nessuna parte	en ninguna parte
number[1] (E)	Anzahl *f*	—	nombre *m*	numero *m*	número *m*
number[2] (E)	numerieren	—	numéroter	numerare	numerar
number[3] (E)	Nummer *f*	—	numéro	numero *m*	número *m*
number[4] (E)	Zahl *f*	—	chiffre *m*	numero *m*	número *m*
number plate (E)	Nummernschild *n*	—	plaque d'immatriculation *f*	targa *f*	matrícula *f*
numerar (Es)	numerieren	number	numéroter	numerare	—
numerare (I)	numerieren	number	numéroter	—	numerar
numerieren (D)	—	number	numéroter	numerare	numerar
número[1] (Es)	Anzahl *f*	number	nombre *m*	numero *m*	—
número[2] (Es)	Nummer *f*	number	numéro	numero *m*	—
número[3] (Es)	Zahl *f*	number	chiffre *m*	numero *m*	—
numéro (F)	Nummer *f*	number	—	numero *m*	número *m*
numero[1] (I)	Anzahl *f*	number	nombre *m*	—	número *m*

	D	E	F	I	Es
numero² (I)	Nummer f	number	numéro	—	número m
numero³ (I)	Zahl f	number	chiffre m	—	número m
número de teléfono (Es)	Telefonnummer f	phone number	numéro de téléphone m	numero telefonico m	—
numéro de téléphone (F)	Telefonnummer f	phone number	—	numero telefonico m	número de teléfono m
numeroso (Es)	zahlreich	numerous	nombreux(-euse)	numeroso(a)	—
numeroso (I)	zahlreich	numerous	nombreux(-euse)	—	numeroso(a)
numero telefonico (I)	Telefonnummer f	phone number	numéro de téléphone m	—	número de teléfono m
numéroter (F)	numerieren	number	—	numerare	numerar
numerous (E)	zahlreich	—	nombreux(-euse)	numeroso(a)	numeroso(a)
Nummer (D)	—	number	numéro	numero m	número m
Nummernschild (D)	—	number plate	plaque d'immatriculation f	targa f	matrícula f
nun (D)	—	now	maintenant	adesso	actualmente
nun (E)	Nonne f	—	religieuse f	suora f	monja f
nuocere (I)	schaden	damage	nuire	—	dañar
nuotare (I)	schwimmen	swim	nager	—	nadar
nuovo (I)	neu	new	nouveau, nouvel, nouvelle	—	nuevo(a)
nur (D)	—	only	seulement	solo	sólo
nurse (E)	Krankenschwester f	—	infirmière f	infermiera f	enfermera f
nursery school (E)	Kindergarten m	—	jardin d'enfants m	asilo (infantile) m	jardín de infancia m
nursing orderly (E)	Krankenpfleger m	—	infirmier m	infermiere m	enfermero m
Nuß (D)	—	nut	noix f	noce f	nuez f
nut (E)	Nuß f	—	noix f	noce f	nuez f
nutrición (Es)	Nahrung f	food	nourriture f	alimentazione f	—
nutrire (I)	ernähren	feed	nourrir	—	alimentar
nützlich (D)	—	useful	utile	utile	útil
nutzlos (D)	—	useless	inutile	inutile	inútil
nuvola (I)	Wolke f	cloud	nuage m	—	nube f
nuvoloso (I)	bewölkt	cloudy	couvert(e)	—	nublado(a)
o (Es)	oder	or	ou	o	—
o (I)	oder	or	ou	—	o
o...o (Es)	entweder...oder	either...or	ou...ou	o...o	—
o...o (I)	entweder...oder	either...or	ou...ou	—	o...o
oar (E)	Ruder n	—	rame f	remo m	remo m
Oase (D)	—	oasis	oasis f	oasi f	oasis m
oasi (I)	Oase f	oasis	oasis f	—	oasis m
oasis (E)	Oase f	—	oasis f	oasi f	oasis m
oasis (Es)	Oase f	oasis	oasis f	oasi f	—
oasis (F)	Oase f	oasis	—	oasi f	oasis m
ob (D)	—	if/whether	si	se	si
obbligare (I)	verpflichten	oblige	obliger	—	obligar

	D	E	F	I	Es
obbligo (I)	Verpflichtung *f*	obligation	obligation *f*	—	obligación *f*
obedecer (Es)	gehorchen	obey	obéir	ubbidire	—
obedient (E)	gehorsam	—	obéissant(e)	ubbidiente	obediente
obediente (Es)	gehorsam	obedient	obéissant(e)	ubbidiente	—
obéir (F)	gehorchen	obey	—	ubbidire	obedecer
obéissant (F)	gehorsam	obedient	—	ubbidiente	obediente
oben (D)	—	above	en haut	sopra	arriba
Ober (D)	—	waiter	garçon *m*	cameriere *m*	camarero *m*
Oberfläche (D)	—	surface	surface *f*	superficie *f*	superficie *f*
oberflächlich (D)	—	superficial	superficiel(le)	superficiale	superficial
obey (E)	gehorchen	—	obéir	ubbidire	obedecer
obgleich (D)	—	although	bien que	benché	aunque
object (E)	Gegenstand *m*	—	objet *m*	oggetto *m*	objeto *m*
objet (F)	Gegenstand *m*	object	—	oggetto *m*	objeto *m*
objeto (Es)	Gegenstand *m*	object	objet *m*	oggetto *m*	—
oblicuo (Es)	schief	sloped	oblique	obliquo(a)	—
obligación[1] (Es)	Pflicht *f*	duty	devoir *m*	dovere *m*	—
obligación[2] (Es)	Verpflichtung *f*	obligation	obligation *f*	obbligo *m*	—
obligar[1] (Es)	verpflichten	oblige	obliger	obbligare	—
obligar[2] (Es)	zwingen	force	forcer	costringere	—
obligation (E)	Verpflichtung *f*	—	obligation *f*	obbligo *m*	obligación *f*
obligation (F)	Verpflichtung *f*	obligation	—	obbligo *m*	obligación *f*
oblige (E)	verpflichten	—	obliger	obbligare	obligar
obligeance (F)	Gefälligkeit *f*	favour	—	favore *m*	complacencia *f*
obliger (F)	verpflichten	oblige	—	obbligare	obligar
obliging (E)	zuvorkommend	—	prévenant(e)	premuroso(a)	cortés
oblique (F)	schief	sloped	—	obliquo(a)	torcido(a)
obliquo (I)	schief	sloped	oblique	—	torcido(a)
obra (Es)	Werk *n*	work	œuvre *f*	opera *f*	—
obrar (Es)	handeln	act	agir	agire	—
obscurité (F)	Finsternis *f*	darkness	—	buio *m*	oscuridad *f*
observar (Es)	beobachten	observe	observer	osservare	—
observe (E)	beobachten	—	observer	osservare	observar
observer[1] (F)	beobachten	observe	—	osservare	observar
observer[2] (F)	beachten	take notice of	—	osservare	prestar atención a
Obst (D)	—	fruit	fruits *m pl*	frutta *f*	fruta *f*
obtain by force (E)	erzwingen	—	forcer	ottenere con la forza	forzar
obtener (Es)	erhalten	receive	recevoir	ricevere	—
obvious (E)	offensichtlich	—	manifeste	evidente	evidente
obwohl (D)	—	although	bien que	benché	aunque
oca (I)	Gans *f*	goose	oie *f*	—	ganso *m*
ocasional (Es)	gelegentlich	occasional	occasionnel(le)	occasionale	—
ocasionar (Es)	verursachen	cause	causer	causare	—
occasion (E)	Gelegenheit *f*	—	occasion *f*	occasione *f*	oportunidad *f*

	D	E	F	I	Es
occasion¹ (F)	Anlaß *m*	occasion	—	occasione *f*	causa *f*
occasion² (F)	Gelegenheit *f*	occasion	—	occasione *f*	oportunidad *f*
occasional (E)	gelegentlich	—	occasionnel(le)	occasionale	ocasional
occasionale (I)	gelegentlich	occasional	occasionnel(le)	—	ocasional
occasione¹ (I)	Anlaß *m*	cause	occasion *f*	—	ocasión *f*
occasione² (I)	Chance *f*	chance	possibilité *f*	—	oportunidad *f*
occasione³ (I)	Gelegenheit *f*	cause	occasion *f*	—	oportunidad *f*
occasionnel (F)	gelegentlich	occasional	—	occasionale	ocasional
occhiali (I)	Brille *f*	glasses	lunettes *f pl*	—	gafas *f pl*
occhiali da sole (I)	Sonnenbrille *f*	sunglasses	lunettes de soleil *f pl*	—	gafas de sol *f pl*
occhio (I)	Auge *n*	eye	œil *m* (yeux *pl*)	—	ojo *m*
occidental (Es)	westlich	western	de l'ouest	ad ovest	—
occupare (I)	beschäftigen	occupy/employ	occuper	—	ocupar
occupato¹ (I)	besetzt	engaged	occupé(e)	—	ocupado(a)
occupato² (I)	beschäftigt	busy	occupé(e)	—	ocupado(a)
occupé¹ (F)	beschäftigt	busy	—	occupato(a)	ocupado(a)
occupé² (F)	besetzt	engaged	—	occupato(a)	ocupado(a)
occuper (F)	beschäftigen	occupy/employ	—	occupare	ocupar
occuper de, se¹ (F)	kümmern, sich	look after	—	interessarsi di	ocuparse de
occuper de, se² (F)	sorgen	worry about	—	prendersi cura di	atender
occupy (E)	beschäftigen	—	occuper	occupare	ocupar
occur (E)	vorkommen	—	exister	accadere	suceder
ocean (E)	Ozean *m*	—	océan *m*	oceano *m*	océano *m*
océan (F)	Ozean *m*	ocean	—	oceano *m*	océano *m*
océano (Es)	Ozean *m*	ocean	océan *m*	oceano *m*	—
oceano (I)	Ozean *m*	ocean	océan *m*	—	océano *m*
ochenta (Es)	achtzig	eighty	quatre-vingts	ottanta	—
ocho (Es)	acht	eight	huit	otto	—
Ochse (D)	—	ox	bœuf *m*	bue *m*	buey *m*
October (E)	Oktober *m*	—	octobre *m*	ottobre *m*	octubre *m*
octobre (F)	Oktober *m*	October	—	ottobre *m*	octubre *m*
octubre (Es)	Oktober *m*	October	octobre *m*	ottobre *m*	—
oculista (Es)	Augenarzt *m*	eye specialist	oculiste *m*	oculista *m*	—
oculista (I)	Augenarzt *m*	eye specialist	oculiste *m*	—	oculista *m*
oculiste (F)	Augenarzt *m*	eye specialist	—	oculista *m*	oculista *m*
ocultar (Es)	verstecken	hide	cacher	nascondere	—
oculto (Es)	heimlich	secret	secret(-ète)	segreto(a)	—
ocupado¹ (Es)	beschäftigt	busy	occupé(e)	occupato(a)	—
ocupado² (Es)	besetzt	engaged	occupé(e)	occupato(a)	—
ocupar (Es)	beschäftigen	occupy/employ	occuper	occupare	—
ocuparse de (Es)	kümmern, sich	look after	occuper de, se	interessarsi di	—
ocurrir (Es)	geschehen	happen	arriver	accadere	—
öde (D)	—	waste	désert(e)	deserto(a)	desierto(a)
oder (D)	—	or	ou	o	o

	D	E	F	I	Es
odeur¹ (F)	Duft *m*	scent	—	profumo *m*	aroma *m*
odeur² (F)	Geruch *m*	smell	—	odore *m*	olor *m*
odiar (Es)	hassen	hate	détester	odiare	—
odiare (I)	hassen	hate	détester	—	odear
odio (Es)	Haß *m*	hate	haine *f*	odio *m*	—
odio (I)	Haß *m*	hate	haine *f*	—	odio *m*
odore (I)	Geruch *m*	smell	odeur *f*	—	olor *m*
œil (F)	Auge *n*	eye	—	occhio *m*	ojo *m*
œillet (F)	Nelke *f*	carnation	—	garofano *m*	clavel *m*
oeste (Es)	Westen *m*	west	ouest *m*	ovest *m*	—
œuf (F)	Ei *n*	egg	—	uovo *m*	huevo *m*
œuvre (F)	Werk *n*	work	—	opera *f*	obra *f*
of age (E)	volljährig	—	majeur(e)	maggiorenne	mayor de edad
of course (E)	selbstverständlich	—	évidemment	naturalmente	por supuesto
Ofen (D)	—	oven	poêle *m*	stufa *f*	estufa *f*
ofender (Es)	beleidigen	insult	offenser	offendere	—
ofensa (Es)	Beleidigung *f*	insult	offense *f*	offesa *f*	—
oferta (Es)	Angebot *n*	offer	offre *f*	offerta *f*	—
oferta especial (Es)	Sonderangebot *n*	special offer	offre spéciale *f*	offerta speciale *f*	—
off¹ (E)	ab	—	à partir de/dès	da	a partir de/de
off² (E)	aus	—	de/par/hors de	da/di	de/por
off! (E)	los!	—	allons-y!	avanti!	¡adelante!
offen (D)	—	open	ouvert(e)	aperto(a)	abierto(a)
offendere (I)	beleidigen	insult	offenser	—	ofender
offense (F)	Beleidigung *f*	insult	—	offesa *f*	ofensa *f*
offenser (F)	beleidigen	insult	—	offendere	ofender
offensichtlich (D)	—	obvious	manifeste	evidente	evidente
öffentlich (D)	—	public	public(-ique)	pubblico(a)	público(a)
Öffentlichkeit (D)	—	public	public *m*	pubblico *m*	público *m*
offer¹ (E)	anbieten	—	offrir	offrire	ofrecer
offer² (E)	Angebot *n*	—	offre *f*	offerta *f*	oferta *f*
offer³ (E)	bieten	—	présenter	offrire	ofrecer
offerta (I)	Angebot *n*	offer	offre *f*	—	oferta *f*
offerta speciale (I)	Sonderangebot *n*	special offer	offre spéciale *f*	—	oferta especial *f*
offesa (I)	Beleidigung *f*	insult	offense *f*	—	ofensa *f*
office¹ (E)	Amt *n*	—	bureau *m*	ufficio *m*	oficio *m*
office² (E)	Büro *n*	—	bureau *m*	ufficio *m*	oficina *f*
office divin (F)	Gottesdienst *m*	service	—	messa *f*	servicio religioso *m*
official¹ (E)	amtlich	—	officiel(le)	ufficiale	oficial
official² (E)	offiziell	—	officiel(le)	ufficiale	oficial
officiel¹ (F)	amtlich	official	—	ufficiale	oficial
officiel² (F)	offiziell	official	—	ufficiale	oficial
officina (I)	Werkstatt *f*	workshop	atelier *m*	—	taller *m*
offiziell (D)	—	official	officiel(le)	ufficiale	oficial

	D	E	F	I	Es
öffnen (D)	—	open	ouvrir	aprire	abrir
Öffnungzeiten (D)	—	business hours	heures d'ouverture *f pl*	orario d'ufficio *m*	horario de oficina *m*
offre (F)	Angebot *n*	offer	—	offerta *f*	oferta *f*
offre spéciale (F)	Sonderangebot *n*	special offer	—	offerta speciale *f*	oferta especial *f*
offrir¹ (F)	anbieten	offer	—	offrire	ofrecer
offrir² (F)	schenken	give	—	regalare	regalar
offrire¹ (I)	anbieten	offer	offrir	—	ofrecer
offrire² (I)	bieten	offer	présenter	—	ofrecer
oficial¹ (Es)	amtlich	official	officiel(le)	ufficiale	—
oficial² (Es)	offiziell	official	officiel(le)	ufficiale	—
oficina (Es)	Büro *n*	office	bureau *m*	ufficio *m*	—
oficina de correos (Es)	Postamt *n*	post office	bureau de poste *m*	ufficio postale *m*	—
oficina de objetos perdidos (Es)	Fundbüro *n*	lost property office	bureau des objets trouvés *m*	ufficio oggetti smarriti *m*	—
oficina de turismo (Es)	Verkehrsbüro *n*	travel agency	bureau touristique *m*	ufficio turistico *m*	—
oficina de viajes (Es)	Reisebüro *f*	travel agency	agence de voyages *f*	agenzia turistica *f*	—
oficio (Es)	Amt *n*	office	bureau *m*	ufficio *m*	—
of it (E)	davon	—	en/de cela	di la/ne	de ello
ofrecer¹ (Es)	anbieten	offer	offrir	offrire	—
ofrecer² (Es)	bieten	offer	présenter	offrire	—
oft (D)	—	often	souvent	spesso	a menudo
often (E)	oft	—	souvent	spesso	a menudo
oggetti antichi (I)	Antiquitäten *pl*	antiques	antiquités *f pl*	—	antigüedades *f pl*
oggetto (I)	Gegenstand *m*	object	objet *m*	—	objeto *m*
oggi (I)	heute	today	aujourd'hui	—	hoy
oggigiorno (I)	heutzutage	nowadays	de nos jours	—	hoy en día
ogni, ognuno (I)	jede(r,s)	each/every	chaque	—	cada
ogni ora (I)	stündlich	hourly	toutes les heures	—	cada hora
ogni volta (I)	jedesmal	each time	chaque fois	—	cada vez
ohne (D)	—	without	sans	senza	sin
Ohnmacht (D)	—	faint	évanouisse-ment *m*	svenimento *m*	desmayo *m*
Ohr (D)	—	ear	oreille *f*	orecchio *m*	oreja *f*
Ohrenarzt (D)	—	ear specialist	spécialiste de l'oreille *m*	otoiatra *m*	médico del oído *m*
Ohren-schmerzen (D)	—	earache	mal d'oreilles *m*	mal d'orecchi *m*	dolor de oídos *m*
oie (F)	Gans *f*	goose	—	oca *f*	ganso *m*
oignon (F)	Zwiebel *f*	onion	—	cipolla *f*	cebolla *f*
oil¹ (E)	Erdöl *n*	—	pétrole *m*	petrolio *m*	petróleo *m*
oil² (E)	Öl *n*	—	huile *f*	olio *m*	aceite *m*
ointment (E)	Salbe *f*	—	onguent *m*	pomata *f*	pomada *f*
oír (Es)	hören	hear	entendre	sentire	—
oiseau (F)	Vogel *m*	bird	—	uccello *m*	pájaro *m*

	D	E	F	I	Es
ojo (Es)	Auge n	eye	œil m (yeux pl)	occhio m	—
ojo de la cerradura (Es)	Schlüsselloch n	keyhole	trou de la serrure m	buco della chiave m	—
Oktober (D)	—	October	octobre m	ottobre m	octubre m
Öl (D)	—	oil	huile f	olio m	aceite m
ola (Es)	Welle f	wave	vague f	onda f	—
old (E)	alt	—	vieux, vieil, vieille	vecchio(a)	viejo(a)
old-fashioned (E)	altmodisch	—	démodé(e)	fuori moda	pasado(a) de moda
oler (Es)	riechen	smell	sentir	sentire	—
Olimpiadi (I)	Olympische Spiele pl	Olympic Games	jeux olympiques m pl	—	Juegos Olímpicos m pl
olio (I)	Öl n	oil	huile f	—	aceite m
olio combustibile (I)	Heizöl n	fuel	mazout m	—	combustible para la calefacción m
oliva (I)	Olive f	olive	olive f	—	aceituna f
Olive (D)	—	olive	olive f	oliva f	aceituna f
olive (E)	Olive f	—	olive f	oliva f	aceituna f
olive (F)	Olive f	olive	—	oliva f	aceituna f
olla¹ (Es)	Kochtopf m	saucepan	casserole f	pentola f	—
olla² (Es)	Topf m	pot	casserole f	pentola f	—
olor (Es)	Geruch m	smell	odeur f	odore m	—
olvidar (Es)	vergessen	forget	oublier	dimenticare	—
Olympic Games (E)	Olympische Spiele pl	—	jeux olympiques m pl	Olimpiadi f pl	Juegos Olímpicos m pl
Olympische Spiele (D)	—	Olympic Games	jeux olympiques m pl	Olimpiadi f pl	Juegos Olímpicos m pl
ombelico (I)	Nabel m	navel	nombril m	—	ombligo m
ombligo (Es)	Nabel m	navel	nombril m	ombelico m	—
ombra (I)	Schatten m	shadow	ombre f	—	sombra f
ombragé (F)	schattig	shady	—	ombroso(a)	a la sombra
ombre (F)	Schatten m	shadow	—	ombra f	sombra f
ombrello¹ (I)	Regenschirm m	umbrella	parapluie m	—	paraguas m
ombrello² (I)	Schirm m	umbrella	parapluie m	—	paraguas m
ombrellone (I)	Sonnenschirm m	parasol	parasol m	—	sombrilla f
ombroso (I)	schattig	shady	ombragé(e)	—	a la sombra
Omelett (D)	—	omelette	omelette f	frittata f	tortilla f
omelette (E)	Omelett n	—	omelette f	frittata f	tortilla f
omelette (F)	Omelett n	omelette	—	frittata f	tortilla f
Omnibus (D)	—	omnibus	autobus m	autobus m	autobús m
omnibus (E)	Omnibus m	—	autobus m	autobus m	autobús m
on (E)	auf	—	sur	su/sopra	sobre/en/hacia
on business (E)	geschäftlich	—	d'affaires	per affari	comercial
once (E)	einmal	—	une fois	una volta	una vez
once (Es)	elf	eleven	onze	undici	—
oncle (F)	Onkel m	uncle	—	zio m	tío m
onda (I)	Welle f	wave	vague f	—	ola f

	D	E	F	I	Es
one[1] (E)	eins	—	un	uno	uno(a)
one[2] (E)	eine(r,s)	—	un(e)	un(a)	una/un/uno
one after the other (E)	hintereinander	—	l'un derrière l'autre	uno dopo l'altro	uno detrás de otro
one and a half (E)	anderthalb	—	un(e) et demi(e)	uno e mezzo	uno(a) y medio(a)
one before last (E)	vorletzte(r,s)	—	avant-dernier (-ère)	penultimo(a)	penúltima(o)
one hundred (E)	einhundert	—	cent	cento	cien
one-sided (E)	einseitig	—	partial(e)	unilaterale	unilateral
onesto[1] (I)	ehrlich	honest	honnête	—	honesto(a)
onesto[2] (I)	aufrichtig	honest	sincère	—	sincero(a)
one upon the other (E)	übereinander	—	l'un(e) sur l'autre	uno sopra l'altro	uno sobre otro
one-way street (E)	Einbahnstraße f	—	rue à sens unique f	senso unico m	calle de dirección única f
ongle (F)	Nagel m	nail	—	unghia f	uña f
onguent (F)	Salbe f	ointment	—	pomata f	pomada f
onion (E)	Zwiebel f	—	oignon m	cipolla f	cebolla f
Onkel (D)	—	uncle	oncle m	zio m	tío m
only[1] (E)	bloß	—	seulement	soltanto	sólo
only[2] (E)	einzig	—	seul(e)	unico(a)	único(a)
only[3] (E)	nur	—	seulement	solo	sólo
on one hand (E)	einerseits	—	d'une part	da un lato	por un lado
onore (I)	Ehre f	honour	honneur m	—	honor m
on the other hand (E)	andererseits	—	d'autre part	d'altra parte	por otra parte
on the way (E)	unterwegs	—	en route	per strada	de camino
on working days (E)	werktags	—	les jours ouvrables	nei giorni feriali	los días laborables
onze (F)	elf	eleven	—	undici	once
opción (Es)	Wahl f	choice	choix m	scelta f	—
open[1] (E)	geöffnet	—	ouvert(e)	aperto(a)	abierto(a)
open[2] (E)	öffnen	—	ouvrir	aprire	abrir
open[3] (E)	offen	—	ouvert(e)	aperto(a)	abierto(a)
open-air swimming pool (E)	Freibad n	—	piscine en plein air f	piscina all'aperto f	piscina al aire libre f
opening (E)	Eröffnung f	—	ouverture f	apertura f	abertura f
Oper (D)	—	opera	opéra m	opera f	ópera f
opera (E)	Oper f	—	opéra m	opera f	ópera f
ópera (Es)	Oper f	opera	opéra m	opera f	—
opéra (F)	Oper f	opera	—	opera f	ópera f
opera[1] (I)	Oper f	opera	opéra m	—	ópera f
opera[2] (I)	Werk n	work	œuvre f	—	obra f
operación (Es)	Operation f	operation	opération f	operazione f	—
operaio (I)	Arbeiter m	worker	ouvrier m	—	trabajador m
opera teatrale (I)	Theaterstück n	play	pièce de théâtre f	—	pieza de teatro f
Operation (D)	—	operation	opération f	operazione f	operación f
operation (E)	Operation f	—	opération f	operazione f	operación f

	D	E	F	I	Es
opération (F)	Operation *f*	operation	—	operazione *f*	operación *f*
operazione (I)	Operation *f*	operation	opération *f*	—	operación *f*
Opfer[1] (D)	—	sacrifice	sacrifice *m*	sacrificio *m*	sacrificio *m*
Opfer[2] (D)	—	victim	victime *f*	vittima *f*	víctima *f*
opinar (Es)	meinen	think	penser	credere	—
opinion[1] (E)	Ansicht *f*	—	avis *m*	opinione *f*	opinión *f*
opinion[2] (E)	Meinung *f*	—	opinion *f*	opinione *f*	opinión *f*
opinión[1] (Es)	Ansicht *f*	opinion	avis *m*	opinione *f*	—
opinión[2] (Es)	Meinung *f*	opinion	opinion *f*	opinione *f*	—
opinion (F)	Meinung *f*	opinion	—	opinione *f*	opinión *f*
opinione[1] (I)	Ansicht *f*	opinion	avis *m*	—	opinión *f*
opinione[2] (I)	Meinung *f*	opinion	opinion *f*	—	opinión *f*
oportunidad[1] (Es)	Chance *f*	chance	possibilité *f*	occasione *f*	—
oportunidad[2] (Es)	Gelegenheit *f*	occasion	occasion *f*	occasione *f*	—
opponent (E)	Gegner *m*	—	adversaire *m*	avversario *m*	adversario *m*
opposé (F)	entgegengesetzt	opposite	—	opposto(a)	opuesto(a)
opposite[1] (E)	entgegengesetzt	—	opposé(e)	opposto(a)	opuesto(a)
opposite[2] (E)	gegenüber	—	en face de	di fronte(a)	en frente
opposite[3] (E)	Gegenteil *n*	—	contraire *m*	contrario *m*	opuesto *m*
opposto (I)	entgegengesetzt	opposite	opposé(e)	—	opuesto(a)
oppress (E)	unterdrücken	—	opprimer	sopprimere	oprimir
opprimer (F)	unterdrücken	oppress	—	sopprimere	oprimir
oprimir (Es)	unterdrücken	oppress	opprimer	sopprimere	—
optician (E)	Optiker *m*	—	opticien *m*	ottico *m*	óptico *m*
opticien (F)	Optiker *m*	optician	—	ottico *m*	óptico *m*
óptico (Es)	Optiker *m*	optician	opticien *m*	ottico *m*	—
Optiker (D)	—	optician	opticien *m*	ottico *m*	óptico *m*
óptimo (Es)	beste(r,s)	best	meilleur(e)	migliore	—
opuesto[1] (Es)	Gegenteil *n*	opposite	contraire *m*	contrario *m*	—
opuesto[2] (Es)	entgegengesetzt	opposite	opposé(e)	opposto(a)	—
or (E)	oder	—	ou	o	o
or (F)	Gold *n*	gold	—	oro *m*	oro *m*
ora (I)	Stunde *f*	hour	heure *f*	—	hora *f*
oración (Es)	Satz *m*	sentence	phrase *f*	frase *f*	—
ora di ricevimento (I)	Sprechstunde *f*	consultation hour	heures de consultation *f pl*	—	hora de consulta *f*
orage (F)	Gewitter *n*	thunderstorm	—	temporale *m*	tormenta *f*
oral (E)	mündlich	—	oral(e)	orale	oral
oral (Es)	mündlich	oral	oral(e)	orale	—
oral (F)	mündlich	oral	—	orale	oral
orale (I)	mündlich	oral	oral(e)	—	oral
ora legale (I)	Sommerzeit *f*	summertime	heure d'été *f*	—	temporada de verano *f*
Orange (D)	—	orange	orange *f*	arancia *f*	naranja *f*
orange[1] (E)	Apfelsine *f*	—	orange *f*	arancia *f*	naranja *f*

	D	E	F	I	Es
orange² (E)	Orange *f*	—	orange *f*	arancia *f*	naranja *f*
orange¹ (F)	Apfelsine *f*	orange	—	arancia *f*	naranja *f*
orange² (F)	Orange *f*	orange	—	arancia *f*	naranja *f*
orario (I)	Fahrplan *m*	timetable	horaire *m*	—	horario *m*
orario di apertura (I)	Öffnungszeiten *pl*	business hours	heures d'ouverture *f pl*	—	horario de abertura *m*
Orchester (D)	—	orchestra	orchestre *m*	orchestra *f*	orquesta *f*
orchestra (E)	Orchester *n*	—	orchestre *m*	orchestra *f*	orquesta *f*
orchestra (I)	Orchester *n*	orchestra	orchestre *m*	—	orquesta *f*
orchestre¹ (F)	Kapelle *f*	band	—	banda *f*	banda *f*
orchestre² (F)	Orchester *n*	orchestra	—	orchestra *f*	orquesta *f*
Orden¹ (D)	—	order	ordre *m*	ordine *m*	orden *m*
Orden² (D)	—	decoration	décoration *f*	decorazione *f*	condecoración *f*
orden¹ (Es)	Ordnung *f*	order	ordre *m*	ordine *m*	—
orden² (Es)	Orden *m*	order	ordre *m*	ordine *m*	—
ordenado (Es)	ordentlich	tidy	rangé(e)	ordinato(a)	—
ordenar (Es)	ordnen	put in order	ordonner	ordinare	—
ordentlich (D)	—	tidy	rangé(e)	ordinato(a)	ordenado(a)
order¹ (E)	bestellen	—	commander	ordinare	pedir
order² (E)	verfügen	—	disposer de	disporre	disponer
order³ (E)	Befehl *m*	—	ordre *m*	ordine *m*	mando *m*
order⁴ (E)	Ordnung *f*	—	ordre *m*	ordine *m*	orden *m*
order⁵ (E)	Orden *m*	—	ordre *m*	ordine *m*	orden *m*
ordinare¹ (I)	bestellen	order	commander	—	pedir
ordinare² (I)	ordnen	put in order	ordonner	—	ordenar
ordinato (I)	ordentlich	tidy	rangé(e)	—	ordenado(a)
ordine¹ (I)	Befehl *m*	order	ordre *m*	—	mando *m*
ordine² (I)	Ordnung *f*	order	ordre *m*	—	orden *m*
ordine³ (I)	Orden *m*	order	ordre *m*	—	orden *m*
ordnen (D)	—	put in order	ordonner	ordinare	ordenar
Ordnung (D)	—	order	ordre *m*	ordine *m*	orden *m*
ordonnance (F)	Rezept *n*	prescription	—	prescrizione *f*	prescripción médica *f*
ordonner (F)	ordnen	put in order	—	ordinare	ordenar
ordre¹ (F)	Befehl *m*	order	—	ordine *m*	mando *m*
ordre² (F)	Ordnung *f*	order	—	ordine *m*	orden *m*
ordre³ (F)	Orden *m*	order	—	ordine *m*	orden *m*
orecchio (I)	Ohr *n*	ear	oreille *f*	—	oreja *f*
oreille (F)	Ohr *n*	ear	—	orecchio *m*	oreja *f*
oreiller (F)	Kopfkissen *n*	pillow	—	guanciale *m*	almohada *f*
oreja¹ (Es)	Gehör *n*	hearing	ouïe *f*	udito *m*	—
oreja² (Es)	Ohr *n*	ear	oreille *f*	orecchio *m*	—
orfano (I)	Waise *f*	orphan	orphelin *m*	—	huérfano *m*
organiser¹ (F)	organisieren	organize	—	organizzare	organizar
organiser² (F)	veranstalten	organize	—	organizzare	organizar

	D	E	F	I	Es
organisieren (D)	—	organize	organiser	organizzare	organizar
organizar¹ (Es)	arrangieren	arrange	arranger	arrangiare	—
organizar² (Es)	organisieren	organize	organiser	organizzare	—
organizar³ (Es)	veranstalten	organize	organiser	organizzare	—
organize¹ (E)	organisieren	—	organiser	organizzare	organizar
organize² (E)	veranstalten	—	organiser	organizzare	organizar
organizzare¹ (I)	organisieren	organize	organiser	—	organizar
organizzare² (I)	veranstalten	organize	organiser	—	organizar
orgoglioso (I)	stolz	proud	fier(-ère)	—	orgulloso(a)
orgulloso (Es)	stolz	proud	fier(-ère)	orgoglioso(a)	—
Orient (D)	—	Orient	Orient *m*	Oriente *m*	oriente *m*
Orient (E)	Orient *m*	—	Orient *m*	Oriente *m*	oriente *m*
Orient (F)	Orient *m*	Orient	—	Oriente *m*	oriente *m*
orientarse (Es)	zurechtfinden, sich	find one's way	retrouver, se	orientarsi	—
orientarsi (I)	zurechtfinden, sich	find one's way	retrouver, se	—	orientarse
oriente (Es)	Orient *m*	Orient	Orient *m*	Oriente *m*	—
Oriente (I)	Orient *m*	Orient	Orient *m*	—	oriente *m*
original¹ (E)	originell	—	original(e)	originale	original
original² (E)	ursprünglich	—	originel(le)	originario(a)	primitivo(a)
original (Es)	originell	original	original(e)	originale	—
original (F)	originell	original	—	originale	original
originale (I)	originell	original	original(e)	—	original
originalidad (Es)	Neuheit *f*	novelty	nouveauté *f*	novità *f*	—
originario (I)	ursprünglich	original	originel(le)	—	primitivo(a)
originel (F)	ursprünglich	original	—	originario(a)	primitivo(a)
originell (D)	—	original	original(e)	originale	original
orilla (Es)	Ufer *n*	shore	bord *m*	riva *f*	—
orina (Es)	Harn *m*	urine	urine *f*	urina *f*	—
orizzontale (I)	waagrecht	horizontal	horizontal(e)	—	horizontal
oro (Es)	Gold *n*	gold	or *m*	oro *m*	—
oro (I)	Gold *n*	gold	or *m*	—	oro *m*
orologio (I)	Uhr *f*	watch	montre *f*	—	reloj *m*
orphan (E)	Waise *f*	—	orphelin *m*	orfano *m*	huérfano *m*
orphelin (F)	Waise *f*	orphan	—	orfano *m*	huérfano *m*
orquesta (Es)	Orchester *n*	orchestra	orchestre *m*	orchestra *f*	—
orso (I)	Bär *m*	bear	ours *m*	—	oso *m*
Ort (D)	—	place	endroit *m*	luogo *m*	lugar *m*
örtlich (D)	—	local	local(e)	locale	local
os (F)	Knochen *m*	bone	—	osso *m*	hueso *m*
osare (I)	wagen	dare	oser	—	atreverse
oscuridad (Es)	Finsternis *f*	darkness	obscurité *f*	buio *m*	—
oscuro¹ (Es)	dunkel	dark	sombre	scuro(a)	—
oscuro² (Es)	finster	dark	sombre	buio(a)	—

	D	E	F	I	Es
oser (F)	wagen	dare	—	osare	atreverse
oso (Es)	Bär *m*	bear	ours *m*	orso *m*	—
ospedale (I)	Krankenhaus *n*	hospital	hôpital *m*	—	hospital *m*
ospitale (I)	gastfreundlich	hospitable	hospitalier(-ière)	—	hospitalario(a)
ospitalità (I)	Gastfreundschaft *f*	hospitality	hospitalité *f*	—	hospitalidad *f*
ospite[1] (I)	Gastgeber *m*	host	hôte *m*	—	anfitrión *m*
ospite[2] (I)	Gast *m*	guest	hôte *m*	—	invitado *m*
osservare[1] (I)	beachten	take notice of	observer	—	prestar atención
osservare[2] (I)	beobachten	observe	observer	—	observar
osso (I)	Knochen *m*	bone	os *m*	—	hueso *m*
oste (I)	Wirt *m*	landlord	patron *m*	—	dueño *m*
Osten (D)	—	east	est *m*	est *m*	este *m*
osteria[1] (I)	Gasthaus *n*	inn	auberge *f*	—	posada *f*
osteria[2] (I)	Kneipe *f*	pub	bistro *m*	—	tasca *f*
osteria[3] (I)	Wirtshaus *n*	inn	auberge *f*	—	restaurante *m*
Ostern (D)	—	Easter	Pâques *f pl*	Pasqua *f*	Pascua *f*
Österreich (D)	—	Austria	Autriche *f*	Austria *f*	Austria *f*
Österreicher (D)	—	Austrian	Autrichien *m*	austriaco *m*	austríaco *m*
österreichisch (D)	—	Austrian	autrichien(ne)	austriaco(a)	austríaco(a)
Osterwoche (D)	—	Holy week	semaine sainte *f*	settimana santa *f*	Semana Santa *f*
östlich (D)	—	eastern	d'est	ad est	al este
ostra (Es)	Auster *f*	oyster	huître *f*	ostrica *f*	—
ostrica (I)	Auster *f*	oyster	huître *f*	—	ostra *f*
other (E)	andere(r,s)	—	autre	altro(a)	otro(a)
otherwise (E)	sonst	—	autrement	altrimenti	por lo demás
otoiatra (I)	Ohrenarzt *m*	ear specialist	spécialiste de l'oreille *m*	—	médico del oído *m*
otoño (Es)	Herbst *m*	autumn	automne *m*	autunno *m*	—
otra vez (Es)	nochmals	again	encore une fois	di nuovo	—
otro (Es)	andere(r,s)	other	autre	altro(a)	—
ottanta (I)	achtzig	eighty	quatre-vingts	—	ochenta
ottenere con la forza (I)	erzwingen	obtain by force	forcer	—	forzar
ottico (I)	Optiker *m*	optician	opticien *m*	—	óptico *m*
otto (I)	acht	eight	huit	—	ocho
ottobre (I)	Oktober *m*	October	octobre *m*	—	octubre *m*
ou (F)	oder	or	—	o	o
où[1] (F)	wohin	where to	—	dove	a dónde
où[2] (F)	wo	where	—	dove	dónde
ouate (F)	Watte *f*	cotton wool	—	ovatta *f*	algodón *m*
oublier (F)	vergessen	forget	—	dimenticare	olvidar
ouest (F)	Westen *m*	west	—	ovest *m*	oeste *m*
oui (F)	ja	yes	—	sì	sí
ouïe (F)	Gehör *n*	hearing	—	udito *m*	oreja *f*
ou...ou (F)	entweder...oder	either...or	—	o...o	o...o

	D	E	F	I	Es
ours (F)	Bär m	bear	—	orso m	oso m
out¹ (E)	hinaus	—	dehors	fuori	hacia afuera
out² (E)	heraus	—	dehors	fuori	hacia afuera
outil (F)	Werkzeug n	tool	—	utensile m	herramienta f
outing (E)	Ausflug m	—	excursion f	gita f	excursión f
outline (E)	Entwurf m	—	esquisse f	abbozzo m	proyecto m
out of (E)	außerhalb	—	hors de	fuori di	fuera de
outside¹ (E)	außen	—	au dehors	fuori	afuera
outside² (E)	draußen	—	dehors	fuori	afuera
outwards (E)	auswärts	—	à l'extérieur	fuori	fuera
ouvert¹ (F)	geöffnet	open	—	aperto(a)	abierto(a)
ouvert² (F)	offen	open	—	aperto(a)	abierto(a)
ouverture (F)	Eröffnung f	opening	—	apertura f	abertura f
ouvre-bouteilles (F)	Flaschenöffner m	bottle opener	—	apribottiglie m	abridor de botellas m
ouvrier (F)	Arbeiter m	worker	—	operaio m	trabajador m
ouvrir (F)	öffnen	open	—	aprire	abrir
ovatta (I)	Watte f	cotton wool	ouate f	—	algodón m
oveja (Es)	Schaf n	sheep	mouton m	pecora f	—
oven (E)	Ofen m	—	poêle m	stufa f	estufa f
over¹ (E)	herüber	—	par ici	da questa parte	a este lado
over² (E)	über	—	sur	su/sopra/per	por/sobre
overestimate (E)	überschätzen	—	surestimer	sopravvalutare	sobrevalorar
over here (E)	hierher	—	par ici	qua	para acá
overnight stay (E)	Übernachtung f	—	logement pour une nuit m	pernottamento m	pernoctación f
overtake (E)	überholen	—	doubler	sorpassare	adelantar
over there (E)	drüben	—	de l'autre côté	dall'altra parte	al otro lado
ovest (I)	Westen m	west	ouest m	—	oeste m
owe (E)	schulden	—	devoir qch à qn	dovere	deber
own (E)	eigen	—	propre	proprio(a)	propio(a)
owner¹ (E)	Besitzer m	—	propriétaire m	proprietario m	propietario m
owner² (E)	Eigentümer m	—	propriétaire m	proprietario m	propietario m
owner³ (E)	Inhaber m	—	propriétaire m	proprietario m	propietario m
ox (E)	Ochse m	—	bœuf m	bue m	buey m
oxidado (Es)	rostig	rusty	rouillé(e)	arrugginito(a)	—
oxidarse (Es)	rosten	rust	rouiller	arrugginire	—
oyente (Es)	Hörer m	listener	auditeur m	ascoltatore m	—
oyster (E)	Auster f	—	huître f	ostrica f	ostra f
Ozean (D)	—	ocean	océan m	oceano m	océano m
Paar (D)	—	pair	paire f	paio m	par m
pacchetto (I)	Päckchen n	small package	petit paquet m	—	paquetito m
pacco (I)	Paket n	parcel	paquet m	—	paquete m
pace (I)	Friede m	peace	paix f	—	paz f
paciencia (Es)	Geduld f	patience	patience f	pazienza f	—

	D	E	F	I	Es
paciente (Es)	Patient *m*	patient	patient *m*	paziente *m*	—
Pacific (E)	Pazifik *m*	—	Pacifique *m*	Pacifico *m*	pacífico *m*
pacífico (Es)	friedlich	peaceful	paisible	pacifico(a)	—
Pacífico (Es)	Pazifik *m*	Pacific	Pacifique *m*	Pacifico *m*	—
pacifico (I)	friedlich	peaceful	paisible	—	pacífico(a)
Pacifico (I)	Pazifik *m*	Pacific	Pacifique *m*	—	pacífico *m*
Pacifique (F)	Pazifik *m*	Pacific	—	Pacifico *m*	pacífico *m*
pack[1] (E)	packen	—	faire les malles	impacchettare	hacer la maleta
pack[2] (E)	verpacken	—	emballer	impacchettare	empaquetar
Päckchen (D)	—	small package	petit paquet *m*	pacchetto *m*	paquetito *m*
packen (D)	—	pack	faire les malles	impacchettare	hacer la maleta
Paddelboot (D)	—	canoe	canoë *m*	canoa *f*	piragua *f*
padella (I)	Pfanne *f*	pan	poêle *f*	—	sartén *f*
padre (Es)	Vater *m*	father	père *m*	padre *m*	—
padre (I)	Vater *m*	father	père *m*	—	padre *m*
padres (Es)	Eltern *pl*	parents	parents *m pl*	genitori *m pl*	—
padrino (Es)	Pate *m*	godfather	parrain *m*	padrino *m*	—
padrino (I)	Pate *m*	godfather	parrain *m*	—	padrino *m*
paesaggio (I)	Landschaft *f*	landscape	paysage *m*	—	paisaje *m*
paese[1] (I)	Dorf *n*	village	village *m*	—	pueblo *m*
paese[2] (I)	Land *n*	land	pays *m*	—	país *m*
Paesi Bassi (I)	Niederlande *f*	Netherlands	Pays-Bas *m pl*	—	los Paìses Bajos *m pl*
pagamento[1] (I)	Bezahlung *f*	payment	paiement *m*	—	pago *m*
pagamento[2] (I)	Zahlung *f*	payment	paiement *m*	—	pago *m*
pagamento contro assegno (I)	Nachnahme *f*	cash on delivery	remboursement *m*	—	entrega contra reembolso *f*
pagar[1] (Es)	bezahlen	pay	payer	pagare	—
pagar[2] (Es)	zahlen	pay	payer	pagare	—
pagare[1] (I)	bezahlen	pay	payer	—	pagar
pagare[2] (I)	zahlen	pay	payer	—	pagar
page (E)	Seite *f*	—	page *f*	pagina *f*	página *f*
page (F)	Seite *f*	page	—	pagina *f*	página *f*
pagella (I)	Zeugnis *n*	report	bulletin *m*	—	informe *m*
página (Es)	Seite *f*	page	page *f*	pagina *f*	—
pagina (I)	Seite *f*	page	page *f*	—	página *f*
paglia (I)	Stroh *n*	straw	paille *f*	—	paja *f*
pago[1] (Es)	Bezahlung *f*	payment	paiement *m*	pagamento *m*	—
pago[2] (Es)	Zahlung *f*	payment	paiement *m*	pagamento *m*	—
paiement[1] (F)	Bezahlung *f*	payment	—	pagamento *m*	pago *m*
paiement[2] (F)	Zahlung *f*	payment	—	pagamento *m*	pago *m*
paille (F)	Stroh *n*	straw	—	paglia *f*	paja *f*
pain (E)	Schmerz *m*	—	douleur *f*	dolore *m*	dolor *m*
pain (F)	Brot *n*	bread	—	pane *m*	pan *m*
painful (E)	schmerzhaft	—	douloureux(-euse)	doloroso(a)	doloroso(a)

	D	E	F	I	Es
paint¹ (E)	malen	—	peindre	dipingere	pintar
paint² (E)	streichen	—	peindre	verniciare	pintar
painter (E)	Maler *m*	—	peintre *m*	pittore *m*	pintor *m*
painting¹ (E)	Gemälde *n*	—	tableau *m*	quadro *m*	cuadro *m*
painting² (E)	Malerei *f*	—	peinture *f*	pittura *f*	pintura *f*
paio (I)	Paar *n*	pair	paire *f*	—	par *m*
pair (E)	Paar *n*	—	paire *f*	paio *m*	par *m*
pair (F)	gerade	even	—	pari	par
paire (F)	Paar *n*	pair	—	paio *m*	par *m*
pair of scissors (E)	Schere *f*	—	ciseaux *m pl*	forbici *f pl*	tijeras *f pl*
país (Es)	Land *n*	land	pays *m*	paese *m*	—
paisaje (Es)	Landschaft *f*	landscape	paysage *m*	paesaggio *m*	—
paisible (F)	friedlich	peaceful	—	pacifico(a)	pacífico(a)
paix (F)	Friede *m*	peace	—	pace *f*	paz *f*
paja (Es)	Stroh *n*	straw	paille *f*	paglia *f*	—
pájaro (Es)	Vogel *m*	bird	oiseau *m*	uccello *m*	—
Paket (D)	—	parcel	paquet *m*	pacco *m*	paquete *m*
pala (Es)	Schaufel *f*	shovel	pelle *f*	pala *f*	—
pala (I)	Schaufel *f*	shovel	pelle *f*	—	pala *f*
palabra (Es)	Wort *n*	word	mot *m*	parola *f*	—
palace (E)	Palast *m*	—	palais	palazzo *m*	palacio *m*
palacio (Es)	Palast *m*	palace	palais	palazzo *m*	—
palais (F)	Palast *m*	palace	—	palazzo *m*	palacio *m*
Palast (D)	—	palace	palais	palazzo *m*	palacio *m*
palazzo (I)	Palast *m*	palace	palais	—	palacio *m*
palco (Es)	Loge *f*	box	loge *f*	palco *m*	—
palco (I)	Loge *f*	box	loge *f*	—	palco *m*
palcoscenico (I)	Bühne *f*	stage	scène *f*	—	escenario *m*
pale (E)	blaß	—	pâle	pallido(a)	pálido(a)
pâle (F)	blaß	pale	—	pallido(a)	pálido(a)
pálido (Es)	blaß	pale	pâle	pallido(a)	—
palla (I)	Ball *m*	ball	balle *f*	—	pelota *f*
pallido (I)	blaß	pale	pâle	—	pálido(a)
pallone (I)	Fußball *m*	football	football *m*	—	fútbol *m*
palma (I)	Palme *f*	palmtree	palmier *m*	—	palmera *f*
Palme (D)	—	palmtree	palmier *m*	palma *f*	palmera *f*
palmera (Es)	Palme *f*	palmtree	palmier *m*	palma *f*	—
palmier (F)	Palme *f*	palmtree	—	palma *f*	palmera *f*
palmtree (E)	Palme *f*	—	palmier *m*	palma *f*	palmera *f*
Pampelmuse (D)	—	grapefruit	pamplemousse *m*	pompelmo *m*	pomelo *m*
pamplemousse (F)	Pampelmuse *f*	grapefruit	—	pompelmo *m*	pomelo *m*
pan (E)	Pfanne *f*	—	poêle *f*	padella *f*	sartén *f*
pan (Es)	Brot *n*	bread	pain *m*	pane *m*	—
panadería (Es)	Bäckerei *f*	bakery	boulangerie *f*	panetteria *f*	—
pañal (Es)	Windel *f*	nappy	lange *m*	pannolino *m*	—
pancia (I)	Bauch *m*	stomach	ventre *m*	—	vientre *m*
pane (E)	Scheibe *f*	—	carreau *m*	vetro *m*	cristal *m*
pane (I)	Brot *n*	bread	pain *m*	—	pan *m*

	D	E	F	I	Es
panecillo (Es)	Brötchen *n*	roll	petit pain *m*	panino *m*	—
panetteria (I)	Bäckerei *f*	bakery	boulangerie *f*	—	panadería *f*
panfilo (I)	Jacht *f*	yacht	yacht *m*	—	yate *m*
panic (E)	Panik *f*	—	panique *f*	panico *m*	pánico *m*
pánico (Es)	Panik *f*	panic	panique *f*	panico *m*	—
panico (I)	Panik *f*	panic	panique *f*	—	pánico *m*
panier (F)	Korb *m*	basket	—	cesto *m*	cesta *f*
Panik (D)	—	panic	panique *f*	panico *m*	pánico *m*
panino (I)	Brötchen *n*	roll	petit pain *m*	—	panecillo *m*
panique (F)	Panik *f*	panic	—	panico *m*	pánico *m*
panna (I)	Sahne *f*	cream	crème *f*	—	nata *f*
Panne (D)	—	breakdown	panne *f*	panna *f*	avería *f*
panne (F)	Panne *f*	breakdown	—	panna *f*	avería *f*
panne (I)	Panne *f*	breakdown	panne *f*	—	avería *f*
panno (I)	Tuch *n*	cloth	étoffe *f*	—	paño *m*
pannolino (I)	Windel *f*	nappy	lange *m*	—	pañal *m*
paño (Es)	Tuch *n*	cloth	étoffe *f*	panno *m*	—
Panorama (D)	—	panorama	panorama *m*	panorama *m*	panorama *m*
panorama (E)	Panorama *n*	—	panorama *m*	panorama *m*	panorama *m*
panorama (Es)	Panorama *n*	panorama	panorama *m*	panorama *m*	—
panorama (F)	Panorama *n*	panorama	—	panorama *m*	panorama *m*
panorama (I)	Panorama *n*	panorama	panorama *m*	—	panorama *m*
pantalón (Es)	Hose *f*	trousers	pantalon *m*	pantaloni *m pl*	—
pantalon (F)	Hose *f*	trousers	—	pantaloni *m pl*	pantalón *m*
pantaloni (I)	Hose *f*	trousers	pantalon *m*	—	pantalón *m*
Pantoffel (D)	—	slipper	pantoufle *f*	pantofola *f*	zapatilla *f*
pantofola (I)	Pantoffel *f*	slipper	pantoufle *f*	—	zapatilla *f*
pantoufle (F)	Pantoffel *f*	slipper	—	pantofola *f*	zapatilla *f*
pañuelo[1] (Es)	Handtuch *n*	towel	serviette *f*	asciugamano *m*	—
pañuelo[2] (Es)	Taschentuch *n*	handkerchief	mouchoir *m*	fazzoletto *m*	—
pañuelo para el cuello (Es)	Halstuch *n*	scarf	écharpe *f*	sciarpa *f*	—
papagayo (Es)	Papagei *m*	parrot	perroquet *m*	pappagallo *m*	—
Papagei (D)	—	parrot	perroquet *m*	pappagallo *m*	papagayo *m*
papavero (I)	Mohn *m*	poppy	coquelicot *m*	—	amapola *f*
papel (Es)	Papier *n*	paper	papier *m*	carta *f*	—
papelería (Es)	Schreibwaren-handlung *f*	stationery shop	papeterie *f*	cartoleria *f*	—
paper (E)	Papier *n*	—	papier *m*	carta *f*	papel *m*
papeterie (F)	Schreibwaren-handlung *f*	stationery shop	—	cartoleria *f*	papelería *f*
Papier (D)	—	paper	papier *m*	carta *f*	papel *m*
papier (F)	Papier *n*	paper	—	carta *f*	papel *m*
papillon (F)	Schmetter-ling *m*	butterfly	—	farfalla *f*	mariposa *f*
pappagallo (I)	Papagei *m*	parrot	perroquet *m*	—	papagayo *m*
Pappe (D)	—	cardboard	carton *m*	cartone *m*	cartón *m*
paprica (I)	Paprika *f*	paprika	paprika *m*	—	pimentón *m*
Paprika (D)	—	paprika	paprika *m*	paprica *f*	pimentón *m*
paprika (E)	Paprika *f*	—	paprika *m*	paprica *f*	pimentón *m*

	D	E	F	I	Es
paprika (F)	Paprika *f*	paprika	—	paprica *f*	pimentón *m*
Pâques (F)	Ostern *n*	Easter	—	Pasqua *f*	Pascua *f*
paquet (F)	Paket *n*	parcel	—	pacco *m*	paquete *m*
paquete (Es)	Paket *n*	parcel	paquet *m*	pacco *m*	—
paquetito (Es)	Päckchen *n*	small package	petit paquet *m*	pacchetto *m*	—
par[1] (Es)	gerade	even	pair(e)	pari	—
par[2] (Es)	Paar *n*	pair	paire *f*	paio *m*	—
par (F)	durch	through	—	per	por
para (Es)	zu	to	de/à	da/di/a	—
para acá (Es)	hierher	over here	par ici	qua	—
parada (Es)	Haltestelle *f*	stop	arrêt *m*	fermata *f*	—
Paradies (D)	—	paradise	paradis *m*	paradiso *m*	paraíso *m*
paradis (F)	Paradies *n*	paradise	—	paradiso *m*	paraíso *m*
paradise (E)	Paradies *n*	—	paradis *m*	paradiso *m*	paraíso *m*
paradiso (I)	Paradies *n*	paradise	paradis *m*	—	paraíso *m*
para ello (Es)	dafür	for it	pour cela	per questo	—
paragonare (I)	vergleichen	compare	comparer	—	comparar
paragone (I)	Vergleich *m*	comparison	comparaison *f*	—	comparación *f*
paraguas[1] (Es)	Regenschirm *m*	umbrella	parapluie *m*	ombrello *m*	—
paraguas[2] (Es)	Schirm *m*	umbrella	parapluie *m*	ombrello *m*	—
paraíso (Es)	Paradies *n*	paradise	paradis *m*	paradiso *m*	—
paralelo (Es)	parallel	parallel	parallèle	parallelo(a)	—
paralítico (Es)	gelähmt	paralysed	paralysé(e)	paralizzato(a)	—
paralizzato (I)	gelähmt	paralysed	paralysé(e)	—	paralítico
parallel (D)	—	parallel	parallèle	parallelo(a)	paralelo(a)
parallel (E)	parallel	—	parallèle	parallelo(a)	paralelo(a)
parallèle (F)	parallel	parallel	—	parallelo(a)	paralelo(a)
parallelo (I)	parallel	parallel	parallèle	—	paralelo(a)
paralysé (F)	gelähmt	paralysed	—	paralizzato(a)	paralítico
paralysed (E)	gelähmt	—	paralysé(e)	paralizzato(a)	paralítico
parapluie[1] (F)	Regenschirm *m*	umbrella	—	ombrello *m*	paraguas *m*
parapluie[2] (F)	Schirm *m*	umbrella	—	ombrello *m*	paraguas *m*
¿para qué?[1] (Es)	wozu	what for	pourquoi	perché	—
¿para qué?[2] (Es)	wofür	what for	pourquoi	per cui	—
parar (Es)	anhalten	stop	arrêter	fermare	—
parasol (E)	Sonnenschirm *m*	—	parasol *m*	ombrellone *m*	sombrilla *f*
parasol (F)	Sonnenschirm *m*	parasol	—	ombrellone *m*	sombrilla *f*
parc (F)	Park *m*	park	—	parco *m*	parque *m*
parcel (E)	Paket *n*	—	paquet *m*	pacco *m*	paquete *m*
parce que (F)	weil	because	—	perché	porque
parcheggiare (I)	parken	park	garer	—	aparcar
parcheggio (I)	Parkplatz *m*	parking place	parking *m*	—	plaza de aparcamiento *f*
parco (I)	Park *m*	park	parc *m*	—	parque *m*
par cœur (F)	auswendig	by heart	—	a memoria	de memoria
pardon (F)	Verzeihung *f*	forgiveness	—	perdono *m*	perdón *m*
pardonner (F)	verzeihen	forgive	—	perdonare	perdonar
parecchi (I)	mehrere	several	plusieurs	—	muchos(as)

	D	E	F	I	Es
parecer (Es)	aussehen	look	avoir l'air	avere l'aspetto	—
parecerse (Es)	ähneln	resemble	ressembler	assomigliare	—
parecido (Es)	ähnlich	similar	semblable	simile	—
pared (Es)	Wand f	wall	mur m	parete f	—
parent¹ (F)	Verwandter m	relative	—	parente m	pariente m
parent² (F)	verwandt	related	—	imparentato(a)	emparentado(a)
parente (I)	Verwandter m	relative	parent m	—	pariente m
parents (E)	Eltern pl	—	parents m pl	genitori m pl	padres m pl
parents (F)	Eltern pl	parents	—	genitori m pl	padres m pl
parents-in-law (E)	Schwiegereltern pl	—	beaux-parents m pl	suoceri m pl	suegros m pl
paresseux (F)	faul	lazy	—	pigro(a)	perezoso(a)
parete (I)	Wand f	wall	mur m	—	pared f
parfait (F)	vollkommen	perfect	—	perfetto(a)	perfecto(a)
Parfüm (D)	—	perfume	parfum m	profumo m	perfume m
parfum (F)	Parfüm n	perfume	—	profumo m	perfume m
par hasard (F)	zufällig	by chance	—	per caso	por casualidad
pari (F)	Wette f	bet	—	scommessa f	apuesta f
pari (I)	gerade	even	pair(e)	—	par
par ici¹ (F)	herüber	over	—	da questa parte	a este lado
par ici² (F)	hierher	over here	—	qua	para acá
pariente (Es)	Verwandter m	relative	parent m	parente m	—
parier (F)	wetten	bet	—	scommettere	apostar
parir (Es)	gebären	give birth to	mettre au monde	partorire	—
Park (D)	—	park	parc m	parco m	parque m
park¹ (E)	parken	—	garer	parcheggiare	aparcar
park² (E)	Park m	—	parc m	parco m	parque m
parken (D)	—	park	garer	parcheggiare	aparcar
Parkett (D)	—	stalls	parquet m	parquet m	entarimado m
parking (F)	Parkplatz m	parking place	—	parcheggio m	plaza de aparcamiento f
parking place (E)	Parkplatz m	—	parking m	parcheggio m	plaza de aparcamiento f
Parkplatz (D)	—	parking place	parking m	parcheggio m	plaza de aparcamiento f
Parkverbot (D)	—	no parking	défense de stationner f	divieto di parcheggio m	estacionamiento prohibido m
parlare¹ (I)	reden	talk	parler	—	hablar
parlare² (I)	sprechen	speak	parler	—	hablar
parler¹ (F)	reden	talk	—	parlare	hablar
parler² (F)	sprechen	speak	—	parlare	hablar
parola (I)	Wort n	word	mot m	—	palabra f
par principe (F)	grundsätzlich	fundamental	—	basilare	en principio
parque (Es)	Park m	park	parc m	parco m	—
parquet (F)	Parkett n	stalls	—	parquet m	entarimado m
parquet (I)	Parkett n	stalls	parquet m	—	entarimado m
parrain (F)	Pate m	godfather	—	padrino m	padrino m
párroco (Es)	Pfarrer m	priest	curé m	parroco m	—
parroco (I)	Pfarrer m	priest	curé m	—	párroco m
parrot (E)	Papagei m	—	perroquet m	pappagallo m	papagayo m

	D	E	F	I	Es
parruchiere (I)	Friseur *m*	hairdresser	coiffeur *m*	—	peluquero *m*
parsimonioso (I)	sparsam	economical	économe	—	económico(a)
par suite de (F)	infolge	as a result of	—	in seguito a	por
part¹ (E)	scheiden	—	séparer	separare	separar
part² (E)	Teil *m*	—	partie *f*	parte *f*	parte *f*
partager (F)	teilen	share	—	dividere	partir
partager en deux (F)	halbieren	halve	—	dimezzare	dividir por la mitad
parte¹ (Es)	Stück *n*	piece	morceau *m*	pezzo *m*	—
parte² (Es)	Teil *m*	part	partie *f*	parte *f*	—
parte (I)	Teil *m*	part	partie *f*	—	parte *f*
partecipare (I)	teilnehmen	take part	participer	—	participar
Partei (D)	—	party	parti *m*	partito *m*	partido *m*
partenza¹ (I)	Abfahrt *f*	departure	départ *m*	—	salida *f*
partenza² (I)	Abreise *f*	departure	départ *m*	—	salida *f*
partenza³ (I)	Start *m*	start	départ *m*	—	partida *f*
Parterre (D)	—	ground floor	rez-de chaussée *m*	pianterreno *m*	planta baja *f*
parti¹ (F)	fort	away	—	via	lejos
parti² (F)	Partei *f*	party	—	partito *m*	partido *m*
partial (F)	einseitig	one-sided	—	unilaterale	unilateral
participar (Es)	teilnehmen	take part	participer	partecipare	—
participer (F)	teilnehmen	take part	—	partecipare	participar
particolarmente (I)	besonders	especially	surtout	—	sobre todo
partida (Es)	Start *m*	start	départ *m*	partenza *f*	—
partido (Es)	Partei *f*	party	parti *m*	partito *m*	—
partie (F)	Teil *m*	part	—	parte *f*	parte *f*
parting (E)	Abschied *m*	—	adieux *m pl*	addio *m*	despedida *f*
partir¹ (Es)	starten	start	démarrer	partire	—
partir² (Es)	teilen	share	partager	dividere	—
partir (F)	abreisen	leave	—	partire	salir
partir (de) (F)	abfahren	depart	—	partire	salir
partire¹ (I)	abfahren	depart	partir (de)	—	salir
partire² (I)	abreisen	leave	partir	—	salir
partire³ (I)	starten	start	démarrer	—	partir
partire in viaggio (I)	verreisen	go away	partir en voyage	—	irse de viaje
partir en voyage (F)	verreisen	go away	—	partire in viaggio	irse de viaje
partito (I)	Partei *f*	party	parti *m*	—	partido *m*
partly (E)	teilweise	—	en partie	in parte	en parte
partorire (I)	gebären	give birth to	mettre au monde	—	parir
partout (F)	überall	everywhere	—	dappertutto	por todas partes
Party (D)	—	party	fête *f*	festa *f*	fiesta *f*
party¹ (E)	Fest *n*	—	fête *f*	festa *f*	fiesta *f*
party² (E)	Party *f*	—	fête *f*	festa *f*	fiesta *f*
party³ (E)	Partei *f*	—	parti *m*	partito *m*	partido *m*
pas (F)	Schritt *m*	step	—	passo *m*	paso *m*
pasada (Es)	vergangene(r,s)	past	dernier(-ère)	passato(a)	—
pasado¹ (Es)	Vergangenheit *f*	past	passé *m*	passato *m*	—
pasado² (Es)	vorüber	past	passé(e)	passato(a)	—
pasado³ (Es)	vergangen	past	passé(e)	passato(a)	—

	D	E	F	I	Es
pasado⁴ (Es)	vorbei	past	passé(e)	passato(a)	—
pasado de moda (Es)	altmodisch	old-fashioned	démodé(e)	fuori moda	—
pasado mañana (Es)	übermorgen	day after tomorrow	après-demain	dopodomani	—
pasajero¹ (Es)	Fahrgast m	passenger	passager m	passeggero m	—
pasajero² (Es)	Passagier m	passenger	passager m	passeggero m	—
pasajero³ (Es)	vorübergehend	temporary	temporaire	temporaneo	—
pasaporte¹ (Es)	Paß m	passport	passeport m	passaporto m	—
pasaporte² (Es)	Reisepaß m	passport	passeport m	passaporto m	—
pasar¹ (Es)	durchgehen	go through	passer à travers	passare	—
pasar² (Es)	passieren	happen	arriver	succedere	—
pasar³ (Es)	vorbeigehen	pass	passer	passare	—
pasar⁴ (Es)	vergehen	pass by	passer	passare	—
pasar⁵ (Es)	verbringen	spend	passer	passare	—
pasar adelante (Es)	vorangehen	go ahead	marcher devant	andare avanti	—
pasar de mano en mano (Es)	herumreichen	pass around	faire passer	far circolare	—
pasarse sin (Es)	entbehren	do without	passer de, se	fare a meno di	—
Pascua (Es)	Ostern n	Easter	Pâques f pl	Pasqua f	—
Pascua de Pentecostés (Es)	Pfingsten n	Whitsun	Pentecôte f	Pentecoste f	—
pas du tout (F)	keineswegs	not at all	—	non affatto	en modo alguno
paseo (Es)	Spaziergang m	walk	promenade f	passeggiata f	—
pasillo (Es)	Korridor m	corridor	corridor m	corridoio m	—
pasión (Es)	Leidenschaft f	passion	passion f	passione f	—
pas là (F)	weg	away	—	via	fuera
paso¹ (Es)	Durchgang m	passage	passage m	passaggio m	—
paso² (Es)	Durchreise f	passing through	passage m	transito m	—
paso³ (Es)	Durchfahrt f	transit	passage m	passaggio m	—
paso⁴ (Es)	Paß m	pass	col m	passo m	—
paso⁵ (Es)	Schritt m	step	pas m	passo m	—
paso⁶ (Es)	Übergang m	crossing	passage m	passaggio m	—
paso inferior (Es)	Unterführung f	subway	passage souterrain m	sottopassaggio m	—
Pasqua (I)	Ostern n	Easter	Pâques f pl	—	Pascua f
Paß¹ (D)	—	passport	passeport m	passaporto m	pasaporte m
Paß² (D)	—	pass	col m	passo m	paso m
pass¹ (E)	Paß m	—	col m	passo m	paso m
pass² (E)	reichen	—	passer	passare	alcanzar
pass³ (E)	vorbeigehen	—	passer	passare	pasar
passage (E)	Durchgang m	—	passage m	passaggio m	paso m
passage¹ (F)	Durchfahrt f	transit	—	passaggio m	paso m
passage² (F)	Durchreise f	passing through	—	transito m	paso m
passage³ (F)	Durchgang m	passage	—	passaggio m	paso m
passage⁴ (F)	Übergang m	crossing	—	passaggio m	paso m
passager¹ (F)	Fahrgast m	passenger	—	passeggero m	pasajero m
passager² (F)	Passagier m	passenger	—	passeggero m	pasajero m
passage souterrain (F)	Unterführung f	subway	—	sottopassaggio m	paso inferior m

	D	E	F	I	Es
passaggio¹ (I)	Durchgang *m*	passage	passage *m*	—	paso *m*
passaggio² (I)	Durchfahrt *f*	transit	passage *m*	—	paso *m*
passaggio³ (I)	Übergang *m*	crossing	passage *m*	—	paso *m*
Passagier (D)	—	passenger	passager *m*	passeggero *m*	pasajero *m*
passaporto¹ (I)	Paß *m*	passport	passeport *m*	—	pasaporte *m*
passaporto² (I)	Reisepaß *m*	passport	passeport *m*	—	pasaporte *m*
passare¹ (I)	durchgehen	go through	passer à travers	—	pasar
passare² (I)	reichen	pass	passer	—	alcanzar
passare³ (I)	vorbeigehen	pass	passer	—	pasar
passare⁴ (I)	verbringen	spend	passer	—	pasar
passare⁵ (I)	vergehen	pass by	passer	—	pasar
pass around (E)	herumreichen	—	faire passer	far circolare	pasar de mano en mano
passato¹ (I)	vorüber	past	passé(e)	—	pasado(a)
passato² (I)	vergangen	past	passé(e)	—	pasado(a)
passato³ (I)	vorbei	past	passé(e)	—	pasado(a)
passato⁴ (I)	Vergangenheit *f*	past	passé *m*	—	pasado *m*
passato⁵ (I)	vergangene(r,s)	past	dernier(-ère)	—	pasada(o)
pass by (E)	vergehen	—	passer	passare	pasar
passé¹ (F)	Vergangenheit *f*	past	—	passato *m*	pasado *m*
passé² (F)	vorbei	past	—	passato(a)	pasado(a)
passé³ (F)	vergangen	past	—	passato(a)	pasado(a)
passé⁴ (F)	vorüber	past	—	passato(a)	pasado(a)
passeggero¹ (I)	Fahrgast *m*	passenger	passager *m*	—	pasajero *m*
passeggero² (I)	Passagier *m*	passenger	passager *m*	—	pasajero *m*
passeggiare (I)	spazierengehen	go for a walk	promener, se	—	ir de paseo
passeggiata (I)	Spaziergang *m*	walk	promenade *f*	—	paseo *m*
passen (D)	—	suit	aller bien	stare bene	venir bien
passend (D)	—	suitable	assorti(e)	adatto(a)	apropiado(a)
passenger¹ (E)	Beifahrer *m*	—	passager *m*	passeggero *m*	pasajero *m*
passenger² (E)	Fahrgast *m*	—	passager *m*	passeggero *m*	pasajero *m*
passenger³ (E)	Passagier *m*	—	passager *m*	passeggero *m*	pasajero *m*
passeport¹ (F)	Paß *m*	passport	—	passaporto *m*	pasaporte *m*
passeport² (F)	Reisepaß *m*	passport	—	passaporto *m*	pasaporte *m*
passer¹ (F)	reichen	pass	—	passare	alcanzar
passer² (F)	verbringen	spend	—	passare	pasar
passer³ (F)	vergehen	pass by	—	passare	pasar
passer⁴ (F)	vorbeigehen	pass	—	passare	pasar
passer à travers (F)	durchgehen	go through	—	passare	pasar
passer de, se (F)	entbehren	do without	—	fare a meno di	pasarse sin
passer la nuit (F)	übernachten	stay the night	—	pernottare	pernoctar
passieren (D)	—	happen	arriver	succedere	pasar
passing through (E)	Durchreise *f*	—	passage *m*	transito *m*	paso *m*
passion (E)	Leidenschaft *f*	—	passion *f*	passione *f*	pasión *f*
passion (F)	Leidenschaft *f*	passion	—	passione *f*	pasión *f*
passione (I)	Leidenschaft *f*	passion	passion *f*	—	pasión *f*
passo¹ (I)	Paß *m*	pass	col *m*	—	paso *m*
passo² (I)	Schritt *m*	step	pas *m*	—	paso *m*

	D	E	F	I	Es
pass on a message (E)	ausrichten	—	transmettre	riferire	comunicar
passport¹ (E)	Ausweis *m*	—	pièce d'identité *f*	documento d'identità *m*	documento de identidad *m*
passport² (E)	Paß *m*	—	passeport *m*	passaporto *m*	pasaporte *m*
passport³ (E)	Reisepaß *m*	—	passeport *m*	passaporto *m*	pasaporte *m*
past¹ (E)	vergangen	—	passé(e)	passato(a)	pasado(a)
past² (E)	vergangene(r,s)	—	dernier(-ère)	passato(a)	pasada(o)
past³ (E)	vorbei	—	passé(e)	passato(a)	pasado(a)
past⁴ (E)	vorüber	—	passé(e)	passato(a)	pasado(a)
past⁵ (E)	Vergangenheit *f*	—	passé *m*	passato *m*	pasado *m*
pasta (E)	Teigwaren *pl*	—	pâtes *f pl*	pasta *f*	pastas *f pl*
pasta¹ (I)	Nudeln *pl*	noodles	nouilles *f pl*	—	pastas *f pl*
pasta² (I)	Teig *m*	dough	pâte *f*	—	masa *f*
pasta³ (I)	Teigwaren *pl*	pasta	pâtes *f pl*	—	pastas *f pl*
pasta dentífrica (Es)	Zahnpasta *f*	toothpaste	dentifrice *m*	dentifricio *m*	—
pastas¹ (Es)	Gebäck *n*	pastry	pâtisserie *f*	biscotti *m pl*	—
pastas² (Es)	Nudeln *pl*	noodles	nouilles *f pl*	pasta *f*	—
pastas³ (Es)	Teigwaren *pl*	pasta	pâtes *f pl*	pasta *f*	—
pastel (Es)	Kuchen *m*	cake	gâteau *m*	dolce *m*	—
pastelería (Es)	Konditorei *f*	cake shop	pâtisserie *f*	pasticceria *f*	—
Pastete (D)	—	pie	pâté *m*	vol-au-vent *m*	empanada *f*
pasticceria (I)	Konditorei *f*	cake shop	pâtisserie *f*	—	pastelería *f*
pastilla (Es)	Tablette *f*	tablet	comprimé *m*	compressa *f*	—
pasto (I)	Mahlzeit *f*	meal	repas *m*	—	comida *f*
pastry (E)	Gebäck *n*	—	pâtisserie *f*	biscotti *m pl*	pastas *f pl*
patata (Es)	Kartoffel *f*	potato	pomme de terre *f*	patata *f*	—
patata (I)	Kartoffel *f*	potato	pomme de terre *f*	—	patata *f*
patatas fritas (Es)	Pommes frites *pl*	French fries	frites *f pl*	patate fritte *f pl*	—
patate fritte (I)	Pommes frites *pl*	French fries	frites *f pl*	—	patatas fritas *f pl*
Pate (D)	—	godfather	parrain *m*	padrino *m*	padrino *m*
pâté (F)	Pastete *f*	pie	—	vol-au-vent *m*	empanada *f*
pâte (F)	Teig *m*	dough	—	pasta *f*	masa *f*
patente (I)	Führerschein *m*	driving licence	permis de conduire *m*	—	permiso de conducir *m*
pâtes (F)	Teigwaren *pl*	pasta	—	pasta *f*	pastas *f pl*
patience (E)	Geduld *f*	—	patience *f*	pazienza *f*	paciencia *f*
patience (F)	Geduld *f*	patience	—	pazienza *f*	paciencia *f*
Patient (D)	—	patient	patient *m*	paziente *m*	paciente *m*
patient¹ (E)	geduldig	—	patient(e)	paziente	con paciencia
patient² (E)	Patient *m*	—	patient *m*	paziente *m*	paciente *m*
patient¹ (F)	geduldig	patient	—	paziente	con paciencia
patient² (F)	Patient *m*	patient	—	paziente *m*	paciente *m*
Patin (D)	—	godmother	marraine *f*	madrina *f*	madrina *f*
patio (Es)	Hof *m*	yard	cour *f*	cortile *m*	—
pâtisserie¹ (F)	Gebäck *n*	pastry	—	biscotti *m pl*	pastas *f pl*
pâtisserie² (F)	Konditorei *f*	cake shop	—	pasticceria *f*	pastelería *f*
pato (Es)	Ente *f*	duck	canard *m*	anatra *f*	—
patria (Es)	Heimat *f*	home	patrie *f*	patria *f*	—

	D	E	F	I	Es
patria (I)	Heimat f	home	patrie f	—	patria f
patrie (F)	Heimat f	home	—	patria f	patria f
patron¹ (F)	Chef m	boss	—	capo m	jefe m
patron² (F)	Wirt m	landlord	—	oste m	dueño m
pattumiera (I)	Abfalleimer m	bin	poubelle f	—	cubo de la basura m
paura (I)	Angst f	fear	peur f	—	miedo m
pauroso (I)	ängstlich	fearful	peureux(-euse)	—	miedoso(a)
pausa (Es)	Pause f	break	pause f	pausa f	—
pausa (I)	Pause f	break	pause f	—	pausa f
Pause (D)	—	break	pause f	pausa f	pausa f
pause (F)	Pause f	break	—	pausa f	pausa f
pauvre (F)	arm	poor	—	povero(a)	pobre
pavé (F)	Pflaster n	pavement	—	lastricato m	adoquinado m
pavement¹ (E)	Gehweg m	—	trottoir m	marciapiede m	acera f
pavement² (E)	Pflaster n	—	pavé m	lastricato m	adoquinado m
pavillon (F)	Flagge f	flag	—	bandiera f	bandera f
pavimento (I)	Fußboden m	floor	sol m	—	suelo m
pavo (Es)	Truthahn m	turkey	dindon m	tacchino m	—
pay¹ (E)	bezahlen	—	payer	pagare	pagar
pay² (E)	zahlen	—	payer	pagare	pagar
pay attention (E)	aufpassen	—	faire attention	fare attenzione	prestar atención
pay back (E)	zurückzahlen	—	rembourser	rimborsare	devolver
payer¹ (F)	bezahlen	pay	—	pagare	pagar
payer² (F)	zahlen	pay	—	pagare	pagar
payment¹ (E)	Bezahlung f	—	paiement m	pagamento m	pago m
payment² (E)	Zahlung f	—	paiement m	pagamento m	pago m
pay off (E)	abbezahlen	—	finir de payer	pagare a rate	pagar a plazos
pays (F)	Land n	land	—	paese m	país m
paysage (F)	Landschaft f	landscape	—	paesaggio m	paisaje m
paysan (F)	Bauer m	farmer	—	contadino m	campesino m
Pays-Bas (F)	Niederlande f	Netherlands	—	Paesi Bassi m pl	los Paìses Bajos m pl
paz (Es)	Friede m	peace	paix f	pace f	—
paziente¹ (I)	geduldig	patient	patient(e)	—	con paciencia
paziente² (I)	Patient m	patient	patient m	—	paciente m
pazienza (I)	Geduld f	patience	patience f	—	paciencia f
Pazifik (D)	—	Pacific	Pacifique m	Pacifico m	pacífico m
pazzo¹ (I)	Narr m	fool	fou m	—	loco m
pazzo² (I)	verrückt	mad	fou (folle)	—	loco(a)
pea (E)	Erbse f	—	pois m	pisello m	guisante m
peace (E)	Friede m	—	paix f	pace f	paz f
peaceful (E)	friedlich	—	paisible	pacifico	pacífico
peach (E)	Pfirsich m	—	pêche f	pesca f	melocotón m
peak (E)	Gipfel m	—	sommet m	cima f	cumbre f
pear (E)	Birne f	—	poire f	pera f	pera f
pearl (E)	Perle f	—	perle f	perla f	perla f
peatón (Es)	Fußgänger m	pedestrian	piéton m	pedone m	—
peau¹ (F)	Haut f	skin	—	pelle f	piel f

pendere

	D	E	F	I	Es
peau² (F)	Schale f	peel	—	buccia f	piel f
pecado (Es)	Sünde f	sin	péché m	peccato m	—
peccato (I)	Sünde f	sin	péché m	—	pecado m
Pech (D)	—	bad luck	malchance f	sfortuna f	mala suerte f
pêche (F)	Pfirsich m	peach	—	pesca f	melocotón m
péché (F)	Sünde f	sin	—	peccato m	pecado m
pêcher¹ (F)	angeln	fish	—	pescare	pescar con caña
pêcher² (F)	fischen	fish	—	pescare	pescar
pêcheur (F)	Fischer m	fisher	—	pescatore m	pescador m
pecho (Es)	Brust f	breast	poitrine f	petto m	—
pecora (I)	Schaf n	sheep	mouton m	—	oveja f
pedazo (Es)	Scherbe f	broken piece	tesson m	coccio m	—
pedestrian (E)	Fußgänger m	—	piéton m	pedone m	peatón m
pedir¹ (Es)	anfordern	request	demander	esigere	—
pedir² (Es)	bestellen	order	commander	ordinare	—
pedone (I)	Fußgänger m	pedestrian	piéton m	—	peatón m
peel¹ (E)	schälen	—	éplucher	sbucciare	pelar
peel² (E)	Schale f	—	peau f	buccia f	piel f
pegar (Es)	kleben	stick	coller	incollare	—
pegno (I)	Pfand n	pledge	gage m	—	prenda f
peigne (F)	Kamm m	comb	—	pettine m	peine m
peigner (F)	kämmen	comb	—	pettinare	peinar
peinado (Es)	Frisur f	hairstyle	coiffure f	pettinatura f	—
peinar (Es)	kämmen	comb	peigner	pettinare	—
peindre¹ (F)	malen	paint	—	dipingere	pintar
peindre² (F)	streichen	paint	—	verniciare	pintar
peine (Es)	Kamm m	comb	peigne m	pettine m	—
peine (F)	Mühe f	effort	—	fatica f	esfuerzo m
peinlich (D)	—	embarrassing	gênant(e)	imbarazzante	desagradable
peintre (F)	Maler m	painter	—	pittore m	pintor m
peinture (F)	Malerei f	painting	—	pittura f	pintura f
pelar (Es)	schälen	peel	éplucher	sbucciare	—
pêle-mêle (F)	durcheinander	in a muddle	—	sottosopra	en desorden
película (Es)	Film m	film	film m	film m	—
peligro (Es)	Gefahr f	danger	danger m	pericolo m	—
peligroso (Es)	gefährlich	dangerous	dangereux(-euse)	pericoloso(a)	—
pelle (F)	Schaufel f	shovel	—	pala f	pala f
pelle (I)	Haut f	skin	peau f	—	piel f
pelliccia (I)	Pelz m	fur	fourrure f	—	piel f
pelo (Es)	Haar n	hair	cheveu m	capello m	—
pelota (Es)	Ball m	ball	balle f	palla f	—
pelouse (F)	Rasen m	lawn	—	prato m	césped m
peluquero (Es)	Friseur m	hairdresser	coiffeur m	parrucchiere m	—
Pelz (D)	—	fur	fourrure f	pelliccia f	piel f
pencil¹ (E)	Bleistift m	—	crayon m	matita f	lápiz m
pencil² (E)	Stift m	—	crayon m	penna f	lápiz m
pendant (F)	während	during	—	durante	durante
pendere (I)	hängen	hang	pendre	—	colgar

	D	E	F	I	Es
pendiente (Es)	Hang *m*	slope	versant *m*	pendio *m*	—
pendio (I)	Hang *m*	slope	versant *m*	—	pendiente *m*
pendre (F)	hängen	hang	—	pendere	colgar
peninsuia (E)	Halbinsel *f*	—	presqu'île *f*	penisola *f*	península *f*
península (Es)	Halbinsel *f*	peninsula	presqu'île *f*	penisola *f*	—
penisola (I)	Halbinsel *f*	peninsula	presqu'île *f*	—	península *f*
penna[1] (I)	Feder *f*	pen nib	plume *f*	—	pluma *f*
penna[2] (I)	Stift *m*	pencil	crayon *m*	—	lápiz *m*
penna stilografica (I)	Füller *m*	fountain pen	stylo *m*	—	pluma *f*
pennello (I)	Pinsel *m*	brush	pinceau *m*	—	pincel *m*
pen nib (E)	Feder *f*	—	plume *f*	penna *f*	pluma *f*
penniless (E)	pleite	—	fauché(e)	fallito(a)	sin dinero
pensamiento (Es)	Gedanke *m*	thought	pensée *f*	pensiero *m*	—
pensar[1] (Es)	denken	think	penser	pensare	—
pensar[2] (Es)	überlegen	consider	réfléchir à	riflettere	—
pensare (I)	denken	think	penser	—	pensar
pensée (F)	Gedanke *m*	thought	—	pensiero *m*	pensamiento *m*
penser[1] (F)	denken	think	—	pensare	pensar
penser[2] (F)	meinen	think	—	credere	opinar
pensiero (I)	Gedanke *m*	thought	pensée *f*	—	pensamiento *m*
Pension (D)	—	boarding house	pension *f*	pensione *f*	pensión *f*
pension (E)	Rente *f*	—	retraite *f*	pensione *f*	pensión *f*
pensión[1] (Es)	Pension *f*	boarding house	pension *f*	pensione *f*	—
pensión[2] (Es)	Rente *f*	pension	retraite *f*	pensione *f*	—
pension (F)	Pension *f*	boarding house	—	pensione *f*	pensión *f*
pensionato (I)	Rentner *m*	pensioner	retraité *m*	—	pensionista *m*
pensión completa (Es)	Vollpension *f*	full board	pension complète *f*	pensione completa *f*	—
pension complète (F)	Vollpension *f*	full board	—	pensione completa *f*	pensión completa *f*
pensione[1] (I)	Pension *f*	boarding house	pension *f*	—	pensión *f*
pensione[2] (I)	Ruhestand *m*	retirement	retraite *f*	—	retiro *m*
pensione[3] (I)	Rente *f*	pension	retraite *f*	—	pensión *f*
pensione completa (I)	Vollpension *f*	full board	pension complète *f*	—	pensión completa *f*
pensioner (E)	Rentner *m*	—	retraité *m*	pensionato *m*	pensionista *m*
pensionista (Es)	Rentner *m*	pensioner	retraité *m*	pensionato *m*	—
Pentecoste (I)	Pfingsten *n*	Whitsun	Pentecôte *f*	—	Pascua de Pentecostés *f*
Pentecôte (F)	Pfingsten *n*	Whitsun	—	Pentecoste *f*	Pascua de Pentecostés *f*
pentirsi (I)	bereuen	regret	regretter	—	arrepentirse
pentola[1] (I)	Kochtopf *m*	saucepan	casserole *f*	—	olla *f*
pentola[2] (I)	Topf *m*	pot	casserole *f*	—	olla *f*
penúltimo (Es)	vorletzte(r,s)	one before last	avant-dernier(-ère)	penultimo(a)	—
penultimo (I)	vorletzte(r,s)	one before last	avant-dernier(-ère)	—	penúltima(o)
people[1] (E)	Leute *pl*	—	gens *m pl*	gente *f*	gente *f*
people[2] (E)	Volk *n*	—	peuple *m*	popolo *m*	pueblo *m*
pepe (I)	Pfeffer *m*	pepper	poivre *m*	—	pimienta *f*

	D	E	F	I	Es
pepino (Es)	Gurke *f*	cucumber	concombre *m*	cetriolo *m*	—
pepper (E)	Pfeffer *m*	—	poivre *m*	pepe *m*	pimienta *f*
pequeño[1] (Es)	gering	slight	minime	poco(a)	—
pequeño[2] (Es)	klein	small/little	petit(e)	piccolo(a)	—
pequeño burgués (Es)	spießig	bourgeois	bourgeois(e)	da piccolo(a) borghese *m*	—
per[1] (I)	durch	through	par	—	por
per[2] (I)	für	for	pour	—	por/para
pera (Es)	Birne *f*	pear	poire *f*	pera *f*	—
pera (I)	Birne *f*	pear	poire *f*	—	pera *f*
per affari (I)	geschäftlich	on business	d'affaires	—	comercial
per caso (I)	zufällig	by chance	par hasard	—	por casualidad
percent (E)	Prozent *n*	—	pour cent	percentuale *f*	por ciento *m*
percentuale (I)	Prozent *n*	percent	pour cent	—	por ciento *m*
perché[1] (I)	denn	for/than	car	—	pues/porque
perché[2] (I)	weil	because	parce que	—	porque
perché[3] (I)	weshalb	why	pourquoi	—	por qué
perché[4] (I)	warum	why	pourquoi	—	por qué
perché[5] (I)	wozu	what for	pourquoi	—	para qué
perció (I)	deshalb	therefore	c'est pourquoi	—	por eso
per cui (I)	wofür	what for	pourquoi	—	para qué
perder[1] (Es)	einbüßen	lose	perdre	perdere	—
perder[2] (Es)	versäumen	miss	manquer	perdere	—
perder[3] (Es)	verlieren	lose	perdre	perdere	—
perdere[1] (I)	einbüßen	lose	perdre	—	perder
perdere[2] (I)	versäumen	miss	manquer	—	perder
perdere[3] (I)	verlegen	mislay	égarer	—	extraviar
perdere[4] (I)	verlieren	lose	perdre	—	perder
perderse (Es)	verlaufen, sich	get lost	perdre, se	perdersi	—
perdersi (I)	verlaufen, sich	get lost	perdre, se	—	perderse
pérdida (Es)	Verlust *m*	loss	perte *f*	perdita *f*	—
perdita (I)	Verlust *m*	loss	perte *f*	—	pérdida *f*
perdón (Es)	Verzeihung *f*	forgiveness	pardon *m*	perdono *m*	—
perdonar (Es)	verzeihen	forgive	pardonner	perdonare	—
perdonare (I)	verzeihen	forgive	pardonner	—	perdonar
perdono (I)	Verzeihung *f*	forgiveness	pardon *m*	—	perdón *m*
perdre[1] (F)	einbüßen	lose	—	perdere	perder
perdre[2] (F)	verlieren	lose	—	perdere	perder
perdre, se (F)	verlaufen, sich	get lost	—	perdersi	perderse
père (F)	Vater *m*	father	—	padre *m*	padre *m*
perezoso (Es)	faul	lazy	paresseux(-euse)	pigro(a)	—
perfect (E)	vollkommen	—	parfait(e)	perfetto(a)	perfecto(a)
perfecto (Es)	vollkommen	perfect	parfait(e)	perfetto(a)	—
perferire (I)	bevorzugen	prefer	préférer	—	preferir
perfetto (I)	vollkommen	perfect	parfait(e)	—	perfecto(a)
perfino (I)	sogar	even	même	—	incluso
performance[1] (E)	Aufführung *f*	—	représentation *f*	recita *f*	representación *f*
performance[2] (E)	Vorstellung *f*	—	représentation *f*	rappresenta-zione *f*	representación *f*

	D	E	F	I	Es
perfume (E)	Parfüm *n*	—	parfum *m*	profumo *m*	perfume *m*
perfume (Es)	Parfüm *n*	perfume	parfum *m*	profumo *m*	—
pericolo (I)	Gefahr *f*	danger	danger *m*	—	peligro *m*
pericoloso (I)	gefährlich	dangerous	dangereux(-euse)	—	peligroso(a)
periódico (Es)	Zeitung *f*	newspaper	journal *m*	giornale *m*	—
periodista (Es)	Journalist *m*	journalist	journaliste *m*	giornalista *m*	—
perjudicar (Es)	benachteiligen	disadvantage	désavantager	svantaggiare	—
perla (Es)	Perle *f*	pearl	perle *f*	perla *f*	—
perla (I)	Perle *f*	pearl	perle *f*	—	perla *f*
Perle (D)	—	pearl	perle *f*	perla *f*	perla *f*
perle (F)	Perle *f*	pearl	—	perla *f*	perla *f*
per lo meno (I)	zumindest	at least	au moins	—	por lo menos
permanent (F)	ständig	permanent	—	fisso(a)	permanente
permanent (E)	ständig	permanent	permanent(e)	fisso(a)	permanente
permanente (Es)	ständig	permanent	permanent(e)	fisso(a)	—
permesso[1] (I)	Erlaubnis *f*	permission	permission *f*	—	permiso *m*
permesso[2] (I)	Genehmigung *f*	authorization	autorisation *f*	—	permiso *m*
permesso[3] (I)	zulässig	permissable	permis(e)	—	permitido(a)
permettere[1] (I)	erlauben	allow	permettre	—	permitir
permettere[2] (I)	gestatten	allow	permettre	—	permitir
permettere[3] (I)	zulassen	permit	admettre	—	permitir
permettre[1] (F)	erlauben	allow	—	permettere	permitir
permettre[2] (F)	gestatten	allow	—	permettere	permitir
permis (F)	zulässig	permissable	—	permesso	permitido(a)
permis de conduire (F)	Führerschein *m*	driving licence	—	patente *f*	permiso de conducir *m*
permiso[1] (Es)	Erlaubnis *f*	permission	permission *f*	permesso *m*	—
permiso[2] (Es)	Genehmigung *f*	authorization	autorisation *f*	permesso *m*	—
permiso de conducir (Es)	Führerschein *m*	driving licence	permis de conduire *m*	patente *f*	—
permissable (E)	zulässig	—	permis(e)	permesso(a)	permitido(a)
permission (E)	Erlaubnis *f*	—	permission *f*	permesso *m*	permiso *m*
permission (F)	Erlaubnis *f*	permission	—	permesso *m*	permiso *m*
permit (E)	zulassen	—	admettre	permettere	permitir
permitido (Es)	zulässig	permissable	permis(e)	permesso(a)	—
permitir[1] (Es)	erlauben	allow	permettre	permettere	—
permitir[2] (Es)	gestatten	allow	permettre	permettere	—
permitir[3] (Es)	genehmigen	approve	autoriser	approvare	—
permitir[4] (Es)	zulassen	permit	admettre	permettere	—
per niente (I)	umsonst	for nothing	en vain	—	en vano
pernoctación (Es)	Übernachtung *f*	overnight stay	logement pour une nuit *m*	pernottamento *m*	—
pernoctar (Es)	übernachten	stay the night	passer la nuit	pernottare	—
pernottamento (I)	Übernachtung *f*	overnight stay	logement pour une nuit *m*	—	pernoctación *f*
pernottare (I)	übernachten	stay the night	passer la nuit	—	pernoctar
pero (Es)	aber	but	mais	ma	—
per questo (I)	dafür	for it	pour cela	—	para ello
perro (Es)	Hund *m*	dog	chien *m*	cane *m*	—
perroquet (F)	Papagei *m*	parrot	—	pappagallo *m*	papagayo *m*

	D	E	F	I	Es
perseguir (Es)	verfolgen	pursue	poursuivre	inseguire	—
Person (D)	—	person	personne *f*	persona *f*	persona *f*
person (E)	Person *f*	—	personne *f*	persona *f*	persona *f*
persona[1] (Es)	Mensch *m*	human being	homme *m*	essere umano *m*	—
persona[2] (Es)	Person *f*	person	personne *f*	persona *f*	—
persona (I)	Person *f*	person	personne *f*	—	persona *f*
Personal (D)	—	personnel	personnel *m*	personale *m*	personal *m*
personal (E)	persönlich	—	personnel(le)	personale	en persona
personal (Es)	Personal *n*	personnel	personnel *m*	personale *m*	—
Personalausweis (D)	—	identity card	carte d'identité *f*	carta d'identitá *f*	documento de identidad *m*
personale[1] (I)	persönlich	personal	personnel(le)	—	en persona
personale[2] (I)	Personal *n*	personnel	personnel *m*	—	personal *m*
persönlich (D)	—	personal	personnel(le)	personale	en persona
personne (F)	Person *f*	person	—	persona *f*	persona *f*
personnel (E)	Personal *n*	—	personnel *m*	personale *m*	personal *m*
personnel[1] (F)	Personal *n*	personnel	—	personale *m*	personal *m*
personnel[2] (F)	persönlich	personal	—.	personale	en persona
per strada (I)	unterwegs	on the way	en route	—	de camino
persuader (F)	überreden	convince	—	persuadere	persuadir
persuadere (I)	überreden	convince	persuader	—	persuadir
persuadir (Es)	überreden	convince	persuader	persuadere	—
perte (F)	Verlust *m*	loss	—	perdita *f*	pérdida *f*
per te (I)	deinetwegen	for your sake	pour toi	—	por ti
pertenecer (Es)	gehören	belong	appartenir	appartenere	—
pesado (Es)	schwer	heavy	lourd(e)	pesante	—
pésame (Es)	Beileid *n*	condolence	condoléances *f pl*	condoglianza *f*	—
pesante (I)	schwer	heavy	lourd(e)	—	pesado(a)
pesar[1] (Es)	Kummer *m*	grief	chagrin *m*	dolore *m*	—
pesar[2] (Es)	wiegen	weigh	peser	pesare	—
pesare (I)	wiegen	weigh	peser	—	pesar
pesca (I)	Pfirsich *m*	peach	pêche *f*	—	melocotón *m*
pescador (Es)	Fischer *m*	fisher	pêcheur *m*	pescatore *m*	—
pescar (Es)	fischen	fish	pêcher	pescare	—
pescar con caña (Es)	angeln	fish	pêcher	pescare	—
pescare[1] (I)	angeln	fish	pêcher	—	pescar con caña
pescare[2] (I)	fischen	fish	pêcher	—	pescar
pescatore (I)	Fischer *m*	fisher	pêcheur *m*	—	pescador *m*
pesce (I)	Fisch *m*	fish	poisson *m*	—	pez *m*
pescecane (I)	Hai *m*	shark	requin *m*	—	tiburón *m*
peser (F)	wiegen	weigh	—	pesare	pesar
peso[1] (Es)	Gewicht *n*	weight	poids *m*	peso *m*	—
peso[2] (Es)	Last *f*	load	charge *f*	carico *m*	—
peso (I)	Gewicht *n*	weight	poids *m*	—	peso *m*
pestaña (Es)	Wimper *f*	eyelash	cil *m*	ciglia *f*	—
pestare (I)	treten	step	mettre le pied sur	—	pisar
petit (F)	klein	small/little	—	piccolo	pequeño(a)
petit-déjeuner (F)	Frühstück *n*	breakfast	—	colazione *f*	desayuno *m*

	D	E	F	I	Es
petite-fille (F)	Enkelin *f*	granddaughter	—	nipote *f*	nieta *f*
petit-enfant (F)	Enkelkind *n*	grandchild	—	nipote *m/f*	nieto *m*
petit-fils (F)	Enkel *m*	grandson	—	nipote *m*	nieto *m*
petit pain (F)	Brötchen *n*	roll	—	panino *m*	panecillo *m*
petit paquet (F)	Päckchen *n*	small package	—	pacchetto *m*	paquetito *m*
petrol (E)	Benzin *n*	—	essence *f*	benzina	gasolina *f*
pétrole (F)	Erdöl *n*	oil	—	petrolio *m*	petróleo *m*
petróleo (Es)	Erdöl *n*	oil	pétrole *m*	petrolio *m*	—
petrolio (I)	Erdöl *n*	oil	pétrole *m*	—	petróleo *m*
pettinare (I)	kämmen	comb	peigner	—	peinar
pettinatura (I)	Frisur *f*	hairstyle	coiffure *f*	—	peinado *m*
pettine (I)	Kamm *m*	comb	peigne *m*	—	peine *m*
petto (I)	Brust *f*	breast	poitrine *f*	—	pecho *m*
peu (F)	wenige	few	—	pochi	pocos(as)
peu aimable (F)	unfreundlich	unfriendly	—	sgarbato(a)	descortés
peu de (F)	wenig	little	—	poco(a)	poco(a)
peuple (F)	Volk *n*	people	—	popolo *m*	pueblo *m*
peur (F)	Angst *f*	fear	—	paura *f*	miedo *m*
peureux (F)	ängstlich	fearful	—	pauroso(a)	miedoso(a)
peut-être (F)	vielleicht	maybe	—	forse	tal vez
pez (Es)	Fisch *m*	fish	poisson *m*	pesce *m*	—
pezzo (I)	Stück *n*	piece	morceau *m*	—	parte *f*
Pfand (D)	—	pledge	gage *m*	pegno *m*	prenda *f*
Pfanne (D)	—	pan	poêle *f*	padella *f*	sartén *f*
Pfarrer (D)	—	priest	curé *m*	parroco *m*	párroco *m*
Pfeffer (D)	—	pepper	poivre *m*	pepe *m*	pimienta *f*
Pfeife[1] (D)	—	whistle	sifflet *m*	fischietto *m*	silbato *m*
Pfeife[2] (D)	—	pipe	pipe *f*	pipa *f*	pipa *f*
Pfeil (D)	—	arrow	flèche *f*	freccia *f*	flecha *f*
Pferd (D)	—	horse	cheval *m*	cavallo *m*	caballo *m*
Pfingsten (D)	—	Whitsun	Pentecôte *f*	Pentecoste *f*	Pascua de Pentecostés *f*
Pfirsich (D)	—	peach	pêche *f*	pesca *f*	melocotón *m*
Pflanze (D)	—	plant	plante *f*	pianta *f*	planta *f*
pflanzen (D)	—	plant	planter	piantare	plantar
Pflaster[1] (D)	—	plaster	emplâtre *m*	cerotto *m*	esparadrapo *m*
Pflaster[2] (D)	—	pavement	pavé *m*	lastricato *m*	adoquinado *m*
Pflaume (D)	—	plum	prune *f*	prugna *f*	ciruela *f*
Pflege (D)	—	care	soins *m pl*	cura *f*	aseo *m*
pflegen (D)	—	look after	soigner	curare	cuidar
Pflicht (D)	—	duty	devoir *m*	dovere *m*	obligación *f*
pflücken (D)	—	pick	cueillir	cogliere	coger
Pförtner (D)	—	porter	concierge *m*	portiere *m*	portero *m*
Pfund (D)	—	pound	livre *f*	mezzo chilo *m*	libra *f*
Pfütze (D)	—	puddle	flaque *f*	pozzanghera *f*	charco *m*
pharmacie (F)	Apotheke *f*	chemist's	—	farmacia *f*	farmacia *f*
phone book (E)	Telefonbuch *n*	—	annuaire du téléphone *m*	elenco telefonico *m*	guía telefónica *f*

	D	E	F	I	Es
phone box (E)	Telefonzelle f	—	cabine téléphonique f	cabina telefonica f	cabina de teléfono f
phone call[1] (E)	Telefongespräch n	—	communication téléphonique f	conversazione telefonica f	conversación telefónica f
phone call[2] (E)	Telefonanruf m	—	coup de téléphone m	telefonata f	llamada telefónica f
phone number (E)	Telefonnummer f	—	numéro de téléphone m	numero telefonico m	número de teléfono m
phoque (F)	Robbe f	seal	—	foca f	foca f
photo (E)	Foto n	—	photo f	foto f	foto f
photo (F)	Foto n	photo	—	foto f	foto f
photocopie (F)	Fotokopie f	photocopy	—	fotocopia f	fotocopia f
photocopy (E)	Fotokopie f	—	photocopie f	fotocopia f	fotocopia f
photograph (E)	aufnehmen	—	photographier	fotografare	fotografiar
photographie (F)	Aufnahme f	photograph	—	fotografia f	fotografía f
photographier[1] (F)	aufnehmen	photograph	—	fotografare	fotografiar
photographier[2] (F)	fotografieren	take pictures	—	fotografare	fotografiar
photographier[3] (F)	knipsen	take a snap	—	scattare una foto	hacer una foto
phrase (F)	Satz m	sentence	—	frase f	oración f
piacere[1] (I)	Belieben n	will	plaisir m	—	placer m
piacere[2] (I)	gefallen	please	plaire	—	gustar
piacere[3] (I)	Genuß m	pleasure	plaisir m	—	deleite m
piacere[4] (I)	Lust f	delight	plaisir m	—	ganas f pl
piacere[5] (I)	mögen	like	aimer	—	querer
piacere[6] (I)	schmecken	taste	sentir	—	gustar
pianeta (I)	Planet m	planet	planète f	—	planeta m
piangere (I)	weinen	cry	pleurer	—	llorar
piano (E)	Klavier n	—	piano m	pianoforte m	piano m
piano (Es)	Klavier n	piano	piano m	pianoforte m	—
piano (F)	Klavier n	piano	—	pianoforte m	piano m
piano[1] (I)	eben	even	plan(e)	—	plano
piano[2] (I)	Etage f	floor	étage m	—	piso m
pianoforte (I)	Klavier n	piano	piano m	—	piano m
pianta (I)	Pflanze f	plant	plante f	—	planta f
piantare (I)	pflanzen	plant	planter	—	plantar
pianterreno[1] (I)	Erdgeschoß n	ground floor	rez-de-chaussée m	—	piso bajo m
pianterreno[2] (I)	Parterre n	ground floor	rez-de chaussée m	—	planta baja f
pianura (I)	Ebene f	plain	plaine f	—	llanura f
piattino (I)	Untertasse f	saucer	soucoupe f	—	platillo m
piatto[1] (I)	flach	flat	plat(e)	—	llano(a)
piatto[2] (I)	Gericht n	dish	plat m	—	comida f
piatto[3] (I)	Teller m	plate	assiette f	—	plato m
piazza (I)	Platz m	place	place f	—	plaza f
picante (Es)	scharf	hot	épicé(e)	piccante	—
picar[1] (Es)	jucken	itch	démanger	prudere	—
picar[2] (Es)	stechen	prick	piquer	pungere	—
piccante (I)	scharf	hot	épicé(e)	—	picante
piccolo (I)	klein	small/little	petit(e)	—	pequeño(a)
pick (E)	pflücken	—	cueillir	cogliere	coger
Picknick (D)	—	picnic	pique-nique m	picnic m	picnic m

	D	E	F	I	Es
pick up (E)	abholen	—	aller chercher	andare a prendere	recoger
picnic (E)	Picknick n	—	pique-nique m	picnic m	picnic m
picnic (Es)	Picknick n	picnic	pique-nique m	picnic m	—
picnic (I)	Picknick n	picnic	pique-nique m	—	picnic m
picture (E)	Bild n	—	image f	immagine f	cuadro m
picture magazine (E)	Illustrierte f	—	illustré m	rivista f	revista
picturesque (E)	malerisch	—	pittoresque	pittoresco(a)	pintoresco(a)
pie (E)	Pastete f	—	pâté m	vol-au-vent m	empanada f
pie (Es)	Fuß m	foot	pied m	piede m	—
piece (E)	Stück n	—	morceau m	pezzo m	parte f
pièce (F)	Raum m	room	—	stanza f	habitación f
pièce de monnaie (F)	Münze f	coin	—	moneta f	moneda f
pièce de théâtre (F)	Theaterstück n	play	—	opera teatrale f	pieza de teatro f
pièce d'identité (F)	Ausweis m	passport	—	documento d'identità m	documento de identidad m
pied (F)	Fuß m	foot	—	piede m	pie m
piede (I)	Fuß m	foot	pied m	—	pie m
piedra (Es)	Stein m	stone	pierre f	sasso m	—
piegare (I)	biegen	bend	plier	—	doblar
piel[1] (Es)	Haut f	skin	peau f	pelle f	—
piel[2] (Es)	Pelz m	fur	fourrure f	pelliccia f	—
pieno (I)	voll	full	plein(e)	—	lleno(a)
pieno di successi (I)	erfolgreich	successful	avec succès	—	afortunado(a)
pieno zeppo (I)	überfüllt	crowded	bondé	—	abarrotado(a)
pierna (Es)	Bein n	leg	jambe f	gamba f	—
pierre (F)	Stein m	stone	—	sasso m	piedra f
piéton (F)	Fußgänger m	pedestrian	—	pedone m	peatón m
pieux (F)	fromm	pious	—	devoto(a)	religioso(a)
pieza de teatro (Es)	Theaterstück n	play	pièce de théâtre f	opera teatrale f	—
pig (E)	Schwein n	—	cochon m	maiale m	cerdo m
pigro (I)	faul	lazy	paresseux(-euse)	—	perezoso(a)
píldora (Es)	Pille f	pill	pilule f	pillola f	—
pill (E)	Pille f	—	pilule f	pillola f	píldora f
pillar (E)	Säule f	—	colonne f	colonna f	columna f
Pille (D)	—	pill	pilule f	pillola f	píldora f
piller (F)	plündern	loot	—	saccheggiare	desvalijar
pillola (I)	Pille f	pill	pilule f	—	píldora f
pillow (E)	Kopfkissen n	—	oreiller m	guanciale m	almohada f
pilule (F)	Pille f	pill	—	pillola f	píldora f
Pilz (D)	—	mushroom	champignon m	fungo m	hongo m
pimentón (Es)	Paprika f	paprika	paprika m	paprica f	—
pimienta (Es)	Pfeffer m	pepper	poivre m	pepe m	—
piña (Es)	Ananas f	pineapple	ananas m	ananas m	—
pinceau (F)	Pinsel m	brush	—	pennello m	pincel m
pincel (Es)	Pinsel m	brush	pinceau m	pennello m	—
pineapple (E)	Ananas f	—	ananas m	ananas m	piña f
ping-pong (F)	Tischtennis n	tabletennis	—	tennis da tavolo m	tenis de mesa m

	D	E	F	I	Es
pink (E)	rosa	—	rose	rosa	de color rosa
Pinsel (D)	—	brush	pinceau *m*	pennello *m*	pincel *m*
pintar¹ (Es)	malen	paint	peindre	dipingere	—
pintar² (Es)	streichen	paint	peindre	verniciare	—
pintor (Es)	Maler *m*	painter	peintre *m*	pittore *m*	—
pintoresco (Es)	malerisch	picturesque	pittoresque	pittoresco(a)	—
pintura (Es)	Malerei *f*	painting	peinture *f*	pittura *f*	—
pioggia (I)	Regen *m*	rain	pluie *f*	—	lluvia *f*
pious (E)	fromm	—	pieux(-euse)	devoto(a)	religioso(a)
piovere (I)	regnen	rain	pleuvoir	—	llover
pip (E)	Kern *m*	—	noyau *m*	nocciolo	hueso *m*
pipa (Es)	Pfeife *f*	pipe	pipe *f*	pipa *f*	—
pipa (I)	Pfeife *f*	pipe	pipe *f*	—	pipa *f*
pipe¹ (E)	Leitung *f*	—	tuyau *m*	conduttura *f*	tubería *f*
pipe² (E)	Pfeife *f*	—	pipe *f*	pipa *f*	pipa *f*
pipe (F)	Pfeife *f*	pipe	—	pipa *f*	pipa *f*
pique-nique (F)	Picknick *n*	picnic	—	picnic *m*	picnic *m*
piquer (F)	stechen	prick	—	pungere	picar
piqûre (F)	Spritze *f*	injection	—	iniezione *f*	inyección *f*
piragua (Es)	Paddelboot *n*	canoe	canoë *m*	canoa *f*	—
pirogue (F)	Paddelboot *n*	canoe	—	canoa *f*	piragua *f*
pisar (Es)	treten	step	mettre le pied sur	pestare	—
piscina (Es)	Schwimmbad *n*	swimming pool	piscine *f*	piscina *f*	—
piscina (I)	Schwimmbad *n*	swimming pool	piscine *f*	—	piscina *f*
piscina al aire libre (Es)	Freibad *n*	open-air swimming pool	piscine en plein air *f*	piscina all'aperto *f*	—
piscina all'aperto (I)	Freibad *n*	open-air swimming pool	piscine en plein air *f*	—	piscina al aire libre *f*
piscina coperta (I)	Hallenbad *n*	indoor swimming pool	piscine *f*	—	piscina cubierta *f*
piscina cubierta (Es)	Hallenbad *n*	indoor swimming pool	piscine *f*	piscina coperta *f*	—
piscine¹ (F)	Hallenbad *n*	indoor swimming pool	—	piscina coperta *f*	piscina cubierta *f*
piscine² (F)	Schwimmbad *n*	swimming pool	—	piscina *f*	piscina *f*
piscine en plein air (F)	Freibad *n*	open-air swimming pool	—	piscina all'aperto *f*	piscina al aire libre *f*
pisello (I)	Erbse *f*	pea	pois *m*	—	guisante *m*
piso¹ (Es)	Etage *f*	floor	étage *m*	piano *m*	—
piso² (Es)	Wohnung *f*	flat	appartement *m*	appartamento *m*	—
piso bajo (Es)	Erdgeschoß *n*	ground floor	rez-de-chaussée *m*	pianterreno *m*	—
pistol (E)	Pistole *f*	—	pistolet *m*	pistola *f*	pistola *f*
pistola (Es)	Pistole *f*	pistol	pistolet *m*	pistola *f*	—
pistola (I)	Pistole *f*	pistol	pistolet *m*	—	pistola *f*
Pistole (D)	—	pistol	pistolet *m*	pistola *f*	pistola *f*
pistolet (F)	Pistole *f*	pistol	—	pistola *f*	pistola *f*
pittore (I)	Maler *m*	painter	peintre *m*	—	pintor *m*
pittoresco (I)	malerisch	picturesque	pittoresque	—	pintoresco(a)
pittoresque (F)	malerisch	picturesque	—	pittoresco(a)	pintoresco(a)
pittura (I)	Malerei *f*	painting	peinture *f*	—	pintura *f*
pity¹ (E)	bemitleiden	—	plaindre	compatire	compadecerse de

	D	E	F	I	Es
pity² (E)	Mitleid *n*	—	compassion *f*	compassione *f*	compasión *f*
più¹ (I)	mehr	more	plus	—	más
più² (I)	plus	plus	plus	—	más
più ampio (I)	weiter	further	plus éloigné(e)	—	adelante
piuma (I)	Feder *f*	feather	plume *f*	—	pluma *f*
piú tardi (I)	später	later	plus tard	—	más tarde
piuttosto (I)	lieber	rather	mieux	—	más bien
più vecchio (I)	ältere(r,s)	elder	aîné(e)	—	mayor
place¹ (E)	Ort *m*	—	endroit *m*	luogo *m*	lugar *m*
place² (E)	Platz *m*	—	place *f*	piazza *f*	plaza *f*
place³ (E)	Stelle *f*	—	place *f*	posto *m*	puesto *m*
place⁴ (E)	stellen	—	mettre	mettere	colocar
place¹ (F)	Platz *m*	place	—	piazza *f*	plaza *f*
place² (F)	Stelle *f*	place	—	posto *m*	puesto *m*
place assise (F)	Sitzplatz *m*	seat	—	posto a sedere *m*	asiento *m*
placer¹ (Es)	Belieben *n*	will	plaisir *m*	piacere *m*	—
placer² (Es)	Vergnügen *n*	pleasure	plaisir *m*	divertimento *m*	—
plage (F)	Strand *m*	beach	—	spiaggia *f*	playa *f*
plain (E)	Ebene *f*	—	plaine *f*	pianura *f*	llanura *f*
plaindre (F)	bemitleiden	pity	—	compatire	compadecerse de
plaindre de, se¹ (F)	beklagen	deplore	—	lamentare	quejarse
plaindre de, se² (F)	reklamieren	complain	—	reclamare	reclamar
plaindre, se (F)	beschweren, sich	complain	—	lamentarsi	quejarse
plaine (F)	Ebene *f*	plain	—	pianura *f*	llanura *f*
plainte¹ (F)	Beschwerde *f*	complaint	—	reclamo *m*	reclamación *f*
plainte² (F)	Klage *f*	complaint	—	lamento *m*	lamento *m*
plaire (F)	gefallen	please	—	piacere	gustar
plaisanter (F)	spaßen	joke	—	scherzare	bromear
plaisanterie¹ (F)	Scherz *m*	joke	—	scherzo *m*	broma *f*
plaisanterie² (F)	Witz *m*	joke	—	barzelletta *f*	chiste *m*
plaisir¹ (F)	Belieben *n*	will	—	piacere *m*	placer *m*
plaisir² (F)	Genuß *m*	pleasure	—	piacere *m*	deleite *m*
plaisir³ (F)	Lust *f*	delight	—	piacere *m*	ganas *f pl*
plaisir⁴ (F)	Spaß *m*	fun	—	scherzo *m*	broma *f*
plaisir⁵ (F)	Vergnügen *n*	pleasure	—	divertimento *m*	placer *m*
plait (E)	Zopf *m*	—	natte *f*	treccia *f*	trenza *f*
Plakat (D)	—	poster	affiche *f*	affisso *m*	cartel *m*
Plan (D)	—	plan	plan *m*	progetto *m*	plan *m*
plan¹ (E)	planen	—	projeter	progettare	planear
plan² (E)	Plan *m*	—	plan *m*	progetto *m*	plan *m*
plan (Es)	Plan *m*	plan	plan *m*	progetto *m*	—
plan¹ (F)	eben	even	—	piano(a)	plano(a)
plan² (F)	Plan *m*	plan	—	progetto *m*	plan *m*
plancha (Es)	Bügeleisen *n*	iron	fer à repasser *m*	ferro da stiro *m*	—
planchar (Es)	bügeln	iron	repasser	stirare	—
planear (Es)	planen	plan	projeter	progettare	—
planen (D)	—	plan	projeter	progettare	planear
Planet (D)	—	planet	planète *f*	pianeta *m*	planeta *m*

	D	E	F	I	Es
planet (E)	Planet *m*	—	planète *f*	pianeta *m*	planeta *m*
planeta (Es)	Planet *m*	planet	planète *f*	pianeta *m*	—
planète (F)	Planet *m*	planet	—	pianeta *m*	planeta *m*
plano (Es)	eben	even	plan(e)	piano(a)	—
plant¹ (E)	Anlage *f*	—	construction *f*	impianto *m*	establecimiento *m*
plant² (E)	Pflanze *f*	—	plante *f*	pianta *f*	planta *f*
plant³ (E)	pflanzen	—	planter	piantare	plantar
planta (Es)	Pflanze *f*	plant	plante *f*	pianta *f*	—
planta baja (Es)	Parterre *n*	ground floor	rez-de chaussée *m*	pianterreno *m*	—
plantar (Es)	pflanzen	plant	planter	piantare	—
plante (F)	Pflanze *f*	plant	—	pianta *f*	planta *f*
planter (F)	pflanzen	plant	—	piantare	plantar
plaque d'immatriculation (F)	Nummernschild *n*	number plate	—	targa *f*	matrícula *f*
plaster (E)	Pflaster *n*	—	emplâtre *m*	cerotto *m*	esparadrapo *m*
plastic (E)	Plastik *n*	—	plastique *m*	plastica *f*	plástico *m*
plastica (I)	Plastik *n*	plastic	plastique *m*	—	plástico *m*
plástico (Es)	Plastik *n*	plastic	plastique *m*	plastica *f*	—
Plastik (D)	—	plastic	plastique *m*	plastica *f*	plástico *m*
plastique (F)	Plastik *n*	plastic	—	plastica *f*	plástico *m*
plat¹ (F)	Gericht *n*	dish	—	piatto *m*	comida *f*
plat² (F)	Gang *m*	course	—	portata *f*	plato *m*
plat³ (F)	flach	flat	—	piatto(a)	llano(a)
plata (Es)	Silber *n*	silver	argent *m*	d'argento	—
plátano (Es)	Banane *f*	banana	banane *f*	banana *f*	—
plate (E)	Teller *m*	—	assiette *f*	piatto *m*	plato *m*
plateado (Es)	silbern	silver	d'argent	argenteo	—
plateau (F)	Tablett *n*	tray	—	vassoio *m*	bandeja *f*
platillo (Es)	Untertasse *f*	saucer	soucoupe *f*	piattino *m*	—
plato¹ (Es)	Gang *m*	course	plat *m*	portata *f*	—
plato² (Es)	Gericht *n*	dish	plat *m*	piatto *m*	—
plato³ (Es)	Teller *m*	plate	assiette *f*	piatto *m*	—
Platte (D)	—	record	disque *m*	disco *m*	disco *m*
Plattenspieler (D)	—	record player	tourne-disque *m*	giradischi *m*	tocadiscos *m*
Platz (D)	—	place	place *f*	piazza *f*	plaza *f*
platzen (D)	—	burst	éclater	scoppiare	reventar
plaudern (D)	—	chat	causer	chiacchierare	conversar
play¹ (E)	spielen	—	jour	giocare	jugar
play² (E)	Schauspiel *n*	—	spectacle *m*	spettacolo *m*	espectáculo *m*
play³ (E)	Theaterstück *n*	—	pièce de théâtre *f*	opera teatrale *f*	pieza de teatro *f*
playa (Es)	Strand *m*	beach	plage *f*	spiaggia *f*	—
player (E)	Spieler *m*	—	joueur *m*	giocatore *m*	jugador *m*
playground (E)	Spielplatz *m*	—	terrain de jeu *m*	campo dei giochi *m*	campo de juego *m*
plaza (Es)	Platz *m*	place	place *f*	piazza *f*	—
plaza de aparcamiento (Es)	Parkplatz *m*	parking place	parking *m*	parcheggio *m*	—
plazo (Es)	Rate *f*	instalment	quote-part *f*	rata *f*	—
pleasant (E)	angenehm	—	agréable	gradevole	agradable

	D	E	F	I	Es
please[1] (E)	bitte	—	s'il vous plaît	prego	por favor
please[2] (E)	gefallen	—	plaire	piacere	gustar
pleasure[1] (E)	Genuß *m*	—	plaisir *m*	piacere *m*	deleite *m*
pleasure[2] (E)	Vergnügen *n*	—	plaisir *m*	divertimento *m*	placer *m*
pledge (E)	Pfand *n*	—	gage *m*	pegno *m*	prenda *f*
plein (F)	voll	full	—	pieno(a)	lleno(a)
pleine saison (F)	Hochsaison *f*	high season	—	alta stagione *f*	temporada alta *f*
pleite (D)	—	penniless	fauché(e)	fallito(a)	sin dinero
pleurer (F)	weinen	cry	—	piangere	llorar
pleuvoir (F)	regnen	rain	—	piovere	llover
plier (F)	biegen	bend	—	piegare	doblar
plonger (F)	tauchen	dive	—	immergere	bucear
plötzlich (D)	—	suddenly	tout à coup	di colpo	de repente
pluie (F)	Regen *m*	rain	—	pioggia *f*	lluvia *f*
plum (E)	Pflaume *f*	—	prune *f*	prugna *f*	ciruela *f*
pluma[1] (Es)	Feder *f*	pen nib	plume *f*	penna *f*	—
pluma[2] (Es)	Feder *f*	feather	plume *f*	piuma *f*	—
pluma[3] (Es)	Füller *m*	fountain pen	stylo *m*	penna stilografica *f*	—
plume[1] (F)	Feder *f*	pen nib	—	penna *f*	pluma *f*
plume[2] (F)	Feder *f*	feather	—	piuma *f*	pluma *f*
plündern (D)	—	loot	piller	saccheggiare	desvalijar
plural (E)	Mehrzahl *f*	—	pluriel *m*	plurale *m*	plural *m*
plural (Es)	Mehrzahl *f*	plural	pluriel *m*	plurale *m*	—
plurale (I)	Mehrzahl *f* .	plural	pluriel *m*	—	plural *m*
pluriel (F)	Mehrzahl *f*	plural	—	plurale *m*	plural *m*
plus (D)	—	plus	plus	più	más
plus (E)	plus	—	plus	più	más
plus[1] (F)	mehr	more	—	più	más
plus[2] (F)	plus	plus	—	più	más
plus éloigné (F)	weiter	further	—	più ampio(a)	adelante
plusieurs (F)	mehrere	several	—	parecchi	muchos(as)
plus tard (F)	später	later	—	piú tardi	más tarde
plus tôt (F)	eher	sooner	—	prima	antes
pneu (F)	Reifen *m*	tyre	—	pneumatico *m*	neumático *m*
pneumatico (I)	Reifen *m*	tyre	pneu *m*	—	neumático *m*
población (Es)	Bevölkerung *f*	population	population *f*	popolazione *f*	—
pobre (Es)	arm	poor	pauvre	povero(a)	—
pochen (D)	—	knock	frapper	battere	golpear
pochi (I)	wenige	few	peu	—	pocos(as)
pocket money (E)	Taschengeld *n*	—	argent de poche *f*	denaro per le piccole spese *m*	dinero de bolsillo *m*
poco (Es)	wenig	little	peu de	poco(a)	—
poco[1] (I)	gering	slight	minime	—	pequeño(a)
poco[2] (I)	wenig	little	peu de	—	poco(a)
poco accogliente (I)	ungemütlich	uncomfortable	désagréable	—	incómodo(a)
poco fa (I)	soeben	just now	à l'instant même	—	ahora mismo
pocos (Es)	wenige	few	peu	pochi	—
poder[1] (Es)	dürfen	be allowed	avoir le droit	potere	—

	D	E	F	I	Es
poder² (Es)	Gewalt f	force	force f	forza f	—
poder³ (Es)	Macht f	power	pouvoir m	potere m	—
poder⁴ (Es)	Vollmacht f	authority	procuration f	delega f	—
podere (I)	Anwesen n	premises	domaine m	—	posesión f
poêle¹ (F)	Ofen m	oven	—	stufa f	estufa f
poêle² (F)	Pfanne f	pan	—	padella f	sartén f
poem (E)	Gedicht n	—	poème m	poesia f	poema m
poema (Es)	Gedicht n	poem	poème m	poesia f	—
poème (F)	Gedicht n	poem	—	poesia f	poema m
poesia (I)	Gedicht n	poem	poème m	—	poema m
poet (E)	Dichter m	—	poète m	poeta m	poeta m
poeta (Es)	Dichter m	poet	poète m	poeta m	—
poeta (I)	Dichter m	poet	poète m	—	poeta m
poète (F)	Dichter m	poet	—	poeta m	poeta m
poi (I)	danach	afterwards	après	—	después
poids (F)	Gewicht n	weight	—	peso m	peso m
poignée (F)	Griff m	handle	—	maniglia f	asidero m
poindre (F)	dämmern	dawn	—	spuntare	amanecer
poing (F)	Faust f	fist	—	pugno m	puño m
point¹ (E)	Punkt m	—	point m	punto m	punto m
point² (E)	Spitze f	—	pointe f	punta f	punta f
point (F)	Punkt m	point	—	punto m	punto m
point de vue (F)	Standpunkt m	standpoint	—	punto di vista m	punto de vista m
pointe (F)	Spitze f	point	—	punta f	punta f
pointed (E)	spitz	—	pointu(e)	appuntito(a)	puntiagudo(a)
pointless (E)	zwecklos	—	inutile	inutile	inútil
pointu (F)	spitz	pointed	—	appuntito(a)	puntiagudo(a)
poire (F)	Birne f	pear	—	pera f	pera f
pois (F)	Erbse f	pea	—	pisello m	guisante m
poison (E)	Gift n	—	poison m	veleno m	veneno m
poison (F)	Gift n	poison	—	veleno m	veneno m
poisonous (E)	giftig	—	toxique	velenoso	venenoso(a)
poisson (F)	Fisch m	fish	—	pesce m	pez m
poitrine (F)	Brust f	breast	—	petto m	pecho m
poivre (F)	Pfeffer m	pepper	—	pepe m	pimienta f
Poland (E)	Polen	—	Pologne f	Polonia f	Polonia f
pole (E)	Stange f	—	barre f	asta f	vara f
Polen (D)	—	Poland	Pologne f	Polonia f	Polonia f
poli (F)	höflich	polite	—	cortese	cortés
police (E)	Polizei f	—	police f	polizia f	policía f
police (F)	Polizei f	police	—	polizia f	policía f
policeman (E)	Polizist m	—	agent de police m	poliziotto m	policía m
policía¹ (Es)	Polizei f	police	police f	polizia f	—
policía² (Es)	Polizist m	policeman	agent de police m	poliziotto m	—
polieren (D)	—	polish	astiquer	lucidare	pulir
polish (E)	polieren	—	astiquer	lucidare	pulir
polite (E)	höflich	—	poli(e)	cortese	cortés
politeness (E)	Höflichkeit f	—	politesse f	cortesia f	cortesía f

	D	E	F	I	Es
politesse (F)	Höflichkeit f	politeness	—	cortesia f	cortesía f
política (Es)	Politik f	politics	politique f	politica f	—
politica (I)	Politik f	politics	politique f	—	política f
politician (E)	Politiker m	—	politicien m	politico m	político m
politicien (F)	Politiker m	politician	—	politico m	político m
político (Es)	Politiker m	politician	politicien m	politico m	—
politico (I)	Politiker m	politician	politicien m	—	político m
politics (E)	Politik f	—	politique f	politica f	política f
Politik (D)	—	politics	politique f	politica f	política f
Politiker (D)	—	politician	politicien m	politico m	político m
politique (F)	Politik f	politics	—	politica f	política f
Polizei (D)	—	police	police f	polizia f	policía f
polizia (I)	Polizei f	police	police f	—	policía f
poliziotto (I)	Polizist m	policeman	agent de police m	—	policía m
Polizist (D)	—	policeman	agent de police m	poliziotto m	policía m
poll (E)	Umfrage f	—	enquête f	inchiesta f	encuesta f
pollame (I)	Geflügel n	poultry	volaille f	—	aves f pl
pollice (I)	Daumen m	thumb	pouce m	—	pulgar m
pollo (I)	Huhn n	chicken	poule f	—	gallina f
polmone (I)	Lunge f	lung	poumon m	—	pulmón m
Pologne (F)	Polen	Poland	—	Polonia f	Polonia f
Polonia (Es)	Polen	Poland	Pologne f	Polonia f	—
Polonia (I)	Polen	Poland	Pologne f	—	Polonia f
polso (I)	Puls m	pulse	pouls m	—	pulso m
poltrona (I)	Sessel m	armchair	fauteuil m	—	sillón m
polvere[1] (I)	Pulver n	powder	poudre f	—	pólvora f
polvere[2] (I)	Staub m	dust	poussière f	—	polvo m
polveroso (I)	staubig	dusty	poussiéreux (-euse)	—	polvoriento(a)
polvo (Es)	Staub m	dust	poussière f	polvere f	—
pólvora (Es)	Pulver n	powder	poudre f	polvere f	—
polvoriento (Es)	staubig	dusty	poussiéreux (-euse)	polveroso(a)	—
polvos (Es)	Puder n	powder	poudre f	cipria f	—
pomada (Es)	Salbe f	ointment	onguent m	pomata f	—
pomata (I)	Salbe f	ointment	onguent m	—	pomada f
pomelo (Es)	Pampelmuse f	grapefruit	pamplemousse m	pompelmo m	—
pomeriggio (I)	Nachmittag m	afternoon	après-midi m	—	tarde f
pomme (F)	Apfel m	apple	—	mela f	manzana f
pomme de terre (F)	Kartoffel f	potato	—	patata f	patata f
Pommes frites (D)	—	French fries	frites f pl	patate fritte f pl	patatas fritas f pl
pomodoro (I)	Tomate f	tomato	tomate f	—	tomate m
pompa (I)	Pumpe f	pump	pompe f	—	bomba f
pompe (F)	Pumpe f	pump	—	pompa f	bomba f
pompelmo (I)	Pampelmuse f	grapefruit	pamplemousse m	—	pomelo m
ponctuel (F)	pünktlich	punctual	—	puntuale	puntual
pond (E)	Teich m	—	étang m	stagno m	estanque m
poner[1] (Es)	anstellen	turn on	mettre en marche	accendere	—
poner[2] (Es)	hinlegen	put down	poser	posare	—

	D	E	F	I	Es
poner³ (Es)	setzen	put	mettre	mettere	—
poner en cuenta (Es)	anrechnen	charge	compter	mettere in conto	—
poner en libertad (Es)	freilassen	release	libérer	mettere in libertà	—
poner las señas en (Es)	adressieren	address	adresser	indirizzare	—
ponerse (Es)	anziehen	dress	mettre	indossare	—
ponerse de acuerdo (Es)	einigen, sich	agree	mettre d'accord, se	accordarsi	—
pont¹ (F)	Brücke f	bridge	—	ponte m	puente m
pont² (F)	Deck n	deck	—	ponte m	cubierta f
ponte¹ (I)	Brücke f	bridge	pont m	—	puente m
ponte² (I)	Deck n	deck	pont m	—	cubierta f
poor (E)	arm	—	pauvre	povero(a)	pobre
popolare (I)	beliebt	popular	populaire	—	estimado(a)
popolazione (I)	Bevölkerung f	population	population f	—	población f
popolo (I)	Volk n	people	peuple m	—	pueblo m
poppy (E)	Mohn m	—	coquelicot m	papavero m	amapola f
populaire (F)	beliebt	popular	—	popolare	estimado(a)
popular (E)	beliebt	—	populaire	popolare	estimado(a)
population (E)	Bevölkerung f	—	population f	popolazione f	población f
population (F)	Bevölkerung f	population	—	popolazione f	población f
por¹ (Es)	durch	through	par	per	—
por² (Es)	für	for	pour	per	—
por³ (Es)	infolge	as a result of	par suite de	in seguito a	—
por⁴ (Es)	über	over/about	sur	su/sopra/per	—
por casualidad (Es)	zufällig	by chance	par hasard	per caso	—
porcelain (E)	Porzellan n	—	porcelaine f	porcellana f	porcelana f
porcelaine (F)	Porzellan n	porcelain	—	porcellana f	porcelana f
porcelana (Es)	Porzellan n	porcelain	porcelaine f	porcellana f	—
porcellana (I)	Porzellan n	porcelain	porcelaine f	—	porcelana f
por ciento (Es)	Prozent n	percent	pour cent	percentuale f	—
por debajo (Es)	darunter	underneath	en dessous	sotto	—
por encima (Es)	darüber	above	au dessus	sopra	—
por escrito (Es)	schriftlich	written	écrit(e)	scritto(a)	—
por eso (Es)	deshalb	therefore	c'est pourquoi	perció	—
¡por favor! (Es)	bitte!	please!	s'il vous plaît!	prego!	—
pork (E)	Schweinefleisch n	—	viande de porc f	carne di maiale f	carne de cerdo f
por la mañana (Es)	vormittags	in the morning	le matin	di mattina	—
por la noche (Es)	nachts	at nighttime	la nuit	di notte	—
por la tarde¹ (Es)	abends	in the evening	le soir m	di sera	—
por la tarde² (Es)	nachmittags	in the afternoon	l'après-midi	di pomeriggio	—
por lo común (Es)	meistens	generally	généralement	di solito	—
por lo demás¹ (Es)	sonst	otherwise	autrement	altrimenti	—
por lo demás² (Es)	übrigens	by the way	d'ailleurs	del resto	—
por lo menos¹ (Es)	mindestens	at least	au moins	almeno	—
por lo menos² (Es)	wenigstens	at least	au moins	almeno	—
por lo menos³ (Es)	zumindest	at least	au moins	per lo meno	—
por medio (Es)	durchschnittlich	average	moyen(ne)	medio(a)	—

	D	E	F	I	Es
por otra parte (Es)	andererseits	on the other hand	d'autre part	d'altra parte	—
porque (Es)	weil	because	parce que	perché	—
¿por qué?[1] (Es)	warum	why	pourquoi	perché	—
¿por qué?[2] (Es)	weshalb	why	pourquoi	perché	—
¿por qué?[3] (Es)	wieso	why	pourquoi	come mai	—
por supuesto (Es)	selbstverständlich	of course	évidemment	naturalmente	—
port (E)	Hafen *m*	—	port *m*	porto *m*	puerto *m*
port[1] (F)	Hafen *m*	port	—	porto *m*	puerto *m*
port[2] (F)	Porto *n*	postage	—	affrancatura *f*	franqueo *m*
porta[1] (I)	Tür *f*	door	porte *f*	—	puerta *f*
porta[2] (I)	Tor *n*	gate	porte *f*	—	puerta *f*
portabagagli (I)	Kofferraum *m*	boot	coffre *m*	—	maletero *m*
portacenere (I)	Aschenbecher *m*	ashtray	cendrier *m*	—	cenicero *m*
portare[1] (I)	bringen	fetch	porter	—	llevar
portare[2] (I)	tragen	carry	porter	—	llevar
portare[3] (I)	überbringen	deliver	remettre	—	transmitir
portare con sé (I)	mitbringen	bring (along)	apporter	—	traer
portata (I)	Gang *m*	course	plat *m*	—	plato *m*
porte[1] (F)	Tür *f*	door	—	porta *f*	puerta *f*
porte[2] (F)	Tor *n*	gate	—	porta *f*	puerta *f*
porte-documents (F)	Aktenmappe *f*	file	—	cartella *f*	cartera *f*
porter[1] (E)	Portier *m*	—	portier *m*	portiere *m*	portero *m*
porter[2] (E)	Pförtner *m*	—	concierge *m*	portiere *m*	portero *m*
porter[1] (F)	anhaben	have on	—	indossare	llevar
porter[2] (F)	bringen	fetch	—	portare	llevar
porter[3] (F)	tragen	carry	—	portare	llevar
portero[1] (Es)	Hausmeister *m*	caretaker	concierge *m*	portinaio *m*	—
portero[2] (Es)	Portier *m*	porter	portier *m*	portiere *m*	—
portero[3] (Es)	Pförtner *m*	porter	concierge *m*	portiere *m*	—
porteur (F)	Träger *m*	carrier	—	facchino *m*	mozo *m*
por ti (Es)	deinetwegen	for your sake	pour toi	per te	—
Portier (D)	—	porter	portier *m*	portiere *m*	portero *m*
portier (F)	Portier *m*	porter	—	portiere *m*	portero *m*
portiere[1] (I)	Portier *m*	porter	portier *m*	—	portero *m*
portiere[2] (I)	Pförtner *m*	porter	concierge *m*	—	portero *m*
portinaio (I)	Hausmeister *m*	caretaker	concierge *m*	—	portero *m*
Porto (D)	—	postage	port *m*	affrancatura *f*	franqueo *m*
porto (I)	Hafen *m*	port	port *m*	—	puerto *m*
por todas partes (Es)	überall	everywhere	partout	dappertutto	—
Portogallo (I)	Portugal	Portugal	Portugal *m*	—	Portugal *m*
Portugal (D)	—	Portugal	Portugal *m*	Portogallo *m*	Portugal *m*
Portugal (E)	Portugal	—	Portugal *m*	Portogallo *m*	Portugal *m*
Portugal (Es)	Portugal	Portugal	Portugal *m*	Portogallo *m*	—
Portugal (F)	Portugal	Portugal	—	Portogallo *m*	Portugal *m*
por último (Es)	zuletzt	finally	finalement	infine	—
por un lado (Es)	einerseits	on one hand	d'une part	da un lato	—
Porzellan (D)	—	porcelain	porcelaine *f*	porcellana *f*	porcelana *f*
posada (Es)	Gasthaus *n*	hotel	auberge *f*	osteria *f*	—

	D	E	F	I	Es
posare (I)	hinlegen	put down	poser	—	poner
poseer (Es)	besitzen	possess	posséder	possedere	—
poser (F)	hinlegen	put down	—	posare	poner
poser sa candidature (F)	bewerben, sich	apply	—	concorrere	presentarse
posesión[1] (Es)	Anwesen *n*	premises	domaine *m*	podere *m*	—
posesión[2] (Es)	Besitz *m*	possession	propriété *f*	proprietà *f*	—
posibilidad (Es)	Möglichkeit *f*	possibility	possibilité *f*	possibilità *f*	—
posible (Es)	möglich	possible	possible	possibile	—
posición (Es)	Stellung *f*	position	position *f*	posizione *f*	—
positif (F)	positiv	positive	—	positivo(a)	positivo(a)
position[1] (E)	Posten *m*	—	poste *m*	posto *m*	puesto *m*
position[2] (E)	Stellung *f*	—	position *f*	posizione *f*	posición *f*
position[3] (E)	Stand *m*	—	état *m*	stato *m*	estado *m*
position (F)	Stellung *f*	position	—	posizione *f*	posición *f*
positiv (D)	—	positive	positif(-ive)	positivo(a)	positivo(a)
positive (E)	positiv	—	positif(-ive)	positivo(a)	positivo(a)
positivo (Es)	positiv	positive	positif(-ive)	positivo(a)	—
positivo (I)	positiv	positive	positif(-ive)	—	positivo(a)
posizione (I)	Stellung *f*	position	position *f*	—	posición *f*
posséder (F)	besitzen	possess	—	possedere	poseer
possedere (I)	besitzen	possess	posséder	—	poseer
possess (E)	besitzen	—	posséder	possedere	poseer
possession (E)	Besitz *m*	—	propriété *f*	proprietà *f*	posesión *f*
possibile (I)	möglich	possible	possible	—	posible
possibilità (I)	Möglichkeit *f*	possibility	possibilité *f*	—	posibilidad *f*
possibilité[1] (F)	Chance *f*	chance	—	occasione *f*	oportunidad *f*
possibilité[2] (F)	Möglichkeit *f*	possibility	—	possibilità *f*	posibilidad *f*
possibility (E)	Möglichkeit *f*	—	possibilité *f*	possibilità *f*	posibilidad *f*
possible[1] (E)	eventuell	—	éventuel(le)	eventuale	eventual
possible[2] (E)	möglich	—	possible	possibile	posible
possible (F)	möglich	possible	—	possibile	posible
Post (D)	—	post	poste *f*	posta *f*	correo *m*
post[1] (E)	einwerfen	—	poster	imbucare	echar
post[2] (E)	Post *f*	—	poste *f*	posta *f*	correo *m*
posta (I)	Post *f*	post	poste *f*	—	correo *m*
posta aerea (I)	Luftpost *f*	air mail	poste aérienne *f*	—	correo aéreo *m*
postage (E)	Porto *n*	—	port *m*	affrancatura *f*	franqueo *m*
postal[1] (Es)	Karte *f*	card	carte *f*	cartolina *f*	—
postal[2] (Es)	Postkarte *f*	postcard	carte postale *f*	cartolina *f*	—
Postamt (D)	—	post office	bureau de poste *m*	ufficio postale *m*	oficina de correos *f*
Postbote (D)	—	postman	facteur *m*	postino *m*	cartero *m*
postcard[1] (E)	Ansichtskarte *f*	—	carte postale *f*	cartolina *f*	tarjeta postal *f*
postcard[2] (E)	Postkarte *f*	—	carte postale *f*	cartolina *f*	postal *f*
poste[1] (F)	Posten *m*	position	—	posto *m*	puesto *m*
poste[2] (F)	Post *f*	post	—	posta *f*	correo *m*
poste aérienne (F)	Luftpost *f*	air mail	—	posta aerea *f*	correo aéreo *m*
poste de télévision (F)	Fernseher *m*	television set	—	televisore *m*	televisor *m*

	D	E	F	I	Es
Posten (D)	—	position	poste *m*	posto *m*	puesto *m*
poster (E)	Plakat *n*	—	affiche *f*	affisso *m*	cartel *m*
poster (F)	einwerfen	post	—	imbucare	echar
postino (I)	Postbote *m*	postman	facteur *m*	—	cartero *m*
Postkarte (D)	—	postcard	carte postale *f*	cartolina *f*	postal *f*
postman (E)	Postbote *m*	—	facteur *m*	postino *m*	cartero *m*
posto¹ (I)	Posten *m*	position	poste *m*	—	puesto *m*
posto² (I)	Stelle *f*	place	place *f*	—	puesto *m*
posto a sedere (I)	Sitzplatz *m*	seat	place assise *f*	—	asiento *m*
post office (E)	Postamt *n*	—	bureau de poste *m*	ufficio postale *m*	oficina de correos *f*
postpone (E)	verschieben	—	remettre	rimandare	aplazar
postre (Es)	Nachtisch *m*	dessert	dessert *m*	desert *m*	—
pot (E)	Topf *m*	—	casserole *f*	pentola *f*	olla *f*
potabile (I)	trinkbar	drinkable	potable	—	potable
potable (Es)	trinkbar	drinkable	potable	potabile	—
potable (F)	trinkbar	drinkable	—	potabile	potable
potato (E)	Kartoffel *f*	—	pomme de terre *f*	patata *f*	patata *f*
potere¹ (I)	dürfen	be allowed	avoir le droit	—	poder
potere² (I)	Macht *f*	power	pouvoir *m*	—	poder *m*
poubelle¹ (F)	Abfalleimer *m*	bin	—	pattumiera *f*	cubo de la basura *m*
poubelle² (F)	Mülleimer *m*	dustbin	—	secchio dei rifiuti *m*	cubo de la basura *m*
pouce (F)	Daumen *m*	thumb	—	pollice *m*	pulgar *m*
poudre¹ (F)	Pulver *n*	powder	—	polvere *f*	pólvora *f*
poudre² (F)	Puder *n*	powder	—	cipria *f*	polvos *m pl*
poule¹ (F)	Huhn *n*	chicken	—	pollo *m*	gallina *f*
poule² (F)	Henne *f*	hen	—	gallina *f*	gallina *f*
pouls (F)	Puls *m*	pulse	—	polso *m*	pulso *m*
poultry (E)	Geflügel *n*	—	volaille *f*	pollame *m*	aves *f pl*
poumon (F)	Lunge *f*	lung	—	polmone *m*	pulmón *m*
pound (E)	Pfund *n*	—	livre *f*	mezzo chilo *m*	libra *f*
poupée (F)	Puppe *f*	doll	—	bambola *f*	muñeca *f*
pour¹ (E)	eingießen	—	verser	versare	echar
pour² (E)	schütten	—	verser	versare	verter
pour (F)	für	for	—	per	por/para
pourboire (F)	Trinkgeld *n*	tip	—	mancia *f*	propina *f*
pour cela (F)	dafür	for it	—	per questo	para ello
pour cent (F)	Prozent *n*	percent	—	percentuale *f*	por ciento *m*
pour l'instant (F)	zunächst	first of all	—	dapprima	en primer lugar
pourquoi¹ (F)	wofür	what for	—	per cui	para qué
pourquoi² (F)	warum	why	—	perché	por qué
pourquoi³ (F)	wieso	why	—	come mai	por qué
pourquoi⁴ (F)	weshalb	why	—	perché	por qué
pourquoi⁵ (F)	wozu	what for	—	perché	para qué
poursuivre (F)	verfolgen	pursue	—	inseguire	perseguir
pousser¹ (F)	stoßen	push	—	spingere	empujar
pousser² (F)	schieben	push	—	spingere	empujar

	D	E	F	I	Es
pousser des cris de joie (F)	jubeln	rejoice	—	giubilare	dar gritos de alegría
poussière (F)	Staub *m*	dust	—	polvere *f*	polvo *m*
poussiéreux (F)	staubig	dusty	—	polveroso(a)	polvoriento(a)
pouvoir¹ (F)	können	can	—	sapere	saber
pouvoir² (F)	Macht *f*	power	—	potere *m*	poder *m*
povero (I)	arm	poor	pauvre	—	pobre
powder¹ (E)	Pulver *n*	—	poudre *f*	polvere *f*	pólvora *f*
powder² (E)	Puder *n*	—	poudre *f*	cipria *f*	polvos *m pl*
power (E)	Macht *f*	—	pouvoir *m*	potere *m*	poder *m*
pozzanghera (I)	Pfütze *f*	puddle	flaque *f*	—	charco *m*
prächtig (D)	—	splendid	magnifique	meraviglioso(a)	magnífico(a)
práctica (Es)	Praxis *f*	practice	pratique *f*	pratica *f*	—
practical (E)	praktisch	—	pratique	pratico(a)	práctico(a)
practical training (E)	Praktikum *n*	—	stage *m*	tirocinio *m*	prácticas *f pl*
practicar (Es)	üben	practise	étudier	esercitarsi	—
prácticas (Es)	Praktikum *n*	practical training	stage *m*	tirocinio *m*	—
practice (E)	Praxis *f*	—	pratique *f*	pratica *f*	práctica *f*
práctico (Es)	praktisch	practical	pratique	pratico(a)	—
practise¹ (E)	ausüben	—	exercer	esercitare	ejercer
practise² (E)	üben	—	étudier	esercitarsi	practicar
practise magic (E)	zaubern	—	faire de la magie	esercitare la magia	hacer magia
prado (Es)	Wiese *f*	meadow	pré *m*	prato *m*	—
praise (E)	loben	—	louer	lodare	elogiar
Praktikum (D)	—	practical training	stage *m*	tirocinio *m*	prácticas *f pl*
praktisch (D)	—	practical	pratique	pratico(a)	práctico(a)
pranzo (I)	Mittagessen *n*	lunch	déjeuner *m*	—	comida *f*
Präsident (D)	—	president	président *m*	presidente *m*	presidente *m*
pratica (I)	Praxis *f*	practice	pratique *f*	—	práctica *f*
pratico (I)	praktisch	practical	pratique	—	práctico(a)
pratique¹ (F)	praktisch	practical	—	pratico(a)	práctico(a)
pratique² (F)	Praxis *f*	practice	—	pratica *f*	práctica *f*
prato¹ (I)	Rasen *m*	lawn	pelouse *f*	—	césped *m*
prato² (I)	Wiese *f*	meadow	pré *m*	—	prado *m*
Praxis (D)	—	practice	pratique *f*	pratica *f*	práctica *f*
pray (E)	beten	—	prier	pregare	rezar
prayer (E)	Gebet *n*	—	prière *f*	preghiera *f*	horación *f*
pré (F)	Wiese *f*	meadow	—	prato *m*	prado *m*
précédent¹ (F)	vorhergehend	preceding	—	precedente	anterior(a)
précédent² (F)	vorig	previous	—	precedente	precedente
precedente (Es)	vorig	previous	précédent(e)	precedente	—
precedente¹ (I)	vorig	previous	précédent(e)	—	precedente
precedente² (I)	vorhergehend	preceding	antécédent	—	anterior
precedenza (I)	Vorfahrt *f*	right of way	priorité *f*	—	preferencia *f*
preceding (E)	vorhergehend	—	antécédent	precedente	anterior
précieux¹ (F)	wertvoll	valuable	—	prezioso(a)	valioso(a)
précieux² (F)	kostbar	precious	—	prezioso(a)	valioso(a)
precio (Es)	Preis *m*	price	prix *m*	prezzo *m*	—

	D	E	F	I	Es
precio máximo (Es)	Höchstpreis *m*	maximum price	prix plafond *m*	prezzo massimo *m*	—
precious (E)	kostbar	—	précieux(-euse)	prezioso(a)	valioso(a)
precipitare (I)	abstürzen	crash	faire une chute	—	caer a tierra
precisione (I)	Genauigkeit *f*	accuracy	exactitude *f*	—	exactitud *f*
preciso (I)	genau	exact	exact(e)	—	exacto(a)
predict (E)	vorhersagen	—	prédire	prognosticare	pronosticar
prédire (F)	vorhersagen	predict	—	prognosticare	pronosticar
preface (E)	Vorwort *n*	—	préface *f*	prefazione *f*	prólogo *m*
préface (F)	Vorwort *n*	preface	—	prefazione *f*	prólogo *m*
prefazione (I)	Vorwort *n*	preface	préface *f*	—	prólogo *m*
prefer[1] (E)	bevorzugen	—	préférer	perferire	preferir
prefer[2] (E)	vorziehen	—	préférer	preferire	preferir
preference (E)	Vorzug *m*	—	préférence *f*	preferenza *f*	preferencia *f*
préférence (F)	Vorzug *m*	preference	—	preferenza *f*	preferencia *f*
preferencia[1] (Es)	Vorfahrt *f*	right of way	priorité *f*	precedenza *f*	—
preferencia[2] (Es)	Vorzug *m*	preference	préférence *f*	preferenza *f*	—
preferenza (I)	Vorzug *m*	preference	préférence *f*	—	preferencia *f*
préférer[1] (F)	bevorzugen	prefer	—	perferire	preferir
préférer[2] (F)	vorziehen	prefer	—	preferire	preferir
preferir[1] (Es)	bevorzugen	prefer	préférer	perferire	—
preferir[2] (Es)	vorziehen	prefer	préférer	preferire	—
preferire (I)	vorziehen	prefer	préférer	—	preferir
prefijo (Es)	Vorwahl *f*	dialling code	indicatif téléphonique *m*	prefisso *m*	—
prefisso (I)	Vorwahl *f*	dialling code	indicatif téléphonique *m*	—	prefijo *m*
pregare[1] (I)	beten	pray	prier	—	rezar
pregare[2] (I)	bitten	request	demander	—	rogar
preghiera (I)	Gebet *n*	prayer	prière *f*	—	oración *f*
pregnant (E)	schwanger	—	enceinte	incinta	embarazada
prego! (I)	bitte!	please!	s'il vous plaît!	—	¡por favor!
pregunta (Es)	Frage *f*	question	question *f*	domanda *f*	—
preguntar (Es)	fragen	ask	demander	domandare	—
Preis (D)	—	price	prix *m*	prezzo *m*	precio *m*
preiswert (D)	—	inexpensive	bon marché	conveniente	económico
premere (I)	drücken	press	presser	—	apretar
premiare (I)	belohnen	reward	récompenser	—	recompensar
premier (F)	erste(r,s)	first	—	primo(a)	primera(o)
Premierminister (D)	—	prime minister	président du Conseil *m*	primo ministro *m*	primer ministro *m*
premises (E)	Anwesen *n*	—	domaine *m*	podere *m*	posesión *f*
premuroso (I)	zuvorkommend	obliging	prévenant(e)	—	cortés
prenda (Es)	Pfand *n*	pledge	gage *m*	pegno *m*	—
prendere[1] (I)	fassen	grasp	saisir	—	coger
prendere[2] (I)	nehmen	take	prendre	—	tomar
prendere alloggio (I)	einziehen	move in	emménager	—	instalarse
prendere con sè (I)	mitnehmen	take along	emmener	—	llevar consigo
prendere indietro (I)	zurücknehmen	take back	retirer	—	retirar
prendere nota di (I)	vormerken	book	prendre note de	—	tomar nota

	D	E	F	I	Es
prendersi cura di (I)	sorgen	worry about	occuper de, se	—	atender
prendre (F)	nehmen	take	—	prendere	tomar
prendre congé de (F)	verabschieden	say goodbye to	—	congedare	despedir
prendre de l'essence (F)	tanken	fill up with petrol	—	fare benzina	llenar de gasolina
prendre note de (F)	vormerken	book	—	prendere nota di	tomar nota
prénom (F)	Vorname *m*	Christian name	—	nome di battesimo *m*	nombre de pila *m*
prenotare[1] (I)	buchen	book[1]	retenir	—	reservar
prenotare[2] (I)	vorbestellen	book	réserver	—	hacer reservar
prensa (Es)	Presse *f*	press	presse *f*	stampa *f*	—
preoccupare (I)	beunruhigen	disturb	inquiéter	—	inquietar
preoccupazione (I)	Sorge *f*	concern	souci *m*	—	preocupación *f*
preocupación (Es)	Sorge *f*	concern	souci *m*	preoccupazione *f*	—
preparar[1] (Es)	vorbereiten	prepare	préparer	preparare	—
preparar[2] (Es)	zubereiten	prepare	préparer	preparare	—
preparare[1] (I)	vorbereiten	prepare	préparer	—	preparar
preparare[2] (I)	zubereiten	prepare	préparer	—	preparar
prepare[1] (E)	vorbereiten	—	préparer	preparare	preparar
prepare[2] (E)	zubereiten	—	préparer	preparare	preparar
préparer[1] (F)	vorbereiten	prepare	—	preparare	preparar
préparer[2] (F)	zubereiten	prepare	—	preparare	preparar
presa (I)	Steckdose *f*	socket	prise électrique *f*	—	enchufe *m*
prescribe (E)	verschreiben	—	prescrire	prescrivere	prescribir
prescribir (Es)	verschreiben	prescribe	prescrire	prescrivere	—
prescripción médica (Es)	Rezept *n*	prescription	ordonnance *f*	prescrizione *f*	—
prescription (E)	Rezept *n*	—	ordonnance *f*	prescrizione *f*	prescripción médica *f*
prescrire (F)	verschreiben	prescribe	—	prescrivere	prescribir
prescrivere (I)	verschreiben	prescribe	prescrire	—	prescribir
prescrizione (I)	Rezept *n*	prescription	ordonnance *f*	—	prescripción médica *f*
près de[1] (F)	neben	beside	—	accanto a	al lado de
près de[2] (F)	nahe	near by	—	vicino(a)	contiguo(a)
present[1] (E)	anwesend	—	présent(e)	presente	presente
present[2] (E)	Geschenk *n*	—	cadeau *m*	regalo *m*	regalo *m*
present[3] (E)	Gegenwart *f*	—	présent *m*	presente *m*	presente *m*
présent[1] (F)	Gegenwart *f*	present	—	presente *m*	presente *m*
présent[2] (F)	anwesend	present	—	presente	presente
présent[3] (F)	vorhanden	available	—	disponibile	presente
presentar[1] (Es)	darstellen	represent	représenter	rappresentare	—
presentar[2] (Es)	vorstellen	introduce	présenter	presentare	—
presentar[3] (Es)	vorzeigen	show	monter	esibire	—
presentare (I)	vorstellen	introduce	présenter	—	presentar
presentarse (Es)	bewerben, sich	apply	poser sa candidature	concorrere	—
presente[1] (Es)	anwesend	present	présent(e)	presente	—
presente[2] (Es)	Gegenwart *f*	present	présent *m*	presente *m*	—
presente[3] (Es)	vorhanden	available	présent(e)	disponibile	—
presente[1] (I)	anwesend	present	présent(e)	—	presente

	D	E	F	I	Es
presente² (I)	Gegenwart *f*	present	présent *m*	—	presente *m*
présenter¹ (F)	bieten	offer	—	offrire	ofrecer
présenter² (F)	überreichen	hand over	—	consegnare	entregar
présenter³ (F)	vorstellen	introduce	—	presentare	presentar
presentiment (E)	Ahnung *f*	—	pressentiment *m*	presentimento *m*	presentimiento *m*
presentimento (I)	Ahnung *f*	presentiment	pressentiment *m*	—	presentimiento *m*
presentimiento (Es)	Ahnung *f*	presentiment	pressentiment *m*	presentimento *m*	—
president (E)	Präsident *m*	—	président *m*	presidente *m*	presidente *m*
président (F)	Präsident *m*	president	—	presidente *m*	presidente *m*
président du Conseil (F)	Premier-minister *m*	prime minister	—	primo ministro *m*	primer ministro *m*
presidente (Es)	Präsident *m*	president	président *m*	presidente *m*	—
presidente (I)	Präsident *m*	president	président *m*	—	presidente *m*
presión (Es)	Zwang *m*	compulsion	contrainte *f*	costrizione *f*	—
presque¹ (F)	beinahe	nearly	—	circa/quasi	casi
presque² (F)	fast	nearly	—	quasi	casi
presqu'île (F)	Halbinsel *f*	peninsula	—	penisola *f*	península *f*
press¹ (E)	drücken	—	presser	premere	apretar
press² (E)	Presse *f*	—	presse *f*	stampa *f*	prensa *f*
pressappoco¹ (I)	etwa	about	environ	—	unos
pressappoco² (I)	ungefähr	about	environ	—	aproximadamente
Presse (D)	—	press	presse *f*	stampa *f*	prensa *f*
presse (F)	Presse *f*	press	—	stampa *f*	prensa *f*
pressé (F)	eilig	hurried	—	frettoloso(a)	rápido(a)
pressentiment (F)	Ahnung *f*	presentiment	—	presentimento *m*	presentimiento *m*
presser (F)	drücken	press	—	premere	apretar
prestar¹ (Es)	ausleihen	lend	prêter	dare in prestito	—
prestar² (Es)	borgen	lend	prêter	prestare	—
prestar³ (Es)	leihen	lend	prêter	prestare	—
prestar⁴ (Es)	verleihen	lend	prêter	prestare	—
prestar atención¹ (Es)	aufpassen	pay attention	faire attention	fare attenzione	—
prestar atención² (Es)	beachten	take notice	observer	osservare	—
prestare¹ (I)	borgen	lend	prêter	—	prestar
prestare² (I)	leihen	lend	prêter	—	prestar
prestare³ (I)	verleihen	lend	prêter	—	prestar
presto¹ (I)	bald	soon	bientôt	—	pronto
presto² (I)	demnächst	shortly	prochainement	—	próximamente
presto³ (I)	früh	early	tôt	—	temprano(a)
presumendo (I)	vorausgesetzt	provided	à condition que	—	supuesto
presunto (I)	angeblich	pretended	prétendu(e)	—	supuesto(a)
presupporre (I)	voraussetzen	assume	supposer	—	suponer
prêt¹ (F)	bereit	ready	—	pronto(a)	dispuesto(a)
prêt² (F)	fertig	ready	—	pronto(a)	listo(a)
prete (I)	Priester *m*	priest	prêtre *m*	—	sacerdote *m*
pretemporada (Es)	Vorsaison *f*	low season	basse saison *f*	bassa stagione *f*	—
pretended (E)	angeblich	—	prétendu(e)	presunto(a)	supuesto(a)
pretendere (I)	zumuten	expect	exiger	—	exigir

	D	E	F	I	Es
prétendu (F)	angeblich	pretended	—	presunto(a)	supuesto(a)
prêter[1] (F)	ausleihen	lend	—	dare in prestito	prestar
prêter[2] (F)	borgen	lend	—	prestare	prestar
prêter[3] (F)	leihen	lend	—	prestare	prestar
prêter[4] (F)	verleihen	lend	—	prestare	prestar
pretesto (I)	Vorwand m	pretext	prétexte m	—	pretexto m
pretext (E)	Vorwand m	—	prétexte m	pretesto m	pretexto m
prétexte (F)	Vorwand m	pretext	—	pretesto m	pretexto m
pretexto (Es)	Vorwand m	pretext	prétexte m	pretesto m	—
prêtre (F)	Priester m	priest	—	prete m	sacerdote m
pretty (E)	hübsch	—	joli(e)	carino(a)	bonito(a)
preuve (F)	Beweis m	proof	—	prova f	prueba f
prévenant (F)	zuvorkommend	obliging	—	premuroso(a)	cortés
prévenir (F)	verständigen	inform	—	informare	informar
prévenir de (F)	warnen	warn	—	ammonire	advertir
prevent (E)	verhindern	—	empêcher	impedire	evitar
previous (E)	vorig	—	précédent(e)	precedente	precedente
previsioni del tempo (I)	Wetter-vorhersage f	weather forecast	prévisions météorologiques f pl	—	pronóstico del tiempo m
prévisions météorologiques (F)	Wetter-vorhersage f	weather forecast	—	previsioni del tempo f pl	pronóstico del tiempo m
prezioso[1] (I)	kostbar	precious	précieux(-euse)	—	valioso(a)
prezioso[2] (I)	wertvoll	valuable	précieux(euse)	—	valioso(a)
prezzo (I)	Preis m	price	prix m	—	precio m
prezzo massimo (I)	Höchstpreis m	maximum price	prix plafond m	—	precio máximo m
price (E)	Preis m	—	prix m	prezzo m	precio m
prick (E)	stechen	—	piquer	pungere	picar
prier (F)	beten	pray	—	pregare	rezar
prière (F)	Gebet n	prayer	—	preghiera f	oración f
priest[1] (E)	Priester m	—	prêtre m	prete m	sacerdote m
priest[2] (E)	Pfarrer m	—	curé	parroco m	párroco m
Priester (D)	—	priest	prêtre m	prete m	sacerdote m
prigione (I)	Gefängnis n	prison	prison f	—	cárcel f
prima (Es)	Cousine f	cousin	cousine f	cugina f	—
prima[1] (I)	eher	sooner	plus tôt	—	antes
prima[2] (I)	früher	earlier	autrefois	—	antes
prima[3] (I)	vorher	before	avant	—	antes
prima[4] (I)	zuvor	before	auparavant	—	antes
prima che[1] (I)	bevor	before	avant que	—	antes que
prima che[2] (I)	ehe	before	avant que	—	antes que
primavera (Es)	Frühjahr n	spring	printemps m	primavera f	—
primavera (I)	Frühjahr n	spring	printemps m	—	primavera f
prime minister (E)	Premier-minister m	—	président du Conseil m	primo ministro m	primer ministro m
primer ministro (Es)	Premier-minister m	prime minister	président du Conseil m	primo ministro m	—
primero[1] (Es)	erst	first	d'abord	dapprima	—
primero[2] (Es)	zuerst	at first	d'abord	dapprima	—
primero[3] (Es)	erste(r,s)	first	premier(-ière)	primo(a)	—

	D	E	F	I	Es
primer pago (Es)	Anzahlung *f*	deposit	acompte *m*	acconto *m*	—
primer plato (Es)	Vorspeise *f*	appetizer	hors-d'œuvre *m*	antipasto *m*	—
primitivo (Es)	ursprünglich	original	originel(le)	originario(a)	—
primo (Es)	Vetter *m*	cousin	cousin *m*	cugino *m*	—
primo (I)	erste(r,s)	first	premier(-ière)	—	primera(o)
primo ministro (I)	Premier-minister *m*	prime minister	président du Conseil *m*	—	primer ministro *m*
prince[1] (E)	Fürst *m*	—	prince *m*	principe *m*	príncipe *m*
prince[2] (E)	Prinz *m*	—	prince *m*	principe *m*	príncipe *m*
prince[1] (F)	Fürst *m*	prince	—	principe *m*	príncipe *m*
prince[2] (F)	Prinz *m*	prince	—	principe *m*	príncipe *m*
principalmente (Es)	hauptsächlich	mainly	surtout	principalmente	—
principalmente (I)	hauptsächlich	mainly	surtout	—	principalmente
principante (Es)	Anfänger *m*	beginner	débutant(e)	principiante *m*	—
príncipe[1] (Es)	Fürst *m*	prince	prince *m*	principe *m*	—
príncipe[2] (Es)	Prinz *m*	prince	prince *m*	principe *m*	—
principe[1] (I)	Fürst *m*	prince	prince *m*	—	príncipe *m*
principe[2] (I)	Prinz *m*	prince	prince *m*	—	príncipe *m*
principiante (I)	Anfänger *m*	beginner	débutant(e)	—	principante *m*
principio (Es)	Beginn *m*	beginning	commencement *m*	inizio *m*	—
printemps (F)	Frühjahr *n*	spring	—	primavera *f*	primavera *f*
Prinz (D)	—	prince	prince *m*	principe *m*	príncipe *m*
priorité (F)	Vorfahrt *f*	right of way	—	precedenza *f*	preferencia *f*
prisa (Es)	Eile *f*	haste	hâte *f*	fretta *f*	—
prise électrique (F)	Steckdose *f*	socket	—	presa *f*	enchufe *m*
prison (E)	Gefängnis *n*	—	prison *f*	prigione *f*	cárcel *f*
prison (F)	Gefängnis *n*	prison	—	prigione *f*	cárcel *f*
privado (Es)	privat	private	privé(e)	privato(a)	—
privat (D)	—	private	privé(e)	privato(a)	privado(a)
private (E)	privat	—	privé(e)	privato(a)	privado(a)
privato (I)	privat	private	privé(e)	—	privado(a)
privé (F)	privat	private	—	privato(a)	privado(a)
prix (F)	Preis *m*	price	—	prezzo *m*	precio *m*
prix plafond (F)	Höchstpreis *m*	maximum price	—	prezzo massimo *m*	precio máximo *m*
probabilmente (I)	wahrscheinlich	probably	probablement	—	probablemente
probablement (F)	wahrscheinlich	probably	—	probabilmente	probablemente
probablemente (Es)	wahrscheinlich	probably	probablement	probabilmente	—
probably (E)	wahrscheinlich	—	probablement	probabilmente	probablemente
probar[1] (Es)	anprobieren	try on	essayer	provare	—
probar[2] (Es)	beweisen	prove	prouver	provare	—
probar[3] (Es)	probieren	try	essayer	assaggiare	—
probar[4] (Es)	testen	test	tester	collaudare	—
probar[5] (Es)	versuchen	try	essayer	assagiare	—
Probe (D)	—	test	essai *m*	prova *f*	prueba *f*
probieren (D)	—	try	essayer	assaggiare	probar
Problem (D)	—	problem	problème *m*	problema *m*	problema *m*
problem (E)	Problem *n*	—	problème *m*	problema *m*	problema *m*
problema (Es)	Problem *n*	problem	problème *m*	problema *m*	—

	D	E	F	I	Es
problema (I)	Problem *n*	problem	problème *m*	—	problema *m*
problème (F)	Problem *n*	problem	—	problema *m*	problema *m*
proceder[1] (Es)	verfahren	act	procéder	procedere	—
proceder[2] (Es)	vorgehen	proceed	avancer	procedere	—
procéder (F)	verfahren	act	—	procedere	proceder
procedere[1] (I)	verfahren	act	procéder	—	proceder
procedere[2] (I)	vorgehen	proceed	avancer	—	proceder
proceed (E)	vorgehen	—	avancer	andare avanti	proceder
procès (F)	Prozeß *m*	trial	—	processo *m*	proceso *m*
proceso[1] (Es)	Fortschritt *m*	progress	progrès *m*	progresso *m*	—
proceso[2] (Es)	Prozeß *m*	trial	procès *m*	processo *m*	—
processo (I)	Prozeß *m*	trial	procès *m*	—	proceso *m*
prochainement (F)	demnächst	shortly	—	presto	próximamente
procurare[1] (I)	beschaffen	get	procurer	—	proporcionar
procurare[2] (I)	besorgen	acquire	procurer	—	conseguir
procurare[3] (I)	verschaffen	procure	procurer	—	procurarse algo
procurarse algo (Es)	verschaffen	procure	procurer	procurare	—
procuration (F)	Vollmacht *f*	authority	—	delega *f*	poder *m*
procure (E)	verschaffen	—	procurer	procurare	procurarse algo
procurer[1] (F)	beschaffen	get	—	procurare	proporcionar
procurer[2] (F)	besorgen	acquire	—	procurare	conseguir
procurer[3] (F)	verschaffen	procure	—	procurare	procurarse algo
prodotto[1] (I)	Erzeugnis *n*	product	produit *m*	—	producto *m*
prodotto[2] (I)	Produkt *n*	product	produit *m*	—	producto *m*
produce[1] (E)	erzeugen	—	produire	fabbricare	producir
produce[2] (E)	produzieren	—	produire	produrre	producir
producir[1] (Es)	erzeugen	produce	produire	fabbricare	—
producir[2] (Es)	herstellen	manufacture	produire	fabbricare	—
producir[3] (Es)	produzieren	produce	produire	produrre	—
product[1] (E)	Erzeugnis *n*	—	produit *m*	prodotto *m*	producto *m*
product[2] (E)	Produkt *n*	—	produit *m*	prodotto *m*	producto *m*
producteur (F)	Hersteller *m*	manufacturer	—	produttore *m*	productor *m*
producto[1] (Es)	Erzeugnis *n*	product	produit *m*	prodotto *m*	—
producto[2] (Es)	Produkt *n*	product	produit *m*	prodotto *m*	—
productor (Es)	Hersteller *m*	manufacturer	producteur *m*	produttore *m*	—
produire[1] (F)	erzeugen	produce	—	fabbricare	producir
produire[2] (F)	herstellen	manufacture	—	fabbricare	producir
produire[3] (F)	produzieren	produce	—	produrre	producir
produit[1] (F)	Erzeugnis *n*	product	—	prodotto *m*	producto *m*
produit[2] (F)	Produkt *n*	product	—	prodotto *m*	producto *m*
produits alimentaires (F)	Eßwaren *pl*	victuals	—	alimentari *m pl*	comestibles *m pl*
Produkt (D)	—	product	produit *m*	prodotto *m*	producto *m*
produrre (I)	produzieren	produce	produire	—	producir
produttore (I)	Hersteller *m*	manufacturer	producteur *m*	—	productor *m*
produzieren (D)	—	produce	produire	produrre	producir
profesión (Es)	Beruf *m*	profession	profession *f*	professione *f*	—
profesor (Es)	Lehrer *m*	teacher	professeur *m*	maestro *m*	—

	D	E	F	I	Es
professeur (F)	Lehrer *m*	teacher	—	maestro *m*	profesor *m*
profession (E)	Beruf *m*	—	profession *f*	professione *f*	profesión *f*
profession (F)	Beruf *m*	profession	—	professione *f*	profesión *f*
professione (I)	Beruf *m*	profession	profession *f*	—	profesión *f*
profit (E)	Gewinn *m*	—	gain *m*	guadagno *m*	ganancia *f*
profond (F)	tief	deep	—	profondo(a)	profundo(a)
profondeur (F)	Tiefe *f*	depth	—	profondità *f*	profundidad *f*
profondità (I)	Tiefe *f*	depth	profondeur *f*	—	profundidad *f*
profondo (I)	tief	deep	profond(e)	—	profundo(a)
profumo[1] (I)	Duft *m*	scent	odeur *f*	—	aroma *m*
profumo[2] (I)	Parfüm *n*	perfume	parfum *m*	—	perfume *m*
profundidad (Es)	Tiefe *f*	depth	profondeur *f*	profondità *f*	—
profundo (Es)	tief	deep	profond(e)	profondo(a)	—
progettare (I)	planen	plan	projeter	—	planear
progetto (I)	Plan *m*	plan	plan *m*	—	plan *m*
prognosticare (I)	vorhersagen	predict	prédire	—	pronosticar
programa (Es)	Programm *n*	programme	programme *m*	programma *m*	—
Programm (D)	—	programme	programme *m*	programma *m*	programa *m*
programma (I)	Programm *n*	programme	programme *m*	—	programa *m*
programme (E)	Programm *n*	—	programme *m*	programma *m*	programa *m*
programme (F)	Programm *n*	programme	—	programma *m*	programa *m*
progrès (F)	Fortschritt *m*	progress	—	progresso *m*	progreso *m*
progress (E)	Fortschritt *m*	—	progrès *m*	progresso *m*	progreso *m*
progresso (I)	Fortschritt *m*	progress	progrès *m*	—	progreso *m*
prohibición (Es)	Verbot *n*	prohibition	défense *f*	divieto *m*	—
prohibido (Es)	verboten	forbidden	interdit(e)	vietato(a)	—
prohibir[1] (Es)	untersagen	forbid	interdire qch à qn	proibire	—
prohibir[2] (Es)	verbieten	forbid	défendre	proibire	—
prohibition (E)	Verbot *n*	—	défense *f*	divieto *m*	prohibición *f*
proibire[1] (I)	untersagen	forbid	interdire qch à qn	—	prohibir
proibire[2] (I)	verbieten	forbid	défendre	—	prohibir
projeter (F)	planen	plan	—	progettare	planear
prólogo (Es)	Vorwort *n*	preface	préface *f*	prefazione *f*	—
prolonger (F)	verlängern	extend	—	allungare	alargar
promenade (F)	Spaziergang *m*	walk	—	passeggiata *f*	paseo *m*
promener, se (F)	spazierengehen	go for a walk	—	passeggiare	ir de paseo
promesa (Es)	Versprechen *n*	promise	promesse *f*	promessa *f*	—
promessa (I)	Versprechen *n*	promise	promesse *f*	—	promesa *f*
promesse (F)	Versprechen *n*	promise	—	promessa *f*	promesa *f*
prometer[1] (Es)	versprechen	promise	promettre	promettere	—
prometer[2] (Es)	zusagen	promise	promettre	promettere	—
prometerse (Es)	verloben	get engaged	fiancer, se	fidanzarsi	—
prometido (Es)	Verlobter *m*	fiancé	fiancé *m*	fidanzato *m*	—
promettere[1] (I)	versprechen	promise	promettre	—	prometer
promettere[2] (I)	zusagen	promise	promettre	—	prometer
promettre[1] (F)	versprechen	promise	—	promettere	prometer
promettre[2] (F)	zusagen	promise	—	promettere	prometer
promise[1] (E)	versprechen	—	promettre	promettere	prometer

	D	E	F	I	Es
promise² (E)	Versprechen *n*	—	promesse *f*	promessa *f*	promesa *f*
promise³ (E)	zusagen	—	promettre	promettere	prometer
prononcer (F)	aussprechen	pronounce	—	pronunciare	pronunciar
prononciation (F)	Aussprache *f*	pronunciation	—	pronuncia *f*	pronunciación *f*
pronosticar (Es)	vorhersagen	predict	prédire	prognosticare	—
pronóstico del tiempo (Es)	Wetter-vorhersage *f*	weather forecast	prévisions météorologiques *f pl*	previsioni del tempo *f pl*	—
pronounce (E)	aussprechen	—	prononcer	pronunciare	pronunciar
pronto (Es)	bald	soon	bientôt	presto	—
pronto¹ (I)	bereit	ready	prêt(e)	—	dispuesto(a)
pronto² (I)	fertig	ready	prêt(e)	—	listo(a)
pronto! (I)	hallo!	hello!	allô!	—	¡diga!
pronuncia (I)	Aussprache *f*	pronunciation	prononciation *f*	—	pronunciación *f*
pronunciación (Es)	Aussprache *f*	pronunciation	prononciation *f*	pronuncia *f*	—
pronunciar (Es)	aussprechen	pronounce	prononcer	pronunciare	—
pronunciare (I)	aussprechen	pronounce	prononcer	—	pronunciar
pronunciation (E)	Aussprache *f*	—	prononciation *f*	pronuncia *f*	pronunciación *f*
proof (E)	Beweis *m*	—	preuve *f*	prova *f*	prueba *f*
propager (F)	verbreiten	spread	—	diffondere	difundir
propietario¹ (Es)	Eigentümer *m*	owner	propriétaire *m*	proprietario *m*	—
propietario² (Es)	Inhaber *m*	owner	propriétaire *m*	proprietario *m*	—
propietario³ (Es)	Besitzer *m*	owner	propriétaire *m*	proprietario *m*	—
propina (Es)	Trinkgeld *n*	tip	pourboire *m*	mancia *f*	—
propio (Es)	eigen	own	propre	proprio(a)	—
proponer (Es)	vorschlagen	propose	proposer	proporre	—
proporcionar (Es)	beschaffen	get	procurer	procurare	—
proporre (I)	vorschlagen	propose	proposer	—	proponer
proposal (E)	Vorschlag *m*	—	proposition *f*	proposta *f*	proposición *f*
propose (E)	vorschlagen	—	proposer	proporre	proponer
proposer (F)	vorschlagen	propose	—	proporre	proponer
proposición (Es)	Vorschlag *m*	proposal	proposition *f*	proposta *f*	—
proposition (F)	Vorschlag *m*	proposal	—	proposta *f*	proposición *f*
proposta (I)	Vorschlag *m*	proposal	proposition *f*	—	proposición *f*
propre¹ (F)	eigen	own	—	proprio(a)	propio(a)
propre² (F)	sauber	clean	—	pulito(a)	limpio(a)
proprietà (I)	Besitz *m*	possession	propriété *f*	—	posesión *f*
propriétaire¹ (F)	Besitzer *m*	owner	—	proprietario *m*	propietario *m*
propriétaire² (F)	Eigentümer *m*	owner	—	proprietario *m*	propietario *m*
propriétaire³ (F)	Inhaber *m*	owner	—	proprietario *m*	propietario *m*
proprietario¹ (I)	Besitzer *m*	owner	propriétaire *m*	—	propietario *m*
proprietario² (I)	Eigentümer *m*	owner	propriétaire *m*	—	propietario *m*
proprietario³ (I)	Inhaber *m*	owner	propriétaire *m*	—	propietario *m*
propriété (F)	Besitz *m*	possession	—	proprietà *f*	posesión *f*
proprio (I)	eigen	own	propre	—	propio(a)
prosciutto (I)	Schinken *m*	ham	jambon *m*	—	jamón *m*
proseguir¹ (Es)	fortsetzen	continue	continuer	continuare	—
proseguir² (Es)	weitergehen	go on	aller plus loin	proseguire	—
proseguire (I)	weitergehen	go on	aller plus loin	—	proseguir

	D	E	F	I	Es
prospecto (Es)	Prospekt *m*	brochure	prospectus *m*	dépliant *m*	—
prospectus (F)	Prospekt *m*	brochure	—	dépliant *m*	prospecto *m*
Prospekt (D)	—	brochure	prospectus *m*	dépliant *m*	prospecto *m*
prossimo (I)	nächste(r,s)	next	suivant(e)	—	siguiente
prost! (D)	—	cheers!	santé!	salute!	¡salud!
protección (Es)	Schutz *m*	protection	protection *f*	protezione *f*	—
protect[1] (E)	beschützen	—	protéger	proteggere	proteger
protect[2] (E)	schützen	—	protéger	proteggere	proteger
protection (E)	Schutz *m*	—	protection *f*	protezione *f*	protección *f*
protection (F)	Schutz *m*	protection	—	protezione *f*	protección *f*
proteger[1] (Es)	beschützen	protect	protéger	proteggere	—
proteger[2] (Es)	schützen	protect	protéger	proteggere	—
protéger[1] (F)	beschützen	protect	—	proteggere	proteger
protéger[2] (F)	schützen	protect	—	proteggere	proteger
proteggere[1] (I)	beschützen	protect	protéger	—	proteger
proteggere[2] (I)	schützen	protect	protéger	—	proteger
Protestant (E)	evangelisch	—	protestant(e)	protestante	protestante
protestant (F)	evangelisch	Protestant	—	protestante	protestante
protestante (Es)	evangelisch	Protestant	protestant(e)	protestante	—
protestante (I)	evangelisch	Protestant	protestant(e)	—	protestante
protezione (I)	Schutz *m*	protection	protection *f*	—	protección *f*
proud (E)	stolz	—	fier(-ère)	orgoglioso(a)	orgulloso(a)
prouver (F)	beweisen	prove	—	provare	probar
prova[1] (I)	Beweis *m*	proof	preuve *f*	—	prueba *f*
prova[2] (I)	Probe *f*	test	essai *m*	—	prueba *f*
provare[1] (I)	anprobieren	try on	essayer	—	probar
provare[2] (I)	beweisen	prove	prouver	—	probar
provare[3] (I)	probieren	try	essayer	—	probar
prove (E)	beweisen	—	prouver	provare	probar
proveer (Es)	versorgen	provide	fournir	approvvigionare	—
proverb (E)	Sprichwort *n*	—	proverbe *m*	proverbio *m*	proverbio *m*
proverbe (F)	Sprichwort *n*	proverb	—	proverbio *m*	proverbio *m*
proverbio (Es)	Sprichwort *n*	proverb	proverbe *m*	proverbio *m*	—
proverbio (I)	Sprichwort *n*	proverb	proverbe *m*	—	proverbio *m*
provide (E)	versorgen	—	fournir	approvvigionare	proveer
provided (E)	vorausgesetzt	—	à condition que	presumendo	supuesto
Provision (D)	—	commission	commission *f*	provvigione *f*	comisión *f*
provisión (Es)	Vorrat *m*	stock	réserves *f pl*	scorte *f pl*	—
provisional (Es)	vorläufig	temporary	provisoire	provvisorio(a)	—
provisoire (F)	vorläufig	temporary	—	provvisorio(a)	provisional
provvigione (I)	Provision *f*	commission	commission *f*	—	comisión *f*
provvisorio (I)	vorläufig	temporary	provisoire	—	provisional
proximamente (Es)	demnächst	shortly	prochainement	presto	—
próximidad (Es)	Nähe *f*	proximity	environs *m pl*	vicinanza *f*	—
proximity (E)	Nähe *f*	—	environs *m pl*	vicinanza *f*	próximidad *f*
proyectar (Es)	beabsichtigen	intend	avoir l'intention de	avere (l')intenzione di	—
proyecto (Es)	Entwurf *m*	outline	esquisse *f*	abbozzo *m*	—

	D	E	F	I	Es
Prozent (D)	—	percent	pour cent	percentuale *f*	por ciento *m*
Prozeß (D)	—	trial	procès *m*	processo *m*	proceso *m*
prudence (F)	Vorsicht *f*	caution	—	prudenza *f*	cuidado *m*
prudent (F)	vorsichtig	careful	—	prudente	cauto(a)
prudente (I)	vorsichtig	careful	prudent(e)	—	cauto(a)
prudenza (I)	Vorsicht *f*	caution	prudence *f*	—	cuidado *m*
prudere (I)	jucken	itch	démanger	—	picar
prueba[1] (Es)	Beweis *m*	proof	preuve *f*	prova *f*	—
prueba[2] (Es)	Probe *f*	test	essai *m*	prova *f*	—
prüfen (D)	—	test	tester	esaminare	examinar
Prüfung (D)	—	examination	examen *m*	esame *m*	examen *m*
prugna (I)	Pflaume *f*	plum	prune *f*	—	ciruela *f*
prune (F)	Pflaume *f*	plum	—	prugna *f*	ciruela *f*
pub[1] (E)	Kneipe *f*	—	bistro *m*	osteria *f*	tasca *f*
pub[2] (E)	Lokal *n*	—	restaurant *m*	locale *m*	local *m*
pubblicare[1] (I)	herausgeben	publish	éditer	—	editar
pubblicare[2] (I)	veröffentlichen	publish	publier	—	publicar
pubblicità (I)	Werbung *f*	advertising	publicité *f*	—	publicidad *f*
pubblico[1] (I)	öffentlich	public	public(-ique)	—	público(a)
pubblico[2] (I)	Öffentlichkeit *f*	public	public *m*	—	público *m*
pubblico[3] (I)	Publikum *n*	audience	spectateurs *m pl*	—	público *m*
public[1] (E)	öffentlich	—	public(-ique)	pubblico(a)	público(a)
public[2] (E)	Öffentlichkeit *f*	—	public *m*	pubblico *m*	público *m*
public[1] (F)	Öffentlichkeit *f*	public	—	pubblico *m*	público *m*
public[2] (F)	öffentlich	public	—	pubblico(a)	público(a)
publicar (Es)	veröffentlichen	publish	publier	pubblicare	—
publicidad (Es)	Werbung *f*	advertising	publicité *f*	pubblicità *f*	—
publicité[1] (F)	Reklame *f*	advertisement	—	réclame *f*	anuncio *m*
publicité[2] (F)	Werbung *f*	advertising	—	pubblicità *f*	publicidad *f*
público[1] (Es)	Öffentlichkeit *f*	public	public *m*	pubblico *m*	—
público[2] (Es)	Publikum *n*	audience	spectateurs *m pl*	pubblico *m*	—
público[3] (Es)	öffentlich	public	public(-ique)	pubblico(a)	—
publier (F)	veröffentlichen	publish	—	pubblicare	publicar
Publikum (D)	—	audience	spectateurs *m pl*	pubblico *m*	público *m*
publish[1] (E)	herausgeben	—	éditer	pubblicare	editar
publish[2] (E)	veröffentlichen	—	publier	pubblicare	publicar
puce (F)	Floh *m*	flea	—	pulce *f*	pulga *f*
Pudding (D)	—	pudding	flan *m*	budino *m*	flan *m*
pudding (E)	Pudding *m*	—	flan *m*	budino *m*	flan *m*
puddle (E)	Pfütze *f*	—	flaque *f*	pozzanghera *f*	charco *m*
Puder (D)	—	powder	poudre *f*	cipria *f*	polvos *m pl*
pueblo[1] (Es)	Dorf *n*	village	village *m*	paese *m*	—
pueblo[2] (Es)	Volk *n*	people	peuple *m*	popolo *m*	—
puente (Es)	Brücke *f*	bridge	pont *m*	ponte *m*	—
puer (F)	stinken	stink	—	puzzare	apestar
puerta[1] (Es)	Tür *f*	door	porte *f*	porta *f*	—
puerta[2] (Es)	Tor *n*	gate	porte *f*	porta *f*	—
puerto (Es)	Hafen *m*	port	port *m*	porto *m*	—

	D	E	F	I	Es
pues (Es)	denn	for/than	car	perchè	—
puesta del sol (Es)	Sonnenunter-gang *m*	sunset	coucher du soleil *m*	tramonto del sole *m*	—
puesto[1] (Es)	Posten *m*	position	poste *m*	posto *m*	—
puesto[2] (Es)	Stelle *f*	place	place *f*	posto *m*	—
pugno (I)	Faust *f*	fist	poing *m*	—	puño *m*
puissance (F)	Stärke *f*	strength	—	forza *f*	fuerza *f*
pulce (I)	Floh *m*	flea	puce *f*	—	pulga *f*
pulga (Es)	Floh *m*	flea	puce *f*	pulce *f*	—
pulgar (Es)	Daumen *m*	thumb	pouce *m*	pollice *m*	—
pulir (Es)	polieren	polish	astiquer	lucidare	—
pulire[1] (I)	putzen	clean	nettoyer	—	limpiar
pulire[2] (I)	reinigen	clean	nettoyer	—	limpiar
pulire[3] (I)	wischen	wipe	essuyer	—	fregar
pulito (I)	sauber	clean	propre	—	limpio(a)
pulitura (I)	Reinigung *f*	cleaning	nettoyage *m*	—	limpieza *f*
pull (E)	ziehen	—	tirer	tirare	tirar
Pullover (D)	—	pullover	pull-over *m*	pullover *m*	jersey *m*
pullover (E)	Pullover *m*	—	pull-over *m*	pullover *m*	jersey *m*
pull-over (F)	Pullover *m*	pullover	—	pullover *m*	jersey *m*
pullover (I)	Pullover *m*	pullover	pull-over *m*	—	jersey *m*
pulmón (Es)	Lunge *f*	lung	poumon *m*	polmone *m*	—
Puls (D)	—	pulse	pouls *m*	polso *m*	pulso *m*
pulse (E)	Puls *m*	—	pouls *m*	polso *m*	pulso *m*
pulsera (Es)	Armband *n*	bracelet	bracelet *m*	bracciale *m*	—
pulso (Es)	Puls *m*	pulse	pouls *m*	polso *m*	—
Pulver (D)	—	powder	poudre *f*	polvere *f*	pólvora *f*
pump (E)	Pumpe *f*	—	pompe *f*	pompa *f*	bomba *f*
Pumpe (D)	—	pump	pompe *f*	pompa *f*	bomba *f*
punctual (E)	pünktlich	—	ponctuel(le)	puntuale	puntual
pungere (I)	stechen	prick	piquer	—	picar
punir (F)	strafen	punish	—	punire	castigar
punire (I)	strafen	punish	punir	—	castigar
punish (E)	strafen	—	punir	punire	castigar
punishment (E)	Strafe *f*	—	punition *f*	punizione *f*	castigo *m*
punition (F)	Strafe *f*	punishment	—	punizione *f*	castigo *m*
punizione (I)	Strafe *f*	punishment	punition *f*	—	castigo *m*
Punkt (D)	—	point	point *m*	punto *m*	punto *m*
pünktlich (D)	—	punctual	ponctuel(le)	puntuale	puntual
puño (Es)	Faust *f*	fist	poing *m*	pugno *m*	—
punta (Es)	Spitze *f*	point	pointe *f*	punta *f*	—
punta (I)	Spitze *f*	point	pointe *f*	—	punta *f*
puntiagudo (Es)	spitz	pointed	pointu(e)	appuntito(a)	—
punto (Es)	Punkt *m*	point	point *m*	punto *m*	—
punto (I)	Punkt *m*	point	point *m*	—	punto *m*

	D	E	F	I	Es
punto de vista (Es)	Standpunkt *m*	standpoint	point de vue *m*	punto di vista *m*	—
punto di vista (I)	Standpunkt *m*	standpoint	point de vue *m*	—	punto de vista *m*
puntual (Es)	pünktlich	punctual	ponctuel(le)	puntuale	—
puntuale (I)	pünktlich	punctual	ponctuel(le)	—	puntual
pupil (E)	Schüler *m*	—	élève *m*	scolaro *m*	alumno *m*
Puppe (D)	—	doll	poupée *f*	bambola *f*	muñeca *f*
pur (D)	—	pure	pur(e)	puro(a)	puro
pur¹ (F)	pur	pure	—	puro(a)	puro
pur² (F)	rein	pure	—	puro(a)	puro(a)
purchase (E)	Kauf *m*	—	achat *m*	acquisto *m*	compra *f*
pure¹ (E)	pur	—	pur(e)	puro(a)	puro
pure² (E)	rein	—	pur(e)	puro(a)	puro(a)
puro¹ (I)	pur	pure	pur(e)	—	puro
puro² (I)	rein	pure	pur(e)	—	puro(a)
puro (Es)	rein	pure	pur(e)	puro(a)	—
purple (E)	lila	—	mauve	lilla	de color lila
purpose (E)	Zweck *m*	—	but *m*	scopo *m*	finalidad *f*
pursue (E)	verfolgen	—	poursuivre	inseguire	perseguir
purtroppo (I)	leider	unfortunately	malheureusement	—	desgraciadamente
push¹ (E)	stoßen	—	pousser	spingere	empujar
push² (E)	schieben	—	pousser	spingere	empujar
put (E)	setzen	—	mettre	mettere	poner
put down (E)	hinlegen	—	poser	posare	poner
put in order (E)	ordnen	—	ordonner	ordinare	ordenar
put on¹ (E)	anmachen	—	allumer	accendere	encender
put on² (E)	anziehen	—	mettre	indossare	ponerse
putzen (D)	—	clean	nettoyer	pulire	limpiar
Putzfrau (D)	—	charwoman	femme de ménage *f*	donna delle pulizie *f*	mujer de la limpieza *f*
puzzare (I)	stinken	stink	puer	—	apestar
qua¹ (I)	hierher	over here	par ici	—	para acá
qua² (I)	her	here/ago	ici	—	aquí
quaderno (I)	Heft *n*	exercise book	cahier *m*	—	cuaderno *m*
Quadrat (D)	—	square	carré *m*	quadrato *m*	cuadrado *m*
quadratisch (D)	—	square	carré(e)	quadrato(a)	cuadrado(a)
Quadratmeter (D)	—	square metre	mètre carré *m*	metro quadrato *m*	metro cuadrado *m*
quadrato¹ (I)	quadratisch	square	carré(e)	—	cuadrado(a)
quadrato² (I)	Quadrat *f*	square	carré *m*	—	cuadrado *m*
quadrato³ (I)	viereckig	square	carré(e)	—	cuadrangular
quadro (I)	Gemälde *n*	painting	tableau *m*	—	cuadro *m*
qualcosa (I)	etwas	something	quelque chose	—	algo
qualcuno¹ (I)	irgend jemand	somebody	n'importe qui	—	alguno(a)
qualcuno² (I)	jemand	somebody	quelqu'un	—	alguien
qualcuno³ (I)	irgendein(e)	some/any	quelconque	—	cualquiera

	D	E	F	I	Es
quälen (D)	—	torture	torturer	tormentare	atormentar
qualità¹ (I)	Eigenschaft f	quality	qualité f	—	atributo m
qualità² (I)	Qualität f	quality	qualité f	—	cualidad f
Qualität (D)	—	quality	qualité f	qualità f	cualidad f
qualité¹ (F)	Eigenschaft f	quality	—	qualità f	atributo m
qualité² (F)	Qualität f	quality	—	qualità f	cualidad f
quality¹ (E)	Eigenschaft f	—	qualité f	qualità f	atributo m
quality² (E)	Qualität f	—	qualité f	qualità f	cualidad f
qualora (I)	falls	in case	au cas où	—	en caso de que
qualsiasi (I)	beliebig	any	n'importe quel	—	a voluntad
qualsiasi cosa (I)	irgend etwas	something	n'importe quoi	—	algo
quand¹ (F)	als	when	—	quando	cuando
quand² (F)	wann	when	—	quando	cuando
quando¹ (I)	als	when	quand	—	cuando
quando² (I)	wann	when	quand	—	cuando
quanti (I)	wieviele	how many	combien	—	¿cuántos(as)?
quantità¹ (I)	Menge f	quantity	quantité f	—	cantidad f
quantità² (I)	Quantität f	quantity	quantité f	—	cantidad f
Quantität (D)	—	quantity	quantité f	quantità f	cantidad f
quantité¹ (F)	Menge f	quantity	—	quantità f	cantidad f
quantité² (F)	Quantität f	quantity	—	quantità f	cantidad f
quantity¹ (E)	Menge f	—	quantité f	quantità f	cantidad f
quantity² (E)	Quantität f	—	quantité f	quantità f	cantidad f
quanto¹ (I)	wieviel	how much	combien	—	¿cuánto?
quanto² (I)	soviel	so much	tant	—	tanto
quaranta (I)	vierzig	forty	quarante	—	cuarenta
quarante (F)	vierzig	forty	—	quaranta	cuarenta
Quark (D)	—	curd cheese	fromage blanc m	ricotta f	requesón m
quarrel (E)	streiten	—	disputer, se	litigare	discutir
quart (F)	Viertel n	a quarter	—	quarto m	barrio m
Quartett (D)	—	quartet	quatuor m	quartetto m	cuarteto m
quartet (E)	Quartett n	—	quatuor m	quartetto m	cuarteto m
quartetto (I)	Quartett n	quartet	quatuor m	—	cuarteto m
quarto (I)	Viertel n	a quarter	quart m	—	barrio m
quasi (I)	fast	nearly	presque	—	casi
quatorze (F)	vierzehn	fourteen	—	quattordici	catorce
quatre (F)	vier	four	—	quattro	cuatro
quatre-vingt-dix (F)	neunzig	ninety	—	novanta	noventa
quatre-vingts (F)	achtzig	eighty	—	ottanta	ochenta
quattordici (I)	vierzehn	fourteen	quatorze	—	catorce
quattro (I)	vier	four	quatre	—	cuatro
quatuor (F)	Quartett n	quartet	—	quartetto m	cuarteto m
que (Es)	daß	that	que	che	—
que (F)	daß	that	—	che	que

	D	E	F	I	Es
¿qué?[1] (Es)	was	what	quoi/ qu'est-ce que	che/cosa	—
¿qué?[2] (Es)	welch	what a	quel(le)	che	—
Quecksilber (D)	—	mercury	mercure *m*	mercurio *m*	mercurio *m*
quedar (Es)	übrigbleiben	be left	rester	avanzare	—
quedarse (Es)	bleiben	stay	rester	rimanere	—
quedarse aquí (Es)	hierbleiben	stay here	rester	restare qui	—
queen (E)	Königin *f*	—	reine *f*	regina *f*	reina *f*
quejarse[1] (Es)	beschweren, sich	complain	plaindre, se	lamentarsi	—
quejarse[2] (Es)	beklagen	deplore	plaindre de, se	lamentare	—
quel (F)	welch	what a	—	che	¿qué?
quelconque (F)	irgendein(e)	some/any	—	qualcuno(a)	cualquiera
Quelle (D)	—	spring	source *f*	sorgente *f*	fuente *f*
quello (I)	jene(r,s)	that, those *pl*	ce, cette, ces *pl*	—	aquella, aquel, aquello
quelque chose (F)	etwas	something	—	qualcosa	algo
quelquefois (F)	manchmal	sometimes	—	talvolta	a veces
quelques[1] (F)	etliche	several	—	alcuni(e)	algunos(as)
quelques[2] (F)	einige	some	—	alcuni(e)	algunos(as)
quelqu'un (F)	jemand	somebody	—	qualcuno	alguien
quemadura solar (Es)	Sonnenbrand *m*	sunburn	coup de soleil *m*	scottatura solare *f*	—
quemar (Es)	verbrennen	burn	brûler	bruciare	—
que puede adquirirse (Es)	erhältlich	available	en vente	acquistabile	—
quer (D)	—	across	en travers	di trasverso	al través
querer[1] (Es)	mögen	like	aimer	piacere	—
querer[2] (Es)	wollen	want	vouloir	volere	—
querido[1] (Es)	Liebling *m*	darling	chéri *m*	tesoro *m*	—
querido[2] (Es)	wert	worth	cher(ère)	che vale	—
Querstraße (D)	—	intersecting road	rue transversale *f*	traversa *f*	travesía *f*
queso (Es)	Käse *m*	cheese	fromage *m*	formaggio *m*	—
question (E)	Frage *f*	—	question *f*	domanda *f*	pregunta *f*
question (F)	Frage *f*	question	—	domanda *f*	pregunta *f*
questo (I)	diese(r,s)	this	ce, cette	—	esta, e
queue (F)	Schwanz *m*	tail	—	coda *f*	rabo *m*
qui[1] (F)	wer	who	—	chi	¿quién?
qui[2] (F)	welche(r,s)	which	—	il(la) quale	¿cuál?
qui[1] (I)	hier	here	ici	—	aquí
qui[2] (I)	da	there	là/ici	—	allí
quick (E)	rasch	—	rapide	rapido(a)	impulsivo(a)
¿quién? (Es)	wer	who	qui	chi	—
quiet[1] (E)	ruhig	—	tranquille	calmo(a)	quieto(a)
quiet[2] (E)	still	—	calme	calmo(a)	tranquilo(a)
quietly (E)	leise	—	à voix basse	a bassa voce	sin ruido
quieto (Es)	ruhig	quiet	tranquille	calmo(a)	—

	D	E	F	I	Es
quietud (Es)	Ruhe *f*	calm	calme *m*	silenzio *m*	—
químico (Es)	chemisch	chemical	chimique	chimico(a)	—
quince (Es)	fünfzehn	fifteen	quinze	quindici	—
quindici (I)	fünfzehn	fifteen	quinze	—	quince
quinze (F)	fünfzehn	fifteen	—	quindici	quince
quitar[1] (Es)	entfernen	remove	éloigner	allontanare	—
quitar[2] (Es)	wegnehmen	take away	enlever	togliere	—
quitarse (Es)	ausziehen	take off	enlever	levare	—
quite (E)	ziemlich	—	assez	abbastanza	bastante
quittance (F)	Quittung *f*	receipt	—	ricevuta *f*	recibo *m*
Quittung (D)	—	receipt	quittance *f*	ricevuta *f*	recibo *m*
quoi (F)	was	what	—	che/cosa	¿qué?
quote-part (F)	Rate *f*	instalment	—	rata *f*	plazo *m*
quotidiano (I)	täglich	daily	quotidien(ne)	—	cotidiano(a)
quotidien (F)	täglich	daily	—	quotidiano(a)	cotidiano(a)
rabais (F)	Rabatt *m*	discount	—	sconto *m*	rebaja *f*
Rabatt (D)	—	discount	rabais *m*	sconto *m*	rebaja *f*
rabbia (I)	Wut *f*	anger	colère *f*	—	rabia *f*
Rabe (D)	—	raven	corbeau *m*	corvo *m*	cuervo *m*
rabia (Es)	Wut *f*	anger	colère *f*	rabbia *f*	—
rabo (Es)	Schwanz *m*	tail	queue *f*	coda *f*	—
raccogliere (I)	sammeln	collect	collecter	—	recolectar
raccoglitore (I)	Mappe *f*	folder	serviette *f*	—	carpeta *f*
raccolta (I)	Sammlung *f*	collection	collection *f*	—	colección *f*
raccolto (I)	Ernte *f*	harvest	moisson *f*	—	cosecha *f*
raccomandare (I)	empfehlen	recommend	recommander	—	recomendar
raccomandazione (I)	Empfehlung *f*	recommendation	recommandation *f*	—	recomendación *f*
raccontare (I)	erzählen	tell	raconter	—	contar
Rache (D)	—	revenge	vengeance *f*	vendetta *f*	venganza *f*
Rachen (D)	—	throat	gorge *f*	faringe *m*	garganta *f*
racine (F)	Wurzel *f*	root	—	radice *f*	raíz *f*
raconter (F)	erzählen	tell	—	raccontare	contar
Rad (D)	—	wheel	roue *f*	ruota *f*	rueda *f*
Radarkontrolle (D)	—	speed trap	contrôle radar *m*	controllo radar *m*	control de radar *m*
radice (I)	Wurzel *f*	root	racine *f*	—	raíz *f*
Radio (D)	—	radio	radio *f*	radio *f*	radio *f*
radio (E)	Radio *n*	—	radio *f*	radio *f*	radio *f*
radio (Es)	Radio *n*	radio	radio *f*	radio *f*	—
radio[1] (F)	Radio *n*	radio	—	radio *f*	radio *f*
radio[2] (F)	Rundfunk *m*	broadcasting	—	radio *f*	radiodifusión *f*
radio[1] (I)	Rundfunk *m*	broadcasting	radio *f*	—	radiodifusión *f*
radio[2] (I)	Radio *n*	radio	radio *f*	—	radio *f*
radiodifusión (Es)	Rundfunk *m*	broadcasting	radio *f*	radio *f*	—
radiografiar (Es)	röntgen	X-ray	radiographier	fare una radiografia	—

	D	E	F	I	Es
radiographier (F)	röntgen	X-ray	—	fare una radiografia	radiografiar
raffreddore[1] (I)	Erkältung *f*	cold	refroidissement *m*	—	catarro *m*
raffreddore[2] (I)	Schnupfen *m*	cold	rhume *m*	—	resfriado *m*
rafraîchissement (F)	Erfrischung *f*	refreshment	—	rinfresco *m*	refresco *m*
ragazza (I)	Mädchen *n*	girl	jeune fille *f*	—	chica *f*
ragazzo[1] (I)	Bursche *m*	fellow	garçon *m*	—	chico *m*
ragazzo[2] (I)	Junge *m*	boy	garçon *m*	—	chico *m*
raggio (I)	Strahl *m*	ray	rayon *m*	—	rayo *m*
raggiungere (I)	erreichen	reach	atteindre	—	alcanzar
ragionevole (I)	vernünftig	sensible	raisonnable	—	razonable
ragno (I)	Spinne *f*	spider	araignée *f*	—	araña *f*
Rahmen (D)	—	frame	cadre *m*	cornice *f*	marco *m*
raid[1] (E)	überfallen	—	attaquer	assalire	asaltar
raid[2] (E)	Überfall *m*	—	attaque *f*	aggressione *f*	asalto *m*
raide (F)	steil	steep	—	ripido(a)	inclinado(a)
railway (E)	Eisenbahn *f*	—	chemin de fer *m*	ferrovia *f*	ferrocarril *m*
rain[1] (E)	regnen	—	pleuvoir	piovere	llover
rain[2] (E)	Regen *m*	—	pluie *f*	pioggia *f*	lluvia *f*
raincoat (E)	Regenmantel *m*	—	imperméable *m*	impermeabile *m*	impermeable *m*
raise[1] (E)	erhöhen	—	augmenter	innalzare	elevar
raise[2] (E)	erheben	—	lever	alzare	elevar
raison (F)	Grund *m*	reason	—	causa *f*	causa *f*
raisonnable (F)	vernünftig	sensible	—	ragionevole	razonable
raíz (Es)	Wurzel *f*	root	racine *f*	radice *f*	—
rallegrarsi (I)	freuen, sich	be glad	être heureux(-euse)	—	alegrarse
rama[1] (Es)	Ast *m*	branch	branche *f*	ramo *m*	—
rama[2] (Es)	Zweig *m*	branch	branche *f*	ramo *m*	—
rame (F)	Ruder *n*	oar	—	remo *m*	remo *m*
ramer (F)	rudern	row	—	remare	remar
ramo (Es)	Strauß *m*	bunch	bouquet *m*	mazzo *m*	—
ramo[1] (I)	Ast *m*	branch	branche *f*	—	rama *f*
ramo[2] (I)	Zweig *m*	branch	branche *f*	—	rama *f*
rana (Es)	Frosch *m*	frog	grenouille *f*	rana *f*	—
rana (I)	Frosch *m*	frog	grenouille *f*	—	rana *f*
Rand (D)	—	brim	bord *m*	margine *m*	borde *m*
Rang (D)	—	rank	rang *m*	ceto *m*	clase *f*
rang (F)	Rang *m*	rank	—	ceto *m*	clase *f*
rangé (F)	ordentlich	tidy	—	ordinato(a)	ordenado(a)
rangée (F)	Reihe *f*	row	—	fila *f*	fila *f*
ranger[1] (F)	aufräumen	clear away	—	mettere in ordine	arreglar
ranger[2] (F)	unterbringen	stow	—	sistemare	colocar
rango (I)	Grad *m*	rank	grade *m*	—	titulo *m*
rank[1] (E)	Grad *m*	—	grade *m*	rango *m*	título *m*
rank[2] (E)	Rang *m*	—	rang *m*	ceto *m*	clase *f*
rape (E)	vergewaltigen	—	violer	violentare	violar
rapide[1] (F)	rasch	quick	—	rapido(a)	impulsivo(a)
rapide[2] (F)	schnell	fast	—	veloce	rápido(a)

	D	E	F	I	Es
rapide³ (F)	Schnellzug *m*	express train	—	treno direttissimo *m*	tren expreso *m*
rapidez (Es)	Schnelligkeit *f*	speed	rapidité *f*	velocità *f*	—
rapidité (F)	Schnelligkeit *f*	speed	—	velocità *f*	rapidez *f*
rapido (I)	rasch	quick	rapide	—	impulsivo(a)
rápido¹ (Es)	eilig	hurried	pressé(e)	frettoloso(a)	—
rápido² (Es)	schnell	fast	rapide	veloce	—
rapinare (I)	rauben	rob	voler	—	robar
rapport¹ (F)	Beziehung *f*	relation	—	relazione *f*	relación *f*
rapport² (F)	Bericht *m*	report	—	relazione *f*	relación *f*
rapporter (F)	zurückbringen	bring back	—	riportare	devolver
rapporto (I)	Beziehung *f*	relationship	relation *f*	—	relaciones *f pl*
rappresentante (I)	Vertreter *m*	representative	représentant *m*	—	representante
rappresentare¹ (I)	darstellen	represent	représenter	—	presentar
rappresentare² (I)	vertreten	represent	représenter	—	representar
rappresentazione (I)	Vorstellung *f*	performance	représentation *f*	—	representación *f*
rare (E)	selten	—	rare	raro(a)	raro(a)
rare (F)	selten	rare	—	raro(a)	raro(a)
rareté (F)	Seltenheit *f*	rarity	—	rarità *f*	rareza *f*
rareza (Es)	Seltenheit *f*	rarity	rareté *f*	rarità *f*	—
rarità (I)	Seltenheit *f*	rarity	rareté *f*	—	rareza *f*
rarity (E)	Seltenheit *f*	—	rareté *f*	rarità *f*	rareza *f*
raro (Es)	selten	rare	rare	raro(a)	—
raro (I)	selten	rare	rare	—	raro(a)
rasch (D)	—	quick	rapide	rapido(a)	impulsivo(a)
Rasen (D)	—	lawn	pelouse *f*	prato *m*	césped *m*
raser (F)	rasieren	shave	—	fare la barba	afeitar
rasgo (Es)	Merkmal *n*	characteristic	signe *m*	caratteristica *f*	—
Rasierapparat (D)	—	shaver	rasoir *m*	rasoio *m*	máquina de afeitar *f*
rasieren (D)	—	shave	raser	fare la barba	afeitar
rasoio (I)	Rasierapparat *m*	shaver	rasoir *m*	—	máquina de afeitar *f*
rasoir (F)	Rasierapparat *m*	shaver	—	rasoio *m*	máquina de afeitar *f*
raspberry (E)	Himbeere *f*	—	framboise *f*	lampone *m*	frambuesa *f*
rassasié (F)	satt	full	—	sazio(a)	satisfecho(a)
rastro (Es)	Flohmarkt *m*	fleamarket	marché aux puces *m*	mercato delle pulci *m*	—
Rat (D)	—	advice	conseil *m*	consiglio *m*	consejo *m*
rat (E)	Ratte *f*	—	rat *m*	ratto *m*	rata *f*
rat (F)	Ratte *f*	rat	—	ratto *m*	rata *f*
rata (Es)	Ratte *f*	rat	rat *m*	ratto *m*	—
rata (I)	Rate *f*	instalment	quote-part *f*	—	plazo *m*
Rate (D)	—	instalment	quote-part *f*	rata *f*	plazo *m*
rate (E)	Kurs *m*	—	cours *m*	corso *m*	curso *m*
raten¹ (D)	—	guess	deviner	indovinare	adivinar
raten² (D)	—	advise	conseiller	consigliare	aconsejar
Rathaus (D)	—	town hall	mairie *f*	municipio *m*	ayuntamiento *m*
rather (E)	lieber	—	mieux	piuttosto	más bien

	D	E	F	I	Es
rato (Es)	Weile *f*	while	moment *m*	momento *m*	—
ratón (Es)	Maus *f*	mouse	souris *f*	topo *m*	—
Rätsel (D)	—	riddle	devinette	enigma *m*	adivinanza *f*
Ratte (D)	—	rat	rat *m*	ratto *m*	rata *f*
ratto (I)	Ratte *f*	rat	rat *m*	—	rata *f*
rauben (D)	—	rob	voler	rapinare	robar
Rauch (D)	—	smoke	fumée *f*	fumo *m*	humo *m*
rauchen (D)	—	smoke	fumer	fumare	fumar
Raucher (D)	—	smoker	fumeur *m*	fumatore *m*	fumador *m*
rauh (D)	—	rough	rêche	ruvido(a)	rudo(a)
Raum (D)	—	room	pièce *f*	stanza *f*	habitación *f*
rauschen (D)	—	rush	bruire	mormorare	susurrar
raven (E)	Rabe *m*	—	corbeau *m*	corvo *m*	cuervo *m*
ravi (F)	entzückt	delighted	—	affascinato(a)	encantado(a)
ravissant (F)	entzückend	delightful	—	affascinante	encantador(a)
raw (E)	roh	—	cru(e)	crudo(a)	crudo(a)
ray (E)	Strahl *m*	—	rayon *m*	raggio *m*	rayo *m*
rayo[1] (Es)	Blitz *m*	lightning	éclair *m*	lampo *m*	—
rayo[2] (Es)	Strahl *m*	ray	rayon *m*	raggio *m*	—
rayon (F)	Strahl *m*	ray	—	raggio *m*	rayo *m*
razón (Es)	Verstand *m*	intelligence	intelligence *f*	intelligenza *f*	—
razonable (Es)	vernünftig	sensible	raisonnable	ragionevole	—
re (I)	König *m*	king	roi *m*	—	rey *m*
reacción (Es)	Reaktion *f*	reaction	réaction *f*	reazione *f*	—
reach (E)	erreichen	—	atteindre	raggiungere	alcanzar
reaction (E)	Reaktion *f*	—	réaction *f*	reazione *f*	reacción *f*
réaction (F)	Reaktion *f*	reaction	—	reazione *f*	reacción *f*
read (E)	lesen	—	lire	leggere	leer
ready[1] (E)	bereit	—	prêt(e)	pronto(a)	dispuesto(a)
ready[2] (E)	fertig	—	prêt(e)	pronto(a)	listo(a)
Reaktion (D)	—	reaction	réaction *f*	reazione *f*	reacción *f*
real (E)	wirklich	—	réel(le)	reale	real
real (Es)	wirklich	real	réel(le)	reale	—
reale (I)	wirklich	real	réel(le)	—	real
realidad (Es)	Wirklichkeit *f*	reality	réalité *f*	realtà *f*	—
réalisateur (F)	Regisseur *m*	director	—	regista *m*	director *m*
réaliser (F)	verwirklichen	realize	—	realizzare	llevar a cabo
réalité (F)	Wirklichkeit *f*	reality	—	realtà *f*	realidad *f*
reality (E)	Wirklichkeit *f*	—	réalité *f*	realtà *f*	realidad *f*
realize (E)	verwirklichen	—	réaliser	realizzare	llevar a cabo
realizzare (I)	verwirklichen	realize	réaliser	—	llevar a cabo
really (E)	tatsächlich	—	vraiment	realmente	realmente
realmente (Es)	tatsächlich	really	vraiment	realmente	—
realmente (I)	tatsächlich	really	vraiment	—	realmente
realtà (I)	Wirklichkeit *f*	reality	réalité *f*	—	realidad *f*
reason (E)	Grund *m*	—	raison *f*	causa *f*	causa *f*
reazione (I)	Reaktion *f*	reaction	réaction *f*	—	reacción *f*
rebaja[1] (Es)	Ermäßigung *f*	reduction	réduction *f*	riduzione *f*	—

	D	E	F	I	Es
rebaja² (Es)	Rabatt m	discount	rabais m	sconto m	—
rebajar (Es)	herabsetzen	lower	baisser	diminuire	—
rebellion (E)	Aufstand m	—	soulèvement m	insurrezione f	revuelta f
receipt (E)	Quittung f	—	quittance f	ricevuta f	recibo m
receive¹ (E)	aufnehmen	—	accueillir	accogliere	recibir
receive² (E)	empfangen	—	recevoir	ricevere	recibir
receive³ (E)	erhalten	—	recevoir	ricevere	obtener
receiver¹ (E)	Empfänger m	—	destinataire f	destinatario m	destinatario m
receiver² (E)	Hörer m	—	récepteur m	ricevitore m	auricular m
récemment (F)	kürzlich	lately	—	recente	reciente
recente (I)	kürzlich	lately	récemment	—	reciente
recentemente (I)	neulich	recently	l'autre jour	—	recientemente
recently (E)	neulich	—	l'autre jour	recentemente	recientemente
recepción (Es)	Empfang m	reception	réception f	ricerzione f	—
recepción de equipajes (Es)	Gepäckannahme f	luggage desk	enregistrement des bagages m	accettazione bagagli f	—
récepteur (F)	Hörer m	receiver	—	ricevitore m	auricular m
reception¹ (E)	Aufnahme f	—	accueil m	accoglienza f	acogida f
reception² (E)	Empfang m	—	réception f	ricezione f	recepción f
réception¹ (F)	Annahme f	acceptance	—	accettazione f	aceptación f
réception³ (F)	Empfang m	reception	—	ricezione f	recepción f
receta (Es)	Rezept n	recipe	recette f	ricetta f	—
recette (F)	Rezept n	recipe	—	ricetta f	receta f
recevoir¹ (F)	bekommen	get	—	ricevere	recibir
recevoir² (F)	erhalten	receive	—	ricevere	obtener
recevoir³ (F)	empfangen	receive	—	ricevere	recibir
rêche (F)	rauh	rough	—	ruvido(a)	rudo(a)
rechercher (F)	forschen	research	—	ricercare	investigar
rechnen (D)	—	calculate	calculer	fare i conti	calcular
Rechnung (D)	—	bill	facture f	fattura f	factura f
Recht (D)	—	right	droit m	diritto m	derecho m
rechts (D)	—	right	à droite	a destra	a la derecha
Rechtsanwalt (D)	—	lawyer	avocat m	avvocato m	abogado m
rechtzeitig (D)	—	in time	à temps	in tempo	a tiempo
recibir¹ (Es)	aufnehmen	receive	accueillir	accogliere	—
recibir² (Es)	bekommen	get	recevoir	ricevere	—
recibir³ (Es)	empfangen	receive	recevoir	ricevere	—
recibo (Es)	Quittung f	receipt	quittance f	ricevuta f	—
reciente (Es)	kürzlich	lately	récemment	recente	—
recientemente (Es)	neulich	recently	l'autre jour	recentemente	—
recinto (I)	Zaun m	fence	clôture f	—	valla f
recipe (E)	Rezept n	—	recette f	ricetta f	receta f
récipient¹ (F)	Behälter m	container	—	recipiente m	recipiente m
récipient² (F)	Gefäß n	container	—	recipiente m	recipiente m
recipiente¹ (Es)	Behälter m	container	récipient m	recipiente m	—
recipiente² (Es)	Gefäß n	container	récipient m	recipiente m	—
recipiente¹ (I)	Behälter m	container	récipient m	—	recipiente m
recipiente² (I)	Gefäß n	container	récipient m	—	recipiente m

	D	E	F	I	Es
recita (I)	Aufführung *f*	performance	représentation *f*	—	representación *f*
réclam (I)	Reklame *f*	advertisement	publicité *f*	—	anuncio *m*
reclamación[1] (Es)	Beschwerde *f*	complaint	plainte *f*	reclamo *m*	—
reclamación[2] (Es)	Reklamation *f*	complaint	réclamation *f*	reclamo *m*	—
reclamar (Es)	reklamieren	complain	plaindre de, se	reclamare	—
reclamare (I)	reklamieren	complain	plaindre de, se	—	reclamar
réclamation (F)	Reklamation *f*	complaint	—	reclamo *m*	reclamación *f*
reclamo[1] (I)	Beschwerde *f*	complaint	plainte *f*	—	reclamación *f*
reclamo[2] (I)	Reklamation *f*	complaint	réclamation *f*	—	reclamación *f*
recoger (Es)	abholen	pick up	aller chercher	andare a prendere	—
recognize (E)	erkennen	—	reconnaître	riconoscere	reconocer
recolectar (Es)	sammeln	collect	collecter	raccogliere	—
recomendación (Es)	Empfehlung *f*	recommendation	recommandation *f*	raccomandazione *f*	—
recomendar (Es)	empfehlen	recommend	recommander	raccomandare	—
recommandation (F)	Empfehlung *f*	recommendation	—	raccomandazione *f*	recomendación *f*
recommander (F)	empfehlen	recommend	—	raccomandare	recomendar
recommend (E)	empfehlen	—	recommander	raccomandare	recomendar
recommendation (E)	Empfehlung *f*		recommandation *f*	raccomandazione *f*	recomendación *f*
recompensa (Es)	Belohnung *f*	reward	récompense *f*	ricompensa *f*	—
recompensar (Es)	belohnen	reward	récompenser	premiare	—
récompense (F)	Belohnung *f*	reward	—	ricompensa *f*	recompensa *f*
récompenser (F)	belohnen	reward	—	premiare	recompensar
reconnaissant (F)	dankbar	grateful	—	grato(a)	agradecido(a)
reconnaître (F)	erkennen	recognize	—	riconoscere	reconocer
reconocer (Es)	erkennen	recognize	reconnaître	riconoscere	—
record[1] (E)	Platte *f*	—	disque *m*	disco *m*	disco *m*
record[2] (E)	Rekord *m*	—	record *m*	record *m*	record *m*
record[3] (E)	Schallplatte *f*	—	disque *m*	disco *m*	disco *m*
record (Es)	Rekord *m*	record	record *m*	record *m*	—
record (F)	Rekord *m*	record	—	record *m*	record *m*
record (I)	Rekord *m*	record	record *m*	—	record *m*
recordar (Es)	erinnern	remember	souvenir	ricordare	—
recorded delivery letter (E)	Einschreibebrief *m*	—	lettre recommandée *f*	lettera raccomandata *f*	carta certificada *f*
record player (E)	Plattenspieler *m*	—	tourne-disque *m*	giradischi *m*	tocadiscos *m*
recouvrer (F)	einkassieren	call in	—	incassare	cobrar
recouvrir (F)	beziehen	cover	—	ricoprire	tapizar
recover (E)	erholen, sich	—	reposer, se	rimettersi	aliviarse
recovery (E)	Erholung *f*	—	repos *m*	riposo *m*	descanso *m*
recruter (F)	einstellen	employ	—	assumere	emplear
red (E)	rot	—	rouge	rosso(a)	rojo(a)
red (Es)	Netz *n*	net	filet *m*	rete *f*	—
Rede (D)	—	speech	discours *m*	discorso *m*	discurso *m*
reden (D)	—	talk	parler	parlare	hablar
Red Indian (E)	Indianer *m*	—	Indien *m*	indiano *m*	indio *m*
redondo (Es)	rund	round	rond(e)	rotondo(a)	—
reduce (E)	verringern	—	diminuer	diminuire	disminuir
reducir (Es)	verkleinern	make smaller	réduire	ridurre	—

	D	E	F	I	Es
reduction (E)	Ermäßigung *f*	—	réduction *f*	riduzione *f*	rebaja *f*
réduction (F)	Ermäßigung *f*	reduction	—	riduzione *f*	rebaja *f*
réduire (F)	verkleinern	make smaller	—	ridurre	reducir
reel (E)	taumeln	—	tituber	barcollare	vacilar
réel (F)	wirklich	real	—	reale	real
reembolso (Es)	Nachnahme *f*	cash on delivery	remboursement *m*	contro assegno	—
referee (E)	Schiedsrichter *m*	—	arbitre *m*	arbitro *m*	árbitro *m*
réfléchi (F)	besonnen	sensible	—	avveduto(a)	sensato(a)
réfléchir (F)	nachdenken	think	—	riflettere	reflexionar
réfléchir à (F)	überlegen	consider	—	riflettere	pensar
reflexionar (Es)	nachdenken	think	réfléchir	riflettere	—
Reformhaus (D)	—	health food shop	magasin diététique *m*	negozio di prodotti dietetici *m*	tienda de productos dietéticos *f*
refresco (Es)	Erfrischung *f*	refreshment	rafraîchissement *m*	rinfresco *m*	—
refreshment (E)	Erfrischung *f*	—	rafraîchissement *m*	rinfresco *m*	refresco *m*
refrigerador (Es)	Eisschrank *m*	freezer	réfrigérateur *m*	frigorifero *m*	—
réfrigérateur[1] (F)	Eisschrank *m*	freezer	—	frigorifero *m*	refrigerador *m*
réfrigérateur[2] (F)	Kühlschrank *m*	fridge	—	frigorifero *m*	nevera *f*
refrigerio (Es)	Imbiß *m*	snack	casse-croûte *m*	spuntino *m*	—
refroidissement (F)	Erkältung *f*	cold	—	raffreddore *m*	catarro *m*
refus (F)	Absage *f*	refusal	—	risposta negativa *f*	negativa *f*
refusal (E)	Absage *f*	—	refus *m*	risposta negativa *f*	negativa *f*
refuse[1] (E)	verweigern	—	refuser	rifiutare	negar
refuse[2] (E)	weigern	—	refuser	rifiutare	resistirse
refuser[1] (F)	ablehnen	reject	—	rifiutare	rehusar
refuser[2] (F)	verweigern	refuse	—	rifiutare	negar
refuser[3] (F)	weigern	refuse	—	rifiutare	resistirse
Regal (D)	—	shelves	étagère *f*	scaffale *m*	estantería *f*
regalar (Es)	schenken	give	offrir	regalare	—
regalare (I)	schenken	give	offrir	—	regalar
regalo (Es)	Geschenk *n*	present	cadeau *m*	regalo *m*	—
regalo (I)	Geschenk *n*	present	cadeau *m*	—	regalo *m*
regar (Es)	gießen	water	arroser	annaffiare	—
regard (F)	Blick *m*	look	—	sguardo *m*	vista *f*
regarder[1] (F)	anschauen	look at	—	guardare	mirar
regarder[2] (F)	ansehen	look at	—	guardare	mirar
regarder[3] (F)	blicken	look	—	guardare	mirar
regarder[4] (F)	schauen	look	—	guardare	mirar
regarder[5] (F)	zusehen	watch	—	stare a guardare	mirar
regarder[6] (F)	zuschauen	watch	—	stare a guardare	mirar
regarder la télévision (F)	fernsehen	watch television	—	guardare la TV	ver la televisión
regelmäßig (D)	—	regular	régulier(-ière)	regolare	regular
regeln (D)	—	regulate	régler	regolare	dirigir
Regen (D)	—	rain	pluie *f*	pioggia *f*	lluvia *f*
Regenmantel (D)	—	raincoat	imperméable *m*	impermeabile *m*	impermeable *m*
Regenschirm (D)	—	umbrella	parapluie *m*	ombrello *m*	paraguas *m*
Regierung (D)	—	government	gouvernement *m*	governo *m*	gobierno *m*

	D	E	F	I	Es
regina (I)	Königin *f*	queen	reine *f*	—	reina *f*
region¹ (E)	Gebiet *n*	—	région *f*	regione *f*	zona *f*
region² (E)	Gegend *f*	—	région *f*	regione *f*	región *f*
región (Es)	Gegend *f*	region	région *f*	regione *f*	—
région¹ (F)	Gegend *f*	region	—	regione *f*	región *f*
région² (F)	Gebiet *n*	region	—	regione *f*	zona *f*
regione¹ (I)	Gegend *f*	region	région *f*	—	región *f*
regione² (I)	Gebiet *n*	region	région *f*	—	zona *f*
Regisseur (D)	—	director	réalisateur *m*	regista *m*	director *m*
regista (I)	Regisseur *m*	director	réalisateur *m*	—	director *m*
registrare (I)	verzeichnen	list	enregistrer	—	hacer una hista
registre (F)	Verzeichnis *n*	list	—	elenco *m*	lista *f*
regla (Es)	Lineal *n*	ruler	règle *f*	riga *f*	—
reglamento (Es)	Vorschrift *f*	regulation	règle *f*	norma *f*	—
règle¹ (F)	Lineal *n*	ruler	—	riga *f*	regla *f*
règle² (F)	Vorschrift *f*	regulation	—	norma *f*	reglamento *m*
régler¹ (F)	erledigen	take care of	—	sbrigare	acabar
régler² (F)	einstellen	adjust	—	regolare	ajustar
régler³ (F)	regeln	regulate	—	regolare	dirigir
regnen (D)	—	rain	pleuvoir	piovere	llover
régner (F)	herrschen	rule	—	dominare	mandar
regolare¹ (I)	einstellen	adjust	régler	—	ajustar
regolare² (I)	regeln	regulate	régler	—	dirigir
regolare³ (I)	regelmäßig	regular	régulier(-ière)	—	regular
regresar¹ (Es)	umkehren	turn back	retourner	ritornare	—
regresar² (Es)	zurückkommen	come back	revenir	ritornare	—
regreso (Es)	Rückkehr *f*	return	retour *m*	ritorno *m*	—
regret¹ (E)	bedauern	—	regretter	deplorare	lamentar
regret² (E)	bereuen	—	regretter	pentirsi	arrepentirse
regret³ (E)	Bedauern *n*	—	regret *m*	dispiacere *m*	compasión *f*
regret (F)	Bedauern *n*	regret	—	dispiacere *m*	compasión *f*
regretter¹ (F)	bedauern	regret	—	deplorare	lamentar
regretter² (F)	bereuen	regret	—	pentirsi	arrepentirse
regular¹ (E)	regelmäßig	—	régulier(-ière)	regolare	regular
regular² (E)	Stammgast *m*	—	habitué *m*	cliente abituale *m*	cliente habitual *m*
regular (Es)	regelmäßig	regular	régulier(-ière)	regolare	—
regulate (E)	regeln	—	régler	regolare	dirigir
regulation (E)	Vorschrift *f*	—	règle	norma *f*	reglamento *m*
régulier (F)	regelmäßig	regular	—	regolare	regular
Reh (D)	—	deer	chevreuil *m*	capriolo *m*	corzo *m*
rehusar (Es)	ablehnen	reject	refuser	rifiutare	—
reiben (D)	—	rub	frotter	sfregare	frotar
reich (D)	—	rich	riche	ricco(a)	rico(a)
reichen (D)	—	pass	passer	passare	alcanzar
reif (D)	—	ripe	mûr(e)	maturo(a)	maduro(a)
Reifen (D)	—	tyre	pneu *m*	pneumatico *m*	neumático *m*
Reihe (D)	—	row	rangée *f*	fila *f*	fila *f*
rein (D)	—	pure	pur(e)	puro(a)	puro(a)

	D	E	F	I	Es
rein (F)	Niere *f*	kidney	—	rene *m*	riñón *m*
reina (Es)	Königin *f*	queen	reine *f*	regina *f*	—
reine (F)	Königin *f*	queen	—	regina *f*	reina *f*
reinigen (D)	—	clean	nettoyer	pulire	limpiar
Reinigung (D)	—	cleaning	nettoyage *m*	pulitura *f*	limpieza *f*
reír (Es)	lachen	laugh	rire	ridere	—
reírse de (Es)	auslachen	laugh at	rire de qn	deridere	—
Reis (D)	—	rice	riz *m*	riso *m*	arroz *m*
Reise (D)	—	journey	voyage *m*	viaggio *m*	viaje *m*
Reisebüro (D)	—	travel agency	agence de voyages *f*	agenzia turistica *f*	oficina de viajes *f*
Reiseführer (D)	—	guide	guide *m*	guida *f*	guía *m*
reisen (D)	—	travel	voyager	viaggiare	viajar
Reisender (D)	—	traveller	voyageur *m*	viaggiatore *m*	viajero *m*
Reisepaß (D)	—	passport	passeport *m*	passaporto *m*	pasaporte *m*
Reiseroute (D)	—	route	itinéraire *m*	itinerario *m*	itinerario *m*
Reisescheck (D)	—	traveller's cheque	chèque de voyage *m*	assegno turistico *m*	cheque de viaje *m*
reißen (D)	—	tear	déchirer, se	strappare	desgarrarse
Reißverschluß (D)	—	zip	fermeture éclair *f*	chiusura lampo *f*	cremallera *f*
reiten (D)	—	ride	monter	cavalcare	cabalgar
reject (E)	ablehnen	—	refuser	rifiutare	rehusar
rejoice (E)	jubeln	—	pousser des cris de joie	giubilare	dar gritos de alegría
réjoui (F)	erfreut	delighted	—	lieto(a)	contento(a)
Reklamation (D)	—	complaint	réclamation *f*	reclamo *m*	reclamación *f*
Reklame (D)	—	advertisement	publicité *f*	réclame *f*	anuncio *m*
reklamieren (D)	—	complain	plaindre de, se	reclamare	reclamar
Rekord (D)	—	record	record *m*	record *m*	record *m*
relación¹ (Es)	Beziehung *f*	relation	rapport *m*	relazione *f*	—
relación² (Es)	Bericht *m*	report	rapport *m*	relazione *f*	—
relación³ (Es)	Verbindung *f*	connection	relation *f*	relazione *f*	—
relaciones (Es)	Beziehung *f*	relationship	relation *f*	rapporto *m*	—
related (E)	verwandt	—	parent(e)	imparentato(a)	emparentado(a)
relation (E)	Beziehung *f*	—	rapport *m*	relazione *f*	relación *f*
relation¹ (F)	Beziehung *f*	relationship	—	rapporto *m*	relaciones *f pl*
relation² (F)	Verbindung *f*	connection	—	relazione *f*	relación *f*
relationship (E)	Beziehung *f*	—	relation *f*	rapporto *m*	relaciones *f pl*
relative (E)	Verwandter *m*	—	parent *m*	parente *m*	pariente *m*
relazione¹ (I)	Bericht *m*	report	rapport *m*	—	relación *f*
relazione² (I)	Beziehung *f*	relation	rapport *m*	—	relación *f*
relazione³ (I)	Verbindung *f*	connection	relation *f*	—	relación *f*
release¹ (E)	entlassen	—	renvoyer	lizenziare	despedir
release² (E)	freilassen	—	libérer	mettere in libertà	poner en libertad
reliable (E)	zuverlässig	—	sûr(e)	affidabile	de confianza
relier (F)	verbinden	connect	—	unire	unir
religieuse (F)	Nonne *f*	nun	—	suora *f*	monja *f*
religieux (F)	religiös	religious	—	religioso(a)	religioso(a)
Religion (D)	—	religion	religion *f*	religione *f*	religión *f*

	D	E	F	I	Es
religion (E)	Religion *f*	—	religion *f*	religione *f*	religión *f*
religión (Es)	Religion *f*	religion	religion *f*	religione *f*	—
religion (F)	Religion *f*	religion	—	religione *f*	religión *f*
religione (I)	Religion *f*	religion	religion *f*	—	religión *f*
religiös (D)	—	religious	religieux(-euse)	religioso(a)	religioso(a)
religioso (I)	religiös	religious	religieux(-euse)	—	religioso(a)
religioso[1] (Es)	fromm	pious	pieux(-euse)	devoto(a)	—
religioso[2] (Es)	religiös	religious	religieux(-euse)	religioso(a)	—
religious (E)	religiös	—	religieux(-euse)	religioso(a)	religioso(a)
reloj (Es)	Uhr *f*	watch	montre *f*	orologio *m*	—
reluctantly (E)	ungern	—	de mauvaise grâce	malvolentieri	de mala gana
remar (Es)	rudern	row	ramer	remare	—
remare (I)	rudern	row	ramer	—	remar
remarquer[1] (F)	bemerken	notice	—	notare	darse cuenta
remarquer[2] (F)	merken	notice	—	accorgersi di	notar
remboursement (F)	Nachnahme *f*	cash on delivery	—	pagamento contro assegno	entrega contra reembolso *f*
rembourser (F)	zurückzahlen	pay back	—	rimborsare	devolver
remember[1] (E)	erinnern	—	souvenir	ricordare	recordar
remember[2] (E)	gedenken	—	souvenir de, se	ricordare	conmemorar
remerciement (F)	Dank *m*	thanks	—	ringraziamento *m*	agradecimiento *m*
remercier[1] (F)	bedanken	say thank you	—	ringraziare	agradecer algo
remercier[2] (F)	danken	thank	—	ringraziare	agradecer
remettre[1] (F)	übergeben	hand over	—	consegnare	transmitir
remettre[2] (F)	überbringen	deliver	—	portare	transmitir
remettre[3] (F)	verschieben	postpone	—	rimandare	aplazar
remitente (Es)	Absender *m*	sender	expéditeur *m*	mittente *m*	—
remo (Es)	Ruder *n*	oar	rame *f*	remo *m*	—
remo (I)	Ruder *n*	oar	rame *f*	—	remo *m*
remolcar (Es)	abschleppen	take in tow	remorquer	rimorchiare	—
remonte-pente (F)	Skilift *m*	skilift	—	sciovia *f*	telesilla *f*
remorquer (F)	abschleppen	take in tow	—	rimorchiare	remolcar
remove (E)	entfernen	—	éloigner	allontanare	quitar
remplacement (F)	Ersatz *m*	substitute	—	sostituzione *f*	sustitución *f*
remplacer (F)	ersetzen	replace	—	sostituire	sustituir
remplir[1] (F)	ausfüllen	fill in	—	riempire	llenar
remplir[2] (F)	erfüllen	fulfil	—	esaudire	conceder
remplir[3] (F)	füllen	fill	—	riempire	llenar
renard (F)	Fuchs *m*	fox	—	volpe *f*	zorro *m*
rencontre (F)	Treffen *n*	meeting	—	incontro *m*	encuentro *m*
rencontrer[1] (F)	begegnen	meet	—	incontrare	encontrar
rencontrer[2] (F)	treffen	meet	—	incontrare	encontrar
rendere possibile (I)	ermöglichen	make possible	rendre possible	—	facilitar
rendez-vous (F)	Verabredung *f*	date	—	appuntamento *m*	cita *f*
rendre[1] (F)	wiedergeben	return	—	restituire	devolver
rendre[2] (F)	zurückgeben	give back	—	restituire	devolver
rendre possible (F)	ermöglichen	make possible	—	rendere possibile	facilitar
rendre visite à (F)	besuchen	visit	—	andare a trovare	visitar

	D	E	F	I	Es
rene (I)	Niere *f*	kidney	rein *m*	—	riñón *m*
renew (E)	erneuern	—	rénover	rinnovare	renovar
renfermer (F)	einschließen	lock up	—	rinchiudere	encerrar
rennen (D)	—	run	courir	correre	correr
renoncer (F)	verzichten	forgo	—	rinunciare	renunciar
renovar¹ (Es)	erneuern	renew	rénover	rinnovare	—
renovar² (Es)	renovieren	renovate	rénover	rinnovare	—
renovate (E)	renovieren	—	rénover	rinnovare	renovar
rénover¹ (F)	erneuern	renew	—	rinnovare	renovar
rénover² (F)	renovieren	renovate	—	rinnovare	renovar
renovieren (D)	—	renovate	rénover	rinnovare	renovar
renseignement (F)	Auskunft *f*	information	—	informazione *f*	información *f*
renseigner, se (F)	erkundigen, sich	inquire	—	informarsi	informarse
rent¹ (E)	mieten	—	louer	affittare	alquilar
rent² (E)	Miete *f*	—	loyer *m*	affitto *m*	alquiler *m*
rent³ (E)	vermieten	—	louer	affittare	alquilar
Rente (D)	—	pension	retraite *f*	pensione *f*	pensión *f*
Rentner (D)	—	pensioner	retraité *m*	pensionato *m*	pensionista *m*
renunciar¹ (Es)	aufgeben	give up	abandonner	rinunciare	—
renunciar² (Es)	verzichten	forgo	renoncer	rinunciare	—
renverser (F)	umschmeißen	throw over	—	rovesciare	derribar
renvoi (F)	Hinweis *m*	hint	—	indicazione *f*	indicación *f*
renvoyer (F)	entlassen	release	—	licenziare	despedir
repair¹ (E)	reparieren	—	réparer	riparare	reparar
repair² (E)	Reparatur *f*	—	réparation *f*	riparazione *f*	reparación *f*
repair shop (E)	Autowerkstatt *f*	—	atelier de réparation d'autos *m*	autofficina *f* reparaciones *m*	taller de
reparación (Es)	Reparatur *f*	repair	réparation *f*	riparazione *f*	—
reparar (Es)	reparieren	repair	réparer	riparare	—
réparation (F)	Reparatur *f*	repair	—	riparazione *f*	reparación *f*
Reparatur (D)	—	repair	réparation *f*	riparazione *f*	reparación *f*
réparer¹ (F)	reparieren	repair	—	riparare	reparar
réparer² (F)	wiedergutmachen	make up for	—	riparare	subsanar
reparieren (D)	—	repair	réparer	riparare	reparar
repartir (Es)	verteilen	distribute	distribuer	distribuire	—
reparto (I)	Abteilung *f*	department	section *f*	—	departamento *m*
repas¹ (F)	Essen *n*	food	—	alimentazione *f*	comida *f*
repas² (F)	Mahlzeit *f*	meal	—	pasto *m*	comida *f*
repasser (F)	bügeln	iron	—	stirare	planchar
repeat (E)	wiederholen	—	répéter	ripetere	repetir
répéter (F)	wiederholen	repeat	—	ripetere	repetir
repetir (Es)	wiederholen	repeat	répéter	ripetere	—
replace (E)	ersetzen	—	remplacer	sostituire	sustituir
répondre (F)	antworten	answer	—	rispondere	responder
répondre à (F)	beantworten	answer	—	rispondere a	responder a
répondre par l'affirmative à (F)	bejahen	agree with	—	approvare	afirmar
réponse (F)	Antwort *f*	answer	—	risposta *f*	respuesta *f*
report¹ (E)	berichten	—	faire un rapport	riferire	informar

	D	E	F	I	Es
report² (E)	Bericht *m*	—	rapport *m*	relazione *f*	relación *f*
report³ (E)	melden	—	annoncer	annunciare	declarar
report⁴ (E)	Meldung *f*	—	annonce *f*	annuncio *m*	aviso *m*
report⁵ (E)	Zeugnis *n*	—	bulletin *m*	pagella *f*	diploma *m*
repos (F)	Erholung *f*	recovery	—	riposo *m*	descanso *m*
reposer, se¹ (F)	ausruhen	rest	—	riposare	descansar
reposer, se² (F)	erholen, sich	recover	—	rimettersi	recuperarse
reposer, se³ (F)	ruhen	rest	—	riposare	descansar
repoussant (F)	widerlich	disgusting	—	ripugnante	repugnante
reprendre (F)	übernehmen	take over	—	accettare	tomar posesión de
represent (E)	vertreten	—	représenter	rappresentare	representar
representación¹ (Es)	Aufführung *f*	performance	représentation *f*	recita *f*	—
representación² (Es)	Veranstaltung *f*	event	manifestation *f*	manifestazione *f*	—
representación³ (Es)	Vorstellung *f*	performance	représentation *f*	rappresentazione *f*	—
représentant (F)	Vertreter *m*	representative	—	rappresentante *m*	representante
representante (Es)	Vertreter *m*	representative	représentant *m*	rappresentante *m*	—
representar (Es)	vertreten	represent	représenter	rappresentare	—
représentation¹ (F)	Aufführung *f*	performance	—	recita *f*	representación *f*
représentation² (F)	Vorstellung *f*	performance	—	rappresentazione *f*	representación *f*
representative (E)	Vertreter *m*	—	représentant *m*	rappresentante *m*	representante
représenter (F)	darstellen	represent	—	rappresentare	representar
reprocher (F)	vorwerfen	blame	—	rimproverare	echar en cara
repugnante (Es)	widerlich	disgusting	repoussant(e)	ripugnante	—
requesón (Es)	Quark *m*	curd cheese	fromage blanc *m*	ricotta *f*	—
request¹ (E)	anfordern	—	demander	esigere	pedir
request² (E)	bitten	—	demander	pregare	rogar
request³ (E)	Bitte *f*	—	demande *f*	domanda *f*	ruego *m*
requin (F)	Hai *m*	shark	—	pescecane *m*	tiburón *m*
resbalar (Es)	rutschen	slide	glisser	scivolare	—
research (E)	forschen	—	rechercher	ricercare	investigar
resemble (E)	ähneln	—	ressembler	assomigliare	parecer
reserva (Es)	Vorbehalt *m*	reservation	réserve *f*	riserva *f*	—
reservar¹ (Es)	buchen	book	retenir	prenotare	—
reservar² (Es)	reservieren	reserve	réserver	riservare	—
reservation (E)	Vorbehalt *m*	—	réserve *f*	riserva *f*	reserva *f*
reserve (E)	reservieren	—	réserver	riservare	reservar
réserve (F)	Vorbehalt *m*	reservation	—	riserva *f*	reserva *f*
réserver¹ (F)	reservieren	reserve	—	riservare	reservar
réserver² (F)	vorbestellen	book	—	prenotare	hacer reservar
réserves (F)	Vorrat *m*	stock	—	scorte *f pl*	provisión *f*
reservieren (D)	—	reserve	réserver	riservare	reservar
resfriado (Es)	Schnupfen *m*	cold	rhume *m*	raffreddore *m*	—
residencia (Es)	Wohnort *m*	domicile	domicile *m*	residenza *f*	—
residenza (I)	Wohnort *m*	domicile	domicile *m*	—	residencia *f*
résilier (F)	kündigen	sack	—	licenziare	despedir
resistance (E)	Widerstand *m*	—	résistance *f*	resistenza *f*	resistencia *f*
résistance (F)	Widerstand *m*	resistance	—	resistenza *f*	resistencia *f*
résistant (F)	haltbar	durable	—	durevole	duradero

	D	E	F	I	Es
resistencia (Es)	Widerstand m	resistance	résistance f	resistenza f	—
resistenza (I)	Widerstand m	resistance	résistance f	—	resistencia f
resistirse (Es)	weigern	refuse	refuser	rifiutare	—
résoudre (F)	lösen	solve	—	sciogliere	desatar
respirar (Es)	atmen	breathe	respirer	respirare	—
respirare (I)	atmen	breathe	respirer	—	respirar
respiration (F)	Atem m	breath	—	fiato m	respiro m
respirer (F)	atmen	breathe	—	respirare	respirar
respiro (Es)	Atem m	breath	respiration f	fiato m	—
responder (Es)	antworten	answer	répondre	rispondere	—
responder a (Es)	beantworten	answer	répondre à	rispondere a	—
responsabile (I)	verantwortlich	responsible	responsable	—	responsable
responsable (Es)	verantwortlich	responsible	responsable	responsabile	—
responsable (F)	verantwortlich	responsible	—	responsabile	responsable
responsible (E)	verantwortlich	—	responsible	responsabile	responsable
respuesta (Es)	Antwort f	answer	réponse f	risposta f	—
ressembler (F)	ähneln	resemble	—	assomigliare	parecer
Rest (D)	—	rest	reste m	resto m	resto m
rest¹ (E)	ausruhen	—	reposer, se	riposare	descansar
rest² (E)	ruhen	—	reposer, se	riposare	descansar
rest³ (E)	Rest m	—	reste m	resto m	resto m
restablecimiento (Es)	Besserung f	improvement	amélioration f	miglioramento m	—
restant (F)	übrig	left	—	restante	restante
restante (Es)	übrig	left	restant(e)	restante	—
restante (I)	übrig	left	restant(e)	—	restante
restar (Es)	abziehen	subtract	retirer	sottrarre	—
restare qui (I)	hierbleiben	stay here	rester	—	quedarse aquí
Restaurant (D)	—	restaurant	restaurant m	ristorante m	restaurante m
restaurant (E)	Restaurant n	—	restaurant m	ristorante m	restaurante m
restaurant¹ (F)	Lokal n	pub	—	locale m	local m
restaurant² (F)	Restaurant n	restaurant	—	ristorante m	restaurante m
restaurante¹ (Es)	Restaurant n	restaurant	restaurant m	ristorante m	—
restaurante² (Es)	Wirtshaus n	inn	auberge f	osteria f	—
reste (F)	Rest m	rest	—	resto m	resto m
rester¹ (F)	bleiben	stay	—	rimanere	quedarse
rester² (F)	hierbleiben	stay here	—	restare qui	quedarse aquí
rester³ (F)	übrigbleiben	be left	—	avanzare	quedar
restituire (I)	zurückgeben	give back	rendre	—	devolver
restless (E)	unruhig	—	inquiet(-ète)	inquieto(a)	intranquilo(a)
restlos (D)	—	completely	complètement	interamente	totalmente
resto (Es)	Rest m	rest	reste m	resto m	—
resto (I)	Rest m	rest	reste m	—	resto m
result (E)	Ergebnis n	—	résultat m	risultato m	resultado m
resultado (Es)	Ergebnis n	result	résultat m	risultato m	—
résultat (F)	Ergebnis n	result	—	risultato m	resultado m
retard (F)	Verspätung f	delay	—	ritardo m	retraso m
rete (I)	Netz n	net	filet m	—	red f

	D	E	F	I	Es
retener¹ (Es)	behalten	keep	garder	tenere	—
retener² (Es)	einbehalten	keep	retenir	trattenere	—
retenir¹ (F)	buchen	book	—	prenotare	reservar
retenir² (F)	einbehalten	keep	—	trattenere	retener
retirar¹ (Es)	zurücknehmen	take back	retirer	prendere indietro	—
retirar² (Es)	zurückziehen	withdraw	retirer	ritirare	—
retire (E)	zurücktreten	—	démissionner	dare le dimissioni	dimitir
retirement (E)	Ruhestand m	—	retraite f	pensione f	descanso m
retirer¹ (F)	abziehen	subtract	—	sottrarre	restar
retirer² (F)	zurückziehen	withdraw	—	ritirare	retirar
retirer³ (F)	zurücknehmen	take back	—	prendere indietro	retirar
retour (F)	Rückkehr f	return	—	ritorno m	regreso m
retourner¹ (F)	umkehren	turn back	—	ritornare	regresar
retourner² (F)	zurückfahren	drive back	—	tornare indietro	retroceder
retract (E)	widerrufen	—	démentir	revocare	revocación f
retraite¹ (F)	Rente f	pension	—	pensione f	pensión f
retraite² (F)	Ruhestand m	retirement	—	pensione f	descanso m
retraité (F)	Rentner m	pensioner	—	pensionato m	pensionista m
retraso (Es)	Verspätung f	delay	retard m	ritardo m	—
retrete (Es)	Klosett n	lavatory	cabinets m pl	gabinetto m	—
retroceder (Es)	zurückfahren	drive back	retourner	tornare indietro	—
retrouver, se (F)	zurechtfinden, sich	find one's way	—	orientarsi	orientarse
retten (D)	—	save	sauver	salvare	salvar
Rettungsring (D)	—	lifebelt	bouée de sauvetage f	salvagente m	salvavidas m
return¹ (E)	Rückkehr f	—	retour m	ritorno m	regreso m
return² (E)	wiedergeben	—	rendre	restituire	devolver
return³ (E)	zurückkehren	—	revenir	ritornare	volver
reunión (Es)	Sitzung f	meeting	séance f	seduta f	—
réussir (F)	gelingen	succeed	—	riuscire	acertar
réussir à faire (F)	schaffen	create	—	creare	crear
rêve (F)	Traum m	dream	—	sogno m	sueño m
réveil (F)	Wecker m	alarm clock	—	sveglia f	despertador m
réveillé (F)	wach	awake	—	sveglio(a)	despierto(a)
réveiller¹ (F)	aufwecken	wake up	—	svegliare	despertar
réveiller² (F)	wecken	wake (up)	—	svegliare	despertar
réveiller, se¹ (F)	aufwachen	wake up	—	svegliarsi	despertarse
réveiller, se² (F)	erwachen	wake up	—	svegliarsi	despertar
revenge (E)	Rache f	—	vengeance f	vendetta f	venganza f
revenir¹ (F)	wiederkommen	come back	—	ritornare	venir de nuevo
revenir² (F)	zurückkommen	come back	—	ritornare	regresar
revenir³ (F)	zurückkehren	return	—	ritornare	volver
reventar (Es)	platzen	burst	éclater	scoppiare	—
revenu (F)	Einkommen n	income	—	entrate f pl	ingresos m pl
revenus (F)	Verdienst n	income	—	guadagno m	ganancia f
rêver (F)	träumen	dream	—	sognare	soñar
réverbère (F)	Laterne f	street light	—	lampione m	farola f
Revier (D)	—	district	district m	distretto m	distrito m

	D	E	F	I	Es
revisor (Es)	Schaffner *m*	conductor	contrôleur *m*	bigliettaio *m*	—
revista¹ (Es)	Illustrierte *f*	illustrated magazine	illustré *m*	rivista *f*	—
revista² (Es)	Zeitschrift *f*	magazine	revue *f*	rivista *f*	—
revocación (Es)	widerrufen	retract	démentir	revocare	—
revocare (I)	widerrufen	retract	démentir	—	revocación *f*
revoir (F)	wiedersehen	see again	—	rivedere	volver a ver
révolté (F)	empört	indignant	—	indignato(a)	indignado(a)
revolución (Es)	Revolution *f*	revolution	révolution *f*	rivoluzione *f*	—
Revolution (D)	—	revolution	révolution *f*	rivoluzione *f*	revolución *f*
revolution (E)	Revolution *f*	—	révolution *f*	rivoluzione *f*	revolución *f*
révolution (F)	Revolution *f*	revolution	—	rivoluzione *f*	revolución *f*
revolver (Es)	wühlen	scrabble	fouiller	rovistare	—
revue (F)	Zeitschrift *f*	magazine	—	rivista *f*	revista *f*
revuelta (Es)	Aufstand *m*	rebellion	soulèvement *m*	insurrezione *f*	—
reward¹ (E)	belohnen	—	récompenser	premiare	recompensar
reward² (E)	Belohnung *f*	—	récompense *f*	ricompensa *f*	recompensa *f*
rey (Es)	König *m*	king	roi *m*	re *m*	—
rezar (Es)	beten	pray	prier	pregare	—
rez-de-chaussée¹ (F)	Parterre *n*	ground floor	—	pianterreno *m*	planta baja *f*
rez-de-chaussée² (F)	Erdgeschoß *n*	ground floor	—	pianterreno *m*	piso bajo *m*
Rezept¹ (D)	—	recipe	recette *f*	ricetta *f*	receta *f*
Rezept² (D)	—	prescription	ordonnance *f*	prescrizione *f*	prescripción médica *f*
rhume (F)	Schnupfen *m*	cold	—	raffreddore *m*	resfriado *m*
rib (E)	Rippe *f*	—	côte *f*	costola *f*	costilla *f*
ribbon (E)	Band *n*	—	bandeau *m*	nastro *m*	cinta *f*
ribes (I)	Johannisbeere *f*	currant	groseille *f*	—	grosella *f*
ricatto (I)	Erpressung *f*	blackmail	chantage *m*	—	chantaje *m*
riccio (I)	Locke *f*	curl	boucle *f*	—	rizo *m*
ricco (I)	reich	rich	riche	—	rico(a)
rice (E)	Reis *m*	—	riz	riso *m*	arroz *m*
ricercare (I)	forschen	research	rechercher	—	investigar
ricetta (I)	Rezept *n*	recipe	recette *f*	—	receta *f*
ricevere¹ (I)	bekommen	get	recevoir	—	recibir
ricevere² (I)	empfangen	receive	recevoir	—	recibir
ricevere³ (I)	erhalten	receive	recevoir	—	obtener
ricevitore (I)	Hörer *m*	receiver	récepteur *m*	—	auricular *m*
ricevuta (I)	Quittung *f*	receipt	quittance *f*	—	recibo *m*
ricezione (I)	Empfang *m*	reception	réception *f*	—	recepción *f*
rich (E)	reich	—	riche	ricco(a)	rico(a)
riche (F)	reich	rich	—	ricco(a)	rico(a)
richiedere (I)	verlangen	demand	demander	—	exigir
richten (D)	—	direct to	diriger	dirigere	dirigir
Richter (D)	—	judge	juge *m*	giudice *m*	juez *m*
richtig (D)	—	correct	juste	giusto(a)	correcto(a)
Richtung (D)	—	direction	direction *f*	direzione *f*	dirección *f*
rico (Es)	reich	rich	riche	ricco(a)	—
ricompensa (I)	Belohnung *f*	reward	récompense *f*	—	recompensa *f*

	D	E	F	I	Es
riconoscere (I)	erkennen	recognize	reconnaître	—	reconocer
ricoprire (I)	beziehen	cover	recouvrir	—	tapizar
ricordare[1] (I)	erinnern	remember	souvenir	—	recordar
ricordare[2] (I)	gedenken	remember	souvenir de, se	—	conmemorar
ricordo[1] (I)	Andenken n	souvenir	souvenir m	—	recuerdo m
ricordo[2] (I)	Erinnerung f	memory	souvenir m	—	memoria f
ricotta (I)	Quark m	curd cheese	fromage blanc m	—	requesón m
ridare (I)	wiedergeben	return	rendre	—	devolver
riddle (E)	Rätsel n	—	devinette	enigma m	adivinanza f
ride (E)	reiten	—	monter	cavalcare	cabalgar
rideau[1] (F)	Gardine f	curtain	—	tenda f	cortina f
rideau[2] (F)	Vorhang m	curtain	—	tenda f	cortina f
ridere (I)	lachen	laugh	rire	—	reír
ridicolo (I)	lächerlich	ridiculous	ridicule	—	ridículo(a)
ridicule (F)	lächerlich	ridiculous	—	ridicolo(a)	ridículo(a)
ridículo (Es)	lächerlich	ridiculous	ridicule	ridicolo(a)	—
ridiculous (E)	lächerlich	—	ridicule	ridicolo(a)	ridículo(a)
ridurre (I)	verkleinern	make smaller	réduire	—	reducir
riduzione (I)	Ermäßigung f	reduction	réduction f	—	rebaja f
riechen (D)	—	smell	sentir	sentire	oler
Riegel (D)	—	bar	verrou m	catenaccio m	cerrojo m
Riemen (D)	—	strap	courroie f	cinghia f	correa f
riempire[1] (I)	ausfüllen	fill in	remplir	—	llenar
riempire[2] (I)	füllen	fill	remplir	—	llenar
rien (F)	nichts	nothing	—	niente	nada
riesgo (Es)	Risiko n	risk	risque m	rischio m	—
riesig (D)	—	huge	énorme	enorme	enorme
riferire[1] (I)	ausrichten	pass on a message	transmettre	—	comunicar
riferire[2] (I)	berichten	report	faire un rapport	—	informar
rifiutare[1] (I)	ablehnen	reject	refuser	—	rehusar
rifiutare[2] (I)	verweigern	refuse	refuser	—	negar
rifiutare[3] (I)	weigern	refuse	refuser	—	resistirse
riflettere[1] (I)	nachdenken	think	réfléchir	—	reflexionar
riflettere[2] (I)	überlegen	consider	réfléchir à	—	pensar
riga[1] (I)	Lineal n	ruler	règle f	—	regla f
riga[2] (I)	Zeile f	line	ligne f	—	línea f
right[1] (E)	rechts	—	à droite	a destra	a la derecha
right[2] (E)	Recht n	—	droit m	diritto m	derecho m
right of way (E)	Vorfahrt f	—	priorité f	precedenza f	preferencia f
rigid (E)	starr	—	rigide	rigido(a)	fijo(a)
rigide[1] (F)	starr	rigid	—	rigido(a)	fijo(a)
rigide[2] (F)	steif	stiff	—	rigido(a)	rígido(a)
rigido[1] (I)	starr	rigid	rigide	—	fijo(a)
rigido[2] (I)	steif	stiff	rigide	—	rígido(a)
rígido (Es)	steif	stiff	rigide	rigido(a)	—
riguardare (I)	betreffen	concern	concerner	—	concernir
riguroso (Es)	streng	strict	sévère	severo(a)	—

	D	E	F	I	Es
rilevante (I)	erheblich	considerable	considérable	—	considerable
rimandare (I)	verschieben	postpone	remettre	—	aplazar
rimanere (I)	bleiben	stay	rester	—	quedarse
rimborsare (I)	zurückzahlen	pay back	rembourser	—	devolver
rimettersi (I)	erholen, sich	recover	reposer, se	—	aliviarse
rimorchiare (I)	abschleppen	take in tow	remorquer	—	remolcar
rimproverare (I)	vorwerfen	blame	reprocher	—	echar en cara
rinchiudere (I)	einschließen	lock up	renfermer	—	encerrar
rincón (Es)	Winkel m	corner	coin m	cantuccio m	—
Rind (D)	—	cow	bœuf m	manzo m	buey m
Rindfleisch (D)	—	beef	viande de bœuf f	carne di manzo f	carne de vaca f
rinfresco (I)	Erfrischung f	refreshment	rafraîchissement m	—	refresco m
Ring (D)	—	ring	bague f	anello m	sortija f
ring¹ (E)	läuten	—	sonner	suonare	tocar
ring² (E)	Ring m	—	bague f	anello m	sortija f
ringraziare¹ (I)	bedanken	say thank you	remercier	—	agradecer algo
ringraziare² (I)	danken	thank	remercier	—	agradecer
ring the bell (E)	klingeln	—	sonner	suonare	tocar el timbre
ring up (E)	anrufen	—	téléphoner	telefonare	llamar por teléfono
rinnovare¹ (I)	erneuern	renew	rénover	—	renovar
rinnovare² (I)	renovieren	renovate	rénover	—	renovar
riñón (Es)	Niere f	kidney	rein m	rene m	—
rinse (E)	spülen	—	rincer	sciacquare	lavar
rinunciare¹ (I)	aufgeben	give up	abandonner	—	renunciar
rinunciare² (I)	verzichten	forgo	renoncer	—	renunciar
río (Es)	Fluß m	river	fleuve m	fiume m	—
rip (E)	zerreißen	—	déchirer	strappare	romper
riparare¹ (I)	reparieren	repair	réparer	—	reparar
riparare² (I)	wiedergutmachen	make up for	réparer	—	subsanar
riparazione (I)	Reparatur f	repair	réparation f	—	reparación f
ripe (E)	reif	—	mûr(e)	maturo(a)	maduro(a)
ripetere (I)	wiederholen	repeat	répéter	—	repetir
ripido (I)	steil	steep	raide	—	inclinado(a)
riportare (I)	zurückbringen	bring back	rapporter	—	devolver
riporto (I)	Umbuchung f	alteration	transfert m	—	cambio m
riposare¹ (I)	ausruhen	rest	reposer, se	—	descansar
riposare² (I)	ruhen	rest	reposer, se	—	descansar
riposo (I)	Erholung f	recovery	repos m	—	descanso m
Rippe (D)	—	rib	côte f	costola f	costilla f
ripugnante (I)	widerlich	disgusting	repoussant(e)	—	repugnante
rire¹ (F)	lachen	laugh	—	ridere	reír
rire² (F)	Lachen n	laughter	—	riso m	risa f
rire de qn (F)	auslachen	laugh at	—	deridere	reírse de
rires (F)	Gelächter n	laughter	—	risata f	risa f

	D	E	F	I	Es
risa¹ (Es)	Gelächter n	laughter	rires m pl	risata f	—
risa² (Es)	Lachen n	laughter	rire m	riso m	—
risata (I)	Gelächter n	laughter	rires m pl	—	risa f
riscaldamento (I)	Heizung f	heating	chauffage m	—	calefacción f
riscaldamento centrale (I)	Zentralheizung f	central heating	chauffage central m	—	calefacción central f
riscaldare¹ (I)	heizen	heat	chauffer	—	calentar
riscaldare² (I)	wärmen	warm	chauffer	—	calentar
rischiare (I)	riskieren	risk	risquer	—	arriesgar
rischio (I)	Risiko n	risk	risque m	—	riesgo m
riserva (I)	Vorbehalt m	reservation	réserve f	—	reserva f
riservare (I)	reservieren	reserve	réserver	—	reservar
Risiko (D)	—	risk	risque m	rischio m	riesgo m
risk¹ (E)	riskieren	—	risquer	rischiare	arriesgar
risk² (E)	Risiko n	—	risque m	rischio m	riesgo m
riskieren (D)	—	risk	risquer	rischiare	arriesgar
riso¹ (I)	Lachen n	laughter	rire m	—	risa f
riso² (I)	Reis m	rice	riz m	—	arroz m
risparmiare (I)	sparen	save	économiser	—	ahorrar
rispondere (I)	antworten	answer	répondre	—	responder
rispondere a (I)	beantworten	answer	répondre à	—	responder a
risposta (I)	Antwort f	answer	réponse f	—	respuesta f
risposta negativa (I)	Absage f	refusal	refus m	—	negativa f
risque (F)	Risiko n	risk	—	rischio m	riesgo m
risquer (F)	riskieren	risk	—	rischiare	arriesgar
ristorante (I)	Restaurant n	restaurant	restaurant m	—	restaurante m
risultato (I)	Ergebnis n	result	résultat m	—	resultado m
ritardare (I)	verspäten	be late	être en retard	—	llevar retraso
ritardo (I)	Verspätung f	delay	retard m	—	retraso m
ritirare (I)	zurückziehen	withdraw	retirer	—	retirar
ritornare¹ (I)	umkehren	turn back	retourner	—	regresar
ritornare² (I)	wiederkommen	come back	revenir	—	venir de nuevo
ritornare³ (I)	zurückkommen	come back	revenir	—	regresar
ritornare⁴ (I)	zurückkehren	return	revenir	—	volver
ritorno (I)	Rückkehr f	return	retour m	—	regreso m
riuscire (I)	gelingen	succeed	réussir	—	acertar
riva (I)	Ufer n	shore	bord m	—	orilla f
rivedere (I)	wiedersehen	see again	revoir	—	volver a ver
river (E)	Fluß m	—	fleuve m	fiume m	río m
rivista¹ (I)	Illustrierte f	picture magazine	illustré m	—	revista
rivista² (I)	Zeitschrift f	magazine	revue f	—	revista f
rivoluzione (I)	Revolution f	revolution	révolution f	—	revolución f
riz (F)	Reis m	rice	—	riso m	arroz m
rizo (Es)	Locke f	curl	boucle f	riccio m	—

	D	E	F	I	Es
roadway (E)	Fahrbahn *f*	—	chaussée *f*	carreggiata *f*	calzada *f*
roast[1] (E)	braten	—	rôtir	arrostire	asar
roast[2] (E)	Braten *m*	—	rôti *m*	arrosto *m*	asado *m*
roast[3] (E)	rösten	—	griller	abbrustolire	tostar
rob (E)	rauben	—	voler	rapinare	robar
robar[1] (Es)	einbrechen	break in	cambrioler	rubare	—
robar[2] (Es)	rauben	rob	voler	rapinare	—
robar[3] (Es)	stehlen	steal	voler	rubare	—
Robbe (D)	—	seal	phoque *m*	foca *f*	foca *f*
robe (F)	Kleid *n*	dress	—	vestito *m*	vestido *m*
rocca (I)	Burg *f*	castle	château *m*	—	fortaleza *f*
Rock (D)	—	skirt	jupe *f*	gonna *f*	falda *f*
rodar (Es)	rollen	roll	rouler	ruotare	—
rodear (Es)	umgeben	surround	entourer	circondare	—
rodeo (Es)	Umweg *m*	detour	détour *m*	deviazione *f*	—
rodilla (Es)	Knie *n*	knee	genou *m*	ginocchio *m*	—
rogar (Es)	bitten	request	demander	pregare	—
roh (D)	—	raw	cru(e)	crudo(a)	crudo(a)
Rohr (D)	—	tube	tube *m*	tubo *m*	tubo *m*
roi (F)	König *m*	king	—	re *m*	rey *m*
rojo (Es)	rot	red	rouge	rosso(a)	—
roll[1] (E)	Brötchen *n*	—	petit pain *m*	panino *m*	panecillo *m*
roll[2] (E)	rollen	—	rouler	ruotare	rodar
rollen (D)	—	roll	rouler	ruotare	rodar
Rolltreppe (D)	—	escalator	escalier roulant *m*	scala mobile *f*	escalera mecánica *f*
Roman (D)	—	novel	roman *m*	romanzo *m*	novela *f*
roman (F)	Roman *m*	novel	—	romanzo *m*	novela *f*
romanzo (I)	Roman *m*	novel	roman *m*	—	novela *f*
romper[1] (Es)	brechen	break	casser	rompere	—
romper[2] (Es)	einschlagen	smash	casser	rompere	—
romper[3] (Es)	zerbrechen	break	casser	rompere	—
romper[4] (Es)	zerreißen	rip	déchirer	strappare	—
rompere[1] (I)	brechen	break	casser	—	romper
rompere[2] (I)	einschlagen	smash	casser	—	romper
rompere[3] (I)	zerbrechen	break	casser	—	romper
roncar (Es)	schnarchen	snore	ronfler	russare	—
rond (F)	rund	round	—	rotondo(a)	redondo(a)
ronfler (F)	schnarchen	snore	—	russare	roncar
röntgen (D)	—	X-ray	radiographier	fare una radiografia	radiografiar
roof (E)	Dach *n*	—	toit *m*	tetto *m*	techo *m*
room[1] (E)	Raum *m*	—	pièce *f*	stanza *f*	habitación *f*
room[2] (E)	Zimmer *n*	—	chambre *f*	camera *f*	habitación *f*
root (E)	Wurzel *f*	—	racine *f*	radice *f*	raíz *f*

	D	E	F	I	Es
ropa (Es)	Wäsche f	washing	linge m	biancheria f	—
ropa interior (Es)	Unterwäsche f	underwear	sous-vêtements m pl	biancheria intima f	—
rope[1] (E)	Strick m	—	corde f	corda f	cuerda f
rope[2] (E)	Seil n	—	corde f	fune f	soga f
rosa (D)	—	pink	rose	rosa	de color rosa
rosa (Es)	Rose f	rose	rose f	rosa f	—
rosa[1] (I)	rosa	pink	rose	—	de color rosa
rosa[2] (I)	Rose f	rose	rose f	—	rosa f
Rose (D)	—	rose	rose f	rosa f	rosa f
rose (E)	Rose f	—	rose f	rosa f	rosa f
rose[1] (F)	rosa	pink	—	rosa	de color rosa
rose[2] (F)	Rose f	rose	—	rosa f	rosa f
rosso (I)	rot	red	rouge	—	rojo(a)
rosten (D)	—	rust	rouiller	arrugginire	oxidarse
rösten (D)	—	roast	griller	abbrustolire	tostar
rostig (D)	—	rusty	rouillé(e)	arrugginito(a)	oxidado(a)
rot (D)	—	red	rouge	rosso	rojo(a)
rôti[1] (F)	Braten m	roast	—	arrosto m	asado m
rôti[2] (F)	gebraten	fried	—	arrosto(a)	asado(a)
rôtir (F)	braten	roast	—	arrostire	asar
roto (Es)	kaputt	broken	cassé(e)	rotto(a)	—
rotondo (I)	rund	round	rond(e)	—	redondo(a)
rotto (I)	kaputt	broken	cassé(e)	—	roto(a)
roue (F)	Rad n	wheel	—	ruota f	rueda f
rouge (F)	rot	red	—	rosso(a)	rojo(a)
rougeole (F)	Masern pl	measles	—	morbillo m	sarampión m
rough (E)	rauh	—	rêche	ruvido(a)	rudo(a)
rouillé (F)	rostig	rusty	—	arrugginito(a)	oxidado(a)
rouiller (F)	rosten	rust	—	arrugginire	oxidarse
rouler (F)	rollen	roll	—	ruotare	rodar
roulotte (I)	Wohnwagen m	caravan	caravane f	—	rulota f
round (E)	rund	—	rond(e)	rotondo(a)	redondo(a)
roundabout (E)	Karussell n	—	manège m	giostra f	tiovivo m
round trip (E)	Rundfahrt f	—	circuit m	giro m	gira f
route (E)	Reiseroute f	—	itinéraire m	itinerario m	itinerario m
route (F)	Landstraße f	country road	—	strada provinciale f	carretera nacional f
route nationale (F)	Bundesstraße f	Federal Highway/main road	—	strada statale f	carretera nacional f
routier (F)	Fernfahrer m	long-distance driver	—	camionista m	camionero m
rovesciare (I)	umschmeißen	throw over	renverser	—	derribar
rovina (I)	Ruine f	ruin	ruine f	—	ruina f
rovinare (I)	verderben	ruin	détruire	—	arrruinar
rovistare (I)	wühlen	scrabble	fouiller	—	revolver

	D	E	F	I	Es
row¹ (E)	rudern	—	ramer	remare	remar
row² (E)	Reihe f	—	rangée f	fila f	fila f
rozzo (I)	grob	coarse	grossier(-ière)	—	tosco(a)
rub (E)	reiben	—	frotter	sfregare	frotar
rubare¹ (I)	einbrechen	break in	cambrioler	—	robar
rubare² (I)	stehlen	steal	voler	—	robar
rubber (E)	Gummi m	—	gomme f	gomma f	goma f
(rubber) dinghy (E)	Schlauchboot n	—	canot pneumatique m	canotto pneumatico m	bote neumático m
rubbish (E)	Abfall m	—	déchets m pl	immondizia f	basura f
rubio (Es)	blond	blond	blond(e)	biondo(a)	—
rücken (D)	—	move	déplacer	muovere	mover
Rücken (D)	—	back	dos m	schiena f	espalda m
Rückkehr (D)	—	return	retour m	ritorno m	regreso m
Rucksack (D)	—	rucksack	sac à dos m	zaino m	mochila f
rucksack (E)	Rucksack m	—	sac à dos m	zaino m	mochila f
rückwärts (D)	—	backwards	en arrière	in dietro	marcha atrás
Ruder (D)	—	oar	rame f	remo m	remo m
rudern (D)	—	row	ramer	remare	remar
rudo (Es)	rauh	rough	rêche	ruvido(a)	—
rue (F)	Straße f	street	—	strada f	calle f
rue à sens unique (F)	Einbahnstraße f	one-way street	—	senso unico m	calle de dirección única f
rueda (Es)	Rad n	wheel	roue f	ruota f	—
ruego (Es)	Bitte f	request	demande f	domanda f	—
ruelle (F)	Gasse f	lane	—	vicolo m	callejón m
rue transversale (F)	Querstraße f	intersecting road	—	traversa f	travesía f
rufen (D)	—	shout	appeler	chiamare	llamar
Ruhe (D)	—	calm	calme m	silenzio m	quietud f
ruhen (D)	—	rest	reposer, se	riposare	descansar
Ruhestand (D)	—	retirement	retraite f	pensione f	retiro m
Ruhetag (D)	—	closing day	jour de repos m	giorno di riposo m	día de descanso m
ruhig (D)	—	quiet	tranquille	calmo(a)	quieto(a)
ruido¹ (Es)	Geräusch n	sound	bruit m	rumore m	—
ruido² (Es)	Krach m	noise	bruit m	chiasso m	—
ruido³ (Es)	Lärm m	noise	bruit m	rumore m	—
ruin¹ (E)	Ruine f	—	ruine f	rovina f	ruina f
ruin² (E)	verderben	—	détruire	rovinare	arrruinar
ruina (Es)	Ruine f	ruin	ruine f	rovina f	—
Ruine (D)	—	ruin	ruine f	rovina f	ruina f
ruine (F)	Ruine f	ruin	—	rovina f	ruina f
ruins (E)	Trümmer pl	—	décombres m pl	macerie f pl	escombros m pl
rule (E)	herrschen	—	régner	dominare	mandar
ruler (E)	Lineal n	—	règle f	riga f	regla f
rulota (Es)	Wohnwagen m	caravan	caravane f	roulotte f	—

	D	E	F	I	Es
rumeur (F)	Gerücht n	rumour	—	voce f	rumor m
rumor (Es)	Gerücht n	rumour	rumeur f	voce f	—
rumore¹ (I)	Geräusch n	sound	bruit m	—	ruido m
rumore² (I)	Lärm m	noise	bruit m	—	ruido m
rumoroso (I)	laut	loud	fort(e)	—	fuerte
rumour (E)	Gerücht n	—	rumeur f	voce f	rumor m
run¹ (E)	laufen	—	courir	correre	correr
run² (E)	rennen	—	courir	correre	correr
rund (D)	—	round	rond(e)	rotondo(a)	redondo(a)
Rundfahrt (D)	—	round trip	circuit m	giro m	gira f
Rundfunk (D)	—	broadcasting	radio f	radio f	radiodifusión f
run over (E)	überfahren	—	écraser	investire	atropellar
ruota (I)	Rad n	wheel	roue f	—	rueda f
ruotare (I)	rollen	roll	rouler	—	rodar
rush (E)	rauschen	—	bruire	mormorare	susurrar
Rusia (Es)	Rußland	Russia	Russie f	Russia f	—
rusk (E)	Zwieback m	—	biscotte f	fette biscottate f pl	bizcocho m
russare (I)	schnarchen	snore	ronfler	—	roncar
Russia (E)	Rußland	—	Russie f	Russia f	Rusia f
Russia (I)	Rußland	Russia	Russie f	—	Rusia f
Russie (F)	Rußland	Russia	—	Russia f	Rusia f
Rußland (D)	—	Russia	Russie f	Russia f	Rusia f
rust (E)	rosten	—	rouiller	arrugginire	oxidarse
rusty (E)	rostig	—	rouillé(e)	arrugginito(a)	oxidado(a)
rutschen (D)	—	slide	glisser	scivolare	resbalar
ruvido (I)	rauh	rough	rêche	—	rudo(a)
Saal (D)	—	hall	salle f	sala f	sala f
sábado¹ (Es)	Sonnabend m	Saturday	samedi m	sabato m	—
sábado² (Es)	Samstag m	Saturday	samedi m	sabato m	—
sábana (Es)	Laken n	sheet	drap m	lenzuolo m	—
sabato¹ (I)	Sonnabend m	Saturday	samedi m	—	sábado m
sabato² (I)	Samstag m	Saturday	samedi m	—	sábado m
sabbia (I)	Sand m	sand	sable m	—	arena f
saber¹ (Es)	können	can	pouvoir	sapere	—
saber² (Es)	wissen	know	savoir	sapere	—
saber³ (Es)	Wissen n	knowledge	savoir m	sapere m	—
sabio (Es)	weise	wise	sage	saggio(a)	—
sable (F)	Sand m	sand	—	sabbia f	arena f
sabor (Es)	Geschmack m	taste	goût m	gusto m	—
sac¹ (F)	Sack m	sack	—	sacco m	saco m
sac² (F)	Tasche f	handbag	—	borsa f	bolso m
sac³ (F)	Tüte f	bag	—	sacchetto m	bolsa f
sacacorchos (Es)	Korkenzieher m	corkscrew	tire-bouchon m	cavatappi m	—
sac à dos (F)	Rucksack m	rucksack	—	zaino m	mochila f

	D	E	F	I	Es
sac à main (F)	Handtasche *f*	handbag	—	borsetta *f*	bolso *m*
sac à provision (F)	Einkaufstasche *f*	shopping bag	—	borsa della spesa *f*	bolsa de compra *f*
saccheggiare (I)	plündern	loot	piller	—	desvalijar
sacchetto (I)	Tüte *f*	bag	sac *m*	—	bolsa *f*
sacco (I)	Sack *m*	sack	sac *m*	—	saco *m*
sacerdote (Es)	Priester *m*	priest	prêtre *m*	prete *m*	—
Sache (D)	—	thing	chose *f*	cosa *f*	cosa *f*
Sack (D)	—	sack	sac *m*	sacco *m*	saco *m*
sack (E)	Sack *m*	—	sac *m*	sacco *m*	saco *m*
saco (Es)	Sack *m*	sack	sac *m*	sacco *m*	—
sacrifice (E)	Opfer *n*	—	sacrifice *m*	sacrificio *m*	sacrificio *m*
sacrifice (F)	Opfer *n*	sacrifice	—	sacrificio *m*	sacrificio *m*
sacrificio (Es)	Opfer *n*	sacrifice	sacrifice *m*	sacrificio *m*	—
sacrificio (I)	Opfer *n*	sacrifice	sacrifice *m*	—	sacrificio *m*
sad (E)	traurig	—	triste	triste	triste
safety (E)	Sicherheit *f*	—	sécurité *f*	sicurezza *f*	seguridad *f*
Saft (D)	—	juice	jus *m*	succo *m*	zumo *m*
Säge (D)	—	saw	scie *f*	sega *f*	sierra *f*
sage (F)	weise	wise	—	saggio	sabio(a)
sagen (D)	—	say	dire	dire	decir
saggio (I)	weise	wise	sage	—	sabio(a)
Sahne (D)	—	cream	crème *f*	panna *f*	nata *f*
saigner (F)	bluten	bleed	—	sanguinare	sangrar
sail (E)	segeln	—	faire de la voile	andare a vela	navegar a vela
sailor (E)	Matrose *m*	—	matelot *m*	marinaio *m*	marinero *m*
sain (F)	gesund	healthy	—	sano(a)	sano(a)
saint (F)	heilig	holy	—	santo(a)	santo(a)
Saint-Sylvestre (F)	Silvester *n*	New Year's Eve	—	San Silvestro *m*	Noche Vieja *f*
saisir¹ (F)	ergreifen	seize	—	afferrare	coger
saisir² (F)	fassen	grasp	—	prendere	coger
saisir³ (F)	greifen	seize	—	afferrare	coger
Saison (D)	—	season	saison *f*	stagione *f*	temporada *f*
saison¹ (F)	Jahreszeit *f*	time of year	—	stagione *f*	estación del año *f*
saison² (F)	Saison *f*	season	—	stagione *f*	temporada *f*
sal (Es)	Salz *n*	salt	sel *m*	sale *m*	—
sala (Es)	Saal *m*	hall	salle *f*	sala *f*	—
sala (I)	Saal *m*	hall	salle *f*	—	sala *f*
salad (E)	Salat *m*	—	salade *f*	insalata *f*	ensalada *f*
sala da pranzo (I)	Eßzimmer *n*	dining room	salle à manger *f*	—	comedor *m*
sala d'attesa (I)	Wartesaal *m*	waiting room	salle d'attente *f*	—	sala de espera *f*
salade (F)	Salat *m*	salad	—	insalata *f*	ensalada *f*
sala de espera (Es)	Wartesaal *m*	waiting room	salle d'attente *f*	sala d'attesa *f*	—
sala de estar (Es)	Wohnzimmer *n*	living room	salle de séjour *f*	salotto *m*	—
salaire¹ (F)	Gehalt *n*	salary	—	stipendio *m*	sueldo *m*
salaire² (F)	Lohn *m*	wages	—	salario *m*	salario *m*
salario (Es)	Lohn *m*	wages	salaire *m*	salario *m*	—
salario (I)	Lohn *m*	wages	salaire *m*	—	salario *m*
salary (E)	Gehalt *n*	—	salaire *m*	stipendio *m*	sueldo *m*

	D	E	F	I	Es
Salat (D)	—	salad	salade *f*	insalata *f*	ensalada *f*
Salbe (D)	—	ointment	onguent *m*	pomata *f*	pomada *f*
saldar (Es)	abbezahlen	pay off	finir de payer	saldare	—
saldare (I)	abbezahlen	pay off	finir de payer	—	saldar
saldi (I)	Ausverkauf *m*	sale	soldes *m pl*	—	liquidación *f*
sale¹ (E)	Ausverkauf *m*	—	soldes *m pl*	saldi *m*	liquidación *f*
sale² (E)	Verkauf *m*	—	vente *f*	vendita *f*	venta *f*
sale¹ (F)	dreckig	dirty	—	sporco(a)	sucio(a)
sale² (F)	schmutzig	dirty	—	sporco(a)	sucio(a)
sale (I)	Salz *n*	salt	sel *m*	—	sal *f*
salesman (E)	Verkäufer *m*	—	vendeur *m*	venditore *m*	vendedor *m*
saleté (F)	Schmutz *m*	dirt	—	sporcizia *f*	suciedad *f*
salida¹ (Es)	Ausgang *m*	exit	sortie *f*	uscita *f*	—
salida² (Es)	Ausreise *f*	departure	départ *m*	partenza *f*	—
salida³ (Es)	Abfahrt *f*	departure	départ *m*	partenza *f*	—
salida⁴ (Es)	Abreise *f*	departure	départ *m*	partenza *f*	—
salida de emergencia (Es)	Notausgang *m*	emergency exit	sortie de secours *f*	uscita di sicurezza *f*	—
salida del sol (Es)	Sonnen-aufgang *m*	sunrise	lever du soleil *m*	sorgere del sole *m*	—
salir¹ (Es)	abfahren	depart	partir (de)	partire	
salir² (Es)	abreisen	leave	partir	partire	
salir³ (Es)	ausgehen	go out	sortir	uscire	
salir⁴ (Es)	heraustreten	step out	sortir	uscire fuori	
salir afuera (Es)	hinausgehen	go out	sortir	uscire	—
salire¹ (I)	aufsteigen	ascend	monter	—	subir
salire² (I)	einsteigen	get in	monter	—	subir a
salire³ (I)	hinaufsteigen	climb	monter	—	subir
salire⁴ (I)	steigen	go up	monter	—	subir
salita d'ingresso (I)	Auffahrt *f*	drive	allée *f*	—	entrada *f*
salle (F)	Saal *m*	hall	—	sala *f*	sala *f*
salle à manger (F)	Eßzimmer *n*	dining room	—	sala da pranzo *f*	comedor *m*
salle d'attente (F)	Wartesaal *m*	waiting room	—	sala d'attesa *f*	sala de espera *f*
salle de bains (F)	Badezimmer *n*	bathroom	—	stanza da bagno *f*	cuarto de baño *m*
salle de séjour (F)	Wohnzimmer *n*	living room	—	salotto *m*	sala de estar *f*
salmon (E)	Lachs *m*	—	saumon *m*	salmone *m*	salmón *m*
salmón (Es)	Lachs *m*	salmon	saumon *m*	salmone *m*	—
salmone (I)	Lachs *m*	salmon	saumon *m*	—	salmón *m*
salotto (I)	Wohnzimmer *n*	living room	salle de séjour *f*	—	sala de estar *f*
salpicar (Es)	spritzen	squirt	asperger	spruzzare	
salsa (Es)	Soße *f*	sauce	sauce *f*	salsa *f*	—
salsa (I)	Soße *f*	sauce	sauce *f*	—	salsa *f*
salsiccia (I)	Wurst *f*	sausage	saucisse *f*	—	salchicha *f*
salt (E)	Salz *n*	—	sel *m*	sale *m*	sal *f*
saltar¹ (Es)	hüpfen	jump	sautiller	saltellare	—
saltar² (Es)	springen	jump	sauter	saltare	—
saltare (I)	springen	jump	sauter	—	saltar
saltellare (I)	hüpfen	jump	sautiller	—	saltar
salto (Es)	Sprung *m*	jump	saut *m*	salto *m*	—

	D	E	F	I	Es
salto (I)	Sprung *m*	jump	saut *m*	—	salto *m*
salud (Es)	Gesundheit *f*	health	santé *f*	salute *f*	—
¡salud! (Es)	prost!	cheers!	santé!	salute!	—
saludar[1] (Es)	begrüßen	greet	saluer	salutare	—
saludar[2] (Es)	grüßen	greet	saluer	salutare	—
saludo (Es)	Gruß *m*	greeting	salut *m*	saluto *m*	—
saluer[1] (F)	begrüßen	greet	—	salutare	saludar
saluer[2] (F)	grüßen	greet	—	salutare	saludar
salut (F)	Gruß *m*	greeting	—	saluto *m*	saludo *m*
salu! (F)	tschüs!	bye!	—	ciao!	¡hasta luego!
salutare[1] (I)	begrüßen	greet	saluer	—	saludar
salutare[2] (I)	grüßen	greet	saluer	—	saludar
salute (I)	Gesundheit *f*	health	santé *f*	—	salud *f*
salute! (I)	prost!	cheers!	santé!	—	¡salud!
saluto (I)	Gruß *m*	greeting	salut *m*	—	saludo *m*
salvagente (I)	Rettungsring *m*	lifebelt	bouée de sauvetage *f*	—	salvavidas *m*
salvaje (Es)	wild	wild	sauvage	selvatico(a)	—
salvar (Es)	retten	save	sauver	salvare	—
salvare (I)	retten	save	sauver	—	salvar
salvavidas (Es)	Rettungsring *m*	lifebelt	bouée de sauvetage *f*	salvagente *m*	—
salvo (Es)	außer	except	hors de	eccetto	—
Salz (D)	—	salt	sel *m*	sale *m*	sal *f*
same (E)	gleich	—	égal(e)	identico(a)	idéntico(a)
samedi[1] (F)	Sonnabend *m*	Saturday	—	sabato *m*	sábado *m*
samedi[2] (F)	Samstag *m*	Saturday	—	sabato *m*	sábado *m*
sammeln (D)	—	collect	collecter	raccogliere	recolectar
Sammlung (D)	—	collection	collection *f*	raccolta *f*	colección *f*
sample (E)	Muster *n*	—	modèle *m*	campione *m*	modelo *m*
Samstag (D)	—	Saturday	samedi *m*	sabato *m*	sábado *m*
Sand (D)	—	sand	sable *m*	sabbia *f*	arena *f*
sand (E)	Sand *m*	—	sable *m*	sabbia *f*	arena *f*
sandal (E)	Sandale *f*	—	sandale *f*	sandalo *m*	sandalia *f*
Sandale (D)	—	sandal	sandale *f*	sandalo *m*	sandalia *f*
sandale (F)	Sandale *f*	sandal	—	sandalo *m*	sandalia *f*
sandalia (Es)	Sandale *f*	sandal	sandale *f*	sandalo *m*	—
sandalo (I)	Sandale *f*	sandal	sandale *f*	—	sandalia *f*
sanft (D)	—	gentle	doux(douce)	dolce	dulce
sang (F)	Blut *n*	blood	—	sangue *m*	sangre *f*
Sänger (D)	—	singer	chanteur *m*	cantante *m*	cantante *m*
sangrar (Es)	bluten	bleed	saigner	sanguinare	—
sangre (Es)	Blut *n*	blood	sang *m*	sangue *m*	—
sangue (I)	Blut *n*	blood	sang *m*	—	sangre *f*
sangue misto (I)	Mischling *m*	halfcaste	métis *m*	—	mestizo *m*
sanguinare (I)	bluten	bleed	saigner	—	sangrar
sano (Es)	gesund	healthy	sain(e)	sano(a)	—
sano (I)	gesund	healthy	sain(e)	—	sano(a)
sans (F)	ohne	without	—	senza	sin

	D	E	F	I	Es
sans doute (F)	zweifellos	doubtless	—	senza dubbio	sin duda
sans engagement (F)	unverbindlich	not binding	—	non impegnativo(a)	sin compromiso
San Silvestro (I)	Silvester n	New Year's Eve	Saint-Sylvestre m	—	noche vieja f
sans importance (F)	unwichtig	unimportant	—	non importante	sin importancia
sans valeur (F)	wertlos	worthless	—	senza valore	sin valor
santé (F)	Gesundheit f	health	—	salute f	salud f
santé! (F)	prost!	cheers!	—	salute!	¡salud!
santo (Es)	heilig	holy	saint(e)	santo(a)	—
santo (I)	heilig	holy	saint(e)	—	santo(a)
sapere[1] (I)	können	can	pouvoir	—	saber
sapere[2] (I)	wissen	know	savoir	—	saber
sapere[3] (I)	Wissen n	knowledge	savoir m	—	saber m
sapeurs-pompiers (F)	Feuerwehr f	fire brigade	—	vigili del fuoco	cuerpo de bomberos m
sapone (I)	Seife f	soap	savon m	—	jabón m
Sarg (D)	—	coffin	cercueil m	bara f	ataúd m
sartén (Es)	Pfanne f	pan	poêle f	padella f	—
sarto (I)	Schneider m	tailor	tailleur m	—	sastre m
sasso (I)	Stein m	stone	pierre f	—	piedra f
sastre (Es)	Schneider m	tailor	tailleur m	sarto m	—
satisfacer (Es)	befriedigen	satisfy	satisfaire	soddisfare	—
satisfaire (F)	befriedigen	satisfy	—	soddisfare	satisfacer
satisfecho[1] (Es)	satt	full	rassasié(e)	sazio(a)	—
satisfecho[2] (Es)	zufrieden	satisfied	content(e)	contento(a)	—
satisfied (E)	zufrieden	—	content(e)	contento(a)	satisfecho(a)
satisfy (E)	befriedigen	—	satisfaire	soddisfare	satisfacer
satt (D)	—	full	rassasié(e)	sazio(a)	satisfecho(a)
Saturday[1] (E)	Sonnabend m	—	samedi m	sabato m	sábado m
Saturday[2] (E)	Samstag m	—	samedi m	sabato m	sábado m
Satz (D)	—	sentence	phrase f	frase f	oración f
sauber (D)	—	clean	propre	pulito(a)	limpio(a)
sauce (E)	Soße f	—	sauce f	salsa f	salsa f
sauce (F)	Soße f	sauce	—	salsa f	salsa f
saucepan (E)	Kochtopf m	—	casserole f	pentola f	olla f
saucer (E)	Untertasse f	—	soucoupe f	piattino m	platillo m
saucisse (F)	Wurst f	sausage	—	salsiccia f	salchicha f
sauer (D)	—	sour	aigre	acido(a)	agrio(a)
Säule (D)	—	pillar	colonne f	colonna f	columna f
saumon (F)	Lachs m	salmon	—	salmone m	salmón m
Säure (D)	—	acid	acide m	acido m	ácido m
sausage (E)	Wurst f	—	saucisse f	salsiccia f	salchicha f
saut (F)	Sprung m	jump	—	salto m	salto m
sauter (F)	springen	jump	—	saltare	saltar
sautiller (F)	hüpfen	jump	—	saltellare	saltar
sauvage (F)	wild	wild	—	selvatico(a)	salvaje
sauver (F)	retten	save	—	salvare	salvar
save[1] (E)	retten	—	sauver	salvare	salvar
save[2] (E)	sparen	—	économiser	risparmiare	ahorrar

	D	E	F	I	Es
savings bank (E)	Sparkasse f	—	caisse d'épargne f	cassa di risparmio f	caja de ahorros f
savings book (E)	Sparbuch n	—	livret de caisse d'épargne m	libretto di risparmio m	libreta de ahorro f
savoir[1] (F)	wissen	know	—	sapere	saber
savoir[2] (F)	Wissen n	knowledge	—	sapere m	saber m
savon (F)	Seife f	soap	—	sapone m	jabón m
savoureux (F)	köstlich	delicious	—	squisito(a)	exquisito(a)
saw (E)	Säge f	—	scie f	sega f	sierra f
say (E)	sagen	—	dire	dire	decir
say goodbye to (E)	verabschieden	—	prendre congé de	congedare	despedir
say thank you (E)	bedanken	—	remercier	ringraziare	agradecer algo
sazio (I)	satt	full	rassasié(e)	—	satisfecho(a)
sbagliare (I)	irren	be mistaken	tromper, se	—	equivocarse
sbagliato (I)	verkehrt	wrong	faux(fausse)	—	equivocado(a)
sbaglio (I)	Fehler m	mistake	faute f	—	falta f
sbarra (I)	Schranke f	barrier	barrière f	—	barrera f
sbocco (I)	Mündung f	mouth	embouchure f	—	desembocadura f
sbrigare (I)	erledigen	take care of	régler	—	acabar
sbucciare (I)	schälen	peel	éplucher	—	pelar
scaffale (I)	Regal n	shelves	étagère f	—	estantería f
scala[1] (I)	Aufgang m	staircase	montée f	—	subida f
scala[2] (I)	Leiter f	ladder	échelle f	—	escalera f
scala[3] (I)	Treppe f	stairs	escalier m	—	escalera f
scala mobile (I)	Rolltreppe f	escalator	escalier roulant m	—	escalera mecánica f
scales (E)	Waage f	—	balance f	bilancia f	balanza f
scalo intermedio (I)	Zwischen- landung f	intermediate landing	escale f	—	escala f
scambiare[1] (I)	austauschen	exchange	échanger	—	cambiar
scambiare[2] (I)	tauschen	swap	échanger	—	cambiar
scambiare[3] (I)	verwechseln	confuse	confondre	—	confundir
scambiare[4] (I)	vertauschen	exchange	échanger	—	cambiar
scambio (I)	Austausch m	exchange	échange m	—	cambio m
scandal (E)	Skandal m	—	scandale m	scandalo m	escándalo m
scandale (F)	Skandal m	scandal	—	scandalo m	escándalo m
scandalo (I)	Skandal m	scandal	scandale m	—	escándalo m
Scandinavia (E)	Skandinavien	—	Scandinavie f	Scandinavia f	Escandinavia f
Scandinavia (I)	Skandinavien	Scandinavia	Scandinavie f	—	Escandinavia f
Scandinavie (F)	Skandinavien	Scandinavia	—	Scandinavia f	Escandinavia f
scapolo (I)	Junggeselle m	bachelor	célibataire m	—	soltero m
scappare[1] (I)	entkommen	escape	échapper	—	escapar
scappare[2] (I)	entfliehen	escape	échapper, se	—	huir
scar (E)	Narbe f	—	cicatrice f	cicatrice f	cicatriz f
scarf[1] (E)	Halstuch n	—	écharpe f	sciarpa f	pañuelo para el cuello m
scarf[2] (E)	Schal m	—	écharpe f	sciarpa f	chal m
scaricare[1] (I)	ausladen	unload	décharger	—	descargar
scaricare[2] (I)	abladen	unload	décharger	—	descargar
scarpa (I)	Schuh m	shoe	chaussure f	—	zapato m

	D	E	F	I	Es
scarso (I)	knapp	tight	étroit(e)	—	estrecho(a)
scatola[1] (I)	Dose *f*	tin	boîte *f*	—	lata *f*
scatola[2] (I)	Schachtel *f*	box	boîte *f*	—	caja *f*
scattare una foto (I)	knipsen	take a snap	photographier	—	hacer una foto
scattered (E)	zerstreut	—	dispersé(e)	disperso(a)	disperso(a)
scavare (I)	graben	dig	creuser	—	cavar
scegliere[1] (I)	aussuchen	select	choisir	—	escoger
scegliere[2] (I)	auswählen	choose	choisir	—	eligir
scelta[1] (I)	Auswahl *f*	choice	choix *m*	—	elección *f*
scelta[2] (I)	Wahl *f*	choice	choix *m*	—	opción *f*
scemo (I)	doof	daft	bête	—	estúpido(a)
scendere[1] (I)	aussteigen	get off	descendre	—	bajar
scendere[2] (I)	absteigen	dismount	descendre	—	descender
scendere[3] (I)	hinuntergehen	descend	descendre	—	bajar
scène (F)	Bühne *f*	stage	—	palcoscenico *m*	escenario *m*
scent (E)	Duft *m*	—	odeur *f*	profumo *m*	aroma *m*
Schachtel (D)	—	box	boîte *f*	scatola *f*	caja *f*
Schädel (D)	—	skull	crâne *m*	cranio *m*	cráneo *m*
schaden (D)	—	damage	nuire	nuocere	dañar
Schaden (D)	—	damage	dommage *m*	danno *m*	daño *m*
schädlich (D)	—	harmful	nuisible	nocivo(a)	nocivo(a)
Schaf (D)	—	sheep	mouton *m*	pecora *f*	oveja *f*
schaffen (D)	—	create	réussir à faire	creare	crear
Schaffner (D)	—	conductor	contrôleur *m*	bigliettaio *m*	revisor *m*
Schal (D)	—	scarf	écharpe *f*	sciarpa *f*	chal *m*
Schale (D)	—	peel	peau *f*	buccia *f*	piel *m*
schälen (D)	—	peel	éplucher	sbucciare	pelar
Schallplatte (D)	—	record	disque *m*	disco *m*	disco *m*
schalten (D)	—	switch	connecter	commutare	conectar
Schalter (D)	—	counter	guichet *m*	sportello *m*	ventanilla *f*
schämen (D)	—	be ashamed	avoir honte	vergognarsi	tener vergüenza
Schande (D)	—	disgrace	honte *f*	vergogna *f*	deshonra *f*
Schar (D)	—	band	bande *f*	schiera *f*	grupo *m*
scharf[1] (D)	—	sharp	tranchant(e)	tagliente	cortante
scharf[2] (D)	—	hot	épicé(e)	piccante	picante
schärfen (D)	—	sharpen	aiguiser	affilare	afilar
Schatten (D)	—	shadow	ombre *f*	ombra *f*	sombra *f*
schattig (D)	—	shady	ombragé(e)	ombroso(a)	a la sombra
Schatz (D)	—	treasure	trésor *m*	tesoro *m*	tesoro *m*
schätzen (D)	—	estimate	estimer	stimare	estimar
schauderhaft (D)	—	horrible	horrible	spaventoso(a)	espantoso(a)
schauen (D)	—	look	regarder	guardare	mirar
Schaufel (D)	—	shovel	pelle *f*	pala *f*	pala *f*
Schaufenster (D)	—	shop window	vitrine *f*	vetrina *f*	escaparate *m*
schaukeln (D)	—	swing	balancer, se	dondolare	columpiarse
Schaum (D)	—	foam	écume *f*	schiuma *f*	espuma *f*
Schauspiel (D)	—	play	spectacle *m*	spettacolo *m*	espectáculo *m*

	D	E	F	I	Es
Schauspieler (D)	—	actor	acteur *m*	attore *m*	actor *m*
Scheck (D)	—	cheque	chèque *m*	assegno *m*	cheque *m*
Scheckbuch (D)	—	cheque book	carnet de chèques *m*	libretto degli assegni *m*	talonario de cheques *m*
Scheibe[1] (D)	—	disc	disque *m*	disco *m*	disco *m*
Scheibe[2] (D)	—	pane	carreau *m*	vetro *m*	cristal *m*
scheiden (D)	—	part	séparer	separare	separar
Schein[1] (D)	—	light	lumière *f*	luce *f*	luz *f*
Schein[2] (D)	—	note	billet *m*	banconota *f*	billete *m*
schenken (D)	—	give	offrir	regalare	regalar
Scherbe (D)	—	broken piece	tesson *m*	coccio *m*	pedazo *m*
Schere (D)	—	pair of scissors	ciseaux *m pl*	forbici *f pl*	tijeras *f pl*
Scherz (D)	—	joke	plaisanterie *f*	scherzo *m*	broma *f*
scherzare (I)	spaßen	joke	plaisanter	—	bromear
scherzo[1] (I)	Scherz *m*	joke	plaisanterie *f*	—	broma *f*
scherzo[2] (I)	Spaß *m*	fun	plaisir *m*	—	broma *f*
scheu (D)	—	shy	timide	timido(a)	tímido(a)
schiavo (I)	Sklave *m*	slave	esclave *m*	—	esclavo *m*
schick (D)	—	stylish	chic	elegante	elegante
schicken (D)	—	send	envoyer	inviare	mandar
Schicksal (D)	—	fate	destin *m*	destino *m*	destino *m*
schieben (D)	—	push	pousser	spingere	empujar
Schiedsrichter (D)	—	referee	arbitre *m*	arbitro *m*	árbitro *m*
schief (D)	—	sloped	oblique	obliquo(a)	torcido(a)
schiena (I)	Rücken *m*	back	dos *m*	—	espalda *m*
schiera (I)	Schar *f*	band	bande *f*	—	grupo *m*
schießen (D)	—	shoot	tirer	sparare	disparar
Schiff (D)	—	ship	navire *m*	nave *f*	barco *m*
Schild (D)	—	shield	bouclier *m*	scudo *m*	escudo *m*
schimpfen (D)	—	scold	gronder	imprecare	insultar
Schinken (D)	—	ham	jambon *m*	prosciutto *m*	jamón *m*
Schirm (D)	—	umbrella	parapluie *m*	ombrello *m*	paraguas *m*
schiuma (I)	Schaum *m*	foam	écume *f*	—	espuma *f*
schizzo (I)	Skizze *f*	sketch	esquisse *f*	—	boceto *m*
Schlaf (D)	—	sleep	sommeil *m*	sonno *m*	sueño *m*
schlafen (D)	—	sleep	dormir	dormire	dormir
Schlafzimmer (D)	—	bedroom	chambre à coucher *f*	camera da letto *f*	dormitorio *m*
Schlag (D)	—	blow	coup *m*	colpo *m*	golpe *m*
schlagen (D)	—	hit	battre	battere	golpear
Schlagzeile (D)	—	headline	manchette *f*	titolo *m*	título *m*
Schlamm (D)	—	mud	boue *f*	fango *m*	barro *m*
Schlange (D)	—	snake	serpent *m*	serpente *m*	serpiente *f*
schlank (D)	—	slim	mince	snello(a)	delgado(a)
schlau (D)	—	clever	astucieux(-euse)	astuto(a)	astuto(a)
Schlauchboot (D)	—	(rubber) dinghy	canot pneumatique *m*	canotto pneumatico *m*	bote neumático *m*
schlecht (D)	—	bad	mauvais(e)	cattivo	malo(a)
schließen (D)	—	close	fermer	chiudere	cerrar

	D	E	F	I	Es
schließlich (D)	—	finally	finalement	finalmente	finalmente
Schloß¹ (D)	—	lock	serrure *f*	serratura *f*	cerradura *f*
Schloß² (D)	—	castle	château *m*	castello *m*	castillo *m*
schlucken (D)	—	swallow	avaler	inghiottire	tragar
Schluß (D)	—	end	fin *f*	fine *f*	conclusión *f*
Schlüssel (D)	—	key	clé *f*	chiave *f*	llave *f*
Schlüsselloch (D)	—	keyhole	trou de la serrure *m*	buco della chiave *m*	ojo de la cerradura *m*
schmecken (D)	—	taste	sentir	piacere	gustar
Schmerz (D)	—	pain	douleur *f*	dolore *m*	dolor *m*
schmerzhaft (D)	—	painful	douloureux(-euse)	doloroso(a)	doloroso(a)
Schmetterling (D)	—	butterfly	papillon *m*	farfalla *f*	mariposa *f*
Schminke (D)	—	make-up	maquillage *m*	trucco *m*	maquillaje *m*
Schmuck (D)	—	jewellery	bijoux *m pl*	gioielli *m pl*	joyas *f pl*
Schmutz (D)	—	dirt	saleté *f*	sporcizia *f*	suciedad *f*
schmutzig (D)	—	dirty	sale	sporco(a)	sucio(a)
Schnaps (D)	—	spirits	eau-de-vie *f*	acquavite *f*	aguardiente *m*
schnarchen (D)	—	snore	ronfler	russare	roncar
Schnee (D)	—	snow	neige *f*	neve *f*	nieve *f*
schneiden (D)	—	cut	couper	tagliare	cortar
Schneider (D)	—	tailor	tailleur *m*	sarto *m*	sastre *m*
schneien (D)	—	snow	neiger	nevicare	nevar
schnell (D)	—	fast	rapide	veloce	rápido(a)
Schnelligkeit (D)	—	speed	rapidité *f*	velocità *f*	rapidez *f*
Schnellstraße (D)	—	expressway	voie rapide *f*	superstrada *f*	carretera de circulación rápida *f*
Schnellzug (D)	—	express train	rapide *m*	treno direttissimo *m*	tren expreso *m*
Schnitt (D)	—	cut	coupe *f*	taglio *m*	corte *m*
Schnupfen (D)	—	cold	rhume *m*	raffreddore *m*	resfriado *m*
Schnur (D)	—	string	ficelle *f*	corda *f*	cordel *m*
Schnurrbart (D)	—	moustache	moustache *f*	baffi *m pl*	bigote *m*
Schokolade (D)	—	chocolate	chocolat *m*	cioccolato *m*	chocolate *m*
schon (D)	—	already	déjà	già	ya
schön (D)	—	beautiful	beau, bel, belle	bello(a)	hermoso(a)
Schönheit (D)	—	beauty	beauté *f*	bellezza *f*	belleza *f*
school (E)	Schule *f*	—	école *f*	scuola *f*	escuela *f*
Schrank (D)	—	cupboard	armoire *f*	armadio *m*	armario *m*
Schranke (D)	—	barrier	barrière *f*	sbarra *f*	barrera *f*
Schraube (D)	—	screw	vis *f*	vite *f*	tornillo *m*
Schraubenzieher (D)	—	screwdriver	tournevis *m*	cacciavite *m*	destornillador *m*
schrecklich (D)	—	terrible	terrible	spaventoso(a)	horrible
Schrei (D)	—	scream	cri *m*	grido *m*	grito *m*
schreiben (D)	—	write	écrire	scrivere	escribir
Schreibmaschine (D)	—	typewriter	machine à écrire *f*	macchina da scrivere *f*	máquina de escribir *f*
Schreibwarenhandlung (D)	—	stationery shop	papeterie *f*	cartoleria *f*	papelería *f*
schreien (D)	—	scream	crier	gridare	gritar
Schrift (D)	—	writing	écriture *f*	scrittura *f*	escritura *f*

	D	E	F	I	Es
schriftlich (D)	—	written	écrit(e)	scritto	por escrito
Schriftsteller (D)	—	writer	écrivain m	scrittore m	escritor m
Schritt (D)	—	step	pas m	passo m	paso m
Schublade (D)	—	drawer	tiroir m	cassetto m	cajón m
schüchtern (D)	—	shy	timide	timido(a)	tímido(a)
Schuh (D)	—	shoe	chaussure f	scarpa f	zapato m
Schuhcreme (D)	—	shoe polish	cirage m	lucido per scarpe m	betún m
Schuhgeschäft (D)	—	shoeshop	magasin de chaussures m	negozio di scarpe m	zapatería f
Schuld (D)	—	fault	culpabilité f	colpa f	culpa f
schulden (D)	—	owe	devoir qch à qn	dovere	deber
Schulden (D)	—	debt	dette f	debiti m pl	deudas f pl
schuldig (D)	—	guilty	coupable	colpevole	culpable
Schule (D)	—	school	école f	scuola f	escuela f
Schüler (D)	—	pupil	élève m	scolaro m	alumno m
schulfrei (D)	—	holiday	de congé	vacanza	sin colegio
Schulter (D)	—	shoulder	épaule f	spalla f	hombro m
Schuß (D)	—	shot	coup m	sparo m	disparo m
Schüssel (D)	—	bowl	jatte f	scodella f	fuente f
Schuster (D)	—	shoemaker	cordonnier m	calzolaio m	zapatero m
schütteln (D)	—	shake	secouer	agitare	agitar
schütten (D)	—	pour	verser	versare	verter
Schutz (D)	—	protection	protection f	protezione f	protección f
schützen (D)	—	protect	protéger	proteggere	proteger
schwach (D)	—	weak	faible	debole	débil
Schwäche (D)	—	weakness	faiblesse f	debolezza f	debilidad f
Schwager (D)	—	brother-in-law	beau-frère m	cognato m	cuñado m
Schwägerin (D)	—	sister-in-law	belle-sœur f	cognata f	cuñada f
Schwamm (D)	—	sponge	éponge f	spugna f	esponja f
schwanger (D)	—	pregnant	enceinte	incinta	embarazada
Schwanz (D)	—	tail	queue f	coda f	rabo m
schwarz (D)	—	black	noir(e)	nero(a)	negro(a)
schwatzen (D)	—	chatter	bavarder	chiacchierare	charlar
Schweden (D)	—	Sweden	Suède f	Svezia f	Suecia f
schweigen (D)	—	be silent	taire, se	tacere	callar
Schwein (D)	—	pig	cochon m	maiale m	cerdo m
Schweine-fleisch (D)	—	pork	viande de porc f	carne di maiale f	carne de cerdo f
Schweiz (D)	—	Switzerland	Suisse f	Svizzera f	Suiza f
Schweizer (D)	—	Swiss	Suisse m	svizzero	suizo m
schwer (D)	—	heavy	lourd(e)	pesante	pesado(a)
Schwester (D)	—	sister	sœur f	sorella f	hermana f
Schwiegereltern (D)	—	parents-in-law	beaux-parents m pl	suoceri m pl	suegros m pl
Schwiegermutter (D)	—	mother-in-law	belle-mère f	suocera f	suegra f
schwierig (D)	—	difficult	difficile	difficile	difícil
Schwierigkeit (D)	—	difficulty	difficulté f	difficoltà f	dificultad f
Schwimmbad (D)	—	swimming pool	piscine f	piscina f	piscina f
schwimmen (D)	—	swim	nager	nuotare	nadar

	D	E	F	I	Es
Schwimmweste (D)	—	life jacket	gilet de sauvetage *m*	giubbotto di salvataggio *m*	chaleco salvavidas *m*
schwitzen (D)	—	sweat	transpirer	sudare	sudar
schwören (D)	—	swear	jurer	giurare	jurar
schwül (D)	—	sultry	lourd(e)	afoso(a)	sofocante
sci (I)	Ski *m*	ski	ski *m*	—	esquí *m*
sciacquare (I)	abspülen	wash up	faire la vaisselle	—	lavar
sciarpa[1] (I)	Halstuch *n*	scarf	écharpe *f*	—	pañuelo para el cuello *m*
sciarpa[2] (I)	Schal *m*	scarf	écharpe *f*	—	chal *m*
scie (F)	Säge *f*	saw	—	sega *f*	sierra *f*
science (E)	Wissenschaft *f*	—	science *f*	scienza *f*	ciencia *f*
science (F)	Wissenschaft *f*	science	—	scienza *f*	ciencia *f*
scientifique (F)	Wissenschaftler *m*	scientist	—	scienziato *m*	científico *m*
scientist (E)	Wissenschaftler *m*	—	scientifique *m*	scienziato *m*	científico *m*
scienza (I)	Wissenschaft *f*	science	science *f*	—	ciencia *f*
scienziato (I)	Wissenschaftler *m*	scientist	scientifique *m*	—	científico *m*
scimmia (I)	Affe *m*	ape	singe *m*	—	mono *m*
sciocco (I)	albern	foolish	sot(te)	—	tonto
sciogliere[1] (I)	auflösen	dissolve	dénouer	—	deshacer
sciogliere[2] (I)	lösen	solve	résoudre	—	desatar
sciogliere[3] (I)	losbinden	free	délier	—	desatar
sciogliersi (I)	tauen	thaw	fondre	—	deshelar
scioperare (I)	streiken	be on strike	faire grève	—	hacer huelga
sciopero (I)	Streik *m*	strike	grève *f*	—	huelga *f*
sciovia (I)	Skilift *m*	skilift	remonte-pente *m*	—	telesilla *f*
scivolare (I)	rutschen	slide	glisser	—	resbalar
scodella (I)	Schüssel *f*	bowl	jatte *f*	—	fuente *f*
scolaro (I)	Schüler *m*	pupil	élève *m*	—	alumno *m*
scold (E)	schimpfen	—	gronder	imprecare	insultar
scommessa (I)	Wette *f*	bet	pari *m*	—	apuesta *f*
scommettere (I)	wetten	bet	parier	—	apostar
scomodo (I)	unbequem	uncomfortable	inconfortable	—	incómodo(a)
scompartimento (I)	Abteil *n*	compartment	compartiment *m*	—	compartimiento *m*
scomparto (I)	Fach *n*	compartment	compartiment *m*	—	compartimiento *m*
sconfitta (I)	Niederlage *f*	defeat	défaite *f*	—	derrota *f*
sconosciuto (I)	unbekannt	unknown	inconnu(e)	—	desconocido(a)
sconsigliare (I)	abraten	warn	déconseiller	—	desaconsejar
scontento (I)	unzufrieden	dissatisfied	mécontent(e)	—	descontento(a)
sconto (I)	Rabatt *m*	discount	rabais *m*	—	rebaja *f*
sconveniente (I)	unpassend	inappropriate	mal à prospos	—	inadecuado(a)
scopa (I)	Besen *m*	broom	balai *m*	—	escoba *f*
scopare[1] (I)	fegen	sweep	balayer	—	barrer
scopare[2] (I)	kehren	sweep	balayer	—	barrer
scopo (I)	Zweck *m*	purpose	but *m*	—	finalidad *f*
scoppiare (I)	platzen	burst	éclater	—	reventar
scoprire (I)	entdecken	discover	découvrir	—	descubrir
scorpion (E)	Skorpion *m*	—	scorpion *m*	scorpione *m*	escorpión *m*
scorpion (F)	Skorpion *m*	scorpion	—	scorpione *m*	escorpión *m*

	D	E	F	I	Es
scorpione (I)	Skorpion *m*	scorpion	scorpion *m*	—	escorpión *m*
scorrere (I)	fließen	flow	couler	—	correr
scorte (I)	Vorrat *m*	stock	réserves *f pl*	—	provisión *f*
scortese (I)	unhöflich	impolite	impoli(e)	—	descortés
scottatura solare (I)	Sonnenbrand *m*	sunburn	coup de soleil *m*	—	quemadura solar *f*
scrabble (E)	wühlen	—	fouiller	rovistare	revolver
scream[1] (E)	schreien	—	crier	gridare	gritar
scream[2] (E)	Schrei *m*	—	cri *m*	grido *m*	grito *m*
screw (E)	Schraube *f*	—	vis *f*	vite *f*	tornillo *m*
screwdriver (E)	Schraubenzieher *m*	—	tournevis *m*	cacciavite *m*	destornillador *m*
scritto (I)	schriftlich	written	écrit(e)	—	por escrito
scrittore (I)	Schriftsteller *m*	writer	écrivain *m*	—	escritor *m*
scrittura (I)	Schrift *f*	writing	écriture *f*	—	escritura *f*
scrivere (I)	schreiben	write	écrire	—	escribir
scudo (I)	Schild *n*	shield	bouclier *m*	—	escudo *m*
sculpteur (F)	Bildhauer *m*	sculptor	—	scultore *m*	escultor(a) *m(f)*
sculptor (E)	Bildhauer *m*	—	sculpteur *m*	scultore *m*	escultor(a) *m(f)*
sculpture (E)	Skulptur *f*	—	sculpture *f*	scultura *f*	escultura *f*
sculpture (F)	Skulptur *f*	sculpture	—	scultura *f*	escultura *f*
scultore (I)	Bildhauer *m*	sculptor	sculpteur *m*	—	escultor(a) *m(f)*
scultura (I)	Skulptur *f*	sculpture	sculpture *f*	—	escultura *f*
scuola (I)	Schule *f*	school	école *f*	—	escuela *f*
scuro (I)	dunkel	dark	sombre	—	oscuro(a)
scusa (I)	Entschuldigung *f*	apology	excuse *f*	—	disculpa *f*
scusarsi (I)	entschuldigen, sich	apologize	excuser, se	—	disculparse
sdoganare (I)	verzollen	declare	dédouaner	—	declarar en la aduana
se[1] (I)	ob	if/whether	si	—	si
se[2] (I)	wenn	when/if	si/quand	—	cuando
sea (E)	Meer *n*	—	mer *f*	mare *m*	mar *m*
seagull (E)	Möwe *f*	—	mouette *f*	gabbiano *m*	gaviota *f*
seal (E)	Robbe *f*	—	phoque *m*	foca *f*	foca *f*
sea level (E)	Meeresspiegel *m*	—	niveau de la mer *m*	livello del mare *m*	nivel del mar *m*
séance (F)	Sitzung *f*	meeting	—	seduta *f*	reunión *f*
season[1] (E)	Saison *f*	—	saison *f*	stagione *f*	temporada *f*
season[2] (E)	würzen	—	épicer	condire	condimentar
seat[1] (E)	Sitz *m*	—	siège *m*	sede *f*	asiento *m*
seat[2] (E)	Sitzplatz *m*	—	place assise *f*	posto a sedere *m*	asiento *m*
seau (F)	Eimer *m*	bucket	—	secchio *m*	cubo *m*
sec (F)	trocken	dry	—	asciutto(a)	seco(a)
secar (Es)	trocknen	dry	sécher	asciugare	—
secchio (I)	Eimer *m*	bucket	seau *m*	—	cubo *m*
secchio dei rifiuti (I)	Mülleimer *m*	dustbin	poubelle *f*	—	cubo de la basura *m*
secco (I)	dürr	skinny	maigre	—	árido(a)
sécher (F)	trocknen	dry	—	asciugare	secar
sechs (D)	—	six	six	sei	seis
sechzehn (D)	—	sixteen	seize	sedici	dieciséis

segretaria

	D	E	F	I	Es
sechzig (D)	—	sixty	soixante	sessanta	sesenta
seco (Es)	trocken	dry	sec(sèche)	asciutto(a)	—
secolo (I)	Jahrhundert n	century	siècle m	—	siglo m
second¹ (E)	Sekunde f	—	seconde f	secondo m	segundo m
second² (E)	zweite(r,s)	—	second(e)	secondo(a)	segunda(o)
second (F)	zweite(r,s)	second	—	secondo(a)	segunda(o)
seconde (F)	Sekunde f	second	—	secondo m	segundo m
secondo¹ (I)	Sekunde f	second	seconde f	—	segundo m
secondo² (I)	zweite(r,s)	second	second(e)	—	segunda(o)
secouer (F)	schütteln	shake	—	agitare	agitar
secret¹ (E)	geheim	—	secret(-ète)	segreto(a)	secreto(a)
secret² (E)	Geheimnis n	—	secret m	segreto m	secreto m
secret³ (E)	heimlich	—	secret(-ète)	segreto(a)	oculto(a)
secret¹ (F)	Geheimnis n	secret	—	segreto m	secreto m
secret² (F)	geheim	secret	—	segreto(a)	secreto(a)
secret³ (F)	heimlich	secret	—	segreto(a)	oculto(a)
secrétaire (F)	Sekretärin f	secretary	—	segretaria f	secretaria f
secretaria¹ (Es)	Sekretärin f	secretary	secrétaire f	segretaria f	—
secretaría² (Es)	Sekretariat n	secretariat	secrétariat m	segretariato m	—
secretariat (E)	Sekretariat n	—	secrétariat m	segretariato m	secretaría f
secrétariat (F)	Sekretariat n	secretariat	—	segretariato m	secretaría f
secretary (E)	Sekretärin f	—	secrétaire f	segretaria f	secretaria f
secreto¹ (Es)	Geheimnis n	secret	secret m	segreto m	—
secreto² (Es)	geheim	secret	secret(-ète)	segreto(a)	—
section (F)	Abteilung f	department	—	reparto m	departamento m
sécurité (F)	Sicherheit f	safety	—	sicurezza f	seguridad f
sed (Es)	Durst m	thirst	soif f	sete f	—
seda (Es)	Seide f	silk	soie f	seta f	—
sede (I)	Sitz m	seat	siège m	—	asiento m
sedersi (I)	hinsetzen	sit down	asseoir, s'	—	sentarse
sedia (I)	Stuhl m	chair	chaise f	—	silla f
sedia a sdraio (I)	Liegestuhl m	deck chair	chaise longue f	—	tumbona f
sedici (I)	sechzehn	sixteen	seize	—	dieciséis
sediento (Es)	durstig	thirsty	assoiffé(e)	assetato(a)	—
seduce (E)	verführen	—	séduire	sedurre	seducir
séduire (F)	verführen	seduce	—	sedurre	seducir
sedurre (I)	verführen	seduce	séduire	—	seducir
seduta (I)	Sitzung f	meeting	séance f	—	reunión f
See (D)	—	lake	lac m	lago m	lago m
see (E)	sehen	—	voir	vedere	ver
see again (E)	wiedersehen	—	revoir	rivedere	volver a ver
seemingly (E)	anscheinend	—	apparemment	apparentemente	aparentemente
Seezunge (D)	—	sole	sole f	sogliola f	lenguado m
sega (I)	Säge f	saw	scie f	—	sierra f
segeln (D)	—	sail	faire de la voile	andare a vela	navegar a vela
segnale (I)	Zeichen n	sign	signe m	—	signo m
segno (I)	Mal n	mark	marque f	—	marca f
segretaria (I)	Sekretärin f	secretary	secrétaire f	—	secretaria f

	D	E	F	I	Es
segretariato (I)	Sekretariat *n*	secretariat	secrétariat *m*	—	secretaría *f*
segreto¹ (I)	geheim	secret	secret(-ète)	—	secreto(a)
segreto² (I)	Geheimnis *n*	secret	secret *m*	—	secreto *m*
segreto³ (I)	heimlich	secret	secret(-ète)	—	oculto(a)
seguente (I)	folgend	following	suivant(e)	—	siguiente
seguir (Es)	folgen	follow	suivre	seguire	—
seguir durmiendo (Es)	weiterschlafen	sleep on	continuer à dormir	continuare a dormire	—
seguire (I)	folgen	follow	suivre	—	seguir
segunda (Es)	zweite(r,s)	second	second(e)	secondo(a)	—
segundo (Es)	Sekunde *f*	second	seconde *f*	secondo *m*	—
seguridad (Es)	Sicherheit *f*	safety	sécurité *f*	sicurezza *f*	—
seguro¹ (Es)	sicher	sure	sûr(e)	sicuro(a)	—
seguro² (Es)	Versicherung *f*	insurance	assurance *f*	assicurazione *f*	—
seguro de sí mismo (Es)	selbstsicher	self-assured	sûr(e) de soi	sicuro di sé	—
sehen (D)	—	see	voir	vedere	ver
Sehenswürdigkeit (D)	—	sight	curiosité *f*	curiosità *f*	lugares de interés *m pl*
sehr (D)	—	very	très	molto	mucho/muy
sei (I)	sechs	six	six	—	seis
seiche (F)	Tintenfisch *m*	cuttlefish	—	seppia *f*	calamar *m*
Seide (D)	—	silk	soie *f*	seta *f*	seda *f*
Seife (D)	—	soap	savon *m*	sapone *m*	jabón *m*
Seil (D)	—	rope	corde *f*	fune *f*	soga *f*
sein (D)	—	be	être	essere	ser/estar
seis (Es)	sechs	six	six	seí	—
seit (D)	—	since/for	depuis	da	de/desde
Seite (D)	—	page	page *f*	pagina *f*	página *f*
seize¹ (E)	ergreifen	—	saisir	afferrare	coger
seize² (E)	festhalten	—	tenir ferme	tener fermo	sujetar
seize³ (E)	greifen	—	saisir	afferrare	coger
seize (F)	sechzehn	sixteen	—	sedici	dieciséis
séjour (F)	Aufenthalt *m*	stay	—	soggiorno *m*	estancia *f*
Sekretariat (D)	—	secretariat	secrétariat *m*	segretariato *m*	secretaría *f*
Sekretärin (D)	—	secretary	secrétaire *f*	segretaria *f*	secretaria *f*
Sekt (D)	—	champagne	champagne *m*	spumante *m*	champán *m*
Sekunde (D)	—	second	seconde *f*	secondo *m*	segundo *m*
sel (F)	Salz *n*	salt	—	sale *m*	sal *f*
selbständig (D)	—	independent	indépendant(e)	indipendente	independiente
Selbstbedienung (D)	—	self service	libre-service *m*	self-service *m*	autoservicio *m*
Selbstmord (D)	—	suicide	suicide *m*	suicidio *m*	suicidio *m*
selbstsicher (D)	—	self-assured	sûr(e) de soi	sicuro di sé	seguro de sí mismo
Selbstsucht (D)	—	selfishness	égoïsme *m*	egoismo *m*	egoísmo *m*
selbstverständlich (D)	—	of course	évidemment	naturalmente	por supuesto
select (E)	aussuchen	—	choisir	scegliere	escoger
self-assured (E)	selbstsicher	—	sûr(e) de soi	sicuro di sé	seguro de sí mismo
selfishness (E)	Selbstsucht *f*	—	égoïsme *m*	egoismo *m*	egoísmo *m*

sensible

	D	E	F	I	Es
self service (E)	Selbstbedienung f	—	libre-service m	self-service m	autoservicio m
self-service (I)	Selbstbedienung f	self service	libre-service m	—	autoservicio m
sell (E)	verkaufen	—	vendre	vendere	vender
sello[1] (Es)	Briefmarke f	stamp	timbre m	francobollo m	—
sello[2] (Es)	Stempel m	stamp	timbre m	timbro m	—
selten (D)	—	rare	rare	raro(a)	raro(a)
Seltenheit (D)	—	rarity	rareté f	rarità f	rareza f
seltsam (D)	—	strange	bizarre	strano(a)	extraño(a)
selvaggina (I)	Wild n	game	gibier m	—	caza f
selvatico (I)	wild	wild	sauvage	—	salvaje
semáforo (Es)	Ampel f	traffic lights	feux m pl	semaforo m	—
semaforo (I)	Ampel f	traffic lights	feux m pl	—	semáforo m
semaine (F)	Woche f	week	—	settimana f	semana f
semaine sainte (F)	Osterwoche f	Holy week	—	settimana santa f	Semana Santa f
semana (Es)	Woche f	week	semaine f	settimana f	—
semanal (Es)	wöchentlich	weekly	hebdomadaire	settimanale	—
Semana Santa (Es)	Osterwoche f	Holy week	semaine sainte f	settimana santa f	—
semblable (F)	ähnlich	similar	—	simile	parecido(a)
semelle (F)	Sohle f	sole	—	suola f	suela f
semilla (Es)	Korn n	corn	grain m	grano m	—
semplice[1] (I)	einfach	simple	simple	—	sencillo(a)
semplice[2] (I)	leicht	easy	facile	—	ligero(a)
sempre[1] (I)	immer	always	toujours	—	siempre
sempre[2] (I)	stets	always	toujours	—	siempre
senape (I)	Senf m	mustard	moutarde f	—	mostaza f
sencillo[1] (Es)	einfach	simple	simple	semplice	—
sencillo[2] (Es)	leicht	light	léger(-ère)	leggero(a)	—
send[1] (E)	schicken	—	envoyer	inviare	mandar
send[2] (E)	übersenden	—	envoyer	spedire	enviar
senden (D)	—	broadcast	transmettre	trasmettere	transmitir
Sender (D)	—	station	émetteur m	trasmettitore m	emisora f
sender (E)	Absender m	—	expéditeur m	mittente m	remitente m
send on (E)	nachsenden	—	faire suivre	inoltrare	enviar a la nueva dirección
Sendung (D)	—	transmission	diffusion f	trasmissione f	emisión f
Senf (D)	—	mustard	moutarde f	senape f	mostaza f
senken (D)	—	lower	baisser	abbassare	bajar
senkrecht (D)	—	vertical	vertical(e)	verticale	vertical
señor (Es)	Herr m	gentleman	monsieur m	signore m	—
señora (Es)	Dame f	lady	dame f	signora f	—
señorita (Es)	Fräulein n	Miss	mademoiselle	signorina f	—
sens (F)	Sinn m	sense	—	senso m	sentido m
sensato (Es)	besonnen	sensible	réfléchi(e)	avveduto(a)	—
sensazione (I)	Gefühl n	feeling	sentiment m	—	sentimiento m
sense (E)	Sinn m	—	sens m	senso m	sentido m
senseless (E)	sinnlos	—	insensé(e)	assurdo(a)	inútil
sensibile (I)	empfindlich	sensitive	sensible	—	sensible
sensible[1] (E)	besonnen	—	réfléchi	avveduto	sensato(a)

	D	E	F	I	Es
sensible² (E)	vernünftig	—	raisonnable	ragionevole	razonable
sensible (Es)	empfindlich	sensitive	sensible	sensibile	—
sensible (F)	empfindlich	sensitive	—	sensibile	sensible
sensitive (E)	empfindlich	—	sensible	sensibile	sensible
senso (I)	Sinn *m*	sense	sens *m*	—	sentido *m*
senso unico (I)	Einbahnstraße *f*	one-way street	rue à sens unique *f*	—	calle de dirección única *f*
sentarse (Es)	hinsetzen	sit down	asseoir, se	sedersi	—
sentence (E)	Satz *m*	—	phrase *f*	frase *f*	oración *f*
sentenciar (Es)	verurteilen	condemn	condamner	condannare	—
sentido (Es)	Sinn *m*	sense	sens *m*	senso *m*	—
sentiment (F)	Gefühl *n*	feeling	—	sensazione *f*	sentimiento *m*
sentimiento (Es)	Gefühl *n*	feeling	sentiment *m*	sensazione *f*	—
sentir (Es)	fühlen	feel	sentir	sentire	—
sentir¹ (F)	fühlen	feel	—	sentire	sentir
sentir² (F)	riechen	smell	—	sentire	oler
sentir³ (F)	schmecken	taste	—	piacere	gustar
sentire¹ (I)	fühlen	feel	sentir	—	sentir
sentire² (I)	hören	hear	entendre	—	oír
sentire³ (I)	riechen	smell	sentir	—	oler
sentire la mancanza (I)	vermissen	miss	manquer	—	echar de menos
senza (I)	ohne	without	sans	—	sin
senza dubbio (I)	zweifellos	doubtless	sans doute	—	sin duda
senza valore (I)	wertlos	worthless	sans valeur	—	sin valor
separación (Es)	Trennung *f*	separation	séparation *f*	separazione *f*	—
separado¹ (Es)	extra	extra	à part	a parte	—
separado² (Es)	getrennt	separate	séparé(e)	separato(a)	—
separar¹ (Es)	scheiden	part	séparer	separare	—
separar² (Es)	trennen	separate	séparer	separare	—
separare¹ (I)	scheiden	part	séparer	—	separar
separare² (I)	trennen	separate	séparer	—	separar
separate¹ (E)	trennen	—	séparer	separare	separar
separate² (E)	getrennt	—	séparé(e)	separato(a)	separado(a)
separation (E)	Trennung *f*	—	séparation *f*	separazione *f*	separación *f*
séparation (F)	Trennung *f*	separation	—	separazione *f*	separación *f*
separato¹ (I)	auseinander	apart	séparé(e)	—	lejos/distante
separato² (I)	getrennt	separate	séparé(e)	—	separado(a)
separazione (I)	Trennung *f*	separation	séparation *f*	—	separación *f*
séparé¹ (F)	getrennt	separate	—	separato(a)	separado(a)
séparé² (F)	auseinander	apart	—	separato(a)	lejos/distante
séparer¹ (F)	scheiden	part	—	separare	separar
séparer² (F)	trennen	separate	—	separare	separar
seppia (I)	Tintenfisch *m*	cuttlefish	seiche *f*	—	calamar *m*
sept (F)	sieben	seven	—	sette	siete
September (D)	—	September	septembre *m*	settembre *m*	septiembre *m*
September (E)	September *m*	—	septembre *m*	settembre *m*	septiembre *m*
septembre (F)	September *m*	September	—	settembre *m*	septiembre *m*
septiembre (Es)	September *m*	September	septembre *m*	settembre *m*	—

	D	E	F	I	Es
ser¹ (Es)	Wesen n	being	être m	essere m	—
ser² (Es)	sein	be	être	essere	—
sera (I)	Abend m	evening	soir m	—	noche f
sereno (Es)	Nachtwächter m	night-watchman	veilleur de nuit m	guardia notturna f	—
sereno (I)	sonnig	sunny	ensoleillé(e)	—	soleado(a)
serie (Es)	Folge f	consequence	suite f	conseguenza f	—
seriedad (Es)	Ernst m	seriousness	sérieux m	serietà f	—
serietà (I)	Ernst m	seriousness	sérieux m	—	seriedad f
sérieux¹ (F)	Ernst m	seriousness	—	serietà f	seriedad f
sérieux² (F)	ernst	serious	—	serio(a)	serio(a)
serio (I)	ernst	serious	sérieux(-ieuse)	—	serio(a)
serio (Es)	ernst	serious	sérieux(-ieuse)	serio(a)	—
serious (E)	ernst	—	sérieux(-ieuse)	serio(a)	serio(a)
seriousness (E)	Ernst m	—	sérieux m	serietà f	seriedad f
serpent (F)	Schlange f	snake	—	serpente m	serpiente f
serpente (I)	Schlange f	snake	serpent m	—	serpiente f
serpiente (Es)	Schlange f	snake	serpent m	serpente m	—
serratura (I)	Schloß n	lock	serrure f	—	cerradura f
serrure (F)	Schloß n	lock	—	serratura f	cerradura f
serve¹ (E)	bedienen	—	servir	servire	servir
serve² (E)	dienen	—	servir	servire	servir
serve³ (E)	servieren	—	servir	servire	servir
service¹ (E)	Bedienung f	—	service m	servizio m	servicio m
service² (E)	Dienst m	—	service m	servizio m	servicio m
service³ (E)	Gottesdienst m	—	office divin m	messa f	servicio religioso m
service¹ (F)	Bedienung f	service	—	servizio m	servicio m
service² (F)	Dienst m	service	—	servizio m	servicio m
service³ (F)	Gefallen m	favour	—	favore m	favor m
servicio¹ (Es)	Bedienung f	service	service m	servizio m	—
servicio² (Es)	Dienst m	service	service m	servizio m	—
servicio religioso (Es)	Gottesdienst m	service	office divin m	messa f	—
servieren (D)	—	serve	servir	servire	servir
Serviette (D)	—	serviette	serviette f	tovagliolo m	servilleta f
serviette (E)	Serviette f	—	serviette f	tovagliolo m	servilleta f
serviette¹ (F)	Handtuch n	towel	—	asciugamano m	pañuelo m
serviette² (F)	Mappe f	folder	—	raccoglitore m	carpeta f
serviette² (F)	Serviette f	serviette	—	tovagliolo m	servilleta f
servilleta (Es)	Serviette f	serviette	serviette f	tovagliolo m	—
servir¹ (Es)	bedienen	serve	servir	servire	—
servir² (Es)	dienen	serve	servir	servire	—
servir³ (Es)	servieren	serve	servir	servire	—
servir¹ (F)	bedienen	serve	—	servire	servir
servir² (F)	dienen	serve	—	servire	servir
servir³ (F)	servieren	serve	—	servire	servir
servire¹ (I)	bedienen	serve	servir	—	servir
servire² (I)	dienen	serve	servir	—	servir
servire³ (I)	servieren	serve	servir	—	servir

	D	E	F	I	Es
servizio¹ (I)	Bedienung f	service	service m	—	servicio m
servizio² (I)	Dienst m	service	service m	—	servicio m
sesenta (Es)	sechzig	sixty	soixante	sessanta	—
sessanta (I)	sechzig	sixty	soixante	—	sesenta
Sessel (D)	—	armchair	fauteuil m	poltrona f	sillón m
sesso (I)	Geschlecht n	sex	sexe m	—	sexo m
seta (I)	Seide f	silk	soie f	—	seda f
setaccio (I)	Sieb n	sieve	tamis m	—	colador m
sete (I)	Durst m	thirst	soif f	—	sed f
setenta (Es)	siebzig	seventy	soixante-dix	settanta	—
settanta (I)	siebzig	seventy	soixante-dix	—	setenta
sette (I)	sieben	seven	sept	—	siete
settembre (I)	September m	September	septembre m	—	septiembre m
settimana (I)	Woche f	week	semaine f	—	semana f
settimanale (I)	wöchentlich	weekly	hebdomadaire	—	semanal
settimana santa (I)	Osterwoche f	Holy week	semaine sainte f	—	Semana Santa f
settle down¹ (E)	einleben, sich	—	acclimater, se	ambientarsi	familiarizarse
settle down² (E)	niederlassen	—	s'installer	stabilirsi	instalarse
settlement (E)	Siedlung f	—	cité f	agglomerato m	colonia f
setzen (D)	—	put	mettre	mettere	poner
seul¹ (F)	allein	alone	—	solo(a)	solo(a)
seul² (F)	einzeln	single	—	singolo(a)	singular
seul³ (F)	einzig	only	—	unico(a)	único(a)
seulement¹ (F)	bloß	only	—	soltanto	sólo
seulement² (F)	nur	only	—	solo	sólo
seven (E)	sieben	—	sept	sette	siete
seventeen (E)	siebzehn	—	dix-sept	diciassette	diecisiete
seventy (E)	siebzig	—	soixante-dix	settanta	setenta
several¹ (E)	etliche	—	quelques	alcuni(e)	algunos(as)
several² (E)	mehrere	—	plusieurs	parecchi	muchos(as)
sévère (F)	streng	strict	—	severo(a)	riguroso(a)
severo (I)	streng	strict	sévère	—	riguroso(a)
sew (E)	nähen	—	coudre	cucire	cocer
sex (E)	Geschlecht n	—	sexe m	sesso m	sexo m
sexe (F)	Geschlecht n	sex	—	sesso m	sexo m
sexo (Es)	Geschlecht n	sex	sexe m	sesso m	—
sfacciato (I)	frech	cheeky	insolent(e)	—	atrevido(a)
sfiducia (I)	Mißtrauen n	distrust	méfiance f	—	desconfianza f
sfortuna (I)	Pech n	bad luck	malchance f	—	mala suerte f
sfortunato (I)	unglücklich	unhappy	malheureux(-euse)	—	desgraciado(a)
sforzarsi (I)	bemühen, sich	make an effort	efforcer, se	—	esforzarse
sforzo (I)	Bemühung f	effort	effort m	—	esfuerzo m
sfregare (I)	reiben	rub	frotter	—	frotar
sgarbato (I)	unfreundlich	unfriendly	peu aimable	—	descortés
sgualcire (I)	zerdrücken	squash	écraser	—	aplastar
sguardo (I)	Blick m	look	regard m	—	vista f
shadow (E)	Schatten m	—	ombre f	ombra f	sombra f
shady (E)	schattig	—	ombragé(e)	ombroso(a)	a la sombra

	D	E	F	I	Es
shake (E)	schütteln	—	secouer	agitare	agitar
share (E)	teilen	—	partager	dividere	partir
shark (E)	Hai *m*	—	requin *m*	pescecane *m*	tiburón *m*
sharp (E)	scharf	—	tranchant(e)	tagliente	cortante
sharpen (E)	schärfen	—	aiguiser	affilare	afilar
shave (E)	rasieren	—	raser	fare la barba	afeitar
shaver (E)	Rasierapparat *m*	—	rasoir *m*	rasoio *m*	máquina de afeitar *f*
she (E)	sie	—	elle	lei	ella
sheep (E)	Schaf *n*	—	mouton *m*	pecora *f*	oveja *f*
sheet (E)	Laken *n*	—	drap *m*	lenzuolo *m*	sábana *f*
sheet metal (E)	Blech *n*	—	tôle *f*	latta *f*	chapa *f*
shelves (E)	Regal *n*	—	étagère *f*	scaffale *m*	estantería *f*
shield (E)	Schild *n*	—	bouclier *m*	scudo *m*	escudo *m*
shine (E)	glänzen, scheinen	—	briller	splendere	brillar
ship (E)	Schiff *n*	—	navire *m*	nave *f*	barco *m*
shirt (E)	Hemd *n*	—	chemise *f*	camicia *f*	camisa *f*
shoe (E)	Schuh *m*	—	chaussure *f*	scarpa *f*	zapato *m*
shoemaker (E)	Schuster *m*	—	cordonnier *m*	calzolaio *m*	zapatero *m*
shoe polish (E)	Schuhcreme *f*	—	cirage *m*	lucido per scarpe *m*	betún *m*
shoeshop (E)	Schuhgeschäft *n*	—	magasin de chaussures *m*	negozio di scarpe *m*	zapatería *f*
shoot (E)	schießen	—	tirer	sparare	disparar
shop¹ (E)	Geschäft *n*	—	magasin *m*	negozio *m*	tienda *f*
shop² (E)	Laden *m*	—	magasin *m*	negozio *m*	tienda *f*
shopping (E)	Einkauf *m*	—	achat *m*	spesa *f*	compra *f*
shopping bag (E)	Einkaufstasche *f*	—	sac à provision *m*	borsa della spesa *f*	bolsa de compra *f*
shop-window (E)	Schaufenster *n*	—	vitrine *f*	vetrina *f*	escaparate *m*
shore (E)	Ufer *n*	—	bord *m*	riva *f*	orilla *f*
short (E)	kurz	—	court(e)	corto(a)	corto(a)
shortly (E)	demnächst	—	prochainement	presto	próximamente
shot¹ (E)	Foto *n*	—	photo *f*	foto *f*	foto *f*
shot² (E)	Schuß *m*	—	coup *m*	sparo *m*	disparo *m*
shoulder (E)	Schulter *f*	—	épaule *f*	spalla *f*	hombro *m*
shout (E)	rufen	—	appeler	chiamare	llamar
shovel (E)	Schaufel *f*	—	pelle *f*	pala *f*	pala *f*
show¹ (E)	vorzeigen	—	monter	esibire	presentar
show² (E)	zeigen	—	montrer	mostrare	indicar
shower (E)	Dusche *f*	—	douche *f*	doccia *f*	ducha *f*
shut (E)	zumachen	—	fermer	chiudere	cerrar
shy¹ (E)	scheu	—	timide	timido(a)	tímido(a)
shy² (E)	schüchtern	—	timide	timido(a)	tímido(a)
sí (Es)	ja	yes	oui	sì	—
si (Es)	ob	if/whether	si	se	—
si¹ (F)	doch	still	—	sì!	sin embargo
si² (F)	ob	if/whether	—	se	si
si³ (F)	wenn	when/if	—	se/quando	cuando
sì (I)	ja	yes	oui	—	sí

	D	E	F	I	Es
si! (I)	doch	still	si	—	sin embargo
sicher (D)	—	sure	sûr(e)	sicuro(a)	seguro(a)
Sicherheit (D)	—	safety	sécurité f	sicurezza f	seguridad f
Sicht (D)	—	view	vue f	vista f	vista f
sichtbar (D)	—	visible	visible	visibile	visible
sicurezza (I)	Sicherheit f	safety	sécurité f	—	seguridad f
sicuro (I)	sicher	sure	sûr(e)	—	seguro(a)
sicuro di sé (I)	selbstsicher	self-assured	sûr(e) de soi	—	seguro de sí mismo
sie (D)	—	she	elle	lei	ella
sie (D)	—	they	ils/elles	loro	ellos, ellas
Sieb (D)	—	sieve	tamis m	setaccio m	colador m
sieben (D)	—	seven	sept	sette	siete
siebzehn (D)	—	seventeen	dix-sept	diciassette	diecisiete
siebzig (D)	—	seventy	soixante-dix	settanta	setenta
siècle (F)	Jahrhundert n	century	—	secolo m	siglo m
Siedlung (D)	—	settlement	cité f	agglomerato m	colonia f
Sieg (D)	—	victory	victoire f	vittoria f	victoria f
siège (F)	Sitz m	seat	—	sede f	asiento m
siegen (D)	—	win	gagner	vincere	vencer
siempre[1] (Es)	immer	always	toujours	sempre	—
siempre[2] (Es)	stets	always	toujours	sempre	—
sierra (Es)	Säge f	saw	scie f	sega f	—
siete (Es)	sieben	seven	sept	sette	—
sieve (E)	Sieb n	—	tamis m	setaccio m	colador m
sifflet (F)	Pfeife f	whistle	—	fischietto m	silbato m
sigaretta (I)	Zigarette f	cigarette	cigarette f	—	cigarrillo m
sigaro (I)	Zigarre f	cigar	cigare m	—	cigarro m
sight (E)	Sehenswürdig-keit f	—	curiosité f	curiosità f	lugares de interés m pl
siglo (Es)	Jahrhundert n	century	siècle m	secolo m	—
sign[1] (E)	unterschreiben	—	signer	firmare	firmar
sign[2] (E)	Zeichen n	—	signe m	segnale m	signo m
signature (E)	Unterschrift f	—	signature f	firma f	firma f
signature (F)	Unterschrift f	signature	—	firma f	firma f
signe[1] (F)	Merkmal n	characteristic	—	caratteristica f	rasgo m
signe[2] (F)	Zeichen n	sign	—	segnale m	signo m
signer (F)	unterschreiben	sign	—	firmare	firmar
significado (Es)	Bedeutung f	meaning	signification f	significato m	—
significant (E)	bedeutend	—	important(e)	importante	importante
significar (Es)	bedeuten	mean	signifier	significare	—
significare (I)	bedeuten	mean	signifier	—	significar
signification (F)	Bedeutung f	meaning	—	significato m	significado m
significato (I)	Bedeutung f	meaning	signification f	—	significado m
signifier (F)	bedeuten	mean	—	significare	significar
signo (Es)	Zeichen n	sign	signe m	segnale m	—
signora (I)	Dame f	lady	dame f	—	señora f
signore (I)	Herr m	gentleman	monsieur m	—	señor m
signorina (I)	Fräulein n	Miss	mademoiselle	—	señorita f

	D	E	F	I	Es
siguiente[1] (Es)	folgend	following	suivant(e)	seguente	—
siguiente[2] (Es)	nächste(r,s)	next	suivant(e)	prossimo(a)	—
silbato (Es)	Pfeife f	whistle	sifflet m	fischietto m	—
Silber (D)	—	silver	argent m	argento m	plata f
silbern (D)	—	silver	d'argent	d'argento	plateado(a)
silenzio (I)	Ruhe f	calm	calme m	—	quietud f
silk (E)	Seide f	—	soie f	seta f	seda f
silla (Es)	Stuhl m	chair	chaise f	sedia f	—
sillabare (I)	buchstabieren	spell	épeler	—	deletrear
sillón (Es)	Sessel m	armchair	fauteuil m	poltrona f	—
silver[1] (E)	silbern	—	d'argent	d'argento	plateado(a)
silver[2] (E)	Silber n	—	argent m	argento m	plata f
Silvester (D)	—	New Year's Eve	Saint-Sylvestre m	San Silvestro m	Noche Vieja f
s'il vous plaît (F)	bitte	please	—	prego	por favor
similar (E)	ähnlich	—	semblable	simile	parecido(a)
simile (I)	ähnlich	similar	semblable	—	parecido(a)
simpatico (I)	sympathisch	likeable	sympathique	—	simpático(a)
simpático (Es)	sympathisch	likeable	sympathique	simpatico(a)	—
simple (E)	einfach	—	simple	semplice	sencillo(a)
simple (F)	einfach	simple	—	semplice	sencillo(a)
simultaneous (E)	gleichzeitig	—	en même temps	contemporaneo(a)	a la vez
sin (E)	Sünde f	—	péché m	peccato m	pecado m
sin (Es)	ohne	without	sans	senza	—
since (E)	seit	—	depuis	da	de/desde
sincère (F)	aufrichtig	honest	—	onesto(a)	sincero(a)
sincero (Es)	aufrichtig	honest	sincère	onesto(a)	—
sin colegio (Es)	schulfrei	holiday	de congé	vacanza	—
sin compromiso (Es)	unverbindlich	not binding	sans engagement	non impegnativo(a)	—
sindacato (I)	Gewerkschaft f	trade union	syndicat m	—	sindicato m
sindaco (I)	Bürgermeister m	mayor	maire m	—	alcalde m
sindicato (Es)	Gewerkschaft f	trade union	syndicat m	sindacato m	—
sin dinero (Es)	pleite	penniless	fauché(e)	fallito(a)	—
sin duda (Es)	zweifellos	doubtless	sans doute	senza dubbio	—
sin embargo[1] (Es)	doch	still	si	si!	—
sin embargo[2] (Es)	dennoch	nevertheless	cependant	tuttavia	—
sin embargo[3] (Es)	jedoch	however	cependant	tutta via	—
sing (E)	singen	—	chanter	cantare	cantar
singe (F)	Affe m	ape	—	scimmia f	mono m
singen (D)	—	sing	chanter	cantare	cantar
singer (E)	Sänger m	—	chanteur m	cantante m	cantante m
singing (E)	Gesang m	—	chant m	canto m	canto m
single[1] (E)	einzeln	—	seul(e)	singolo(a)	singular
single[2] (E)	ledig	—	célibataire	celibe m/nubile f	soltero(a)
singolo (I)	einzeln	single	seul(e)	—	singular
singular (Es)	einzeln	single	seul(e)	singolo(a)	—
singulier (F)	eigenartig	strange	—	strano(a)	extraño(a)
sin importancia (Es)	unwichtig	unimportant	sans importance	non importante	—

	D	E	F	I	Es
sink¹ (E)	sinken	—	couler	affondare	hundirse
sink² (E)	versinken	—	enfoncer, se	affondare	hundirse
sinken (D)	—	sink	couler	affondare	hundirse
Sinn (D)	—	sense	sens *m*	senso *m*	sentido *m*
sinnlos (D)	—	senseless	insensé(e)	assurdo(a)	inútil
sino (Es)	sondern	but	mais	ma/bensì	—
sin ruido (Es)	leise	quietly	à voix basse	a bassa voce	—
sin valor (Es)	wertlos	worthless	sans valeur	senza valore	—
sistema (Es)	System *n*	system	système *m*	sistema *m*	—
sistema (I)	System *n*	system	système *m*	—	sistema *m*
sistemare (I)	unterbringen	stow	ranger	—	colocar
sister (E)	Schwester *f*	—	sœur *f*	sorella *f*	hermana *f*
sister-in-law (E)	Schwägerin *f*	—	belle-sœur *f*	cognata *f*	cuñada *f*
sit (E)	sitzen	—	être assis(e)	stare seduto(a)	estar sentado(a)
sit down (E)	hinsetzen	—	asseoir, se	sedersi	sentarse
Sitte (D)	—	custom	coutume *f*	usanza *f*	costumbre *f*
sittlich (D)	—	moral	moral(e)	morale	moral
situación¹ (Es)	Lage *f*	situation	situation *f*	situazione *f*	—
situación² (Es)	Situation *f*	situation	situation *f*	situazione *f*	—
Situation (D)	—	situation	situation *f*	situazione *f*	situación *f*
situation¹ (E)	Lage *f*	—	situation *f*	situazione *f*	situación *f*
situation² (E)	Situation *f*	—	situation *f*	situazione *f*	situación *f*
situation¹ (F)	Lage *f*	situation	—	situazione *f*	situación *f*
situation² (F)	Situation *f*	situation	—	situazione *f*	situación *f*
situazione¹ (I)	Lage *f*	situation	situation *f*	—	situación *f*
situazione² (I)	Situation *f*	situation	situation *f*	—	situación *f*
Sitz (D)	—	seat	siège *m*	sede *f*	asiento *m*
sitzen (D)	—	sit	être assis(e)	stare seduto(a)	estar sentado(a)
Sitzplatz (D)	—	seat	place assise *f*	posto a sedere *m*	asiento *m*
Sitzung (D)	—	meeting	séance *f*	seduta *f*	reunión *f*
six (E)	sechs	—	six	sei	seis
six (F)	sechs	six	—	sei	seis
sixteen (E)	sechzehn	—	seize	sedici	dieciseis
sixty (E)	sechzig	—	soixante	sessanta	sesenta
size (E)	Größe *f*	—	taille *f*	taglia *f*	talla *f*
Skandal (D)	—	scandal	scandale *m*	scandalo *m*	escándalo *m*
Skandinavien (D)	—	Scandinavia	Scandinavie *f*	Scandinavia *f*	Escandinavia *f*
sketch (E)	Skizze *f*	—	esquisse *f*	schizzo *m*	boceto *m*
Ski (D)	—	ski	ski *m*	sci *m*	esquí *m*
ski (E)	Ski *m*	—	ski *m*	sci *m*	esquí *m*
ski (F)	Ski *m*	ski	—	sci *m*	esquí *m*
Skilift (D)	—	skilift	remonte-pente *m*	sciovia *f*	telesilla *f*
skilift (E)	Skilift *m*	—	remonte-pente *m*	sciovia *f*	telesilla *f*
skillful (E)	geschickt	—	habile	abile	mañoso(a)
skin (E)	Haut *f*	—	peau *f*	pelle *f*	piel *f*
skinny¹ (E)	dürr	—	maigre	secco(a)	árido(a)
skinny² (E)	mager	—	maigre	magro(a)	delgado(a)
skirt (E)	Rock *m*	—	jupe *f*	gonna *f*	falda *f*

	D	E	F	I	Es
Skizze (D)	—	sketch	esquisse *f*	schizzo *m*	boceto *m*
Sklave (D)	—	slave	esclave *m*	schiavo *m*	esclavo *m*
Skorpion (D)	—	scorpion	scorpion *m*	scorpione *m*	escorpión *m*
skull (E)	Schädel *m*	—	crâne *m*	cranio *m*	cráneo *m*
Skulptur (D)	—	sculpture	sculpture *f*	scultura *f*	escultura *f*
sky (E)	Himmel *m*	—	ciel *m*	cielo *m*	cielo *m*
slacken (E)	nachlassen	—	apaiser, se	allentare	aflojar
slave (E)	Sklave *m*	—	esclave *m*	schiavo *m*	esclavo *m*
sleep[1] (E)	schlafen	—	dormir	dormire	dormir
sleep[2] (E)	Schlaf *m*	—	sommeil *m*	sonno *m*	sueño *m*
sleep on (E)	weiterschlafen	—	continuer à dormir	continuare a dormire	seguir durmiendo
sleeve (E)	Ärmel *m*	—	manche *f*	manica *f*	manga *f*
slide[1] (E)	Dia *n*	—	diapositive *f*	diapositiva *f*	diapositiva *f*
slide[2] (E)	rutschen	—	glisser	scivolare	resbalar
slight (E)	gering	—	minime	poco(a)	pequeño(a)
slim (E)	schlank	—	mince	snello(a)	delgado(a)
slip (E)	Unterrock *m*	—	jupon *m*	sottoveste *f*	combinación *f*
slip (F)	Unterhose *f*	underpants	—	mutande *f pl*	calzoncillos *m pl*
slip de bain (F)	Badehose *f*	swimming trunks	—	costume da bagno *m*	bañador *m*
slipper (E)	Pantoffel *f*	—	pantoufle *f*	pantofola *f*	zapatilla *f*
slip road (E)	Auffahrt *f*	—	bretelle d'accès *f*	entrata *f*	vía de acceso *f*
sloggiare (I)	ausziehen	move out	déménager	—	mudarse
slope (E)	Hang *m*	—	versant *m*	pendio *m*	pendiente *m*
sloped (E)	schief	—	en pente	obliquo(a)	torcido(a)
slow (E)	langsam	—	lent(e)	lento(a)	despacio(a)
small (E)	klein	—	petit(e)	piccolo(a)	pequeño(a)
small change (E)	Kleingeld *n*	—	monnaie *f*	spiccioli *m pl*	cambio *m*
small package (E)	Päckchen *n*	—	petit paquet *m*	pacchetto *m*	paquetito *m*
Smaragd (D)	—	emerald	émeraude *f*	smeraldo *m*	esmeralda *f*
smash (E)	einschlagen	—	casser	rompere	romper
smell[1] (E)	Geruch *m*	—	odeur *f*	odore *m*	olor *m*
smell[2] (E)	riechen	—	sentir	sentire	oler
smeraldo (I)	Smaragd *m*	emerald	émeraude *f*	—	esmeralda *f*
smile[1] (E)	lächeln	—	sourire	sorridere	sonreír
smile[2] (E)	Lächeln *n*	—	sourire *m*	sorriso *m*	sonrisa *f*
smoke[1] (E)	rauchen	—	fumer	fumare	fumar
smoke[2] (E)	Rauch *m*	—	fumée *f*	fumo *m*	humo *m*
smoker (E)	Raucher *m*	—	fumeur *m*	fumatore *m*	fumador *m*
smooth (E)	glatt	—	lisse	liscio(a)	liso(a)
snack (E)	Imbiß *m*	—	casse-croûte *m*	spuntino *m*	refrigerio *m*
snake (E)	Schlange *f*	—	serpent *m*	serpente *m*	serpiente *f*
sneeze (E)	niesen	—	éternuer	starnutire	estornudar
snello (I)	schlank	slim	mince	—	delgado(a)
snore (E)	schnarchen	—	ronfler	russare	roncar
snow[1] (E)	schneien	—	neiger	nevicare	nevar
snow[2] (E)	Schnee *m*	—	neige *f*	neve *f*	nieve *f*
so (D)	—	like this	ainsi	così	así

	D	E	F	I	Es
soap (E)	Seife *f*	—	savon *m*	sapone *m*	jabón *m*
sobald (D)	—	as soon as	dès que	appena	tan pronto como
sobborgo (I)	Vorort *m*	suburb	faubourg *m*	—	suburbio *m*
sober (E)	nüchtern	—	sobre	sobrio(a)	sobrio(a)
sobre[1] (Es)	Umschlag *m*	envelope	enveloppe *f*	busta *f*	—
sobre[2] (Es)	auf	on/on top/onto	sur	su/sopra	—
sobre (F)	nüchtern	sober	—	sobrio(a)	sobrio(a)
sobre todo (Es)	besonders	especially	surtout	particolarmente	—
sobrevalorar (Es)	überschätzen	overestimate	surestimer	sopravvalutare	—
sobrevivir (Es)	überleben	survive	survivre	sopravvivere	—
sobrina (Es)	Nichte *f*	niece	nièce *f*	nipote *f*	—
sobrino (Es)	Neffe *m*	nephew	neveu *m*	nipote *m*	—
sobrio (Es)	nüchtern	sober	sobre	sobrio(a)	—
sobrio (I)	nüchtern	sober	sobre	—	sobrio(a)
soccombere (I)	unterliegen	be defeated	être vaincu(e) par qn	—	sucumbir
sociedad (Es)	Gesellschaft *f*	society	société *f*	società *f*	—
società (I)	Gesellschaft *f*	society	société *f*	—	sociedad *f*
société (F)	Gesellschaft *f*	society	—	società *f*	sociedad *f*
society (E)	Gesellschaft *f*	—	société *f*	società *f*	sociedad *f*
sock (E)	Socke *f*	—	chausette *f*	calzino *m*	calcetín *m*
Socke (D)	—	sock	chausette *f*	calzino *m*	calcetín *m*
socket (E)	Steckdose *f*	—	prise électrique *f*	presa *f*	enchufe *m*
soddisfare (I)	befriedigen	satisfy	satisfaire	—	satisfacer
soeben (D)	—	just now	à l'instant même	poco fa	ahora mismo
sœur (F)	Schwester *f*	sister	—	sorella *f*	hermana *f*
Sofa (D)	—	sofa	canapé *m*	sofà *m*	sofá *m*
sofa (E)	Sofa *n*	—	canapé *m*	sofà *m*	sofá *m*
sofá (Es)	Sofa *n*	sofa	canapé *m*	sofà *m*	—
sofà (I)	Sofa *n*	sofa	canapé *m*	—	sofá *m*
so far (E)	bisher	—	jusqu'à présent	finora	hasta ahora
soffiare (I)	blasen	blow	souffler	—	soplar
soffrire (I)	leiden	suffer	souffrir	—	sufrir
sofocante (Es)	schwül	sultry	lourd(e)	afoso(a)	—
sofort (D)	—	immediately	immédiatement	subito	en seguida
soft[1] (E)	weich	—	doux(douce)	morbido(a)	tierno(a)
soft[2] (E)	zart	—	doux (douce)	tenero(a)	suave
soga (Es)	Seil *n*	rope	corde *f*	fune *f*	—
sogar (D)	—	even	même	perfino	incluso
soggiorno (I)	Aufenthalt *m*	stay	séjour *m*	—	estancia *f*
sogliola (I)	Seezunge *f*	sole	sole *f*	—	lenguado *m*
sognare (I)	träumen	dream	rêver	—	soñar
sogno (I)	Traum *m*	dream	rêve *m*	—	sueño *m*
Sohle (D)	—	sole	semelle *f*	suola *f*	suela *f*
Sohn (D)	—	son	fils *m*	figlio *m*	hijo *m*
soie (F)	Seide *f*	silk	—	seta *f*	seda *f*
soif (F)	Durst *m*	thirst	—	sete *f*	sed *f*
soigné (F)	gepflegt	looked-after	—	curato(a)	cuidado(a)

	D	E	F	I	Es
soigner (F)	pflegen	look after	—	curare	cuidar
soigneux (F)	sorgfältig	careful(ly)	—	accurato(a)	cuidadoso(a)
soins (F)	Pflege *f*	care	—	cura *f*	aseo *m*
soir (F)	Abend *m*	evening	—	sera *f*	noche *f*
soixante (F)	sechzig	sixty	—	sessanta	sesenta
soixante-dix (F)	siebzig	seventy	—	settanta	setenta
sol (Es)	Sonne *f*	sun	soleil *m*	sole *m*	—
sol (F)	Fußboden *m*	floor	—	pavimento *m*	suelo *m*
solange (D)	—	as long	tant que	finché	en tanto que
solche (D)	—	such	tel(le)	tale(i)	un(a) tal
soldado (Es)	Soldat *m*	soldier	soldat *m*	soldato *m*	—
Soldat (D)	—	soldier	soldat *m*	soldato *m*	soldado *m*
soldat (F)	Soldat *m*	soldier	—	soldato *m*	soldado *m*
soldato (I)	Soldat *m*	soldier	soldat *m*	—	soldado *m*
soldes (F)	Ausverkauf *m*	sale	—	saldi *m*	liquidación *f*
soldier (E)	Soldat *m*	—	soldat *m*	soldato *m*	soldado *m*
sold out (E)	ausverkauft	—	épuisé(e)	esaurito(a)	vendido(a)
sole[1] (E)	Sohle *f*	—	semelle *f*	suola *f*	suela *f*
sole[2] (E)	Seezunge *f*	—	sole *f*	sogliola *f*	lenguado *m*
sole (F)	Seezunge *f*	sole	—	sogliola *f*	lenguado *m*
sole (I)	Sonne *f*	sun	soleil *m*	—	sol *m*
soleado (Es)	sonnig	sunny	ensoleillé(e)	sereno(a)	—
soleil (F)	Sonne *f*	sun	—	sole *m*	sol *m*
solicitud (Es)	Antrag *m*	application	demande *f*	domanda *f*	—
solid (E)	fest	—	solide	solido(a)	firme
solide (F)	fest	solid	—	solido(a)	firme
solido (I)	fest	solid	solide	—	firme
solitaire (F)	einsam	lonely	—	solitario(a)	solitario(a)
solitario (Es)	einsam	lonely	solitaire	solitario(a)	—
solitario (I)	einsam	lonely	solitaire	—	solitario(a)
solito (I)	üblich	usual	habituel(le)	—	usual
sollen (D)	—	have to	devoir	dovere	deber
solo[1] (Es)	allein	alone	seul	solo(a)	—
sólo[2] (Es)	bloß	only	seulement	soltanto	—
sólo[3] (Es)	nur	only	seulement	solo	—
solo[1] (I)	allein	alone	seul	—	solo(a)
solo[2] (I)	nur	only	seulement	—	sólo
soltanto (I)	bloß	only	seulement	—	sólo
soltero[1] (Es)	Junggeselle *m*	bachelor	célibataire *m*	scapolo *m*	—
soltero[2] (Es)	ledig	single	célibataire	celibe *m*/nubile *f*	—
soltero[3] (Es)	unverheiratet	unmarried	non marié(e)	celibe *m*/nubile *f*	—
solución (Es)	Lösung *f*	solution	solution *f*	soluzione *f*	—
solution (E)	Lösung *f*	—	solution *f*	soluzione *f*	solución *f*
solution (F)	Lösung *f*	solution	—	soluzione *f*	solución *f*
soluzione (I)	Lösung *f*	solution	solution *f*	—	solución *f*
solve (E)	lösen	—	résoudre	sciogliere	desatar
sombra (Es)	Schatten *m*	shadow	ombre *f*	ombra *f*	—
sombre[1] (F)	dunkel	dark	—	scuro(a)	oscuro(a)

	D	E	F	I	Es
sombre² (F)	finster	dark	—	buio(a)	oscuro(a)
sombrero (Es)	Hut m	hat	chapeau m	cappello m	—
sombrilla (Es)	Sonnenschirm m	parasol	parasol m	ombrellone m	—
some¹ (E)	einige	—	quelques	alcuni(e)	algunos(as)
some² (E)	irgendein(e)	—	quelconque	qualcuno(a)	cualquiera
somebody¹ (E)	irgend jemand	—	n'importe qui	qualcuno(a)	alguno(a)
somebody² (E)	jemand	—	quelqu'un	qualcuno(a)	alguien
somehow (E)	irgendwie	—	n'importe comment	in qualche modo	de alguna manera
someter (Es)	unterwerfen	subject	soumettre	sottomettere	—
something¹ (E)	etwas	—	quelque chose	qualcosa	algo
something² (E)	irgend etwas	—	n'importe quoi	qualsiasi cosa	algo
sometimes (E)	manchmal	—	quelquefois	talvolta	a veces
somewhere (E)	irgendwo	—	n'importe où	in qualche posto	en alguna parte
somma¹ (I)	Betrag m	amount	montant m	—	importe m
somma² (I)	Summe f	sum	somme f	—	suma f
sommare (I)	addieren	add up	additionner	—	sumar
somme (F)	Summe f	sum	—	somma f	suma f
sommeil (F)	Schlaf m	sleep	—	sonno m	sueño m
Sommer (D)	—	summer	été m	estate f	verano m
Sommerzeit (D)	—	summertime	heure d'été f	ora legale f	temporada de verano f
sommet (F)	Gipfel m	peak	—	cima f	cumbre f
so much (E)	soviel	—	tant	quanto/tanto	tanto
son (E)	Sohn m	—	fils m	figlio m	hijo m
son¹ (F)	Klang m	sound	—	suono m	sonido m
son² (F)	Ton m	sound	—	suono m	sonido m
soñar (Es)	träumen	dream	rêver	sognare	—
Sonderangebot (D)	—	special offer	offre spéciale f	offerta speciale f	oferta especial f
sondern (D)	—	but	mais	ma/bensì	sino
song (E)	Lied n	—	chanson f	canzone f	canción f
sonido¹ (Es)	Klang m	sound	son m	suono m	—
sonido² (Es)	Ton m	sound	son m	suono m	—
Sonnabend (D)	—	Saturday	samedi m	sabato m	sábado m
Sonne (D)	—	sun	soleil m	sole m	sol m
Sonnenaufgang (D)	—	sunrise	lever du soleil m	sorgere del sole m	salida del sol f
Sonnenbrand (D)	—	sunburn	coup de soleil m	scottatura solare f	quemadura solar f
Sonnenbrille (D)	—	sunglasses	lunettes de soleil f pl	occhiali da sole m pl	gafas de sol f pl
Sonnenschirm (D)	—	parasol	parasol m	ombrellone m	sombrilla f
Sonnen-untergang (D)	—	sunset	coucher du soleil m	tramonto del sole m	puesta del sol f
sonner¹ (F)	klingeln	ring the bell	—	suonare	tocar el timbre
sonner² (F)	läuten	ring	—	suonare	tocar
sonnette (F)	Klingel f	bell	—	campanello m	timbre m
sonnig (D)	—	sunny	ensoleillé(e)	sereno(a)	soleado(a)
sonno (I)	Schlaf m	sleep	sommeil m	—	sueño m
Sonntag (D)	—	Sunday	dimanche m	domenica f	domingo m
sonreír (Es)	lächeln	smile	sourire	sorridere	—
sonrisa (Es)	Lächeln n	smile	sourire m	sorriso m	—

	D	E	F	I	Es
sonst (D)	—	otherwise	autrement	altrimenti	por lo demás
soon (E)	bald	—	bientôt	presto	pronto
sooner (E)	eher	—	plus tôt	prima	antes
sopa (Es)	Suppe *f*	soup	soupe *f*	zuppa *f*	—
soplar (Es)	blasen	blow	souffler	soffiare	—
soportar (Es)	ertragen	bear	supporter	sopportare	—
sopportare[1] (I)	aushalten	bear	supporter	—	aguantar
sopportare[2] (I)	ertragen	bear	supporter	—	soportar
sopprimere (I)	unterdrücken	oppress	opprimer	—	oprimir
sopra[1] (I)	darüber	above	au dessus	—	por encima
sopra[2] (I)	oben	above	en haut	—	arriba
sopravvalutare (I)	überschätzen	overestimate	surestimer	—	sobrevalorar
sopravvivere (I)	überleben	survive	survivre	—	sobrevivir
sorcière (F)	Hexe *f*	witch	—	strega *f*	bruja *f*
sordo (Es)	taub	deaf	sourd(e)	sordo(a)	—
sordo (I)	taub	deaf	sourd(e)	—	sordo(a)
sorella (I)	Schwester *f*	sister	sœur *f*	—	hermana *f*
sore throat (E)	Halsschmerzen *pl*	—	mal de gorge *m*	mal di gola *m*	dolor de garganta *m*
Sorge (D)	—	concern	souci *m*	preoccupazione *f*	preocupación *f*
sorgen (D)	—	worry about	occuper de, se	prendersi cura di	atender
sorgente (I)	Quelle *f*	spring	source *f*	—	fuente *f*
sorgere del sole (I)	Sonnenaufgang *m*	sunrise	lever du soleil *m*	—	salida del sol *f*
sorgfältig (D)	—	careful(ly)	soigneux(-euse)	accurato(a)	cuidadoso(a)
sorpassare (I)	überholen	overtake	doubler	—	adelantar
sorprender (Es)	überraschen	surprise	surprendre	sorprendere	—
sorprendere (I)	überraschen	surprise	surprendre	—	sorprender
sorprendido (Es)	überrascht	surprised	surpris(e)	sorpreso(a)	—
sorpresa (Es)	Überraschung *f*	surprise	surprise *f*	sorpresa *f*	—
sorpresa (I)	Überraschung *f*	surprise	surprise *f*	—	sorpresa *f*
sorpreso (I)	überrascht	surprised	surpris(e)	—	sorprendido(a)
sorridere (I)	lächeln	smile	sourire	—	sonreír
sorriso (I)	Lächeln *n*	smile	sourire *m*	—	sonrisa *f*
sort[1] (E)	sortieren	—	trier	assortire	clasificar
sort[2] (E)	Sorte *f*	—	sorte *f*	specie *f*	clase *f*
Sorte (D)	—	sort	sorte *f*	specie *f*	clase *f*
sorte (F)	Sorte *f*	sort	—	specie *f*	clase *f*
sortie (F)	Ausgang *m*	exit	—	uscita *f*	salida *f*
sortie de secours (F)	Notausgang *m*	emergency exit	—	uscita di sicurezza *f*	salida de emergencia *f*
sortieren (D)	—	sort	trier	assortire	clasificar
sortija (Es)	Ring *m*	ring	bague *f*	anello *m*	—
sortir[1] (F)	ausgehen	go out	—	uscire	salir
sortir[2] (F)	hinausgehen	go out	—	uscire	salir afuera
sortir[3] (F)	heraustreten	step out	—	uscire fuori	salir
sorvegliare[1] (I)	bewachen	guard	garder	—	vigilar
sorvegliare[2] (I)	überwachen	supervise	surveiller	—	vigilar
soso (Es)	fade	dull	fade	insipido(a)	—
sospechoso (Es)	verdächtig	suspicious	suspect(e)	sospetto(a)	—

	D	E	F	I	Es
sospetto (I)	verdächtig	suspicious	suspect(e)	—	sospechoso(a)
Soße (D)	—	sauce	sauce *f*	salsa *f*	salsa *f*
sostegno (I)	Unterstützung *f*	support	soutien *m*	—	apoyo *m*
sostituire (I)	ersetzen	replace	remplacer	—	sustituir
sostituzione (I)	Ersatz *m*	substitute	remplacement *m*	—	sustitución *f*
sot (F)	albern	foolish	—	sciocco(a)	tonto(a)
sótano (Es)	Keller *m*	cellar	cave *f*	cantina *f*	—
sottile (I)	fein	fine	fin(e)	—	fino(a)
sotto[1] (I)	darunter	underneath	en dessous	—	por debajo
sotto[2] (I)	unten	downstairs	dessous	—	abajo
sottolineare (I)	unterstreichen	underline	souligner	—	subrayar
sottomettere (I)	unterwerfen	subject	soumettre	—	someter
sottopassaggio (I)	Unterführung *f*	subway	passage souterrain *m*	—	paso inferior *m*
sottosopra (I)	durcheinander	in a muddle	pêle-mêle	—	en desorden
sottoveste (I)	Unterrock *m*	slip	jupon *m*	—	combinación *f*
sottrarre[1] (I)	abziehen	subtract	retirer	—	restar
sottrarre[2] (I)	unterschlagen	embezzle	soustraire	—	sustraer
souci (F)	Sorge *f*	concern	—	preoccupazione *f*	preocupación *f*
soucoupe (F)	Untertasse *f*	saucer	—	piattino *m*	platillo *m*
souffler[1] (F)	abblasen	call off	—	disdire	anular
souffler[2] (F)	blasen	blow	—	soffiare	soplar
souffrir (F)	leiden	suffer	—	soffrire	sufrir
souhait (F)	Wunsch *m*	wish	—	desiderio *m*	deseo *m*
souhaiter (F)	wünschen	wish	—	desiderare	desear
soûl (F)	betrunken	drunk	—	ubriaco	borracho(a)
soulèvement (F)	Aufstand *m*	rebellion	—	insurrezione *f*	revuelta *f*
soulever (F)	heben	lift	—	alzare	levantar
souligner (F)	unterstreichen	underline	—	sottolineare	subrayar
soumettre (F)	unterwerfen	subject	—	sottomettere	someter
sound[1] (E)	Geräusch *n*	—	bruit *m*	rumore *m*	ruido *m*
sound[2] (E)	Klang *m*	—	son *m*	suono *m*	sonido *m*
sound[3] (E)	Ton *m*	—	son *m*	suono *m*	sonido *m*
soup (E)	Suppe *f*	—	soupe *f*	zuppa *f*	sopa *f*
soupe (F)	Suppe *f*	soup	—	zuppa *f*	sopa *f*
sour (E)	sauer	—	aigre	acido(a)	agrio(a)
source (F)	Quelle *f*	spring	—	sorgente *f*	fuente *f*
sourd (F)	taub	deaf	—	sordo(a)	sordo(a)
sourire[1] (F)	lächeln	smile	—	sorridere	sonreír
sourire[2] (F)	Lächeln *n*	smile	—	sorriso *m*	sonrisa *f*
souris (F)	Maus *f*	mouse	—	topo *m*	ratón *m*
sous (F)	unter	under	—	al di sotto di	debajo de
sous-louer (F)	untervermieten	sublet	—	subaffittare	realquilar
soustraire (F)	unterschlagen	embezzle	—	sottrarre	sustraer
sous-vêtements (F)	Unterwäsche *f*	underwear	—	biancheria intima *f*	ropa interior *f*
soutenir (F)	unterstützen	support	—	assistere	apoyar
South (E)	Süden *m*	—	sud *m*	sud	sur *m*
southern (E)	südlich	—	du sud	a sud	al sur

special

	D	E	F	I	Es
soutien (F)	Unterstützung f	support	—	sostegno m	apoyo m
souvenir (E)	Andenken n	—	souvenir m	ricordo m	recuerdo m
souvenir¹ (F)	Andenken n	souvenir	—	ricordo m	recuerdo m
souvenir² (F)	erinnern	remember	—	ricordare	recordar
souvenir³ (F)	Erinnerung f	memory	—	ricordo m	memoria f
souvenir de, se (F)	gedenken	remember	—	ricordare	conmemorar
souvent (F)	oft	often	—	spesso	a menudo
soviel (D)	—	so much	tant	quanto/tanto	tanto
soweit (D)	—	as far as	autant que	fin dove	hasta tanto
sowohl (D)	—	as well as	aussi bien	tanto...quanto	tanto...
space (E)	Zwischenraum m	—	espace m	spazio m	espacio intermedio m
spacieux (F)	geräumig	spacious	—	spazioso(a)	espacioso(a)
spacious (E)	geräumig	—	spacieux(-euse)	spazioso(a)	espacioso(a)
Spagna (I)	Spanien n	Spain	Espagne f	—	España f
spagnolo¹ (I)	spanisch	Spanish	espagnol(e)	—	español(a)
spagnolo² (I)	Spanier m	Spaniard	Espagnol m	—	español m
Spain (E)	Spanien n	—	Espagne f	Spagna f	España f
spalla (I)	Schulter f	shoulder	épaule f	—	hombro m
Spaniard (E)	Spanier m	—	Espagnol m	spagnolo m	español m
Spanien (D)	—	Spain	Espagne f	Spagna f	España f
Spanier (D)	—	Spaniard	Espagnol m	spagnolo m	español m
spanisch (D)	—	Spanish	espagnol(e)	spagnolo(a)	español(a)
Spanish (E)	spanisch	—	espagnol(e)	spagnolo(a)	español(a)
sparare (I)	schießen	shoot	tirer	—	disparar
Sparbuch (D)	—	savings book	livret de caisse d'épargne m	libretto di risparmio m	libreta de ahorro f
sparen (D)	—	save	économiser	risparmiare	ahorrar
sparire (I)	verschwinden	disappear	disparaître	—	desaparecer
Sparkasse (D)	—	savings bank	caisse d'épargne f	cassa di risparmio f	caja de ahorros f
sparo (I)	Schuß m	shot	coup m	—	disparo m
sparsam (D)	—	economical	économe	parsimonioso(a)	económico(a)
Spaß (D)	—	fun	plaisir m	scherzo m	broma f
spaßen (D)	—	joke	plaisanter	scherzare	bromear
spät (D)	—	late	tard	tardi	tarde
später (D)	—	later	plus tard	piú tardi	más tarde
spaventare (I)	erschrecken	frighten	effrayer	—	asustar
spaventoso¹ (I)	schrecklich	terrible	terrible	—	horrible
spaventoso² (I)	schauderhaft	horrible	horrible	—	espantoso(a)
spazierengehen (D)	—	go for a walk	promener, se	passeggiare	ir de paseo
Spaziergang (D)	—	walk	promenade f	passeggiata f	paseo m
spazio (I)	Zwischenraum m	space	espace m	—	espacio intermedio m
spazioso (I)	geräumig	spacious	spacieux(-euse)	—	espacioso(a)
spazzola (I)	Bürste f	brush	brosse f	—	cepillo m
spazzolino da denti (I)	Zahnbürste f	toothbrush	brosse à dents f	—	cepillo de dientes m
speak (E)	sprechen	—	parler	parlare	hablar
specchio (I)	Spiegel m	mirror	miroir m	—	espejo m
special¹ (E)	besondere(r,s)	—	spécial(e)	straordinario(a)	extraordinario(a)

	D	E	F	I	Es
special² (E)	speziell	—	spécial(e)	speciale	especial
spécial¹ (F)	besondere(r,s)	special	—	straordinario(a)	extraordinario(a)
spécial² (F)	speziell	special	—	speciale	especial
speciale (I)	speziell	special	spécial(e)	—	especial
spécialiste de l'oreille (F)	Ohrenarzt m	ear specialist	—	otoiatra m	médico del oído m
special offer (E)	Sonderangebot n	—	offre spéciale f	offerta speciale f	oferta especial f
specie¹ (I)	Art f	species	espèce f	—	especie f
specie² (I)	Sorte f	sort	sorte f	—	clase f
species (E)	Art f	—	espèce f	specie f	especie f
Speck (D)	—	bacon	lard m	lardo m	tocino m
spectacle (F)	Schauspiel n	play	—	spettacolo m	espectáculo m
spectateur (F)	Zuschauer m	spectator	—	spettatore m	espectador m
spectateurs (F)	Publikum n	audience	—	pubblico m	público m
spectator (E)	Zuschauer m	—	spectateur m	spettatore m	espectador m
spedire (I)	übersenden	send	envoyer	—	enviar
speech (E)	Rede f	—	discours m	discorso m	discurso m
speed¹ (E)	Geschwindigkeit f	—	vitesse f	velocità f	velocidad f
speed² (E)	Schnelligkeit f	—	rapidité f	velocità f	rapidez f
speed³ (E)	Tempo n	—	vitesse f	velocità f	velocidad f
speed trap (E)	Radarkontrolle f	—	contrôle radar m	controllo radar m	control de radar m
spegnere¹ (I)	ausmachen	switch off	éteindre	—	apagar
spegnere² (I)	ausschalten	switch off	arrêter	—	desconectar
spegnere³ (I)	abschalten	switch off	éteindre	—	desconectar
spegnere⁴ (I)	abstellen	turn off	arrêter	—	desconectar
spegnere⁵ (I)	löschen	extinguish	éteindre	—	apagar
Speise (D)	—	food	aliment m	cibo m	comida f
Speisekarte (D)	—	menu	menu m	menu m	lista de platos f
speisen (D)	—	dine	manger	mangiare	comer
Speisewagen (D)	—	dining car	wagon-restaurant m	vagone ristorante m	vagón restaurante m
spell (E)	buchstabieren	—	épeler	sillabare	deletrear
spend (E)	verbringen	—	passer	passare	pasar
Spende (D)	—	donation	don m	donazione f	donativo m
spensierato (I)	leichtsinnig	careless	étourdi(e)	—	imprudente
sperare (I)	hoffen	hope	espérer	—	esperar
speriamo che (I)	hoffentlich	hopefully	espérons	—	espero que
spesa (I)	Einkauf m	shopping	achat m	—	compra f
spese¹ (I)	Kosten pl	expenses	coûts m pl	—	costas m pl
spese² (I)	Spesen pl	expenses	frais m pl	—	gastos m pl
spese³ (I)	Unkosten pl	expenses	frais m pl	—	gastos m pl
Spesen (D)	—	expenses	frais m pl	spese f pl	gastos m pl
spesso (I)	oft	often	souvent	—	a menudo
spettacolo (I)	Schauspiel n	play	spectacle m	—	espectáculo m
spettatore (I)	Zuschauer m	spectator	spectateur m	—	espectador m
spezia (I)	Gewürz n	spice	épice f	—	especia f
speziell (D)	—	special	spécial(e)	speciale	especial
spiacevole (I)	unangenehm	unpleasant	désagréable	—	desagradable
spiaggia (I)	Strand m	beach	plage f	—	playa f

	D	E	F	I	Es
spiccioli (I)	Kleingeld n	small change	monnaie f	—	cambio m
spice (E)	Gewürz n	—	épice f	spezia f	especia f
spicy (E)	würzig	—	épicé(e)	aromatico(a)	aromático(a)
spider (E)	Spinne f	—	araignée f	ragno m	araña f
spiegare (I)	erklären	explain	expliquer	—	explicar
Spiegel (D)	—	mirror	miroir m	specchio m	espejo m
Spiel (D)	—	game	jeu m	gioco m	juego m
spielen (D)	—	play	jouer	giocare	jugar
Spieler (D)	—	player	joueur m	giocatore m	jugador m
Spielplatz (D)	—	playground	terrain de jeu m	campo dei giochi m	campo de juego m
spießig (D)	—	bourgeois	bourgeois(e)	da piccolo(a) borghese m	pequeño(a) burgués(-esa)
spinach (E)	Spinat m	—	épinard m	spinaci m pl	espinacas f pl
spinaci (I)	Spinat m	spinach	épinard m	—	espinacas f pl
Spinat (D)	—	spinach	épinard m	spinaci m pl	espinacas f pl
spine (E)	Wirbelsäule f	—	colonne vertébrale f	colonna vertebrale f	columna vertebral f
spingere[1] (I)	stoßen	push	pousser	—	empujar
spingere[2] (I)	schieben	push	pousser	—	empujar
spingere[3] (I)	treiben	drive	mener	—	estimular
Spinne (D)	—	spider	araignée f	ragno m	araña f
spinta (I)	Stoß m	blow	coup m	—	empujón m
spirit (E)	Geist m	—	esprit m	spirito m	espíritu m
spirito (I)	Geist m	spirit	esprit m	—	espíritu m
spirits (E)	Schnaps m	—	eau-de-vie f	acquavite f	aguardiente m
spit (E)	spucken	—	cracher	sputare	escupir
spitz (D)	—	pointed	pointu(e)	appuntito(a)	puntiagudo(a)
Spitze (D)	—	point	pointe f	punta f	punta f
splendere (I)	glänzen	shine	briller	—	brillar
splendid (E)	prächtig	—	magnifique	meraviglioso(a)	magnífico(a)
spoil (E)	verwöhnen	—	gâter	viziare	mimar
sponge (E)	Schwamm m	—	éponge f	spugna f	esponja f
spoon (E)	Löffel m	—	cuiller f	cucchiaio m	cuchara f
sporcizia (I)	Schmutz m	dirt	saleté f	—	suciedad f
sporco[1] (I)	dreckig	dirty	sale	—	sucio(a)
sporco[2] (I)	schmutzig	dirty	sale	—	sucio(a)
Sport (D)	—	sport	sport m	sport m	deporte m
sport (E)	Sport m	—	sport m	sport m	deporte m
sport (F)	Sport m	sport	—	sport m	deporte m
sport (I)	Sport m	sport	sport m	—	deporte m
sportello (I)	Schalter m	counter	guichet m	—	ventanilla f
sposa (I)	Braut f	bride	mariée f	—	novia f
sposarsi (I)	heiraten	marry	marier, se		casarse
sposato (I)	verheiratet	married	marié(e)	—	casado(a)
Sprache (D)	—	language	langage m	lingua f	lengua f
spread (E)	verbreiten	—	propager	diffondere	difundir
sprecare (I)	verschwenden	waste	gaspiller	—	desperdiciar
sprechen (D)	—	speak	parler	parlare	hablar

	D	E	F	I	Es
Sprechstunde (D)	—	consultation hour	heures de consultation *f pl*	ora di ricevimento *f*	hora de consulta *f*
Sprichwort (D)	—	proverb	proverbe *m*	proverbio *m*	proverbio *m*
spring¹ (E)	Frühjahr *n*	—	printemps *m*	primavera *f*	primavera *f*
spring² (E)	Quelle *f*	—	source *f*	sorgente *f*	fuente *f*
springen (D)	—	jump	sauter	saltare	saltar
Spritze (D)	—	injection	piqûre *f*	iniezione *f*	inyección *f*
spritzen (D)	—	squirt	asperger	spruzzare	salpicar
Sprung (D)	—	jump	saut *m*	salto *m*	salto *m*
spruzzare (I)	spritzen	squirt	asperger	—	salpicar
spucken (D)	—	spit	cracher	sputare	escupir
spugna (I)	Schwamm *m*	sponge	éponge *f*	—	esponja *f*
spülen (D)	—	rinse	rincer	sciacquare	lavar
spumante (I)	Sekt *m*	champagne	champagne *m*	—	champán *m*
spuntare (I)	dämmern	dawn	poindre	—	amanecer
spuntino (I)	Imbiß *m*	snack	casse-croûte *m*	—	refrigerio *m*
sputare (I)	spucken	spit	cracher	—	escupir
squadra (I)	Mannschaft *f*	team	équipe *f*	—	equipo *m*
square¹ (E)	quadratisch	—	carré(e)	quadrato(a)	cuadrado(a)
square² (E)	Quadrat *n*	—	carré *m*	quadrato *m*	cuadrado *m*
square³ (E)	viereckig	—	carré(e)	quadrato(a)	cuadrangular
square metre (E)	Quadratmeter *m*	—	mètre carré *m*	metro quadrato *m*	metro cuadrado *m*
squash (E)	zerdrücken	—	écraser	sgualcire	aplastar
squirt (E)	spritzen	—	asperger	spruzzare	salpicar
squisito (I)	köstlich	delicious	savoureux(-euse)	—	exquisito(a)
Staat (D)	—	state	état *m*	stato *m*	estado *m*
Staatsangehörig- keit (D)	—	nationality	nationalité *f*	cittadinanza *f*	nacionalidad *f*
stabilire¹ (I)	ausmachen	agree	convenir	—	convenir
stabilire² (I)	festsetzen	fix	fixer	—	fijar
stabilirsi (I)	niederlassen	settle down	s'installer	—	instalarse
staccare (I)	abnehmen	take away	décrocher	—	descolgar
Stadt (D)	—	town	ville *f*	città *f*	ciudad *f*
stage¹ (E)	Bühne *f*	—	scène *f*	palcoscenico *m*	escenario *m*
stage² (E)	inszenieren	—	mettre en scène	mettere in scena	escenificar
stage (F)	Praktikum *n*	practical training	—	tirocinio *m*	prácticas *f pl*
stagger (E)	wanken	—	chanceller	barcollare	vacilar
stagione¹ (I)	Jahreszeit *f*	time of year	saison *f*	—	estación del año *f*
stagione² (I)	Saison *f*	season	saison *f*	—	temporada *f*
stagno (I)	Teich *m*	pond	étang *m*	—	estanque *m*
Stahl (D)	—	steel	acier *m*	acciaio *m*	acero *m*
stain (E)	Fleck *m*	—	tache *f*	macchia *f*	mancha *f*
staircase (E)	Aufgang *m*	—	montée *f*	scala *f*	subida *f*
stairs (E)	Treppe *f*	—	escalier *m*	scala *f*	escalera *f*
stalls (E)	Parkett *n*	—	parquet *m*	parquet *m*	entarimado *m*
Stammgast (D)	—	regular	habitué *m*	cliente abituale *m*	cliente habitual *m*
stamp¹ (E)	Briefmarke *f*	—	timbre *m*	francobollo *m*	sello *m*
stamp² (E)	frankieren	—	affranchir	affrancare	franquear
stamp³ (E)	Stempel *m*	—	timbre *m*	timbro *m*	sello *m*

	D	E	F	I	Es
stampa (I)	Presse f	press	presse f	—	prensa f
stancarsi (I)	ermüden	tire	fatiguer	—	cansar
stanco (I)	müde	tired	fatigué(e)	—	cansado(a)
Stand (D)	—	position	état m	stato m	estado m
stand (E)	stehen	—	être debout	stare in piedi	estar en pie
stand by s.b. (E)	beistehen	—	assister	assistere	asistir a
ständig (D)	—	permanent	permanent(e)	fisso(a)	permanente
standpoint (E)	Standpunkt m	—	point de vue m	punto di vista m	punto de vista m
Standpunkt (D)	—	standpoint	point de vue m	punto di vista m	punto de vista m
Stange (D)	—	pole	barre f	asta f	vara f
stanza (I)	Raum m	room	pièce f	—	habitación f
stanza da bagno (I)	Badezimmer n	bathroom	salle de bains f	—	cuarto de baño m
star (E)	Stern m	—	étoile f	stella f	estrella f
stare a guardare[1] (I)	zusehen	watch	regarder	—	mirar
stare a guardare[2] (I)	zuschauen	watch	regarder	—	mirar
stare bene (I)	passen	suit	aller bien	—	venir bien
stare in piedi (I)	stehen	stand	être debout	—	estar en pie
stare seduto (I)	sitzen	sit	être assis(e)	—	estar sentado(a)
stark (D)	—	strong	fort(e)	forte	fuerte
Stärke (D)	—	strength	puissance f	forza f	fuerza f
starnutire (I)	niesen	sneeze	éternuer	—	estornudar
starr (D)	—	rigid	rigide	rigido(a)	fijo(a)
Start (D)	—	start	départ m	partenza f	partida f
start[1] (E)	anfangen	—	commencer	cominciare	empezar
start[2] (E)	starten	—	démarrer	partire	partir
start[3] (E)	Start m	—	départ m	partenza f	partida f
starten (D)	—	start	démarrer	partire	partir
starve (E)	verhungern	—	mourir de faim	morire di fame	morir de hambre
state (E)	Staat m	—	état m	stato m	estado m
statement (E)	Aussage f	—	déclaration f	dichiarazione f	afirmación f
Station (D)	—	station	station f	stazione f	estación f
station[1] (E)	Bahnhof m	—	gare f	stazione f	estación f
station[2] (E)	Station f	—	station f	stazione f	estación f
station[3] (E)	Sender m	—	émetteur m	trasmettitore m	emisora f
station (F)	Station f	station	—	stazione f	estación f
stationery shop (E)	Schreibwaren-handlung f	—	papeterie f	cartoleria f	papelería f
station-service (F)	Tankstelle f	filling station	—	distributore di benzina m	gasolinera f
Stati Uniti (I)	Vereinigte Staaten pl	United States	Etats-Unis m pl	—	Estados Unidos m pl
stato[1] (I)	Staat m	state	état m	—	estado m
stato[2] (I)	Stand m	position	état m	—	estado m
stato[3] (I)	Zustand m	condition	état m	—	estado m
statt (D)	—	instead	au lieu de	invece di	en vez de
stattfinden (D)	—	take place	avoir lieu	avere luogo	tener lugar
Stau (D)	—	traffic jam	embouteillage m	ingorgo m	embotellamiento m
Staub (D)	—	dust	poussière f	polvere f	polvo m
staubig (D)	—	dusty	poussiéreux(-euse)	polveroso(a)	polvoriento(a)

	D	E	F	I	Es
Staubsauger (D)	—	vacuum-cleaner	aspirateur *m*	aspirapolvere *m*	aspirador *m*
staunen (D)	—	be astonished	étonner, s'	stupirsi	asombrarse
stay[1] (E)	Aufenthalt *m*	—	séjour *m*	soggiorno *m*	estancia *f*
stay[2] (E)	bleiben	—	rester	rimanere	quedarse
stay here (E)	hierbleiben	—	rester	restare qui	quedarse aquí
stay the night (E)	übernachten	—	passer la nuit	pernottare	pernoctar
stazione[1] (I)	Bahnhof *m*	station	gare *f*	—	estación *f*
stazione[2] (I)	Station *f*	station	station *f*	—	estación *f*
stazione centrale (I)	Hauptbahnhof *m*	central station	gare centrale *f*	—	estación central *f*
steal (E)	stehlen	—	voler	rubare	robar
steam (E)	Dampf *m*	—	vapeur *f*	vapore *m*	vapor *m*
stechen (D)	—	prick	piquer	pungere	picar
Steckdose (D)	—	socket	prise électrique *f*	presa *f*	enchufe *m*
stecken (D)	—	insert	enfoncer	inserire	introducir
steel (E)	Stahl *m*	—	acier *m*	acciaio *m*	acero *m*
steep (E)	steil	—	raide	ripido(a)	inclinado(a)
steer (E)	lenken	—	conduire	guidare	encauzar
steering wheel (E)	Lenkrad *n*	—	volant *m*	volante *m*	volante *m*
stehen (D)	—	stand	être debout	stare in piedi	estar en pie
stehlen (D)	—	steal	voler	rubare	robar
steif (D)	—	stiff	rigide	rigido(a)	rígido(a)
steigen (D)	—	go up	monter	salire	subir
steil (D)	—	steep	raide	ripido(a)	inclinado(a)
Stein (D)	—	stone	pierre *f*	sasso *m*	piedra *f*
stella (I)	Stern *m*	star	étoile *f*	—	estrella *f*
Stelle (D)	—	place	place *f*	posto *m*	puesto *m*
stellen (D)	—	place	mettre	mettere	colocar
Steilung (D)	—	position	position *f*	posizione *f*	posición *f*
Stempel (D)	—	stamp	timbre *m*	timbro *m*	sello *m*
stendere (I)	strecken	stretch	allonger	—	alargar
step[1] (E)	Stufe *f*	—	marche *f*	gradino *m*	escalón *m*
step[2] (E)	Schritt *m*	—	pas *m*	passo *m*	paso *m*
step[3] (E)	treten	—	mettre le pied sur	pestare	pisar
step out (E)	heraustreten	—	sortir	uscire fuori	salir
sterben (D)	—	die	mourir	morire	morir
Stern (D)	—	star	étoile *f*	stella *f*	estrella *f*
stets (D)	—	always	toujours	sempre	siempre
Steuern (D)	—	tax	impôt *m*	imposte *f pl*	impuesto *m*
Stewardeß (D)	—	stewardess	hôtesse de l'air *f*	hostess *f*	azafata *f*
stewardess (E)	Stewardeß *f*	—	hôtesse de l'air *f*	hostess *f*	azafata *f*
stick[1] (E)	kleben	—	coller	incollare	pegar
stick[2] (E)	Stock *m*	—	bâton *m*	bastone *m*	bastón *m*
Stiefel (D)	—	boot	botte *f*	stivale *m*	bota *f*
Stier (D)	—	bull	taureau *m*	toro *m*	toro *m*
stiff (E)	steif	—	rigide	rigido(a)	rígido(a)
Stift (D)	—	pencil	crayon *m*	penna *f*	lápiz *m*
still (D)	—	quiet	calme	calmo(a)	tranquilo(a)
still[1] (E)	doch	—	si	si	sin embargo

straight

	D	E	F	I	Es
still² (E)	noch	—	encore	ancora	aún/todavía
stimare (I)	schätzen	estimate	estimer	—	estimar
Stimme (D)	—	voice	voix f	voce f	voz f
stink (E)	stinken	—	puer	puzzare	apestar
stinken (D)	—	stink	puer	puzzare	apestar
stipendio (I)	Gehalt n	salary	salaire m	—	sueldo m
stirare (I)	bügeln	iron	repasser	—	planchar
Stirn (D)	—	forehead	front m	fronte f	frente f
stivale (I)	Stiefel m	boot	botte f	—	bota f
Stock (D)	—	stick	bâton m	bastone m	bastón m
stock (E)	Vorrat m	—	réserves f pl	scorte f pl	provisión f
stocking (E)	Strumpf m	—	bas m	calza f	media f
Stoff (D)	—	cloth	tissu m	stoffa f	tela f
stoffa (I)	Stoff m	cloth	tissu m	—	tela f
stolpern (D)	—	stumble	trébucher	inciampare	tropezar
stolz (D)	—	proud	fier(-ère)	orgoglioso(a)	orgulloso(a)
stomach¹ (E)	Bauch m	—	ventre m	pancia f	vientre m
stomach² (E)	Magen m	—	estomac m	stomaco m	estómago m
stomach-ache (E)	Magen-schmerzen pl	—	mal d'estomac m	mal di stomaco m	dolor de estómago m
stomaco (I)	Magen m	stomach	estomac m	—	estómago m
stone (E)	Stein m	—	pierre f	sasso m	piedra f
stop¹ (E)	aufhören	—	arrêter	cessare	terminar
stop² (E)	anhalten	—	arrêter	fermare	parar
stop² (E)	beenden	—	terminer	terminare	terminar
stop⁴ (E)	Haltestelle f	—	arrêt m	fermata f	parada f
stop! (E)	halt!	—	stop!	alt!	¡alto!
stop! (F)	halt!	stop!	—	alt!	¡alto!
store (E)	Lager n	—	magasin m	magazzino m	almacén m
stören (D)	—	disturb	déranger	disturbare	molestar
storia (I)	Geschichte f	history	histoire f	—	historia f
storm (E)	Sturm m	—	tempête f	tempesta f	tempestad f
storto (I)	krumm	crooked	tordu(e)	—	torcido(a)
Störung (D)	—	interference	trouble m	disturbo m	molestia f
Stoß (D)	—	blow	coup m	spinta f	empujón m
stoßen (D)	—	push	pousser	spingere	empujar
stottern (D)	—	stutter	bégayer	balbettare	tartamudear
stoviglie (I)	Geschirr n	crockery	vaisselle f	—	vajilla f
stow (E)	unterbringen	—	ranger	sistemare	colocar
strada (I)	Straße f	street	rue f	—	calle f
strada principale (I)	Hauptstraße f	main street	grand-rue f	—	calle central f
strada provinciale (I)	Landstraße f	country road	route f	—	carretera nacional f
strada statale (I)	Bundesstraße f	Federal Highway/main road	route nationale f	—	carretera nacional f
Strafe (D)	—	punishment	punition f	punizione f	castigo m
strafen (D)	—	punish	punir	punire	castigar
Strahl (D)	—	ray	rayon m	raggio m	rayo m
straight (E)	gerade	—	droit(e)	diritto(a)	derecho(a)

	D	E	F	I	Es
straight ahead (E)	geradeaus	—	tout droit	dritto	todo derecho
strain (E)	Anstrengung *f*	—	effort *m*	fatica *f*	esfuerzo *m*
Strand (D)	—	beach	plage *f*	spiaggia *f*	playa *f*
strange[1] (E)	eigenartig	—	singulier(-ière)	strano(a)	extraño(a)
strange[2] (E)	merkwürdig	—	curieux(-euse)	curioso(a)	curioso(a)
strange[3] (E)	seltsam	—	bizarre	strano(a)	extraño(a)
straniero[1] (I)	ausländisch	foreign	étranger(-ère)	—	extranjero(a)
straniero[2] (I)	Ausländer *m*	foreigner	étranger *m*	—	extranjero *m*
straniero[3] (I)	Fremder *m*	foreigner	étranger *m*	—	extranjero *m*
strano[1] (I)	eigenartig	strange	singulier(-ière)	—	extraño(a)
strano[2] (I)	seltsam	strange	bizarre	—	extraño(a)
straordinario[1] (I)	außerordentlich	extraordinary	exeptionnel(le)	—	extraordinario(a)
straordinario[2] (I)	außergewöhnlich	exceptional	extraordinaire	—	excepcional
straordinario[3] (I)	besondere(r,s)	special	exeptionnel(le)	—	extraordinario(a)
strap (E)	Riemen *m*	—	courroie *f*	cinghia *f*	correa *f*
strappare[1] (I)	zerreißen	rip	déchirer	—	romper
strappare[2] (I)	reißen	tear	déchirer, se	—	desgarrarse
Straße (D)	—	street	rue *f*	strada *f*	calle *f*
Straßenbahn (D)	—	tram	tramway *m*	tram *m*	tranvía *m*
Strauch (D)	—	bush	buisson *m*	cespuglio *m*	arbusto *m*
Strauß (D)	—	bunch	bouquet *m*	mazzo *m*	ramo *m*
straw (E)	Stroh *n*	—	paille *f*	paglia *f*	paja *f*
strawberry (E)	Erdbeere *f*	—	fraise *f*	fragola *f*	fresa *f*
Strecke (D)	—	stretch	trajet *m*	tratto *m*	trayecto *m*
strecken (D)	—	stretch	allonger	stendere	alargar
street (E)	Straße *f*	—	rue *f*	strada *f*	calle *f*
street light (E)	Laterne *f*	—	réverbère *m*	lampione *m*	farola *f*
strega (I)	Hexe *f*	witch	sorcière *f*	—	bruja *f*
streichen (D)	—	paint	peindre	verniciare	pintar
Streichholz (D)	—	match	allumette *f*	fiammifero *m*	cerilla *f*
Streik (D)	—	strike	grève *f*	sciopero *m*	huelga *f*
streiken (D)	—	be on strike	faire grève	scioperare	hacer huelga
Streit (D)	—	argument	dispute *f*	lite *f*	disputa *f*
streiten (D)	—	quarrel	disputer, se	litigare	discutir
streng (D)	—	strict	sévère	severo(a)	riguroso(a)
strength[1] (E)	Kraft *f*	—	force *f*	forza *f*	fuerza *f*
strength[2] (E)	Stärke *f*	—	puissance *f*	forza *f*	fuerza *f*
stretch[1] (E)	strecken	—	allonger	stendere	alargar
stretch[2] (E)	Strecke *f*	—	trajet *m*	tratto *m*	trayecto *m*
stretcher (E)	Bahre *f*	—	brancard *m*	barella *f*	camilla *f*
stretto (I)	eng	narrow	étroit(e)	—	estrecho(a)
Strich (D)	—	line	trait *m*	linea *f*	línea *f*
Strick (D)	—	rope	corde *f*	corda *f*	cuerda *f*
stricken (D)	—	knit	tricoter	lavorare a maglia	hacer punto
Strickjacke (D)	—	cardigan	veste en tricot *f*	giacca di maglia	chaqueta de punto *f*
strict (E)	streng	—	sévère	severo	riguroso(a)
strike (E)	Streik *m*	—	grève *f*	sciopero *m*	huelga *f*

	D	E	F	I	Es
string (E)	Schnur f	—	ficelle f	corda f	cordel m
Stroh (D)	—	straw	paille f	paglia f	paja f
stroll (E)	bummeln	—	flâner	girellare	callejear
Strom (D)	—	current	courant m	corrente f	corriente f
strong¹ (E)	kräftig	—	fort(e)	forte	fuerte
strong² (E)	stark	—	fort(e)	forte	fuerte
strumento (I)	Instrument n	instrument	instrument m	—	instrumento m
Strumpf (D)	—	stocking	bas m	calza f	media f
Strumpfhose (D)	—	tights	collants m pl	calzamaglia f	leotardos m pl
Stück (D)	—	piece	morceau m	pezzo m	parte f
Student (D)	—	student	étudiant m	studente m	estudiante m
student (E)	Student m	—	étudiant m	studente m	estudiante m
studente (I)	Student m	student	étudiant m	—	estudiante m
studi (I)	Studium n	studies	études f pl	—	estudio m
studiare (I)	studieren	study	étudier	—	estudiar
studieren (D)	—	study	étudier	studiare	estudiar
studies (E)	Studium n	—	études f pl	studi m pl	estudio m
Studium (D)	—	studies	études f pl	studi m pl	estudio m
study (E)	studieren	—	étudier	studiare	estudiar
stufa (I)	Ofen m	oven	poêle m	—	estufa f
Stufe (D)	—	step	marche f	gradino m	escalón m
stuff (E)	Zeug n	—	truc m	cose f pl	cosa f
Stuhl (D)	—	chair	chaise f	sedia f	silla f
stumble (E)	stolpern	—	trébucher	inciampare	tropezar
stumm (D)	—	dumb	muet(te)	muto(a)	mudo(a)
Stunde (D)	—	hour	heure f	ora f	hora f
stündlich (D)	—	hourly	toutes les heures	ogni ora	cada hora
stuoia (I)	Matte f	mat	natte f	—	colchoneta f
stupendo (I)	herrlich	marvellous	magnifique	—	maravilloso(a)
stupid (E)	dumm	—	bête	stupido(a)	tonto(a)
stupido (I)	dumm	stupid	bête	—	tonto(a)
stupire (I)	wundern	wonder	étonner	—	asombrar
stupirsi (I)	staunen	be astonished	étonner, se	—	asombrarse
Sturm (D)	—	storm	tempête f	tempesta f	tempestad f
Sturz (D)	—	fall	chute f	caduta f	caída f
stürzen (D)	—	fall	tomber	cadere	caer
stutter (E)	stottern	—	bégayer	balbettare	tartamudear
stylish (E)	schick	—	chic	elegante	elegante
stylo (F)	Füller m	fountain pen	—	penna stilografica f	pluma f
stylo à bille (F)	Kugelschreiber m	biro	—	biro f	bolígrafo m
su¹ (I)	auf	on/on top/onto	sur	—	sobre/en/hacia
su² (I)	herauf	up	vers le haut	—	hacia arriba
su³ (I)	hinauf	up	vers le haut	—	hacia arriba
su⁴ (I)	über	over/about	sur	—	por/sobre
suave (Es)	zart	soft	doux (douce)	tenero(a)	—
subaffittare (I)	untervermieten	sublet	sous-louer	—	subarrendar
subarrendar (Es)	untervermieten	sublet	sous-louer	subaffittare	—

	D	E	F	I	Es
subida[1] (Es)	Auffahrt f	drive	allée f	salita d'ingresso f	—
subida[2] (Es)	Aufgang m	staircase	montée f	scala f	—
subir[1] (Es)	aufsteigen	ascend	monter	salire	—
subir[2] (Es)	hinaufsteigen	climb	monter	salire	—
subir[3] (Es)	steigen	go up	monter	salire	—
subir a (Es)	einsteigen	get in	monter	salire	—
subit (F)	abrupt	abrupt	—	improvviso(a)	súbito(a)
súbito (Es)	abrupt	abrupt	subit(e)	improvviso(a)	—
subito (I)	sofort	immediately	immédiatement	—	en seguida
subject[1] (E)	Fach n	—	matière f	materia f	materia f
subject[2] (E)	unterwerfen	—	soumettre	sottomettere	someter
sublet (E)	untervermieten	—	sous-louer	subaffittare	realquilar
subrayar (Es)	unterstreichen	underline	souligner	sottolineare	—
subsanar (Es)	wiedergut-machen	make up for	réparer	riparare	—
substitute (E)	Ersatz m	—	remplacement m	sostituzione f	sustitución f
subtract (E)	abziehen	—	retirer	sottrarre	restar
suburb (E)	Vorort m	—	faubourg m	sobborgo m	suburbio m
suburbio (Es)	Vorort m	suburb	faubourg m	sobborgo m	—
subway (E)	Unterführung f	—	passage souterrain m	sottopassaggio m	paso inferior m
succedere (I)	passieren	happen	arriver	—	pasar
succeed (E)	gelingen	—	réussir	riuscire	acertar
succès (F)	Erfolg m	success	—	successo m	éxito m
success (E)	Erfolg m	—	succès m	successo m	éxito m
successful (E)	erfolgreich	—	avec succès	pieno(a) di successi	afortunado(a)
successo (I)	Erfolg m	success	succès m	—	éxito m
succhiare (I)	lutschen	suck	sucer	—	chupar
succo (I)	Saft m	juice	jus m	—	zumo m
succursale (F)	Filiale f	branch	—	filiale f	sucursal f
suceder (Es)	vorkommen	occur	exister	accadere	—
sucer (F)	lutschen	suck	—	succhiare	chupar
suceso[1] (Es)	Ereignis n	event	événement m	avvenimento m	—
suceso[2] (Es)	Vorfall m	incident	cas m	caso m	—
such (E)	solche(r,s)	—	tel(le)	tale(i)	un(a) tal
suchen (D)	—	look for	chercher	cercare	buscar
suciedad (Es)	Schmutz m	dirt	saleté f	sporcizia f	—
sucio[1] (Es)	dreckig	dirty	sale	sporco(a)	—
sucio[2] (Es)	schmutzig	dirty	sale	sporco(a)	—
suck (E)	lutschen	—	sucer	succhiare	chupar
sucre (F)	Zucker m	sugar	—	zucchero m	azúcar m
sucré (F)	süß	sweet	—	dolce	dulce
sucumbir (Es)	unterliegen	be defeated	être vaincu(e) par qn	soccombere	—
sucursal (Es)	Filiale f	branch	succursale f	filiale f	—
sud (F)	Süden m	South	—	sud	sur m
sud (I)	Süden m	South	sud m	—	sur m
sudar (Es)	schwitzen	sweat	transpirer	sudare	—
sudare (I)	schwitzen	sweat	transpirer	—	sudar

	D	E	F	I	Es
suddenly (E)	plötzlich	—	tout à coup	di colpo	de repente
Süden (D)	—	South	sud *m*	sud	sur *m*
südlich (D)	—	southern	du sud	a sud	al sur
Suecia (Es)	Schweden	Sweden	Suède *f*	Svezia *f*	—
Suède (F)	Schweden	Sweden	—	Svezia *f*	Suecia *f*
suegra (Es)	Schwieger-mutter *f*	mother-in-law	belle-mère *f*	suocera *f*	—
suegros (Es)	Schwieger-eltern *pl*	parents-in-law	beaux-parents *m pl*	suoceri *m pl*	—
suela (Es)	Sohle *f*	sole	semelle *f*	suola *f*	—
sueldo (Es)	Gehalt *n*	salary	salaire *m*	stipendio *m*	—
suelo[1] (Es)	Boden *m*	floor	terre *f*	terra *f*	—
suelo[2] (Es)	Fußboden *m*	floor	sol *m*	pavimento *m*	—
sueño[1] (Es)	Schlaf *m*	sleep	sommeil *m*	sonno *m*	—
sueño[2] (Es)	Traum *m*	dream	rêve *m*	sogno *m*	—
suerte (Es)	Glück *n*	luck	chance *f*	fortuna *f*	—
suffer (E)	leiden	—	souffrir	soffrire	sufrir
suffice (E)	genügen	—	suffire	bastare	bastar
suffire (F)	genügen	suffice	—	bastare	bastar
sufrir (Es)	leiden	suffer	souffrir	soffrire	—
sugar (E)	Zucker *m*	—	sucre *m*	zucchero *m*	azúcar *m*
suicide (E)	Selbstmord *m*	—	suicide *m*	suicidio *m*	suicidio *m*
suicide (F)	Selbstmord *m*	suicide	—	suicidio *m*	suicidio *m*
suicidio (Es)	Selbstmord *m*	suicide	suicide *m*	suicidio *m*	—
suicidio (I)	Selbstmord *m*	suicide	suicide *m*	—	suicidio *m*
Suisse[1] (F)	Schweizer *m*	Swiss	—	svizzero *m*	suizo *m*
Suisse[2] (F)	Schweiz *f*	Switzerland	—	Svizzera *f*	Suiza *f*
suit[1] (E)	Anzug *m*	—	costume *m*	vestito *m*	traje *m*
suit[2] (E)	passen	—	aller bien	stare bene	venir bien
suitable[1] (E)	geeignet	—	approprié(e)	adatto(a)	indicado(a)
suitable[2] (E)	passend	—	assorti(e)	adatto(a)	apropiado(a)
suitable[3] (E)	zweckmäßig	—	approprié(e)	adatto(a)	adecuado(a)
suitcase (E)	Koffer *m*	—	valise *f*	valigia *f*	maleta *f*
suite (F)	Folge *f*	consequence	—	conseguenza *f*	serie *f*
suivant[1] (F)	folgend	following	—	seguente	siguiente
suivant[2] (F)	nächste(r,s)	next	—	prossimo(a)	siguiente
suivre (F)	folgen	follow	—	seguire	seguir
Suiza (Es)	Schweiz *f*	Switzerland	Suisse *f*	Svizzera *f*	—
suizo (Es)	Schweizer *m*	Swiss	Suisse *m*	svizzero *m*	—
sujet (F)	Thema *n*	topic	—	tema *m*	tema *m*
sujetar[1] (Es)	befestigen	fasten	fixer	fissare	
sujetar[2] (Es)	festhalten	seize	tenir ferme	tener fermo	
sujetar[3] (Es)	halten	hold	tenir	tenere	
sultry (E)	schwül	—	lourd(e)	afoso(a)	sofocante
sum (E)	Summe *f*	—	somme *f*	somma *f*	suma *f*
suma (Es)	Summe *f*	sum	somme *f*	somma *f*	
sumar (Es)	addieren	add up	additionner	sommare	
suministrar (Es)	liefern	deliver	livrer	fornire	
suministro (Es)	Lieferung *f*	delivery	livraison *f*	fornitura *f*	

	D	E	F	I	Es
Summe (D)	—	sum	somme *f*	somma *f*	suma *f*
summer (E)	Sommer *m*	—	été *m*	estate *f*	verano *m*
summertime (E)	Sommerzeit *f*	—	heure d'été *f*	ora legale *f*	temporada de verano *f*
summon (E)	vorladen	—	assigner	citare in giudizio	citar
sun (E)	Sonne *f*	—	soleil *m*	sole *m*	sol *m*
sunburn (E)	Sonnenbrand *m*	—	coup de soleil *m*	scottatura solare *f*	quemadura solar *f*
Sunday (E)	Sonntag *m*	—	dimanche *m*	domenica *f*	domingo *m*
Sünde (D)	—	sin	péché *m*	peccato *m*	pecado *m*
sunglasses (E)	Sonnenbrille *f*	—	lunettes de soleil *f pl*	occhiali da sole *m pl*	gafas de sol *f pl*
sunny (E)	sonnig	—	ensoleillé(e)	sereno(a)	soleado(a)
sunrise (E)	Sonnenaufgang *m*	—	lever du soleil *m*	sorgere del sole *m*	salida del sol *f*
sunset (E)	Sonnenuntergang *m*	—	coucher du soleil *m*	tramonto del sole *m*	puesta del sol *f*
suocera (I)	Schwiegermutter *f*	mother-in-law	belle-mère *f*	—	suegra *f*
suoceri (I)	Schwiegereltern *pl*	parents-in-law	beaux-parents *m pl*	—	suegros *m pl*
suola (I)	Sohle *f*	sole	semelle *f*	—	suela *f*
suonare[1] (I)	klingeln	ring the bell	sonner	—	tocar el timbre
suonare[2] (I)	läuten	ring	sonner	—	tocar
suono[1] (I)	Klang *m*	sound	son *m*	—	sonido *m*
suono[2] (I)	Ton *m*	sound	son *m*	—	sonido *m*
suora (I)	Nonne *f*	nun	religieuse *f*	—	monja *f*
superficial (E)	oberflächlich	—	superficiel(le)	superficiale	superficial
superficial[1] (Es)	äußerlich	external	externe	esterno(a)	—
superficial[2] (Es)	oberflächlich	superficial	superficiel(le)	superficiale	—
superficiale (I)	oberflächlich	superficial	superficiel(le)	—	superficial
superficie (Es)	Oberfläche *f*	surface	surface *f*	superficie *f*	—
superficie (I)	Oberfläche *f*	surface	surface *f*	—	superficie *f*
superficiel (F)	oberflächlich	superficial	—	superficiale	superficial
superflu (F)	überflüssig	superfluous	—	superfluo(a)	superfluo(a)
superfluo (I)	überflüssig	superfluous	superflu(e)	—	superfluo(a)
superfluo (Es)	überflüssig	superfluous	superflu(e)	superfluo(a)	—
superfluous (E)	überflüssig	—	superflu(e)	superfluo(a)	superfluo(a)
supermarché (F)	Supermarkt *m*	supermarket	—	supermercato *m*	supermercado *m*
supermarket (E)	Supermarkt *m*	—	supermarché *m*	supermercato *m*	supermercado *m*
Supermarkt (D)	—	supermarket	supermarché *m*	supermercato *m*	supermercado *m*
supermercado (Es)	Supermarkt *m*	supermarket	supermarché *m*	supermercato *m*	—
supermercato (I)	Supermarkt *m*	supermarket	supermarché *m*	—	supermercado *m*
supersticioso (Es)	abergläubisch	superstitious	superstitieux (-euse)	superstizioso(a)	—
superstitieux (F)	abergläubisch	superstitious	—	superstizioso(a)	supersticioso(a)
superstitious (E)	abergläubisch	—	superstitieux (-euse)	superstizioso(a)	supersticioso(a)
superstizioso (I)	abergläubisch	superstitious	superstitieux (-euse)	—	supersticioso(a)
superstrada (I)	Schnellstraße *f*	expressway	voie rapide *f*	—	carretera de circulación rápida *f*
supervise (E)	überwachen	—	surveiller	sorvegliare	vigilar
suplemento[1] (Es)	Beilage *f*	supplement	supplément *m*	supplemento *m*	—

	D	E	F	I	Es
suplemento² (Es)	Zuschlag *m*	extra charge	supplément *m*	supplemento *m*	—
suponer¹ (Es)	annehmen	suppose	supposer	supporre	—
suponer² (Es)	ahnen	suspect	douter, se	supporre	—
suponer³ (Es)	voraussetzen	assume	supposer	presupporre	—
suponer⁴ (Es)	vermuten	suppose	supposer	supporre	—
suposición¹ (Es)	Annahme *f*	assumption	supposition *f*	supposizione *f*	—
suposición² (Es)	Vermutung *f*	supposition	supposition *f*	supposizione *f*	—
Suppe (D)	—	soup	soupe *f*	zuppa *f*	sopa *f*
supper (E)	Abendessen *n*	—	dîner *m*	cena *f*	cena *f*
supplement (E)	Beilage *f*	—	supplément *m*	supplemento *m*	suplemento *m*
supplément¹ (F)	Beilage *f*	supplement	—	supplemento *m*	suplemento *m*
supplément² (F)	Zuschlag *m*	extra charge	—	supplemento *m*	suplemento *m*
supplémentaire (F)	zusätzlich	in addition	—	supplementare	adicional
supplementare (I)	zusätzlich	in addition	supplémentaire	—	adicional
supplemento¹ (I)	Beilage *f*	supplement	supplément *m*	—	suplemento *m*
supplemento² (I)	Zuschlag *m*	extra charge	supplément *m*	—	suplemento *m*
supporre¹ (I)	ahnen	suspect	douter, se	—	suponer
supporre² (I)	annehmen	suppose	supposer	—	suponer
supporre³ (I)	vermuten	suppose	supposer	—	suponer
support¹ (E)	unterstützen	—	soutenir	assistere	apoyar
support² (E)	Unterstützung *f*	—	soutien *m*	sostegno *m*	apoyo *m*
supporter¹ (F)	aushalten	bear	—	sopportare	aguantar
supporter² (F)	ertragen	bear	—	sopportare	soportar
suppose¹ (E)	annehmen	—	supposer	supporre	suponer
suppose² (E)	vermuten	—	supposer	supporre	suponer
supposer¹ (F)	annehmen	suppose	—	supporre	suponer
supposer² (F)	vermuten	suppose	—	supporre	suponer
supposer³ (F)	voraussetzen	assume	—	presupporre	suponer
supposition (E)	Vermutung *f*	—	supposition *f*	supposizione *f*	suposición *f*
supposition¹ (F)	Annahme *f*	assumption	—	supposizione *f*	suposición *f*
supposition² (F)	Vermutung *f*	supposition	—	supposizione *f*	suposición *f*
supposizione¹ (I)	Annahme *f*	assumption	supposition *f*	—	suposición *f*
supposizione² (I)	Vermutung *f*	supposition	supposition *f*	—	suposición *f*
supuesto¹ (Es)	vorausgesetzt	provided	à condition que	presumendo	—
supuesto² (Es)	angeblich	pretended	prétendu(e)	presunto(a)	—
sur (Es)	Süden *m*	South	sud *m*	sud	—
sur¹ (F)	auf	on/on top/onto	—	su/sopra	sobre/en/hacia
sur² (F)	über	over/about	—	su/sopra/per	por/sobre
sûr¹ (F)	sicher	sure	—	sicuro(a)	seguro(a)
sûr² (F)	zuverlässig	reliable	—	affidabile	de confianza
sûr de soi (F)	selbstsicher	self-assured	—	sicuro di sé	seguro de sí mismo
sure (E)	sicher	—	sûr(e)	sicuro(a)	seguro(a)
surestimer (F)	überschätzen	overestimate	—	sopravvalutare	sobrevalorar
surface (E)	Oberfläche *f*	—	surface *f*	superficie *f*	superficie *f*
surface¹ (F)	Fläche *f*	area	—	area *f*	áera *f*
surface² (F)	Oberfläche *f*	surface	—	superficie *f*	superficie *f*
surgeon (E)	Chirurg *m*	—	chirurgien *m*	chirurgo *m*	cirujano *m*
surgir (Es)	entstehen	arise	naître	nascere	—

	D	E	F	I	Es
surname (E)	Nachname m	—	nom de famille m	cognome m	apellido m
surprendre (F)	überraschen	surprise	—	sorprendere	sorprender
surpris (F)	überrascht	surprised	—	sorpreso(a)	sorprendido(a)
surprise¹ (E)	überraschen	—	surprendre	sorprendere	sorprender
surprise² (E)	Überraschung f	—	surprise f	sorpresa f	sorpresa f
surprise (F)	Überraschung f	surprise	—	sorpresa f	sorpresa f
surprised (E)	überrascht	—	surpris(e)	sorpreso(a)	sorprendido(a)
surround (E)	umgeben	—	entourer	circondare	rodear
surroundings (E)	Umgebung f	—	environs m pl	dintorni m pl	alrededores m pl
surtout¹ (F)	besonders	especially	—	particolarmente	sobre todo
surtout² (F)	hauptsächlich	mainly	—	principalmente	principalmente
surveiller (F)	überwachen	supervise	—	sorvegliare	vigilar
survive (E)	überleben	—	survivre	sopravvivere	sobrevivir
survivre (F)	überleben	survive	—	sopravvivere	sobrevivir
suspect (E)	ahnen	—	douter, se	supporre	suponer
suspect (F)	verdächtig	suspicious	—	sospetto(a)	sospechoso(a)
suspicious (E)	verdächtig	—	suspect(e)	sospetto(a)	sospechoso(a)
süß (D)	—	sweet	sucré(e)	dolce	dulce
sustitución (Es)	Ersatz m	substitute	remplacement m	sostituzione f	—
sustituir (Es)	ersetzen	replace	remplacer	sostituire	—
sustraer (Es)	unterschlagen	embezzle	soustraire	sottrarre	—
susurrar (Es)	rauschen	rush	bruire	mormorare	—
svantaggiare (I)	benachteiligen	disadvantage	désavantager	—	perjudicar
svantaggio (I)	Nachteil m	disadvantage	désavantage m	—	desventaja f
sveglia (I)	Wecker m	alarm clock	réveil m	—	despertador m
svegliare¹ (I)	aufwecken	wake up	réveiller	—	despertar
svegliare² (I)	wecken	wake (up)	réveiller	—	despertar
svegliarsi¹ (I)	aufwachen	wake up	réveiller, se	—	despertarse
svegliarsi² (I)	erwachen	wake up	réveiller, se	—	despertar
sveglio (I)	wach	awake	réveillé(e)	—	despierto(a)
svenimento (I)	Ohnmacht f	faint	évanouissement m	—	desmayo m
Svezia (I)	Schweden	Sweden	Suède f	—	Suecia f
sviluppare (I)	entwickeln	develop	développer	—	desarrollar
sviluppo (I)	Entwicklung f	development	développement m	—	desarrollo m
Svizzera (I)	Schweiz f	Switzerland	Suisse f	—	Suiza f
svizzero (I)	Schweizer m	Swiss	Suisse m	—	suizo m
svoltare¹ (I)	abbiegen	turn off	tourner	—	torcer
svoltare² (I)	einbiegen	turn	tourner	—	doblar
swallow (E)	schlucken	—	avaler	inghiottire	tragar
swap (E)	tauschen	—	échanger	scambiare	cambiar
swear (E)	schwören	—	jurer	giurare	jurar
sweat (E)	schwitzen	—	transpirer	sudare	sudar
Sweden (E)	Schweden	—	Suède f	Svezia f	Suecia f
sweep¹ (E)	fegen	—	balayer	scopare	barrer

	D	E	F	I	Es
sweep² (E)	kehren	—	balayer	scopare	barrer
sweet¹ (E)	Bonbon *n*	—	bonbon *m*	caramella *f*	caramelo *m*
sweet² (E)	lieb	—	gentil(le)	caro(a)	amable
sweet³ (E)	niedlich	—	mignon(ne)	carino(a)	gracioso(a)
sweet⁴ (E)	süß	—	sucré(e)	dolce	dulce
swim (E)	schwimmen	—	nager	nuotare	nadar
swimming pool (E)	Schwimmbad *n*	—	piscine *f*	piscina *f*	piscina *f*
swimming trunks (E)	Badehose *f*	—	slip de bain *m*	costume da bagno *m*	bañador *m*
swimsuit (E)	Badeanzug *m*	—	maillot de bain *m*	costume da bagno *m*	traje de baño *m*
swing (E)	schaukeln	—	balancer, se	dondolare	columpiarse
Swiss (E)	Schweizer *m*	—	Suisse *m*	svizzero	suizo *m*
switch (E)	schalten	—	connecter	commutare	conectar
switch off¹ (E)	ausschalten	—	arrêter	spegnere	desconectar
switch off² (E)	abschalten	—	éteindre	spegnere	desconectar
switch off⁴ (E)	ausmachen	—	éteindre	spegnere	apagar
switch on (E)	einschalten	—	allumer	accendere	conectar
Switzerland (E)	Schweiz *f*	—	Suisse *f*	Svizzera *f*	Suiza *f*
swollen (E)	geschwollen	—	enflé(e)	gonfio(a)	hinchado(a)
sympathique (F)	sympathisch	likeable	—	simpatico(a)	simpático(a)
sympathisch (D)	—	likeable	sympathique	simpatico(a)	simpático(a)
syndicat (F)	Gewerkschaft *f*	trade union	—	sindacato *m*	sindicato *m*
syndicat d'initiative (F)	Verkehrsbüro *n*	travel agency	—	ufficio turistico *m*	oficina de turismo *f*
System (D)	—	system	système *m*	sistema *m*	sistema *m*
system (E)	System *n*	—	système *m*	sistema *m*	sistema *m*
système (F)	System *n*	system	—	sistema *m*	sistema *m*
tabac (F)	Tabak *m*	tabacco	—	tabacco *m*	tabaco *m*
tabacco (E)	Tabak *m*	—	tabac *m*	tabacco *m*	tabaco *m*
tabacco (I)	Tabak *m*	tabacco	tabac *m*	—	tabaco *m*
tabaco (Es)	Tabak *m*	tabacco	tabac *m*	tabacco *m*	—
Tabak (D)	—	tabacco	tabac *m*	tabacco *m*	tabaco *m*
table (E)	Tisch *m*	—	table *f*	tavolo *m*	mesa *f*
table (F)	Tisch *m*	table	—	tavolo *m*	mesa *f*
tableau (F)	Gemälde *n*	painting	—	quadro *m*	cuadro *m*
table des matières (F)	Inhalts- verzeichnis *n*	table of contents	—	indice *m*	índice *m*
table of contents (E)	Inhalts- verzeichnis *n*	—	table des matières *f*	indice *m*	índice *m*
tablespoon (E)	Eßlöffel *m*	—	cuiller *f*	cucchiaio *m*	cuchara *f*
tablet (E)	Tablette *f*	—	comprimé *m*	compressa *f*	pastilla *f*
tabletennis (E)	Tischtennis *n*	—	ping-pong *m*	tennis da tavolo *m*	tenis de mesa *m*
Tablett (D)	—	tray	plateau *m*	vassoio *m*	bandeja *f*
Tablette (D)	—	tablet	comprimé *m*	compressa *f*	pastilla *f*
tacchino (I)	Truthahn *m*	turkey	dindon *m*	—	pavo *m*
tacere (I)	schweigen	be silent	taire, se	—	callar

	D	E	F	I	Es
tache (F)	Fleck *m*	stain	—	macchia *f*	mancha *f*
tâche (F)	Aufgabe *f*	task	—	incarico *m*	tarea *f*
Tag (D)	—	day	jour *m*	giorno *m*	día *m*
taglia (I)	Größe *f*	size	taille *f*	—	talla *f*
tagliare (I)	schneiden	cut	couper	—	cortar
täglich (D)	—	daily	quotidien(ne)	quotidiano(a)	cotidiano(a)
tagliente (I)	scharf	sharp	tranchant(e)	—	cortante
taglio (I)	Schnitt *m*	cut	coupe *f*	—	corte *m*
tail (E)	Schwanz *m*	—	queue *f*	coda *f*	rabo *m*
taille (F)	Größe *f*	size	—	taglia	talla *f*
tailleur (F)	Schneider *m*	tailor	—	sarto *m*	sastre *m*
tailleur (I)	Kostüm *n*	costume	costume *m*	—	vestido *m*
tailor (E)	Schneider *m*	—	tailleur *m*	sarto *m*	sastre *m*
taire, se (F)	schweigen	be silent	—	tacere	callar
take[1] (E)	kassieren	—	encaisser	incassare	cobrar
take[2] (E)	nehmen	—	prendre	prendere	tomar
take along (E)	mitnehmen	—	emmener	prendere con sè	llevar consigo
take a snap (E)	knipsen	—	photographier	scattare	hacer una foto
take away[1] (E)	abnehmen	—	décrocher	staccare	descolgar
take away[2] (E)	wegnehmen	—	enlever	togliere	quitar
take back (E)	zurücknehmen	—	retirer	prendere indietro	retirar
take care (E)	achtgeben	—	faire attention	badare	atender
take care of (E)	erledigen	—	régler	sbrigare	acabar
take in tow (E)	abschleppen	—	remorquer	rimorchiare	remolcar
take notice of (E)	beachten	—	observer	osservare	prestar atención a
take off (E)	ausziehen	—	enlever	levare	quitarse
take-off (E)	Abflug *m*	—	décollage *m*	partenza *f*	despegue *m*
take over (E)	übernehmen	—	reprendre	accettare	aceptar
take part (E)	teilnehmen	—	participer	partecipare	participar
take pictures (E)	fotografieren	—	photographier	fotografare	fotografiar
take place (E)	stattfinden	—	avoir lieu	avere luogo	tener lugar
take turns (E)	abwechseln	—	alterner	alternarsi	alternar
Tal (D)	—	valley	vallée *f*	valle *f*	valle *m*
tale (I)	solche(r,s)	such	tel(le)	—	un(a) tal
talk[1] (E)	reden	—	parler	parlare	hablar
talk[2] (E)	unterhalten, sich	—	entretenir, se	conversare	conversar
talk[3] (E)	Unterredung *f*	—	entrevue *f*	colloquio *m*	entrevista *f*
talla (Es)	Größe *f*	size	taille *f*	taglia *f*	—
taller (Es)	Werkstatt *f*	workshop	atelier *m*	officina *f*	—
taller de reparaciones (Es)	Autowerkstatt *f*	repair shop	atelier de réparation d'autos *m*	autofficina *f*	—
talonario de cheques (Es)	Scheckbuch *n*	cheque book	carnet de chèques *m*	libretto degli assegni *m*	—
tal vez (Es)	vielleicht	maybe	peut-être	forse	—
talvolta (I)	manchmal	sometimes	quelquefois	—	a veces
también[1] (Es)	auch	also/too	aussi	anche/pure	—
también[2] (Es)	ebenfalls	likewise	aussi	altrettanto	—
tamis (F)	Sieb *n*	sieve	—	setaccio *m*	colador *m*

	D	E	F	I	Es
tanken (D)	—	fill up with petrol	prendre de l'essence	fare benzina	llenar de gasolina
Tankstelle (D)	—	filling station	station-service *f*	distributore di benzina *m*	gasolinera *f*
tan pronto... como (Es)	sobald	as soon as	dès que	appena	—
tant (F)	soviel	so much	—	quanto/tanto	tanto
Tante (D)	—	aunt(ie)	tante *f*	zia *f*	tía *f*
tante (F)	Tante *f*	aunt(ie)	—	zia *f*	tía *f*
tanto (Es)	soviel	so much	tant	quanto/tanto	—
tanto... (Es)	sowohl	as well as	aussi bien	tanto...quanto	—
tanto...quanto (I)	sowohl	as well as	aussi bien	—	tanto...
tant que (F)	solange	as long	—	finché	en tanto que
Tanz (D)	—	dance	danse *f*	ballo *m*	baile *f*
tanzen (D)	—	dance	danser	ballare	bailar
tapa (Es)	Deckel *m*	lid	couvercle *m*	coperchio *m*	—
tapar (Es)	zudecken	cover (up)	couvrir	coprire	—
tape (E)	Tonband *n*	—	bande magnétique *f*	nastro magnetico *m*	cinta magnetofónica *f*
taper (à la machine) (F)	tippen	type	—	battere a macchina	escribir a máquina
tapfer (D)	—	brave	courageux(-euse)	coraggioso(a)	valiente
tapis (F)	Teppich *m*	carpet	—	tappeto *m*	alfombra *f*
tapizar (Es)	beziehen	cover	recouvrir	ricoprire	—
tappeto (I)	Teppich *m*	carpet	tapis *m*	—	alfombra *f*
tard (F)	spät	late	—	tardi	tarde
tarde¹ (Es)	Nachmittag *m*	afternoon	après-midi *m*	pomeriggio *m*	—
tarde² (Es)	spät	late	tard	tardi	—
tardi (I)	spät	late	tard	—	tarde
tarea (Es)	Aufgabe *f*	task	tâche *f*	incarico *m*	—
targa (I)	Nummernschild *n*	number plate	plaque d'immatriculation *f*	—	matrícula *f*
tarifa (Es)	Gebühr *f*	fee	droit *m*	tassa *f*	—
tarjeta postal (Es)	Ansichtskarte *f*	postcard	carte postale *f*	cartolina *f*	—
tarta (Es)	Torte *f*	cake	gâteau *m*	torta *f*	—
tartamudear (Es)	stottern	stutter	bégayer	balbettare	—
tas (F)	Haufen *m*	heap	—	mucchio *m*	montón *m*
tasca (Es)	Kneipe *f*	pub	bistro *m*	osteria *f*	—
Tasche (D)	—	handbag	sac *m*	borsa *f*	bolso *m*
Taschengeld (D)	—	pocket money	argent de poche *f*	denaro per le piccole spese *m*	dinero de bolsillo *m*
Taschenlampe (D)	—	torch	lampe de poche *f*	lampadina tascabile *f*	linterna *f*
Taschentuch (D)	—	handkerchief	mouchoir *m*	fazzoletto *m*	pañuelo *m*
task (E)	Aufgabe *f*	—	tâche *f*	incarico *m*	tarea *f*
tassa (I)	Gebühr *f*	fee	droit *m*	—	tarifa *f*
Tasse (D)	—	cup	tasse *f*	tazza *f*	taza *f*
tasse (F)	Tasse *f*	cup	—	tazza *f*	taza *f*
tassì (I)	Taxi *n*	taxi	taxi *m*	—	taxi *m*
taste¹ (E)	Geschmack *m*	—	goût *m*	gusto *m*	sabor *m*
taste² (E)	schmecken	—	sentir	piacere	gustar

	D	E	F	I	Es
Tat (D)	—	deed	action f	azione f	acción f
tätig (D)	—	active	actif(-ive)	attivo(a)	activo(a)
Tätigkeit (D)	—	activity	activité f	attività f	actividad f
Tatsache (D)	—	fact	fait m	fatto m	hecho m
tatsächlich (D)	—	really	vraiment	realmente	realmente
taub (D)	—	deaf	sourd(e)	sordo(a)	sordo(a)
tauchen (D)	—	dive	plonger	immergere	bucear
tauen (D)	—	thaw	fondre	sciogliersi	deshelar
Taufe (D)	—	baptism	baptême m	battesimo m	bautizo m
taugen (D)	—	be of use	convenir pour	essere portato(a)	valer
taumeln (D)	—	reel	tituber	barcollare	vacilar
taureau (F)	Stier m	bull	—	toro m	toro m
tauschen (D)	—	swap	échanger	scambiare	cambiar
täuschen (D)	—	deceive	tromper	ingannare	engañar
tausend (D)	—	thousand	mille	mille	mil
tavolo (I)	Tisch m	table	table f	—	mesa f
tax (E)	Steuern pl	—	impôt m	imposte f pl	impuesto m
taxe sur la valeur ajoutée (F)	Mehrwertsteuer f	value added tax	—	imposta sul'valore aggiunto f	impuesto sobre el valor añadido m
Taxi (D)	—	taxi	taxi m	tassì m	taxi m
taxi (E)	Taxi n	—	taxi m	tassì m	taxi m
taxi (Es)	Taxi n	taxi	taxi m	tassì m	—
taxi (F)	Taxi n	taxi	—	tassì m	taxi m
taza (Es)	Tasse f	cup	tasse f	tazza f	—
tazza (I)	Tasse f	cup	tasse f	—	taza f
Tchécoslovaquie (F)	Tschecho-slowakei f	Czechoslovakia	—	Cecoslovacchia f	Checoslovaquia f
té (Es)	Tee m	tea	thé m	tè m	—
tè (I)	Tee m	tea	thé m	—	té m
tea (E)	Tee m	—	thé m	tè m	té m
teach (E)	lehren	—	enseigner	insegnare	enseñar
teacher (E)	Lehrer m	—	professeur m	maestro m	profesor m
team (E)	Mannschaft f	—	équipe f	squadra f	equipo m
teapot (E)	Teekanne f	—	théière f	teiera f	tetera f
tear[1] (E)	reißen	—	déchirer, se	strappare	desgarrarse
tear[2] (E)	Träne f	—	larme f	lacrima f	lágrima f
teaspoon (E)	Teelöffel m	—	cuiller à thé f	cucchiaino da tè m	cucharilla f
teatro (Es)	Theater n	theatre	théâtre m	teatro m	—
teatro (I)	Theater n	theatre	théâtre m	—	teatro m
Technik (D)	—	technology	technique f	tecnica f	técnica f
technique (F)	Technik f	technology	—	tecnica f	técnica f
technology (E)	Technik f	—	technique f	tecnica f	técnica f
techo[1] (Es)	Dach n	roof	toit m	tetto m	—
techo[2] (Es)	Decke f	blanket	couverture f	coperta f	—
técnica (Es)	Technik f	technology	technique f	tecnica f	—
tecnica (I)	Technik f	technology	technique f	—	técnica f
tedesco[1] (I)	Deutscher m	German	Allemand m	—	alemán m
tedesco[2] (I)	deutsch	German	allemand(e)	—	alemán(a)
Tee (D)	—	tea	thé m	tè m	té m

	D	E	F	I	Es
Teekanne (D)	—	teapot	théière f	teiera f	tetera f
Teelöffel (D)	—	teaspoon	cuiller à thé f	cucchiaino da tè m	cucharilla f
teeth (E)	Gebiß n	—	dents f pl	denti m pl	dentadura f
Teich (D)	—	pond	étang m	stagno m	estanque m
teiera (I)	Teekanne f	teapot	théière f	—	tetera f
Teig (D)	—	dough	pâte f	pasta f	masa f
Teigwaren (D)	—	pasta	pâtes f pl	pasta f	pastas f pl
Teil (D)	—	part	partie f	parte f	parte f
teilen (D)	—	share	partager	dividere	partir
teilnehmen (D)	—	take part	participer	partecipare	participar
teilweise (D)	—	partly	en partie	in parte	en parte
tel (F)	solche(r,s)	such	—	tale(i)	un(a) tal
tela¹ (Es)	Gewebe n	fabric	tissu m	tessuto m	—
tela² (Es)	Stoff m	cloth	tissu m	stoffa f	—
Telefon (D)	—	telephone	téléphone m	telefono m	teléfono m
Telefonanruf (D)	—	phone call	coup de téléphone m	telefonata f	llamada telefónica f
telefonare¹ (I)	anrufen	ring up	téléphoner	—	llamar por teléfono
telefonare² (I)	telefonieren	telephone	téléphoner	—	llamar por teléfono
telefonata (I)	Telefonanruf m	phone call	coup de téléphone m	—	llamada telefónica f
telefonata interurbana (I)	Ferngespräch n	long-distance call	communication interurbaine f	—	llamada interurbana f
Telefonbuch (D)	—	phone book	annuaire du téléphone m	elenco telefonico m	guía telefónica f
Telefongespräch (D)	—	phone call	communication téléphonique f	conversazione telefonica f	conversación telefónica f
telefonieren (D)	—	telephone	téléphoner	telefonare	llamar por teléfono
Telefonnummer (D)	—	phone number	numéro de téléphone m	numero telefonico m	número de teléfono m
teléfono (Es)	Telefon n	telephone	téléphone m	telefono m	—
telefono (I)	Telefon n	telephone	téléphone m	—	teléfono m
Telefonzelle (D)	—	phone box	cabine téléphonique f	cabina telefonica f	cabina de teléfono f
telegram (E)	Telegramm n	—	télégramme m	telegramma f	telegrama f
telegrama (Es)	Telegramm n	telegram	télégramme m	telegramma f	—
Telegramm (D)	—	telegram	télégramme m	telegramma f	telegrama f
telegramma (I)	Telegramm n	telegram	télégramme m	—	telegrama f
télégramme (F)	Telegramm n	telegram	—	telegramma f	telegrama f
telephone¹ (E)	telefonieren	—	téléphoner	telefonare	llamar por teléfono
telephone² (E)	Telefon n	—	téléphone m	telefono m	teléfono m
téléphone (F)	Telefon n	telephone	—	telefono m	teléfono m
téléphoner¹ (F)	anrufen	ring up	—	telefonare	llamar por teléfono
téléphoner² (F)	telefonieren	telephone	—	telefonare	llamar por teléfono
telesilla (Es)	Skilift m	skilift	remonte-pente m	sciovia f	—
television (E)	Fernsehen n	—	télévision f	televisione f	televisión f
televisión (Es)	Fernsehen n	television	télévision f	televisione f	—
télévision (F)	Fernsehen n	television	—	televisione f	televisión f
televisione (I)	Fernsehen n	television	télévision f	—	televisión f
television set (E)	Fernseher m	—	poste de télévision m	televisore m	televisor m

	D	E	F	I	Es
televisor (Es)	Fernseher *m*	television set	poste de télévision *m*	televisore *m*	—
televisore (I)	Fernseher *m*	television set	poste de télévision *m*	—	televisor *m*
tell (E)	erzählen	—	raconter	raccontare	contar
Teller (D)	—	plate	assiette *f*	piatto *m*	plato *m*
tema (Es)	Thema *n*	topic	sujet *m*	tema *m*	—
tema (I)	Thema *n*	topic	sujet *m*	—	tema *m*
temer¹ (Es)	befürchten	fear	craindre	temere	—
temer² (Es)	fürchten	fear	craindre	temere	—
temere¹ (I)	befürchten	fear	craindre	—	temer
temere² (I)	fürchten	fear	craindre	—	temer
témoin (F)	Zeuge *m*	witness	—	testimone *m*	testigo *m*
Temperatur (D)	—	temperature	température *f*	temperatura *f*	temperatura *f*
temperatura (Es)	Temperatur *f*	temperature	température *f*	temperatura *f*	—
temperatura (I)	Temperatur *f*	temperature	température *f*	—	temperatura *f*
temperature (E)	Temperatur *f*	—	température *f*	temperatura *f*	temperatura *f*
température (F)	Temperatur *f*	temperature	—	temperatura *f*	temperatura *f*
tempesta (I)	Sturm *m*	storm	tempête *f*	—	tempestad *f*
tempestad (Es)	Sturm *m*	storm	tempête *f*	tempesta *f*	—
tempête¹ (F)	Sturm *m*	storm	—	tempesta *f*	tempestad *f*
tempête² (F)	Unwetter *n*	thunderstorm	—	maltempo *m*	tormenta *f*
templado (Es)	lauwarm	lukewarm	tiède	tiepido(a)	—
Tempo (D)	—	speed	vitesse *f*	velocità *f*	velocidad *f*
tempo¹ (I)	Wetter *n*	weather	temps *m*	—	tiempo *m*
tempo² (I)	Zeit *f*	time	temps *m*	—	tiempo *m*
tempo libero (I)	Freizeit *f*	free time	loisirs *m pl*	—	tiempo libre *m*
temporada (Es)	Saison *f*	season	saison *f*	stagione *f*	—
temporada alta (Es)	Hochsaison *f*	high season	pleine saison *f*	alta stagione *f*	—
temporada de verano (Es)	Sommerzeit *f*	summertime	heure d'été *f*	ora legale *f*	—
temporaire (F)	vorübergehend	temporar	—	temporaneo(a)	pasajero(a)
temporale (I)	Gewitter *n*	thunderstorm	orage *m*	—	tormenta *f*
temporaneo (I)	vorübergehend	temporary	temporaire	—	pasajero(a)
temporary¹ (E)	vorläufig	—	provisoire	temporaneo(a)	pasajero(a)
temporary² (E)	vorübergehend	—	temporaire	provvisorio(a)	provisional
temprano (Es)	früh	early	tôt	presto	—
temps¹ (F)	Wetter *n*	weather	—	tempo *m*	tiempo *m*
temps² (F)	Zeit *f*	time	—	tempo *m*	tiempo *m*
ten (E)	zehn	—	dix	dieci	diez
tenant (E)	Mieter *m*	—	locataire *m*	inquilino *m*	inquilino *m*
tenda¹ (I)	Gardine *f*	curtain	rideau *m*	—	cortina *f*
tenda² (I)	Vorhang *m*	curtain	rideau *m*	—	cortina *f*
tenda³ (I)	Zelt *n*	tent	tente *f*	—	tienda *f*
tenderness (E)	Zärtlichkeit *f*	—	tendresse *f*	tenerezza *f*	cariño *m*
tendresse (F)	Zärtlichkeit *f*	tenderness	—	tenerezza *f*	cariño *m*
tendu (F)	gespannt	tense	—	teso(a)	tenso(a)
tenedor (Es)	Gabel *f*	fork	fourchette *f*	forchetta *f*	—
tener (Es)	haben	have	avoir	avere	—

	D	E	F	I	Es
tenere¹ (I)	behalten	keep	garder	—	retener
tenere² (I)	halten	hold	tenir	—	sujetar
tenerezza (I)	Zärtlichkeit *f*	tenderness	tendresse *f*	—	cariño *m*
tener fermo (I)	festhalten	seize	tenir ferme	—	sujetar
tener frío (Es)	frieren	be cold	avoir froid	avere freddo	—
tener la intención de (Es)	vorhaben	intend	avoir l'intention de	avere intenzione	—
tener lugar (Es)	stattfinden	take place	avoir lieu	avere luogo	—
tenero (I)	zart	soft	doux (douce)	—	suave
tener vergüenza (Es)	schämen	be ashamed	avoir honte	vergognarsi	—
tenir (F)	halten	hold	—	tenere	sujetar
tenir ferme (F)	festhalten	seize	—	tener fermo	sujetar
tenis (Es)	Tennis *n*	tennis	tennis *m*	tennis *m*	—
tenis de mesa (Es)	Tischtennis *n*	tabletennis	ping-pong *m*	tennis da tavolo *m*	—
Tennis (D)	—	tennis	tennis *m*	tennis *m*	tenis *m*
tennis (E)	Tennis *n*	—	tennis *m*	tennis *m*	tenis *m*
tennis (F)	Tennis *n*	tennis	—	tennis *m*	tenis *m*
tennis (I)	Tennis *n*	tennis	tennis *m*	—	tenis *m*
tennis da tavolo (I)	Tischtennis *n*	tabletennis	ping-pong *m*	—	tenis de mesa *m*
tense (E)	gespannt	—	tendu(e)	teso(a)	tenso(a)
tenso (Es)	gespannt	tense	tendu(e)	teso(a)	—
tent (E)	Zelt *n*	—	tente *f*	tenda *f*	tienda *f*
tentativo (I)	Versuch *m*	try	essai *m*	—	intento *m*
tente (F)	Zelt *n*	tent	—	tenda *f*	tienda *f*
Teppich (D)	—	carpet	tapis *m*	tappeto *m*	alfombra *f*
tercera (Es)	dritte(r,s)	third	troisième	terzo(a)	—
tercio (Es)	Drittel *n*	a third	tiers *m*	terzo *m*	—
terme (F)	Termin *m*	date	—	termine *m*	fecha *f*
Termin (D)	—	date	terme *m*	termine *m*	fecha *f*
terminar¹ (Es)	aufhören	stop	arrêter	cessare	—
terminar² (Es)	beenden	stop	terminer	terminare	—
terminare (I)	beenden	stop	terminer	—	terminar
termine (I)	Termin *m*	date	terme *m*	—	fecha *f*
terminer (F)	beenden	stop	—	terminare	terminar
término (Es)	Ausdruck *m*	expression	expression *f*	espressione *f*	—
terminus (E)	Endstation *f*	—	terminus *m*	capolinea *m*	estación terminal *f*
terminus (F)	Endstation *f*	terminus	—	capolinea *m*	estación terminal *f*
termo (Es)	Thermosflasche *f*	thermos flask	thermos *m*	thermos *m*	—
termómetro (Es)	Thermometer *n*	thermometer	thermomètre *m*	termometro *m*	—
termometro (I)	Thermometer *n*	thermometer	thermomètre *m*	—	termómetro *m*
ternera (Es)	Kalb *n*	calf	veau *m*	vitello *m*	—
terra¹ (I)	Boden *m*	floor	terre *f*	—	suelo *m*
terra² (I)	Erde *f*	earth	terre *f*	—	tierra *f*
terrace (E)	Terrasse *f*	--	terrasse *f*	terrazza *f*	terraza *f*
terraferma (I)	Festland *n*	mainland	continent *m*	—	tierra firme *f*
terrain (E)	Gelände *n*	—	terrain *m*	terreno *m*	terreno *m*
terrain (F)	Gelände *n*	terrain	—	terreno *m*	terreno *m*

	D	E	F	I	Es
terrain de camping (F)	Campingplatz m	campsite	—	campeggio m	camping m
terrain de jeu (F)	Spielplatz m	playground	—	campo dei giochi m	campo de juego m
Terrasse (D)	—	terrace	terrasse f	terrazza f	terraza f
terrasse (F)	Terrasse f	terrace	—	terrazza f	terraza f
terraza (Es)	Terrasse f	terrace	terrasse f	terrazza f	—
terrazza (I)	Terrasse f	terrace	terrasse f	—	terraza f
terre¹ (F)	Boden m	floor	—	terra f	suelo m
terre² (F)	Erde f	earth	—	terra f	tierra f
terremoto (Es)	Erdbeben n	earthquake	tremblement de terre m	terremoto m	—
terremoto (I)	Erdbeben n	earthquake	tremblement de terre m	—	terremoto m
terreno (Es)	Gelände n	terrain	terrain m	terreno m	—
terreno (I))	Gelände n	terrain	terrain m	—	terreno m
terribile (I)	fürchterlich	terrible	terrible	—	terrible
terrible¹ (E)	fürchterlich	—	terrible	terribile	terrible
terrible² (E)	schrecklich	—	terrible	spaventoso(a)	horrible
terrible (Es)	fürchterlich	terrible	terrible	terribile	—
terrible¹ (F)	fürchterlich	terrible	—	terribile	terrible
terrible² (F)	schrecklich	terrible	—	spaventoso(a)	horrible
territorio nacional (Es)	Inland n	inland	intérieur m	territorio nazionale m	—
territorio nazionale (I)	Inland n	inland	intérieur m	—	territorio nacional m
terzo¹ (I)	Drittel n	a third	tiers m	—	tercio m
terzo² (I)	dritte(r,s)	third	troisième	—	tercera(o)
teso (I)	gespannt	tense	tendu(e)	—	tenso(a)
tesoro (Es)	Schatz m	treasure	trésor m	tesoro m	—
tesoro¹ (I)	Liebling m	darling	chéri m	—	querido m
tesoro² (I)	Schatz m	treasure	trésor m	—	tesoro m
tesson (F)	Scherbe f	broken piece	—	coccio m	pedazo m
tessuto (I)	Gewebe n	fabric	tissu m	—	tela f
Test (D)	—	test	test m	test m	test m
test¹ (E)	prüfen	—	tester	esaminare	examinar
test² (E)	Probe f	—	essai m	prova f	prueba f
test³ (E)	testen	—	tester	collaudare	probar
test⁴ (E)	Test m	—	test m	test m	test m
test (Es)	Test m	test	test m	test m	—
test (F)	Test m	test	—	test m	test m
test (I)	Test m	test	test m	—	test m
testa (I)	Kopf m	head	tête f	—	cabeza f
Testament (D)	—	will	testament m	testamento m	testamento m
testament (F)	Testament n	will	—	testamento m	testamento m
testamento (Es)	Testament n	will	testament m	testamento m	—
testamento (I)	Testament n	will	testament m	—	testamento m
testen (D)	—	test	tester	collaudare	probar
tester¹ (F)	prüfen	test	—	esaminare	examinar
tester² (F)	testen	test	—	collaudare	probar
testigo (Es)	Zeuge m	witness	témoin m	testimone m	—

	D	E	F	I	Es
testimone (I)	Zeuge *m*	witness	témoin *m*	—	testigo *m*
tête (F)	Kopf *m*	head	—	testa *f*	cabeza *f*
tetera (Es)	Teekanne *f*	teapot	théière *f*	teiera *f*	—
tetto (I)	Dach *n*	roof	toit *m*	—	techo *m*
teuer (D)	—	expensive	cher, chère	caro(a)	caro(a)
Teufel (D)	—	devil	diable *m*	diavolo *m*	diablo *m*
thank (E)	danken	—	remercier	ringraziare	agradecer
thanks (E)	Dank *m*	—	remerciement *m*	ringraziamento *m*	agradecimiento *m*
thank you (E)	danke	—	merci	grazie	¡gracias!
that¹ (E)	daß	—	que	che	que
that² (E)	jene(r,s)	—	ce, cette	quello(a)	aquella, aquel, aquello
that³ (E)	das	—	le, la	il, la	lo
thaw (E)	tauen	—	fondre	sciogliersi	deshelar
the (E)	der, die, das	—	le, la	il, la	el, la, lo
thé (F)	Tee *m*	tea	—	tè *m*	té *m*
Theater (D)	—	theatre	théâtre *m*	teatro *m*	teatro *m*
Theaterstück (D)	—	play	pièce de théâtre *f*	opera teatrale *f*	pieza de teatro *f*
theatre (E)	Theater *n*	—	théâtre *m*	teatro *m*	teatro *m*
théâtre (F)	Theater *n*	theatre	—	teatro *m*	teatro *m*
théière (F)	Teekanne *f*	teapot	—	teiera *f*	tetera *f*
Thema (D)	—	topic	sujet *m*	tema *m*	tema *m*
then (E)	dann	—	ensuite	in seguito	luego
there¹ (E)	dort	—	là/y	là	allí
there² (E)	da	—	là/ici	qui/là	allí
there³ (E)	hin	—	jusqu'à/vers	là	hacia allá/hasta
therefore¹ (E)	also	—	donc	dunque/quindi	así
therefore² (E)	deshalb	—	c'est pourquoi	perció	por eso
Thermo-meter (D)	—	thermometer	thermomètre *m*	termometro *m*	termómetro *m*
thermometer (E)	Thermometer *n*	—	thermomètre *m*	termometro *m*	termómetro *m*
thermomètre (F)	Thermometer *n*	thermometer	—	termometro *m*	termómetro *m*
thermos (F)	Thermosflasche *f*	thermos flask	—	thermos *m*	termo *m*
thermos (I)	Thermosflasche *f*	thermos flask	thermos *m*	—	termo *m*
Thermosflasche (D)	—	thermos flask	thermos *m*	thermos *m*	termo *m*
thermos flask (E)	Thermosflasche *f*	—	thermos *m*	thermos *m*	termo *m*
the same¹ (E)	derselbe	—	le même	lo stesso	el mismo
the same² (E)	dasselbe	—	la même chose	lo stesso	lo mismo
they (E)	sie (pl)	—	ils/elles	loro	ellos, ellas
thief (E)	Dieb *m*	—	voleur *m*	ladro *m*	ladrón *m*
thin (E)	dünn	—	mince	magro(a)	delgado(a)
thing¹ (E)	Ding *n*	—	chose *f*	cosa *f*	cosa *f*
thing² (E)	Sache *f*	—	chose *f*	cosa *f*	cosa *f*
think¹ (E)	denken	—	penser	pensare	pensar
think² (E)	meinen	—	penser	credere	opinar
think³ (E)	nachdenken	—	réfléchir	riflettere	reflexionar
third (E)	dritte(r,s)	—	troisième	terzo(a)	tercera(o)
thirst (E)	Durst *m*	—	soif *f*	sete *f*	sed *f*
thirsty (E)	durstig	—	assoiffé(e)	assetato(a)	sediento(a)

	D	E	F	I	Es
thirteen (E)	dreizehn	—	treize	tredici	trece
thirty (E)	dreißig	—	trente	trenta	treinta
this (E)	diese(r,s)	—	ce, cette	questo(a)	esta, este, esto
thon (F)	Thunfisch *m*	tuna	—	tonno *m*	atún *m*
thorough (E)	gründlich	—	a fond	a fondo	a fondo
thought (E)	Gedanke *m*	—	pensée *f*	pensiero *m*	pensamiento *m*
thousand (E)	tausend	—	mille	mille	mil
thread (E)	Faden *m*	—	fil *m*	filo *m*	hilo *m*
threaten[1] (E)	bedrohen	—	menacer	minacciare	amenazar
threaten[2] (E)	drohen	—	menacer	minacciare	amenazar (a alguien)
threaten s.b. (E)	androhen	—	menacer	minacciare	amenazar
three (E)	drei	—	trois	tre	tres
throat (E)	Rachen *m*	—	gorge *f*	faringe *m*	garganta *f*
through[1] (E)	durch	—	par	per	por
through[2] (E)	hindurch	—	à travers	attraverso	a través de
through train (E)	D-Zug *m*	—	express *m*	direttissimo *m*	tren expreso *m*
throw (E)	werfen	—	lancer	lanciare	tirar
throw over (E)	umschmeißen	—	renverser	rovesciare	derribar
thumb (E)	Daumen *m*	—	pouce *m*	pollice *m*	pulgar *m*
thunder (E)	Donner *m*	—	tonnerre *m*	tuono *m*	trueno *m*
thunderstorm[1] (E)	Gewitter *n*	—	orage *m*	temporale *m*	tormenta *f*
thunderstorm[2] (E)	Unwetter *n*	—	tempête *f*	maltempo *m*	tormenta *f*
Thunfisch (D)	—	tuna	thon *m*	tonno *m*	atún *m*
Thursday (E)	Donnerstag *m*	—	jeudi *m*	giovedì *m*	jueves *m*
tía (Es)	Tante *f*	aunt(ie)	tante *f*	zia *f*	—
tiburón (Es)	Hai *m*	shark	requin *m*	pescecane *m*	—
ticket[1] (E)	Fahrschein *m*	—	ticket *m*	biglietto *m*	billete *m*
ticket[2] (E)	Fahrkarte *f*	—	billet *m*	biglietto *m*	billete *m*
ticket (F)	Fahrschein *m*	ticket	—	biglietto *m*	billete *m*
tidy (E)	ordentlich	—	rangé(e)	ordinato(a)	ordenado(a)
tie (E)	Krawatte *f*	—	cravate *f*	cravatta *f*	corbata *f*
tiède (F)	lauwarm	lukewarm	—	tiepido(a)	templado(a)
tief (D)	—	deep	profond(e)	profondo(a)	profundo(a)
Tiefe (D)	—	depth	profondeur *f*	profondità *f*	profundidad *f*
tiempo[1] (Es)	Wetter *n*	weather	temps *m*	tempo *m*	—
tiempo[2] (Es)	Zeit *f*	time	temps *m*	tempo *m*	—
tiempo libre (Es)	Freizeit *f*	free time	loisirs *m pl*	tempo libero *m*	—
tienda[1] (Es)	Geschäft *n*	shop	magasin *m*	negozio *m*	—
tienda[2] (Es)	Laden *m*	shop	magasin *m*	negozio *m*	—
tienda[3] (Es)	Zelt *n*	tent	tente *f*	tenda *f*	—
tienda de productos dietéticos (Es)	Reformhaus *n*	health food shop	magasin diététique *m*	negozio di prodotti dietetici *m*	—
tienda de ultramarinos (Es)	Lebensmittel-geschäft *n*	grocer's	magasin d'alimentation *m*	negozio di alimentari *m*	—
tiepido (I)	lauwarm	lukewarm	tiède	—	templado(a)
Tier (D)	—	animal	animal *m*	animale *m*	animal *m*
Tierarzt (D)	—	vet	vétérinaire *m*	veterinario *m*	veterinario *m*

	D	E	F	I	Es
tierno (Es)	weich	soft	doux(douce)	morbido(a)	—
tierra (Es)	Erde f	earth	terre f	terra f	—
tierra firme (Es)	Festland n	mainland	continent m	terraferma f	—
tiers (F)	Drittel n	a third	—	terzo m	tercio m
tight (E)	knapp	—	étroit(e)	scarso(a)	estrecho(a)
tights (E)	Strumpfhose f	—	collants m pl	calzamaglia f	leotardos m pl
tijeras (Es)	Schere f	pair of scissors	ciseaux m pl	forbici f pl	—
tilgen (D)	—	erase	effacer	estinguere	anular
till (E)	Kasse f	—	caisse f	cassa f	caja f
timbre (Es)	Klingel f	bell	sonnette f	campanello m	—
timbre[1] (F)	Briefmarke f	stamp	—	francobollo m	sello m
timbre[2] (F)	Stempel m	stamp	—	timbro m	sello m
timbro (I)	Stempel m	stamp	timbre m	—	sello m
time (E)	Zeit f	—	temps m	tempo m	tiempo m
time of year (E)	Jahreszeit f	—	saison f	stagione f	estación del año f
timetable (E)	Fahrplan m	—	horaire m	orario m	horario m
timide[1] (F)	schüchtern	shy	—	timido(a)	tímido(a)
timide[2] (F)	scheu	shy	—	timido(a)	tímido(a)
timido[1] (I)	scheu	shy	timide	—	tímido(a)
timido[2] (I)	schüchtern	shy	timide	—	tímido(a)
tímido[1] (Es)	schüchtern	shy	timide	timido(a)	—
tímido[2] (Es)	scheu	shy	timide	timido(a)	—
tin (E)	Dose f	—	boîte f	scatola f	lata f
tingere (I)	färben	dye	colorer	—	colorear
Tintenfisch (D)	—	cuttlefish	seiche f	seppia f	calamar m
tío (Es)	Onkel m	uncle	oncle m	zio m	—
tíovivo (Es)	Karussell n	roundabout	manège m	giostra f	—
tip (E)	Trinkgeld n	—	pourboire m	mancia f	propina f
tipico (I)	typisch	typical	typique	—	típico(a)
típico (Es)	typisch	typical	typique	tipico	—
tippen (D)	—	type	taper (à la machine)	battere a macchina	escribir a máquina
tirar[1] (Es)	werfen	throw	lancer	lanciare	—
tirar[2] (Es)	ziehen	pull	tirer	tirare	—
tirare (I)	ziehen	pull	tirer	—	tirar
tirare in avanti (I)	vorziehen	draw	tirer	—	correr
tire (E)	ermüden	—	fatiguer	stancarsi	cansar
tire-bouchon (F)	Korkenzieher m	corkscrew	—	cavatappi m	sacacorchos m
tired (E)	müde	—	fatigué(e)	stanco	cansado(a)
tirer[1] (F)	schießen	shoot	—	sparare	disparar
tirer[2] (F)	vorziehen	draw	—	tirare in avanti	correr
tirer[3] (F)	ziehen	pull	—	tirare	tirar
tiring (E)	anstrengend	—	fatigant(e)	faticoso(a)	fatigoso(a)
tiritar (Es)	zittern	tremble	trembler	tremare	—
tirocinio (I)	Praktikum n	practical training	stage m	—	prácticas f pl
tiroir (F)	Schublade f	drawer	—	cassetto m	cajón m
Tisch (D)	—	table	table f	tavolo m	mesa f
Tischler (D)	—	carpenter	menuisier m	falegname m	carpintero m

	D	E	F	I	Es
Tischtennis (D)	—	tabletennis	ping-pong *m*	tennis da tavolo *m*	tenis de mesa *m*
tissu[1] (F)	Gewebe *n*	fabric	—	tessuto *m*	tela *f*
tissu[2] (F)	Stoff *m*	cloth	—	stoffa *f*	tela *f*
Titel (D)	—	title	titre *m*	titolo *m*	título *m*
title (E)	Titel *m*	—	titre *m*	titolo *m*	título *m*
titolo[1] (I)	Schlagzeile *f*	headline	manchette *f*	—	título *m*
titolo[2] (I)	Titel *m*	title	titre *m*	—	título *m*
titolo[3] (I)	Überschrift *f*	heading	titre *m*	—	título *m*
titre[1] (F)	Titel *m*	title	—	titolo *m*	título *m*
titre[2] (F)	Überschrift *f*	heading	—	titolo *m*	título *m*
tituber (F)	taumeln	reel	—	barcollare	vacilar
título[1] (Es)	Grad *m*	rank	grade *m*	rango *m*	—
título[2] (Es)	Schlagzeile *f*	headline	manchette *f*	titolo *m*	—
título[3] (Es)	Titel *m*	title	titre *m*	titolo *m*	—
título[4] (Es)	Überschrift *f*	heading	titre *m*	titolo *m*	—
to (E)	zu	—	de/á	da/di/a	para
tobillo (Es)	Knöchel *m*	ankle	cheville *f*	caviglia *f*	—
tocadiscos (Es)	Plattenspieler *m*	record player	tourne-disque *m*	giradischi *m*	—
tocar[1] (Es)	berühren	touch	toucher	toccare	—
tocar[2] (Es)	läuten	ring	sonner	suonare	—
tocar el timbre (Es)	klingeln	ring the bell	sonner	suonare	—
toccare (I)	berühren	touch	toucher	—	tocar
Tochter (D)	—	daughter	fille *f*	figlia *f*	hija *f*
tocino (Es)	Speck *m*	bacon	lard *m*	lardo *m*	—
Tod (D)	—	death	mort *f*	morte *f*	muerte *f*
today (E)	heute	—	aujourd'hui	oggi	hoy
todo[1] (Es)	alles	everything	tout	tutto	—
todo[2] (Es)	Ganze(s) *n*	lot	le tout	insieme *m*	—
todo derecho (Es)	geradeaus	straight ahead	tout droit	dritto	—
todos (Es)	alle	all	tous(toutes)	tutti(e)	—
toe (E)	Zehe *f*	—	doigt du pied *m*	dito del piede *m*	dedo del pie *m*
together[1] (E)	gemeinsam	—	ensemble	comune	juntos(as)
together[2] (E)	miteinander	—	ensemble	insieme	juntos(as)
together[3] (E)	zusammen	—	ensemble	insieme	juntos(as)
togliere (I)	wegnehmen	take away	enlever	—	quitar
toilet (E)	Toilette *f*	—	toilette *f*	toilette *f*	lavabo *m*
Toilette (D)	—	toilet	toilette *f*	toilette *f*	lavabo *m*
toilette (F)	Toilette *f*	toilet	—	toilette *f*	lavabo *m*
toilette (I)	Toilette *f*	toilet	toilette *f*	—	lavabo *m*
toit (F)	Dach *n*	roof	—	tetto *m*	techo *m*
tôle (F)	Blech *n*	sheet metal	—	latta *f*	chapa *f*
tomar (Es)	nehmen	take	prendre	prendere	—
tomar nota (Es)	vormerken	book	prendre note de	prendere nota di	—
Tomate (D)	—	tomato	tomate *f*	pomodoro *m*	tomate *m*
tomate (Es)	Tomate *f*	tomato	tomate *f*	pomodoro *m*	—
tomate (F)	Tomate *f*	tomato	—	pomodoro *m*	tomate *m*
tomato (E)	Tomate *f*	—	tomate *f*	pomodoro *m*	tomate *m*
tomba (I)	Grab *n*	grave	tombe *f*	—	tumba *f*

	D	E	F	I	Es
tombe (F)	Grab *n*	grave	—	tomba *f*	tumba *f*
tomber[1] (F)	fallen	fall	—	cadere	caer
tomber[2] (F)	stürzen	fall	—	cadere	caer
tomber[3] (F)	umfallen	fall over	—	cadere	caerse
tomber amoureux (F)	verlieben	fall in love	—	innamorarsi	enamorarse
tomber malade (F)	erkranken	get ill	—	ammalarsi	enfermar
tomorrow (E)	morgen	—	demain	domani	mañana
Ton (D)	—	sound	son *m*	suono *m*	sonido *m*
ton (E)	Tonne *f*	—	tonne *f*	tonnellata *f*	tonelada *f*
Tonband (D)	—	tape	bande magnétique *f*	nastro magnetico *m*	cinta magnetofónica *f*
tonelada (Es)	Tonne *f*	ton	tonne *f*	tonnellata *f*	—
tongue (E)	Zunge *f*	—	langue *f*	lingua *f*	lengua *f*
Tonne[1] (D)	—	barrel	tonneau *m*	botte *f*	barril *m*
Tonne[2] (D)	—	ton	tonne *f*	tonnellata *f*	tonelada *f*
tonne (F)	Tonne *f*	ton	—	tonnellata *f*	tonelada *f*
tonneau (F)	Tonne *f*	barrel	—	botte *f*	barril *m*
tonnellata (I)	Tonne *f*	ton	tonne *f*	—	tonelada *f*
tonnerre (F)	Donner *m*	thunder	—	tuono *m*	trueno *m*
tonno (I)	Thunfisch *m*	tuna	thon *m*	—	atún *m*
tonto[1] (Es)	albern	foolish	sot(te)	sciocco(a)	—
tonto[2] (Es)	dumm	stupid	bête	stupido(a)	—
tool (E)	Werkzeug *n*	—	outil *m*	utensile *m*	herramienta *f*
too little (E)	zuwenig	—	trop peu	troppo poco	demasiado poco
too many (E)	zuviele	—	trop	troppi(e)	demasiados(as)
too much (E)	zuviel	—	trop	troppo	demasiado
tooth (E)	Zahn *m*	—	dent *f*	dente *m*	diente *m*
toothache (E)	Zahn-schmerzen *pl*	—	mal de dents *m*	mal di denti *m*	dolor de muelas *m*
toothbrush (E)	Zahnbürste *f*	—	brosse à dents *f*	spazzolino da denti *m*	cepillo de dientes *m*
toothpaste (E)	Zahnpasta *f*	—	dentifrice *m*	dentifricio *m*	pasta dentífrica *f*
Topf (D)	—	pot	casserole *f*	pentola *f*	olla *f*
topic (E)	Thema *n*	—	sujet *m*	tema *m*	tema *m*
topo (I)	Maus *f*	mouse	souris *f*	—	ratón *m*
Tor (D)	—	gate	porte *f*	porta *f*	puerta *f*
torbido (I)	trüb	dull	trouble	—	turbio(a)
torcer (Es)	abbiegen	turn off	tourner	svoltare	—
torch (E)	Taschenlampe *f*	—	lampe de poche *f*	lampadina tascabile *f*	linterna *f*
torcido (Es)	krumm	crooked	tordu(e)	storto(a)	—
tordu (F)	krumm	crooked	—	storto(a)	torcido(a)
tormenta[1] (Es)	Gewitter *n*	thunderstorm	orage *m*	temporale *m*	—
tormenta[2] (Es)	Unwetter *n*	thunderstorm	tempête *f*	maltempo *m*	—
tormentare (I)	quälen	torture	torturer	—	atormentar
tornare indietro (I)	zurückfahren	drive back	retourner	—	retroceder
tornillo (Es)	Schraube *f*	screw	vis *f*	vite *f*	—
toro (Es)	Stier *m*	bull	taureau *m*	toro *m*	—
toro (I)	Stier *m*	bull	taureau *m*	—	toro *m*

	D	E	F	I	Es
torpe (Es)	ungeschickt	clumsy	maladroit(e)	impacciato(a)	—
torre (Es)	Turm *m*	tower	tour *f*	torre *f*	—
torre (I)	Turm *m*	tower	tour *f*	—	torre *f*
torta (I)	Torte *f*	cake	gâteau *m*	—	tarta *f*
Torte (D)	—	cake	gâteau *m*	torta *f*	tarta *f*
tortilla (Es)	Omelett *n*	omelette	omelette *f*	frittata *f*	—
torto (I)	Unrecht *n*	wrong	injustice *f*	—	injusticia *f*
torture (E)	quälen	—	torturer	tormentare	atormentar
torturer (F)	quälen	torture	—	tormentare	atormentar
tos (Es)	Husten *m*	cough	toux *m*	tosse *f*	—
tosco (Es)	grob	coarse	grossier(-ière)	rozzo(a)	—
toser (Es)	husten	cough	tousser	tossire	—
tosse (I)	Husten *m*	cough	toux *m*	—	tos *f*
tossire (I)	husten	cough	tousser	—	toser
tostar (Es)	rösten	roast	griller	abbrustolire	—
tot (D)	—	dead	mort(e)	morto(a)	muerto(a)
tôt (F)	früh	early	—	presto	temprano
totale (I)	gesamt	entire	tout(e)	—	entero(a)
totalmente (Es)	restlos	completely	complètement	interamente	—
töten (D)	—	kill	tuer	uccidere	matar
touch (E)	berühren	—	toucher	toccare	tocar
toucher¹ (F)	berühren	touch	—	toccare	tocar
toucher² (F)	treffen	hit	—	colpire	alcanzar
tough (E)	zäh	—	coriace	duro(a)	duro(a)
toujours¹ (F)	immer	always	—	sempre	siempre
toujours² (F)	stets	always	—	sempre	siempre
Tour (D)	—	tour	excursion *f*	giro *m*	excursión *f*
tour (E)	Tour *f*	—	excursion *f*	giro *m*	excursión *f*
tour (F)	Turm *m*	tower	—	torre *f*	torre *f*
Tourist (D)	—	tourist	touriste *m*	turista *m*	turista *m*
tourist (E)	Tourist *m*	—	touriste *m*	turista *m*	turista *m*
touriste (F)	Tourist *m*	tourist	—	turista *m*	turista *m*
tourne-disque (F)	Plattenspieler *m*	record player	—	giradischi *m*	tocadiscos *m*
tourner¹ (F)	abbiegen	turn off	—	svoltare	torcer
tourner² (F)	drehen	turn	—	girare	girar
tourner³ (F)	einbiegen	turn	—	svoltare	doblar
tourner⁴ (F)	herumdrehen	turn around	—	girare	dar vuelta
tourner⁵ (F)	umdrehen	turn around	—	girare	volver
tourner⁶ (F)	wenden	turn	—	voltare	volver
tourner la page (F)	umblättern	turn over	—	voltare pagina	volver la hoja
tournevis (F)	Schrauben-zieher *m*	screwdriver	—	cacciavite *m*	destornillador *m*
tous (F)	alle	all	—	tutti(e)	todos(as)
tous les deux (F)	beide	both	—	entrambi(e)	ambos(as)
tousser (F)	husten	cough	—	tossire	tocer
tout¹ (F)	ganz	whole	—	intero(a)	entero(a)
tout² (F)	gesamt	entire	—	totale	entero(a)
tout³ (F)	alles	everything	—	tutto	todo

	D	E	F	I	Es
tout à coup (F)	plötzlich	suddenly	—	di colpo	de repente
tout au plus (F)	höchstens	at the most	—	al massimo	a lo sumo
tout droit (F)	geradeaus	straight ahead	—	dritto	todo derecho
toutes les heures (F)	stündlich	hourly	—	ogni ora	cada hora
toux (F)	Husten *m*	cough	—	tosse *f*	tos *f*
tovagliolo (I)	Serviette *f*	serviette	serviette *f*	—	servilleta *f*
towel (E)	Handtuch *n*	—	serviette *f*	asciugamano *m*	pañuelo *m*
tower (E)	Turm *m*	—	tour *f*	torre *f*	torre *f*
town (E)	Stadt *f*	—	ville *f*	città *f*	ciudad *f*
town centre (E)	Innenstadt *f*	—	centre ville *m*	centro città *m*	centro de ciudad *m*
town hall (E)	Rathaus *n*	—	mairie *f*	municipio *m*	ayuntamiento *m*
toxique (F)	giftig	poisonous	—	velenoso(a)	venenoso(a)
tra (I)	zwischen	between	entre	—	entre
trabajador (Es)	Arbeiter *m*	worker	ouvrier *m*	operaio *m*	—
trabajar (Es)	arbeiten	work	travailler	lavorare	—
trabajo (Es)	Arbeit *f*	work	travail *m*	lavoro *m*	—
track (E)	Gleis *n*	—	voie *f*	binario *m*	vía *f*
trade union (E)	Gewerkschaft *f*	—	syndicat *m*	sindacato *m*	sindicato *m*
tradire (I)	verraten	betray	trahir	—	traicionar
traducción (Es)	Übersetzung *f*	translation	traduction *f*	traduzione *f*	—
traducir (Es)	übersetzen	translate	traduire	tradurre	—
traduction (F)	Übersetzung *f*	translation	—	traduzione *f*	traducción *f*
traduire (F)	übersetzen	translate	—	tradurre	traducir
tradurre (I)	übersetzen	translate	traduire	—	traducir
traduzione (I)	Übersetzung *f*	translation	traduction *f*	—	traducción *f*
traer[1] (Es)	holen	fetch	aller chercher	andare a prendere	—
traer[2] (Es)	mitbringen	bring (along)	apporter	portare con sé	—
traffic (E)	Verkehr *m*	—	circulation *f*	traffico *m*	tráfico *m*
traffic jam (E)	Stau *m*	—	embouteillage *m*	ingorgo *m*	embotella-miento *m*
traffic lights (E)	Ampel *f*	—	feux *m pl*	semaforo *m*	semáforo *m*
traffico (I)	Verkehr *m*	traffic	circulation *f*	—	tráfico *m*
tráfico (Es)	Verkehr *m*	traffic	circulation *f*	traffico *m*	—
tragar (Es)	schlucken	swallow	avaler	inghiottire	—
tragedia (Es)	Tragödie *f*	tragedy	tragédie *f*	tragedia *f*	—
tragedia (I)	Tragödie *f*	tragedy	tragédie *f*	—	tragedia *f*
tragédie (F)	Tragödie *f*	tragedy	—	tragedia *f*	tragedia *f*
tragedy (E)	Tragödie *f*	—	tragédie *f*	tragedia *f*	tragedia *f*
tragen (D)	—	carry	porter	portare	llevar
Träger (D)	—	carrier	porteur *m*	facchino *m*	mozo *m*
traghetto (I)	Fähre *f*	ferry	bac *m*	—	transbordador *m*
Tragödie (D)	—	tragedy	tragédie *f*	tragedia *f*	tragedia *f*
trahir (F)	verraten	betray	—	tradire	traicionar
traicionar (Es)	verraten	betray	trahir	tradire	—
train (E)	Zug *m*	—	train *m*	treno *m*	tren *m*
train (F)	Zug *m*	train	—	treno *m*	tren *m*
trait (F)	Strich *m*	line	—	linea *f*	línea *f*
traitement (F)	Behandlung *f*	treatment	—	trattamento *m*	tratamiento *m*

	D	E	F	I	Es
traiter (F)	behandeln	treat	—	trattare	tratar
traje (Es)	Anzug *m*	suit	costume *m*	vestito *m*	—
traje de baño (Es)	Badeanzug *m*	swimsuit	maillot de bain *m*	costume da bagno *m*	—
trajet (F)	Strecke *f*	stretch	—	tratto *m*	trayecto *m*
tram (E)	Straßenbahn *f*	—	tramway *m*	tram *m*	tranvía *m*
tram (I)	Straßenbahn *f*	tram	tramway *m*	—	tranvía *m*
tramonto del sole (I)	Sonnen-untergang *m*	sunset	coucher du soleil *m*	—	puesta del sol *f*
tramway (F)	Straßenbahn *f*	tram	—	tram *m*	tranvía *m*
tranchant (F)	scharf	sharp	—	tagliente	cortante
Träne (D)	—	tear	larme *f*	lacrima *f*	lágrima *f*
tranquille (F)	ruhig	quiet	—	calmo(a)	quieto(a)
tranquilo (Es)	still	quiet	calme	calmo(a)	—
transbordador (Es)	Fähre *f*	ferry	bac *m*	traghetto *m*	—
transbordar[1] (Es)	umsteigen	change	changer (de train)	cambiare	—
transbordar[2] (Es)	umladen	transfer	transborder	trasbordare	—
transborder (F)	umladen	transfer	—	trasbordare	transbordar
transfer[1] (E)	überweisen	—	virer	trasferire	transferir
transfer[2] (E)	umladen	—	transborder	trasbordare	transbordar
transfer[3] (E)	Überweisung *f*	—	virement *m*	trasferimento *m*	transferencia *f*
transferencia (Es)	Überweisung *f*	transfer	virement *m*.	trasferimento *m*	—
transferir[1] (Es)	überschreiben	make over	céder	cedere	—
transferir[2] (Es)	überweisen	transfer	virer	trasferire	—
transfert (F)	Umbuchung *f*	alteration	—	riporto *m*	cambio *m*
transformer (F)	verändern	change	—	mutare	cambiar
Transit (D)	—	transit	transit *m*	transito *m*	tránsito *m*
transit[1] (E)	Durchfahrt *f*	—	passage *m*	passaggio *m*	paso *m*
transit[2] (E)	Transit *m*	—	transit *m*	transito *m*	tránsito *m*
transit (F)	Transit *m*	transit	—	transito *m*	tránsito *m*
tránsito (Es)	Transit *m*	transit	transit *m*	transito *m*	—
transito[1] (I)	Durchreise *f*	passing through	passage *m*	—	paso *m*
transito[2] (I)	Transit *m*	transit	transit *m*	—	tránsito *m*
translate (E)	übersetzen	—	traduire	tradurre	traducir
translation (E)	Übersetzung *f*	—	traduction *f*	traduzione *f*	traducción *f*
transmettre[1] (F)	ausrichten	pass on a message	—	riferire	comunicar
transmettre[2] (F)	senden	broadcast	—	trasmettere	transmitir
transmettre[3] (F)	übermitteln	convey	—	trasmettere	transmitir
transmission (E)	Sendung *f*	—	diffusion *f*	trasmissione *f*	emisión *f*
transmitir[1] (Es)	senden	broadcast	transmettre	trasmettere	—
transmitir[2] (Es)	überbringen	deliver	remettre	portare	—
transmitir[3] (Es)	übermitteln	convey	transmettre	trasmettere	—
transmitir[4] (Es)	übergeben	hand over	remettre	consegnare	—
transmitir hereditariamente (Es)	vererben	bequeath	léguer	lasciare in eredità	—
transpirer (F)	schwitzen	sweat	—	sudare	sudar
Transport (D)	—	transport	transport *m*	trasporto *m*	transporte *m*
transport[1] (E)	transportieren	—	transporter	trasportare	transportar
transport[2] (E)	Transport *m*	—	transport *m*	trasporto *m*	transporte *m*

	D	E	F	I	Es
transport (F)	Transport *m*	transport	—	trasporto *m*	transporte *m*
transportar (Es)	transportieren	transport	transporter	trasportare	—
transporte (Es)	Transport *m*	transport	transport *m*	trasporto *m*	—
transporter (F)	transportieren	transport	—	trasportare	transportar
transportieren (D)	—	transport	transporter	trasportare	transportar
tranvía (Es)	Straßenbahn *f*	tram	tramway *m*	tram *m*	—
trasbordare (I)	umladen	transfer	transborder	—	transbordar
trascurare (I)	vernachlässigen	neglect	négliger	—	descuidar
trasferimento (I)	Überweisung *f*	transfer	virement *m*	—	tranferencia *f*
trasferire (I)	überweisen	transfer	virer	—	transferir
trasferirsi (I)	übersiedeln	move	émigrer	—	trasladarse
trasladarse (Es)	übersiedeln	move	émigrer	trasferirsi	—
trasloco (I)	Umzug *m*	move	déménagement *m*	—	mudanza *f*
trasmettere[1] (I)	senden	broadcast	transmettre	—	transmitir
trasmettere[2] (I)	übermitteln	convey	transmettre	—	transmitir
trasmettitore (I)	Sender *m*	station	émetteur *m*	—	emisora *f*
trasmissione (I)	Sendung *f*	transmission	diffusion *f*	—	emisión *f*
trasportare (I)	transportieren	transport	transporter	—	transportar
trasporto (I)	Transport *m*	transport	transport *m*	—	transporte *m*
tratamiento (Es)	Behandlung *f*	treatment	traitement *m*	trattamento *m*	—
tratar (Es)	behandeln	treat	traiter	trattare	—
trattamento (I)	Behandlung *f*	treatment	traitement *m*	—	tratamiento *m*
trattare (I)	behandeln	treat	traiter	—	tratar
trattenere (I)	einbehalten	keep	retenir	—	retener
tratto (I)	Strecke *f*	stretch	trajet *m*	—	trayecto *m*
Traube (D)	—	grape	grappe *f*	uva *f*	uva *f*
Traum (D)	—	dream	rêve *m*	sogno *m*	sueño *m*
träumen (D)	—	dream	rêver	sognare	soñar
traurig (D)	—	sad	triste	triste	triste
travail (F)	Arbeit *f*	work	—	lavoro *m*	trabajo *m*
travailler (F)	arbeiten	work	—	lavorare	trabajar
travailleur (F)	fleißig	diligent	—	diligente	activo(a)
travel (E)	reisen	—	voyager	viaggiare	viajar
travel agency[1] (E)	Reisebüro *n*	—	agence de voyages *f*	agenzia turistica *f*	oficina de viajes *f*
travel agency[2] (E)	Verkehrsbüro *n*	—	bureau touristique *m*	ufficio turistico *m*	oficina de turismo *f*
traveller (E)	Reisender *m*	—	voyageur *m*	viaggiatore *m*	viajero *m*
traveller's cheque (E)	Reisescheck *m*	—	chèque de voyage *m*	assegno turistico *m*	cheque de viaje *m*
traversa (I)	Querstraße *f*	intersecting road	rue transversale *f*	—	travesía *f*
traversata (I)	Überfahrt *f*	crossing	traversée *f*	—	travesía *f*
traversée (F)	Überfahrt *f*	crossing	—	traversata *f*	travesía *f*
traverser (F)	überqueren	cross	—	attraversare	atraveasar
travesía[1] (Es)	Querstraße *f*	intersecting road	rue transversale *f*	traversa *f*	—
travesía[2] (Es)	Überfahrt *f*	crossing	traversée *f*	traversata *f*	—
tray (E)	Tablett *n*	—	plateau *m*	vassoio *m*	bandeja *f*
trayecto (Es)	Strecke *f*	stretch	trajet *m*	tratto *m*	—
tre (I)	drei	three	trois	—	tres

	D	E	F	I	Es
treasure (E)	Schatz *m*	—	trésor *m*	tesoro *m*	tesoro *m*
treat (E)	behandeln	—	traiter	trattare	tratar
treatment[1] (E)	Behandlung *f*	—	traitement *m*	trattamento *m*	tratamiento *m*
treatment[2] (E)	Kur *f*	—	cure *f*	cura *f*	cura *f*
trébucher (F)	stolpern	stumble	—	inciampare	tropezar
treccia (I)	Zopf *m*	plait	natte *f*	—	trenza *f*
trece (Es)	dreizehn	thirteen	treize	tredici	—
tredici (I)	dreizehn	thirteen	treize	—	trece
tree (E)	Baum *m*	—	arbre *m*	albero *m*	árbol *m*
treffen[1] (D)	—	hit	toucher	colpire	alcanzar
treffen[2] (D)	—	meet	rencontrer	incontrare	encontrar
Treffen (D)	—	meeting	rencontre *f*	incontro *m*	encuentro *m*
treiben (D)	—	drive	mener	spingere	estimular
treinta (Es)	dreißig	thirty	trente	trenta	—
treize (F)	dreizehn	thirteen	—	tredici	trece
tremare (I)	zittern	tremble	trembler	—	tiritar
tremble (E)	zittern	—	trembler	tremare	tiritar
tremblement de terre (F)	Erdbeben *n*	earthquake	—	terremoto *m*	terremoto *m*
trembler (F)	zittern	tremble	—	tremare	tiritar
tremendous (E)	gewaltig	—	énorme	enorme	formidable
tren (Es)	Zug *m*	train	train *m*	treno *m*	—
tren expreso[1] (Es)	D-Zug *m*	through train	express *m*	direttissimo *m*	—
tren expreso[2] (Es)	Eilzug *m*	limited stop train	express *m*	treno diretto *m*	—
tren expreso[3] (Es)	Schnellzug *m*	express train	rapide *m*	treno direttissimo *m*	—
trennen (D)	—	separate	séparer	separare	separar
Trennung (D)	—	separation	séparation *f*	separazione *f*	separación *f*
treno (I)	Zug *m*	train	train *m*	—	tren *m*
treno direttissimo (I)	Schnellzug *m*	express train	rapide *m*	—	tren expreso *m*
treno diretto (I)	Eilzug *m*	limited stop train	express *m*	—	tren expreso *m*
trenta (I)	dreißig	thirty	trente	—	treinta
trente (F)	dreißig	thirty	—	trenta	treinta
trenza (Es)	Zopf *m*	plait	natte *f*	treccia *f*	—
Treppe (D)	—	stairs	escalier *m*	scala *f*	escalera *f*
tres (Es)	drei	three	trois	tre	—
très (F)	sehr	very	—	molto	mucho/muy
trésor (F)	Schatz *m*	treasure	—	tesoro *m*	tesoro *m*
treten (D)	—	kick	mettre le pied sur	pestare	pisar
treu (D)	—	faithful	fidèle	fedele	fiel
trial (E)	Prozeß *m*	—	procès *m*	processo *m*	proceso *m*
tribunal (Es)	Gericht *n*	court	tribunal *m*	tribunale *m*	—
tribunal (F)	Gericht *n*	court	—	tribunale *m*	tribunal *m*
tribunale (I)	Gericht *n*	court	tribunal *m*	—	tribunal *m*
tricot (F)	Unterhemd *n*	vest	—	canottiera *f*	camiseta *f*

	D	E	F	I	Es
tricoter (F)	stricken	knit	—	lavorare a maglia	hacer punto
trier (F)	sortieren	sort	—	assortire	clasificar
trigo (Es)	Weizen *m*	wheat	blé *m*	frumento *m*	—
trinkbar (D)	—	drinkable	potable	potabile	potable
trinken (D)	—	drink	boire	bere	beber
Trinkgeld (D)	—	tip	pourboire *m*	mancia *f*	propina *f*
Trinkwasser (D)	—	drinking water	eau potable *f*	acqua potabile *f*	agua potable *f*
triste (Es)	traurig	sad	triste	triste	—
triste (F)	traurig	sad	—	triste	triste
triste (I)	traurig	sad	triste	—	triste
trocken (D)	—	dry	sec(sèche)	asciutto(a)	seco(a)
trocknen (D)	—	dry	sécher	asciugare	secar
trois (F)	drei	three	—	tre	tres
troisième (F)	dritte(r,s)	third	—	terzo(a)	tercera(o)
tromper¹ (F)	betrügen	cheat	—	ingannare	engañar
tromper² (F)	täuschen	deceive	—	ingannare	engañar
tromper, se (F)	irren	be mistaken	—	sbagliare	equivocarse
tromperie (F)	Betrug *m*	fraud	—	inganno *m*	engaño *m*
trop¹ (F)	zuviel	too much	—	troppo	demasiado
trop² (F)	zuviele	too many	—	troppi(e)	demasiados(as)
tropezar (Es)	stolpern	stumble	trébucher	inciampare	—
tropfen (D)	—	drip	dégoutter	gocciolare	gotear
Tropfen (D)	—	drop	goutte *f*	goccia *f*	gota *f*
tropical (E)	tropisch	—	tropical(e)	tropicale	tropical
tropical (Es)	tropisch	tropical	tropical(e)	tropicale	—
tropical (F)	tropisch	tropical	—	tropicale	tropical
tropicale (I)	tropisch	tropical	tropical(e)	—	tropical
tropisch (D)	—	tropical	tropical(e)	tropicale	tropical
trop peu (F)	zuwenig	too little	—	troppo poco	demasiado poco
troppi (I)	zuviele	too many	trop	—	demasiados(as)
troppo (I)	zuviel	too much	trop	—	demasiado
troppo poco (I)	zuwenig	too little	trop peu	—	demasiado poco
Trost (D)	—	consolation	consolation *f*	consolazione *f*	consuelo *m*
trösten (D)	—	comfort	consoler	consolare	consolar
trota (I)	Forelle *f*	trout	truite *f*	—	trucha *f*
trottoir (F)	Gehweg *m*	pavement	—	marciapiede *m*	acera *f*
trotz (D)	—	despite	malgré	nonostante	a pesar de
trotzdem (D)	—	nevertheless	malgré tout	tuttavia	no obstante
trou (F)	Loch *n*	hole	—	buco *m*	agujero *m*
trouble (E)	Not *f*	—	détresse *f*	miseria *f*	necesidad *f*
trouble¹ (F)	Störung *f*	interference	—	disturbo *m*	molestia *f*
trouble² (F)	trüb	dull	—	torbido(a)	turbio(a)
troublesome (E)	lästig	—	importun(e)	molesto(a)	desagradable
trou de la serrure (F)	Schlüsselloch *n*	keyhole	—	buco della chiave *m*	ojo de la cerradura *m*

	D	E	F	I	Es
trousers (E)	Hose *f*	—	pantalon *m*	pantaloni *m pl*	pantalón *m*
trout (E)	Forelle *f*	—	truite *f*	trota *f*	trucha *f*
trouver (F)	finden	find	—	trovare	encontrar
trouver, se[1] (F)	befinden, sich	feel	—	trovarsi	encontrarse
trouver, se[2] (F)	liegen	lie	—	giacere	estar tumbado(a)
trovare (I)	finden	find	trouver	—	encontrar
trovarsi (I)	befinden, sich	feel	trouver, se	—	encontrarse
trüb (D)	—	dull	trouble	torbido(a)	turbio(a)
truc (F)	Zeug *n*	stuff	—	cose *f pl*	cosa *f*
trucco (I)	Schminke *f*	make-up	maquillage *m*	—	maquillaje *m*
trucha (Es)	Forelle *f*	trout	truite *f*	trota *f*	—
true (E)	wahr	—	vrai(e)	vero	verdadero(a)
trueno (Es)	Donner *m*	thunder	tonnerre *m*	tuono *m*	—
truite (F)	Forelle *f*	trout	—	trota *f*	trucha *f*
Trümmer (D)	—	ruins	décombres *m pl*	macerie *f pl*	escombros *m pl*
trust (E)	vertrauen	—	avoir confiance	fidarsi	confiar
truth (E)	Wahrheit *f*	—	vérité *f*	verità *f*	verdad *f*
Truthahn (D)	—	turkey	dindon *m*	tacchino *m*	pavo *m*
try[1] (E)	probieren	—	essayer	assaggiare	probar
try[2] (E)	Versuch *m*	—	essai *m*	tentativo *m*	intento *m*
try[3] (E)	versuchen	—	essayer	provare	probar
try on (E)	anprobieren	—	essayer	provare	probar
Tschecho-slowakei (D)	—	Czechoslovakia	Tchécoslovaquie *f*	Cecoslovacchia *f*	Checoslovaquia *f*
tschüs! (D)	—	bye!	salut!	ciao!	¡hasta luego!
tú (Es)	du	you	tu/toi	tu	—
tu (I)	du	you	tu/toi	—	tú
tu (F)	du	you	—	tu	tú
tube (E)	Rohr *n*	—	tube *m*	tubo *m*	tubo *m*
tube (F)	Rohr *n*	tube	—	tubo *m*	tubo *m*
tubería (Es)	Leitung *f*	pipe	tuyau *m*	conduttura *f*	—
tubo (Es)	Rohr *n*	tube	tube *m*	tubo *m*	—
tubo (I)	Rohr *n*	tube	tube *m*	—	tubo *m*
Tuch (D)	—	cloth	étoffe *f*	panno *m*	paño *m*
tuer[1] (F)	töten	kill	—	uccidere	matar
tuer[2] (F)	umbringen	kill	—	uccidere	matar
Tuesday (E)	Dienstag *m*	—	mardi *m*	martedì *m*	martes *m*
tulip (E)	Tulpe *f*	—	tulipe *f*	tulipano *m*	tulipán *m*
tulipán (Es)	Tulpe *f*	tulip	tulipe *f*	tulipano *m*	—
tulipano (I)	Tulpe *f*	tulip	tulipe *f*	—	tulipán *m*
tulipe (F)	Tulpe *f*	tulip	—	tulipano *m*	tulipán *m*
Tulpe (D)	—	tulip	tulipe *f*	tulipano *m*	tulipán *m*
tumba (Es)	Grab *n*	grave	tombe *f*	tomba *f*	—
tumbona (Es)	Liegestuhl *m*	deck chair	chaise longue *f*	sedia a sdraio *f*	—
tun (D)	—	do	faire	fare	hacer

	D	E	F	I	Es
tuna (E)	Thunfisch *m*	—	thon *m*	tonno *m*	atún *m*
túnel (Es)	Tunnel *m*	tunnel	tunnel *m*	galleria *f*	—
Tunnel (D)	—	tunnel	tunnel *m*	galleria *f*	túnel *m*
tunnel (E)	Tunnel *m*	—	tunnel *m*	galleria *f*	túnel *m*
tunnel (F)	Tunnel *m*	tunnel	—	galleria *f*	túnel *m*
tuono (I)	Donner *m*	thunder	tonnerre *m*	—	trueno *m*
Tür (D)	—	door	porte *f*	porta *f*	puerta *f*
turbio (Es)	trüb	dull	trouble	torbido(a)	—
Turchia (I)	Türkei *f*	Turkey	Turquie *f*	—	Turquía *f*
turista (Es)	Tourist *m*	tourist	touriste *m*	turista *m*	—
turista (I)	Tourist *m*	tourist	touriste *m*	—	turista *m*
Türkei (D)	—	Turkey	Turquie *f*	Turchia *f*	Turquía *f*
turkey (E)	Truthahn *m*	—	dindon *m*	tacchino *m*	pavo *m*
Turkey (E)	Türkei *f*	—	Turquie *f*	Turchia *f*	Turquía *f*
Turm (D)	—	tower	tour *f*	torre *f*	torre *f*
turn[1] (E)	drehen	—	tourner	girare	girar
turn[2] (E)	einbiegen	—	tourner	svoltare	doblar
turn[3] (E)	wenden	—	tourner	voltare	volver
turn around[1] (E)	herumdrehen	—	tourner	girare	dar vuelta
turn around[2] (E)	umdrehen	—	tourner	girare	volver
turn back (E)	umkehren	—	retourner	ritornare	regresar
turnen (D)	—	do gymnastic exercises	faire de la gymnastique	fare ginnastica	hacer gimnasia
turn off[1] (E)	abstellen	—	arrêter	spegnere	desconectar
turn off[2] (E)	abbiegen	—	tourner	svoltare	torcer
turn off[3] (E)	zudrehen	—	fermer	chiudere	cerrar
turn on (E)	anstellen	—	mettre en marche	accendere	poner
turn over (E)	umblättern	—	tourner la page	voltare pagina	volver la hoja
Turquía (Es)	Türkei *f*	Turkey	Turquie *f*	Turchia *f*	—
Turquie (F)	Türkei *f*	Turkey	—	Turchia *f*	Turquía *f*
Tüte (D)	—	bag	sac *m*	sacchetto *m*	bolsa *f*
tutear (Es)	duzen	use the familiar form	tutoyer	dare del tu	—
tutoyer (F)	duzen	use the familiar form	—	dare del tu	tutear
tuttavia[1] (I)	jedoch	however	cependant	—	sin embargo
tuttavia[2] (I)	dennoch	nevertheless	cependant	—	sin embargo
tuttavia[3] (I)	trotzdem	nevertheless	malgré tout	—	no obstante
tutti (I)	alle	all	tous(toutes)	—	todos(as)
tutto (I)	alles	everything	tout	—	todo
tuyau (F)	Leitung *f*	pipe	—	conduttura *f*	tubería *f*
twelve (E)	zwölf	—	douze	dodici	doce
twenty (E)	zwanzig	—	vingt	venti	veinte
twice (E)	zweimal	—	deux fois	due volte	dos veces
twins (E)	Zwillinge *pl*	—	jumeaux *m pl*	gemelli *m pl*	gemelos *m pl*

	D	E	F	I	Es
two (E)	zwei	—	deux	due	dos
type (E)	tippen	—	taper (à la machine)	battere a macchina	escribir a máquina
typewriter (E)	Schreibmaschine f	—	machine à écrire f	macchina da scrivere f	máquina de escribir f
typical (E)	typisch	—	typique	tipico(a)	típico(a)
typique (F)	typisch	typical	—	tipico(a)	típico(a)
typisch (D)	—	typical	typique	tipico(a)	típico(a)
tyre (E)	Reifen m	—	pneu m	pneumatico m	neumático m
U-Bahn (D)	—	underground	métro m	metropolitana f	metro m
ubbidiente (I)	gehorsam	obedient	obéissant(e)	—	obediente
ubbidire (I)	gehorchen	obey	obéir	—	obedecer
übel (D)	—	bad	mauvais(e)	cattivo(a)	malo(a)
Übelkeit (D)	—	nausea	nausée f	nausea f	náuseas f pl
üben (D)	—	practise	étudier	esercitarsi	practicar
über (D)	—	over/about	sur	su/sopra/per	por/sobre
überall (D)	—	everywhere	partout	dappertutto	por todas partes
überbringen (D)	—	deliver	remettre	portare	transmitir
übereinander (D)	—	one upon the other	l'un(e) sur l'autre	uno sopra l'altro	uno sobre otro
übereinstimmen (D)	—	agree	être d'accord	concordare	estar de acuerdo
überfahren (D)	—	run over	écraser	investire	atropellar
Überfahrt (D)	—	crossing	traversée f	traversata f	travesía f
Überfall (D)	—	raid	attaque f	aggressione f	asalto m
überfallen (D)	—	raid	attaquer	assalire	asaltar
überflüssig (D)	—	superfluous	superflu(e)	superfluo(a)	superfluo(a)
überfüllt (D)	—	crowded	bondé(e)	pieno(a) zeppo(a)	abarrotado(a)
Übergang (D)	—	crossing	passage m	passaggio m	paso m
übergeben (D)	—	hand over	remettre	consegnare	transmitir
überhaupt (D)	—	at all	en général	in genere	en general
überholen (D)	—	overtake	doubler	sorpassare	adelantar
überleben (D)	—	survive	survivre	sopravvivere	sobrevivir
überlegen (D)	—	consider	réfléchir à	riflettere	pensar
übermitteln (D)	—	convey	transmettre	trasmettere	transmitir
übermorgen (D)	—	day after tomorrow	après-demain	dopodomani	pasado mañana
übernachten (D)	—	stay the night	passer la nuit	pernottare	pernoctar
Übernachtung (D)	—	spending the night	logement pour une nuit m	pernottamento m	pernoctación f
übernehmen (D)	—	take over	reprendre	accettare	aceptar
überprüfen (D)	—	check	contrôler	esaminare	examinar
überqueren (D)	—	cross	traverser	attraversare	atraveasar
überraschen (D)	—	surprise	surprendre	sorprendere	sorprender
überrascht (D)	—	surprised	surpris(e)	sorpreso(a)	sorprendido(a)
Überraschung (D)	—	surprise	surprise f	sorpresa f	sorpresa f
überreden (D)	—	convince	persuader	persuadere	persuadir
überreichen (D)	—	hand over	présenter	consegnare	entregar
überschätzen (D)	—	overestimate	surestimer	sopravvalutare	sobrevalorar
überschreiben (D)	—	make over	céder	cedere	transferir
Überschrift (D)	—	heading	titre m	titolo m	título m

umbringen

	D	E	F	I	Es
Über-schwemmung (D)	—	flood	inondation *f*	inondazione *f*	inundación *f*
übersehen (D)	—	ignore	ignorer	non vedere	no ver
übersenden (D)	—	send	envoyer	spedire	envíar
übersetzen (D)	—	translate	traduire	tradurre	traducir
Übersetzung (D)	—	translation	traduction *f*	traduzione *f*	traducción *f*
übersiedeln (D)	—	move	émigrer	trasferirsi	transladarse
übertreiben (D)	—	exaggerate	exagérer	esagerare	exagerar
Übertreibung (D)	—	exaggeration	exagération *f*	esagerazione *f*	exageración *f*
übertrieben (D)	—	exaggerated	exagéré(e)	esagerato(a)	exagerado(a)
überwachen (D)	—	supervise	surveiller	sorvegliare	vigilar
überweisen (D)	—	transfer	virer	trasferire	transferir
Überweisung (D)	—	transfer	virement *m*	versamento *m*	transferencia *f*
überzeugen (D)	—	convince	convaincre	convincere	convencer
üblich (D)	—	usual	habituel(le)	solito(a)	usual
ubriacarsi (I)	betrinken, sich	get drunk	enivrer, se	—	emborracharse
ubriaco (I)	betrunken	drunk	soûl(e)	—	borracho(a)
übrig (D)	—	left	restant(e)	restante	restante
übrigbleiben (D)	—	be left	rester	avanzare	quedar
übrigens (D)	—	by the way	d'ailleurs	del resto	por lo demás
übriglassen (D)	—	leave	laisser	lasciare	dejar
Übung (D)	—	exercise	exercice *m*	esercizio *f*	ejercicio *m*
uccello (I)	Vogel *m*	bird	oiseau *m*	—	pájaro *m*
uccidere¹ (I)	töten	kill	tuer	—	matar
uccidere² (I)	umbringen	kill	tuer	—	matar
udito (I)	Gehör *n*	hearing	ouïe *f*	—	oreja *f*
Ufer (D)	—	shore	bord *m*	riva *f*	orilla *f*
ufficiale¹ (I)	amtlich	official	officiel(le)	—	oficial
ufficiale² (I)	offiziell	official	officiel(le)	—	oficial
ufficio¹ (I)	Amt *n*	office	bureau *m*	—	oficio *m*
ufficio² (I)	Büro *n*	office	bureau *m*	—	oficina *f*
ufficio di cambio (I)	Wechselstube *f*	bureau de change	bureau de change *m*	—	casa de cambio *f*
ufficio oggetti smarriti (I)	Fundbüro *n*	lost property office	bureau des objets trouvés *m*	—	oficina de objetos perdidos *f*
ufficio postale (I)	Postamt *n*	post office	bureau de poste *m*	—	oficina de correos *f*
ufficio turistico (I)	Verkehrsbüro *n*	travel agency	bureau touristique *m*	—	oficina de turismo *f*
ugly (E)	häßlich	—	laid(e)	brutto(a)	feo(a)
uguale (I)	egal	all the same	égal(e)	—	igual
Uhr (D)	—	watch	montre *f*	orologio *m*	reloj *m*
última (Es)	letzte(r,s)	last	dernier(-ière)	ultimo(a)	—
ultimo (I)	letzte(r,s)	last	dernier(-ière)	—	última(o)
um (D)	—	at/around	autour de/à	intorno a/a	alrededor de/a las
umano (I)	menschlich	human	humain(e)	—	humano(a)
umarmen (D)	—	embrace	embrasser	abbracciare	abrazar
umblättern (D)	—	turn over	tourner la page	voltare pagina	volver la hoja
umbrella¹ (E)	Regenschirm *m*	—	parapluie *m*	ombrello *m*	paraguas *m*
umbrella² (E)	Schirm *m*	—	parapluie *m*	ombrello *m*	paraguas *m*
umbringen (D)	—	kill	tuer	uccidere	matar

	D	E	F	I	Es
Umbuchung (D)	—	alteration	transfert *m*	riporto *m*	cambio *m*
umdrehen (D)	—	turn around	tourner	girare	volver
umfallen (D)	—	fall over	tomber	cadere	caerse
Umfrage (D)	—	poll	enquête *f*	inchiesta *f*	encuesta *f*
Umgangssprache (D)	—	colloquial language	langue familière *f*	linguaggio corrente *m*	lenguaje coloquial *m*
umgeben (D)	—	surround	entourer	circondare	rodear
Umgebung (D)	—	surroundings	environs *m pl*	dintorni *m pl*	alrededores *m pl*
umgekehrt (D)	—	vice versa	vice versa	inverso(a)	contrario(a)
umido (I)	feucht	damp	humide	—	húmedo(a)
umkehren (D)	—	turn back	retourner	ritornare	regresar
umkleiden (D)	—	change	changer de vêtements	cambiarsi	cambiarse de ropa
umladen (D)	—	transfer	transborder	trasbordare	transbordar
Umleitung (D)	—	diversion	déviation *f*	deviazione *f*	desviación *f*
umore (I)	Laune *f*	mood	humeur *f*	—	humor *m*
umrechnen (D)	—	convert	convertir	convertire	convertir
Umschlag (D)	—	envelope	enveloppe *f*	busta *f*	sobre *m*
umschmeißen (D)	—	throw over	renverser	rovesciare	derribar
umsonst (D)	—	for nothing	en vain	per niente	en vano
Umstände (D)	—	circumstances	circonstances *f pl*	circostanze *f pl*	circunstancias *f pl*
umständlich (D)	—	complicated	compliqué(e)	complicato(a)	complicado(a)
umsteigen (D)	—	change	changer (de train)	cambiare	transbordar
umtauschen (D)	—	exchange	échanger	cambiare	cambiar
umwechseln (D)	—	change	changer	cambiare	cambiar
Umweg (D)	—	detour	détour *m*	deviazione *f*	rodeo *m*
Umwelt (D)	—	environment	environnement *m*	ambiente *m*	medio ambiente *m*
umziehen¹ (D)	—	change	changer, se	cambiarsi	cambiarse
umziehen² (D)	—	move	déménager	cambiare casa	cambiar
Umzug (D)	—	move	déménagement *m*	trasloco *m*	mudanza *f*
un¹ (F)	eins	one	—	uno(a)	uno(a)
un² (F)	eine(r,s)	one	—	un(a)	una/un/uno
un (I)	eine(r,s)	one	un(e)	—	una/un/uno
una (Es)	eine(r,s)	one	un(e)	un(a)	—
uña (Es)	Nagel *m*	nail	ongle *m*	unghia *f*	—
unabhängig (D)	—	independent	indépendant(e)	indipendente	independiente
unable to make it (E)	verhindert	—	empêché(e)	impedito(a)	impedido(a)
unangenehm (D)	—	unpleasant	désagréable	spiacevole	desagradable
unanständig (D)	—	indecent	indécent(e)	indecente	inmoral
unauthorized (E)	unbefugt	—	non autorisé(e)	non autorizzato(a)	no autorizado(a)
una vez (Es)	einmal	once	une fois	una volta	—
una volta (I)	einmal	once	une fois	—	una vez
unbearable (E)	unerträglich	—	insupportable	insopportabile	inaguantable
unbedingt (D)	—	absolutely	absolument	assolutamente	absolutamente
unbefugt (D)	—	unauthorized	non autorisé(e)	non autorizzato(a)	no autorizado(a)
unbegrenzt (D)	—	unlimited	illimité(e)	illimitato(a)	ilimitado(a)
unbekannt (D)	—	unknown	inconnu(e)	sconosciuto(a)	desconocido(a)

	D	E	F	I	Es
unbequem (D)	—	uncomfortable	inconfortable	scomodo(a)	incómodo(a)
unbesetzt (D)	—	unoccupied	vacant(e)	libero(a)	desocupado(a)
unbestimmt (D)	—	uncertain	indéfini(e)	incerto(a)	indeterminado(a)
uncertain[1] (E)	unsicher	—	incertain(e)	incerto(a)	inseguro(a)
uncertain[2] (E)	unbestimmt	—	indéfini(e)	incerto(a)	indeterminado(a)
uncertain[3] (E)	ungewiß	—	incertain(e)	incerto(a)	incierto(a)
uncle (E)	Onkel m	—	oncle m	zio m	tío m
uncomfortable[1] (E)	ungemütlich	—	désagréable	poco accogliente	incómodo(a)
uncomfortable[2] (E)	unbequem	—	inconfortable	scomodo(a)	incómodo(a)
und (D)	—	and	et	e	y
undankbar (D)	—	ungrateful	ingrat(e)	ingrato(a)	desagradecido(a)
undecided (E)	unentschlossen	—	irrésolu(e)	indeciso(a)	irresoluto(a)
under (E)	unter	—	sous	al di sotto di	debajo de
underground (E)	U-Bahn f	—	métro m	metropolitana f	metro m
underline (E)	unterstreichen	—	souligner	sottolineare	subrayar
underneath (E)	darunter	—	en dessous	sotto	por debajo
underpants (E)	Unterhose f	—	slip m	mutande f pl	calzoncillos m pl
understand (E)	verstehen	—	comprendre	capire	entender
understanding (E)	Verständnis n	—	compréhension f	comprensione f	comprensión f
undertake (E)	unternehmen	—	entreprendre	intraprendere	emprender
underwear (E)	Unterwäsche f	—	sous-vêtements m pl	biancheria intima f	ropa interior f
undici (I)	elf	eleven	onze	—	once
unecht (D)	—	fake	imité(e)	falso(a)	falso(a)
une fois (F)	einmal	once	—	una volta	una vez
unemployed (E)	arbeitslos	—	en chômage	disoccupato(a)	desempleado(a)
unemployment (E)	Arbeitslosigkeit f	—	chômage m	disoccupazione f	desempleo m
unentbehrlich (D)	—	indispensable	indispensable	indispensabile	indispensable
unentschlossen (D)	—	undecided	irrésolu(e)	indeciso(a)	irresoluto(a)
unequivocal (E)	eindeutig	—	incontestable	univoco(a)	evidente
unerfahren (D)	—	inexperienced	inexpérimenté(e)	inesperto(a)	inexperto(a)
unerträglich (D)	—	unbearable	insupportable	insopportabile	inaguantable
unerwartet (D)	—	unexpected	inattendu(e)	inatteso(a)	inesperado(a)
unerwünscht (D)	—	unwelcome	inopportun(e)	indesiderato(a)	indeseado(a)
un et demi (F)	anderthalb	one and a half	—	uno(a) e mezzo	uno(a) y medio(a)
uneven (E)	ungerade	—	impair(e)	dispari	impar
unexpected (E)	unerwartet	—	inattendu(e)	inatteso(a)	inesperado(a)
unfähig (D)	—	incapable	incapable	incapace	incapaz
Unfall (D)	—	accident	accident m	incidente m	accidente m
unfit (E)	untauglich	—	incapable	incapace	inútil
unfortunately (E)	leider	—	malheureusement	purtroppo	desgraciadamente
unfreundlich (D)	—	unfriendly	peu aimable	sgarbato(a)	descortés
unfriendly (E)	unfreundlich	—	peu aimable	sgarbato(a)	descortés
ungeduldig (D)	—	impatient	impatient(e)	impaziente	inpaciente
ungefähr (D)	—	about	environ	pressappoco	aproximadamente
ungemütlich (D)	—	uncomfortable	désagréable	poco accogliente	incómodo(a)
ungenau (D)	—	inaccurate	inexact(e)	impreciso(a)	inexacto(a)
ungenügend (D)	—	insufficient	insuffisant(e)	insufficiente	insuficiente

ungerade

	D	E	F	I	Es
ungerade (D)	—	uneven	impair(e)	dispari	impar
ungerecht (D)	—	unjust	injuste	ingiusto(a)	injusto(a)
Ungerechtigkeit (D)	—	injustice	injustice f	ingiustizia f	injusticia f
ungern (D)	—	reluctantly	de mauvaise grâce	malvolentieri	de mala gana
ungeschickt (D)	—	clumsy	maladroit(e)	impacciato(a)	torpe
ungesund (D)	—	unhealthy	malsain(e)	malsano(a)	enfermizo(a)
ungewiß (D)	—	uncertain	incertain(e)	incerto(a)	incierto(a)
ungewöhnlich (D)	—	unusual	exceptionnel(le)	insolito(a)	desacostumbrado(a)
unghia (I)	Nagel m	nail	ongle m	—	uña f
unglaublich (D)	—	incredible	incroyable	incredibile	increíble
Unglück (D)	—	misfortune	malheur m	disgrazia f	desgracia f
unglücklich (D)	—	unhappy	malheureux (-euse)	sfortunato(a)	desgraciado(a)
ungrateful (E)	undankbar	—	ingrat(e)	ingrato(a)	desagradecido(a)
ungültig (D)	—	invalid	non valable	non valido(a)	caducado(a)
unhappy (E)	unglücklich	—	malheureux (-euse)	sfortunato(a)	desgraciado(a)
unhealthy (E)	ungesund	—	malsain(e)	malsano(a)	enfermizo(a)
unhöflich (D)	—	impolite	impoli(e)	scortese	descortés
uni (F)	einfarbig	all one colour	—	monocolore	de un solo color
unico (I)	einzig	only	seul(e)	—	único(a)
único (Es)	einzig	only	seul(e)	unico(a)	—
Uniform (D)	—	uniform	uniforme m	divisa f	uniforme m
uniform (E)	Uniform f	—	uniforme m	divisa f	uniforme m
uniforme (F)	Uniform f	uniform	—	divisa f	uniforme m
uniforme (Es)	Uniform f	uniform	uniforme m	divisa f	—
unilateral (Es)	einseitig	one-sided	partial(e)	unilaterale	—
unilaterale (I)	einseitig	one-sided	partial(e)	—	unilateral
unimportant (E)	unwichtig	—	sans importance	non importante	sin importancia
unir¹ (Es)	vereinigen	unite	unir	unire	—
unir² (Es)	verbinden	connect	relier	unire	—
unir (F)	vereinigen	unite	—	unire	unir
unire¹ (I)	verbinden	connect	relier	—	unir
unire² (I)	vereinigen	unite	unir	—	unir
unite (E)	vereinigen	—	unir	unire	unir
United States (E)	Vereinigte Staaten pl	—	Etats-Unis m pl	Stati Uniti m pl	Estados Unidos m pl
univers (F)	Weltall n	universe	—	universo m	universo m
universe (E)	Weltall n	—	univers m	universo m	universo m
universidad (Es)	Universität f	university	université f	università f	—
università (I)	Universität f	university	université f	—	universidad f
Universität (D)	—	university	université f	università f	universidad f
université¹ (F)	Hochschule f	university	—	istituto superiore m	escuela superior f
université² (F)	Universität f	university	—	università f	universidad f
university¹ (E)	Hochschule f	—	université f	istituto superiore m	escuela superior f
university² (E)	Universität f	—	université f	università f	universidad f
universo (Es)	Weltall n	universe	univers m	universo m	—
universo (I)	Weltall n	universe	univers m	—	universo m

	D	E	F	I	Es
univoco (I)	eindeutig	unequivocal	incontestable	—	evidente
unjust (E)	ungerecht	—	injuste	ingiusto(a)	injusto(a)
unknown (E)	unbekannt	—	inconnu(e)	sconosciuto(a)	desconocido(a)
Unkosten (D)	—	expenses	frais *m pl*	spese *f pl*	gastos *m pl*
unlawful (E)	unrechtmäßig	—	illégitime	illegale	ilegítimo(a)
unlikely (E)	unwahrscheinlich	—	invraisemblable	improbabile	improbable
unlimited (E)	unbegrenzt	—	illimité(e)	illimitato(a)	ilimitado(a)
unload¹ (E)	abladen	—	décharger	scaricare	descargar
unload² (E)	ausladen	—	décharger	scaricare	descargar
unmarried (E)	unverheiratet	—	non marié(e)	celibe *m*/nubile *f*	soltero(a)
unmittelbar (D)	—	immediate	immédiat(e)	immediato(a)	directo(a)
unmöglich (D)	—	impossible	impossible	impossibile	imposible
unnecessary (E)	unnötig	—	inutile	inutile	inútil
unnötig (D)	—	unnecessary	inutile	inutile	inútil
uno (Es)	eins	one	un	uno	—
uno (I)	eins	one	un	—	uno(a)
unoccupied (E)	unbesetzt	—	vacant(e)	libero(a)	desocupado(a)
uno detras de otro (Es)	hintereinander	one after the other	l'un derrière l'autre	uno dopo l'altro	—
uno dopo l'altro (I)	hintereinander	one after the other	l'un derrière l'autre	—	uno detras de otro
uno e mezzo (I)	anderthalb	one and a half	un(e) et demi(e)	—	uno(a) y medio(a)
uno en otro (Es)	ineinander	into one another	l'un dans l'autre	l'uno nell'altro	—
unordentlich (D)	—	untidy	désordonné(e)	disordinato(a)	desordenado(a)
Unordnung (D)	—	mess	désordre *m*	disordine *m*	desorden *m*
unos (Es)	etwa	about	environ	pressappoco	—
uno sobre otro (Es)	übereinander	one upon the other	l'un(e) sur l'autre	uno sopra l'altro	—
uno sopra l'altro (I)	übereinander	one upon the other	l'un(e) sur l'autre	—	uno sobre otro
uno y medio (Es)	anderthalb	one and a half	un(e) et demi(e)	uno(a) e mezzo	—
unpack (E)	auspacken	—	défaire	disfare	deshacer
unpassend (D)	—	inappropriate	mal à propos	sconveniente	inadecuado(a)
un peu (F)	bißchen	a little	—	un po'	un poquito
unpleasant (E)	unangenehm	—	désagréable	spiacevole	desagradable
un po (I)	bißchen	a little	un peu	—	un poquito
un poquito (Es)	bißchen	a little	un peu	un po'	—
Unrecht (D)	—	wrong	injustice *f*	torto *m*	injusticia *f*
unrechtmäßig (D)	—	unlawful	illégitime	illegale	ilegítimo(a)
unregelmäßig (D)	—	irregular	irrégulier(ère)	irregolare	irregular
unruhig (D)	—	restless	inquiet(-iète)	inquieto(a)	intranquilo(a)
unschuldig (D)	—	innocent	innocent(e)	innocente	inocente/puro(a)
unsicher (D)	—	uncertain	incertain(e)	incerto(a)	inseguro(a)
Unsinn (D)	—	nonsense	bêtises *f pl*	nonsenso *m*	absurdo *m*
unsinnig (D)	—	nonsensical	insensé(e)	insensato(a)	absurdo(a)
un tal (Es)	solche(r,s)	such	tel(le)	tale(i)	—
Untat (D)	—	crime	méfait *m*	misfatto *m*	crimen *m*
untauglich (D)	—	unfit	incapable	incapace	inútil
unten (D)	—	downstairs	dessous	sotto/giù	abajo
unter (D)	—	under	sous	al di sotto di	debajo de

	D	E	F	I	Es
unterbrechen (D)	—	interrupt	interrompre	interrompere	interrumpir
Unterbrechung (D)	—	interruption	interruption *f*	interruzione *f*	interrupción *f*
unterbringen (D)	—	stow	ranger	sistemare	colocar
unterdrücken (D)	—	oppress	opprimer	sopprimere	oprimir
Unterführung (D)	—	subway	passage souterrain *m*	sottopassaggio *m*	paso inferior *m*
unterhalten (D)	—	entertain	entretenir	divertire	entretener
unterhalten, sich (D)	—	talk	entretenir, se	conversare	conversar
Unterhaltung (D)	—	conversation	entretien *m*	conversazione *f*	conversación *f*
Unterhemd (D)	—	vest	tricot *m*	canottiere *f*	camiseta *f*
Unterhose (D)	—	underpants	slip *m*	mutande *f pl*	calzoncillos *m pl*
Unterkunft (D)	—	accommodation	logement *m*	alloggio *m*	hospedaje *m*
unterliegen (D)	—	be defeated	être vaincu(e) par qn	soccombere	sucumbir
unternehmen (D)	—	undertake	entreprendre	intraprendere	emprender
Unternehmen (D)	—	company	entreprise *f*	impresa *f*	empresa *f*
Unterredung (D)	—	talk	entrevue *f*	colloquio *m*	entrevista *f*
Unterricht (D)	—	lessons	cours	lezione *f*	enseñanza *f*
unterrichten (D)	—	teach	enseigner	insegnare	enseñar
Unterrichts-stunde (D)	—	lesson	leçon *f*	lezione *f*	clase *f*
Unterrock (D)	—	slip	jupon *m*	sottoveste *f*	combinación *f*
untersagen (D)	—	forbid	interdire qch à qn	proibire	prohibir
unterscheiden (D)	—	distinguish	distinguer	distinguere	distinguir
Unterschied (D)	—	difference	différence *f*	differenza *f*	diferencia *f*
unterschiedlich (D)	—	different	différent(e)	diverso(a)	distinto(a)
unterschlagen (D)	—	embezzle	soustraire	sottrarre	sustraer
unterschreiben (D)	—	sign	signer	firmare	firmar
Unterschrift (D)	—	signature	signature *f*	firma *f*	firma *f*
unterste (D)	—	lowest	inférieur(e)	inferiore	inferior
unterstreichen (D)	—	underline	souligner	sottolineare	subrayar
unterstützen (D)	—	support	soutenir	assistere	apoyar
Unterstützung (D)	—	support	soutien *m*	sostegno *m*	apoyo *m*
untersuchen (D)	—	examine	examiner	esaminare	examinar
Untertasse (D)	—	saucer	soucoupe *f*	piattino *m*	platillo *m*
untervermieten (D)	—	sublet	sous-louer	subaffittare	realquilar
Unterwäsche (D)	—	underwear	sous-vêtements *m pl*	biancheria intima *f*	ropa interior *f*
unterwegs (D)	—	on the way	en route	per strada	de camino
unterwerfen (D)	—	subject	soumettre	sottomettere	someter
untidy (E)	unordentlich	—	désordonné(e)	disordinato(a)	desordenado(a)
until (E)	bis	—	jusqu'à	fino a	hasta
unusual (E)	ungewöhnlich	—	exceptionnel(le)	insolito(a)	desacostumbrado(a)
unverbindlich (D)	—	not binding	sans engagement	non impegnativo(a)	sin compromiso
unverheiratet (D)	—	unmarried	non marié(e)	celibe m/nubile *f*	soltero(a)
unvermeidlich (D)	—	inevitable	inévitable	inevitabile	inevitable
unvollständig (D)	—	incomplete	incomplet(-ète)	incompleto(a)	incompleto(a)
unvorsichtig (D)	—	careless	imprudent(e)	imprudente	descuidado(a)

	D	E	F	I	Es
unwahr-scheinlich (D)	—	unlikely	invraisemblable	improbabile	improbable
unwelcome (E)	unerwünscht	—	inopportun(e)	indesiderato(a)	indeseado(a)
unwell (E)	unwohl	—	indisposé(e)	indisposto(a)	indispuesto(a)
Unwetter (D)	—	thunderstorm	tempête *f*	maltempo *m*	tormenta *f*
unwichtig (D)	—	unimportant	sans importance	non importante	sin importancia
unwohl (D)	—	unwell	indisposé(e)	indisposto(a)	indispuesto(a)
unzufrieden (D)	—	dissatisfied	mécontent(e)	scontento(a)	descontento(a)
uomo (I)	Mann *m*	man	homme *m*	—	hombre *m*
uovo (I)	Ei *n*	egg	œuf *m*	—	huevo *m*
up[1] (E)	hinauf	—	vers le haut	su	hacia arriba
up[2] (E)	herauf	—	vers le haut	su	hacia arriba
up[3] (E)	hoch	—	haut(e)	alto(a)	alto(a)
uphill (E)	bergauf	—	en montant	in salita	cuesta arriba
upright (E)	aufrecht	—	droit(e)	diritto(a)	derecho(a)
upwards (E)	aufwärts	—	vers le haut	in su	hacia arriba
urbe (Es)	Großstadt *f*	large town	grande ville *f*	grande città *f*	—
urgent (E)	dringend	—	urgent(e)	urgente	urgente
urgent (F)	dringend	urgent	—	urgente	urgente
urgente (Es)	dringend	urgent	urgent(e)	urgente	—
urgente (I)	dringend	urgent	urgent(e)	—	urgente
Urgroßeltern (D)	—	great-grandparents	arrière-grands-parents *m pl*	bisnonni *m pl*	bisabuelos *m pl*
urina (I)	Harn *m*	urine	urine *f*	—	orina *f*
urine (E)	Harn *m*	—	urine *f*	urina *f*	orina *f*
urine (F)	Harn *m*	urine	—	urina *f*	orina *f*
Urkunde (D)	—	document	document *m*	documento *m*	documento *m*
Urlaub (D)	—	vacation	vacances *f pl*	vacanze *f pl*	vacaciones *f pl*
urn (E)	Urne *f*	—	urne *f*	urna *f*	urna *f*
urna (Es)	Urne *f*	urn	urne *f*	urna *f*	—
urna (I)	Urne *f*	urn	urne *f*	—	urna *f*
Urne (D)	—	urn	urne *f*	urna *f*	urna *f*
urne (F)	Urne *f*	urn	—	urna *f*	urna *f*
Ursache (D)	—	cause	cause *f*	causa *f*	causa *f*
ursprünglich (D)	—	original	originel(le)	originario(a)	primitivo(a)
urtare (I)	anstoßen	bump	heurter	—	empujar
Urteil (D)	—	judgement	jugement *m*	giudizio *m*	juicio *m*
urteilen (D)	—	judge	juger	giudicare	juzgar
usado (Es)	gebraucht	used	d'occasion	usato(a)	—
usage (F)	Gebrauch *m*	custom	—	uso *m*	uso *m*
usanza (I)	Sitte *f*	custom	coutume *f*	—	costumbre *f*
usar[1] (Es)	anwenden	apply	employer	impiegare	—
usar[2] (Es)	benutzen	use	utiliser	usare	—
usar[3] (Es)	gebrauchen	use	utiliser	usare	—
usare[1] (I)	benutzen	use	utiliser	—	usar
usare[2] (I)	gebrauchen	use	utiliser	—	usar
usare[3] (I)	verwenden	use	employer	—	utilizar
usato (I)	gebraucht	used	d'occasion	—	usado(a)
uscire[1] (I)	ausgehen	go out	sortir	—	salir

	D	E	F	I	Es
uscire² (I)	hinausgehen	go out	sortir	—	salir afuera
uscire fuori (I)	heraustreten	step out	sortir	—	salir
uscita (I)	Ausgang *m*	exit	sortie *f*	—	salida *f*
uscita di sicurezza (I)	Notausgang *m*	emergency exit	sortie de secours *f*	—	salida de emergencia *f*
use¹ (E)	benutzen	—	utiliser	usare	usar
use² (E)	gebrauchen	—	utiliser	usare	usar
use³ (E)	verwenden	—	employer	usare	utilizar
use⁴ (E)	Verwendung *f*	—	emploi *m*	uso *m*	utilización *f*
used (E)	gebraucht	—	d'occasion	usato(a)	usado(a)
useful (E)	nützlich	—	utile	utile	útil
useless (E)	nutzlos	—	inutile	inutile	inútil
user (F)	abnutzen	wear out	—	consumare	desgastar
use the familiar form (E)	duzen	—	tutoyer	dare del tu	tutear
usine (F)	Fabrik *f*	factory	—	fabbrica *f*	fábrica *f*
uso (Es)	Gebrauch *m*	custom	usage *m*	uso *m*	—
uso¹ (I)	Gebrauch *m*	custom	usage *m*	—	uso *m*
uso² (I)	Verwendung *f*	use	emploi *m*	—	utilización *f*
usual¹ (E)	gewöhnlich	—	habituel(le)	abituale	habitual
usual² (E)	üblich	—	habituel(le)	solito(a)	usual
usual (Es)	üblich	usual	habituel(le)	solito(a)	—
utensile (I)	Werkzeug *n*	tool	outil *m*	—	herramienta *f*
utensilio (Es)	Gerät *n*	appliance	appareil *m*	apparecchio *m*	—
útil (Es)	nützlich	useful	utile	utile	—
utile (F)	nützlich	useful	—	utile	útil
utile (I)	nützlich	useful	utile	—	útil
utiliser¹ (F)	benutzen	use	—	usare	usar
utiliser² (F)	gebrauchen	use	—	usare	usar
utilización (Es)	Verwendung *f*	use	emploi *m*	uso *m*	—
utilizar (Es)	verwenden	use	employer	usare	—
uva (Es)	Traube *f*	grape	grappe *f*	uva *f*	—
uva (I)	Traube *f*	grape	grappe *f*	—	uva *f*
vaca (Es)	Kuh *f*	cow	vache *f*	mucca *f*	—
vacaciones¹ (Es)	Ferien *f*	holidays	vacances *f pl*	vacanze *f pl*	—
vacaciones² (Es)	Urlaub *m*	vacation	vacances *f pl*	vacanze *f pl*	—
vacances¹ (F)	Ferien *f*	holidays	—	vacanze *f pl*	vacaciones *f pl*
vacances² (F)	Urlaub *m*	vacation	—	vacanze *f pl*	vacaciones *f pl*
vacant (F)	unbesetzt	unoccupied	—	libero(a)	desocupado(a)
vacanza (I)	schulfrei	holiday	de congé	—	sin colegio
vacanze¹ (I)	Ferien *f*	holidays	vacances *f pl*	—	vacaciones *f pl*
vacanze² (I)	Urlaub *m*	vacation	vacances *f pl*	—	vacaciones *f pl*
vacation (E)	Urlaub *m*	—	vacances *f pl*	vacanze *f pl*	vacaciones *f pl*
vaccinare (I)	impfen	vaccinate	vacciner	—	vacunar
vaccinate (E)	impfen	—	vacciner	vaccinare	vacunar
vaccination (E)	Impfung *f*	—	vaccination *f*	vaccinazione *f*	vacunación *f*
vaccination (F)	Impfung *f*	vaccination	—	vaccinazione *f*	vacunación *f*
vaccinazione (I)	Impfung *f*	vaccination	vaccination *f*	—	vacunación *f*
vacciner (F)	impfen	vaccinate	—	vaccinare	vacunar

	D	E	F	I	Es
vache (F)	Kuh *f*	cow	—	mucca *f*	vaca *f*
vacilar[1] (Es)	taumeln	reel	tituber	barcollare	—
vacilar[2] (Es)	wanken	stagger	chanceller	barcollare	—
vacilar[3] (Es)	zögern	hesitate	hésiter	esitare	—
vacío (Es)	leer	empty	vide	vuoto(a)	—
vacunación (Es)	Impfung *f*	vaccination	vaccination *f*	vaccinazione *f*	—
vacunar (Es)	impfen	vaccinate	vacciner	vaccinare	—
vacuum-cleaner (E)	Staubsauger *m*	—	aspirateur *m*	aspirapolvere *m*	aspirador *m*
vagón (Es)	Waggon *m*	carriage	wagon *m*	vagone *m*	—
vagone (I)	Waggon *m*	carriage	wagon *m*	—	vagón *m*
vagone ristorante (I)	Speisewagen *m*	dining car	wagon-restaurant *m*	—	vagón restaurante *m*
vagón restaurante (Es)	Speisewagen *m*	dining car	wagon-restaurant *m*	vagone ristorante *m*	—
vague (F)	Welle *f*	wave	—	onda *f*	ola *f*
vain (E)	eitel	—	vaniteux(-euse)	vanitoso(a)	vanidoso(a)
vaisselle (F)	Geschirr *n*	crockery	—	stoviglie *f pl*	vajilla *f*
vajilla (Es)	Geschirr *n*	crockery	vaisselle *f*	stoviglie *f pl*	—
valable (F)	gültig	valid	—	valido(a)	válido(a)
vale (Es)	Gutschein *m*	voucher	bon *m*	buono *m*	—
valer[1] (Es)	gelten	be worth	valoir	valere	—
valer[2] (Es)	taugen	be of use	convenir pour	essere portato(a)	—
valere (I)	gelten	be worth	valoir	—	valer
valere la pena (I)	lohnen	be worth while	en valoir la peine	—	valer la pena
valer la pena (Es)	lohnen	be worth while	en valoir la peine	valere la pena	—
valeur (F)	Wert *m*	value	—	valore *m*	valor *m*
valid (E)	gültig	—	valable	valido(a)	válido(a)
validez (Es)	Gültigkeit *f*	validity	validité *f*	validità *f*	—
validità (I)	Gültigkeit *f*	validity	validité *f*	—	validez *f*
validité (F)	Gültigkeit *f*	validity	—	validità *f*	validez *f*
validity (E)	Gültigkeit *f*	—	validité *f*	validità *f*	validez *f*
valido (I)	gültig	valid	valable	—	válido(a)
válido (Es)	gültig	valid	valable	valido(a)	—
valiente (Es)	tapfer	brave	courageux(-euse)	coraggioso(a)	—
valigia (I)	Koffer *m*	suitcase	valise *f*	—	maleta *f*
valioso[1] (Es)	kostbar	precious	précieux(-euse)	prezioso(a)	—
valioso[2] (Es)	wertvoll	valuable	précieux(-euse)	prezioso(a)	—
valise (F)	Koffer *m*	suitcase	—	valigia *f*	maleta *f*
valla (Es)	Zaun *m*	fence	clôture *f*	recinto *m*	—
valle (Es)	Tal *n*	valley	vallée *f*	valle *f*	—
valle (I)	Tal *n*	valley	vallée *f*	—	valle *m*
vallée (F)	Tal *n*	valley	—	valle *f*	valle *m*
valley (E)	Tal *n*	—	vallée *f*	valle *f*	valle *m*
valoir (F)	gelten	be worth	—	valere	valer
valor (Es)	Wert *m*	value	valeur *f*	valore *m*	—
valore (I)	Wert *m*	value	valeur *f*	—	valor *m*
valuable (E)	wertvoll	—	précieux(-euse)	prezioso(a)	valioso(a)
value (E)	Wert *m*	—	valeur *f*	valore *m*	valor *m*

	D	E	F	I	Es
value added tax (E)	Mehrwertsteuer f	—	taxe sur la valeur ajoutée f	imposta sul'valore aggiunto f	impuesto sobre el valor añadido m
valuta (I)	Währung f	currency	monnaie f	—	moneda f
vanidoso (Es)	eitel	vain	vaniteux(-euse)	vanitoso(a)	—
vaniteux (F)	eitel	vain	—	vanitoso(a)	vanidoso(a)
vanitoso (I)	eitel	vain	vaniteux(-euse)	—	vanidoso(a)
vantaggio (I)	Vorteil m	advantage	avantage m	—	ventaja f
vapeur (F)	Dampf m	steam	—	vapore m	vapor m
vapor (Es)	Dampf m	steam	vapeur f	vapore m	—
vapore (I)	Dampf m	steam	vapeur f	—	vapor m
vara (Es)	Stange f	pole	barre f	asta f	—
variabile (I)	veränderlich	changeable	variable	—	variable
variable (Es)	veränderlich	changeable	variable	variabile	—
variable (F)	veränderlich	changeable	—	variabile	variable
variopinto (I)	bunt	coloured	coloré(e)	—	de colores
vasca da bagno (I)	Badewanne f	bath tub	baignoire f	—	bañera f
Vase (D)	—	vase	vase m	vaso m	florero m
vase (E)	Vase f	—	vase m	vaso m	florero m
vase (F)	Vase f	vase	—	vaso m	florero m
vaso (Es)	Glas n	glass	verre m	bicchiere m	—
vaso (I)	Vase f	vase	vase m	—	florero m
vassoio (I)	Tablett n	tray	plateau m	—	bandeja f
Vater (D)	—	father	père m	padre m	padre m
veau (F)	Kalb n	calf	—	vitello m	ternera f
vecchio (I)	alt	old	vieux , vieil, vieille	—	viejo(a)
vecino[1] (Es)	Nachbar m	neighbour	voisin m	vicino m	—
vecino[2] (Es)	benachbart	neighbouring	avoisinant(e)	vicino(a)	—
vedere (I)	sehen	see	voir	—	ver
vedova (I)	Witwe f	widow	veuve f	—	viuda f
vedovo (I)	Witwer m	widower	veuf m	—	viudo m
vegetables (E)	Gemüse n	—	légumes m pl	verdura f	legumbres f pl
vegetarian (E)	Vegetarier m	—	végétarien m	vegetariano m	vegetariano m
vegetariano (Es)	Vegetarier m	vegetarian	végétarien m	vegetariano m	—
vegetariano (I)	Vegetarier m	vegetarian	végétarien m	—	vegetariano m
végétarien (F)	Vegetarier m	vegetarian	—	vegetariano m	vegetariano m
Vegetarier (D)	—	vegetarian	végétarien m	vegetariano m	vegetariano m
vehicle (E)	Fahrzeug n	—	véhicule m	veicolo m	vehículo m
véhicule (F)	Fahrzeug n	vehicle	—	veicolo m	vehículo m
vehículo (Es)	Fahrzeug n	vehicle	véhicule m	veicolo m	—
veicolo (I)	Fahrzeug n	vehicle	véhicule m	—	vehículo m
veille (F)	Vorabend m	evening before	—	vigilia f	víspera f
veilleur de nuit (F)	Nachtwächter m	night-watchman	—	guardia notturna f	sereno m
vein (E)	Ader f	—	veine f	vena f	vena f
veine (F)	Ader f	vein	—	vena f	vena f
veinte (Es)	zwanzig	twenty	vingt	venti	—
vejiga (Es)	Blase f	bladder	vessie f	vescica f	—
vela (Es)	Kerze f	candle	bougie f	candela f	—
veleno (I)	Gift n	poison	poison m	—	veneno m

	D	E	F	I	Es
velenoso (I)	giftig	poisonous	toxique	—	venenoso(a)
veloce (I)	schnell	fast	rapide	—	rápido(a)
velocidad[1] (Es)	Geschwindigkeit f	speed	vitesse f	velocità f	—
velocidad[2] (Es)	Tempo n	speed	vitesse f	velocità f	—
velocidad máxima (Es)	Höchstgeschwindigkeit f	maximum speed	vitesse maximum f	velocità massima f	—
velocità[1] (I)	Geschwindigkeit f	speed	vitesse f	—	velocidad f
velocità[2] (I)	Schnelligkeit f	speed	rapidité f	—	rapidez f
velocità[3] (I)	Tempo n	speed	vitesse f	—	velocidad f
velocità massima (I)	Höchstgeschwindigkeit f	maximum speed	vitesse maximum f	—	velocidad máxima f
vena (Es)	Ader f	vein	veine f	vena f	—
vena (I)	Ader f	vein	veine f	—	vena f
vencer (Es)	siegen	win	gagner	vincere	—
vendedor (Es)	Verkäufer m	salesman	vendeur m	venditore m	—
vender (Es)	verkaufen	sell	vendre	vendere	—
vendere (I)	verkaufen	sell	vendre	—	vender
vendetta (I)	Rache f	revenge	vengeance f	—	venganza f
vendeur (F)	Verkäufer m	salesman	—	venditore m	vendedor m
vendido (Es)	ausverkauft	sold out	épuisé(e)	esaurito(a)	—
vending machine (E)	Automat m	—	distributeur automatique m	distributore automatico m	distribuidor automático m
vendita (I)	Verkauf m	sale	vente f	—	venta f
vendita anticipata (I)	Vorverkauf m	advance booking	location f	—	venta anticipada f
venditore (I)	Verkäufer m	salesman	vendeur m	—	vendedor m
vendre (F)	verkaufen	sell	—	vendere	vender
vendredi (F)	Freitag m	Friday	—	venerdì m	viernes m
veneno (Es)	Gift n	poison	poison m	veleno m	—
venenoso (Es)	giftig	poisonous	toxique	velenoso(a)	—
venerdì (I)	Freitag m	Friday	vendredi	—	viernes m
venganza (Es)	Rache f	revenge	vengeance f	vendetta f	—
vengeance (F)	Rache f	revenge	—	vendetta f	venganza f
venir (Es)	kommen	come	venir	venire	—
venir (F)	kommen	come	—	venire	venir
venir à la rencontre (F)	entgegenkommen	approach	—	venire incontro	venir al encuentro
venir al encuentro (Es)	entgegenkommen	approach	venir à la rencontre	venire incontro	—
venir bien (Es)	passen	suit	aller bien	stare bene	—
venir de nuevo (Es)	wiederkommen	come back	revenir	ritornare	—
venire (I)	kommen	come	venir	—	venir
venire a sapere (I)	erfahren	learn	apprendre	—	enterarse
venire incontro (I)	entgegenkommen	approach	venir à la rencontre	—	venir al encuentro
vent (F)	Wind m	wind	—	vento m	viento m
venta (Es)	Verkauf m	sale	vente f	vendita f	—
venta anticipada (Es)	Vorverkauf m	advance booking	location f	vendita anticipata f	—
ventaja (Es)	Vorteil m	advantage	avantage m	vantaggio m	—
ventana (Es)	Fenster n	window	fenêtre f	finestra f	—
ventanilla (Es)	Schalter m	counter	guichet m	sportello m	—

	D	E	F	I	Es
vente (F)	Verkauf *m*	sale	—	vendita *f*	venta *f*
venti (I)	zwanzig	twenty	vingt	—	veinte
ventilar (Es)	lüften	air	aérer	arrieggiare	—
vento (I)	Wind *m*	wind	vent *m*	—	viento *m*
ventoso (I)	windig	windy	éventé(e)	—	ventoso
ventoso (Es)	windig	windy	éventé(e)	ventoso(a)	—
ventre (F)	Bauch *m*	stomach	—	pancia *f*	vientre *m*
ver (Es)	sehen	see	voir	vedere	—
verabreden (D)	—	arrange to meet	prendre rendez-vous	darsi appuntamento	concertar una cita
Verabredung (D)	—	date	rendez-vous *m*	appuntamento *m*	cita *f*
verabschieden (D)	—	say goodbye to	prendre congé de	congedare	despedir
veränderlich (D)	—	changeable	variable	variabile	variable
verändern (D)	—	change	transformer	mutare	cambiar
Veränderung (D)	—	change	changement *m*	cambiamento *m*	cambio *m*
verano (Es)	Sommer *m*	summer	été *m*	estate *f*	—
veranstalten (D)	—	organize	organiser	organizzare	organizar
Veranstaltung (D)	—	event	manifestation *f*	manifestazione *f*	representación *f*
verantwortlich (D)	—	responsible	responsable	responsabile	responsable
verbergen (D)	—	hide	dissimuler	nascondere	esconder
verbessern (D)	—	improve	améliorer	migliorare	mejorar
verbieten (D)	—	forbid	défendre	proibire	prohibir
verbinden (D)	—	connect	relier	unire	unir
Verbindung (D)	—	connection	relation *f*	relazione *f*	relación *f*
Verbot (D)	—	prohibition	défense *f*	divieto *m*	prohibición *f*
verboten (D)	—	forbidden	interdit(e)	vietato(a)	prohibido(a)
Verbrauch (D)	—	consumption	consommation *f*	consumo *m*	consumo *m*
verbrauchen (D)	—	consume	consommer	consumare	consumir
Verbrechen (D)	—	crime	crime *m*	delitto *m*	crimen *m*
verbreiten (D)	—	spread	propager	diffondere	difundir
verbrennen (D)	—	burn	brûler	bruciare	quemar
verbringen (D)	—	spend	passer	passare	pasar
verdächtig (D)	—	suspicious	suspect(e)	sospetto(a)	sospechoso(a)
verdad (Es)	Wahrheit *f*	truth	vérité *f*	verità *f*	—
verdadero[1] (Es)	echt	genuine	vrai(e)	vero(a)	—
verdadero[2] (Es)	wahr	true	vrai(e)	vero(a)	—
verdauen (D)	—	digest	digérer	digerire	digerir
verde (Es)	grün	green	vert(e)	verde	—
verde (I)	grün	green	vert(e)	—	verde
verderben (D)	—	ruin	détruire	rovinare	arrruinar
verdienen (D)	—	earn	gagner	guadagnare	ganar
Verdienst[1] (D)	—	merit	mérite *m*	merito *m*	mérito *m*
Verdienst[2] (D)	—	income	revenus *m pl*	guadagno *m*	ganancia *f*
verdura (I)	Gemüse *n*	vegetables	légumes *m pl*	—	legumbres *f pl*
Verein (D)	—	club	association *f*	associazione *f*	asociación *f*
vereinbaren (D)	—	agree upon	convenir de	fissare	convenir
vereinigen (D)	—	unite	unir	unire	unir
Vereinigte Staaten (D)	—	United States	Etats-Unis *m pl*	Stati Uniti *m pl*	Estados Unidos *m pl*

	D	E	F	I	Es
vererben (D)	—	bequeath	léguer	lasciare in eredità	transmitir hereditariamente
verfahren (D)	—	act	procéder	procedere	proceder
Verfassung[1] (D)	—	constitution	état m	condizioni f pl	estado m
Verfassung[2] (D)	—	constitution	constitution f	costituzione f	constitución f
verfolgen (D)	—	pursue	poursuivre	inseguire	perseguir
verfügen (D)	—	order	disposer de	disporre	disponer
verführen (D)	—	seduce	séduire	sedurre	seducir
vergangen (D)	—	past	passé(e)	passato(a)	pasado(a)
vergangene (D)	—	past	dernier(-ère)	passato(a)	pasada(o)
Vergangenheit (D)	—	past	passé m	passato m	pasado m
vergehen (D)	—	pass by	passer	passare	pasar
vergessen (D)	—	forget	oublier	dimenticare	olvidar
vergewaltigen (D)	—	rape	violer	violentare	violar
vergine (I)	Jungfrau f	virgin	vierge f	—	virgen f
Vergleich (D)	—	comparison	comparaison f	paragone m	comparación f
vergleichen (D)	—	compare	comparer	paragonare	comparar
Vergnügen (D)	—	pleasure	plaisir m	divertimento m	placer m
vergogna (I)	Schande f	disgrace	honte f	—	deshonra f
vergognarsi (I)	schämen	be ashamed	avoir honte	—	tener vergüenza
vergrößern (D)	—	enlarge	agrandir	ingrandire	agrandar
verhaften (D)	—	arrest	arrêter	arrestare	detener
verheiratet (D)	—	married	marié(e)	sposato(a)	casado(a)
verhindern (D)	—	prevent	empêcher	impedire	evitar
verhindert (D)	—	unable to make it	empêché(e)	impedito(a)	impedido(a)
verhungern (D)	—	starve	mourir de faim	morire di fame	morir de hambre
vérifier (F)	nachsehen	check	—	controllare	examinar
verità (I)	Wahrheit f	truth	vérité f	—	verdad f
vérité (F)	Wahrheit f	truth	—	verità f	verdad f
Verkauf (D)	—	sale	vente f	vendita f	venta f
verkaufen (D)	—	sell	vendre	vendere	vender
Verkäufer (D)	—	salesman	vendeur m	venditore m	vendedor m
Verkehr (D)	—	traffic	circulation f	traffico m	tráfico m
Verkehrsbüro (D)	—	travel agency	bureau touristique m	ufficio turistico m	oficina de turismo f
verkehrt (D)	—	wrong	faux (fausse)	sbagliato(a)	equivocado(a)
verkleinern (D)	—	make smaller	réduire	ridurre	reducir
verladen (D)	—	load	charger	caricare	cargar
verlangen (D)	—	demand	demander	richiedere	exigir
verlängern (D)	—	extend	prolonger	allungare	alargar
verlassen (D)	—	leave	abandonner	lasciare	dejar
ver la televisión (Es)	fernsehen	watch television	regarder la télévision	guardare la TV	—
verlaufen (D)	—	get lost	perdre, se	perdersi	perderse
verlegen (D)	—	mislay	égarer	perdere	extraviar
Verlegenheit (D)	—	embarrassment	gêne f	imbarazzo m	contratiempo m
verleihen (D)	—	lend	prêter	prestare	prestar
verletzen (D)	—	injure	blesser	ferire	herir
Verletzung (D)	—	injury	blessure f	ferita f	herida f

	D	E	F	I	Es
verlieben (D)	—	fall in love	tomber amoureux(-euse)	innamorarsi	enamorarse
verliebt (D)	—	in love	amoureux(-euse)	innamorato	enamorado(a)
verlieren (D)	—	lose	perdre	perdere	perder
verloben (D)	—	get engaged	fiancer, se	fidanzarsi	prometerse
Verlobter (D)	—	fiancé	fiancé *m*	fidanzato *m*	prometido *m*
Verlust (D)	—	loss	perte *f*	perdita *f*	pérdida *f*
vermehren (D)	—	increase	augmenter	aumentare	aumentar
vermeiden (D)	—	avoid	éviter	evitare	evitar
vermieten (D)	—	rent	louer	affittare	alquilar
vermissen (D)	—	miss	manquer	sentire la mancanza	echar de menos
vermuten (D)	—	suppose	supposer	supporre	suponer
Vermutung (D)	—	supposition	supposition *f*	supposizione *f*	suposición *f*
vernachlässigen (D)	—	neglect	négliger	trascurare	descuidar
vernichten (D)	—	destroy	détruire	distruggere	destruir
verniciare (I)	streichen	paint	peindre	—	pintar
vernünftig (D)	—	sensible	raisonnable	ragionevole	razonable
vero¹ (I)	echt	genuine	vrai(e)	—	verdadero(a)
vero² (I)	wahr	true	vrai(e)	—	verdadero(a)
veröffentlichen (D)	—	publish	publier	pubblicare	publicar
verpachten (D)	—	lease out	affermer	affittare	arrendar
verpacken (D)	—	pack	emballer	impacchettare	empaquetar
Verpflegung (D)	—	catering	nourriture *f*	vitto *m*	alimentación *f*
verpflichten (D)	—	oblige	obliger	obbligare	obligar
Verpflichtung (D)	—	obligation	obligation *f*	obbligo *m*	obligación *f*
verraten (D)	—	betray	trahir	tradire	traicionar
verre (F)	Glas *n*	glass	—	bicchiere *m*	vaso *m*
verreisen (D)	—	go away	partir en voyage	partire in viaggio	irse de viaje
verringern (D)	—	reduce	diminuer	diminuire	disminuir
verrou (F)	Riegel *m*	bar	—	catenaccio *m*	cerrojo *m*
verrückt (D)	—	mad	fou (folle)	pazzo(a)	loco(a)
versant (F)	Hang *m*	slope	—	pendio *m*	pendiente *m*
versare¹ (I)	eingießen	pour	verser	—	echar
versare² (I)	schütten	pour	verser	—	verter
versäumen (D)	—	miss	manquer	perdere	perder
verschaffen (D)	—	procure	procurer	procurare	procurarse algo
verschieben (D)	—	postpone	remettre	rimandare	aplazar
verschieden (D)	—	different	différent(e)	diverso(a)	diferente
verschließen (D)	—	lock (up)	fermer à clé	chiudere	cerrar con llave
Verschluß (D)	—	lock	fermeture *f*	chiusura *f*	cierre *m*
verschreiben (D)	—	prescribe	prescrire	prescrivere	prescribir
verschwenden (D)	—	waste	gaspiller	sprecare	desperdiciar
verschwinden (D)	—	disappear	disparaître	sparire	desaparecer
verser¹ (F)	eingießen	pour	—	versare	echar
verser² (F)	schütten	pour	—	versare	verter
versichern (D)	—	assure	assurer	assicurare	asegurar
Versicherung (D)	—	insurance	assurance *f*	assicurazione *f*	seguro *m*
versinken (D)	—	sink	enfoncer, se	affondare	hundirse

	D	E	F	I	Es
vers le bas (F)	herab/hinab	down	—	giù	hacia abajo
vers le haut[1] (F)	aufwärts	upwards	—	in su	hacia arriba
vers le haut[2] (F)	herauf	up	—	su	hacia arriba
vers le haut[3] (F)	hinauf	up	—	su	hacia arriba
vers l'intérieur (F)	herein	in	—	dentro	adentro
versorgen (D)	—	provide	fournir	approvvigionare	proveer
verspäten (D)	—	be late	être en retard	ritardare	llevar retraso
Verspätung (D)	—	delay	retard m	ritardo m	retraso m
versprechen (D)	—	promise	promettre	promettere	prometer
Versprechen (D)	—	promise	promesse f	promessa f	promesa f
Verstand (D)	—	intelligence	intelligence f	intelligenza f	razón f
verständigen (D)	—	inform	prévenir	informare	informar
Verständigung (D)	—	agreement	accord m	accordo m	acuerdo m
Verständnis (D)	—	understanding	compréhension f	comprensione f	comprensión f
verstecken (D)	—	hide	cacher	nascondere	ocultar
verstehen (D)	—	understand	comprendre	capire	entender
Versuch (D)	—	try	essai m	tentativo m	intento m
versuchen (D)	—	try	essayer	assaggiare	probar
vert (F)	grün	green	—	verde	verde
vertauschen (D)	—	exchange	échanger	scambiare	cambiar
verteidigen (D)	—	defend	défendre	difendere	defender
Verteidigung (D)	—	defence	défense f	difesa f	defensa f
verteilen (D)	—	distribute	distribuer	distribuire	repartir
verter (Es)	schütten	pour	verser	versare	—
vertical (E)	senkrecht	—	vertical(e)	verticale	vertical
vertical (Es)	senkrecht	vertical	vertical(e)	verticale	—
vertical (F)	senkrecht	vertical	—	verticale	vertical
verticale (I)	senkrecht	vertical	vertical(e)	—	vertical
Vertrag (D)	—	contract	contrat m	contratto m	contrato m
vertrauen (D)	—	trust	avoir confiance	fidarsi	confiar
Vertrauen (D)	—	confidence	confiance f	fiducia f	confianza f
vertreten (D)	—	represent	représenter	rappresentare	representar
Vertreter (D)	—	representative	représentant m	rappresentante m	representante
verursachen (D)	—	cause	causer	causare	ocasionar
verurteilen (D)	—	condemn	condamner	condannare	sentenciar
Verwaltung (D)	—	administration	administration f	amministrazione f	administración f
verwandt (D)	—	related	parent(e)	imparentato(a)	emparentado(a)
Verwandter (D)	—	relative	parent m	parente m	pariente m
verwechseln (D)	—	confuse	confondre	scambiare	confundir
verweigern (D)	—	refuse	refuser	rifiutare	negar
verwenden (D)	—	use	employer	usare	utilizar
Verwendung (D)	—	use	emploi m	uso m	utilización f
verwirklichen (D)	—	realize	réaliser	realizzare	llevar a cabo
verwirrt (D)	—	confused	confus(e)	confuso(a)	confundido(a)
Verwirrung (D)	—	confusion	confusion f	confusione f	confusión f
verwöhnen (D)	—	spoil	gâter	viziare	mimar
verwunden (D)	—	wound	blesser	ferire	herir
very (E)	sehr	—	très	molto	mucho/muy

	D	E	F	I	Es
verzeichnen (D)	—	list	enregistrer	registrare	hacer una lista
Verzeichnis (D)	—	list	registre *m*	elenco *m*	lista *f*
verzeihen (D)	—	forgive	pardonner	perdonare	perdonar
Verzeihung (D)	—	forgiveness	pardon *m*	perdono *m*	perdón *m*
verzichten (D)	—	forgo	renoncer	rinunciare	renunciar
verzollen (D)	—	clear through customs	dédouaner	sdoganare	pagar la aduana
verzweifelt (D)	—	desperate	désespéré(e)	disperato(a)	desesperado(a)
vescica (I)	Blase *f*	bladder	vessie *f*	—	vejiga *f*
vespa (I)	Wespe *f*	wasp	guêpe *f*	—	avispa *f*
vessie (F)	Blase *f*	bladder	—	vescica *f*	vejiga *f*
vest (E)	Unterhemd *n*	—	tricot *m*	canottiera *f*	camiseta *f*
veste (F)	Jacke *f*	jacket	—	giacca *f*	chaqueta *f*
veste en tricot (F)	Strickjacke *f*	cardigan	—	giacca di maglia *f*	chaqueta de punto *f*
vestiaire (F)	Garderobe *f*	wardrobe	—	guardaroba *m*	guardaropa *m*
vestibule (F)	Diele *f*	hall	—	corridoio *m*	vestíbulo *m*
vestíbulo (Es)	Diele *f*	hall	vestibule *m*	corridoio *m*	—
vestido¹ (Es)	Kleid *n*	dress	robe *f*	vestito *m*	—
vestido² (Es)	Kostüm *n*	costume	costume *m*	tailleur *m*	—
vestir (Es)	kleiden	dress	habiller	vestire	—
vestire (I)	kleiden	dress	habiller	—	vestir
vestito¹ (I)	Anzug *m*	suit	costume *m*	—	traje *m*
vestito² (I)	Kleid *n*	dress	robe *f*	—	vestido *m*
vestuario (Es)	Kleidung *f*	clothing	habits *m pl*	abbigliamento *m*	—
vet (E)	Tierarzt *m*	—	vétérinaire *m*	veterinario *m*	veterinario *m*
veta (Es)	Masern *pl*	speckle	rougeole *f*	morbillo *m*	—
vétérinaire (F)	Tierarzt *m*	vet	—	veterinario *m*	veterinario *m*
veterinario (Es)	Tierarzt *m*	vet	vétérinaire *m*	veterinario *m*	—
veterinario (I)	Tierarzt *m*	vet	vétérinaire *m*	—	veterinario *m*
vetrina (I)	Schaufenster *n*	shop window	vitrine *f*	—	escaparate *m*
vetro (I)	Scheibe *f*	pane	carreau *m*	—	cristal *m*
Vetter (D)	—	cousin	cousin *m*	cugino *m*	primo *m*
vettura (I)	Wagen *m*	car	voiture *f*	—	coche *m*
veuf (F)	Witwer *m*	widower	—	vedovo *m*	viudo *m*
veuve (F)	Witwe *f*	widow	—	vedova *f*	viuda *f*
vía (Es)	Gleis *n*	track	voie *f*	binario *m*	—
via¹ (I)	fort	away	parti	—	lejos
via² (I)	weg	away	pas là	—	fuera
via³ (I)	Weg *m*	way	chemin *m*	—	camino *m*
vía de acceso (Es)	Auffahrt *f*	slip road	bretelle d'accès *f*	entrata *f*	—
viaggiare (I)	reisen	travel	voyager	—	viajar
viaggiatore (I)	Reisender *m*	traveller	voyageur *m*	—	viajero *m*
viaggio¹ (I)	Fahrt *f*	journey	voyage *f*	—	viaje *m*
viaggio² (I)	Reise *f*	journey	voyage *m*	—	viaje *m*
viajar (Es)	reisen	travel	voyager	viaggiare	—
viaje¹ (Es)	Fahrt *f*	journey	voyage *f*	viaggio *m*	—
viaje² (Es)	Reise *f*	journey	voyage *m*	viaggio *m*	—
viajero (Es)	Reisender *m*	traveller	voyageur *m*	viaggiatore *m*	—

	D	E	F	I	Es
viande (F)	Fleisch *n*	meat	—	carne *f*	carne *f*
viande de bœuf (F)	Rindfleisch *n*	beef	—	carne di manzo *f*	carne de vaca *f*
viande de porc (F)	Schweinefleisch *n*	pork	—	carne di maiale *f*	carne de cerdo *f*
viande hachée (F)	Hackfleisch *n*	minced meat	—	carne tritata *f*	carne picada *f*
vice versa (E)	umgekehrt	—	vice versa	inverso(a)	contrario(a)
vice versa (F)	umgekehrt	vice versa	—	inverso(a)	contrario(a)
vicinanza (I)	Nähe *f*	proximity	environs *m pl*	—	proximidad *f*
vicino[1] (I)	benachbart	neighbouring	avoisinant(e)	—	vecino(a)
vicino[2] (I)	nahe	near	près de	—	contiguo(a)
vicino[3] (I)	Nachbar *m*	neighbour	voisin *m*	—	vecino *m*
vicolo (I)	Gasse *f*	lane	ruelle *f*	—	callejón *m*
victim (E)	Opfer *n*	—	victime *f*	vittima *f*	víctima *f*
víctima (Es)	Opfer *n*	victim	victime *f*	vittima *f*	—
victime (F)	Opfer *n*	victim	—	vittima *f*	víctima *f*
victoire (F)	Sieg *m*	victory	—	vittoria *f*	victoria *f*
victoria (Es)	Sieg *m*	victory	victoire *f*	vittoria *f*	—
victory (E)	Sieg *m*	—	victoire *f*	vittoria *f*	victoria *f*
victuals (E)	Eßwaren *pl*	—	produits alimentaires *m pl*	alimentari *m pl*	comestibles *m pl*
vida (Es)	Leben *n*	life	vie *f*	vita *f*	—
vida cotidiana (Es)	Alltag *m*	everyday life	vie quotidienne *f*	vita quotidiana *f*	—
vide (F)	leer	empty	—	vuoto(a)	vacío(a)
vie (F)	Leben *n*	life	—	vita *f*	vida *f*
viejo (Es)	alt	old	vieux, vieil, vieille	vecchio(a)	—
viel (D)	—	a lot of	beaucoup de	molto(a)	mucho(a)
viele (D)	—	many/a lot of	beaucoup de	molti(e)	muchos(as)
vielleicht (D)	—	maybe	peut-être	forse	tal vez
viento (Es)	Wind *m*	wind	vent *m*	vento *m*	—
vientre (Es)	Bauch *m*	stomach	ventre *m*	pancia *f*	—
vie quotidienne (F)	Alltag *m*	everyday life	—	vita quotidiana *f*	vida cotidiana *f*
vier (D)	—	four	quatre	quattro	cuatro
viereckig (D)	—	square	carré(e)	quadrato(a)	cuadrangular
vierge (F)	Jungfrau *f*	virgin	—	vergine *f*	virgen *f*
viernes (Es)	Freitag *m*	Friday	vendredi	venerdì *m*	—
Viertel (D)	—	a quarter	quart *m*	quarto *m*	barrio *m*
vierzehn (D)	—	fourteen	quatorze	quattordici	catorce
vierzig (D)	—	forty	quarante	quaranta	cuarenta
vietato (I)	verboten	forbidden	interdit(e)	—	prohibido(a)
vieux (F)	alt	old	—	vecchio(a)	viejo(a)
view[1] (E)	Aussicht *f*	—	vue *f*	vista *f*	vista *f*
view[2] (E)	Sicht *f*	—	vue *f*	vista *f*	vista *f*
vif (F)	lebhaft	lively	—	vivace	vivaz
vigilante (Es)	Aufseher *m*	guard	gardien *m*	custode *m*	—
vigilar[1] (Es)	bewachen	guard	garder	sorvegliare	—
vigilar[2] (Es)	überwachen	supervise	surveiller	sorvegliare	—
vigilia (I)	Vorabend *m*	evening before	veille *f*	—	víspera *f*
vigilia di Natale (I)	Heiligabend *m*	Christmas Eve	nuit de Noël *f*	—	Nochebuena *f*

	D	E	F	I	Es
vigili del fuoco (I)	Feuerwehr f	fire brigade	sapeurs-pompiers m pl	—	cuerpo de bomberos m
vile (I)	feig	cowardly	lâche	—	cobarde
village (E)	Dorf n	—	village m	paese m	pueblo m
village (F)	Dorf n	village	—	paese m	pueblo m
ville (F)	Stadt f	town	—	città f	ciudad f
vin (F)	Wein m	wine	—	vino m	vino m
vinagre (Es)	Essig m	vinegar	vinaigre m	aceto m	—
vinaigre (F)	Essig m	vinegar	—	aceto m	vinagre m
vincere[1] (I)	gewinnen	win	gagner	—	ganar
vincere[2] (I)	siegen	win	gagner	—	vencer
vinegar (E)	Essig m	—	vinaigre m	aceto m	vinagre m
vingt (F)	zwanzig	twenty	—	venti	veinte
vino (Es)	Wein m	wine	vin m	vino m	—
vino (I)	Wein m	wine	vin m	—	vino m
violar (Es)	vergewaltigen	rape	violer	violentare	—
violent (F)	heftig	fierce	—	violento	fuerte
violentare (I)	vergewaltigen	rape	violer	—	violar
violento (I)	heftig	fierce	violent(e)	—	fuerte
violer (F)	vergewaltigen	rape	—	violentare	violar
violin (E)	Geige f	—	violon m	violino m	violín m
violín (Es)	Geige f	violin	violon m	violino m	—
violino (I)	Geige f	violin	violon m	—	violín m
violon (F)	Geige f	violin	—	violino m	violín m
virage (F)	Kurve f	bend	—	curva f	curva f
virement (F)	Überweisung f	transfer	—	trasferimento m	transferencia f
virer (F)	überweisen	transfer	—	trasferire	transferir
virgen (Es)	Jungfrau f	virgin	vierge f	vergine f	—
virgin (E)	Jungfrau f	—	vierge f	vergine f	virgen f
vis (F)	Schraube f	screw	—	vite f	tornillo m
visa (E)	Visum n	—	visa m	visto m	visado m
visa (F)	Visum n	visa	—	visto m	visado m
visado (Es)	Visum n	visa	visa m	visto m	—
visage (F)	Gesicht n	face	—	faccia f	cara f
visibile (I)	sichtbar	visible	visible	—	visible
visible (E)	sichtbar	—	visible	visibile	visible
visible (Es)	sichtbar	visible	visible	visibile	—
visible (F)	sichtbar	visible	—	visibile	visible
visit[1] (E)	besuchen	—	rendre visite à	andare a trovare	visitar
visit[2] (E)	Besuch m	—	visite f	visita f	visita f
visita (Es)	Besuch m	visit	visite f	visita f	—
visita (I)	Besuch m	visit	visite f	—	visita f
visita guidata (I)	Führung f	guided tour	visite guidée f	—	vista guiada f
visitante (Es)	Besucher m	visitor	visiteur m	visitatore m	—
visitar[1] (Es)	besuchen	visit	rendre visite à	andare a trovare	—
visitar[2] (Es)	besichtigen	have a look at	visiter	visitare	—
visitare (I)	besichtigen	have a look at	visiter	—	visitar
visitatore (I)	Besucher m	visitor	visiteur m	—	visitante m

	D	E	F	I	Es
visite (F)	Besuch *m*	visit	—	visita *f*	visita *f*
visite guidée (F)	Führung *f*	guided tour	—	visita guidata *f*	vista guiada *f*
visiter (F)	besichtigen	have a look at	—	visitare	visitar
visiteur (F)	Besucher *m*	visitor	—	visitatore *m*	visitante *m*
visitor (E)	Besucher *m*	—	visiteur *m*	visitatore *m*	visitante *m*
víspera (Es)	Vorabend *m*	evening before	veille *f*	vigilia *f*	—
vista[1] (Es)	Aussicht *f*	view	vue *f*	vista *f*	—
vista[2] (Es)	Blick *m*	look	regard *m*	sguardo *m*	—
vista[3] (Es)	Sicht *f*	view	vue *f*	vista *f*	—
vista[1] (I)	Aussicht *f*	view	vue *f*	—	vista *f*
vista[2] (I)	Sicht *f*	view	vue *f*	—	vista *f*
visto (I)	Visum *n*	visa	visa *m*	—	visado *m*
Visum (D)	—	visa	visa *m*	visto *m*	visado *m*
vita (I)	Leben *n*	life	vie *f*	—	vida *f*
Vitamin (D)	—	vitamin	vitamine *f*	vitamina *f*	vitamina *f*
vitamin (E)	Vitamin *n*	—	vitamine *f*	vitamina *f*	vitamina *f*
vitamina (Es)	Vitamin *n*	vitamin	vitamine *f*	vitamina *f*	—
vitamina (I)	Vitamin *n*	vitamin	vitamine *f*	—	vitamina *f*
vitamine (F)	Vitamin *n*	vitamin	—	vitamina *f*	vitamina *f*
vita quotidiana (I)	Alltag *m*	everyday life	vie quotidienne *f*	—	vida cotidiana *f*
vite (I)	Schraube *f*	screw	vis *f*	—	tornillo *m*
vitello (I)	Kalb *n*	calf	veau *m*	—	ternera *f*
vitesse[1] (F)	Gang *m*	gear	—	marcia *f*	marcha *f*
vitesse[2] (F)	Geschwindigkeit *f*	speed	—	velocità *f*	velocidad *f*
vitesse[3] (F)	Tempo *n*	speed	—	velocità *f*	velocidad *f*
vitesse maximum (F)	Höchst- geschwindigkeit *f*	maximum speed	—	velocità massima *f*	velocidad máxima *f*
vitrine (F)	Schaufenster *n*	shop window	—	vetrina *f*	escaparate *m*
vittima (I)	Opfer *n*	victim	victime *f*	—	víctima *f*
vitto (I)	Verpflegung *f*	catering	nourriture *f*	—	alimentación *f*
vittoria (I)	Sieg *m*	victory	victoire *f*	—	victoria *f*
viuda (Es)	Witwe *f*	widow	veuve *f*	vedova *f*	—
viudo (Es)	Witwer *m*	widower	veuf *m*	vedovo *m*	—
vivace[1] (I)	lebhaft	lively	vif(vivre)	—	vivaz
vivace[2] (I)	munter	lively	éveillé(e)	—	alegre
vivant (F)	lebendig	alive	—	vivo(a)	vivo(a)
vivaz (Es)	lebhaft	lively	vif(vivre)	vivace	—
vivere[1] (I)	erleben	experience	être témoin de	—	experimentar
vivere[2] (I)	leben	live	vivre	—	vivir
vivir[1] (Es)	leben	live	vivre	vivere	—
vivir[2] (Es)	wohnen	live	habiter	abitare	—
vivo (I)	lebendig	alive	vivant(e)	—	vivo(a)
vivre (F)	leben	live	—	vivere	vivir
viziare (I)	verwöhnen	spoil	gâter	—	mimar
voce[1] (I)	Gerücht *n*	rumour	rumeur *f*	—	rumor *m*
voce[2] (I)	Stimme *f*	voice	voix *f*	—	voz *f*
Vogel (D)	—	bird	oiseau *m*	uccello *m*	pájaro *m*
voi (I)	ihr	you	vous	—	vosotros

	D	E	F	I	Es
voice (E)	Stimme *f*	—	voix *f*	voce *f*	voz *f*
voie (F)	Gleis *n*	track	—	binario *m*	vía *f*
voie rapide (F)	Schnellstraße *f*	expressway	—	superstrada *f*	carretera de circulación rápida *f*
voir (F)	sehen	see	—	vedere	ver
voisin (F)	Nachbar *m*	neighbour	—	vicino *m*	vecino *m*
voiture[1] (F)	Auto *n*	car	—	automobile *f* / macchina *f*	coche *m*
voiture[2] (F)	Wagen *m*	car	—	vettura *f*	coche *m*
voix (F)	Stimme *f*	voice	—	voce *f*	voz *f*
vol (F)	Flug *m*	flight	—	volo *m*	vuelo *m*
volaille (F)	Geflügel *n*	poultry	—	pollame *m*	aves *f pl*
volant (F)	Lenkrad *n*	steering wheel	—	volante *m*	volante *m*
volante (Es)	Lenkrad *n*	steering wheel	volant *m*	volante *m*	—
volante (I)	Lenkrad *n*	steering wheel	volant *m*	—	volante *m*
volar (Es)	fliegen	fly	voler	volare	—
volare (I)	fliegen	fly	voler	—	volar
vol-au-vent (I)	Pastete *f*	pie	pâté *m*	—	empanada *f*
volentieri (I)	gern	willingly	avec plaisir	—	con gusto
voler[1] (F)	fliegen	fly	—	volare	volar
voler[2] (F)	rauben	rob	—	rapinare	robar
voler[3] (F)	stehlen	steal	—	rubare	robar
volere (I)	wollen	want	vouloir	—	querer
voleur (F)	Dieb *m*	thief	—	ladro *m*	ladrón *m*
volgare (I)	gemein	mean	méchant(e)	—	vulgar
Volk (D)	—	people	peuple *m*	popolo *m*	pueblo *m*
voll (D)	—	full	plein(e)	pieno(a)	lleno(a)
völlig (D)	—	completely	complètement	completamente	completamente
volljährig (D)	—	of age	majeur(e)	maggiorenne	mayor de edad
vollkommen (D)	—	perfect	parfait(e)	perfetto(a)	perfecto(a)
Vollmacht (D)	—	authority	procuration *f*	delega *f*	poder *m*
Vollpension (D)	—	full board	pension complète *f*	pensione completa *f*	pensión completa *f*
vollständig (D)	—	complete	complet(-ète)	completo(a)	completo(a)
volo (I)	Flug *m*	flight	vol *m*	—	vuelo *m*
volontaire (F)	freiwillig	voluntary	—	volontario(a)	voluntario(a)
volontario (I)	freiwillig	voluntary	volontaire	—	voluntario(a)
volpe (I)	Fuchs *m*	fox	renard *m*	—	zorro *m*
voltare (I)	wenden	turn	tourner	—	volver
voltare pagina (I)	umblättern	turn over	tourner la page	—	volver la hoja
voluntario (Es)	freiwillig	voluntary	volontaire	volontario(a)	—
voluntary (E)	freiwillig	—	volontaire	volontario(a)	voluntario(a)
volver[1] (Es)	umdrehen	turn around	tourner	girare	—
volver[2] (Es)	wenden	turn	tourner	voltare	—
volver[3] (Es)	zurückkehren	return	revenir	ritornare	—
volver a ver (Es)	wiedersehen	see again	revoir	rivedere	—
volver la hoja (Es)	umblättern	turn over	tourner la page	voltare pagina	—
von (D)	—	from/by	de	di/da	de
vor (D)	—	before/ in front of	devant/avant	davanti a	delante de

	D	E	F	I	Es
Vorabend (D)	—	evening before	veille *f*	vigilia *f*	víspera *f*
vorangehen (D)	—	go ahead	marcher devant	andare avanti	pasar adelante
voraus (D)	—	ahead	en avant	avanti	delante
vorausgesetzt (D)	—	provided	à condition que	presumendo	supuesto
voraussetzen (D)	—	assume	supposer	presupporre	suponer
Vorbehalt (D)	—	reservation	réserve *f*	riserva *f*	reserva *f*
vorbei (D)	—	past	passé(e)	passato(a)	pasado(a)
vorbeigehen (D)	—	pass	passer	passare	pasar
vorbereiten (D)	—	prepare	préparer	preparare	preparar
vorbestellen (D)	—	book	réserver	prenotare	hacer reservar
Vorbild (D)	—	ideal	modèle *m*	modello *m*	modelo *m*
Vorfahrt (D)	—	right of way	priorité *f*	precedenza *f*	preferencia *f*
Vorfall (D)	—	incident	cas *m*	caso *m*	suceso *m*
vorgehen (D)	—	proceed	avancer	procedere	proceder
vorgestern (D)	—	day before yesterday	avant-hier	l'altro ieri	anteayer
vorhaben (D)	—	intend	avoir l'intention de	avere intenzione	tener la intención de
vorhanden (D)	—	available	présent(e)	disponibile	presente
Vorhang (D)	—	curtain	rideau *m*	tenda *f*	cortina *f*
vorher (D)	—	before	avant	prima	antes
vorhergehend (D)	—	preceding	précédent(e)	precedente	anterior
vorhersagen (D)	—	predict	prédire	prognosticare	pronosticar
vorig (D)	—	previous	précédent(e)	precedente	precedente
vorkommen (D)	—	occur	exister	accadere	suceder
vorladen (D)	—	summon	assigner	citare in giudizio	citar
vorläufig (D)	—	temporary	provisoire	provvisorio(a)	provisional
Vorlesung (D)	—	lecture	cours magistral *m*	lezione *f*	clase *f*
vorletzter (D)	—	one before last	avant-dernier(-ère)	penultimo(a)	penúltima(o)
vormerken (D)	—	book	prendre note de	prendere nota di	tomar nota
Vormittag (D)	—	before noon	matinée *f*	mattina *f*	mañana *f*
vormittags (D)	—	in the morning	le matin	di mattina	por la mañana
vorn(e) (D)	—	at the front	devant	davanti	delante
Vorname (D)	—	Christian name	prénom *m*	nome di battesimo *m*	nombre *m*
vornehm (D)	—	distinguished	distingué(e)	distinto(a)	distinguido(a)
Vorort (D)	—	suburb	faubourg *m*	sobborgo *m*	suburbio *m*
Vorrat (D)	—	stock	réserves *f pl*	scorte *f pl*	provisión *f*
Vorsaison (D)	—	low season	basse saison *f*	bassa stagione *f*	pretemporada *f*
Vorschlag (D)	—	proposal	proposition *f*	proposta *f*	proposición *f*
vorschlagen (D)	—	propose	proposer	proporre	proponer
Vorschrift (D)	—	regulation	règle *f*	norma *f*	reglamento *m*
Vorsicht (D)	—	caution	prudence *f*	prudenza *f*	cuidado *m*
vorsichtig (D)	—	careful	prudent(e)	prudente	cauto(a)
Vorspeise (D)	—	appetizer	hors-d'œuvre *m*	antipasto *m*	primer plato *m*
vorstellen (D)	—	introduce	présenter	presentare	presentar
Vorstellung¹ (D)	—	idea	idée *f*	idea *f*	idea *f*
Vorstellung² (D)	—	performance	représentation *f*	rappresentazione *f*	representación *f*
Vorteil (D)	—	advantage	avantage *m*	vantaggio *m*	ventaja *f*
vorüber (D)	—	past	passé(e)	passato(a)	pasado(a)

	D	E	F	I	Es
vorübergehend (D)	—	temporary	temporaire	temporaneo(a)	pasajero(a)
Vorverkauf (D)	—	advance booking	location *f*	vendita anticipata *f*	venta anticipada *f*
Vorwahl (D)	—	dialling code	indicatif téléphonique *m*	prefisso *m*	prefijo *m*
Vorwand (D)	—	pretext	prétexte *m*	pretesto *m*	pretexto *m*
vorwärts (D)	—	forward(s)	en avant	avanti	adelante
vorwerfen (D)	—	blame	reprocher	rimproverare	echar en cara
Vorwort (D)	—	preface	préface *f*	prefazione *f*	prólogo *m*
vorzeigen (D)	—	show	monter	esibire	presentar
vorziehen¹ (D)	—	draw	tirer	tirare in avanti	correr
vorziehen² (D)	—	prefer	préférer	preferire	preferir
Vorzug (D)	—	preference	préférence *f*	preferenza *f*	preferencia *f*
vosotros (Es)	ihr	you	vous	voi	—
voto (I)	Note *f*	mark	note *f*	—	calificación *f*
voucher (E)	Gutschein *m*	—	bon *m*	buono *m*	vale *m*
vouloir (F)	wollen	want	—	volere	querer
vous (F)	ihr	you	—	voi	vosotros
voyage¹ (F)	Fahrt *f*	journey	—	viaggio *m*	viaje *m*
voyage² (F)	Reise *f*	journey	—	viaggio *m*	viaje *m*
voyager (F)	reisen	travel	—	viaggiare	viajar
voyageur (F)	Reisender *m*	traveller	—	viaggiatore *m*	viajero *m*
voz (Es)	Stimme *f*	voice	voix *f*	voce *f*	—
vrai¹ (F)	echt	genuine	—	vero(a)	verdadero(a)
vrai² (F)	wahr	true	—	vero(a)	verdadero(a)
vraiment (F)	tatsächlich	really	—	realmente	realmente
vue¹ (F)	Aussicht *f*	view	—	vista *f*	vista *f*
vue² (F)	Sicht *f*	view	—	vista *f*	vista *f*
vuelo (Es)	Flug *m*	flight	vol *m*	volo *m*	—
vulgar (Es)	gemein	mean	méchant(e)	volgare	—
vuoto (I)	leer	empty	vide	—	vacío(a)
Waage (D)	—	scales	balance *f*	bilancia *f*	balanza *f*
waagrecht (D)	—	horizontal	horizontal(e)	orizzontale	horizontal
wach (D)	—	awake	réveillé(e)	sveglio(a)	despierto(a)
wachsen (D)	—	grow	grandir	crescere	crecer
Waffe (D)	—	weapon	arme *f*	arma *f*	arma *m*
wagen (D)	—	dare	oser	osare	atreverse
Wagen (D)	—	car	voiture *f*	vettura *f*	coche *m*
wages (E)	Lohn *m*	—	salaire *m*	salario *m*	salario *m*
Waggon (D)	—	carriage	wagon *m*	vagone *m*	vagón *m*
wagon (F)	Waggon *m*	carriage	—	vagone *m*	vagón *m*
wagon-couchette (F)	Liegewagen *m*	couchette	—	cuccetta *f*	coche cama *m*
wagon-restaurant (F)	Speisewagen *m*	dining car	—	vagone ristorante *m*	vagón restaurante *m*
Wahl¹ (D)	—	choice	choix *m*	scelta *f*	opción *f*
Wahl² (D)	—	election	élection *f*	elezioni *f pl*	elección *f*
wählen (D)	—	elect	élire	eleggere	elegir
wahr (D)	—	true	vrai(e)	vero(a)	verdadero(a)
während (D)	—	during	pendant	durante	durante

	D	E	F	I	Es
Wahrheit (D)	—	truth	vérité f	verità f	verdad f
wahrscheinlich (D)	—	probably	probablement	probabile	probablemente
Währung (D)	—	currency	monnaie f	valuta f	moneda f
Waise (D)	—	orphan	orphelin m	orfano m	huérfano m
wait (E)	warten	—	attendre	aspettare	esperar
waiter (E)	Kellner m/ Ober m	—	garçon m	cameriere m	camarero m
waiting room (E)	Wartesaal m	—	salle d'attente f	sala d'attesa f	sala de espera f
wake (up) (E)	wecken	—	réveiller	svegliare	despertar
wake up[1] (E)	aufwachen	—	réveiller, se	svegliarsi	despertarse
wake up[2] (E)	aufwecken	—	réveiller	svegliare	despertar
wake up[3] (E)	erwachen	—	réveiller, se	svegliarsi	despertar
Wald (D)	—	forest	forêt f	bosco m	bosque m
walk (E)	Spaziergang m	—	promenade f	passeggiata f	paseo m
wall[1] (E)	Mauer f	—	mur m	muro m	muro m
wall[2] (E)	Wand f	—	mur m	parete f	pared f
Wand (D)	—	wall	mur m	parete f	pared f
wandern (D)	—	hike	marcher	fare escursioni a piedi	hacer excursiones
Wange (D)	—	cheek	joue f	guancia f	mejilla f
wanken (D)	—	stagger	chanceller	barcollare	vacilar
wann (D)	—	when	quand	quando	cuando
want (E)	wollen	—	vouloir	volere	querer
war (E)	Krieg m	—	guerre f	guerra f	guerra f
wardrobe[1] (E)	Garderobe f	—	vestiaire m	guardaroba m	guardaropa m
wardrobe[2] (E)	Kleiderschrank m	—	garde-robe f	armadio m	armario ropero m
Ware (D)	—	goods	marchandise f	merce f	mercancía f
warm (D)	—	warm	chaud(e)	caldo(a)	caliente
warm[1] (E)	wärmen	—	chauffer	riscaldare	calentar
warm[2] (E)	warm	—	chaud(e)	caldo(a)	caliente
Wärme (D)	—	warmth	chaleur f	calore m	calor m
wärmen (D)	—	warm	chauffer	riscaldare	calentar
warmth (E)	Wärme f	—	chaleur f	calore m	calor m
warn[1] (E)	abraten	—	déconseiller	sconsigliare	desaconsejar
warn[2] (E)	mahnen	—	exhorter	ammonire	notificar
warn[3] (E)	warnen	—	prévenir de	ammonire	advertir
warnen (D)	—	warn	prévenir de	ammonire	advertir
warten (D)	—	wait	attendre	aspettare	esperar
Wärter (D)	—	attendant	gardien m	custode m	guarda m
Wartesaal (D)	—	waiting room	salle d'attente f	sala d'attesa f	sala de espera f
warum (D)	—	why	pourquoi	perché	por qué
was (D)	—	what	quoi/qu'est-ce que	che/cosa	qué
waschbar (D)	—	washable	lavable	lavabile	lavable
Waschbecken (D)	—	wash-basin	lavabo m	lavandino m	lavabo m
Wäsche (D)	—	washing	linge m	biancheria f	ropa f
waschen (D)	—	wash	laver	lavare	lavar
Wäscherei (D)	—	laundry	blanchisserie f	lavanderia f	lavandería f
Waschmaschine (D)	—	washing machine	machine à laver f	lavatrice f	lavadora f
Waschmittel (D)	—	detergent	lessive f	detersivo m	detergente m

	D	E	F	I	Es
wash (E)	waschen	—	laver	lavare	lavar
wash up (E)	abspülen	—	faire la vaissèlle	sciacquare	lavar
washable (E)	waschbar	—	lavable	lavabile	lavable
wash-basin (E)	Waschbecken *n*	—	lavabo *m*	lavandino *m*	lavabo *m*
washing (E)	Wäsche *f*	—	linge *m*	biancheria *f*	ropa *f*
washing machine (E)	Waschmaschine *f*	—	machine à laver *f*	lavatrice *f*	lavadora *f*
wash off (E)	abwaschen	—	laver	lavar via	lavar
wasp (E)	Wespe *f*	—	guêpe *f*	vespa *f*	avispa *f*
Wasser (D)	—	water	eau *f*	acqua *f*	agua *f*
waste¹ (E)	öde	—	désert(e)	deserto(a)	desierto(a)
waste² (E)	verschwenden	—	gaspiller	sprecare	desperdiciar
watch¹ (E)	Uhr *f*	—	montre *f*	orologio *m*	reloj *m*
watch² (E)	zuschauen	—	regarder	stare a guardare	mirar
watch³ (E)	zusehen	—	regarder	stare a guardare	mirar
watch television (E)	fernsehen	—	regarder la télévision	guardare la TV	ver la televisión
water¹ (E)	gießen	—	arroser	annaffiare	regar
water² (E)	Wasser *n*	—	eau *f*	acqua *f*	agua *f*
waters (E)	Gewässer *n*	—	eaux *f pl*	acque *f pl*	aguas *f pl*
Watte (D)	—	cotton wool	ouate *f*	ovatta *f*	algodón *m*
wave¹ (E)	winken	—	faire signe	chiamare con cenni	llamar con gestos
wave² (E)	Welle *f*	—	vague *f*	onda *f*	ola *f*
way¹ (E)	Art *f*	—	manière *f*	modo *m*	manera *f*
way² (E)	Weise *f*	—	manière *f*	maniera *f*	manera *f*
way³ (E)	Weg *m*	—	chemin *m*	via *f*	camino *m*
we (E)	wir	—	nous	noi	nosotros(as)
weak (E)	schwach	—	faible	debole	débil
weakness (E)	Schwäche *f*	—	faiblesse *f*	debolezza *f*	debilidad *f*
weapon (E)	Waffe *f*	—	arme *f*	arma *f*	arma *m*
wear out (E)	abnutzen	—	user	consumare	desgastar
weather (E)	Wetter *n*	—	temps *m*	tempo *m*	tiempo *m*
weather forecast (E)	Wetter-vorhersage *f*	—	prévisions météorologiques *f pl*	previsioni del tempo *f pl*	pronóstico del tiempo *m*
weather report (E)	Wetterbericht *m*	—	bulletin météorologique *m*	bollettino metereologico *m*	informe metereológico *m*
Wechsel (D)	—	change	changement *m*	cambiamento *m*	cambio *m*
wechseln (D)	—	change	changer	cambiare	cambiar
Wechselstube (D)	—	bureau de change	bureau de change *m*	ufficio di cambio *m*	casa de cambio *f*
wecken (D)	—	wake (up)	réveiller	svegliare	despertar
Wecker (D)	—	alarm clock	réveil *m*	sveglia *f*	despertador *m*
wedding (E)	Hochzeit *f*	—	mariage *m*	nozze *f pl*	boda *f*
weder (D)	—	neither	ni	né…né	ni
Wednesday (E)	Mittwoch *m*	—	mercredi *m*	mercoledì *m*	miércoles *m*
week (E)	Woche *f*	—	semaine *f*	settimana *f*	semana *f*
weekend (E)	Wochenende *n*	—	week-end *m*	fine settimana *m*	fin de semana *m*
week-end (F)	Wochenende *n*	weekend	—	fine settimana *m*	fin de semana *m*
weekly (E)	wöchentlich	—	hebdomadaire	settimanale	semanal
weg (D)	—	away	pas là	via	fuera

	D	E	F	I	Es
Weg (D)	—	way	chemin m	via f	camino m
wegen (D)	—	because of	à cause de	a causa di	a causa de
weggehen (D)	—	go away	s'en aller	andare via	marcharse
wegnehmen (D)	—	take away	enlever	togliere	quitar
weh (D)	—	hurt	douloureux(-euse)	dolente	doloroso(a)
wehren, sich (D)	—	defend	défendre, se	difendersi	defenderse
weiblich (D)	—	feminine	féminin(e)	femminile	femenino
weich (D)	—	soft	doux (douce)	morbido(a)	tierno(a)
weigern (D)	—	refuse	refuser	rifiutare	resistirse
weigh (E)	wiegen	—	peser	pesare	pesar
weight (E)	Gewicht n	—	poids m	peso m	peso m
Weihnachten (D)	—	Christmas	Noël m	Natale m	Navidad(es) f *(pl)*
weil (D)	—	because	parce que	perché	porque
Weile (D)	—	while	moment m	momento m	rato m
Wein (D)	—	wine	vin m	vino m	vino m
weinen (D)	—	cry	pleurer	piangere	llorar
weise (D)	—	wise	sage	saggio(a)	sabio(a)
Weise (D)	—	way	manière f	maniera f	manera f
weiß (D)	—	white	blanc, blanche	bianco(a)	blanco(a)
weit (D)	—	far	éloigné(e)	largo(a)	ancho(a)
weiter (D)	—	further	plus éloigné(e)	più ampio(a)	adelante
weitergehen (D)	—	go on	aller plus loin	proseguire	proseguir
weitermachen (D)	—	carry on	continuer	continuare	continuar
weiterschlafen (D)	—	sleep on	continuer à dormir	continuare a dormire	seguir durmiendo
Weizen (D)	—	wheat	blé m	frumento m	trigo m
welch (D)	—	what a	quel(le)	che	¿qué?
welche (D)	—	which	qui/que	il(la) quale	¿cual?
welcome (E)	willkommen	—	bienvenu(e)	benvenuto(a)	bienvenido(a)
welfare (E)	Wohl n	—	bien m	benessere m	bienestar m
welken (D)	—	wither	faner, se	appassire	machitarse
well (E)	wohl	—	bien	bene/forse	bien
Welle (D)	—	wave	vague f	onda f	ola f
well known (E)	bekannt	—	connu(e)	conosciuto(a)	conocido(a)
Welt (D)	—	world	monde m	mondo m	mundo m
Weltall (D)	—	universe	univers m	universo m	universo m
Weltsprache (D)	—	world language	langue internationale f	lingua mondiale f	lengua universal f
wenden (D)	—	turn	tourner	voltare	volver
wenig (D)	—	little	peu de	poco	poco(a)
wenige (D)	—	few	peu	pochi	pocos(as)
weniger (D)	—	less	moins	di meno	menos
wenigstens (D)	—	at least	au moins	almeno	por lo menos
wenn (D)	—	when/if	si/quand	se/quando	cuando
wer (D)	—	who	qui	chi	quién
werben (D)	—	advertise	faire de la publicité	fare propaganda	hacer publicidad
Werbung (D)	—	advertising	publicité f	pubblicità f	publicidad f
werden (D)	—	become	devenir	diventare	llegar
werfen (D)	—	throw	lancer	lanciare	tirar

	D	E	F	I	Es
Werk (D)	—	work	œuvre *f*	opera *f*	obra *f*
Werkstatt (D)	—	workshop	atelier *m*	officina *f*	taller *m*
Werktag (D)	—	working day	jour ouvrable *m*	giorno feriale *m*	día laborable *m*
werktags (D)	—	on working days	les jours ouvrables	nei giorni feriali	los días laborables
Werkzeug (D)	—	tool	outils *m pl*	utensile *m*	herramienta *f*
wert (D)	—	worth	cher, chère	che vale	querido(a)
Wert (D)	—	value	valeur *f*	valore *m*	valor *m*
wertlos (D)	—	worthless	sans valeur	senza valore	sin valor
wertvoll (D)	—	valuable	précieux(-euse)	prezioso(a)	valioso(a)
Wesen (D)	—	being	être *m*	essere *m*	ser *m*
wesentlich (D)	—	essential	essentiel(-le)	essenziale	esencial
weshalb (D)	—	why	pourquoi	perché	por qué
Wespe (D)	—	wasp	guêpe *f*	vespa *f*	avispa *f*
wessen (D)	—	whose	de qui	di chi	de quién
west (E)	Westen *m*	—	ouest *m*	ovest *m*	oeste *m*
Westen (D)	—	west	ouest *m*	ovest *m*	oeste *m*
western (E)	westlich	—	de l'ouest	ad ovest	del oeste
westlich (D)	—	western	de l'ouest	ad ovest	del oeste
wet (E)	naß	—	mouillé(e)	bagnato	húmedo(a)
Wettbewerb (D)	—	competition	concours *m*	concorso *m*	concurso *m*
Wette (D)	—	bet	pari *m*	scommessa *f*	apuesta *f*
wetten (D)	—	bet	parier	scommettere	apostar
Wetter (D)	—	weather	temps *m*	tempo *m*	tiempo *m*
Wetterbericht (D)	—	weather report	bulletin météorologique *m*	bollettino metereologico *m*	informe metereológico *m*
Wetter-vorhersage (D)	—	weather forecast	prévisions météorologiques *f pl*	previsioni del tempo *f pl*	pronóstico del tiempo *m*
what (E)	was	—	quoi/qu'est-ce que	che/cosa	qué
what a (E)	welch	—	quel(le)	che	qué
what for[1] (E)	wofür	—	pourquoi	per cui	para qué
what for[2] (E)	wozu	—	pourquoi	perché	para qué
wheat (E)	Weizen *m*	—	blé *m*	frumento *m*	trigo *m*
wheel (E)	Rad *n*	—	roue *f*	ruota *f*	rueda *f*
when[1] (E)	als	—	quand	quando	cuando
when[2] (E)	wann	—	quand	quando	cuando
when[3] (E)	wenn	—	si/quand	se/quando	cuando
where (E)	wo	—	où	dove	dónde
where from (E)	woher	—	d'où	da dove	de dónde
where to (E)	wohin	—	où	dove	a dónde
which (E)	welche(r,s)	—	qui/que	il(la) quale	cual
while (E)	Weile *f*	—	moment *m*	momento *m*	rato *m*
whisper (E)	flüstern	—	chuchoter	bisbigliare	cuchichear
whistle (E)	Pfeife *f*	—	sifflet *m*	fischietto *m*	silbato *m*
white (E)	weiß	—	blanc(he)	bianco(a)	blanco(a)
Whitsun (E)	Pfingsten *n*	—	Pentecôte *f*	Pentecoste *f*	Pascua de Pentecostés *f*
who (E)	wer	—	qui	chi	quién
whole (E)	ganz	—	tout(e)	intero(a)	entero(a)
whose (E)	wessen	—	de qui	di chi	de quién

	D	E	F	I	Es
why[1] (E)	warum	—	pourquoi	perché	por qué
why[2] (E)	wieso	—	pourquoi	come mai	por qué
why[3] (E)	weshalb	—	pourquoi	perché	por qué
wichtig (D)	—	important	important(e)	importante	importante
wicked (E)	böse	—	méchant(e)	cattivo(a)	malo(a)
wickeln (D)	—	wind	enrouler	avvolgere	envolver
widerlich (D)	—	disgusting	repoussant(e)	ripugnante	repugnante
widerrufen (D)	—	retract	démentir	revocare	revocación f
widersprechen (D)	—	contradict	contredire	contraddire	contradecir
Widerstand (D)	—	resistance	résistance f	resistenza f	resistencia f
widmen (D)	—	dedicate	dédier	dedicare	dedicar
widow (E)	Witwe f	—	veuve f	vedova f	viuda f
widower (E)	Witwer m	—	veuf m	vedovo m	viudo m
width (E)	Breite f	—	largeur f	larghezza f	extensión f
wie (D)	—	how	comment	come	cómo
wieder (D)	—	again	de nouveau	di nuovo	de nuevo
wiedergeben (D)	—	return	rendre	restituire	devolver
wiedergut-machen (D)	—	make up for	réparer	riparare	subsanar
wiederholen (D)	—	repeat	répéter	ripetere	repetir
wiederhören! (D)	—	good-bye!	au revoir!	a risentirci!	¡adiós!
wieder-kommen (D)	—	come back	revenir	ritornare	venir de nuevo
wiedersehen (D)	—	see again	revoir	rivedere	volver a ver
wiedersehen! (D)	—	good-bye!	au revoir!	arrivederci!	¡adiós!
wiegen (D)	—	weigh	peser	pesare	pesar
Wiese (D)	—	meadow	pré m	prato m	prado m
wieso (D)	—	why	pourquoi	come mai	por qué
wieviel (D)	—	how much	combien	quanto	cuánto
wieviele (D)	—	how many	combien	quanti(e)	cuántos(as)
wife (E)	Ehefrau f	—	épouse f	moglie f	mujer f
wild (D)	—	wild	sauvage	selvatico(a)	salvaje
Wild (D)	—	game	gibier m	selvaggina f	caza f
wild (E)	wild	—	sauvage	selvatico(a)	salvaje
will[1] (E)	Belieben n	—	plaisir m	piacere m	placer m
will[2] (E)	Testament n	—	testament m	testamento m	testamento m
willingly (E)	gern	—	avec plaisir	volentieri	con gusto
willkommen (D)	—	welcome	bienvenu(e)	benvenuto(a)	bienvenido(a)
Wimper (D)	—	eyelash	cil m	ciglia f	pestaña f
win[1] (E)	gewinnen	—	gagner	vincere	ganar
win[2] (E)	siegen	—	gagner	vincere	vencer
Wind (D)	—	wind	vent m	vento m	viento m
wind[1] (E)	wickeln	—	enrouler	avvolgere	envolver
wind[2] (E)	Wind m	—	vent m	vento m	viento m
Windel (D)	—	nappy	lange m	pannolino m	pañal m
windig (D)	—	windy	éventé(e)	ventoso(a)	ventoso
window (E)	Fenster n	—	fenêtre f	finestra f	ventana f
windy (E)	windig	—	éventé(e)	ventoso	ventoso
wine (E)	Wein m	—	vin m	vino m	vino m

	D	E	F	I	Es
wing (E)	Flügel *m*	—	aile *f*	ala *f*	ala *f*
Winkel (D)	—	corner	coin *m*	cantuccio *m*	rincón *m*
winken (D)	—	wave	faire signe	chiamare con cenni	llamar con gestos
Winter (D)	—	winter	hiver *m*	inverno *m*	invierno *m*
winter (E)	Winter *m*	—	hiver *m*	inverno *m*	invierno *m*
wipe (E)	wischen	—	essuyer	pulire	fregar
wir (D)	—	we	nous	noi	nosotros(as)
Wirbelsäule (D)	—	spine	colonne vertébrale *f*	colonna vertebrale *f*	columna vertebral *f*
wire (E)	Draht *m*	—	fil de fer *m*	filo metallico *m*	alambre *m*
wirklich (D)	—	real	réel(le)	reale	real
Wirklichkeit (D)	—	reality	réalité *f*	realtà *f*	realidad *f*
wirksam (D)	—	effective	efficace	efficace	eficaz
Wirkung (D)	—	effect	effet *m*	effetto *m*	efecto *m*
Wirt (D)	—	landlord	patron *m*	oste *m*	dueño *m*
Wirtshaus (D)	—	inn	auberge *f*	osteria *f*	restaurante *m*
wischen (D)	—	wipe	essuyer	pulire	fregar
wise (E)	weise	—	sage	saggio(a)	sabio(a)
wish[1] (E)	wünschen	—	souhaiter	desiderare	desear
wish[2] (E)	Wunsch *m*	—	souhait *m*	desiderio *m*	deseo *m*
wissen (D)	—	know	savoir	sapere	saber
Wissen (D)	—	knowledge	savoir *m*	sapere *m*	saber *m*
Wissenschaft (D)	—	science	science *f*	scienza *f*	ciencia *f*
Wissenschaftler (D)	—	scientist	scientifique *m*	scienziato *m*	científico *m*
witch (E)	Hexe *f*	—	sorcière *f*	strega *f*	bruja *f*
with (E)	mit	—	avec	con	con
withdraw (E)	zurückziehen	—	retirer	ritirare	retirar
wither (E)	welken	—	faner, se	appassire	marchitarse
within (E)	innerhalb	—	à l'intérieur de	entro	dentro de
with it (E)	damit	—	avec cela	con questo	con ello
without (E)	ohne	—	sans	senza	sin
witness (E)	Zeuge *m*	—	témoin *m*	testimone *m*	testigo *m*
Witwe (D)	—	widow	veuve *f*	vedova *f*	viuda *f*
Witwer (D)	—	widower	veuf *m*	vedovo *m*	viudo *m*
Witz (D)	—	joke	plaisanterie *f*	barzelletta *f*	chiste *m*
wo (D)	—	where	où	dove	dónde
woanders (D)	—	elsewhere	ailleurs	altrove	en otra parte
Woche (D)	—	week	semaine *f*	settimana *f*	semana *f*
Wochenende (D)	—	weekend	week-end *m*	fine settimana *m*	fin de semana *m*
wochentags (D)	—	during the week	en semaine	nei giorni feriali	entre semana
wöchentlich (D)	—	weekly	hebdomadaire	settimanale	semanal
wofür (D)	—	what for	pourquoi	per cui	para qué
woher (D)	—	where from	d'où	da dove	de dónde
wohin (D)	—	where to	où	dove	a dónde
wohl (D)	—	well	bien	bene/forse	bien
Wohl (D)	—	welfare	bien *m*	benessere *m*	bienestar *m*
wohnen (D)	—	live	habiter	abitare	vivir
Wohnmobil (D)	—	camper	caravane *f*	camper *m*	caravana *f*

Würfel

	D	E	F	I	Es
Wohnort (D)	—	domicile	domicile *m*	residenza *f*	residencia *f*
Wohnung (D)	—	flat	appartement *m*	appartamento *m*	piso *m*
Wohnwagen (D)	—	caravan	caravane *f*	roulotte *f*	rulota *f*
Wohnzimmer (D)	—	living room	salle de séjour *f*	salotto *m*	sala de estar *f*
Wolke (D)	—	cloud	nuage *m*	nuvola *f*	nube *f*
Wolle (D)	—	wool	laine *f*	lana *f*	lana *f*
wollen (D)	—	want	vouloir	volere	querer
woman (E)	Frau *f*	—	femme *f*	donna *f*	mujer *f*
wonder (E)	wundern	—	étonner	stupire	asombrar
wonderful (E)	wunderbar	—	miraculeux (-euse)	meraviglioso(a)	maravilloso(a)
wood (E)	Holz *n*	—	bois *m*	legno *m*	madera *f*
wool (E)	Wolle *f*	—	laine *f*	lana *f*	lana *f*
word (E)	Wort *n*	—	mot *m*	parola *f*	palabra *f*
work[1] (E)	arbeiten	—	travailler	lavorare	trabajar
work[2] (E)	Arbeit *f*	—	travail *m*	lavoro *m*	trabajo *m*
work[3] (E)	funktionieren	—	fonctionner	funzionare	funcionar
work[4] (E)	Werk *n*	—	œuvre *f*	opera *f*	obra *f*
worker (E)	Arbeiter *m*	—	ouvrier *m*	operaio *m*	trabajador *m*
working day (E)	Werktag *m*	—	jour ouvrable *m*	giorno feriale *m*	día laborable *m*
workshop (E)	Werkstatt *f*	—	atelier *m*	officina *f*	taller *m*
world (E)	Welt *f*	—	monde *m*	mondo *m*	mundo *m*
world language (E)	Weltsprache *f*	—	langue internationale *f*	lingua mondiale *f*	lengua universal *f*
worry about (E)	sorgen	—	occuper de, se	prendersi cura di	atender
worship (E)	anbeten	—	adorer	adorare	adorar
Wort (D)	—	word	mot *m*	parola *f*	palabra *f*
Wörterbuch (D)	—	dictionary	dictionnaire *m*	dizionario *m*	diccionario *m*
worth (E)	wert	—	cher, chère	che vale	querido(a)
worthless (E)	wertlos	—	sans valeur	senza valore	sin valor
wound[1] (E)	verwunden	—	blesser	ferire	herir
wound[2] (E)	Wunde *f*	—	blessure *f*	ferita *f*	herida *f*
wozu (D)	—	what for	pourquoi	perchè	¿para qué?
wrap up (E)	einwickeln	—	envelopper	avvolgere	envolver
write (E)	schreiben	—	écrire	scrivere	escribir
writer (E)	Schriftsteller *m*	—	écrivain *m*	scrittore *m*	escritor *m*
writing (E)	Schrift *f*	—	écriture *f*	scrittura *f*	escritura *f*
written (E)	schriftlich	—	écrit(e)	scritto(a)	por escrito
wrong[1] (E)	falsch	—	faux (fausse)	falso(a)	falso(a)
wrong[2] (E)	Unrecht *n*	—	injustice *f*	torto *m*	injusticia *f*
wrong[3] (E)	verkehrt	—	faux (fausse)	sbagliato(a)	equivocado(a)
wühlen (D)	—	scrabble	fouiller	rovistare	revolver
Wunde (D)	—	wound	blessure *f*	ferita *f*	herida *f*
Wunder (D)	—	miracle	miracle *m*	miracolo *m*	milagro *m*
wunderbar (D)	—	wonderful	miraculeux(-euse)	meraviglioso(a)	maravilloso(a)
wundern (D)	—	wonder	étonner	stupire	asombrar
Wunsch (D)	—	wish	souhait *m*	desiderio *m*	deseo *m*
wünschen (D)	—	wish	souhaiter	desiderare	desear
Würfel (D)	—	dice	dé *m*	dado *m*	dado *m*

	D	E	F	I	Es
Wurst (D)	—	sausage	saucisse *f*	salsiccia *f*	salchichón *m*
Wurzel (D)	—	root	racine *f*	radice *f*	raíz *f*
würzen (D)	—	season	épicer	condire	condimentar
würzig (D)	—	spicy	épicé(e)	aromatico(a)	aromático(a)
Wüste (D)	—	desert	désert *m*	deserto *m*	desierto *m*
Wut (D)	—	anger	colère *f*	rabbia *f*	rabia *f*
wütend (D)	—	furious	furieux(-euse)	arrabbiato(a)	furioso(a)
X-ray (E)	röntgen	—	radiographier	fare una radiografia	radiografiar
y (Es)	und	and	et	e	—
ya (Es)	bereits/schon	already	déjà	già	—
yacht (E)	Jacht *f*	—	yacht *m*	panfilo *m*	yate *m*
yacht (F)	Jacht *f*	yacht	—	panfilo *m*	yate *m*
yaourt (F)	Joghurt *m*	yogurt	—	yoghurt *m*	yogur(t) *m*
yard (E)	Hof *m*	—	cour *f*	cortile *m*	patio *m*
yate (Es)	Jacht *f*	yacht	yacht *m*	panfilo *m*	—
y compris (F)	einschließlich	including	—	incluso(a)	incluído
year (E)	Jahr *n*	—	année *f*	anno *m*	año *m*
yellow (E)	gelb	—	jaune	giallo(a)	amarillo(a)
yema (Es)	Knospe *f*	bud	bourgeon *m*	bocciolo *m*	—
yes (E)	ja	—	oui	sì	sí
yesterday (E)	gestern	—	hier	ieri	ayer
yield (E)	nachgeben	—	céder	cedere	ceder
yo (Es)	ich	I	je/moi	io	—
yoghurt (I)	Joghurt *m*	yogurt	yaourt *m*	—	yogur(t) *m*
yogur(t) (Es)	Joghurt *m*	yogurt	yaourt *m*	yoghurt *m*	—
yogurt (E)	Joghurt *m*	—	yaourt *m*	yoghurt *m*	yogur(t) *m*
you¹ (E)	du	—	tu/toi	tu	tú
you² (E)	ihr	—	vous	voi	vosotros
young (E)	jung	—	jeune	giovane	joven
youth (E)	Jugend *f*	—	jeunesse *f*	gioventù *f*	juventud *f*
zäh (D)	—	tough	coriace	duro(a)	duro(a)
Zahl (D)	—	number	chiffre *m*	numero *m*	número *m*
zahlen (D)	—	pay	payer	pagare	pagar
zählen (D)	—	count	compter	contare	contar
zahlreich (D)	—	numerous	nombreux (-euse)	numeroso(a)	numeroso(a)
Zahlung (D)	—	payment	paiement *m*	pagamento *m*	pago *m*
Zahn (D)	—	tooth	dent *f*	dente *m*	diente *m*
Zahnarzt (D)	—	dentist	dentiste *m*	dentista *m*	dentista *m*
Zahnbürste (D)	—	toothbrush	brosse à dents *f*	spazzolino da denti *m*	cepillo de dientes *m*
Zahnpasta (D)	—	toothpaste	dentifrice *m*	dentifricio *m*	pasta dentífrica *f*
Zahnschmerzen (D)	—	toothache	mal de dents *m*	mal di denti *m*	dolor de muelas *m*
zaino (I)	Rucksack *m*	rucksack	sac à dos *m*	—	mochila *f*

	D	E	F	I	Es
zanahoria (Es)	Karotte *f* / Möhre *f*	carrot	carotte *f*	carota *f*	—
zanzara (I)	Mücke *f*	mosquito	moustique *m*	—	mosquito *m*
zapatería (Es)	Schuhgeschäft *n*	shoeshop	magasin de chaussures *m*	negozio di scarpe *m*	—
zapatero (Es)	Schuster *m*	shoemaker	cordonnier *m*	calzolaio *m*	—
zapatilla (Es)	Pantoffel *f*	slipper	pantoufle *f*	pantofola *f*	—
zapato (Es)	Schuh *m*	shoe	chaussure *f*	scarpa *f*	—
zart (D)	—	soft	doux(douce)	tenero(a)	suave
Zärtlichkeit (D)	—	tenderness	tendresse *f*	tenerezza *f*	cariño *m*
zarzamora (Es)	Brombeere *f*	blackberry	mûre *f*	mora *f*	—
Zauberer (D)	—	magician	magicien *m*	mago *m*	mago *m*
zaubern (D)	—	practise magic	faire de la magie	esercitare la magia	hacer magia
Zaun (D)	—	fence	clôture *f*	recinto *m*	valla *f*
Zehe (D)	—	toe	doigt de pied *m*	dito del piede *m*	dedo del pie *m*
zehn (D)	—	ten	dix	dieci	diez
Zeichen (D)	—	sign	signe *m*	segnale *m*	signo *m*
zeichnen (D)	—	draw	dessiner	disegnare	dibujar
Zeichnung (D)	—	drawing	dessin *m*	disegno *m*	dibujo *m*
zeigen (D)	—	show	montrer	mostrare	indicar
Zeile (D)	—	line	ligne *f*	riga *f*	línea *f*
Zeit (D)	—	time	temps *m*	tempo *m*	tiempo *m*
zeitgenössisch (D)	—	contemporary	contemporain(e)	contemporaneo(a)	contemporáneo(a)
Zeitschrift (D)	—	magazine	revue *f*	rivista *f*	revista *f*
Zeitung (D)	—	newspaper	journal *m*	giornale *m*	periódico *m*
zélé (F)	eifrig	keen	—	diligente	diligente
Zelt (D)	—	tent	tente *f*	tenda *f*	tienda *f*
zelten (D)	—	camp	camper	campeggiare	acampar
zentral (D)	—	central	central(e)	centrale	céntrico(a)
Zentralheizung (D)	—	central heating	chauffage central *m*	riscaldamento centrale *m*	calefacción central *f*
Zentrum (D)	—	centre	centre *m*	centro *m*	centro *m*
zerbrechen (D)	—	break	casser	rompere	romper
zerbrechlich (D)	—	fragile	fragile	fragile	frágil
zerdrücken (D)	—	squash	écraser	sgualcire	aplastar
zero (E)	Null *f*	—	zéro	zero	cero
zéro (F)	Null *f*	zero	—	zero	cero
zero (I)	Null *f*	zero	zéro	—	cero
zerreißen (D)	—	rip	déchirer	strappare	romper
zerstören (D)	—	destroy	détruire	distruggere	destruir
zerstreut (D)	—	scattered	dispersé(e)	disperso(a)	disperso(a)
Zeug (D)	—	stuff	truc *m*	cose *f pl*	cosa *f*
Zeuge (D)	—	witness	témoin *m*	testimone *m*	testigo *m*
Zeugnis (D)	—	report	bulletin *m*	pagella *f*	informe *m*
zia (I)	Tante *f*	aunt(ie)	tante *f*	—	tía *f*

	D	E	F	I	Es
Ziege (D)	—	goat	chèvre *f*	capra *f*	cabra *f*
Ziegel (D)	—	brick	brique *f*	mattone *m*	ladrillo *m*
ziehen (D)	—	pull	tirer	tirare	tirar
Ziel (D)	—	goal	but *m*	meta *f*	intención *f*
ziemlich (D)	—	quite	assez	abbastanza	bastante
Zigarette (D)	—	cigarette	cigarette *f*	sigaretta *f*	cigarrillo *m*
Zigarre (D)	—	cigar	cigare *m*	sigaro *m*	cigarro *m*
Zimmer (D)	—	room	chambre *f*	camera *f*	habitación *f*
zio (I)	Onkel *m*	uncle	oncle *m*	—	tío *m*
zip (E)	Reiß-verschluß *m*	—	fermeture *f*	chiusura lampo *f*	cremallera *f*
Zirkus (D)	—	circus	cirque *m*	circo *m*	circo *m*
Zitrone (D)	—	lemon	citron *m*	limone *m*	limón *m*
zittern (D)	—	tremble	trembler	tremare	tiritar
Zivilisation (D)	—	civilisation	civilisation *f*	civiltà *f*	civilización *f*
zögern (D)	—	hesitate	hésiter	esitare	vacilar
Zoll¹ (D)	—	customs	douane *f*	dogana *f*	aduana *f*
Zoll² (D)	—	duty	droits de douane *m pl*	dazio *m*	arbitrio *m*
zona (Es)	Gebiet *n*	region	région *f*	regione *f*	—
Zopf (D)	—	plait	natte *f*	treccia *f*	trenza *f*
zorro (Es)	Fuchs *m*	fox	renard *m*	volpe *f*	—
zu (D)	—	to	de/à	da/di/a	para
zubereiten (D)	—	prepare	préparer	preparare	preparar
zucchero (I)	Zucker *m*	sugar	sucre *m*	—	azúcar *m*
züchten (D)	—	breed	élever	allevare	críar
Zucker (D)	—	sugar	sucre *m*	zucchero *m*	azúcar *m*
zudecken (D)	—	cover (up)	couvrir	coprire	tapar
zudrehen (D)	—	turn off	fermer	chiudere	cerrar
zuerst (D)	—	at first	d'abord	dapprima	primero
Zufall (D)	—	chance	hasard *m*	caso *m*	casualidad *f*
zufällig (D)	—	by chance	par hasard	per caso	por casualidad
zufrieden (D)	—	satisfied	content(e)	contento(a)	satisfecho(a)
Zug (D)	—	train	train *m*	treno *m*	tren *m*
Zugang (D)	—	access	accès *m*	entrata *f*	entrada *f*
zuhören (D)	—	listen	écouter	ascoltare	escuchar
Zukunft (D)	—	future	avenir *m*	futuro *m*	futuro *m*
zukünftig (D)	—	future	futur(e)	futuro(a)	en el futuro
zulassen (D)	—	permit	admettre	permettere	permitir
zulässig (D)	—	permissable	permis(e)	permesso(a)	permítido(a)
zuletzt (D)	—	finally	finalement	infine	por último
zumachen (D)	—	shut	fermer	chiudere	cerrar
zumindest (D)	—	at least	au moins	per lo meno	por lo menos
zumo (Es)	Saft *m*	juice	jus *m*	succo *m*	—
zumuten (D)	—	expect	exiger	pretendere	exigir

	D	E	F	I	Es
zunächst (D)	—	first of all	pour l'instant	dapprima	en primer lugar
zünden (D)	—	ignite	allumer, se	accendersi	encender
zunehmen (D)	—	increase	augmenter	aumentare	aumentar
Zunge (D)	—	tongue	langue f	lingua f	lengua f
zuppa (I)	Suppe f	soup	soupe f	—	sopa f
zurechtfinden, sich (D)	—	find one's way	retrouver, se	orientarsi	orientarse
zurück (D)	—	back	de retour	indietro	atrás
zurückbringen (D)	—	bring back	rapporter	riportare	devolver
zurückfahren (D)	—	drive back	retourner	tornare indietro	retroceder
zurückgeben (D)	—	give back	rendre	restituire	devolver
zurückkehren (D)	—	return	revenir	ritornare	volver
zurückkommen (D)	—	come back	revenir	ritornare	regresar
zurücknehmen (D)	—	take back	retirer	prendere indietro	retirar
zurücktreten (D)	—	retire	démissionner	dare le dimissioni	dimitir
zurückzahlen (D)	—	pay back	rembourser	rimborsare	devolver
zurückziehen (D)	—	withdraw	retirer	ritirare	retirar
zusagen (D)	—	promise	promettre	promettere	prometer
zusammen (D)	—	together	ensemble	insieme	juntos
zusammenbrechen (D)	—	collapse	s'éffondrer	crollare	desmayarse
zusätzlich (D)	—	in addition	supplémentaire	supplementare	adicional
zuschauen (D)	—	watch	regarder	stare a guardare	mirar
Zuschauer (D)	—	spectator	spectateur m	spettatore m	espectador m
Zuschlag (D)	—	extra charge	supplément m	supplemento m	suplemento m
zuschließen (D)	—	lock (up)	fermer à clé	chiudere a chiave	cerrar con llave
zusehen (D)	—	watch	regarder	stare a guardare	mirar
Zustand (D)	—	condition	état m	stato m	estado m
zuständig (D)	—	competent	compétent(e)	competente	competente
zustimmen (D)	—	agree	être d'accord	acconsentire	consentir
Zutritt (D)	—	admission	accès m	accesso m	acceso m
zuverlässig (D)	—	reliable	sûr(e)	affidabile	de confianza
zuviel (D)	—	too much	trop	troppo	demasiado
zuviele (D)	—	too many	trop	troppi(e)	demasiados(as)
zuvor (D)	—	before	auparavant	prima	antes
zuvorkommend (D)	—	obliging	prévenant(e)	premuroso(a)	cortés
zuwenig (D)	—	too little	trop peu	troppo poco	demasiado poco
Zwang (D)	—	compulsion	contrainte f	costrizione f	presión f
zwanzig (D)	—	twenty	vingt	venti	veinte
Zweck (D)	—	purpose	but m	scopo m	finalidad f
zwecklos (D)	—	useless	inutile	inutile	inútil
zweckmäßig (D)	—	suitable	approprié(e)	adatto	adecuado(a)
zwei (D)	—	two	deux	due	dos
zweifach (D)	—	double	double	duplice	doble

	D	E	F	I	Es
Zweifel (D)	—	doubt	doute *m*	dubbio *m*	duda *f*
zweifelhaft (D)	—	doubtful	douteux(-euse)	dubbioso(a)	dudoso(a)
zweifellos (D)	—	doubtless	sans doute	senza dubbio	sin duda
zweifeln (D)	—	doubt	douter	dubitare	dudar
Zweig (D)	—	branch	branche *f*	ramo *m*	rama *f*
zweimal (D)	—	twice	deux fois	due volte	dos veces
zweisprachig (D)	—	bilingual	bilingue	bilingue	bilingüe
zweiter (D)	—	second	second(e)	secondo(a)	segunda(o)
Zwieback (D)	—	rusk	biscotte *f*	fette biscottate *f pl*	bizcocho *m*
Zwiebel (D)	—	onion	oignon *m*	cipolla *f*	cebolla *f*
Zwillinge (D)	—	twins	jumeaux *m pl*	gemelli *m pl*	gemelos *m pl*
zwingen (D)	—	force	forcer	costringere	obligar
zwischen (D)	—	between	entrer	tra/fra	entre
Zwischen-landung (D)	—	intermediate landing	escale *f*	scalo intermedio *m*	escala *f*
Zwischenraum (D)	—	space	espace *m*	spazio *m*	espacio intermedio *m*
zwölf (D)	—	twelve	douze	dodici	doce